Governemt Printing Office

Labor in America, Asia, Africa, Australasia, and Polynesia

Governemt Printing Office

Labor in America, Asia, Africa, Australasia, and Polynesia

ISBN/EAN: 9783744755931

Printed in Europe, USA, Canada, Australia, Japan

Cover: Foto ©Suzi / pixelio.de

More available books at **www.hansebooks.com**

LABOR

IN

AMERICA, ASIA, AFRICA, AUSTRALASIA, AND POLYNESIA.

REPORTS FROM CONSULS OF THE UNITED STATES IN THE SEVERAL
COUNTRIES OF AMERICA, ASIA, AFRICA, AUSTRALASIA, AND
POLYNESIA, ON THE STATE OF LABOR IN THEIR SEVERAL
DISTRICTS, IN RESPONSE TO A CIRCULAR FROM
THE DEPARTMENT OF STATE.

WASHINGTON:
GOVERNMENT PRINTING OFFICE.
1885.

CONTENTS.

CONTINENT OF AMERICA.

!NORTH AMERICA.

DOMINION OF CANADA.

PROVINCE OF ONTARIO.

AMHERSTBURG.

REPORT BY CONSUL TURNER.

I. GENERAL TRADES.

Wages per week of sixty hours in Amherstburg.

Occupations.	Average.	Occupations.	Average.
BUILDING TRADES.		**OTHER TRADES—Continued.**	
Bricklayers...........................	$21 00	Printers	$9 00
Hod-carriers......................	9 00	Teachers public schools	*500 00
Masons	18 00	Teachers public schools	†300 00
Tenders	7 50	Saddle and harness makers	6 00
Plasterers	21 00	Stevedores	12 00
Tenders	7 50	Tailors	10 00
Slaters..............................	15 00	Telegraph operators................	10 00
Roofers	12 00	Tinsmiths	15 00
Tenders	7 50	Butchers	6 00
Plumbers	18 00	Drivers...........................	3 00
Assistants........................	9 00	Draymen and teamsters	5 00
Carpenters	10 00	Cab and carriage	5 00
		Gardeners	6 00
OTHER TRADES.		Horseshoers	9 00
		Jewelers	15 00
Bakers..............................	7 00	Laborers, porters, &c..............	5 00
Blacksmiths	9 00		

* Males per year.   † Females per year.

The prices paid for the necessaries of life.

Articles.	Cost.	Articles.	Cost.
Flour................. .....per pound..	$0 03	Salt ....per pound..	02
Tea ....do....	40	Potatoes ....per bushel..	50
Sugar ....do....	08	Corn-meal..................per pound..	03
Rice...........................do....	05	Pork ....do....	10
Butter.........................do....	20	Oatmeal.........................do....	03
Sirup......................per gallon..	75	Coffee ....do....	?5
Prunes ....per pound..	08	Clothing outfits	15 00
Soap ....do....	05	Rent (average for laboring classes) per	
Vinegar ....per gallon..	25	month	4 00
Crackers ....per pound..	08		

The habits of the working class, as a general thing, are good and trustworthy and saving, and the causes which affect their habits good.

The feeling between the employé and the employer, as a general rule, is good and prosperous.

There are no organized conditions of labor in this district.

In regard to strikers in this district, there are none.

The working people purchase where they choose, paid weekly in Canada funds.

There are no co-operative societies in this district.

As to the general condition of the working people, their homes are comfortable, food good, clothes good; their chances for bettering their condition good, if they would take the advantages offered.

As a general rule, no provisions are made for the working people in case of accident. The general relations prevailing between the employer and employed are good.

II. FACTORIES, MILLS, ETC.

Wages paid per week of seventy-two hours in factories or mills.

Occupations.	Average wages.	Occupations.	Average wages.
Clerks	$12 00	Workmen	$9 00

III. FOUNDRIES, MACHINE-SHOPS, AND IRON WORKS.

Wages paid per week in foundries, machine-shops, and iron works in this district.

Occupations.	Average wages.	Occupations.	Average wages.
Foremen	$12 00	Workmen	$9 00

VI. RAILWAY EMPLOYÉS.

Wages paid per month to railway employés (those engaged about stations, as well as those engaged on the engines and cars, linemen, railroad laborers, &c.) in Amherstburg.

Occupations.	Average wages.	Occupations.	Average wages.
Station-master	$75 00	Fireman	$50 00
Conductors	75 00	Telegraph operators	45 00
Engineers	90 00	Clerks	50 00
Brakeman	50 00		

VIII. Seamen's Wages.

Wages paid per eight months to seamen (officers and men)—distinguishing between ocean, coast, and river navigation, and between sail and steam—in the Amherstburg district.

Occupations.	Average wages.	Occupations.	Average wages.
STEAM CRAFTS.		**SAILING.**	
Captain	$1,000 00	Captain	$900 00
Mate	720 00	Mate	800 00
Engineer	840 00	Seaman	300 00
Second mate	600 00		
Seaman	240 00		

IX. Store and Shop Wages.

Wages paid per week of sixty hours in stores, to males and females, in Amherstburg.

Occupations.	Average wages.	Occupations.	Average wages.
Clerks, male	$8 00	Clerks, female	None.

X. Household Wages in Towns and Cities.

Wages paid per week to household servants (towns and cities) in this district.

Occupations.	Average wages.	Occupations.	Average wages.
HOTELS.		**PRIVATE HOUSES.**	
Clerk			
Waiters	$12 00	Male	
Chambermaids	2 50	Female	
Porter	2 00		$3 00
Cook	3 00		2 00

XI. Agricultural Wages.

Wages paid to agricultural laborers and household (country) servants in Amherstburg district, with board and lodging.

Occupations.	Average wages.	Occupations.	Average wages.
Farm laborers, male, per month	$30 00	Household servants, female, per week	$3 00

XII. Government Departments and Offices.

Wages paid per year to employés in Government departments and offices—exclusive of tradesmen and laborers—in Amherstburg, Canada.

Occupations.	Average wages.	Occupations.	Average wages.
Collector of customs	$1,500	Postmaster	$800
Surveyor of customs	1,000	Light-house keeper	500
Landing masters	600		

XV. PRINTERS AND PRINTING OFFICES.

Statement showing the wages paid per week of sixty hours to printers (compositors, pressmen, proof-readers, &c.) in Amherstburg.

Occupations.	Lowest wages.	Highest wages.
Printers	$8 00	$9 00
Compositors	8 00	9 00
Pressmen	8 00	9 00
Proof-readers	8 00	9 00

JOSIAH TURNER,
United States Consul.

UNITED STATES CONSULATE,
Amherstburg, April 23, 1884.

BELLEVILLE.

REPORT BY CONSUL PRINCE.

As a rule, labor in this district is less than it is in the United States for same class, and as far as I am able to procure information prices are rather better than in 1878. I can give no reason for this, only that in 1878 the depression in business then prevailing no doubt affected the price of labor in Canada.

As a rule, also, the service is of a poorer nature than with us in the United States. The laborer here seems to dictate, so far as his manner of service is concerned, as competition is not keen enough to keep him up to what would be called first-class service.

As a generality, ordinary work is slowly done; in many instances imperfectly unless closely superintended. Many who could earn more do not seem to care to.

In the department of home servants the service is poor; farm labor but ordinary. The usual causes for destitution, mainly drink, prevail to a great extent here, and a sort of desire to do as little as possible for the amounts paid is, I think, a fault quite prevalent. A mechanic or laborer can live here at a moderate expense, though food prices are higher in the same proportion—about as labor—than in 1878.

Rents are moderate; a good tenement in a "terrace or block," with from five to seven rooms, can be had from $5 to $7 per month. I have also lately inspected some houses, newly built—brick, 44 by 24 feet, in lot of 64 by 32 feet—containing three rooms and hall on first floor and six bedrooms on second floor; house well finished; good cellar, hard and soft water (cistern and well), wood-house and shed; very neat, comfortable tenement, that rented for $10 and $12 per month.

These are, of course, exceptional, yet there are others equally roomy though not quite so well finished, and some of them in better locations, to be had at the same price.

The poorer classes of tenements, say from two to four rooms, can be had from $2 to $3.50 per month. Very few of these tenements have any ground attached.

The Knights of Labor have an organization here, but I do not see that it has any appreciable effect. The Molders' Union regulate prices in the stove works.

No strikes have occurred since I have resided here. The laboring classes are free to purchase their necessaries where they choose, very little being done in the way of "store pay."

No co-operative societies are in operation in this district.

The hours of labor are 10 hours per day, although on Saturday laborers are dismissed from 4 to 5 o'clock. The public offices here—customs, internal revenue, and inspector of weights and measures—are open from 9 a. m. to 4 p. m.; the post-office from 7.30 a. m. to 6.30 p. m.

The banks and the custom-house close at 1 o'clock on Saturday.

The right of suffrage here is given to all who own, rent, or occupy a tenement, the value of which in cities must be $400, for townships $300, and incorporated villages $200, or if he be assessed on an income of $400.

The rate of taxation in this city the present year is 15 mills, and it has been as high as 19 mills; about 17 to 18 is the average. This includes all taxes—city, school, and state. The rate of taxation in the county, outside of city, for all purposes, is about 13 mills.

A system of promotion exists here in some branches, based to a great extent in length of service. It is confined mostly to the railways and banks, and a benefit fund exists amongst the employers of the Grand Trunk Railway. The Bank of Montreal has a superannuation and pension fund, now amounting to several hundred thousand dollars. The salaries of all employés are taxed 3 per cent. for this fund.

A system of superannuation and gratuities exist in the civil service of Canada, a certain per cent. of each employé's pay being retained for the fund. This insures a certain annual allowance or a fixed gratuity on retirement.

I have thought it well, in view of the interest attaching to the movement for civil service in our own country, to present an epitome of the acts relating to the civil service, and the superannuation allowances of Canada. It will be observed that the act covers about all the employés of the Government except the heads of departments, who are supposed to retire on a change of Government.

THE CIVIL SERVICE IN CANADA.

The act providing for the civil service in Canada divides the service into two divisions:

The first, or "inside departmental division," comprises the employés mentioned in Schedule A employed in the several departments at Ottawa and in the office of the auditor-general.

The second, or "outside departmental division," comprises employés of classes mentioned in Schedule B, and who are employed otherwise than on the departmental staffs at Ottawa.

Schedule A.—(a) Deputy heads of departments; (b) officers who have special, professional, or testimonial qualifications; (c) chief clerks; (d) first-class clerks; (e) second-class clerks; (f) third-class clerks; (g) messengers, packers, and sorters.

The yearly salaries of this division are as follows:

Occupations.	Lowest.	Highest.
Deputy heads of departments	$3,200	$4,000
Chief clerks	1,800	2,400
First-class clerks	*1,400	1,800
Second-class clerks	†1,100	1,400
Third-class clerks	‡400	1,000
Messengers, packers, and sorters	§300	500

* An annual increase of $50 till the pay reaches $1,800.
† An annual increase of $50 till the pay reaches $1,400.
‡ An annual increase of $50 till the pay reaches $1,000.
§ An annual increase of $30 till the pay reaches $500.

Schedule B comprises all the officers, clerks, and employés here enumerated, and such other officers in the lower grades as may be determined by order in council.

Occupations.	Lowest.	Highest.
Customs department.		
Inspectors..	$1, 600	$2, 000
Collectors	400	4, 000
Surveyors	1, 200	2, 500
Chief clerks	1, 200	2, 000
Clerks	600	1, 200
Chief landing waiters...............................	800	1, 200
Landing waiters....................................	600	1, 000
Gaugers	600	1, 200
Chief lockers	800	1, 200
Lockers	400	800
Tide surveyors	800	1, 000
Tide waiters.......................................	400	600
Preventive officers.................................	400	600
Messengers..	200	500
Appraisers	800	2, 000
Assistant appraisers................................	600	1, 500
Inland revenue department.		
Chief inspector.....................................	....	3, 000
Inspector of distilleries.............................	....	2, 500
District inspectors..................................	2, 000	2, 500
Collectors	500	2, 200
Deputy collectors..................................	400	1, 500
Clerks (accountants)	600	1, 200
Special class excisemen............................	....	1, 200
First, second, and third-class excisemen	600	1, 000
Probationary excisemen............................	....	500
Messengers..	200	500

For surveys of important manufacturing establishments an additional salary for the special class excisemen who perform that duty, not exceeding $200 per annum.

Occupations.	Annual pay.
Post-office department.	
Chief inspector.....................................	$2, 800
First class :	
On appointment................................	2, 200
After ten years' service.......................	2, 400
After twenty years' service....................	2, 600
Second class :	
On appointment................................	2, 000
After ten years' service	2, 200
After twenty years' service	2, 400
Assistant post-office inspector :	
On appointment................................	1, 000
After ten years' service.......................	1, 200
After twenty years' service	1, 500

Salaries of clerks in post-office inspector's office the same as for clerks in city post-offices.

RAILWAY MAIL CLERKS.

Class.	On appointment.		After two years' service.		After five years' service.		After ten years' service.	
	Day service.	Night service.	Day service.	Night service.	Day service.	Night service.	Day service.	Night service.
First class..........	$720	$880	$800	$1, 000	$800	$1, 100	$960	$1, 200
Second class.......	600	720	640	800	720	880	800	1, 000
Third class	480	660	520	640	560	700	640	800

In addition to regular salary an allowance not exceeding half a cent a mile for every mile traveled on duty in the post-office cars.

MARINE MAIL CLERKS.

Class.	On appointment.		After two years.		After five years.		After ten years.		After fifteen years.	
	Salary.	*Trip allowance.	Salary.	Trip allowance.	Salary.	Trip allowance.	Salary.	Trip allowance.	Salary.	Trip allowance.
First class.......	$480	$80	$560	$80	$600	$80	$800	$100	$1,000	$100
Second class.....	360	†50	420	50	....	....	....	....	....	....

* "Trip" means the round voyage from Quebec or Halifax to Liverpool and return.
† Only one-half, or $25, to be allowed whilst learning duty.

POST-OFFICES.

	Lowest.	Highest.
City postmasters.		
Class 1, where postage collections exceed $80,000	....	$2,600
Class 2, where postage collections are from $60,000 to $80,000	....	2,400
Class 3, where postage collections are from $40,000 to $60,000....	....	2,200
Class 4, where postage collections are from $20,000 to $40,000......	....	2,000
Class 5, where postage collections are less than $20,000	*$1,400	1,800
Assistant postmasters.		
Class 1......................	....	2,000
Class 2......................	....	1,800
Class 3......................	....	1,600
Class 4......................	....	1,400
Class 5......................	1,100	1,400
Clerks in city post-offices.		
Third class†......................	400	800
Second class ‡......................	900	1,200
First class §......................	1,200	1,500
Letter-carriers and messengers.		
Box collectors and porters ‖	300	600

*$1,400 to $1,800, as the postmaster-general may determine. These salaries are not supplemented by any allowance or perquisite whatever.
† By annual increment of $40.
‡ By annual increment of $50.
§ Specific duties in each case, with fixed salaries, to be determined by the postmaster-general. No salary shall be less than $1,200 or more than $1,500.
‖ By annual increment of $30.

INSPECTOR OF PENITENTIARIES.

The same scale as post-office inspector. The salaries of the employés belonging to the second or "outside division" of other departments than those enumerated above shall be fixed by the governors in council.

SUPERANNUATION.

The superannuation of persons employed in the civil service of Canada is provided for by statute, a general digest of which is as follows:

The superannuation of any civil servant shall be preceded by an inquiry by the treasury board:

Whether the person it is proposed to superannuate is eligible within the meaning of the act.

Whether his superannuation will result in benefit to the service, and is therefore in the public interest; or

Whether it has become necessary in consequence of his mental or physical infirmity. And no civil servant shall be superannuated unless the board report that he is eligible within the meaning of the act, and that such superannuation will be in the public interest.

The different sections of the act provide as follows:

First. Superannuation may be granted to any person having served ten years and upward, or being incapacitated by bodily infirmity, the allowance being calculated on his average yearly salary during the then last three years, not exceeding the following rates: If he has served ten years, and less than eleven years, an annual allowance of ten-fiftieths of such average salary; if for eleven years, and under twelve years, an annual allowance of eleven-fiftieths thereof, and a further addition of one-fiftieth of such average for each additional year of service up to thirty-five years, when an annual allowance of thirty-five-fiftieths may be granted, but no addition can be made for any service beyond thirty-five years. If the service has not been continuous, the periods during interruption are not to be counted.

Second. Provides that in case of any person who has entered the service over 40 years of age and who is possessed of some peculiar professional or other qualification requisite for the office to which appointed and not ordinarily to be acquired in the service, there may be added to his actual years of service, any number of years not exceeding ten, for the purpose of superannuation.

Third. Provides that for the payment of superannuations, there shall be an abatement made from all salaries under this act of 4 per cent. on each salary of $600 and upward, and of $2\frac{1}{2}$ per cent. on all less than $600, but such abatement shall not be made after thirty-six years of service.

Fourth. Provides that full superannuation allowance shall be granted only to those who shall have been subject to such abatement during ten years and upward. The allowance to any person who has not paid it, or have paid for a less period, is subject to a diminution of one-twentieth for every year less than ten during which he has not paid it.

Fifth. Retirement is compulsory on any person to whom the superannuation allowance is offered, and such offer is not considered as implying censure; nor shall any person be considered as having any absolute right to such allowance, but it is granted only on condition of good and faithful service during the time on which it is calculated. Nothing, however, is understood to impair the right of dismissal.

Sixth. Provides that if any person is constrained to apply through infirmity of mind or body to quit the service before the period at which a superannuation allowance ought to be granted to him, the council may allow him a grant not exceeding one month's pay for each year of his service; and if in case of bodily injury received without his own fault while in the public service, he may be allowed by the council a gratuity not exceeding three months' pay for every two years' service, or a superannuation allowance not exceeding one-fifth of his average salary during the then last three years.

Seventh. Provides that if any person to whom the foregoing enactments apply is removed from office in consequence of its abolition, the governor in council may grant him such gratuity or superannuation allowance as will fairly compensate him for his loss of office, not exceeding such as he would have been entitled to had he retired in consequence of permanent infirmity of body or mind after adding ten years to his actual term of service.

Eighth. Provides that any person receiving a superannuation allowance, and being under sixty years of age, and not disabled bodily or mentally, shall be liable to be called upon to fill in any part of Canada any public office or situation for which his previous services render him eligible, and not lower in rank or emolument than that from which he retired ; and if he refuse or neglect so to do, his allowance is forfeited.

All allowance and gratuities under this act are payable out of the consolidated revenue fund of Canada, and a statement thereof made before Parliament the session next after grant or payment.

A civil servant in Canada is prohibited from voting for members of Parliament; *i. e.*, if he is in the provincial service he may not vote for a provincial member, if in the Dominion service he may not vote for the members of the Dominion Parliament. He has the right to vote for municipal officers. It is held that thus divorcing them from politics assures a more faithful service, and it is not expected they will be in any way active in politics, even in municipal matters.

The rates of compensation fixed for the majority of the positions seem low, yet it seems that the positions are coveted by and filled with persons of ability, and the social position of a Government employé is good.

As a class I have found the employés in the civil service of Canada intelligent, capable, and obliging, and while the positions are sought for, the manner of appointment—depending mainly on fitness—deprives it of much of the indiscriminate application that has characterized our service.

FREDERICK W. PRINCE,

Consul.

CONSULATE OF THE UNITED STATES,
Belleville, Canada, December 29, 1884.

I. GENERAL TRADES.

Wages paid per week of sixty hours, in Belleville, Canada.

Occupations.	Lowest.	Highest.	Average.
BUILDING TRADES.			
Bricklayers	$12 00	$15 00	$13 50
Hod-carriers			7 50
Masons	12 00	15 00	13 50
Tenders			7 50
Plasterers			12 00
Tenders			7 56
Slaters	10 50	12 00	11 00
Roofers	9 00	10 50	10 00
Tenders			7 50
Plumbers	10 50	13 50	12 00
Assistants			9 00
Carpenters			12 00
Gas-fitters			12 00
OTHER TRADES.			
Blacksmiths	9 00	13 50	12 00
Strikers			9 00
Brickmakers	6 50	9 00	7 50
Cigar-makers	8 00	12 00	10 00
Drivers:			
Draymen and teamsters	7 00	10 50	8 00
Cab, carriage, &c.	6 00	7 00	6 50
Horseshoers	9 00	13 50	12 00
Jewelers	10 00	15 00	12 50
Laborers, porters, &c.	5 40	7 50	6 00
Printers	5 50	10 00	8 50
Teachers, public schools			
Saddle and harness makers	9 00	12 00	10 00

Wages paid per week of sixty hours, in Belleville, Canada—Continued.

Occupation.	Lowest.	Highest.	Average.
OTHER TRADES – Continued.			
Stevedores	$6 00	$9 00	$7 50
Telegraph operators	7 50	15 00	12 50
Tinsmiths	9 00	13 50	12 00
Teachers, public schools, male per year	3 00	5 50	4 50
Teachers, public schools, female per year	2 75	4 50	3 50
Teachers, public schools, city, female	3 00	4 50	3 75
Teachers, city, male	6 00	7 50	6 50
Teachers, city high school	6 00	11 00	8 50
Lumbermen, winter wages in camps:			
Chopper ⎫			
Skidder ⎬ Per month with board	10 00	15 00	12 50
Sawyer ⎭			
Summer wages, driving logs	26 00	35 00	30 00
Cooks for above	30 00	37 50	35 00
Foremen, both winter and summer	50 00	65 00	55 00

*In the high schools of Ontario if the amount of wages exceeds $2,000, 45 per cent. of the amount is paid by the provincial government.

III. FOUNDRIES, MACHINE-SHOPS, AND IRON WORKS.

Wages paid per week of fifty-eight hours in foundries, machine-shops, and iron works in Belleville, Canada.

Occupations.	Lowest.	Highest.	Average.
Stove foundry.			
Engineer			$12 00
Melter			12 00
Polisher			10 50
Tinsmiths ⎫			
Carpenters ⎬			9 00
Blacksmiths ⎭			
Pattern makers ⎫			13 50
Finishers ⎭			
Molders	$15 00	$18 00	16 50
Mounters	13 50	15 00	14 00
Iron foundry.			
Molders	9 00	12 00	10 50
Foreman			15 00
Pattern makers	12 00	15 00	13 00
Machinists	10 00	12 00	11 50
Blacksmiths	10 50	13 50	12 50
Boiler makers	12 00	13 50	13 00

VI. RAILWAY EMPLOYÉS.

Wages paid to railway employés (those engaged about stations as well as those engaged on the engines and cars, linemen, railroad laborers, &c.) in Belleville, Canada.

Occupations.	Lowest.	Highest.	Average.
Railway baggagemen	per day..	$1 00	$1 50	$1 25
Ticket clerk	do....	1 00	2 00	1 50
Freight checkers	do....	1 00	2 00	1 50
Porters	do....	1 00	1 50	1 25
Yard foremen	do....	1 00	2 00	1 50
Switchmen	do....	90	1 50	1 20
Conductors	do....	1 30	2 50	1 90
Brakemen	do....	90	1 80	1 35
Laborers	do....	90	1 50	1 20
Station agents	per annum..	500 00	1,500 00	....
Telegraph operators	do....	400 00	1,000 00	....
Freight clerks	do....	300 00	850 00	....

IX. STORE AND SHOP WAGES.

Wages paid per week of sixty-four hours in dry goods and grocery stores, wholesale or retail, to males and females, in Belleville, Canada.

Occupations.	Lowest.	Highest.	Average.
Salesmen	$7 50	$12 50	$10 00
Bookkeepers	10 50	12 50	11 00
MILLINERY DEPARTMENT.			
Milliners	4 00	8 00	5 50
Dressmakers	2 00	5 00	4 00
Tailoress			6 00
Fur sewers	3 50	5 00	4 00
Knitting factory girls	2 50	5 00	4 00

X. HOUSEHOLD WAGES IN TOWNS AND CITIES.

Wages paid per month or year to household servants (towns and cities) in Belleville, Canada.

Occupations.	Lowest.	Highest.	Average.
House servants (female)	$6 00	$8 00	$6 50

XI. AGRICULTURAL WAGES.

Wages paid to agricultural laborers and household (country) servants in Belleville, Canada; with or without board and lodging.

Occupations.	Lowest.	Highest.	Average.
Farm hand, with board...............per month..	$16 00	$20 00	$18 50
Farm hands, without board...............do....			25 50
Farm domestics, with board...............per week..	1 25	1 63	1 50
Farm hands during harvest, with board...............per day..	1 00	1 25	1 20

XII. CORPORATION EMPLOYÉS.

Wages paid to the corporation employés in the city of Belleville.

[A week of 58 hours.]

Occupations.	Lowest.	Highest.	Average.
Ordinary street hands...............per week..	$4 80	$7 50	$6 00
Sidewalk hands...............do....	1 00	1 75	9 00
Culvert hands...............do....	1 00	1 75	9 00
Engineers fire steamers, with residence, fuel, and lights, per annum ...			450 00
Stokers fire steamers...............do....			50 00

XIII. GOVERNMENT DEPARTMENTS AND OFFICES.

Wages paid per year to employés in Government departments and offices—exclusive of tradesmen and laborers—in Belleville, Canada.

Occupations.	Lowest.	Highest.	Average
Customs.			
Collector	....	....	1,200
Clerk	....	....	900
Landing waiter	....	....	600
Do.......	....	....	300
Preventive officer...	....	....	200
Internal revenue.			
Collector...	....	....	1,200
Deputy	....	....	1,000
Exciseman	....	....	980
Do...do....	....	....	600
Post-office.			
Postmaster	....	....	1,400
Assistant postmaster	....	....	800
Third-class clerk..	....	....	600
Do	....	....	560
Letter-carrier...	....	....	360
Inspector of weights and measures.........................	....	....	1,200

XIV. TRADES AND LABOR—GOVERNMENT EMPLOY.

Wages paid by the year to the trades and laborers in Government employ in Belleville, Canada.

Occupations.	Lowest.	Highest.	Average.
Janitor to public building, with residence in building	....	....	$600

XV. PRINTERS AND PRINTING OFFICES.

Statement showing the wages paid per week of sixty hours to printers (compositors, pressmen, proof-readers, &c.) in Belleville, Canada.

Occupations.	Lowest.	Highest.	Average.
Compositors, news..	$5 50	$10 00	$8 50
Pressmen	....	....	9 00
Foremen	12 00	14 00	13 00
Foremen, job..	....	....	12 00
Engineers, power press	....	....	7 00

CHATHAM.

REPORT BY COMMERCIAL AGENT BUFFINGTON.

I have the honor to submit herewith such information as I have been able to obtain on the subjects referred to in the "Labor Circular" of February 15th ultimo.

RATES OF WAGES.

The rates of wages current in the various trades and labor departments, represented in my district, will be found in the accompanying schedules, which have, as far as practicable, been prepared from data furnished by the employers of the labor specified and gleaned from inquiries among the workmen themselves. While an "average" is very difficult to arrive at, in some cases, the figures quoted will be a close approximation to the prevailing rates, the highest rates being rarely paid.

THE COST OF LIVING.

The prices of the necessaries of life in this part of Canada, when compared with the current rates of wages, are exceedingly high, and it is a matter for wonder how the more poorly paid among the workingmen, and multitudes who have been unable to obtain employment during the past severe winter, contrived to subsist. It is generally conceded that the season just past has been the hardest one on laborers for many years; in this part of Canada the failure in crops was more marked than in the east, and, of course, intensified their sufferings.

Clothing is rather cheaper than two or three years ago, but the decline in prices has been consequent on the general stagnation of trade and the glut in the cotton and woolen market of the Dominion; so that it can scarcely be said that the decline in the prices of wearing material, under the circumstances, inured to the benefit of labor, as with that decline came sweeping reductions in the number of men employed and in the hours of labor, as well as the general reduction in wages. A decline in the cost of the commodities used by the wage earners is little to their advantage when the causes which combine to bring it about take from them the greater proportion of the scanty means at their disposal for their purchase.

I quote a few of the prices of the staple articles of food by way of illustrating the necessary narrowness of the margin between receipts and expenditure, even in the case of the most economical and steady wage worker who has a family depending upon him for a livelihood: Flour, $3 to $3.50 per hundred weight; beefsteak, 12½c. to 15c.; beef, roast, 12½c. to 15c.; ditto, boiling, 8c. to 10c.; pork, per quarter, 9c. to 10c.; retail, roast, 12½c. to 15c.; bacon, 15c. to 17c.; hams, 17c. to 18c.; mutton, 12½c. to 15c.; potatoes, 50c. to 60c. per bushel; apples, 25c. to 30c. per peck; onions, $1 per bushel; parsnips, 75c. to $1 per bushel; eggs, per dozen, 25c. to 35c.; butter, 25c. to 32c. When these prices are taken into consideration it becomes evident that with a large number of the wage earners the practice of economy is not a matter of choice but rather of stern necessity.

WAGES PAST AND PRESENT.

Compared with that of the year 1878, the condition and prospects of labor are not as encouraging as could be wished for. That year was the culmination of a lengthened period of crop failures, local and general, and intensified by the prevailing world-wide financial stringency. But living expenses were light, the prices of food and clothing, fuel and rent being at a minimum, so that the wages paid—small though they were—bore at least a kind of proportion to the laborers' necessities. Thus it happens that although the wages paid are, in some instances, higher than those of 1878, the increase in the cost of living is such as to more than deprive the laborer of any advantage arising from that circumstance. Wages are rather lower now than a few months ago and the indications are that should anything occur to blight the crop prospects they will drop still lower. It is a common remark that "times are very tight" for labor, and if anything was required to convince of the fact the number of unemployed men to be seen walking the streets of the towns and villages would furnish sufficient evidence. The Dominion Government has agreed to advance the Canada Pacific Railway Company a loan of $30,000,000 to enable them to proceed with the construction of their road and branches, one of which is expected to pass through this town and connect their Credit Valley road, at Ingersoll, with the American system at Detroit, and without going out of my province to speculate on the wisdom of the grant or otherwise, or the probable effect of a road calculated to compete with other lines being heavily bonused by the Federal Government, I may say that it is the general opinion that in certain portions of the country the expenditure will act as a stimulus. In the meantime large numbers of the more enterprising workmen, recognizing the difficulties to be overcome, are betaking themselves to the prairies of the West, a goodly proportion settling on the American side in consequence of the greater liberality, stability, and more judicious administration of the settlement regulatious as compared with those of the Canadian Northwest.

HABITS OF THE WORKING CLASSES.

The habits of the working classes, generally speaking, are regular, and, as a rule, they are industrious, intelligent, and reliable. The only evil which afflicts them in any marked degree is that of intemperance; and that, perhaps, as slightly as in any portion of the continent where intoxicants are sold under license. Vigorous efforts are being put forth to bring a prohibitory measure before the people of this county, and, it is admitted by its opponents, with reasonable hopes of success. From the general satisfaction its operation has given in other counties in which it has been in force, and the fact that after lenghtened trial the attempts to repeal it have been overwhelmingly voted down, I incline to the opinion that its introduction will be beneficial.

FEELING BETWEEN EMPLOYER AND EMPLOYÉ.

The feeling between employer and employé is generally of the most cordial character. The desire for reciprocal benefits seems to influence both in their dealings.

LABOR ORGANIZATIONS.

With the single exception of the railway employés, I know of no organization of labor, in my district, comprising more than a few members of some of the more widely scattered associations. Organizations of capital to affect labor are equally conspicuous by their absence.

STRIKES AND THEIR EFFECTS.

It follows that there being no organizations of labor, and good feeling between employer and employé prevailing, such a contingency as a strike must be an untoward occurrence. With the exception of the railway hands there has been no striking in this district. The strike of the Grand Trunk Railway employés, some time ago, did not result in obtaining the concessions asked; but it has been the means of bringing about many reforms in the service. Wages have, however, even during the most active period, remained low, and at present the management propose a cut of 10 per cent. all around, and this after largely reducing the staff employed. I am informed that, profiting by the experiences of the last strike, and believing they were unfairly paid during the intervening period of the road's prosperity, the men have intimated that sooner than submit to the proposed cut (which would reduce some men's wages to considerably under $1 per day) the employés will go out on strike, and that in event of such an occurrence the Brotherhood of Locomotive Engineers will be with them. As the company, at this season of the year, is not in a position to cope with such a strike, it is extremely improbable that they will attempt to carry into effect the proposed reduction.

FREEDOM OF PURCHASE.

Workingmen are generally in the enjoyment of the fullest liberty to purchase where and how they please—customs regulations, of course, excepted. Some few firms who own stores and employ labor exercise an implied restraint in this particular; but the number is rapidly decreasing, and the system is unpopular.

PAYMENT OF LABOR.

When no contract is made specifying other terms, payments are made weekly, usually Saturdays. Railway hands are paid monthly, fifteen days' pay being held. Farm laborers seldom have regular times of payment, and in many cases draw what they require to use as wanted and the residue at the end of their term. Payments in bank notes, silver, or gold. American currency passes at par in all transactions, Government departments excepted, in this part of Canada. Such is not the case further east, where United States silver is subjected to a discount.

CO-OPERATIVE SOCIETIES.

Co-operative societies are represented in my district by a solitary specimen, the Grange, a kind of farmers' club and association for co-operative purchase. Mechanics and laborers have not found those ventures warranted, and the indifferent success attending the Grange, in which no small amount of capital has been invested, has not been calculated to promote experiments in that direction. The, at one time, dreaded effect of the "Grange stores" on general trade has passed away, and as far as relates to their influence on prices of or demand for merchandise they are a nullity.

GENERAL CONDITION.

The general condition of the laboring classes is not dissimilar to that of those of our Northern States. Wages, I believe, rule lower. Workmen interviewed say that it is next to impossible to save anything; and from the figures obtainable I am led to indorse the view that only in the most remunerative of the occupations named can a man of family maintain them in comfort and lay away a reserve fund.

SAFETY OF EMPLOYÉS.

The provisions for the safety of employés in mills and factories are wofully inadequate. I would scarcely overstate the case if I said there were none. In fact some of the railway companies oblige their employés, on hiring, to sign an agreement intended to release them from liability should the employé be injured or killed, while in their service, by any cause whatever. The courts, however, have decided that, in cases of carelessness on the part of the servants of the road at least, such contract shall be no bar to a suit for damages.

In mills and factories a very unsatisfactory neglect of the employés' interest is manifested. I note that acts for providing for the safety and general regulation of factory employés are now receiving eg slative consideration.

The sanitary influences to which labor is subjected come under the scrutiny of the local and provincial boards of health, and sanitation is so carefully attended to that it is almost a science in execution as well as theory. The police are health officers under the direction of the municipal and medical advisory boards and inspectors, armed with all necessary authority to make weekly visits to every part of the towns and villages. This house-to-house inspection—the inspectors being changed from one beat to another weekly—is productive of general cleanliness and conducive to the well-being of the community.

POLITICAL RIGHTS.

The workingmen enjoy all the rights and privileges political of the country. If a man's name appears on the assessment roll of the municipality of which he is a resident, as tenant or occupant of premises that entitles the owner thereof to a vote, he also is entitled to vote; and as his liberty is religiously guarded by the ballot system of voting, he has the privilege—and exercises it—of making himself felt in the country's legislation. The tendency of recent legislation has been to increase these privileges.

EMIGRATION.

The general cause of emigration is the settled conviction that in the existing condition and apparent prospects for the future there is but little hope that labor can secure a profit. The causes influencing their selection of objective points are varied, but the central one is to secure a home and a means of subsistence which will render them independent of the many circumstances which go to immediately affect labor. Many go to the manufacturing districts of the United States to seek a more liberal remuneration for their toil and skill—and it is an axiom here that first class men are better paid "in the States"—but large numbers go, as I have previously intimated, to settle and secure homes. I cannot speak for other parts of the country, but from this district the majority emigrating go to become American citizens. No less than six or eight railway agents devote their whole time to organizing and taking out parties from this locality. Thus early in the season several large parties have left for Dakota, Minnesota, and Iowa. There is considerble dissatisfaction with the regulations affecting Canadian northwest lands and their administration, the result of which is the diverting of the stream of very desirable emigrants into our northern States and Territories, where the regulations work more smoothly.

FEMALE LABOR.

The extent to which female labor is employed in my district is so limited that I would scarcely be justified in lengthening out this report by extended remarks on the subject. The number employed is small, and chiefly confined to public school teachers, clerks, music teachers, hotel and household cooks, laundresses, &c. In these employments they are subject to the same conditions and perform the same work as for service of a like nature in the United States. Their remuneration, however, is less generous and the field is much more circumscribed. They are not employed to such a degree as to affect the wages of male labor. To obtain employment outside of household service women require to possess a fair education.

GENERAL SUMMARY.

The general condition of labor in this district, which is pre-eminently an agricultural one, is unhealthy. Wages are low and employment scarce, while the necessaries of life are high. An improvement is looked for in the opening of the season, but I see no reason for anticipating more than a slight and temporary improvement at best. My opinion is based on the fact that the market for manufactures is glutted, and in consequence of that a surplus of labor is already at hand, so that a great increase in the rates of wages paid is not to be expected. Add to this the fact that the Canadian Government have already arranged for a large importation of "assisted emigrants" during the season, and the various British societies are preparing to supplement their efforts, and it will be admitted that the outlook for the wage-earner is not the most inviting. True, a great number of these emigrants soon find their way across the lines, while some go to the Northwest, but the fact remains that their continuous introduction on a market already overstocked cannot but be displacing and depressing to labor.

H. C. BUFFINGTON,
Commercial Agent.

UNITED STATES COMMERCIAL AGENCY,
Chatham, July, 1884.

I. GENERAL TRADES.

Wages paid per week of sixty hours in Chatham.

Occupations.	Lowest.	Highest.	Average.
BUILDING TRADES.			
Bricklayers	$10 00	$18 00	$12 00
Hod-carriers	6 00	8 00	7 50
Masons	12 00	20 00	13 50
Tenders	6 00	8 00	7 50
Plasterers	9 00	13 50	10 00
Tenders	6 00	8 00	7 50
Slaters	8 00	12 00	9 00
Roofers	7 50	10 00	9 00
Tenders	6 00	8 00	7 00
Plumbers	10 00	12 00	10 00
Assistants	7 00	8 50	7 50
Carpenters	9 00	12 00	10 00
Gas-fitters	9 00	12 00	10 00
OTHER TRADES.			
Bakers	7 50	10 00	9 00
Blacksmiths	8 50	12 00	9 00
Strikers	7 00	9 00	7 50
Book-binders	7 25	10 00	8 00
Brick-makers	8 00	12 00	9 00
Butchers	6 00	9 00	7 50
Cabinet-makers	7 50	12 00	9 00
Confectioners	8 00	12 00	8 50
Coopers	7 50	10 00	8 00
Draymen and teamsters, and cab and carriage drivers	6 00	9 00	7 50
Dyers	7 00	9 00	8 50
Gardeners	5 00	7 50	7 00
Horse-shoers	8 00	12 00	9 00
Jewelers	7 50	12 00	10 00
Laborers, porters, &c	6 00	8 50	7 25
Millwrights	8 00	12 00	10 00

Wages paid per week of sixty hours in Chatham—Continued.

Occupations.	Lowest.	Highest.	Average.
OTHER TRADES—Continued.			
Printers	$7 00	$12 00	$8 50
Teachers, public school	*200 00	*1, 000 00	*450 00
Saddle and harness makers	8 00	10 00	9 00
Tanners	7 50	10 00	9 00
Tailors	7 50	10 00	9 00
Telegraph operators	6 00	10 00	7 50
Weavers (outside of mills)	8 00	10 00	9 00
Shoemakers	7 50	9 00	8 25

* Per annum.

II. FACTORIES, MILLS, ETC.

Wages paid per week of sixty hours in factories or mills in Kent County, Ontario, Canada.

Occupations.	Lowest.	Highest.	Average.
Head sawyer or filer	$9 00	$15 00	$10 00
Engineer	7 50	10 00	8 50
General saw-mill hands	6 00	9 00	7 50
Stave-cutters	9 00	13 50	10 00
Handlers	4 00	6 00	5 00
Wood-working machine hands	7 50	9 00	8 00
Woolen-factory spinners	4 00	6 00	5 00
Weavers	4 00	8 00	7 50
Dyers and finishers	7 00	9 00	8 50

III.—FOUNDRIES, MACHINE-SKOPS, ANDIRON WORKS.

Wages paid per week of sixty hours in foundries, machine-shops, and iron works in Ken County, Ontario, Canada.

Occupations.	Lowest.	Highest.	Average.
Molders	$8 00	$10 00	$9 00
Laborers and assistants	7 50	9 00	8 00
Lathe hands	9 00	12 00	10 00
Vise-hands	8 00	11 00	9 00
Painters (fancy)	9 00	12 00	10 00
Wood-workers	8 00	10 00	9 00

VI. RAILWAY EMPLOYÉS.

Wages paid per month to railway employés (those engaged about stations, as well as those engaged on the engines and cars, linemen, railroad laborers, &c.) in Ontario, westerly part.

Occupations.	Lowest.	Highest.	Average.
Brakemen .... per month..	$22 00	$40 00	$32 00
Baggagemen .... do...	26 00	35 00	30 00
Conductors .... do...	40 00	65 00	50 00
Engineers .... do...	40 00	100 00	65 00
Firemen .... do...	30 00	45 00	35 00
Flag and switch men .... do...	26 00	32 00	30 00
Oilers .... do...	26 00	32 00	30 00
Operators .... do...	20 00	40 00	26 00
Section-men .... do...	26 00	35 00	30 00
Repairers (machinists) .... per day..	1 75	3 00	2 25
Station-masters .... per annum..	500 00	1, 000 00	....

IX. STORE AND SHOP WAGES.

Wages paid per week of sixty hours in dry goods and other stores, wholesale or retail, to males and females, in Kent County, Ontario, Canada.

Occupations.	Lowest.	Highest.	Average.
Salesmen	$6 50	$10 00	$7 50
Junior salesmen	3 50	6 00	4 50
Lady clerks	3 00	6 00	5 00
Milliners	6 00	9 00	7 00
Bookkeepers ....per annum	400 00	1,000 00	600 00

Tailoresses usally paid piece-work, as follows: Coat, $1.50; pants, 75 cents; vest, 75 cents.

X. HOUSEHOLD WAGES IN TOWNS AND CITIES.

Wages paid per week to household servants (towns and cities) in Kent County, Ontario, Canada.

Occupations.	Lowest.	Highest.	Average.
Laundresses	$2 00	$6 00	$3 00
Cooks (in hotels)	3 00	7 00	4 00
Cooks (private houses)	1 75	3 50	2 50
General household servants	1 50	2 50	2 00

XI. AGRICULTURAL WAGES.

Wages paid to agricultural laborers and household (country) servants in Kent County, Ontario, with or without board and lodging.

Occupations.	Lowest.	Highest.	Average.
Farm laborers when engaged by year (with board)	$150 00	$250 00	$200 00
Farm laborers when engaged for term of 6 months (with board) from April 1 to October 1	100 00	125 00	(*)
Farm laborers when engaged for harvest only, per day (with board)	1 25	2 50	1 75
Female household servants (per week)	1 00	2 00	1 50

* About $18 per month.

NOTE.—The number of females employed in household service in the farm residence is small.

XII. CORPORATION EMPLOYÉS.

Wages paid to the corporation employés in the city of Chatham, Ontario.

Occupations.	Lowest.	Highest.	Average.
Clerk ....per annum			$1,000 00
Police magistrate ....do			1,000 00
Treasurer ....do			600 00
Collector (commission)			½ of 1 p.c.
Assessors (three) each ....per annum			133 33
Chief of police ....do			750 00
Policemen ....do			450 00
Street surveyor ....do			450 00
Firemen ....do	$350 00	$450 00	
Workmen ....per week	6 00	8 00	7 50

XIII. GOVERNMENT DEPARTMENTS AND OFFICES.

*Wages paid per annum to employés in Government departments and offices (exclusive of trades-
men and laborers) in Chatham and Kent generally.*

Occupations.	Lowest.	Highest.	Average.
AT CHATHAM.			
Customs collector			$1,100 00
Landing waiter			800 00
Subcollectors	$400 00	$600 00	
AT WALLACEBURG.			
Customs collector			700 00
Landing waiter			600 00
Subcollector			400 00
District weights and measures inspection:			
Inspector			900 00
Subinspectors			500 00
District inland revenue:			
Collector			1,764 00
Two deputies, each at			980 04
Eight deputies, each at	686 00	900 00	
Gas inspector			508 81
Chatham postmaster			*2,100 00
County offices	10 00	300 00	
Clerk of Crown			†450 00
School inspectors	500 00	1,000 00	600 00
Light-house keepers	150 00	400 00	
Fishery officers	50 00	50 00	

       * And allowances of $640.   † And fees.

The above are actual salaries as given in the Government returns.

XV. PRINTERS AND PRINTING OFFICES.

*Wages paid per week of sixty hours to printers (compositors, pressmen, proof-readers, &c.)
in Kent County, Ontario.*

Occupations.	Lowest.	Highest.	Average.
Foreman	$9 00	$12 00	$10 00
Compositors	7 00	10 00	8 50
Compositors, per thousand ems	21	25	
Job printers	8 00	12 00	9 00
Pressmen	7 00	9 00	8 00
Feeders (youths)	4 50	6 00	5 00
Proof-readers	8 00	12 00	9 00
Apprentices	2 50	4 00	

HAMILTON.

REPORT BY CONSUL HAZLETON.

The rate of wages paid to the several classes of laborers employed
in this consular district I have been unable to obtain fully, as there is
no published statement giving the same in detail, and business men
whom I have asked for the information have varied considerably as to
the rates paid by them for labor of the same class, while others have
declined to furnish any statement of rates paid when requested to do so.

ACKNOWLEDGMENTS.

I am greatly indebted to the following parties for information kindly
furnished which appears in the inclosed tables, viz, Charles Stiff, manager of the Great Western Division of the Grand Trunk Railroad;

John Smith, agent of the Ontario Immigration Society; the Ontario Cotton Mills Company at Hamilton, the Dundas cotton mills at Dundas, the Stewart Stove Manufactory, and the Wanzer Sewing Machine Company at Hamilton, as shown by the tables inclosed.

COST OF LIVING.

The cost of living to the laboring classes varies considerably, owing to the kind of employment, habits, &c., of the employed. In this consular district most of the industrial pursuits demand hard labor. In this city are ten iron foundries employing about nine hundred workmen; cotton mills employing six hundred workmen; glass companies employing one hundred workmen; the Wanzer Sewing Machine Company employing two hundred and fifty workmen, besides many smaller manufactories of various kinds giving employment to a large number of laborers; all of whom require substantial living, consisting usually of meat with potatoes and bread twice a day. The third meal consists of some kind of bread with butter, or something taking its place. Nearly all use tea and coffee.

The retail prices of ordinary articles of food and raiment used by the working classes in this district are as follows, viz:

Articles.	Cost.	Articles.	Cost
Bacon ....per pound..	$0 10 to $0 13	Salt...................60 pounds..	$0 60 to $0 65
Ham ....do	12 to 15	Herrings ....barrel..	5 50 to 7 00
Shoulder ....do....	9 to 12	Fire-wood ....cords..	4 50 to 7 00
Beef..................... do....	8 to 12	Coal ....2,000..	6 00 to 6 50
Mutton....................do....	10 to 12	Coats, over	7 00 to 12 00
Veal......................do	8 to 12	Coats, under	4 50 to 6 50
Butter ....do....	15 to 22	Pants...........................	2 00 to 4 50
Cheese ....do....	10 to 13	Vests...........................	1 00 to 2 00
Coffee............... do....	25 to 40	Shirts, flannel.................	1 50 to 2 00
Codfish ....do....	7 to 8	Shirts, cotton	75 to 1 00
Mustard...................do....	30 to 35	Shirts, under..................	25 to 35
Pepper....................do....	20 to 25	Drawers, woolen	90 to 1 00
Rice ....do....	5 to 6	Hats, felt	75 to 1 25
Soap .... do ...	5 to 6	Socks, worsted................	25 to 35
Sugar ....do....	6 to 9	Socks, cotton	10 to 15
Tea, green................ do....	40 to 50	Blankets..................pair..	3 00 to 4 50
Tea, black................do....	25 to 50	Flannel ....yard..	30 to 35
Tobacco ....do....	30 to 50	Cotton shirtings..........do....	10 to 12
Corn meal ....100 pounds..	1 75 to 2 00	Cotton sheetings, wide..........	20 to 25
Flour.....................do ...	2 50 to 2 75	Canadian Tweed cloth	60 to 1 00
Buckwheat flour ....do....	3 00 to 3 50	Shoes, men's .... per pair..	2 00 to 2 50
Bread ....2-pound loaf..	5 to 6	Shoes, women's.............do	1 25 to 1 75
Milk .... quart..		Boots, men's ....do...	2 00 to 4 00
Eggs ....dozen..	6	Boots, women's ....do ...	1 75 to 3 00
Oatmeal ....100 pounds..	15 to 17	Rubbers, men's	80 to 1 00
Potatoes..............60 pounds..	2 00 to 2 25	Rubbers, women's	70 to 80
	60 to 80		

Those who have families and keep house, rent dwellings with four room for $8 per month; with six rooms, from $9 to $12 per month. Board may be obtained for $4 per week.

WAGES PAST AND PRESENT.

As between the rates of wages now and those which prevailed in 1878 and since that time the present rates are somewhat higher than in 1878. After the depression of 1878 business steadily improved until 1883, when it began to decline and has so continued until the present time, producing great depression in manufactures generally. The price of labor, however, does not seem to decline materially in consequence. The employers have retained their best men as a general rule, expecting

an increase of business in the early autumn, while the discharged employés have found temporary employment on the land and are stimulated by the hope, which is very strong, that business will soon revive.

HABITS OF THE WORKING CLASSES.

The habits of the working classes are generally to be commended.
Many of them are steady and trustworthy, saving something for sickness
and old age. The causes which affect their habits for good or evil are
various. On the one hand are strong religious influences, excellent public
schools, an active, earnest feeling in favor of temperance and good conduct; while on the other hand is much vice, much licentiousness, many
dram-shops and gaming-places.

FEELING BETWEEN EMPLOYER AND EMPLOYÉ.

The feeling which prevails between the employer and employé is generally kindly. The Canadian law authorizes the arrest and imprisonment of indentured apprentices for absence without leave. Public
sentiment, however, is generally opposed to its enforcement, and it is
seldom resorted to for punishment. The effect of this feeling on the
general and particular community is good.

LABOR ORGANIZATIONS.

In this district until last year there was no organized condition of
labor. Then for the first time laboring men of every class, numbering
about two thousand, marched in procession through the streets of Hamilton to Dundwin Park, where they passed a day of enjoyment, listened
in the evening to an address on "the dignity of labor," and returned to
their duties on the day following. This year the same programme has
been repeated without increase of numbers. I cannot learn that this
organization has attempted to change the status of anything. Persons
are employed and discharged without reference to other employés.

STRIKES AND FOOD PURCHASES AND CO-OPERATION.

Strikes have never occurred in this consular district.
Working people are free to purchase the necessaries of life wherever
they choose. No conditions in this regard are imposed by the employers. Wages are paid weekly or monthly to the laborer in Canadian
currency. There are no co-operative societies here.

GENARAL CONDITION OF THE WORKING CLASSES.

The general condition of the working people here is comfortable.
The cities and large manufacturing villages in this district afford a substantial market for the produce of the farms, and give employment to
a great variety of laborers at rates of wages which enables them to provide comfortable homes with good food and clothing for themselves and
families, and to save something for sickness and old age.

SAFETY OF EMPLOYÉS.

No means are provided for the safety of employés in factories, mills,
or railroads, &c., in case of accident, excepting the ordinary stairways,
doors, and windows. In case of accident, hospitals and other suitable
places are provided where the injured may be taken and cared for.

I am unable to learn that the employer gives especial consideration to the moral and physical well-being of the employés, the ability to perform acceptably the duties required of the employé being generally satisfactory to the employer. Their general relations are not intimate.

POLITICAL RIGHTS.

Political rights in this country are enjoyed principally through property, so that the workingman rarely has anything to do with politics.

CAUSES OF EMIGRATION.

The causes which lead to the emigration of the working people are various, the desire to better their condition being the principal. Farmers know that land is cheaper in certain parts of the United States than here. Mechanics also realize that every class of labor is demanded in the United States, and when overcrowded here emigrate with full confidence as to the result.

FEMALE LABOR.

I am unable, because I can find no statistics, to give a satisfactory statement showing the number or approximate number of women and children employed in my district. In the cities they are employed in considerable numbers as saleswomen in dry-good stores at wages ranging from $4 to $6 a week. Many find employment in making clothing of all kinds by the piece for ready-made clothing houses, taking the cut garments to their homes, where, with the sewing-machines, they earn from $6 to $10 a week. The tobacco paper bag, and cotton factories of the district also afford employment to a large number at from $4 to $6 a week.

In the Hamilton public schools one hundred female teachers are employed at salaries running from $188 to $435 a year, and forty at salaries running from $75 to $133 a year.

The employment of women has no perceptible effect upon the wages of men. Its effect on general social and industrial conditions is beneficial.

J. F. HAZLETON,
Consul.

UNITED STATES CONSULATE,
Hamilton, August 4, 1884.

I. GENERAL TRADES.

Wages paid per week of sixty hours in Hamilton.

Occupations.	Lowest.	Highest.	Average.
BUILDING TRADES.			
Bricklayers	$15 00	$16 50	$15 50
Hod-carriers	6 00	7 50	7 00
Masons	15 00	16 50	15 50
Tenders	6 00	7 50	7 00
Plasterers	9 00	12 00	10 00
Tenders	6 00	7 50	7 00
Slaters	15 00	16 50	15 50
Roofers	9 00	12 00	10 50
Tenders	6 00	7 50	7 00
Plumbers	9 00	12 00	10 50
Assistants	6 00	7 50	7 00
Carpenters	10 50	12 00	11 00
Gas-fitters	9 00	15 00	12 00
OTHER TRADES.			
Bakers	7 50	10 50	9 00
Blacksmiths	9 00	15 00	10 50
Strikers	6 00	7 50	7 00
Bookbinders	9 00	15 00	12 00
Brickmakers	9 00	12 00	10 00
Brewers	9 00	15 00	10 50
Butchers	7 50	9 00	8 00
Brass founders	10 50	15 00	12 00
Cabinet-makers	9 00	15 00	10 50
Confectioners	7 50	9 00	8 00
Cigar-makers	6 00	9 00	7 50
Coopers	9 00	10 50	9 50
Drivers:			
Draymen and teamsters	6 00	9 00	7 50
Cab, carriage	6 00	9 00	7 50
Street railways	*7 50	7 50	7 50
Dyers	4 50	15 00	6 75
Gardeners	6 00	9 00	7 50
Hatters	7 50	10 50	8 00
Horseshoers	10 50	18 00	12 00
Jewelers	7 50	10 50	9 00
Laborers, porters, &c	1 00	1 25	1 10
Millwrights	12 00	15 00	13 50
Printers	10 00	10 00	10 00
Teachers, public schools	†75 00	†833 36	†303 58
Saddle and harness makers	8 00	12 00	10 00
Sailmakers	8 00	12 00	10 00
Stevedores	9 00	13 50	11 00
Tanners	8 00	12 00	10 00
Tailors	9 00	12 00	10 50
Telegraph operators	9 00	15 00	12 00
Tinsmiths	8 00	12 00	10 00
Weavers (outside of mills)	3 00	7 50	6 00

* Of 84 hours.   † Per year.

II. FACTORIES, MILLS, ETC.

Wages paid per week of sixty hours in factories or mills in Hamilton, Canada.

Occupations.	Lowest.	Highest.	Average.
Card room:			
Overseers	$9 25	15 85	12 00
Carders	3 00	8 10	6 00
Scutchers	5 40	6 75	5 70
Drawers	3 00	5 00	4 20
Stubbers	3 50	6 00	4 80
Rovers	3 50	6 00	5 00
Throstle room:			
Overseers	4 80	11 00	8 00
Dolphers	1 25	3 60	1 50
Spinners	2 75	5 40	3 60
Ruling room:			
Overseers	3 00	18 00	5 00
Packers	2 70	4 50	3 25
Dressers	7 00	10 80	8 75
Winders	2 00	5 00	3 75
Reelers	3 50	5 50	5 00
Doublers	4 50	4 50	4 50
Spoolers	2 00	3 50	2 75
Warpers	2 00	5 50	4 75
Twisters	3 75	6 50	5 50
Weaving room:			
Overseers	5 40	15 00	9 50
Weavers	3 00	8 00	4 75
Mule room:			
Overseers	2 00	13 50	4 50
Spinners	6 00	13 50	10 75
Wareroom	4 50	9 25	5 00
Dye house	4 50	15 00	6 75
Mechanics	6 00	13 50	12 00
Laborers	4 00	6 50	5 00
Firemen	6 00	9 00	7 50
Engineers	7 50	18 00	10 50

III. FOUNDRIES, MACHINE-SHOPS, AND IRON WORKS.

Wages paid per week of sixty hours in foundries, machine-shops, and iron works in Hamilton, Canada.

Occupations.	Lowest.	Highest.	Average.
Molders	$10 50	16 50	12 00
Pattern-fitters	10 50	16 50	12 00
Stove-mounters	7 50	14 00	9 00
Machinists	7 50	14 00	8 25
Scale-makers	7 50	17 50	9 00
Polishers	9 00	12 00	10 50
Japanners	12 00	13 50	12 00
Tinsmiths	9 00	11 25	10 50
Nickel-platers	4 50	9 00	6 00
Laborers	6 75	7 50	7 20
Sewing-machines:			
Foremen	12 00	24 00	17 22
Machinists	12 00	15 00	13 32
Fitters	9 00	20 40	14 58
Polishers	5 40	18 00	11 40
Laborers	7 50	9 00	1 37
Carpenters	11 25	11 25	11 25
Varnishers, iron	6 00	9 00	7 50
Molders	9 00	18 00	12 00
Packers	7 50	14 22	9 72
Varnishers, wood	9 00	19 50	10 74
Blacksmiths	10 50	15 00	12 96
Storekeepers	10 50	12 00	11 00
Japanners	7 50	14 00	9 00
Nickel-platers	7 50	13 50	9 00

IV. GLASS WORKERS.

Wages paid per week of forty-two hours to glass-workers in Hamilton, Canada.

Occupations.	Lowest.	Highest.	Average.
Blowers	$11	$35	....
Laborers (boys)	3	5	....

VI. RAILWAY EMPLOYÉS.

Wages paid to railway employés (those engaged about stations, as well as those engaged on the engines and cars, linemen, railroad laborers, &c.), in Hamilton, Canada.

Occupations.	Lowest.	Highest.	Average.
Conductors ......per day..	$2 00	$2 50	$2 25
Brakemen ......do....	1 30	1 60	1 40
Baggagemen, train ......do....	1 40	1 60	1 50
Baggagemen, station ......do ...	1 15	1 50	1 25
Engineers ......do....	2 75	3 00	2 87½
Firemen ......do....	1 60	1 80	1 70
Engine cleaners ......do....	1 00	1 00	1 00
Switchmen ......do....	1 15	1 60	1 40
Yardmen ......do....	1 60	2 25	1 75
Trackmen ......do....	1 10	1 10	1 10
Porters ......do....	1 00	1 25	1 10
Section foremen ......do ...	1 50	1 50	1 50
Track foremen ......per year..	900 00	1,000 00	850 00
Train dispatchers ......do....	600 00	1,260 00	1,000 00
Station agents ......do....	420 00	1,000 00	600 00
Clerks ......do....	300 00	1,000 00	600 00
Telegraph operators ......do....	360 00	600 00	480 00

IX. STORE AND SHOP WAGES.

Wages paid per week of sixty hours in dry goods stores, wholesale or retail, to males and females, in Hamilton, Canada.

Occupations.	Lowest.	Highest.	Average.
Clerks	$2 00	$20 00	$7 00
Dress-making	2 00	8 00	5 00
Mantle-making	2 00	8 00	5 00
Shirt-making	2 00	8 00	5 00
Quilt-making	2 00	8 00	5 00
Underclothing making	2 00	8 00	5 00

X. HOUSEHOLD WAGES IN TOWNS AND CITIES.

Wages paid per month to household servants (towns and cities) in Hamilton consular district.

Occupations.	Lowest.	Highest.	Average.
Cooks	$9 00	$12 00	$10 50
General servants	7 00	8 00	7 50
Dairy maids	7 00	8 00	7 50
Laundry maids	8 00	9 00	8 50
Housemaids	7 00	9 00	8 00

XI. Agricultural Wages.

Wages paid per month to agricultural laborers and household (country) servants in Hamilton consular district, with board and lodging.

Occupations.	Lowest.	Highest.	Average.
Farm laborers	$12	$15	
Harvest hands	25	35	
Household servants	6	10	

XII. Corporation Employés.

Wages paid to the corporation employés in the city of Hamilton, Canada.

Occupations.	Lowest.	Highest.	Average.
Fire department ....per annum..	$122 10	$1,000 00	$433 00
Police magistrate...........................do....	2,000 00	2,000 00	2,000 00
Chief of police.............................do....	1,200 00	1,200 00	1,200 00
Policemen (54) ....do ..	91 24	723 00	460 00
Teachers, high school (17) ....do....	60 00	1,433 00	702 00
Teachers, public schools (112) ....do....	75 00	833 36	303 58
Clerk, public schools......................do....	300 00	300 00	300 00
Treasurer, public schools..................do ..	300 00	300 00	300 00
Mayor ....do....			1,200 00
City clerk.................................do....			1,800 00
Assistant clerk ....do....			540 00
Do ....do....			100 00
City treasurer ....do....			1,100 00
Do ....do....			437 00
Assistant treasurer ....do....			413 00
Tax collector ....do....			1,100 00
Assistant collector........................do ..			600 00
Do ....do .			550 00
Do ....do....			500 00
City messenger ....do....			600 00
City engineer ....do....			650 00
Street laborers ....per day...	1 25	1 25	1 25
Street inspector...........................per annum..			624 00
Superintendent cemetery ....do....			713 00
Pound-keeper ....do....			256 00
Superintendent house of refuge ....do....			350 00
Superintendent wood market ....do....			600 00

XIII. Government Departments and Offices.

Wages paid per annum to employés in Government departments and offices—exclusive of tradesmen and laborers—in Hamilton, Canada.

Occupations.	Lowest.	Highest.	Average.
Collector of customs......................	$2,600	$2,600	$2,600
Surveyor of customs	1,500	1,500	1,500
Clerks, customs (7).......................	600	1,400	943
Appraisers, customs......................	1,000	1,200	1,100
Landing waiters (5).......................	600	850	683
Searcher and packer......................	600	600	600
Messenger	450	450	450
Packer	550	550	550
Inspectors	1,600	2,000	1,800
Gaugers..................................	600	1,200	900
Lockers..................................	400	1,200	800
Inland revenue :			
Chief inspector.....................	3,000	3,000	3,000
Inspector of distilleries..............	2,500	2,500	2,500
District inspectors...................	2,000	2,500	2,250
Collectors	500	2,200	1,350
Clerks (accountants)	600	1,200	
Post-office :			
Postmaster...........................	2,400	2,400	2,400
Assistant postmaster.................	1,500	1,500	1,500
Clerks in city post-office............	400	1,400	

XV. PRINTERS AND PRINTING OFFICES.

Statement showing the wages paid to printers (compositors, pressmen, proof-readers, &c.) in Hamilton, Canada.

[Per week of sixty hours.]

Occupations.	Lowest.	Highest.	Average.
Compositors:			
Evening papers ....per M..	$0 28	$0 28	$0 28
Morning papers ....do...	30	30	30
Weekly papers ....per week..	10 00	10 00	10 00
All weekly employés ....do....	10 00	10 00	10 00

KINGSTON.

REPORT BY CONSUL TWITCHELL.

I. GENERAL TRADES.

Wages paid per week of sixty hours in Kingston, Canada.

Occupations.	Lowest.	Highest.	Average.
BUILDING TRADES.			
Bricklayers	$12 00	$16 50	$14 40
Hod-carriers	7 50	7 50	7 50
Masons	12 00	16 50	14 40
Tenders	7 50	7 50	7 50
Plasterers..	12 00	16 50	14 40
Tenders...	7 50	7 50	7 50
Slaters	12 00	15, 00	13 50
Roofers ...	7 50	12 00	9 60
Tenders..	7 50	7 50	7 50
Plumbers	9 00	15 00	10 50
Assistants	6 00	6 00	6 00
Carpenters	7 50	12 00	9 60
Gas-fitters..	9 00	15 00	10 50
OTHER TRADES.			
Bakers	8 00	12 00	10 00
Blacksmiths..	7 50	10 50	9 00
Strikers..	4 50	6 00	5 10
Bookbinders	7 00	12 00	9 00
Malsters	11 00	11 00	11 00
Butchers......	6 25	7 50	7 00
Cabinet-makers	6 00	15 00	9 00
Confectioners	10 00	18 00	14 00
Draymen and teamsters..	7 50	8 75	8 10
Cab, carriage	7 50	8 75	8 10
Furriers	10 00	10 00	10 00
Gardeners..	6 00	9 00	7 50
Hatters	10 00	10 00	10 00
Horseshoers	7 50	10 50	9 00
Laborers, porters..	6 00	7 50	6 50
Millwrights	9 00	15 00	12 00
Harness-makers	7 00	9 00	8 00
Sailmakers..	9 00	12 00	10 50
Tanners..	6 00	15 00	8 50
Tailors	10 00	13 00	11 50
Telegraph operators	7 50	15 00	11 25
Telegraph messengers	2 50	2 50	2 50
Tinsmiths..	7 50	12 00	9 60
Painters	9 00	12 00	10 50
Brickmakers..per thousand..	....	....	1 25
Brewers	....	....	*1, 300 00
Cigar-makers ....per thousand..	6 00	10 00	7 00
Street car driverst	6 00	6 00	6 00
Jewelers;	10 00	15 00	13 00
Stevedores§			
Raftsmen‖	6 50	8 00	7 25

* Per annum; no fixed hours.
† 78 hours per week.
‡ 54 hours per week.
§ 20 cents per hour; 25 cents per thousand bushels grain; 10 cents per ton of coal or ore.
‖ 8 months in year.

II. Factories, Mills, etc.

Wages paid per week of sixty hours in factories or mills in Kingston, Canada.

Occupations.	Lowest.	Highest.	Average.
Cotton factory :			
Mule spinners...............................	$9 00	$12 00	$11 10
Ring spinners.............................	1 50	4 80	2 40
Twisters	1 80	4 50	3 00
Grinders	6 00	7 50	6 60
Drawers	1 80	4 20	3 00
Warping tenders.........................	5 40	7 50	6 60
Cloth-room hands ..	3 00	6 00	4 50
Four-loom weavers.......	6 00	6 00	6 00
Shubbers ....per hank..	....	....	08
Rovers............................ do ..	06	10	....
Winders ....per frame..	....	....	07
Twisting ....per thousand ends..	....	....	07
Knitting mill * :			
Foremen	15 00	15 00	15 00
Laborers	6 00	6 00	6 00
Knitting girls	4 50	4 50	4 50
Card-room boys	3 00	3 00	3 00
Finishing girls	3 00	3 00	3 00
Piano factory † :			
Machinists	5 00	12 00	8 00
Varnishers.............................	2 00	10 50	6 00

* Wages same as in 1878.
† Pianos made by piece-work. Piano-makers average about $4 per day. Wages higher than 1878.

III. Foundries, Machine-Shops, and Iron Works.

Wages paid in foundries, machine-shops, car works, and iron works in Kingston, Canada.

[Per week of sixty hours.]

Occupations.	Lowest.	Highest.	Average.
Stove foundries * :			
Molders ....per week..	$9 00	$12 00	$11 10
Stove molders ....do ...	7 50	10 50	9 00
Laborers .... do ...	6 00	7 50	6 80
Carpenters.......................do...	8 40	11 40	9 90
Blacksmiths ....do....	10 50	10 50	10 50
Car works † :			
Blacksmiths ....do....	10 50	11 40	10 80
Molders.......................do ...	9 00	12 00	10 50
Carpenters.......................do...	8 40	11 40	9 90
Laborers.........................do....	6 60	9 00	7 80
Painters ....do ...	7 80	10 20	9 00
Foremen.........................do....	12 00	16 50	14 40
Machine-shops :			
Machinists ....do....	10 50	12 00	11 25
Locomotive works ‡ :			
Fitters ....per day..	2 00	2 50	2 25
Boiler-makers.....................do...|	2 00	2 50	2 25
Blacksmiths ....do....|	2 00	2 50	2 25
Molders ....do....|	2 00	2 25	2 00
Laborers.........................do ...|	1 00	1 50	1 25
Carpenters.......................do....|	2 00	2 25	2 00
Apprentices ....do....|	30	80	60
Turners ....do....|	1 85	2 25	2 00
Erecters ....do....|	2 00	2 50	2 25
Planers or drillers ....do....|	1 50	2 00	1 75
Pattern makers.....................do....	2 00	2 50	2 25

* Wages higher than 1878.
† Car works not built in 1878.
‡ Wages lower than the above by 25 per cent. in 1878.

V. Mines and Mining.

Wages paid per week of sixty hours in and in connection with iron mines in consular district of Kingston, Canada.

Occupations.	Lowest.	Highest.	Average.
Superintendent..	$37 50	$37 50	$37 50
Drillers...	10 50	10 50	10 50
Engineers...	12 00	12 00	12 00
Laborers...	7 50	7 50	7 20

VI. Railway Employés.

Wages paid per week to railway employés (those engaged about stations, as well as those engaged on the engines and cars, linemen, railroad laborers, &c.), in Kingston, Canada.

Occupations.	Lowest.	Highest.	Average.
Station hands...	$6 75	$6 75	$6 75
Line men..	6 75	8 45	7 45
Laborers..	6 75	6 75	6 75
Engineers...	11 80	16 90	14 35
Firemen...	9 45	9 45	9 45
Brakemen...	8 10	8 10	8 10
Clerks	5 60	8 45	7 00
Conductors*..	10 15	13 50	11 80

* 120 miles per day.

VII. Ship-Yards and Ship-Building.

Wages paid per week of sixty hours in ship-yards, in Kingston, Canada.

Occupations.	Lowest.	Highest.	Average.
Building wooden ships:			
Foremen	$15 00	$15 00	$15 00
Men	9 00	10 50	9 75
Fasteners..	9 00	9 00	9 00
Joiners.	8 40	10 20	9 30
Blacksmiths..	10 50	10 50	10 50
Helpers..	7 50	7 50	7 50
Laborers...	6 90	6 90	6 90

VIII. Seamen's Wages.

Wages paid to seamen, (officers and men)—distinguishing between ocean, coast, and river navigation, and between sail and steam—in Kingston, Canada.

Occupations.	Lowest.	Highest	Average.
SAIL.			
Lake and river navigation:			
Captain................................per month..	$40 00	$80 00	$60 00
Cook.. do ...	20 00	30 00	25 00
First mate...........................per day..	1 75	2 00	1 85
Second mate.............................do....	1 50	1 75	1 65
Able seamen.............................do....	1 25	1 50	1 35
Ordinary seamen........................do....	1 00	1 25	1 15
STEAM.			
Captain................................per month..	40 00	80 00	60 00
Purser or clerk........................do....	30 00	50 00	40 00
Steward ....do....	30 00	50 00	40 00
First mate.............................do....	30 00	50 00	40 00
Second mate............................do....	25 00	35 00	30 00
Engineer...............................do....	50 00	75 00	62 50
Assistant engineer.....................do....	40 00	50 00	45 00
Firemen................................do....	15 00	30 00	22 50
Deck-hands.............................do....	14 00	20 00	17 00
Cook...................................do....	20 00	30 00	25 00
Waiters................................do....	10 00	10 00	10 00

Seaman's Union organized in 1879, since which time wages have averaged as above.
Able seamen in 1879, $25 per month.

IX. Store and Shop Wages.

Wages paid in stores, wholesale or retail, to males and females, in Kingston, Canada.

[Per week of fifty-seven hours.]

Occupations.	Lowest.	Highest.	Average.
Wholesale clerks (male) ....per annum..	$1,000 00	$1,800 00	$1,200 00
Retail clerks (male)........................do....	300 00	600 00	450 00
Retail clerks (female) ....per week..	6 00	14 00	10 00

X. Household Wages in Towns and Cities.

Wages paid per month to household servants (towns and cities) in Kingston, Canada.

Occupations.	Lowest.	Highest.	Average.
Cooks.....................................	$10 00	$35 00	$15 00
Housemaids................................	5 00	10 00	8 00
Coachmen..................................	20 00	30 00	25 00

Wages higher than in 1878.

XI. Agricultural Wages.

Wages paid to agricultural laborers and household (country) servants in Kingston, Canada, with board and lodging.

Occupations.	Lowest.	Highest.	Average.
Men ....per annum...	$120 00	$156 00	$138 00
Household servants.........................do....	60 00	72 00	66 00
Men.......................................	*90 00	*108 00	*99 00
Men ....per day..	†1 25	†1 75	†1 50

* For best six months in the year.　　†Harvesting season.

XII. Corporation Employés.

Wages paid to the corporation employés in the city of Kingston, Canada.

Occupations.	Lowest.	Highest.	Average.
Mayor ..... per annum.			$800 00
Treasurer ..... do ..			1,100 00
City clerk ..... do ...			1,400 00
Collector ..... do...			1,100 00
Assessor ..... do...			800 00
Messenger ..... do...			450 00
Solicitor ..... do...			700 00
Engineer ..... do...			700 00
Chief engineer fire department ..... do...			200 00
Assistant engineer fire department ..... do...			175 00
Police magistrate ..... do ...			1,400 00
Chief of police ..... do...			800 00
Sergeant of police ..... per month..			*42 50
First class policeman ..... do ...			*40 00
Second class policeman ..... do ...			*35 00
Clerks ... . per annum..	$100 00	$400 00	300 00
City laborers ..... per day..			1 00

*In addition allowed $45 per annum for clothing.

XIII. Government Departments and Offices.

Wages paid per annum to employés in Government departments and offices, exclusive of tradesmen and laborers, in Kingston, Canada.

Occupations.	Lowest.	Highest.	Average.
Collector of customs			$1,600 00
Surveyor			1,100 00
Chief clerk and deputy collector			1,000 00
Clerks	$550 00	$800 00	650 00
Appraiser			900 00
Landing waiters			600 to
Preventive officers	150 00	450 00	300 00
Collector of inland revenue			1,400 00
Excisemen	235 00	1,000 00	600 00
Warden, penitentiary			2,600 00
Deputy warden, penitentiary			1,400 00
Chaplain			1,200 00
Surgeon			1,800 00
Accountant			1,000 00
Storekeeper			900 00
Schoolmaster			600 00
Steward			650 00
Trade instructors	400 00	1,000 00	700 00
Keepers	500 00	700 00	600 00
Guards			450 00
Teamsters			350 00
Matrons	250 00	500 00	375 00
Postmaster			1,800 00
Assistant postmaster			1,400 00
Clerks	400 00	1,200 00	800 00
Letter-carriers... ...	300 00	480 00	390 00

XV. Printers and Printing Offices.

Statement showing the wages paid per week of sixty hours to printers (compositors, pressmen, proof-readers, &c.) in Kingston, Canada.

Occupations.	Lowest.	Highest.	Average.
Compositors	$8 00	$12 00	$10 00
Pressmen	8 00	12 00	10 00
Reporters	10 00	16 00	13 00
Apprentices	1 00	3 00	2 00

COST OF LIVING.

Cost of living to the laboring classes, the prices paid for the necessaries of life, clothing, rent, &c., in Kingston.

Articles.	Cost.	Articles.	Cost.
Rent of quarters for laborer, consisting of from 3 to 5 rooms .. per annum..	$45 00	Potatoes ....per bushel..	60
Flour.................per 100 pounds..	2 75	Apples ....do ...	1 70
Oat meal ....do ...	5 50	Turnips.........................do...	40
Corn meal ....do....	1 75	Carrots.........................do....	38
Buckwheat.........................do ..	3 00	Beets...........................do....	38
Beef ....do....	8 50	Onions ....do ...	65
Mutton ....do....	8 00	Coal....................... per ton..	7 00
Pork (fresh).......................do....	8 00	Wood (hard) ....per cord..	5 25
Pork (salt) ....per pound..	11	Turkeys........................	1 75
Bacon ....do	14	Geese..........................	1 00
Veal ....do....	06	Ducks	75
Butter.............................do....	18	Chickens	60

WAGES, PAST AND PRESENT.

Since 1878 cost of living shows a material enlargement; price of labor advancing in a slightly increased proportion, with the following exceptions: Sail making and ship-building, on account of competition from the railroads in the carrying trade, has been steadily declining.

HABITS OF THE WORKING-CLASSES.

The working-classes are steady and trustworthy; 20 per cent. are estimated as having deposits in some savings institution, making payments upon homes, or in other ways saving money; intemperance seems to be the only prominent cause of evil and suffering among them.

FEELING BETWEEN EMPLOYER AND EMPLOYÉ.

There is the best of feeling between the employer and employé.

ORGANIZATION OF LABOR.

No organization of labor with the exception of the sailors' union. I am of the opinion that the union advantageously effects the condition of the seamen; at all events it relieves the consulate of much trouble and the Government of considerable expense.

STRIKES.

Strikes are very unusual and quite limited in their effects. There is no special system of dealing with disagreements between capital and labor.

FOOD PURCHASES.

No restraints upon the employé by his employer in reference to purchases. The laborer is paid in Canadian currency weekly, semi-monthly, and monthly.

CO-OPERATIVE SOCIETIES.

I think there are no co-operative societies in the district.

GENERAL CONDITION OF THE WORKING-CLASSES.

The condition and surroundings of the working-people are good; they are well clothed, well housed, and well fed. Their opportunity for saving is much better than their inclination. In seeking an answer to No. 4, I, in common with prominent citizens of the district, am surprised at the small number of laborers who are saving money. I have been unable to find any laborer who keeps an account of his expenses.

SAFETY OF EMPLOYÉS.

The safety of employés is carefully guarded.

POLITICAL RIGHTS.

All citizens assessed on $400 in the city or $200 in the country, and paying taxes thereon, without regard to the ownership of the property, are voters. The right of suffrage gives him a much better position as a laborer, securing for him better treatment and more steady employment. The tendency of legislation is towards suffrage without property or qualification.

EMIGRATION.

The general prosperity of their friends and relations living in the United States; the ease with which good homes on fertile lands may be procured; the policy of our Government in encouraging the laborer in owning his land; with the feeling that in the United States all positions of trust and profit are open to him and his children without regard to nationality, birth, or religion. Canadian emigrants proper are mostly agriculturists. There is quite an emigration, of which but little is known, taking advantage of the facilities given emigrants to Canada from Great Britain, who stop here a few months on their way to the United States.

M. H. TWITCHELL,
Consul.

United States Consulate,
  Kingston, Canada, May 21, 1884.

OTTAWA.

REPORT BY COMMERCIAL AGENT ROBBINS.

THE DOMINION GOVERNMENT.

The executive authority of the Government of Canada is vested in the sovereign of Great Britain and Ireland, and carried on in her name by a governor-general and privy council. The legislative power is exercised by a Parliament composed of two houses, viz, the Senate and House of Commons. The Senate consists of 77 members who are recommended by the privy council and confirmed by the governor-general as representative of the Crown, and are appointed for life. The House of Commons is composed of 213 members elected by ballot, and for the term of 5 years.

The salary of the governor-general is $48,666.66 per annum, and paid by Canada. The pay of the members of the Senate and House of Commons is $10 per day up to the end of 30 days, and if the session is longer, the sum of $1,000, with traveling expenses of 10 cents per mile. Eight dollars per day is deducted for every day's absence unless the same is caused by sickness.

OFFICIAL SALARIES.

The privy council consists of a premier, whose salary is $8,000 per annum, and twelve members, who are also heads of departments, at a salary of $7,000 each per annum.

Occupations.	Lowest.	Highest.	Average.
Commissioners, deputy heads, secretaries, &c.			
1 High commissioner to England ....per annum..			$10,000 00
1 Deputy head secretary of treasury board ....do..			4,200 00
1 Deputy head of railways and canals ....do..			4,100 00
1 Auditor-general ....do..			3,200 00
9 Deputy heads and secretaries (each) ....do..			3,200 00
1 Assistant auditor ....do..			2,450 00
1 Commissioner of inland revenue ....do..			3,200 00
1 Assistant of inland revenue ....do..			2,400 00
1 Commissioner of customs ....do..			3,200 00
1 Engineer of canals ....do..			4,500 00
1 Engineer of railways ....do..			4,000 00
1 Engineer of public works ....do..			3,000 00
1 Architect ....do..			3,000 00
Department clerks.			
Chief clerks...............per annum..	$1,800 00	$2,800 00	$2,175 00
First-class clerks...............do....	1,200 00	1,800 00	1,593 00
Senior second-class clerks...............do....	1,100 00	1,450 00	1,271 00
Junior second-class clerks...............do....	700 00	1,000 00	884 00
Third-class clerks...............do....	400 00	650 00	530 00
Messengers.			
Messengers ....per annum..	300 00	500 00	449 00
Laborers.			
Gardeners...............per week..	7 50	8 40	8 10
Laborers ....do....	6 00	7 25	6 75

CORPORATION EMPLOYÉS.

Official salaries paid by the city of Ottawa.

Occupations.	Average wages.	Occupations.	Average wages.
POLICE.		ASSESSMENT OFFICE.	
Police magistrate........per annum..	$1,600 00	Commissioner ....per annum..	$1,400 00
Police clerk ....do....	640 00	Assessors...............do....	400 00
Chief...............do....	1,200 00	Assistants ....do....	180 00
Sergeants...............do ...	*720 00	Clerk...............do....	650 00
Policemen...............per month..	*45 00		
		MARKETS.	
FIRE DEPARTMENT.		Inspector and constable..per annum..	1,240 00
Chief ....per annum..	1,240 00		
Deputy chief ....do ...	720 00	BOARD OF HEALTH.	
1 foreman ....per month..	45 00		
2 foremen ....do....	40 00	Medical officer...........per annum..	1,000 00
		Inspectors ....do....	420 00
CITY CLERK'S OFFICE.			
		LABORERS.	
City clerk...............per annum..	1,700 00		
Deputy...............do....	1,200 00	Laborers on streets........per day..	1 25
Clerk...............do....	560 00	Coal-weighers...........per month..	25 00
Messenger ....do....	200 00		
		PUBLIC SCHOOLS.	
CITY TREASURER'S OFFICE.		2 teachers (male)........per annum..	1,000 00
City treasurer ....per annum..	2,000 00	1 teacher (male)...............do....	850 00
Accountant...............do....	1,500 00	4 teachers (male)...............do....	750 00
Bailiff...............do ...	600 00	2 teachers (male)...............do....	650 00
		2 teachers (male)...............do....	600 00
CITY ENGINEER'S OFFICE.		1 teacher (male)...............do....	450 00
		1 teacher (female) ....do....	450 00
City engineer...............per annum..	2,000 00	9 teachers (female)...............do....	400 00
Street foreman ....do....	840 00	6 teachers (female) ....do....	350 00
Clerk ....do....	660 00		

* With uniform.

CONDITION OF LABORING PEOPLE IN OTTAWA.

The condition of the laboring people in Ottawa has improved since 1878, as I am advised, and especially within the last three years, so that at present all kinds of labor are in good demand at fair wages. The habits of the working-people are, as a rule, good—the result of religious influences, good schools, and steady employment. There exists a kindly feeling between the employers and employed, and no organized bodies of workingmen exist, except among printers and telegraphers. Strikes are not prevalent. No restrictions are placed to prevent laborers from purchasing goods in the cheapest market. Rents are moderate. The emigrants from this section are mostly young men who hope to better their condition, and enterprising farmers of limited means; most of the latter go to the Western States and largely to Dakota.

FOOD AND RAIMENT.

List of retail prices of the ordinary articles of food and raiment required by the working-classes in Ottawa, April 8, 1884.

Articles.	Cost.		Articles.	Cost.	
PROVISIONS.			**CLOTHING—Continued.**		
Bacon:					
Smoked ....per pound..	$0 15		Undercoats, tweed	$4 00 to	$8 00
Green ....do....	12		Trousers	2 00	5 50
Butter...................do....	25		Vests.........................	1 25	2 00
Mutton..................do....	$0 08 to	10	Shirts:		
Veal ....do....	10	12	Flannel......................	1 50	2 25
Pork ....do....	10		Cotton	75	1 00
Candles ....do....	13		Underwear	50	1 00
Cheese ....do....	16		Drawers, woolen	50	1 00
Eggs..................per dozen..	23		Socks:		
Flour.................per barrel..	6 00	6 25	Worsted......................	25	35
Fish:			Cotton......................	10	20
Cod ....per pound..	06		Blankets...............per pair..	2 50	5 00
Haddock .... do	06		Flannel ....per yard..	30	40
Ham ....do....	15		Cotton shirting ... . do....	12	17
Shoulders .... do	10		Cotton sheeting, double ...do....	20	25
Milk ....per quart..	08		Canadian cloth .... do....	50	1 00
Potatoes ....per bushel..	40		Hats, felt....................	1 00	2 50
Rice..................per pound..	05		Shoes:		
Soap, yellow ....do....	05		Men's	1 00	5 00
Sugar, brown..............do....	08		Women's	1 25	2 75
Tea:			Long boots	2 00	4 00
Black ....do....	40		India-rubber overshoes:		
Green ....do....	40		Men's	1 05	2 10
			Women's	1 30	1 05
CLOTHING.			India-rubbers:		
			Men's	80	1 15
Overcoats	5 00	15 00	Women's	55	75

VARIOUS OCCUPATIONS.

Wages paid per week of sixty hours in Ottawa.

Occupations.	Lowest.	Highest.	Average.
Planing-mills	$9 00	$10 00	$9 50
Sash and door factories	7 50	12 00	10 00
Laborers in	6 00	7 50	6 10
Saw-mills	6 50	10 00	7 50
Foundries and machine-shops:			
Machinists............................	9 95	16 00	12 00
Molders.............................	7 50	16 50	10 00
Blacksmiths	9 00	12 00	10 50
Helpers	6 00	7 50	6 60

Wages paid per week of sixty hours in Ottawa—Continued.

Occupations.	Lowest.	Highest.	Average.
Printers:			
Job hands..	$10 00	$15 00	$11 00
Pressmen	10 00	12 00	11 00
Proof-readers	10 00	12 00	11 00
Compositors.............................per thousand ems..	30	....	†12 00
Lumbermen:			
Log-makers..per month..	*18 00	20 00	....
Scorers ....do...	*24 00	26 00	....
Lauers ....do...	*28 00	32 00	....
Hewers ....do...	*36 00	45 00	....
Cooks in camp ....do...	*30 00	45 00	....
Railway employés:			
Conductors, passenger ....per annum..	....	....	600 00
Conductors, freight.................................do...	....	....	700 00
Engineers, passenger.........................per month..	....	....	90 00
Engineers, freight ....do ..	....	....	75 00
Station-agents ....do...	....	....	35 00
Firemen ....do...	....	....	45 00
Brakemen ....do...	....	....	40 00
Flagmen ....do...	....	....	22 00
Trackmen ....do...	....	....	26 00
Agricultural:			
Farm hands ....per month..	15 00	24 00	18 00
Female servants..................................do....	5 00	8 00	6 00

* With board. † Per week.

I. GENERAL TRADES.

Wages paid per week of sixty hours in Ottawa.

Occupations.	Lowest.	Highest.	Average.
Building trades...	$9 00	$15 00	$12 00
Bricklayers	15 00	21 00	18 00
Hod-carriers..	7 50	9 00	8 40
Masons, stone	12 00	15 00	13 50
Tenders	7 80	9 00	8 40
Plasterers	12 00	15 00	13 50
Tenders	7 80	9 00	8 40
Roofers.	12 00	15 00	13 50
Tenders	7 50	9 00	8 40
Plumbers..	12 00	15 00	13 50
Assistants..	7 50	9 00	8 40
Carpenters	9 00	12 00	11 00
Gas-fitters..	12 00	15 00	13 50
Bakers	9 00	12 00	10 50
Blacksmiths...	9 00	12 00	10 50
Strikers	6 00	7 50	7 00
Bookbinders:			
Male	9 00	15 00	10 00
Female	3 00	5 00	4 00
Brickmakers	7 50	9 00	8 10
Brewers	7 50	18 00	15 00
Butchers	9 00	10 50	9 60
Cabinet-makers	10 50	12 00	11 40
Confectioners	3 00	15 00	10 00
Coopers	7 50	12 00	9 00
Clerks in stores:			
Male	3 00	12 00	5 00
Female	2 00	6 00	4 00
Drivers:			
Draymen and teamsters	7 50	9 00	8 40
Cab and carriage	7 50	9 00	8 40
Street railway.....................................	10 00	10 00	10 00
Dyers:			
Male	5 00	10 00	7 00
Female	3 50	5 00	4 50
Engravers...	8 00	25 00	15 00
Furriers:			
Male	7 00	18 00	14 00
Female	3 00	7 50	6 00

Wages paid per week of sixty hours in Ottawa.

Occupations.	Lowest.	Highest.	Average.
Gardeners	$7 50	$9 00	$8 00
Horseshoers	9 00	15 00	12 00
Jewelers	8 00	14 00	12 00
Laborers and porters	6 00	9 00	7 00
Lithographers	6 00	15 00	12 00
Millwrights	10 50	15 00	12 00
Printers	10 00	15 00	11 00
Teachers:			
Male	4 00	12 00	6 00
Female	2 00	4 00	3 00
Saddle and harness makers	6 00	10 00	7 00
Ship-carpenters	10 00	16 00	12 00
Tanners	7 50	9 00	8 25
Tailors	8 00	10 00	9 00
Telegraph operators	6 00	12 50	8 50
Tinsmiths	4 00	10 00	8 00

R. B. ROBBINS,
Commercial Agent.

UNITED STATES COMMERCIAL AGENCY,
Ottawa, April 8, 1884.

PORT HOPE.

REPORT BY COMMERCIAL AGENT DUTCHER.

I have the honor to transmit to the Department the following "labor report," as called for by the Department's circular of February 15, 1884. I have made it as complete as it was possible from the resources at hand. In many cases it was impossible to ascertain with any degree of accuracy the number of each class of employés. I have, therefore, found it impossible to strike the average on the data given by the Department, and thus have left that column partially blank. Where, however, it has been filled, the average may be relied on as correct, as the figures were given me by the employés. In many branches of business the proprietors employ no help, and as a consequence no wages are paid. The laboring class, as a whole, are industrious, frugal, and sober ; many of them own comfortable little homes of their own, and they are free to procure the necessaries of life where they please. No provision, however, is made by the authorities for indigence or old age. The major portion of the females employed in shops, and as clerks in stores, are unmarried and young, and are members of respectable families, and as a whole, are intelligent and lady-like in their deportment.

In my inquiries for information on these several points, I have been greatly aided through the kindness of Mr. Sanders, town clerk ; Mr. Fairbairn, station agent of Grand Trunk Railway; J. F. Clark, merchant; S. B. Talter, miller, and others.

JACOB C. DUTCHER,
Commercial Agent.

UNITED STATES COMMERCIAL AGENCY,
Port Hope, May 6, 1884.

I. General Trades.

Wages paid in Port Hope.

[Per week of sixty hours.]

Occupations.	Lowest.	Highest.	Average.
BUILDING TRADES.			
Bricklayers............per week..	$16 50	$16 50	$16 50
Hod-carriers............do....	9 00	9 00	9 00
Masons ....do....	16 50	16 50	16 50
Tenders............do....	9 00	9 00	9 00
Plasterers ....do....	12 00	15 00	13 50
Tenders............do....	9 00	9 00	9 00
Roofers............do....	12 00	15 00	13 50
Tenders............do....	9 00	9 00	9 00
Plumbers............do....	15 00	15 00	15 00
Assistants............do....	6 00	6 00	6 00
Carpenters............do....	10 50	13 50	12 00
Gas-fitters............do....	12 00	12 00	12 00
OTHER TRADES.			
Blacksmiths............per week..	12 00	15 00	13 50
Strikers............do....	7 80	9 60	9 00
Brickmakers ....do ..	9 00	18 00	15 00
Brewers............per annum..	*1,000 00	*1,000 00	*1,000 00
Butchers............per week..	6 00	6 00	6 00
Cabinet-makers ....per day..	1 25	1 75	....
Drivers, draymen, and teamsters............do....	1 00	1 00	1 00
Horseshoers ....per week..	9 00	9 00	9 00
Jewelers............do....	8 00	20 00	14 00
Laborers, porters, &c ....do....	6 00	6 00	6 00
Teachers (public schools) ....per year..	200 00	1,150 00	415 89
Saddle and harness makers............per week..	6 00	8 00	....
Tanners ....do ...	9 00	9 00	9 00
Telegraph operators............per month..	20 00	40 00	30 00
Tinsmiths............per week..	9 00	12 00	....

* And one-half the profits.

II. Factories, Mills, Etc.

Wages paid per week of sixty hours in factories or mills in Port Hope consular district.

Occupations.	Lowest.	Highest.	Average.
Miller......	$10 00	$12 50	$10 87
Packer......	7 50	7 50	7 50
Shovelers......	7 50	7 50	7 50
Salesman....	7 50	7 50	7 50
Teamster and team	18 00	18 00	18 00

III. Foundries, Machine-Shops, and Iron Works.

Wages paid per week of sixty hours in railroad company's machine-shop in Port Hope consular district.

Occupations.	Lowest.	Highest.	Occupations.	Lowest.	Highest.
Machinist..................	$12 00	$13 50	Boiler-makers	$15 00	$18 00
Turners..................	12 00	13 50	Carpenters	9 00	10 50
Blacksmith	9 00	13 50	Fitters....................	12 00	13 50

VI. Railway Employés.

Wages paid per day to railway employés (those engaged about stations, as well as those engaged on the engines and cars, linemen, railroad laborers, &c.) in Port Hope consular district.

Occupations.	Lowest.	Highest.	Average.
Conductors	$2 25	$2 50	
Freightmen	1 75	2 00	
Engineers	2 00	2 65	
Firemen	1 15	1 40	
Trackmen	1 10	1 10	$1 10
Switchmen	1 25	1 25	1 25
Porters	1 00	1 00	1 00
Freight clerks	1 25	1 25	1 25
Telegraph operators	1 25	1 50	

VIII. Seamen's Wages.

Wages paid to seamen (officers and men)—distinguishing between sail and steam—in Port Hope consular district.

Occupations.	Lowest.	Highest.	Average.
Captains............per month..	$60 00	$60 00	$60 00
Mates............do....	52 50	75 00	63 75
Sailors............do....	30 00	60 00	43 13
Cooks............do ...	20 00	20 00	20 00
STEAMERS.			
Captain............per month..	*75 00		
1 engineer............do....	*65 00		
2 engineers............do....	*45 00		
Mate............do....	*45 00		
Firemen............per day..	*1 00		
Wheelmen............do....	*1 00		
Deck hands............per month..	*22 00		
Watchman............do ...	*20 00		
Cook............per day..	*1 00		

For season of 8 months.

IX. Store and Shop Wages.

Wages paid per week of sixty hours in stores, wholesale or retail, to males and females, in Port Hope consular district.

Occupations.	Lowest.	Highest.	Average.
Clerks	$2 50	$14 25	$7 50
Tailoring department	7 50	11 00	9 00
FEMALES.			
Clerks	2 50	5 00	3 50
Tailoresses	2 50	5 00	3 50

X. Household Wages in Towns and Cities.

Wages paid per month to household servants (towns and cities) in Port Hope consular district.

Occupations.	Lowest.	Highest.
Ordinary household servants	$5 00	$8 00

XI. Agricultural Wages.

Wages paid per month to agricultural laborers and household (country) servants in Port Hope consular district, with board and lodging.

Occupations.	Lowest.	Highest.
Ordinary farm hands	$10 00	$20 00
Household servants, same as in town	5 00	8 00

XII. Corporation Employés.

Wages paid to the corporation employés in the town of Port Hope.

Occupations.	Lowest.	Highest.	Average.
Town clerk ....per year	$900 00	$900 00	$900 00
Police magistrate ....do	800 00	800 00	800 00
Chief constable ....do	700 00	700 00	700 00
Treasurer ....do	225 00	225 00	225 00
Market clerk ....do	450 00	450 00	450 00
Street surveyor ....do	400 00	400 00	400 00
Collector taxes ....do	300 00	300 00	300 00
Auditors ....do	50 00	50 00	50 00
Assessors ....do	125 00	125 00	125 00
Laborers ....per day	1 00	1 00	1 00

XIII. Government Departments and Offices.

Wages paid per year to employés in Government departments and offices (exclusive of tradesmen and laborers) in Port Hope consular district.

Occupations.	Lowest.	Highest.	Average.
Collectors of customs	$1,000 00	$1,000 00	$1,000 00
Clerk of customs	800 00	800 00	800 00
Landing waitor	600 00	600 00	600 00

XV. Printers and Printing Offices.

Statement showing the wages paid per week of sixty hours to printers (compositors, pressmen, proof-readers, &c.) in Port Hope consular district.

Occupations.	Lowest.	Highest.	Average.
Foreman	$12 00	$12 00	$12 00
Reporters	8 00	8 00	8 00
Compositors	8 00	8 00	8 00
Pressmen	5 00	5 00	5 00
Apprentice	2 00	2 00	2 00

PORT ROWAN.

REPORT BY COMMERCIAL AGENT JANES.

I. GENERAL TRADES.

Wages paid per day of ten hours in Simcoe.

Occupations.	Lowest.	Highest.	Average.
BUILDING TRADES.			
Bricklayers	$2 00	$3 00	$2 50
Hod-carriers	1 00	1 50	1 25
Masons	2 00	3 00	2 50
Tenders	1 00	1 50	1 25
Plasterers	2 00	3 00	2 50
Tenders	1 00	1 50	1 25
Carpenters	1 50	2 00	1 75
OTHER TRADES.			
Bakers	1 00	1 50	1 25
Blacksmiths	1 50	2 00	1 75
Brick-makers	1 00	1 50	1 25
Brewers	1 00	3 00	1 50
Butchers	1 00	1 50	1 25
Cabinet-makers	1 00	1 50	1 25
Confectioners	1 50	2 50	2 00
Cigar-makers	1 25	2 00	1 50
Coopers	1 00	1 50	1 25
Distillers	1 00	3 00	1 50
Drivers (draymen and teamsters)	*12 00	*16 00	....
Dyers	2 00	3 50	2 50
Gardeners	1 00	1 50	1 25
Horseshoers	1 50	2 00	1 75
Jewelers	1 50	2 50	2 00
Laborers, porters, &c	1 00	1 50	1 25
Millwrights	2 50	3 00	2 75
Printers	†7 00	†12 00	†9 00
Teachers public schools	1 00	2 00	1 50
Saddle and harness makers	1 00	1 50	1 25
Tanners	....	1 25	1 00
Tailors	1 50	2 50	....
Telegraph operators	1 00	1 50	1 00
Tinsmiths	1 25	1 75	1 50

*Per month, with board.   †Per week.

II. FACTORIES, MILLS, ETC.

Wages paid per day of ten hours in factories or mills in Simcoe.

Occupations.	Lowest.	Highest.	Average.
Carders	$1 50	$2 00	$1 75
Spinners	1 25	1 50	1 37
Weavers	75	1 00	
Finishers	1 00	2 00	1 50
Dye-house hands	75	1 00	
Dyer	2 00	3 50	2 75

III. FOUNDRIES, MACHINE-SHOPS, AND IRON WORKS.

Wages paid per day of ten hours in foundries, machine-shops, and iron works in Simcoe.

Occupations.	Lowest.	Highest.	Average.
Molders	$1 50	$2 00	$1 75
Machinists	1 50	2 00	1 75
Boiler-makers	1 25	1 75	1 50

Apprentices receive $3 per week and board themselves.

VI. RAILWAY EMPLOYÉS.

Wages paid to railway employés (those engaged about stations, as well as those engaged on the engines and cars, linemen, railroad laborers, &c.) in Simcoe, Ontario.

Occupations.	Lowest.	Highest.	Average.
Clerks ....per day..	$1 00	$1 25	$1 12½
Engine-drivers......do....	2 90	3 10	3 00
Conductors.........do....	1 90	2 25	2 10
Baggage-men, train......do....	1 50	1 60	1 55
Station agents......do....	1 00	2 50	1 75
Station baggage-men......do....	1 00	1 20	1 10
Station telegraph operators......per month..	30 00	40 00	35 00
Station porter......per day..	1 00	1 00	1 00
Track foreman......do....	1 75	1 75	1 75
Track-men......do....	1 15	1 20	1 12½
Flag-men......do....	90	1 00	95
Switch-men......do....	1 15	1 35	1 25
Pumpers......do..	1 15	1 35	1 25
Track superintendents......per month..	75 00	85 00	80 00

VIII. SEAMEN'S WAGES.

Wages paid to seamen (officers and men) on Lake Erie, Canada.

Occupations.	Lowest.	Highest.	Average.
Captain ....per month..	$75 00	$100 00	$85 00
Mate......do....	40 00	60 00	50 00
Crew......per day..	1 00	1 50	1 25

IX. STORE AND SHOP WAGES.

Wages paid per year in stores, to males and females, in Simcoe and vicinity.

Occupations.	Lowest.	Highest.	Average.
Dry-goods clerks	$150 00	$650 00	$350 00
Grocers.........	300 00	450 00	325 00
Milliners.........	200 00	800 00	400 00
Cutters.........	700 00	1,000 00	800 00

X. HOUSEHOLD WAGES IN TOWNS AND CITIES.

Wages paid per month to household servants (town and cities) in Simcoe and vicinity, Ontario

Occupations.	Lowest.	Highest.	Average.
Household servants	$4 00	$8 00	$6 00

XI. AGRICULTURAL WAGES.

Wages paid to agricultural laborers and household (country) servants in Norfolk County, Ontario, with board and lodging.

Occupations.	Lowest.	Highest.	Average.
Agricultural laborers......per month..	$12 00	$16 00	$14 00
Household servants......per week..	75	1 50	1 00

XII. CORPORATION EMPLOYÉS.

Wages paid per day of ten hours to the corporation employés in the town of Simcoe, Ontario.

Occupations.	Lowest.	Highest.	Average.
Common laborers	$1 00	$1 00	$1 00

XV. PRINTERS AND PRINTING OFFICES.

Statement showing the wages paid per week of sixty hours to printers.

Occupations.	Lowest.	Highest.	Average.
Printers	$7 00	$12 00	$9 00

HENRY M. JANES,
Commercial Agent.
UNITED STATES CONSULAR AGENCY,
Port Rowan, May 30, 1884.

PORT SARNIA.

REPORT BY CONSUL PACE.

DESCRIPTION OF DISTRICT.

In compliance with Department circular under date of February 15, 1884, I have the honor to submit the following information relating to labor and the condition of the laboring classes in the consular district of Port Sarnia. Manufacturing establishments are not numerous in this district, and they are principally confined to the three cities of London, Strathroy, and Port Sarnia. The factories of London give permanent employment to about 1,500 men, whilst Strathroy, and Port Sarnia, employ about two hundred each. The principal articles of manufacture are machinery, stoves, plows, agricultural implements, ale, and woolen cloths. Several oil refineries are also established in this district, the principal ones being located at London. During the past ten years several steamers and schooners have been built at this port, but at the present nothing whatever is being done in the way of ship-building or repairing. The people of this district are for the most part employed in the pursuits of agriculture. Stock-raising and cheese-making are fast becoming permanent and profitable employments.

RATES OF WAGES.

As to the rate of wages, I must refer to the accompanying tabular statement, which is as full and complete as I could make it from information furnished me by both employers and employés.

COST OF LIVING.

There are represented in the laboring classes of Canada most of the countries of Europe as well as the native Canadian. The habits of economy practiced by the European laborer, and which he of necessity inherited from his home beyond the sea, give him an advantage in the battle of life over those who were born in Canada, where wages are higher and food more easily obtained. In the rural districts the farm laborer has usually assigned to him a small piece of land sufficient for his use as a vegetable garden, and I am informed that it is also customary to provide for him pasture for a cow. Under these circumstances I have known men to accumulate capital sufficient to make a first payment on a new farm, and finally become landed proprietors themselves. Whilst I would not recommend Canada as a country where fortunes are easily or rapidly made, yet I am fully persuaded, by inquiry and observation, that in this country industry and economy seldom seek in vain for a reward.

WAGES PAST AND PRESENT.

In every department of skilled labor there has been an advance in wages since 1878. The protective policy inaugurated by the Government of Sir John A. McDonald, commonly known as the national policy, has stimulated all branches of manufacturing industry, and, as a matter of course, a greater demand for labor has had the effect to increase the rate of wages paid; the increase in wages is estimated at the present time to be 20 per cent. in advance of 1878. With agricultural labor, much depends upon the prospect for crops, and the prices realized for the various products of the farm, as to the increase or decrease in the rate of wages paid for hired help.

HABITS OF THE WORKING CLASSES.

As a rule, the habits of the Canadian working classes will compare favorably with the same class of citizens in the United States; to be sure, there are evidences of shiftlessness, and drunkenness, and squalid poverty to be observed here and there, but the opposite is also apparent. The crime of drunkenness, I am glad to say, is decreasing. The sale of intoxicating liquors is now regulated by a license system, and in some localities the sale of intoxicants is very much restricted by a local option law, known as the Scott act. It is not claimed, even by the most enthusiastic advocates of temperance, that drunkenness is entirely restrained by this measure, but it is doubtless true that drunkenness and its attendant evils are greatly restricted in localities where the Scott act, by a vote of the people, has been placed upon the statute books.

FEELING BETWEEN EMPLOYER AND EMPLOYÉ.

So far as my observation goes I should say the most amicable relations exist between the laborer and the man who employs him, and especially is this true in the rural districts. To judge by what we can see, it is hard to distinguish the farm laborer from the proprietor of the soil upon which he labors. The hired man and the hired girl, as they are termed on the farm, dine at the same table with the proprietor and his family, and to all outward appearances they fare as well as do the owners of real estate.

ORGANIZATION OF LABOR.

There are but few labor organizations in this district, and they are confined to London. They consist of a railroad engineers' society and a lodge of the "Knights of Labor." I cannot observe that these organizations have any further effect upon labor than to assist the laborer in a social and intellectual manner. At the present time there does not appear to be any antagonism—at least any marked antagonism—between capital and labor.

THE PREVALENCY OF STRIKES.

Strikes do not frequently occur in this country. A mechanic said to me recently, in reply to the question, "Do you operatives ever strike?" "No," said he with a smile, "we do not strike; we emigrate. The United States is too near to make strikes necessary. When we cannot agree with our employers on the subject of wages we go to that larger country across the border."

FOOD PURCHASES.

"Are working-people free to purchase the necessaries of life wherever they choose?"

To this question I say yes. I believe the workingman has no conditions imposed upon him in this regard. He is paid in cash once a week and sometimes oftener.

CO-OPERATIVE SOCIETIES.

These societies do not prosper in Canada. A few have been established from time to time, but they die early. For some reason they do not carry out in practice what they promise in theory.

GENERAL CONDITION OF WORKING-PEOPLE.

To visit the home of the Canadian laborer one does not discover enough of difference between it and the home of the laborer in the United States to make the description of it a matter of interest to our people; and the same is true in reference to their moral and physical condition.

"What means are furnished for the safety of employés in factories and mines?"

There are no mines in this district, and I cannot learn that any special provisions are made for the safety of working-people in factories.

POLITICAL RIGHTS.

Since the adoption of the ballot in 1874, the Canadian voter may express his choice at the polls, without the slightest interference on the part of anybody. The voter, on reaching the polls, procures a ballot, which has printed upon it the names of all the candidates—the candidates of his choice and those who are opposed to him politically. With this paper he retires to a room by himself, and, being previously provided with a pencil, he makes a mark on the margin of the ballot, opposite the name of the candidate of his choice; he then folds the ballot, and handing it to the returning officer he sees that it is deposited in the ballot-box precisely as he prepared it. The tendency of legislation in Canada is to extend rather than curtail the voting privilege.

EMIGRATION.

"What are the causes that lead to emigration?"

Canadian emigrants to the United States come principally from the rural districts, and their object generally is to procure cheaper lands. Available farming lands in Canada are high, as compared to lands in Michigan and other Western States, and as the native Canadian has no national prejudice to surrender, he as readily assimilates with our people as he would with the people of an adjoining county in Canada; he desires to better his condition financially, and for that purpose he seeks and finds a congenial home in the United States. When once across the border the Canadian emigrant seldom returns to remain permanently. Occasionally, however, a discontented person will find his way back. In such an event he is quite apt to be gratified by seeing his name in print. He is usually interviewed by some press reporter, or he is induced to write a letter. In these literary efforts I have been frequently struck with the evident similarity of style. He tells how he was lured away from Canada by false representations; how he expected to find an Eldorado, instead of which he found the ague, and now that he is safely back again he declares his intention never again to wander from British institutions. Notwithstanding these solemn declarations and pledges, I have known them to be violated over and over again. One man whom I chanced to meet as he was re-crossing into Canada after a six months' sojourn in Michigan, said he had got quite enough of the United States, and that he was glad to get back again to Canada. Notwithstanding all this, in less than six months he again emigrated to Michigan.

SAM'L D. PACE, Consul.

UNITED STATES CONSULATE,
Port Sarnia, June 28, 1884.

1. GENERAL TRADES.

Wages paid per week in Port Sarnia.

Occupations.	Lowest.	Highest.	Average.
Building trades	$9 00	$12 00	$10 50
Bricklayers	12 00	15 00	13 50
Hod-carriers	6 00	7 50	6 75
Masons	12 00	15 00	13 50
Tenders	6 00	7 50	6 75
Plasterers	12 00	15 00	13 50
Tenders	6 00	7 50	6 75
Slaters	12 00	15 00	13 50
Roofers	12 00	15 00	13 50
Tenders	6 00	7 50	6 75
Plumbers	12 00	15 00	13 50
Assistants	6 00	7 50	6 75
Carpenters	12 00	15 00	13 50
Gas-fitters	12 00	15 00	13 50
Bakers	9 00	12 00	10 50
Blacksmiths	9 00	10 50	9 75
Strikers	6 00	7 50	6 75
Bookbinders	15 00	20 00	17 50
Brickmakers	9 00	12 00	10 50
Brewers	12 00	15 00	13 50
Butchers	6 00	12 00	9 00
Brass founders	12 00	15 00	13 50
Cabinet-makers	9 00	10 50	9 75
Confectioners	9 00	12 00	10 50
Cigar-makers	12 00	15 00	13 50
Coopers	9 00	12 00	10 50
Dyers	12 00	15 00	13 50
Gardeners	9 00	12 00	10 50
Horse-shoers	12 00	15 00	13 50
Laborers, porters, &c	6 00	7 50	6 75
Millwrights	12 00	15 00	13 50
Printers	12 00	15 00	13 50
Teachers, public schools	7 50	15 00	10 00
Saddle and harness makers	9 00	12 00	10 50
Sailmakers	9 00	12 00	10 50
Tanners	9 00	12 00	10 50
Tailors	12 00	15 00	13 50
Telegraph operators	9 00	15 00	12 00
Tinsmiths	9 00	10 00	9 50

PRESCOTT.

REPORT BY CONSUL SLAGHT.

I have the honor to report on the labor interest of this district as follows:

Agricultural interests being so largely in excess of all others labor is mostly applied to the production of crude material. Farm implements of a useful and substantial class are quite largely manufactured, cloths of the more serviceable kinds are produced. The building trades of the ordinary class are fairly represented. Skilled or artistic labor is in very limited demand; many branches of the latter class are wholly unrepresented. Hence the very meager scope of this report. The constant intercourse existing among the people of American cities in this vicinity, together with the continuous interchange of commodities, renders the cost of living in this part of Canada very nearly if not quite equal to places of like size in the United States.

HARRY L. SLAGHT,
Consul.

UNITED STATES CONSULATE,
Prescott, 1884.

I. GENERAL TRADES.

Wages paid per day in Prescott.

Occupations.	Lowest.	Highest.	Average.
BUILDING TRADES.			
Bricklayers	$1 50	$3 00	$2 00
Hod-carriers	1 00	1 50	1 25
Masons	1 50	3 00	1 25
Tenders	1 00	1 50	1 25
Plasterers	2 00	3 50	2 50
Tenders	1 00	1 50	1 25
Slaters	2 50	3 00	2 00
Roofers	2 50	3 00	2 00
Tenders	1 00	1 50	1 00
Plumbers	2 00	4 00	3 00
Assistants	1 00	2 00	1 50
Carpenters	1 50	3 00	2 00
Gas-fitters	1 50	3 00	2 00
OTHER TRADES.			
Bakers	1 25	2 50	2 00
Blacksmiths	1 25	2 50	1 50
Strikers	1 25	1 50	1 50
Bookbinders	1 00	1 50	1 25
Brickmakers	1 50	2 50	2 00
Brewers	2 00	5 00	3 00
Butchers	1 00	1 50	1 50
Cabinet-makers	1 50	3 00	2 00
Confectioners	1 50	3 00	2 00
Cigar-makers ....per M.	2 50	8 00	....
Distillers	2 00	5 00	3 00
Drivers:			
Draymen and teamsters	1 00	1 50	1 25
Cab, carriage, and street railways	1 00	1 50	1 25
Dyers	1 50	3 00	2 00
Engravers	2 00	4 00	3 00
Furriers	2 00	4 00	3 00
Gardeners	1 50	2 00	1 50
Horseshoers	1 50	3 00	2 00
Jewelers	2 00	3 00	2 50
Laborers, porters, &c	1 00	2 00	1 50

Wages paid per day in Prescott—Continued.

Occupations.	Lowest.	Highest.	Average.
OTHER TRADES—Continued.			
Millwrights	$2 00	$4 00	$3 00
Printers..	1 50	2 50	2 00
Teachers (public schools) ....per annum..	500 00	1,200 00	720 00
Saddle and harness maker ....per week..	9 00	12 00	10 00
Stevedores ....per hour..	25	40	25
Tanners (board and lodging) ....per month..	....	....	25 00
Tailors ....per week..	9 00	15 00	10 00
Telegraph operators ....per month..	40 00	100 00	75 00
Tinsmiths...per week..	7 50	15 00	10 00
Weavers (outside of mills)................................	....	....	2 00

II. FACTORIES, MILLS, ETC.

Wages paid per week of sixty hours in factories or mills in Prescott consular district.

Occupations.	Lowest.	Highest.	Average.
Carders	$6 00	$10 00	$9 00
Overseers	12 00	18 00	15 00
Weavers	5 00	7 50	6 00
Loom-fixers	6 00	10 00	8 00
Fullers..	7 00	11 00	9 00
Finishers	12 00	18 00	15 00
Dyers..	12 00	18 00	15 00
Wool-sorters..	6 00	9 00	7 50
Spinners	9 00	15 00	12 00

III. FOUNDRIES, MACHINE-SHOPS, AND IRON WORKS.

Wages paid per week of sixty hours in foundries, machine-shops, and iron works in Prescott consular district.

Occupations.	Lowest.	Highest.	Average.
Molders...	$12 00	$18 00	$15 00
Machinists	9 00	12 00	10 00
Tinsmiths..	9 00	12 00	10 00
Helpers and laborers....................................	7 00	9 00	8 00

VI. RAILWAY EMPLOYÉS.

Wages paid to railway employés (those engaged about stations, as well as those engaged on the engines and cars, linemen, railroad laborers, &c.) in Prescott consular district.

Occupations.	Average.	Occupations.	Average.
Charge of stations ....per year..	$800 00	Linemen ....per year..	$400 00
Senior office clerks ....do....	600 00	Conductors ....per month..	60 00
Junior office clerks ....do....	400 00	Engine-drivers ....do....	75 00
Employés in freight-sheds ....do ...	500 00	Brakemen.........................do....	40 00

VIII. SEAMEN'S WAGES.

Wages paid to seamen (officers and men)—distinguishing between ocean, coast, and river navigation, and between sail and steam—in Prescott consular district.

Occupations.	Lowest.	Highest.
Captain of sailing vessels ....per month..	$50 00	$60 00
Mate of sailing vessels... do....	30 00	40 00
Sailors of sailing vessels ....do.....	25 00	30 00
River navigation.		
Captain of steamers...per year..	700 00	1,000 00
First mate and pilot...per month..	60 00	70 00
Second mate...do....	40 00	50 00
Engineers...do....	40 00	60 00
Deck-hands and firemen..do....	20 00	30 00

IX. STORE AND SHOP WAGES.

Wages paid per month in stores, wholesale or retail, to males and females, in Prescott consular district, per month.

Occupations.	Lowest.	Highest.	Average.
Dry goods clerks..	$25 00	$50 00	$38 00
Hardware clerks...	25 00	50 00	40 00
Grocery clerks	20 00	35 00	30 00
Shoe clerks..	25 00	40 00	30 00
Drug clerks..	25 00	50 00	35 00

X. HOUSEHOLD WAGES IN TOWNS AND CITIES.

Wages paid per month to household servants (towns and cities) in Prescott consular district, with board.

Occupations.	Lowest.	Highest.	Average.
Male servants..	$10 00	$20 00	$12 00
Female servants...	5 00	9 00	7 00

XI. AGRICULTURAL WAGES.

Wages paid per month to agricultural laborers and household (country) servants in Prescott consular district, with board and lodging.

Occupations.	Lowest.	Highest.	Average.
Farm hands, men	$18 00	$30 00	$23 00
Gardeners and florists, men	15 00	25 00	20 00
Manager dairy department, men	25 00	35 00	30 00
Dairy helpers, men	10 00	18 00	15 00
Dairy helpers, women.....................................	5 00	8 00	7 00
General house work, women................................	5 00	8 00	6 00

XII. CORPORATION EMPLOYÉS.

Wages paid per day and year to the corporation employés in the cities of Prescott consular district.

Occupations.	Lowest.	Highest.
Police magistrates...per year..	$200 00	$1,000 00
Chief police ....do....	450 00	800 00
Regular police force..do....	400 00	500 00
Laborers...per day..	1 00	1 25

XIII. Government Departments and Offices.

*Wages paid per year to employés in Government departments and offices—exclusive of trades-
men and laborers—in Prescott consular district.*

Occupations.	Lowest.	Highest.
Postmasters	$1,400 00	$2,700 00
Assistants, clerks, &c	400 00	1,000 00
Collectors of customs	1,300 00	1,500 00
Under officers	600 00	1,200 00
Colloctors, inland revenue	....	1,400 00
Assistants	600 00	1,200 00

XV.—Printers and Printing Offices.

*Statement showing the wages paid per week of sixty hours to printers (compositors, press-
men, proof-readers, &c.) in Prescott consular district.*

Occupations.	Lowest.	Highest.	Average.
Typesetters	$8 00	$10 00	$9 00
Pressmen	10 00	15 00	12 00
Jobmen	10 00	15 00	12 00
Proof-readers	10 00	12 00	11 00
Common hands	6 00	8 00	7 00

SHERBROOKE.

REPORT BY CONSUL PARKER.

BUSINESS DEPRESSION.

I have the honor to transmit herewith, in response to the circular of
February 15, 1884, the fullest and most reliable information that I have
been able to obtain relative to the condition of labor and the industrial
pursuits in the consular district of Sherbrooke. Before entering upon
the matters directly connected with the inclosed statements it seems
proper to remark that there is, at this time, a temporary depression in
the market for certain lines of skilled labor, owing to the fact that the
stimulating influence of the Canadian tariff on imports caused an
overproduction of cotton, leather, woolen, and a few other kinds of manufactured goods, thus embarrassing operations, crippling some manufacturers, and causing a few to suspend, and many to curtail production.
This is, however, but the natural result, which was foreseen by many
as inevitable in a country of such comparatively limited population, and
so rich in cheap water-power and other natural advantages that invite
manufacturing enterprise. This evil effect of the "National Policy"
as it is termed here, will, in all probability, work its own cure; and the
condition of the laborer, while not so favored as in the United States,
will continue to be greatly in advance of that of his fellow workers in
the principal countries of Europe. In the city of Sherbrooke the effects
of this depression has been most severely felt by the woolen mills operatives. The woolen mills of A. G. Loomis & Co., that employ from
100 to 150 people, have been closed for the past five months and will not
reopen until the stock on hand is sold, while the mills of the Paton
Manufacturing Company—the largest woolen mills in Canada—have

been running for many months on three-fourths time. As these mills employ over 500 people, the loss of one-fourth their time amounts to a very considerable sum in the aggregate.

AREA AND DIVISION OF LABOR.

This consular district embraces about 4,098 square miles of territory, containing, as nearly as I can determine, 95,500 inhabitants, of whom 49,048 are males and 46,452 are females. The occupation of the people is largely agricultural. Many of those, however, classified as agriculturists, are, a portion of the time, engaged in other pursuits—many in connection with the lumbering and mining interests. The following partial classification of the adults is the best that I have been able to procure, and may serve to indicate, with sufficient accuracy, the facts in the case :

Agricultural pursuits	18,774
Commercial	1,199
Industrial	3,304
Professional	1,022
Domestic service	999
Unclassified	4,073

Of these 13,230 are owners and occupiers of farms. The mills and principal manufacturing establishments of Sherbrooke, the principal city of the consular district, are given in detail in the tabular statements transmitted herewith ; but outside of these there are in various parts of the district many large industrial establishments from which it has been impossible to obtain anything like exact information. Among these latter may be mentioned a number of saw-mills which employ a great many laborers both in the work of cutting the timber in the forests and driving it down the streams to the mills, and at the mills themselves. Hundreds of men also find employment during the winter in cutting logs for shipment to the mills of the United States, in getting ship-timber and ship-knees for the ship-builders of Maine and Massachusetts, and in peeling hemlock bark for the American and other tanneries. The copper, sulphur, and nickel mines of Capleton give employment to probably 1,000 men. A tabular statement of the wages paid at the largest of these mines will be found among the inclosed papers, and the schedule of wages, methods of work, and cost of living are so nearly the same that one may serve the whole. The extensive asbestos mines of Thetford, and the production of vast quantities of quicklime from the quarries at Dudswell, also consume the labor of many people, but the wages at these places are very little in excess of those prevailing for ordinary labor. The gentlemen who compiled, under my direction, the statistics transmitted herewith, and who made diligent and careful inquiries at all the mills and manufactories within reach, places the average of earnings of skilled labor at $8 per week.

COST OF LIVING

to this class of workers per week as follows, to wit:

Rent	$1 50
Clothing	2 50
Food	3 50
Incidentals	50
Total	8 00

I think, however, that the cost of living is very generally less than the figures he has given and that laborers who receive $8 per week often save something beyond supporting themselves and the dependent members of their families, but the savings are necessarily very small. This relates to men's earnings, and in all such cases the other members of the family are put to earning something for their own support as soon as their ages and strength will permit. The wages of women and children are so varied that each kind of labor must stand for itself; no correct average can be given. In lumbering, ordinary woodsmen and choppers average $1 per day, and unusually board themselves in the woods; head sawyers and managers of planing and clapboard machines receive from $1.50 to $1.75 per day. The rate of ordinary unskilled labor varies from 75 cents to $1.20 for men, and from 25 cents to 50 cents per day for women.

The tenements occupied by laborers are generally somewhat poorer and their comforts considerably less than those enjoyed by the same classes in those portions of the United States with which I am best acquainted, to wit, the North and West.

BENJ. S. PARKER,
Consul.

UNITED STATES CONSULATE,
Sherbrooke, June 23, 1884.

I. GENERAL TRADES.

Wages paid per week of sixty hours in Sherbrooke.

Occupations.	Lowest.	Highest.	Average.
BUILDING TRADES.			
Bricklayers	$12 00	$18 00	$15 00
Hod-carriers	6 00	8 00	7 00
Masons	10 50	15 00	12 00
Tenders	6 00	8 00	7 00
Plasterers	8 00	12 00	10 50
Tenders	6 00	8 00	7 00
Plumbers	8 00	12 00	10 00
Assistants	6 00	6 00	6 00
Carpenters	6 60	12 00	9 00
Gas-fitters	8 00	12 00	10 00
OTHER TRADES.			
Bakers	7 00	12 00	8 00
Blacksmiths	7 50	10 50	9 00
Strikers	6 00	6 00	6 00
Brick-makers	6 60	12 00	9 00
Brewers	20 00	20 00	20 00
Cabinet-makers	6 00	12 00	10 00
Confectioners	7 00	12 00	8 00
Cigar-makers	9 00	20 00	12 00
Drivers: Draymen and teamsters	7 50	12 00	9 00
Gardeners	6 00	12 00	9 00
Horseshoers	6 00	10 00	9 00
Laborers, porters, &c	5 40	8 00	6 00
Printers	6 00	10 00	8 00
Teachers, public schools	*200 00	*1,000 00	*500 00
Saddle and harness makers	8 00	14 00	10 00
Tailors	1 50	2 00	1 75
Telegraph operators	†40 00	†60 00	†50 00
Tinsmiths	6 00	12 00	8 00
Painters	8 00	12 00	9 00
Sawyers	8 00	12 00	10 50
Lumbermen	6 00	8 00	7 00

* Per annum.　　　　　† Per month.

II. FACTORIES, MILLS, ETC.

Wages paid per week of sixty hours in factories or mills in Sherbrooke.

Occupations.	Lowest.	Highest.	Average.
PATON'S WOOLEN MILLS.			
Men.			
5 pickers, waste................................	$6 00	$7 50	$6 40
7 wool-sorters.................................	4 50	7 50	6 10
16 dyers......................................	5 10	9 00	6 42
7 pickers.....................................	5 40	9 00	6 30
11 carders....................................	5 40	10 50	6 90
7 spinners....................................	6 00	9 00	8 16
1 spooler.....................................	1 25	1 25	1 25
4 warpers.....................................	6 00	12 00	8 00
24 weavers....................................	6 00	12 00	7 25
28 finishers..................................	4 50	10 50	6 27
10 pattern-makers.............................	6 00	18 00	8 68
8 machinists..................................	6 00	10 50	7 56
13 carpenters.................................	6 00	9 00	7 56
Women.			
8 washers.....................................	2 70	3 00	2 82
13 carders....................................	3 00	3 60	3 14
25 winders....................................	2 40	3 80	3 17
3 spoolers....................................	2 10	4 00	3 20
21 twisters...................................	3 00	3 00	3 00
6 weavers.....................................	....	....	4 50
5 finishers...................................	....	....	5 00
3 pattern-makers..............................	5 00	5 00	5 00
Boys.			
12 pickers, waste.............................	2 10	3 90	2 61
1 wool sorter.................................	....	....	3 00
1 dyer..	....	....	3 00
1 picker......................................	3 00	4 12	3 56
2 corders.....................................	3 00	3 00	3 00
8 spinners....................................	2 10	3 50	2 50
1 spooler.....................................	....	....	2 70
2 twisters....................................	....	....	2 50
9 weavers.....................................	2 00	3 00	2 50
18 finishers..................................	2 25	3 50	2 50
1 pattern-maker...............................	....	....	3 00
1 machinist...................................	....	....	4 50
Girls.			
4 pickers, waste..............................	2 10	3 00	2 70
27 carders....................................	....	....	3 00
24 spinners...................................	....	....	2 70
5 winders.....................................	2 40	2 88	2 60
9 spoolers....................................	4 20	8 00	5 05
8 warpers.....................................	3 00	4 50	3 45
123 weavers...................................	....	....	4 00
45 finishers..................................	2 25	5 00	3 00
4 pattern-makers..............................	3 00	5 00	4 25
A. L. GUINOD & CO., WOOLEN MANUFACTURERS.			
Women.			
Weavers.......................................	3 75	5 00	4 50
Spinners......................................	2 75	4 00	3 00
Carders.......................................	2 00	4 00	3 00
Men.			
Dyers...	....	....	6 00
Finishers.....................................	....	....	6 00
CORSET MANUFACTURERS.			
Corset-makers.................................	1 25	7 50	4 50
DOMINION SNATH COMPANY.			
Snath-makers..................................	6 00	9 00	7 50
PULP-MAKERS.			
Sawyer..	9 00	9 00	9 00
Laborers......................................	6 00	6 00	6 00
Boys..	2 10	2 10	2 10
Paper-makers..................................	....	....	8 10

III. FOUNDRIES, MACHINE-SHOPS, AND IRON WORKS.

Wages paid per week of sixty hours in foundries, machine shops, and iron works in Sherbrooke.

Occupations.	Lowest.	Highest.	Average.
Machinists	$9 00	$12 00	$10 50
Strikers	6 00	10 50	7 50
Blacksmiths	10 50	16 50	14 50
Boys			3 00

V. MINES AND MINING.

Wages paid per week of sixty hours in and in connection with copper mines in Capelon.

Occupations.	Lowest.	Highest.	Average.
Strikers and miners	$7 50	$9 00	$8 00
Trammers and laborers	6 00	7 50	6 75
DUDSWELL LIME QUARRIES.			
Quarry men	6 60	12 00	8 10

VI. RAILWAY EMPLOYÉS.

Wages paid to railway employés (those engaged about stations, as well as those engaged on the engines and cars, linemen, railroad laborers, &c.), in Sherbrooke.

Occupations.	Lowest.	Highest.	Average.
Superintendents ....per month..			$100 00
Night agents ....per week..			7 50
Telegraph operators................do....			7 50
Porters................do....	$6 00	$6 80	6 60
Switchmen ....do....	7 00	9 00	7 50
Clerks ....per annum..	300 00	500 00	450 00
Agent .... do....	800 00	800 00	800 00
Brakesmen ....per week..	7 50	9 30	9 00
Conductors ....per month..	40 00	65 00	50 00
Engine drivers................do....	55 00	70 00	60 00
Firemen................do....			40 00
Section men foreman ....do....			40 00
Laborers,................per week..			6 60
Fitters................do....			15 00
Engine turners................do....			9 00
Laborers ....do....			6 60

IX. STORE AND SHOP WAGES.

Wages paid in all kinds of stores, wholesale or retail, to males and females in Sherbrooke.

[Per week of sixty hours.]

Occupations.	Lowest.	Highest.	Average.
Clerks ....per annum..	$160 00	$800 00	$420 00

X. Household Wages in Towns and Cities.

Wages paid per month to household servants in Sherbrooke.

Occupations.	Lowest.	Highest.	Average.
Servants..	$5 00	$12 00	$8 00

XI. Agricultural Wages.

Wages paid per month to agricultural laborers and household (country) servants in St. Francis district with board.

Occupations.	Lowest.	Highest.	Average.
Farm hands, men	$12 00	$20 00	$16 00

XII. Corporation Employés.

Wages paid to the corporation employés in the city of Sherbrooke.

[[Per week of sixty hours.]

Occupations.		Lowest.	Highest.	Average.
Secretary treasurer ....per annum..				$1, 500 00
Chief of police and fire...do....				*1, 200 00
Five policemen ....per week..		$8 00	$12 00	9 00
Five firemen...do....		8 00	12 00	9 00
Inspector of roads...do....				12 00
Forty laborers...do....		6 00	7 50	6 75

* With house, &c.

XV. Printers and Printing Offices.

Statement showing the wages paid per week of sixty hours to printers (compositors, pressmen, proof-readers, &c.) in Sherbrooke.

Occupation.	Lowest.	Highest.	Average.
Printers..	$6 00	$10 00	$8 00

STRATFORD.

REPORT BY CONSULAR AGENT BENEDICT.

I. GENERAL TRADES.

Wages paid per week of sixty hours in Stratford, Ontario.

Occupations.	Lowest.	Highest.	Average.
BUILDING TRADES.			
Bricklayers	$9 00	$15 00	$13 50
Hod-carriers	7 50	9 00	7 50
Masons	9 00	15 00	13 50
Tenders	7 50	9 00	7 50
Plasterers	12 00	18 00	15 00
Tenders	7 50	10 50	9 00
Roofers	12 00	12 00	12 00
Tenders	7 50	9 00	7 50
Plumbers	10 00	14 00	12 00
Assistants	3 00	5 00	4 00
Carpenters	7 50	13 50	10 50
Gas-fitters	10 00	14 00	12 00
OTHER TRADES.			
Bakers	8 00	12 00	10 00
Blacksmiths	7 50	12 00	9 00
Strikers	5 00	7 70	6 00
Brickmakers	10 50	13 50	12 00
Butchers	5 00	10 00	7 00
Cabinet-makers	7 50	12 00	9 00
Confectioners	8 00	12 00	10 00
Cigar-makers	7 00	20 00	12 00
Coopers	7 50	12 00	10 50
Draymen and teamsters	6 00	9 00	7 50
Furriers:			
Females	3 00	5 00	3 50
Males	10 00	25 00	15 00
Gardeners	6 00	10 50	7 50
Horse shoers	7 50	10 50	9 00
Jewelers	7 00	12 00	10 00
Laborers, porters, &c	6 00	9 00	7 50
Millwrights	9 00	12 00	10 50
Potters	6 00	12 00	9 00
Printers	6 00	12 00	7 50
Saddle and harness makers	6 00	12 00	8 00
Tanners	6 00	7 50	7 50
Tailors	8 00	12 00	10 00
Telegraph operators	6 00	12 00	10 00
Tinsmiths	9 00	12 00	10 00

II. FACTORIES, MILLS, ETC.

Wages paid per week of sixty hours in factories or mills in Stratford, Ontario.

Occupations.	Lowest.	Highest.	Average.
Woolen mill:			
Dyers	$7 50	$12 00	$9 00
Carders	7 20	10 50	7 50
Carders, boys	2 40	3 00	2 70
Spinners	9 00	10 50	9 00
Winders, girls	2 40	3 00	2 70
Weavers	4 00	7 50	6 00
Fullers	7 20	7 50	7 50
Finishers	9 00	10 50	9 00
Engineer			7 50
Flour mills:			
Millers	9 00	15 00	12 00
Packers	7 00	7 50	7 00
Laborers	6 00	7 50	7 00
Engineers	7 00	9 00	8 00
Cabinet shops:			
Cabinet-makers	7 50	12 00	10 50
Upholsterers	7 50	13 50	10 50
Finishers	7 50	9 00	9 00

III. Foundries, Machine-shops, and Iron Works.

Wages paid per week of fifty-four to sixty hours in foundries, machine-shops, and iron works in Stratford, Ontario.

Occupations.	Lowest.	Highest.	Average.
Grand Trunk Railway repair shops.			
Machinists	$9 72	$11 88	$11 34
Boiler-makers	9 18	13 50	12 96
Blacksmiths	11 34	11 88	11 34
Carpenters	9 72	9 72	9 72
Pattern-makers	11 88	11 88	11 88
Laborers	6 00	6 00	6 00
Dominion Agricultural works.			
Machinist	9 00	12 00	10 50
Molders	9 00	12 00	10 50
Blacksmiths	9 00	10 50	9 00
Strikers	4 80	6 75	5 40
Woodworkers	7 50	10 50	9 00
Mill-furnishing works.			
Machinist	9 00	16 50	10 50
Molders	10 50	10 50	10 50
Blacksmiths	9 00	10 50	9 00
Strikers	6 00	7 50	6 00
Woodworkers	4 50	16 50	9 00
Laborers	6 00	12 00	7 50
Iron foundry.			
Machinists	9 00	10 50	9 00
Boiler-makers	9 00	12 00	10 50
Blacksmiths	9 00	10 50	9 00
Molders	9 00	10 50	9 00
Millwrights	9 00	12 00	10 50

IX. Store and Shop Wages.

Wages paid per week of sixty to sixty-five hours in stores, wholesale or retail, to males and females, in Stratford, Ontario.

Occupations.	Lowest.	Highest.	Average.
Groceries.			
Clerks	$5 00	$9 00	$7 00
Waresmen	5 00	8 00	7 00
Bookkeepers	6 00	12 00	8 00
Jewelry, watches, and clocks.			
Watchmakers	7 00	12 00	10 00
Apprentices	1 00	3 00	1 50
Men's furnishing and clothing.			
Clerks	6 00	12 00	9 00
Tailors	8 00	12 00	10 00
Tailoresses	3 00	9 00	5 00
Cutters	12 00	20 00	15 00
Dry-goods and millinery.			
Clerks:			
Males	6 00	12 00	9 00
Females	3 00	6 00	4 00
Milliners	6 00	12 00	9 00
Trimmers	2 00	6 00	4 50
Bookkeepers	6 00	15 00	10 00
Hardware.			
Clerks	5 00	12 00	8 00
Hats, boots and shoes, and furs.			
Clerks	5 00	9 00	6 00
Shoemakers	4 00	10 00	8 00
Furriers:			
Males	10 00	25 00	15 00
Females	3 00	5 00	3 50
Drugs, &c.			
Drug clerks	7 00	12 00	9 00

X. HOUSEHOLD WAGES IN TOWNS AND CITIES.

Wages paid per month to household servants (towns and cities) in Stratford, Ontario.

Occupations.	Lowest.	Highest	Average.
Private residences:			
General servant	$4 00	$9 00	$7 00
Cook	6 00	8 00	7 00
Nurse girls	3 00	5 00	4 00
Hotels:			
Porters	12 00	25 00	18 00
Bell-boys	4 00	7 00	6 00
Cooks	8 00	15 00	10 00
Waitresses and chamber maids	5 00	7 00	6 00

XI. AGRICULTURAL WAGES.

Wages paid to agricultural laborers and household (country) servants in county of Perth, Ontario, with board and lodging.

Occupations.	Lowest.	Highest.	Average.
General farm hands.........................per year	$100 00	$200 00	$180 00
Laborers, during harvest..................per day	1 25	2 25	1 75
Servants, female.........................per month	3 00	6 00	4 50

XII. CORPORATION EMPLOYÉS.

Wages paid to the corporation employés in the town of Stratford, Ontario.

Occupations.	Lowest.	Highest.	Average.
Laborers ....per week	$6	$10 50	$7 50
Foreman..........................per year			450 00
Chief of police......................do			500 00
Night police........................do			450 00
Day police.........................do			300 00
Police magistrate ....do			1,200 00
Foreman of fire-brigade...............do			200 00
Town clerk.........................do			500 00
Assessor...........................do			350 00
Collector...........................do			300 00
Treasurer..........................do			350 00
PUBLIC SCHOOLS.			
Head master.......................per year			800 00
First assistant.......................do			475 00
Teachers ....do	250 00	300 00	275 00
High school:			
Principal			1,500 00
First assistant			1,050 00
Second assistant			1,000 00
Two teachers, at			700 00
COUNTY SCHOOLS.			
Teachers:			
Male	375 00	550 00	420 00
Female.........................	200 00	375 00	300 00

XIII. GOVERNMENT DEPARTMENTS AND OFFICES.

Wages paid per year to employés in Government departments and offices—exclusive of tradesmen and laborers.

Occupations.	Lowest.	Highest.	Average.
Collector of customs			$1,200
Inspector of customs			700
Collector of internal revenue			1,200
Clerk			750
Postmaster			2,000
Post-office clerks	$150	$600	

XV. PRINTERS AND PRINTING OFFICES.

Statement showing the wages paid per week of sixty hours to printers (compositors, pressmen, proof-readers, &c.) in Stratford.

Occupations.	Lowest.	Highest.	Average.
Printers, compositors, pressman	$6	$10 50	$7 50

Retail food and fuel prices in Stratford, Ontario, May 1, 1884.

Articles.	Cost.	Articles.	Cost.
Beef..................per lb..	$0 07 to $0 15	Coffee, green............ per lb..	$0 15 to $0 20
Beef (best roasting pieces) .do....	12	Coffee, roasted ....do....	30 to 40
Mutton.....................do....	7 to 12½	Tea.......................do....	20 to 80
Lamb ....per quarter..	1 00 to 1 50	Cheese ....do....	15 to 16
Veal...... ....per lb..	5 to 12½	Eggs ....do....	13 to 14
Pork, fresh................do....	10 to 14	Potatoes ....per bush..	55 to 60
Pork, salt................do....	14	Turkeys ....each..	75 to 1 75
Bacon and ham............ do....	15	Geese and ducks ....do....	50 to 75
Butter....................do....	16 to 18	Chickens ....per pair..	40 to 60
Lard ....do..	14	Wood, soft............per cord..	2 25 to 2 75
Cornmeal..................do....	2 to 2½	Wood, hard ....do....	4 50 to 5 00
Oatmeal ....do....	3 to 3½	Coal ....per ton..	7 00 to 7 50
Flour ....per 100 lbs..	2 75 to 3 10		

J. S. BENEDICT,

Consular Agent.

UNITED STATES CONSULAR AGENCY,

Stratford, May 19, 1884.

TORONTO.

REPORT BY CONSUL HOWARD.

RATE OF WAGES.

The rate of wages paid to laborers of every class in the month of May of the present year is given in the tables accompanying this report.

COST OF LIVING.

The cost of living to the laboring classes is shown to some extent in the tables submitted herewith. The table containing the prices for the years of 1877, 1878, and 1884 shows the wholesale prices for these years, and is chiefly valuable for the purpose of comparing the cost of living one year with another; the relative cost being shown as well by wholesale as retail prices. The quotations from the Saint Lawrence market are retail prices, and all the tables are for the middle of May in each year. Ready-made clothing is fully as cheap now as in 1878. Higher class clothing is dearer, and domestic cottons are dearer. Boots and shoes are no more expensive now than in 1878. Rent has not advanced much, if any, except, possibly, in the higher class of houses. In this connection it may be well to remark that these inquiries are of special force in Canada, for the reason that in 1878 the national policy, so called, or the policy of protecting home industries, was adopted here, and the question of the relative advancement of the price of labor and the cost of living is an interesting and a disputed one. It will be seen, by reference to the tables, that meats have nearly doubled in price. This is doubtless due, in a large measure, to the extensive export trade to England that has lately sprung up, and which would have caused an increase in prices independently of the national policy. It will also be observed that there is a sharp decline in the price of flour and some other kinds of farinaceous foods—in the price of sugar and other groceries. It must be concluded, however, that as compared with the year 1878, the cost of living, as a whole, has considerably advanced. As compared with the year 1877, however, the prices are more nearly even. There is a duty of 50 cents per ton on coal, and as the coal consumed in this part of Canada comes from the United States, the price of fuel has advanced almost directly in proportion with that duty. In conversation with many laboring men they have universally stated as their impression that the cost of living has advanced out of all proportion with the advance of wages. As one man put it, "To get along as easily now as I did in reciprocity times, when I was getting $1.60 per day, I ought now to be getting $3 per day." I doubt, however, if the impressions of these men are to be relied upon. In an interval of even ten years the average man's expenses are greatly increased. His family is larger in number, or older in years, and requires more money. Besides, if a man gets $1.60 per day and spends it all, when he gets $3 per day and spends it all he at once concludes that there is a want of proportion somewhere. And the laboring men here, as a class, spend all they earn. It is evident, at all events, that both the wages in Canada and the cost of living have advanced since 1878, and the tables submitted herewith give better data for comparison than any one's impressions.

COMPARISON OF WAGES.

As compared with 1878, wages have advanced from 20 to 30 per cent. The conditions affecting the labor market now and in 1878 are very different. Then the wages were lower, but not so much competition was noticed in the various avocations as at the present time. Men found employment the year around. Now there have come into Canada thousands of Italians and other foreign laborers who compete with the native Canadians for the coarser kinds of manual labor and weaken the price of mere muscular exertion, while hundreds of young Englishmen seeking clerkships, mechanical and the various forms of lighter manual labor have, by crowding the market with men eager to accept any wages for a temporary expedient, brought down also the price of skilled labor to a minimum. The natural flow of immigration has been unduly stimulated by assisted passages, the rivalry of transportation lines, and the efforts of immigration agents. The assisted immigrants have, for the most part, been dwellers in cities, and when they reach Canada gravitate instinctively into the cities and towns, and shun the lonesome fields and farms. Thus there is produced in all the large cities in Canada a plethora of labor, which shows its effect not so much in smaller wages, the natural result of competition, as in keeping down the natural and even increase with the increased cost of living, which the advocates of the national policy reasonably expected, in reduced time and scarcity of employment. The efforts of the trades unions have also to some extent counteracted the natural effect of competition. During the summer there is usually employment for all who are determined to work, but the winter soon comes with enforced idleness, want, and distress. Last winter was one of unusual hardship and destitution, demanding public and private charity to prevent absolute starvation. Soup kitchens were maintained for months to give the hungry one meagre meal a day, and various schemes were devised to give employment to those who were able and willing to work. But the difficulty of carrying on public works and improvements during the winter months in this climate is obvious, and resort was had to private benevolence rather than to public enterprises.

HABITS OF THE WORKING CLASSES.

The laboring classes in Toronto and in Ontario differ but little from those of corresponding classes in the United States. There is about the same proportion of saving and improvident, of temperate and intemperate, of virtuous and vicious. I think there is more time given to recreation and more money spent on amusements here, and that intemperance is the vice that steals away the savings and destroys the comfort of the homes. There are licensed saloons on every corner, and I think the drinking habit is much more common than with us. Whisky, gin, and brandy are so cheap that even the poorest man can indulge in a drunk at a very trifling expense, and so easily obtained that a drunken woman is by no means an uncommon sight, and children easily learn to taste and tipple. All this might be said of an American city of equal size, to our shame. It is quite apparent to my mind that the laboring classes do not own their own homes to the same extent that the same classes do in the United States, and that the almost universal ambition of the American laborer to possess the title to his own house and lot is largely wanting here. The absence of this incentive to saving may account for much of the recklessness and apathy that one sees among the working classes in Canada. As a class I should say that they are honest and faithful, but more plodding and less ambitious than the same classes with us. The hope of bettering their condition or the desire to give their children a better position in life than their own seems to me to be less a vital and constant force than with the working classes in the United States. The cause of this is due in large measure, I believe, to the old-country idea of the son walking in the footsteps of his father, inheriting his social position and his trade, and therewith being content. A man is a "gentleman" here by act of Parliament.

EMPLOYÉ AND EMPLOYER.

The relation between the laborers and their employers is purely selfish—each looking out for what he supposes to be his individual interest without very much consideration of the idea that their interests are in any degree mutual. The laborer aims to give as little work as possible for his wages and the employer designs to give as little wages as possible for his work. This feeling has undoubtedly been fostered by labor organizations, counter organizations of capital, strikes, surrenders, or compromises. These contests have an accelerating tendency to reduce the problem of labor and capital to an inhuman question of pure political economy, and the law of supply and demand finds an excuse for amending the golden rule. So that when business is dull and times are slack the employer discharges his employés or cuts down their wages without compunction because when business was active, when orders were brisk and labor had capital on the hip, it exacted the utmost farthing. All this creates an antagonism between labor and capital, and more and more crushes out all faithfulness and loyalty—all sentiment, sympathy, or pity. Except for a few philanthropists, the employers have no consideration for the moral or intellectual improvement of the laboring classes, and the general feeling is that there is very little in common between them.

LABOR ORGANIZATIONS.

Nearly every leading industry or trade has its union. These unions are productive of some good in redressing the absolute wrongs of the working classes and in promoting unity of action, community of interest, fostering mutual aid, and to some extent in stimulating thought, though in many cases wrong thinking rather than right. On the other hand it is questionable if these labor organizations do not intensify the natural antagonisms between labor and capital, foster unnecessary class distinctions, encourage foolish struggles against the laws of trade, and often serve as an excuse for the tyranny of capital. The trades unions have forced capital, in its turn, to organize, and in nearly all lines of industry there are here powerful counter organizations of employers, and as business has been for some time in Canada a lock-out, even though it may end in an advance of wages, has been on the whole an advantage to the employers, while the trifling increase of wages, finally temporarily secured, has poorly compensated the workmen for weeks of enforced idleness. Strikes are of frequent occurrence, and it is the general testimony of all classes that the strikers usually carry their point as far as the bare demand is concerned. Many of these unions have a large reserve fund upon which they can draw while the strike continues, and are also usually assisted by kindred unions. I am not aware that arbitration by reference of the cause of difference to a third party is prevalent, although in some organizations there is a provision for such a method of settlement.

LIBERTY OF TRADE.

The working people are free to purchase their supplies where they please. A few years ago it was customary to pay laborers one-half in money and one-half in store orders, but that practice has been abolished and all are paid in the paper and silver currency of the country and usually every Saturday, though some pay on Monday, thinking it better for the men, and that the money will be less likely to be squandered. Few employers, however, take sufficient interest in their employés to adopt this system, and many workingmen would resent the attempt. Saturday afternoon is largely given up to recreation, all the banks and most of the business houses being closed.

CO-OPERATIVE SOCIETIES.

There are in Toronto two regular co-operative societies with branch stores, besides a bakers' co-operative society and a co-operative sewing machine society. The first society of this kind was started in 1877, and is modeled upon the English co-operative system. Each member subscribes for two shares of capital stock of $5 each. A board of directors and other officers are elected. Goods are purchased and sold to members and others at the same price at which goods of the same quality are sold in other stores. At the end of six months the expenses are computed, such as cost of goods, rent, wages, taxes, and as part of the expenses a certain rate of interest on the share capital is allowed. If there is then any balance, a dividend is declared and paid upon the amount each member has traded at the store. The first society started here has been quite successful. They have paid 8 per cent upon their share capital and some years have declared a dividend as high as 17 per cent. There is no effort directly made to sell goods at a lower price than other dealers, and indeed I have an impression that some things often cost the members more than if purchased elsewhere, but the advantage is supposed to be in the interest on the share capital and the dividend upon the amount of the individual purchase. One real advantage and merit of these societies is their teaching of business methods and the encouragement they offer to habits of saving. They urge their members to leave their dividends in the treasury of the society at interest, and in that way become a kind of savings institutions for small sums. They foster industry, economy, and the satisfaction of accumulating something for a rainy day. They also make some effort for the intellectual growth of their members. There are about one thousand members of the different societies in this city. They have had no effect on general trade.

GENERAL CONDITION OF THE WORKING PEOPLE.

Of course, in such a country as Canada, comparatively new as it is, and in such a city as Toronto, growing steadily, if not rapidly, the general condition of the masses differs but little from the condition of the same classes in the United States. Their methods of life, their homes, their food, their clothes are all similar to those of the working-people across the line, varying, as among us, with nationality, habits, amount of income, education, and general character. As I have before remarked, there seems to be less personal ambition among the working classes here—less push and nerve, less desire to rise in the world, less hope of wealth, less determination to "succeed," more lethargy, more acquiescence in fate, more torpor. Consequently there is less chance of bettering their condition, subjectively. Objectively, the traditions of society and the conservative habits of business are in the way; wages are too low, taking the year together; business too dull and slow; foreign laborers too eager to work for bread alone. All these things are obstacles in the way of the laboring men bettering their condition, and their ability to lay up something for a rainy day or for old age is bounded by the narrow rim of their daily toil, which gathers through the short summer but barely enough, and often not enough, to take them meagerly through the long winter. Physically, the Canadian people are fine, strong specimens of mankind, healthy and robust. There is, however, less nimbleness and dexterity among the workingmen than is seen among the native Americans, and the Canadians will be a week at a job that the same number of Americans would have accomplished in half the time. It would be strong, however, when completed, perhaps unnecessarily strong. Morally, the working classes partake of the general character of the mixed Anglo Saxon and Keltic races the world over. Vice and crime have about the same percentage here as in the Western cities of the same size in the United States, and, as in the United States, are chiefly due to rum. Cheap whisky and a low license law, houses of ill-fame, promiscuous public dances, vicious and demoralizing amusements, brutal contests of strength and endurance—these are the evil influences that surround the common people—these the enemies that exist for them at the street corners and in the alleys, that offer to satisfy the universal human demand for amusement and entertainment, and which will continue to charm and brutalize and destroy until some more powerful influence for good, recognizing the facts of human nature, provides an antidote. Reading rooms and libraries, free to all, have been this year established and are doing a good work. But it is to be considered that people who need uplifting most are not readers and are not attracted by such things as books and newspapers. Several philanthropic men in Toronto—notably Mr. W. H. Howland—have done and are doing much to improve the conditions of the lower classes. Coffee-houses, where cheap and clean food, served in atmosphere of physical and moral cleanliness, have been established in different sections of the city, and some attempts have been made to provide cheap and pure amusements to the working people. But the great defect in this has been that all their efforts have flown too high. The promoters have ignored the flutterings of moral and intellectual infancy. They have advertised amusements and given a lecture on astronomy; they have given notice of a free entertainment and furnished Beethoven piano recitals. Still the intention has been good, if not wisely executed; and has done the promoters good, if it has failed to touch the people for whom the efforts were made.

MEANS OF SAFETY.

The means furnished for fire-escapes are chiefly gravitation, which has the merit of cheapness. With few exceptions the only fire-escapes in factories and large buildings are the windows and an unobstructed passage to the ground. On the 24th day of last May the Mail newspaper building, in which are the offices of this consulate, caught fire. The fire ran swiftly up the elevator about which the stairs were constructed, and then spread rapidly through the top of the building where about twenty-five girls were usually employed. It being a holiday only six girls were there. Their exit from the building was completely cut off via the stairs and elevator, and they made their perilous passage from the fifth story window by walking along a narrow gutter a hundred feet above the pavement to the end of the building, whence they escaped by a ladder to a contiguous structure and thence to the ground. Had the usual number of girls been present or had there been any hesitation on the part of their rescuers there would inevitably have been a panic and disaster. As it was, the girls were with difficulty restrained from throwing themselves into the street. This was a new building, constructed upon a modern plan at great expense, and with a few exceptions was as well equipped with fire-escapes as any building in the city. As far as I know there is no provision made by employers for work-people in case of accident, and the general hospital, which is provided at the public expense, is the only resort for the wounded. On the 2d of January last a frightful accident occurred to a suburban train loaded with operatives employed in the bolt-works about 5 miles from the city, by which about thirty men and boys lost their lives. The wounded were taken to the hospital. The city and the public contributed with great liberality for the assistance of the families of the unfortunates, and the Grand Trunk Railway Company paid out $70,000 in settlement of claims.

GENERAL RELATIONS BETWEEN MEN.

Little, if any, consideration is given by the employers of labor to the moral and physical well-being of their workmen, and when there is it is not because of any recognition of their duty as employers. The general relation prevailing between the two classes is purely "practical."

POLITICAL RIGHTS.

The right of suffrage is granted to all native or naturalized citizens of Canada who are freeholders or householders, to those having an income of $400 per year, and to farmers' sons living at home. Taxation is based upon practically the same conditions. Until recently legislation has been in the interest of capital rather than of labor, but the laboring man is coming to be more and more regarded in legislation, though if the interests of capital and labor should conflict doubtless the interests of capital would be first considered. A large class of laboring men are now without the franchise, but all indications point to an early broadening of the right of suffrage, and when that time comes it is presumed the rights of laboring men will receive their proper consideration.

' EMIGRATION.

The causes that lead the Canadians to emigrate to the United States are, in the first instance, purely business and commercial interests. They think they can better their condition, make more money, secure a home. To a large extent the emigrant who is successful induces his relatives and friends to join him. Neither political nor governmental ideas have any influence upon emigration from Canada. The occupation of the emigrants is various. Many business men with a small capital seek the United States; many young men with business training; many common laborers. But probably by far the largest class are farmers and mechanics.

FEMALE LABOR.

The number of women and children employed in the various industrial pursuits in this consular district is approximately stated below:

Manufacturing and mechanical	3,500
Commercial, &c	1,000
Professional	500

WAGES.

The rate of wages, as near as can be ascertained, is as follows: Minimum, $1.50 per week; maximum, $20; average, $5.

HOURS OF LABOR.

The hours of labor vary. In factories, mills, and shops working on full time the usual day's work is ten hours. In retail stores the duties commence at about 8 o'clock in the morning and continue often to midnight. In offices the time is usually less than ten hours.

MORAL AND PHYSICAL CONDITION.

The working women of Toronto are generally intelligent, virtuous, and respectable. They are not the people who appear in police courts or are found in dance-houses and in slums. Doubtless they partake to some extent of the general character of their individual surroundings, but as a rule they are women who are trying to live clean and honest lives. There is the same idiotic idea among the higher classes here that may possibly prevail in some circles in the United States, that work is degrading to a woman; and I am told that even school-teachers are not good enough for the " best society " here. Among the coarser kinds of labor, as in mills and factories, the women are overworked. A right amount of labor ennobles and dignifies; too great a burden deadens and brutalizes, and in the more menial employments the women show in their faces the marks of excessive labor, a lack of proper nutrition, and the benumbing effects of hopeless toil.

SANITARY MEASURES.

The work-rooms of those who ply the needle and the mills and factories where women work are often vilely ventilated, poorly lighted, and improperly heated. No provisions, other than such as common decency demands, has been made by employers, except in a few instances, in regard to sanitary measures, and none whatever, so far as I am aware, for the care of the sick and disabled.

WAGES OF WOMEN.

There has been an increase during the past five years in women's wages, but less relatively than in wages paid to men, while the price of the necessaries of life has advanced alike for all classes. Where women have competed directly for men's work, as in the case of bookkeepers, typewriters, short-hand writers, telegraph operators, clerks, &c., wages have diminished for that class of labor—that is to say, women receive less money than men for doing the same work equally well, and the knowledge that this is so and that women will work for less than men is taken advantage of by employers to reduce the wages of men engaged in the same class of work.

EDUCATION.

The education of working-women varies, of course, among the different classes; the higher grades, demanding a higher degree of intelligence, have a higher degree of education. But even among the lower class of laboring women there are comparatively few natives of the Province of Ontario that cannot read and write. Their children have the advantages of free schools and generally attend them.

EFFECTS OF EMPLOYMENT.

The effect of the employment of mothers in mills, stores, and factories is bad as regards the family. Most of these women are obliged to perform their domestic duties in addition to the work of the day—prepare food for themselves and their families in the morning before starting for their work, give such attention to the house as their time will permit, and complete the absolutely necessary duties upon their return exhausted from their day's toil abroad. They eat a cold and meager lunch at noon and at night consume a hastily-prepared and ill-cooked supper. During the day the younger children are carried with them to their work, left in the careless charge of older ones, or turned loose in the streets. Overworked mothers produce weak and sickly children, and those naturally robust become lean and wan from insufficient or unsuitable food. The want of a mother's companionship and care early hardens the child to the necessities of its life, and the vicious associations of the street sow in fruitful soil the seeds of vice and crime. The jaded, discouraged, perplexed, and hopeless women often seek temporary relief and oblivion in the rum bottle, and the children have that added to their other dangers and temptations. The life of the poor, especially in the cities, is full of hardship and want and wretchedness, and for which they can find no help. They were born, and they must work or die. The unmarried women have a freer and less wearisome life, but they are slaves in many cases to the avarice and cold-blooded selfishness of their employers. Girls working in stores and shops are obliged to work till late at night, and are required to stand upon their feet behind counters where there is little movement, which is the most wearisome of all work, and this constant standing still, much more dangerous to health than walking, often brings on those diseases peculiar to women and a train of incurable evils.

CONCLUSION.

From what has been said it will be observed that the condition of labor in Canada is very similar to that in the United States. Many evils that prevail in Canada prevail also there; many rights and advantages enjoyed there are also blessings here. The people themselves are not dissimilar. Their origin, their speech, their laws, their customs, and their sturdy, industrious character are the marks of a kindred race.

WALTER E. HOWARD,
Consul.

CONSULATE OF THE UNITED STATES,
Toronto, Ontario, Canada, June 10, 1884.

I. GENERAL TRADES.

Wages paid per week of sixty hours in Toronto.

Occupations.	Lowest.	Highest.	Average.
BUILDING TRADES.			
Bricklayers	$10 00	$10 50	$10 00
Hod-carriers	9 50	9 50	9 50
Masons	10 50	10 50	10 50
Tenders	9 50	9 50	9 50
Plasterers	15 00	15 00	15 00
Tenders	9 60	10 80	10 20
Slaters	12 00	12 00	12 00
Roofers	9 50	10 50	10 00
Tenders	7 50	7 75	7 50
Plumbers	10 50	15 00	12 00
Assistants	1 50	5 00	1 50 to 5 00
Carpenters	9 00	15 00	12 00
Gas-fitters	10 50	15 00	12 00

Wages paid per week of sixty hours in Toronto—Continued.

Occupations.	Lowest.	Highest.	Average.
OTHER TRADES.			
Bakers	$6 00	$12 00	$10 00
Blacksmiths	9 00	10 00	9 00
Strikers	6 00	7 00	6 00
Brick-makers.....................................	10 00	20 00	14 00
Bookbinders......................................	9 00	18 00	15 00
Brewers	7 00	9 00	8 00
Butchers...	7 00	10 00	8 50
Cabinet-makers...................................	10 00	15 00	10 00
Confectioners	6 00	13 00	11 00
Cigar-makers.....................................	7 00	13 00	12 00
Coopers	9 00	16 00	12 00
Distillers..	9 00	18 00	14 00
Drivers:			
Drayman and teamsters..........................	8 00	9 00	8 00
Cab and carriage...............................	8 00	9 00	8 00
Street railways................................	8 00	8 50	8 00
Dyers	6 00	15 00	11 00
Engravers..	6 00	22 00	20 00
Furriers...	12 00	25 00	15 00
Gardeners..	6 00	10 50	9 00
Hatters	9 00	20 00	12 00
Horseshoers	6 00	9 00	9 00
Jewelers	8 00	20 00	15 00
Laborers, porters, &c............................	8 00	10 00	8 00
Lithographers....................................	10 00	40 00	35 00
Printers...	11 00	15 00	11 00
Teachers public schools:			
Counties	*120 00	900 00	385 00
Cities	*400 00	1,100 00	742 00
Towns	*240 00	1,000 00	576 00
Saddle and harness makers	9 00	14 00	12 00
Tanners..	....	....	12 00
Tailors..	10 00	20 00	12 00
Telegraph operators..............................	6 00	20 00	15 00
Tinsmiths..	8 00	10 00	9 00

* Per annum.

II. FACTORIES, MILLS, ETC.

Wages paid in factories or mills in Toronto, Canada.

Occupations.	Lowest.	Highest.	Average.
CORSET FACTORY.*			
Steam stitchers, &c. (girls) .... per week..	$2 50	$12 00	$4 75
Label-marking.............................do ..	3 00	3 00	3 00
KNITTING FACTORY.			
Knitters, girls.......................do....	2 00	6 00	5 00
Small girls, ordinary work ....do....	1 00	1 50	1 00
Overseers, women.......................do ...	5 00	6 00	5 00
Finishers ....do ...	2 00	4 00	4 00
FLOUR MILLS.†			
Head millers.......................per month..	90 00	110 00	100 00
Assistant millers.......................do ...	40 00	50 00	45 00
Weighmen ....do ...	35 00	45 00	35 00
Teamsters ....do....	35 00	40 00	35 00

* Fifty-four hours per week.   Sixty hours per week.

III. FOUNDRIES, MACHINE-SHOPS, AND IRON WORKS.

Wages paid per day in foundries, machine-shops, and iron works in Toronto, Canada.

[Week of fifty-four hours.]

Occupations.	Lowest.	Highest.	Average.
Carpenters and joiners	$1 25	$2 50	$2 00
Machine hands	1 50	1 75	1 50
Special work	2 25	2 50	2 25
Molders	2 25	2 50	2 25
Core-makers	1 25	1 50	1 25
Trimmers	1 75	2 25	1 75
Blacksmiths	1 75	2 25	1 75
Painters	1 75	2 25	2 00
Laborers	1 00	1 40	1 25

VI. RAILWAY EMPLOYÉS.

Wages paid to railway employés (those engaged about stations, as well as those engaged on the engines and cars, linemen, railroad laborers, &c.) in Toronto.

Occupations.	Lowest.	Highest.	Average.
Ballasting and track-work ....per day..	$1 00	$1 25	$1 00
Regular trackmen ....do....	1 10	1 10	1 10
Smiths ....do....	1 75	1 75	1 75
Smiths' helpers ....do....	1 25	1 25	1 25
Carpenters ....do....	1 50	1 60	1 50
Engine drivers, freight ....per month..	70 00	80 00	70 00
Engine drivers, passenger ....do....	90 00	100 00	90 00
Firemen ....do....	45 00	45 00	45 00
Engine fitters ....per day..	1 80	1 80	1 80
Engine cleaners ....do....	90	90	90
General laborers ....do....	1 00	1 00	1 00
Conductors, passenger ....do....	1 75	2 23	1 75
Conductors, freight ....do....	1 75	2 15	1 75
Brakemen ....do....	1 10	1 55	1 30
Baggagemen ....do....	1 90	1 90	1 90

Mileage base for drivers: 25 miles, one-quarter of a day; 50 miles, one-half of a day; 75 miles, three-quarters of a day; 100 miles, one day. All fractions over the quarters count in favor of the drivers to make up one-half, three-quarters, or whole day; for instance, 26 miles counts one-half a day, &c.

VIII. SEAMEN'S WAGES.

Wages paid to seamen (officers and men) on Lake Ontario.

Occupations.	Lowest.	Highest.	Average.
Sailors ....per day..	$1 25	$1 50	$1 25
Masters ....per month..	60 00	100 00	75 00
Mates ....do....	50 00	70 00	60 00
Cooks ....do....	16 00	25 00	20 00
Stewards ....do....	16 00	25 00	20 00

IX. STORE AND SHOP WAGES.

Wages paid per week of sixty hours in retail stores to males and females, in Toronto, Canada.

Occupations.	Lowest.	Highest.	Average.
Shop girls in store, counter	$4 00	$10 00	$7 00
Shop men in store, counter	8 00	15 00	10 00
Dressmakers, women	4 00	6 00	5 00
Tailoring, girls	3 00	10 00	6 00
Tailors, men	8 00	18 00	12 00
Messengers	2 50	6 25	6 00

X. HOUSEHOLD WAGES IN TOWNS AND CITIES.

Wages paid per month to household servants in Toronto, Canada.

Occupations.	Lowest.	Highest.	Average.
Nurse girls	$2 00	$5 00	$4 00
General servants	7 00	10 00	8 00
Cooks	8 00	10 00	9 00
Parlor maids	6 00	8 00	7 00
Men, general work	15 00	30 00	25 00
Grooms	30 00	45 00	40 00

XI. AGRICULTURAL WAGES.

Wages paid to agricultural laborers and household (country) servants in Toronto district with board.

Occupations.	Lowest.	Highest.	Average.
First-class farm hands ....per year..			$200 00
Ordinary farm hands ....do			150 00
Farm hands ....per month..	$15 00	$30 00	25 00

XII. CORPORATION EMPLOYÉS.

Wages paid per year to the corporation employés in the city of Toronto, Canada.

Occupations.	Lowest.	Highest.	Average.
TREASURER'S DEPARTMENT.			
City treasurer		$3,550 00	$3,500 00
Assistant city treasurer		2,000 00	2,000 00
Clerks	$720 00	1,500 00	1,200 00
CITY CLERK'S DEPARTMENT.			
City clerk		2,000 00	2,000 00
Assistant city clerk		1,200 00	1,200 00
Clerks	400 00	800 00	500 00
CITY ENGINEER'S DEPARTMENT.			
City engineer		2,800 00	2,800 00
Assistant city engineer		1,200 00	1,200 00
Clerks	720 00	1,100 00	1,000 00
City solicitor's clerk		600 00	600 00
WATER-WORKS DEPARTMENT.			
Secretary and receiver		1,100 00	1,100 00
Accountant and receiver		1,050 00	1,050 00
ENGINEER AND RATING BRANCH.			
Clerks	590 00	1,300 00	800 00
City auditors		1,100 00	1,100 00
Tax collectors	500 00	787 50	600 00
Assessment commissioner		1,600 00	1,600 00
Assessment clerks	450 00	800 00	600 00
THE JAIL.			
Governor		1,500 00	1,500 00
Deputy governor		800 00	800 00
Physician		1,000 00	1,000 00
Clerks, turnkeys, watchmen, &c	280 00	1,000 00	450 00
THE CITY SCALES.			
Weighmaster		1,000 00	1,000 00
Caretaker of market, including attendance at scales		520 00	520 00
Market constable		500 00	500 00

XIII. GOVERNMENT DEPARTMENTS AND OFFICES.

Wages paid per year to employés in Government departments and offices (exclusive of tradesmen and laborers) in Toronto, Canada.

Occupations.	Lowest.	Highest.	Average.
EDUCATION DEPARTMENT.			
Chief clerk and accountant		$1,300 00	$1,300 00
Clerks	$250 00	1,250 00	1,050 00
Messenger		365 00	365 00
Caretaker		500 00	500 00
CROWN LANDS DEPARTMENT.			
Clerks	800 00	1,700 00	1,200 00
SECRETARY AND REGISTRAR DEPARTMENT.			
Clerks	800 00	1,800 00	1,200 00
Messenger		400 00	400 00
LEGISLATION.			
Clerk of the House		1,800 00	1,800 00
Assistant clerk of the House		1,400 00	1,400 00
Librarian		1,400 00	1,400 00
Assistant librarian		700 00	700 00
Clerks	400 00	600 00	500 00

XIV. TRADES AND LABOR—GOVERNMENT EMPLOY.

Wages paid by the year to the trades and laborers in Government employ in Toronto, Canada.

Occupations.	Lowest.	Highest.	Average.
GOVERNMENT HOUSE.			
Messengers		$480 00	$480 00
Gardener and caretaker		450 00	450 00
Fireman and assistant gardener		550 00	550 00
Assistant gardeners and caretakers		400 00	400 00
Messengers in the civil service	$350 00	500 00	350 00
Night watchmen		450 00	450 00

XV. PRINTERS AND PRINTING OFFICES.

Statement showing the wages paid per week of fifty-four hours to printers (compositors, pressmen, proof-readers, &c.) in Toronto, Canada.

Occupations.	Lowest.	Highest.	Average.
Compositors	$11 00	$12 00	$11 00
Pressmen	7 00	15 00	12 00
Proof-readers	10 00	15 00	12 00
Apprentices	1 50	6 00	
Message boys	1 50	2 00	
Canvasser		12 00	
Traveler		12 00	
Shipping clerk	6 00	8 00	

FOOD PRICES.

Retail prices of produce at Saint Lawrence market, Toronto.

Articles.	Price.	Articles.	Price.
Beef, roast .... per pound..	$0 11 to$0 14	Bacon .... per pound..	$0 11 to$0 14
Sirloin steak..................do...	14 to 16	Eggs....................per dozen..	14 to 15
Round steak..................do...	11 to 13	Turkeys	2 00 to 3 00
Mutton, legs and chops ......do...	13 to 15	Chickens.................per pair..	65 to 90
Inferior cuts.................do...	9 to 11	Potatoes ....per bushel..	60 to 65
Lamb.........................do...	15 to 17	Onions...................per peck..	40 to 45
Veal, best joints..............do...	13 to 14	Parsnips....................do....	20 to 25
Veal, inferior cuts ....do...	9 to 10	Beets ....do....	20
Pork, chops and roasts ......do...	11 to 12	Carrots.....................do....	20
Butter:		Beans .... per bushel..	1 20 to 1 50
Pound rolls...............do...	14 to 17	Turnips....................do ...	35 to 40
Large rolls................do...	13 to 14	Asparagus.............per dozen..	30 to 40
Cooking ....do ...	10 to 11	Rhubarb ....do....	15 to 20
Lard ....do ...	13 to 14	Radishes ....do ..	30 to 35
Cheese, new...............do...	12 to 14	Spinach............. per barrel..	40 to 45

Statement showing difference between cost of living in 1877-'78-'84.

Articles.	Value 1877.	Value 1878.	Value 1884.
Dressed hogs..................per 100 pounds..	$7 00 to $7 75	$5 50 to $6 00	$8 00 to $8 25
Beef, hind quarters.................. do....	6 00 to 7 00	4 00 to 5 00	10 00 to 11 00
Mutton .... do	7 00 to 8 50	8 00 to 9 00	8 50 to 10 00
Butter ....per pound..	23 to 25	17 to 18	19 to 21
Eggs ....per dozen..	11	11	15 to 16
Apples...........................per barrel..	2 50 to 3 25	4 00 to 4 50	3 50 to 4 25
Potatoes.........................per bushel..	90 to 1 00	30 to 40	50 to 60
Onions................................do....	90 to 1 00	85 to 90	90 to 1 00
Turnips ....do....	30 to 35	25 to 30	30 to 40
Parsnips...............................do....	55 to 70	30 to 40	65 to 80
Flour:			
Sup. extra.....................per barrel..	8 75 to 9 00	5 50 to 5 75	5 00 to 5 25
Extra ....do....	8 25 to 8 50	5 10 to 5 20	4 65 to 4 80
Spring extra....................do....	7 50 to 7 80	4 50 to 4 75	4 35 to 4 50
No. 1 superfine.................do....	6 75	3 90 to 4 10	3 75 to 4 00
Oatmeal ....do....	6 00	4 00 to 4 10	4 25 to 4 50
Cornmeal ....do ...	3 50 to 3 60	2 65	3 50
Sugar ....per pound..	9¾ to 12¼	7¼ to 11	5½ to 9
Coffee ....do....	22 to 34	21 to 30	25 to 50
Tea..................................do....	26 to 75	25 to 70	20 to 90
Fish, cod..................per 112 pounds..	5 50 to 5 75	5 00 to 5 25	5 50 to 6 00
Raisins ....per pound..	3 to 10½	4 to 8	5 to 6
Rice ....do....	4 60 to 5 00	4 50 to 4 75	3 65 to 3 90
Sirups ....per gallon..	54 to 75	45 to 65	30 to 70
Cheese...........................per pound..	14	11½ to 13	16
Bacon ....do....	8½ to 10½	6½ to 7¾	11 to 14
Hams:			
Smoked..........................do....	11	9 to 10	10 to 11
Pickled..........................do....	10	7 to 8	7 to 9
Lard ....do....	10½ to 12	8½ to 10	14
Apples, dried.........................do....	5½ to 6½	6 to 7½	8½ to 9½
Coal:			
Large egg ....per ton..	5 50	5 50	6 25
Small egg.......................do....	5 50	5 50	6 25
Wood:			
Hard ....per cord..	5 50	5 50	4 50 to 5 50
Pine................................do....	4 50	4 50	4 00

WINDSOR.

REPORT BY CONSUL EWERS.

RATES OF WAGES.

The rates of wages paid to laborers of every class—mechanical, mining, factory, public works, and railway, domestic, agricultural—are given in the tables herewith.

COST OF LIVING.

The prices of the necessaries of life do not vary greatly in Windsor from those prevailing in Detroit, just across the border on the American side. There was formerly considerable business done here in ready-made clothing of the cheaper grades, but this has now almost entirely disappeared, workingmen and others in moderate circumstances finding that they can buy better goods at much lower prices in Detroit. Fine broadcloths, imported woolens, and silks are about the only articles of clothing that are cheaper on this side. House-rent for working people ranges from $6 to $16 per month.

The following list will give a fair idea of the prevailing prices for articles of food, viz:

Articles.	Cost.		Articles.	Cost.
Flour................ per bbl..	$5 00 to $6 25		Mutton, stewing......... per lb..	$0 07 to $0 08
Butter....................per lb..	20		Corn-meal................ do....	2½
Tea ....do...:	25 to 50		Eggs ....per doz..	16
Sugar ....do...'	7 to 8		Coffee .... per lb..	25
Rice....................do ...	5		Oat-meal ....do....	3½
Tobacco....................do....	50		Crackers ....do....	8
Currants ....do....	8		Raisins ....do....	6
Starch....................do....	8		Lard ....do....	14
Beefsteak ....do....	10 to 15		Pork, roast ....per lb..	10 to 12
Beef, roast ....do....	10 to 15		Pork chops ....do....	10 to 12½
Beef, corned ....do....	6 to 8		Pork, salt ....do....	10 to 12
Beef, for soup ....do....	6 to 7		Ham ....do....	16
Mutton leg ....do....	12½		Shoulder ....do....	11
Mutton shoulder ....do....	10		Bacon ....do....	14
Mutton chops ....do ..	12½		Veal.....................do....	8 to 15
Mutton carcass............. do....	9			

Board in private families can be had at $3 and $3.50 per week, and in hotels at from $3.50 to $9 and $12 per week.

WAGES PAST AND PRESENT.

There has been a slight advance in the price of labor since 1878, following the advance on the other side of the border.

HABITS OF THE WORKING CLASSES.

As a general rule, the laboring classes here are sober and industrious. A considerable number of them are negroes, being those, and the descendants of those, who came here for refuge in slavery days. Some are unthrifty, and spend their money as fast or faster than they get it. But nearly all have an opportunity, by frugality, of laying up something for old age. Many avail themselves of the Government savings system connected with the post-office department.

FEELING BETWEEN EMPLOYER AND EMPLOYÉ.

There are very few institutions here where many men are employed, the principal one being a distillery and works connected therewith, owned and operated by an American citizen and resident of Detroit. In this and the other institutions here a good feeling prevails between employers and employed, manifested by continuous service of employés and by presents given them each year at Christmas time by employers.

LABOR ORGANIZATIONS.

There are no labor organizations here, but Windsor mechanics partake of whatever advantages accrue to workingmen in Detroit through labor organizations. Employers here pay without question the scale of wages adopted by the various trades unions in Detroit and in vogue there.

STRIKES.

As there is no organization in labor, there are no strikes. Windsor mechanics are content to let their Detroit brethren fight the battles, while they (the Windsor mechanics) reap the benefit thereof. It is even the case, in certain instances, when some of the trades in Detroit have been "out" that Windsor mechanics have joined with those of London, Chatham, and other parts of Canada, and taken the places of the striking mechanics in Detroit.

FOOD PURCHASES.

They are free to purchase where they please. Hiram Walker has a store in connection with his large distillery interests, but imposes no conditions on his employés to purchase therefrom. Payments are made weekly or monthly in Canada or American money, both being current, here at their face value.

CO-OPERATIVE SOCIETIES.

There are no co-operative societies in Essex County.

GENERAL CONDITION OF THE WORKING PEOPLE.

The condition of the working people in Windsor and Walkerville is one of comparative independence. They all claim that their wages (including those of clerks) are higher here than in any other part of Canada. They attribute this state of things to their close proximity to a large and prosperous American city (Detroit). Indeed, many who are residents here find employment on the other side of the river.

A careful estimate develops the fact that nearly one-half of all the wage-workers of Windsor either own or are in a way to own their own homes. This is not the case, however, in Walkerville, as there all real property is owned by one man, who will not sell, but leases on favorable terms to his employés.

Their clothing, as before mentioned, is mostly purchased in Detroit, where a good suit of clothes can be bought for from $10 to $15. There is very little chance for a working man to rise above the sphere in life he has chosen, or which has been chosen for him, but there are excellent public schools here, and he can give his children a good education. There are numerous protective societies among workingmen, which pay something in case of death or accident.

SAFETY OF EMPLOYÉS.

No special means of safety, except fire-escapes (in one or two instances), are provided for employés in factories. I cannot ascertain that employers give themselves any special concern over either the moral or the physical condition of their employés. An exception, perhaps, exists in the case of the American distiller before mentioned, who, at his own expense, built a church opposite his distillery. The general relations between employers and employed are harmonious.

POLITICAL RIGHTS.

The elective franchise is bestowed only on those who pay taxes on an assessed valuation of $400 in towns and cities, and on $200 in the country. This, it is claimed, gives nearly every man of family who is a house-renter, a vote, because in most cases the renter pays the taxes.

It was through the influence of the workingmen's votes that the policy of protection was adopted by the Canadian Government six years ago.

There is very little special legislation in regard to workingmen.

There is a law as to mechanic's liens.

EMIGRATION.

The emigrants from Essex County are mostly farmers who are seeking homes in the Western States. A belief in their ability to do better in the "States" influences them. Some are mechanics, who have secured permanent work in Detroit, or in some of the cities of interior Michigan.

FEMALE LABOR.

The number of women and children employed in Essex County, outside of their homes, is so small that no statistics of any value can be given concerning it.

Many young women, however, whose homes are in Windsor, find employment in Detroit as saleswomen and workers in knitting and other factories. A great many women and children throughout the country find employment at home in the manufacture of straw braid for hats.

There being so few women employed in factories, &c., their employment has no visible effect on the wages of men.

Canadian girls are in great demand in Detroit as household servants, in which capacity they receive good wages.

This demand keeps up the rate of wages for household servants in Windsor.

CHARLES EWERS,
Consul.

UNITED STATES CONSULATE,
Windsor, Ontario.

I. GENERAL TRADES.

Wages paid in Windsor.

[Per day of ten hours.]

Occupations.	Lowest.	Highest.	Average.
BUILDING TRADES.			
Bricklayers..per day..	$3 50	$3 50	$3 50
Hod-carriers................................do....	1 50	1 75	1 50
Masons ....do....	3 00	3 50	3 25
Tenders..................................do....	1 50	1 50	1 50
Plasterers...............................do ...	3 50	3 50	3 50
Tenders...............................do....,	1 75	1 75	1 75
Plumbers.................................do....,	1 75	2 50	2 00
Assistants.............................do ...'	1 00	1 50	1 25
Carpenters...............................do ..	2 00	2 25	2 00
Gas-fitters ....do....	1 75	2 50	2 00
Helpers.................................do....	1 00	1 50	1 25
OTHER TRADES.			
Bakers...................................do ..	1 00	2 00	1 67
Blacksmiths ....do....	1 00	2 00	1 50
Strikers...............................do....	1 25	1 25	1 25
Butchers ....per week..	*5 00	*10 00	*7 00
Cabinet-makers ....per day..	1 00	2 33	2 00
Confectioners ....do....	1 00	2 00	1 67
Cigar-makers ....per week..	4 00	12 00	7 00
Coopers................................do....	6 00	12 00	10 00
Distillers..............................per day....	2 00	4 00	3 50
Drivers:			
Draymen and teamsters................per week..	6 00	8 00	7 00
Street railways......................per day..	†1 00	†1 00	†1 00
Gardeners‡...............................			
Horseshoers ....do ...	1 00	2 00	1 50
Jewelers..............................per week..	8 00	15 00	12 00
Laborers, porters, &c.................per day..	1 00	1 50	1 25
Printers ....per week..	7 00	14 00	10 00
Teachers public schools ....per annum..	300 00	1,280 00	425 00
Saddle and harness makers ....per week..	6 00	12 00	7 50
Tailors.................................do ..	§10 00	§15 00	§12 00
Helpers ....do ..	4 00	6 00	5 00
Telegraph operators ....per month..	25 00	40 00	35 00
Tinsmiths ....per day..	1 50	2 00	1 75

* With board.   †Sixteen hours per day.
‡ There are many small market gardeners in the vicinity of Sandwich who contribute largely to supply the Detroit market. They hire no labor, however, the work being done by themselves and members of their families.
§ Piece work.

II. FACTORIES, MILLS, ETC.

Wages paid per week in factories or mills in Windsor and Walkerville, Ontario, Canada.

Occupations.	Lowest.	Highest.	Average.
Cigar factory:			
Strippers...................................	$1 50	$6 00	$2 00
Bunch-breakers	4 00	8 00	5 15
Cigar-makers..............................	4 00	12 00	7 00
Packers...................................	8 00	12 00	10 00

III. FOUNDRIES, MACHINE SHOPS, AND IRON WORKS.

Wages paid per week in foundries, machine shops, and iron works in Windsor, Ontario, Canada.

Occupations.	Lowest.	Highest.	Average.
Iron and wire workers:			
Wire department..	$3 00	$18 00	$10 00
Iron workers (fences)	3 00	18 00	10 00
Blacksmiths	12 00	12 00	12 00

VI. RAILWAY EMPLOYÉS.

Wages paid to railway employés (those engaged about stations, as well as those engaged on the engines and cars, linemen, railroad laborers, &c.) in Windsor, Ontario, Canada.

Occupations.	Lowest.	Highest.	Average.
Engine drivers..per month..	$75 00	$130 00	$85 00
Firemen ....do....	46 00	75 00	{ 68 00 / 70 00
Wipers in shop ....do ...	30 00	30 00	30 00
Fitters ....per hour..	23	23	23
Car repairers outside ....do....	12½	12½	12½
Car repairers in shop ....do....	17½	17½	17½
Car examiners ....do....	15	18	16½
Watchmen ....per day..	1 25	1 25	1 25
Switchmen ....do ...	1 75	2 25	2 00
Brakemen ....per month..	35 00	55 00	45 00
Freight conductors ....do ...	65 00	80 00	70 00
Passenger conductors.....................................do ...	75 00	75 00	75 00
Office clerks ....do....	35 00	65 00	50 00
Bridge men...per day..	1 75	1 80	1 77
Laborers...do....	1 25	1 25	1 25
Several large steam ferry-boats are operated by the railway companies in carrying cars across the Detroit River. Wages on them are as follows:			
Captains ....per annum..	1,000 00	1,200 00	1,100 00
Mates ....per day..	2 50	2 50	2 50
Engineers ....do ...	1 75	3 00	2 25
Firemen ....do....	1 50	1 50	1 50
Ship carpenters ....do ...	2 50	2 75	2 60
Deck hands...do....	1 15	1 15	1 15

IX. STORE AND SHOP WAGES.

Wages paid per week of seventy-two hours in stores, wholesale or retail, to males and females, in Windsor, Ontario, Canada.

Occupations.	Lowest.	Highest.	Average.
Clerks and salesmen:			
Retail groceries	$10 00	$15 00	$12 00
Retail dry goods	9 00	15 00	12 00

XI. AGRICULTURAL WAGES.

Wages paid to agricultural laborers and household (country) servants in Essex County, Ontario, Canada, with board and lodging.

Occupations.	Lowest.	Highest.	Average.
Female household ....per week..	$1 00	$2 00	$1 60
Farm hands (summer) ....per month..	15 00	20 00	17 00
Farm hands (all year) ....do....	12 00	15 00	13 00

XII. CORPORATION EMPLOYÉS.

Wages paid per year to the corporation employés in the city of Windsor, Ontario, Canada.

Occupations.	Lowest.	Highest.	Average.
Town clerk			$1,000 00
Town treasurer			400 00
Secretary water board			750 00
Chief of police			*700 00
Policeman			†480 00

*And fees.
†The members of the police force also receive two suits of clothes each year, and an overcoat every two years from the city. Also fees for making arrests, which makes their yearly receipts $600.

XIII. GOVERNMENT DEPARTMENTS AND OFFICES.

Wages paid per month to employés in Government departments and offices—exclusive of tradesmen and laborers—in Windsor, Ontario, Canada.

Occupations.	Lowest.	Highest.	Average.
Post-office	$33 33	$110 66	$54 17
Inland revenue	18 33	150 00	70 75
Custom-house	41 67	133 33	50 00

XV. PRINTERS AND PRINTING OFFICES.

Statement showing the wages paid per week of sixty hours to printers (compositors, pressmen, proof-readers, &c.) in Windsor, Ontario, Canada.

Occupations.	Lowest.	Highest.	Average.
Compositors	$7 00	$14 00	$10 00
Pressmen	7 00	14 00	10 00
Apprentices	3 00	4 00	3 50
Reporters	9 00	12 00	10 00
Proof-readers	7 00	14 00	10 00

PROVINCE OF QUEBEC.

MONTREAL.

REPORT BY CONSUL-GENERAL STEARNS.

In reply to your circular, under date of February 15, 1884, I have the honor to report as follows:

WAGES PAST AND PRESENT.

It has been a difficult matter to ascertain the actual increase or decrease, if any, since 1878, in the rates of wages paid.

I do not learn of any decrease in wages from those paid in 1878, except in the case of sail-makers, whose wages are reported to be about 20 per cent. less now than in 1878.

The cause of this is said to be overproduction and the falling off in the shipping interests.

The majority of the firms and manufacturers called upon for information state that the rates of wages in most of the trades now and in 1878 are about the same, and nearly all claimed that the cost of living had advanced about 10 per cent., although some were of the opinion that it had advanced 20 or 25 per cent.

In the following trades, however, the rates of wages were reported to me as being higher than in 1878, to wit:

	Per cent.
Metal and cement roofers	10
Plumbers, gas and steam fitters	about.. 20
Bell-hangers, locksmiths, and blacksmiths	15 to 20
Brass-founders, finishers, &c	about.. 20
Horseshoers	do.... 10
Dyers	do.... 10
Printers	10 to 12½
Boiler-makers (in some shops)	10 to 20
Boot and shoe makers (in factories)	about.. 10
Book-binders	do.... 10
Marble and stone-cutters	10 to 15
Coopers	about.. 20
Cigar-makers, about	do.... 45

In some branches of manufacture wages had advanced considerably beyond these rates a year or two ago, but owing to a general depression in business at the present time they have receded.

In the Protestant public schools in this city the average salary paid to a male teacher is $114, and to a female teacher $34 per month of 100 hours. About six years ago the school board, in consequence of financial depression and a decrease in the proceeds of the school tax, was compelled to lower the scale of salaries paid, so that the present scale (the one given above) falls short by about $5 a month from that which obtained in 1878. There are at present twenty-three male teachers and ninety female teachers in the employ of the Protestant board of school commissioners for this city. The cost of board of teachers is stated as being from $10 to $14 per month. I have not been able to obtain any reliable information as to the rate of wages paid to teachers in the Catholic schools of the city, but as they are generally ecclesiastics the average salaries paid to them are no doubt much less than in the Protestant schools.

In comparing the present rates of wages and cost of living with those in 1878, the following facts should be borne in mind as important influences affecting both.

In 1879 the Dominion of Canada adopted a protective tariff by which the rates of duties on almost all articles were largely increased. Manufacturing establishments multiplied all over the country, home industries expanded, the kinds of articles manufactured greatly diversified, and the demand for skilled labor, and, indeed, all kinds of labor, increased in a corresponding ratio. At about the same time the construction of the Canadian Pacific Railway was begun, and has been pushed forward with great rapidity, offering employment to large numbers of skilled and unskilled laborers. Since 1878 the "great northwest country" has been opened to settlement, and great efforts have been put forth to attract emigrants from the older provinces and from Europe.

HABITS OF THE WORKING CLASSES.

The habits of the working classes here are very much like those ot the same classes in the United States; there is a fair degree of providence among them, and in trustworthiness and steadiness they compare favorably with their fellows across the line. A considerable number of the mechanics and the great majority of the unskilled laborers in this city, and the farm hands in the country adjoining it, are French Canadians; they are a hard-working, economical people, who live very plainly, rear large families, contribute largely to the support of the church, and manage to lay up something from their small earnings. There are, too, in this city a large body of Irish, who are, most of them, laborers of one kind and another. The mechanics are in general—although, of course, there are many exceptions—not of the highest class in point of skill, the best workmen being drawn off by higher wages to the United States.

FEELING BETWEEN EMPLOYER AND EMPLOYÉ.

The feeling which prevails between employé and employer is, so far as I know, generally very pleasant and harmonious. There has been for a few years past a great deal of trouble with domestic servants, especially the female portion, who have been very independent in their ways and very inefficient and unsatisfactory in their work.

LABOR ORGANIZATION.

There has been in the past very little tendency on the part of labor to organize, and but few of the mechanics and employés in the various branches of trade and manufacture in this city are members of trades unions or similar societies. The coopers and cigar-makers are notable exceptions to the general rule in this respect. In the printing offices, both union and non-union men are employed, and no distinction is made between them on the part of the proprietors, or insisted upon on the part of the men. On the other hand there are few organizations of capital except in one or two trades where the various large establishments have associated themselves together to resist strikes and for mutual help in their relations towards their employés.

STRIKES.

Very few strikes have occurred among the mechanics and laborers in this city during the past few years, and where they have occurred, in nearly every instance the employés have been compelled to submit to the terms of their employers. In the great strike of telegraph operators last year those in this city took part and shared the fate of their co-strikers in other parts of the continent.

FOOD PURCHASES.

The working people are generally free to purchase the necessaries of life where they choose, and only in rare cases do the employers impose conditions in this regard.

The laborer is paid weekly or monthly, as the case may be, and for the most part in cash in the currency of the country, which is similar in value and kind to that in the United States.

CO-OPERATIVE SOCIETIES.

There are many associations composed wholly or in part of the laboring classes, but they are generally national or religious societies having for their object mutual aid in times of sickness or distress, or the culti-

vation of closer social relations. There is one co-operative society, so
called, in the city, which has taken the form of a large grocery and
dry goods store. It is a stock concern and claims to sell to its stockholders and subscribers at an advance upon cost only sufficient to pay
expenses and a fair dividend upon its stock. Its nominal capital is
divided into a large number of shares of the par value of $5, but I
understand a considerable part of it has not been taken up. Subscribers are admitted to the advantages of the society upon payment
of $1 per annum. All sales are for cash. It is largely used by the
rich and middle classes, but my impression is it receives very little patronage from mechanics and laborers. It has had, however, the effect of
reducing prices somewhat in the ordinary stores. It has once failed
and been reorganized, and it is generally understood that it is not now
very firmly established and is not profitable to the stockholders.

GENERAL CONDITION OF THE WORKING CLASSES.

The general condition of the working people in this city is quite up
to the average in the United States. I have selected, as I was directed
to do by your circular, a workingman whom I thought fairly representative, and have asked him the questions suggested by you. There are
comparatively few large tenement houses, but there are many smaller
ones capable of containing two or three families. A considerable part
of the laboring population, especially the French Canadians, dwell in
small houses, a story or a story and a half high, either in the city or in
the outlying municipalities, of which there are a number immediately
adjoining the city.

Through the efforts of the Montreal Horticultural Society considerable interest has been excited in the cultivation of flowers and plants
and the windows and small door-plats of even the poorest are often
filled with geraniums, verbenas, and similar bright flowers. The
Mountain Park, which can be easily reached on foot, and Saint Helen's
Island, to which a ferry-boat carries pleasure seekers for a small toll,
are much frequented by the laboring classes, and furnish a means of
health and amusement.

The poor and sick are looked after by the various charitable societies,
the ecclesiastical institutions, the Roman Catholic brotherhood and sis-
terhood, the church organizations, &c. There is a flourishing Young
Men's Christian Association, and societies for the prevention of cruelty
to women and children, who are active in their efforts to secure both
classes against oppression and to ameliorate their condition. Temperance societies are numerous; and great efforts are made both by Roman
Catholics and Protestants to put down drunkenness among all classes
and restrict the sale of intoxicating liquors.

There are two or three savings banks in this city, and there is a Government savings bank in connection with the post office-department.
The character and amount of deposits indicate a very satisfactory
tendency among the working classes towards the laying up of money.

SAFETY OF EMPLOYÉS.

The laws require that the large buildings shall be provided with fire
escapes and be built of brick or stone.

In some of the factories the hoistways have automatically-acting doors,
and sprinklers for use in case of fire are arranged at frequent intervals
on every floor.

In one at least of the largest cotton-mills medical attendance is furnished by the owners, each operative being assessed 10 cents a month therefor. A number of those employing many hands give them an excursion once or twice during the summer. It is becoming more and more the custom in all branches of business to close early on Saturday and give the employés a half holiday on that day. In the course of the year there are a goodly number of feast, or holy, days, upon which the Roman Catholic portion of the community abstain, so far as they are able, from work.

CAUSES OF EMIGRATION.

Emigration from this part of the province of Quebec is either to the northwestern portion of Canada or to the United States. The emigrants to the United States are principally French Canadians, who go to the manufacturing cities of New England to find employment in the mills and workshops. They generally take their families with them, that they may utilize the labor of all who are old enough to work, and many of them go with the idea of returning when they have accumulated something. In times past many have returned and, buying farms in the places from which they originally went forth, have enjoyed the fruits of their hard and confining work in the mills in the comparative comfort of farm-life here; but of late fewer of those who go return to their old homes and more settle permanently in the United States. The emigrants to the Northwest, on the other hand, are for the most part English-speaking people of Scotch, English, and Irish origin, who hope to better their condition in a newer country.

NUMBER OF EMPLOYED FEMALES.

I do not think it possible—I certainly have not been able to obtain the information that would enable me—to answer with any degree of fullness or accuracy the questions asked in regard to female labor.

In the cotton-mills, of which there are several in this district, a large number of women are employed. There are also a few in the printing establishments and newspaper offices and in the boot and shoe and clothing manufactories. In the retail dry goods and fancy stores it is quite common to employ female hands, and so in the restaurants and small hotels. Most of the laundrying is done by women, and there are many female teachers in the public schools, both Protestant and Roman Catholic. The great religious houses are full of "sisters," who do sewing, act as nurses, &c. There are no females in any of the professions.

WAGES AND HOURS OF LABOR.

The wages paid vary according to the work. The hours of labor correspond with those of males. In the retail stores attendance from 7 in the morning until 6 at night is required, and the hours in the trades are about the same. There is in all cases a noon intermission for rest and refreshment.

MORAL AND PHYSICAL CONDITION OF FEMALE EMPLOYÉS.

The remarks made under the head of male labor in regard to the moral and physical condition of the employés, the means provided in cases of fire and other danger, for their safety, the provisions made by the employés in regard to sanitary measures, and for the care of the sick and disabled, will apply equally well to female laborers of every kind.

FEMALE WAGES PAST AND PRESENT.

It is only within the past few years that women have been employed to any great extent. and a comparison of wages paid them now and five years ago is not possible. I do not think their employment has had any appreciable effect on the wages paid men, or the general, social, and industrial conditions.

EDUCATION OF FEMALE EMPLOYÉS.

The schools here are fairly good, and the attendance upon them is quite general, so that the female employés have sufficient education to perform their duties satisfactorily. Very few children are employed in the large establishments. There are no laws which regulate their employment, although an effort was made last year to secure the passage of an act for that purpose.

SEARGENT P. STEARNS,

Consul-General.

UNITED STATES CONSULATE-GENERAL,
Montreal, July 1, 1884.

I. GENERAL TRADES.

Wages paid per week in the city and district of Montreal.

Occupations.	Hours.	Lowest.	Highest.	Average.
BUILDING TRADES.				
Bricklayers (summer)	60	$21 00	$21 00	$21 00
Bricklayers (winter)	60	18 00	18 00	18 00
Hod-carriers	60	6 90	9 00	7 50
Masons (summer)	60	10 50	18 00	12 00
Masons (winter)	60	9 00	12 00	10 50
Tenders or laborers	60	6 60	9 00	8 40
Plasterers (winter)	60	13 50	13 50	13 50
Plasterers (summer)	60	15 00	15 00	15 00
Tenders or laborers	60	6 60	9 00	8 40
Slaters	60	10 50	13 50	12 00
Roofers:				
Metal	60	9 00	15 00	10 80
Gravel	60	7 00	9 00	7 50
Cement	60	7 50	12 00	9 00
Tenders or laborers	60	7 00	9 00	7 50
Plumbers	60	9 00	13 00	11 00
Assistants	60	2 00	4 00	3 00
Carpenters	60	7 50	15 00	10 50
Gas and steam fitters	60	9 00	13 00	11 00
Electricians and bell-hangers	60	12 00	19 50	13 50
OTHER TRADES.				
Bakers:				
Biscuit-makers	60	7 00	12 00	9 00
Bread-makers	60	10 50	15 00	12 00
Blacksmiths	60	9 00	15 00	10 50
Blacksmiths, locksmiths, &c.	60	10 00	13 50	11 00
Book-binders:				
Males	60	7 00	12 00	10 00
Females	60	2 00	5 00	3 38
Brewers:				
Maltsters	60	6 00	9 00	6 75
Coopers	60	10 75	10 75	10 75
Bottlers	60	6 00	9 00	7 50
Laborers	60	6 00	9 00	6 75
Butchers	60	7 00	15 00	10 50
Brass-founders	60	6 00	14 00	9 00
Cabinet makers	60	9 00	15 00	11 00
Confectioners	60	5 00	15 00	9 00

Wages paid per week in the city and district of Montreal—Continued.

Occupations.	Hours.	Lowest.	Highest.	Average.
OTHER TRADES—Continued.				
Cigar-makers:				
Males	60	$9 00	$16 00	$13 00
Females	60	3 00	7 00	4 50
Coopers (summer)	60	12 00	12 00	12 00
Coopers (winter)	60	10 50	10 50	10 50
Coopers employed in sugar refineries	60	10 50	10 50	10 50
Drivers:				
Draymen and teamsters	60	6 00	9 00	7 50
Cab and carriage	72	8 00	10 50	9 00
Street railway employés:				
Conductors	87½	7 00	8 00	7 75
Drivers	87½	7 00	8 00	7 75
Stablemen	87½	7 00	7 00	7 00
Trackmen	60	6 00	6 00	6 25
Car-builders	60	8 00	12 00	10 00
Blacksmiths	60	8 00	10 00	9 00
Horseshoers	60	8 00	10 00	9 00
Painters	60	8 00	10 00	9 00
Dyers, males	60	9 00	15 00	12 00
Dyers, helpers, males	60	4 00	8 00	6 00
Dyers, helpers, girls and boys	60	3 00	6 00	4 00
Engravers:				
Jewelers	60	10 00	18 00	15 00
Watch-makers	60	10 00	18 00	15 00
Working jewelers	60	7 00	20 00	12 00
Engravers, lithographic:				
Stone and copper-plate	60	12 00	25 00	20 00
Steam-press printers	54	10 00	15 00	12 00
Furriers:				
Males	60	4 00	15 00	9 00
Females	60	2 00	8 00	4 00
Gardeners	60	6 00	9 00	7 50
Hatters:				
Males	60	7 00	15 00	10 00
Females	60	3 00	6 00	4 50
Horseshoers	60	8 00	10 00	9 00
Laborers, porters, &c	60	6 00	9 00	6 75
Millwrights	60	10 00	18 00	13 50
Printers, newspaper offices:				
Compositors:				
Males	58½	6 00	17 00	12 00
Females	58½	4 00	14 00	9 00
Proof-readers	58½	3 00	12 00	8 00
Pressmen	58½	10 00	15 00	12 00
Printers, job offices:				
Compositors:				
Males	58½	9 00	12 00	10 00
Females	58½	3 00	8 00	6 00
Pressmen	58½	9 00	12 00	10 00
Teachers, public schools:				
Males	(*)	†50 00	†220 00	†114 00
Females	(*)	†24 00	†90 00	†34 00
Saddle and harness makers	57	6 00	15 00	9 00
Sail-makers	60	7 00	10 00	9 00
Stevedores:				
Trimmers	60	9 00	21 00	15 00
Employed on decks	60	9 00	15 00	12 00
Tanners	60	7 00	9 00	8 00
Tanners, curriers	60	9 00	12 00	10 00
Tailors:				
Cutters, custom work	60	12 00	35 00	18 00
Cutters, shop work	60	12 00	20 00	15 00
Journeymen	60	9 00	14 00	12 00
Telegraph operators		†30 00	†70 00	†50 00
Telegraph operators, apprentices just completed their time		†15 00	†15 00	†15 00
Tinsmiths	60	6 00	12 00	9 50
Marble cutters, common work	60	7 50	12 00	9 00
Granite cutters	60	12 00	18 00	13 50
Limestone cutters	60	9 00	15 00	12 00
Marble and stone cutters, artists	60	18 00	60 00	25 00

    * 100 hours per month.   † Per month.

II. FACTORIES, MILLS, ETC.

Wages paid per week of sixty hours in factories or mills in the city of Montreal, Canada.

Occupations.	Lowest.	Highest.	Average.
BOOT AND SHOE FACTORIES.			
Cutters	$6 00	$9 00	$8 00
Lasters	6 00	10 00	8 00
Peggers and sole sewers	8 00	10 00	9 00
Finishers and buffers	7 00	15 00	10 50
Heelers	6 00	9 00	8 00
Burnishers	6 00	9 00	8 00
Edge setters	7 00	10 00	9 00
Fitters and closers, females	2 50	6 00	4 50
Table hands, females	1 50	3 00	2 50
CLOTHING ESTABLISHMENTS.			
Machine operators, females	3 00	8 00	5 00
Finishers, females	3 00	6 00	4 50
Cutters	12 00	20 00	15 00
*Ready-made clothing.**			
Sack overcoats, fine ...... each	2 00	2 00	2 00
Sack overcoats, cheap ...... do	1 20	1 20	1 20
Broadcloth frock coats ...... do	2 50	2 50	2 50
Cassimere business coats ...... do	1 50	1 50	1 50
Cassimere sack coats ...... do	1 50	1 50	1 50
Vests, woolen ...... do	40	40	40
Pantaloons ...... per pair	35	35	35
Shirts, woolen ...... per dozen	1 40	3 00	1 75
Custom-made clothing.			
Sack overcoats ...... each	5 00	5 00	5 00
Broadcloth dress coats ...... do	6 00	6 00	6 00
Cassimere business coats ...... do	2 50	4 50	3 50
Cassimere sack coats ...... do	2 00	3 75	2 75
Vests ...... do	1 00	1 00	1 00
Pantaloons ...... per pair	1 00	1 00	1 00
Shirts ...... per dozen	6 00	6 00	6 00

* Outside piecework for females.

III. FOUNDRIES, MACHINE-SHOPS, AND IRON WORKS.

Wages paid per week of sixty hours in foundries, machine-shops, and iron works, in Montreal, Canada.

Occupations.	Lowest.	Highest.	Average.
Iron molders	$6 00	$15 00	$10 00
Iron finishers	6 50	12 00	9 00
Machinists	7 00	15 00	10 50
Boiler-makers	9 00	18 00	10 50
Blacksmiths	10 00	13 00	11 00
Brass molders	6 00	14 00	9 00
Brass finishers	7 00	14 00	10 00
Platers, silver	9 00	12 00	10 50
Buffers	7 00	11 50	10 00
Telegraph instrument makers	6 50	14 50	11 00
Pattern-makers	9 00	15 00	10 50
Laborers or helpers in shops	6 00	8 50	7 00

VI. Railway Employés.

Wages paid to railway employés (those engaged about stations, as well as those engaged on the engines and cars, linemen, railroad laborers, &c.), in Montreal.

Occupations.	Lowest.	Highest.	Average.
Agents and cashiers................................per annum..	$500 00	$1,000 00	....
Operators and clerks...............................do....	400 00	1,200 00	....
Yardmen and switchmen............................do....	400 00	600 00	....
Conductors :			
Passenger ....do....	600 00	800 00	....
Freight..do....	500 00	700 00	....
Brakemen :			
Passenger......................................do....	400 00	600 00	....
Freight..do....	350 00	600 00	....
Baggagemen.......................................do ..	500 00	500 00	....
Checkers...per day..	1 15	1 75	....
Freight-porters..................................do....	1 00	1 15	....
ENGINEER'S DEPARTMENT.			
Track foremen....................................per day..	1 62½	2 12½	....
Track laborers...................................do....	....	....	$1 00
Carpenters.......................................do....	1 40	1 60	....
Painters...do....	....	....	1 75
Smiths...per hour..	....	....	20
Helpers..do....	....	....	14

NOTE.—The above are the wages paid by the Canadian Pacific Railway, as given to me by one of their officials, and the rates are probably about the same on other roads.

VIII. Seamen's Wages.

Wages paid per month to seamen (officers and men), distinguishing between ocean, coast, and river navigation, and between sail and steam, in the port of Montreal, Canada.

Occupations.	Lowest.	Highest.	Average.
Ocean steamers.			
Mate...........	$53 53	$53 53	$53 53
Second mate............	43 79	43 79	43 79
Third mate.........	38 93	38 93	38 93
Fourth mate.........	34 06	34 06	34 06
Carpenters...........	29 19	29 19	29 19
Seamen, able...........	14 00	16 00	15 00
Seamen, ordinary...........	14 00	14 00	14 00
Steamers, local trade, gulf ports.			
Mate.............	40 00	50 00	45 00
Second mate........	35 00	45 00	40 00
Third mate.........	28 00	35 00	30 00
Firemen............	25 00	25 00	25 00
Seamen, able...........	20 00	20 00	20 00
Seamen, ordinary.........	16 00	16 00	16 00
Trimmers.............	19 50	19 50	19 50
Engineers, first-class ocean steamships.			
First engineer, chief..........	87 59	87 59	87 59
Second-class engineer...........	68 13	68 13	68 13
Third-class engineer...........	53 53	53 53	53 53
Fourth-class engineer...........	48 66	48 66	48 66
Sailing-vessels.			
Mates..........	32 00	35 00	33 33
Mates, second..........	20 00	30 00	25 00
Stewards...........	27 00	30 00	28 50
Seamen, able..........	15 00	18 00	16 00
Seamen, ordinary...........	15 00	18 00	16 00

IX. STORE AND SHOP WAGES.

Wages paid in shops and stores, wholesale or retail, to males and females in the city of Montreal, Canada.

(Week of sixty hours.)

Occupations.	Lowest.	Highest.	Average.
WHOLESALE.			
Commercial travelers................................per annum..	$600 00	$3,000 00	$1,000 00
House salesmen, experienced .... do....	600 00	900 00	750 00
House salesmen, juniors .... do....	200 00	800 00	400 00
Book-keepers ....do....	900 00	1,200 00	1,000 00
Invoice clerks....................................do....	400 00	600 00	500 00
Entry clerks ....do....	400 00	600 00	500 00
Packers and porters ....do...	350 00	550 00	450 00
RETAIL.			
Salesmen or clerks, males ....per week..	7 00	18 00	10 50
Salesmen or clerks, females......................do....	3 00	9 00	5 00
Office clerks and cashiers, females...............do....	4 00	8 00	6 00
Clerks in offices, males..........................do....	5 00	10 00	7 50

The majority of wholesale establishments close their places of business on Saturdays at 1 p. m. and several of the retail stores and shops close at that time also.
The rates of wages paid in the different branches of trade will average about the same.

X. HOUSEHOLD WAGES IN TOWNS AND CITIES.

Wages paid to household servants (towns and cities) in the city of Montreal, Canada.

Occupations.	Lowest.	Highest.	Average.
Cooks ....per month..	$10 00	$15 00	$12 00
General servants ....do....	7 00	10 00	8 00
Housemaids. ....do ...	6 00	9 00	7 00
Washerwomen ....per day..	60	1 00	75
Scrubbers and charwomen.........................do....	60	1 00	75

XI. AGRICULTURAL WAGES.

Wages paid to agricultural laborers and household (country) servants in the district of Montreal.

Occupations.	Lowest.	Highest.	Average.
Laborers ....per day..	....	....	$1 25
Farm hands, summer...............................do....	....	....	1 25
Farm hands, winter ....do....	....	....	80
Household servants, cook ....per month..	$7 00	$10 00	8 00
Household servants, maid ....do....	5 00	7 00	6 00
Farm hands ....do....	....	....	*25 00
Laborers ....do....	....	....	*25 00

*With house-rent.

NOTE.—The above figures, except in the case of household servants, are without board or lodging. If boarded and lodged, as is sometimes the case, 75 cents per day is paid to farm hands and laborers.

XII. Corporation Employés.

Wages paid per annum to the corporation employés in the city of Montreal, Canada.

Occupations.	Lowest.	Highest.	Average.
City clerk	$3,500 00	$3,500 00	$3,500 00
Assistant clerk	1,800 00	1,800 00	1,800 00
City treasurer	3,500 00	3,500 00	3,500 00
Cashier	1,200 00	1,200 00	1,200 00
Accountants	1,000 00	1,600 00	1,325 00
Tellers	800 00	1,000 00	900 00
Clerks in departments	180 00	1,000 00	650 00
City auditor	2,800 00	2,800 00	2,800 00
Assistant auditor	1,200 00	1,200 00	1,200 00
City attorney	5,000 00	5,000 00	5,000 00
Assistant attorneys	1,000 00	1,000 00	1,000 00
City assessors	1,400 00	1,400 00	1,400 00
City surveyor	2,800 00	2,800 00	2,800 00
Deputy surveyor	1,600 00	1,600 00	1,600 00
Assistant surveyor	1,500 00	1,500 00	1,500 00
Inspector of sewers	1,250 00	1,250 00	1,250 00
Chief of police	2,800 00	2,800 00	2,800 00
Deputy chief of police	1,400 00	1,400 00	1,400 00
Subchiefs of police	1,000 00	1,000 00	1,000 00
Chief detective	900 00	900 00	900 00
Detectives	800 00	850 00	807 14
Sergeants of police	700 00	700 00	700 00
Acting sergeants of police	600 00	600 00	600 00
Subconstables (policemen)	416 00	468 00	455 92
City recorder	3,000 00	3,000 00	3,000 00
Recorder's clerk	1,600 00	1,600 00	1,600 00
Chief of fire brigade *	1,400 04	1,400 00	1,400 00
Assistant chiefs of fire brigade	1,000 00	1,000 00	1,000 00
Guardians or chiefs of stations*	600 00	600 00	600 00
Engineers	600 00	600 00	600 00
Foreman of salvage corps	700 00	700 00	700 00
Foreman of Skinner ladder	550 00	550 00	550 00
Hose-maker	600 00	600 00	600 00
Men for salvage corps	550 00	550 00	550 00
Firemen	500 00	500 00	500 00
Superintendent of fire-alarm	1,800 00	1,800 00	1,800 00
Assistant superintendents of fire-alarm	750 00	1,000 00	916 67
Building inspector	1,200 00	1,200 00	1,200 00
Boiler inspector	†1,000 00	†1,000 00	†1,000 00
Superintendent of water-works	2,800 00	2,800 00	2,800 00
Deputy superintendent of water-works	2,000 00	2,000 00	2,000 00
Meter inspectors of water-works	600 00	600 00	600 00
Engineer of water-works wheel-house	1,600 00	1,600 00	1,600 00
Assistant engineers of water-works wheel-house	700 00	700 00	700 00
Oilers of water-works wheel-house	440 00	440 00	440 00
Engineer of water-works engine-house	1,000 00	1,000 00	1,000 00
Guardian of reservoir	700 00	700 00	700 00
Keeper of aqueduct	600 00	600 00	600 00
Laborers in water-works department	‡8 00	‡8 40	‡7 50
Laborers in road department	‡6 00	‡8 40	‡7 50
Clerks of markets	500 00	1,200 00	700 00
Assistant clerks of markets	500 00	600 00	550 00
Medical health officer	1,200 00	1,200 00	1,200 00
Superintendents parks and ferries	600 00	1,000 00	800 00
Guardians parks and ferries	450 00	450 00	450 00
Carpenters parks and ferries	450 00	450 00	450 00
Blacksmiths parks and ferries	450 00	450 00	450 00
Gardeners parks and ferries	450 00	450 00	450 00

* Furnished with dwelling.   † With fees.   ‡ Per week.

XIII. GOVERNMENT DEPARTMENTS AND OFFICES.

Wages paid per annum to employes in Government departments and offices—exclusive of tradesmen and laborers—in the city of Montreal, Canada.

Occupations.	Lowest.	Highest.	Average.
CUSTOMS SERVICE.			
Collector	$4,000 00	$4,000 00	$4,000 00
Surveyor	2,400 00	2,400 00	2,400 00
Chief landing waiter	1,400 00	1,400 00	1,400 00
Landing waiters	750 00	1,400 00	978 57
Tide surveyor	1,000 00	1,000 00	1,000 00
Chief clerk	2,000 00	2,000 00	2,000 00
Cashier	1,600 00	1,600 00	1,600 00
Assistant cashier	1,000 00	1,000 00	1,000 00
Clerks	600 00	1,400 00	875 00
Appraisers	1,200 00	1,800 00	1,650 00
Assistant appraisers	900 00	1,200 00	1,080 00
Assistant appraiser and packer	600 00	600 00	600 00
Ex-warehouse keeper	1,000 00	1,000 00	1,000 00
Weigher and gauger	1,000 00	1,000 00	1,000 00
Assistant weigher and gauger	600 00	600 00	600 00
Packers	500 00	500 00	500 00
First-class tide waiters	600 00	600 00	600 00
Second-class tide waiters	550 00	550 00	550 00
Acting inspector of bonds	750 00	750 00	750 00
POST-OFFICE.			
Postmaster	4,000 00	4,000 00	4,000 00
Assistant postmaster	2,000 00	2,000 00	2,000 00
First-class clerks	1,200 00	1,500 00	1,333 33
Second-class clerks	940 00	1,100 00	1,060 00
Third-class clerks	400 00	840 00	641 31
Letter-carriers	300 00	560 00	468 63
Letter stamper	560 00	560 00	560 00
Messenger	300 00	500 00	433 33
Porter	438 00	438 00	438 00
Firemen and night-watchman	365 00	365 00	365 00

XV. PRINTERS AND PRINTING OFFICES.

Statement showing the wages paid per week of fifty-eight and one-half hours to printers (compositors, pressmen, proof-readers, &c.) in the city of Montreal, Canada.

Occupations.	Lowest.	Highest.	Average.
IN NEWSPAPER OFFICES.			
Morning papers.			
Compositors, day work	$11 75	$13 50	$12 50
Compositors, night work	13 50	15 50	14 50
Proof-readers	8 00	12 00	10 00
Pressmen	10 00	15 00	12 00
Evening papers.			
Compositors	6 00	17 00	12 00
Compositors, females	4 00	14 00	9 00
Proof-readers, females	3 00	8 00	6 00
Pressman	10 00	15 00	12 00
JOB OFFICES.			
Compositors	9 00	12 00	10 00
Compositors, females	3 00	8 00	6 00
Pressmen	9 00	12 00	10 00
Feeders in job room, females	3 00	4 50	4 00
BOOK AND NEWS WORK.			
Compositors, females	3 00	8 00	6 00
Proof-readers, females	5 00	7 00	6 00

RECAPITULATION.

Statement, condensed from the report of the Canadian census of 1880-'81, showing the number of hands employed, the total yearly wages, total value of raw material, and the total value of articles produced of the leading industries of the city of Montreal, in the province of Quebec and Dominion of Canada.

Industries.	Number of industries.	Over sixteen years. Men.	Over sixteen years. Women.	Under sixteen years. Boys.	Under sixteen years. Girls.	Total yearly wages.	Total value of raw material.	Total value of articles produced.
Agricultural implements....	4	63	......	6	......	$17,800	$28,900	$62,000
Bakeries of all sorts	57	321	30	43	3	113,972	842,777	1,265,358
Blacksmithing	49	92	......	6	......	27,620	36,655	93,454
Boots and shoes	171	3,199	1,832	253	155	1,428,223	3,811,214	6,703,386
Brick and tile making	6	186	......	88	......	72,050	54,500	243,000
Cabinet and furniture	73	667	9	34	......	289,269	377,048	1,057,846
Carpenters and joiners.......	24	270	......	8	......	82,716	123,400	204,460
Carriage-making	39	240	......	20	......	95,166	141,425	343,520
Cooperage	18	130	......	3	......	43,915	70,430	138,380
Dress-making and millinery..	126	8	548	1	138	84,069	270,421	516,011
Flour and grist mills	4	187	5	......	......	206,500	2,215,250	2,499,170
Foundries and machine-shops.	18	657	3	37	......	240,962	378,130	774,360
Lime-kilns	1	14	......	......	......	4,200	36,000	44,510
Saddle and harness making..	38	138	14	26	1	46,856	153,950	290,656
Saw-mills	3	218	......	14	......	81,400	327,000	497,000
Tanneries	11	574	30	5	3	171,600	1,094,550	2,445,000
Tailors and clothiers.........	136	1,043	3,895	123	193	678,059	2,389,332	3,770,201
Tin and sheet-iron working..	40	208	20	32	1	61,368	143,010	290,112
Breweries....................	7	182	10	1	......	81,960	432,000	725,000
Broom and brush making....	8	156	8	8	1	19,920	74,000	110,200
Furriers, hatters, &c	45	401	771	24	21	319,070	1,127,720	2,050,750
Jewelers and watchmakers ..	26	119	18	22	1	54,746	127,493	291,927
Meat-curing....	16	72	......	1	......	18,490	536,961	654,121
Painters, glaziers, &c........	12	119	......	6	......	38,606	58,178	156,378
Photographic galleries........	11	59	22	8	......	32,570	25,810	112,300
Printing offices	33	694	84	77	20	333,640	335,000	983,860
Ship-yards	2	91	......	12	......	27,500	87,000	120,000
Stone and marble cutting...	14	140	......	12	......	59,707	49,055	203,700
Book-binding..................	9	135	125	15	5	72,800	58,700	209,140
Chemical establishments	8	51	20	......	......	37,100	141,400	223,500
Dyeing and scouring.........	6	16	12	2	4	7,586	10,700	36,600
Miscellaneous wares.........	27	109	44	32	29	63,952	149,120	310,787
Oil refineries	2	37	......	......	......	13,280	116,500	142,500
Soap and candle making.....	11	134	19	20	8	91,838	560,020	815,300
Tobacco factories and cigars.	22	897	806	341	249	392,279	945,055	1,637,403
Aerated-water making	7	106	15	17	......	21,450	61,400	134,000
Carving and gilding	11	91	8	10	......	34,120	50,900	171,200
Engine-building	1	100	......	50	......	50,000	45,000	145,000
Engraving and lithographing	10	206	56	26	12	90,450	131,100	326,000
Gas-works	1	126	......	......	......	60,000	78,000	312,000
Gold and silver smithing ...	5	55	2	1	......	18,400	67,320	117,640
Musical-instrument making .	4	44	6	......	......	21,900	38,700	140,700
Paint and varnish works	7	115	28	......	......	75,365	533,000	809,500
Paper manufactories	5	253	86	5	3	106,700	362,000	627,746
Patent medicine manufactories ..	8	48	49	1	......	34,700	193,850	343,200
Preserved articles of food....	2	44	21	1	......	10,200	128,800	152,800
Saw and file cutting.........	4	135	......	17	......	25,500	182,000	534,000
Straw-works	1	15	60	......	......	25,000	10,000	50,000
Trunk and box making......	12	170	168	9	12	69,209	211,900	483,400
Wig-making	3	7	18	......	2	5,860	5,200	15,100
Baking-powder making.......	1	4	5	......	......	3,900	50,970	71,200
Bank-note engraving	1	43	51	......	......	55,000	33,000	100,000
Belting and hose making	1	12	......	......	......	4,160	48,000	64,000
Car and locomotive works ...	1	1,190	......	20	......	553,588	959,571	1,513,159
Card-box manufactories	1	2	2	6	6	3,900	15,000	30,000
Chocolate factory............	2	7	5	......	......	3,700	11,500	27,000
Church decorations...........	4	29	13	5	1	16,100	62,200	160,300
Coffee and spice mills........	7	41	12	8	2	26,800	345,000	479,000
Cork-cutting.................	1	15	......	5	......	5,000	35,000	60,000
Cotton factories	1	214	393	62	55	134,200	478,000	860,000
Corset factories..............	2	2	41	5	......	4,300	24,000	34,000
Fittings and foundry working in brass, iron, lead, &c.	24	598	3	81	......	237,304	299,100	660,100
Fire-proof safe manufactories	2	42	......	......	......	13,000	12,000	38,000

Statement, condensed from the report of the Canadian census of 1880–'81, *&c.*—Continued.

Industries.	Number of industries.	Men.	Women.	Boys.	Girls.	Total yearly wages.	Total value of raw material.	Total value of articles produced.
		Over sixteen years.		Under sixteen years.				
Glass-works	3	210	20	79		$108,200	$83,400	$230,000
Glove and mitt manufactories	3	39	74		8	25,600	76,070	108,670
Glue-making	4	25		2		3,700	31,650	58,920
India-rubber factories	2	133	154	21	106	154,612	437,604	679,500
Iron-smelting furnaces and steel	4	94		16		32,918	31,800	142,000
Lamp and chandelier factories	3	34	4	1	4	15,400	19,400	46,000
Last factories	3	34		7		12,300	12,000	36,000
Nail and tack factories	4	561	48	71	21	245,000	590,000	930,000
Nut and bolt works	1	130				45,000	80,000	200,000
Paper bag and box making	4	44	21	10	6	16,230	31,300	79,050
Paper-collar factories	1	4	20	1	17	7,000	9,500	25,000
Planing and molding mills	3	76				32,200	41,000	98,000
Rolling mills (iron)	1	325		50		120,000	320,000	500,000
Roofing-felt manufactories	5	95		6		30,000	150,500	205,000
Scale factories	4	23		3		9,060	20,000	43,000
Sewing-machine factories	8	515	32	25		231,571	220,500	521,031
Shirt, collar, and tie making	17	70	985	8	175	217,196	386,842	935,394
Ship-material making	3	16	15			12,040	37,500	61,000
Shook and box making	2	25		7		7,400	18,500	32,500
Silk-mills	2	50	144	6	11	35,600	158,000	275,000
Spike and railway chair factories	1	29		12		11,000	75,000	144,000
Sugar refineries	2	460		33		240,000	6,100,000	6,800,000
Type foundries	2	18	20			21,100	16,000	64,500
Vermicelli and macaroni factories	2	9	4	3	6	2,260	15,000	22,500
Vinegar factories	1	12				6,000	50,000	90,000
Wall-paper factories	1	20			30	20,000	60,000	100,000
Wire-works	4	33	10	4		14,100	147,000	191,000
Grand total	1,296	18,425	10,927	1,974	1,309	8,795,165	31,620,981	51,219,360

PRICES OF THE NECESSARIES OF LIFE.

Statement showing the retail prices of provisions, groceries, and other leading articles of consumption and of house-rent and board in the city of Montreal, Canada.

Articles.	1878.	1884.
PROVISIONS.		
Flour:		
Wheat, extra superfine ....per barrel..	$4 60	$5 00
superfine ....do....	4 10	3 50
city bags, delivered......................100 pounds..	2 30	2 80
Oatmeal ....do....	2 10	2 50
Cornmeal..do....	1 10	1 75
Buckwheat...do....	2 00	1 60
Pease ....per bushel..	80	1 15
Butter, in the tub.............................. per pound..	$0 13 to 20	$0 15 to 18
Cheese..do ..	07½ 08	15 10
Lard, in pails...do....	08½ 09½	10½ 12
Eggs ....per dozen..	12 14	16 22
Potatoes................................per bag of 1½ bushels..	35 45	85 90
Milk:		
Summer...per quart..	05	06
Winter..do....	07	08
Tea:		
Oolong, or other good black ....per pound..	50 70	50 70
Green and Japan ....do ..	50 80	50 80
Coffee:		
Roasted ....do....	30 40	30 40
Ground..do....	25 35	25 35

Statement showing the retail prices of provisions, groceries, &c.—Continued.

Articles.	1878.		1884.	
PROVISIONS—Continued.				
Sugar:				
Good brown .... per pound..	$0 06 to	$0 07	$0 05 to	$0 06
Yellow "C" .... do....		07½	06	06½
Coffee "B" .... do....		08	07	08
Molasses:				
Barbadoes .... per gallon..	70	75	60	70
Common .... do....	50	60	45	50
Sirups .... do....	75	1 00	75	1 00
Soap, common .... do....	03½	07	03½	07
Starch .... do....	06	07	07	08
Bread, white, good .... per loaf 4 pounds..	16	18	18	20
Rice .... per pound..	05	06	04	05
Beans .... do....	04	05	04	05
Coal oil .... per gallon..	20	25	22	25
MEATS.				
Beef, fresh:				
Roasting pieces .... per pound..	10	12½	12½	15
Soup pieces .... do....	05	08	05	08
Round steaks .... do....	12½	15		15
Sirloin steaks .... do....	15	18	15	18
Corned .... do....	10	12	10	12
Veal:				
Fore-quarters .... do....	04	07	05	07
Hind-quarters .... do....	08	10	10	12
Cutlets .... do....	10	12	12½	15
Mutton:				
Fore-quarters .... do....	09	10		10
Leg .... do....	12	15	12½	15
Chops .... do....	12	15	12½	15
Pork:				
Fresh .... do....		10		12
Corned or salted .... do....		10		12
Bacon .... do....	12	15	13	16
Hams, smoked .... do....	12	15	14	16
Shoulders .... do....	10	12	10	15
Sausages .... do....	10	12		12
Codfish, dry .... do....	06	08	06	08
Mackerel, pickled or salt .... do....	08	10	08	10
DRY GOODS.				
Shirtings:				
Brown, 4/4 standard .... per yard..	10	12	06	10
Bleached, 4/4 standard .... do....	12	18	10	15
Sheetings:				
Brown, 10/4 standard .... do....	30	38	28	30
Bleached, 10/4 standard .... do....	40	45	38	55
Canton (cotton) flannel, medium .... do....	20	25	16	23
Ticking, good .... do....	25	35	22	30
Prints:				
American, good .... do....	12½	18	07½	10
English, good .... do....	15	25	12	20
Mousseline de laines, good .... do....	20	40	15	30
Satinets, medium .... do....	50	75	40	60
Boots, men's heavy .... per pair..	2 50	3 50	2 00	3 00
FUEL.				
Coal, anthracite:				
Stove .... per net ton..		5 50		6 00
Egg .... do....		5 25		5 75
Chestnut .... do....		5 00		6 00
Wood (French measure):				
Maple .... per cord..	5 50	6 50		7 50
Birch .... do....	5 00	6 25		7 00
Beech .... do....	4 50	5 50		6 50
Tamarack .... do....	4 00	5 00		6 00
Hemlock .... do....	4 00	4 50		5 00

House-rent in the city of Montreal, Canada.

Per month.	1878.	1879.	1880.	1881.	1882.	1883.	1884.
Three-room tenements.....................	$2 50 to 3 00	$2 50 to 3 00	$3 00 to 3 50	$3 00 to 3 75	$3 50 to 4 00	$4 00 to 5 00	$4 00 to 5 00
Four-room tenements.....................	3 00 to 3 50	3 00 to 3 50	3 00 to 4 00	3 50 to 4 00	3 50 to 4 50	4 00 to 5 50	5 00 to 7 00
Five-room tenements.....................	5 00 to 5 50	5 00 to 5 50	6 00 to 6 50	6 00 to 6 50	6 00 to 7 00	6 00 to 7 00	6 40 to 8 00

The rate of house-rents depends upon whether the tenement is situated in the first, second, or third flats, and according to the location and condition of the building.

In most instances in addition to the house-rent the tenant has to pay the city taxes on the property, and in all cases the tenant is assessed and is called upon to pay the water-tax. The water rates are based upon the rental.

Board.	1878.	1884.
For men—mechanics, &c..per week..	$3 00 to $3 50	$3 00 to $4 00
For women employed in factories, &c........................do....	2 00 2 75	2 00 3 00

A BLACKSMITH'S STATEMENT.

Question. How old are you?—Answer. I am forty years old.
Q. What is your business?—A. I am a blacksmith.
Q. Have you a family?—A. Yes, a wife and four children.
Q. What wages do you receive?—A. Eleven dollars a week.
Q. How many hours a day do you work?—A. Ten hours a day.
Q. How much time are you allowed for meals?—A. One hour for dinner.
Q. Can you support your family upon such wages?—A. Yes.
Q. What do the united earnings of yourself and family amount to in a year?—A. About $600.
Q. Will you explain in detail the uses you make of this money?—A. Yes.

For rent of six rooms, $9 per month..	$108 00
For clothing for self and family, about..................................	200 00
For food and fuel per day, about 65c....................................	237 25
For taxes, about	10 00
For dues to society...	3 00
For school books, doctors' bills, and incidentals, about...............	25 00
	583 25
Balance for other purposes..	16 75
	600 00

Q. Of what kind of food do your daily meals consist?—A. For breakfast, oatmeal porridge and molasses, bread and butter, tea or coffee; sometimes we take a steak; other times we take some hash made from the meat left over the day previous; for dinner, soup, beef, and potatoes, bread; pudding or sirup for dessert; and for supper, bread and butter and tea, sometimes a piece of cake or crackers or a piece of pie.

Q. Are you able to save any portion of your earnings for days of sickness or old age?—A. No.

SAINT HYACINTHE.

REPORT BY COMMERCIAL AGENT FISH.

The following are the wages paid per day of ten hours for services of laborers in the city of Saint Hyacinthe and the consular district in which it is embraced.

Occupations.	Lowest.	Highest.
Thrashing-machine and horse-rake works.		
Lathe and vice hands:		
First class		$2 00
Second class		80
Blacksmiths	$1 00	1 75
Helper		80
Wood-working hands:		
First class		2 00
Second class		1 50
Helper		65
Molders:		
First class		2 50
Second class		1 50
Painters	75	1 50
Common laborers		1 00
Sash, door, and blind factory.		
Foreman		2 50
Laborers	1 00	1 50
Tanners and curriers	1 00	1 50
Saw-mills.		
Laborers:		
First class		1 75
Second class		1 25
Common	80	1 00
Knitting mills.		
Laborers:		
Male	1 00	2 50
Female	40	1 00
Woolen mills.		
Carders		2 75
Weavers		2 00
Helpers		1 00
Carders and weavers—female	40	80
Railroads.		
Track foreman		1 50
Telegraph operators		1 25
Porters and trackmen		1 25
Station laborers		1 25
Farms.		
Laborers	*5 00	*16 00
Household—female	†1 00	†1 25
General trades.		
Brick-layers, masons	2 00	2 25
Tenders		1 00
Tin roofers		3 00
Plumbers	2 00	2 25
Carpenters		2 00
Gas-fitters		3 00
Tinsmith	1 25	1 50
Painters	1 50	2 00
Saddle and harness makers		1 25
Tailors	1 00	2 25
Bakers	1 00	1 50
Cabinet-makers:		
First-class		1 50
Second class	1 00	1 25
Furriers:		
Male		1 00
Female		50

* Per month. † Per week.

Wages paid per day of ten hours for services of laborers, &c.—Continued.

Occupations.	Lowest.	Highest.
General trades—Continued,		
Foundries and machine-shops :		
First class		$3 00
Second class	$1 50	2 00
Plow factory		1 50
Molders		1 25
Planing mill		1 25
Grist mill :		
First class		1 50
Second class	1 00	1 20
Clerks	75	1 50

ALLEN FISH,
Commercial Agent.

United States Commercial Agency,
Saint Hyacinthe, May 6, 1884.

THREE RIVERS.

REPORT BY CONSUL WILSON.

In answer to your labor circular of the 15th February last relative to the prices paid for wages, &c., in this consular district, I have the honor to report that the only apology I have to offer for my apparent procrastination has arisen from the fact that I was suffering from inflammatory rheumatism during the entire winter past, and I am still afflicted with this painful disease.

I regret I cannot give you a more satisfactory report, but there being no factories or workshops of any importance in this city I am unable to furnish as full a report as I would like to do.

It may be stated, however, that this consular district, comprising 20,000 inhabitants, more or less, since the earliest times has contributed largely of both male and female laborers to the factories and workshops of New England.

Although the demand for mechanics and factory hands is not so great as formerly in New England, yet the weekly and daily wages are to-day full 50 per cent. more in New England than are paid here for the same kinds of labor.

This people as a race are very hardy and never had any of the comforts and luxuries of life, are quite like their horses, they are capable of enduring more hardships and subsisting on meaner food than any people on earth.

The real labor of this district is performed by the "shanty" men, the wood choppers and lumbermen, who have commanded the best wages. But during the past year or two there has been a great falling off in lumber operations, causing real distress among the poorer classes; not so much on account of the low wages paid as for the want of work. It is estimated that not more than one-third of the hands were given work the past season that sought for it, and the present outlook is very dark indeed for that class of laborers.

JAMES M. WILSON,
Consul.

United States Consulate,
Three Rivers, August 4, 1884.

I. GENERAL TRADES.

Wages paid in Three Rivers.

[Per week of sixty hours.]

Occupations.	Lowest.	Highest.
BUILDING TRADES.		
Bricklayers...per week..	$9 00	$12 00
Hod-carriers...do....	4 80	6 00
Masons...do....	9 00	12 00
Tenders...do....	4 80	6 00
Plasterers...do....	9 00	12 00
Tenders...do....	4 80	6 00
Slaters...do....	12 00	15 00
Roofers...do....	12 00	15 00
Tenders...do....	4 80	6 00
Plumbers...do....	15 00	18 00
Assistants...do....	6 00	9 00
Carpenters...do....	9 00	12 00
Gas-fitters...do....	15 00	18 00
OTHER TRADES.		
Bakers...do....	7 50	9 00
Blacksmiths..do....	7 50	9 00
Strikers..do....	7 50	9 00
Book-binders...do....	9 00	12 00
Brick-makers...do....	9 00	12 00
Butchers..do....	7 50	9 00
Brass-founders...do....	9 00	12 00
Cabinet-makers...do....	9 00	12 00
Confectioners..do....	9 00	10 50
Cigar-makers...do....	6 00	9 00
Coopers..do....	9 00	12 00
Drivers..do....	6 00	7 50
Draymen and teamsters.......................................do....	7 50	9 00
Dyers..do....	9 00	12 00
Engravers..do....	15 00	24 00
Furriers...do....	12 00	18 00
Gardeners..do....	7 50	9 00
Hatters..do....	7 50	9 00
Horseshoers..do....	9 00	12 00
Jewelers...do....	15 00	18 00
Laborers, porters, &c..do....	4 80	6 00
Millwrights..do....	21 00	24 00
Saddle and harness makers......................................do....	7 50	9 00
Sail-makers..do....	7 50	9 00
Tanners..do....	9 00	12 00
Tailors..do....	9 00	12 00
Telegraph operators, male...................................per month..	40 00	60 00
Telegraph operators, female....................................do....	25 00	40 00
Tinsmiths...per week..	9 00	10 50
Weavers..do....	7 50	9 00
TEACHERS, PUBLIC SCHOOLS.		
Protestant:		
Male principal...do....		*800 00
Female principal...do....		*275 00
Catholic:		
Male professors..do....		*200 00
Female professors..do....		*144 00
Corporation employés.		
Secretary-treasurer..do....		1,250 00
Assistant secretary-treasurer..................................do....		600 00
Second assistant secretary-treasurer...........................do....		375 00
Third assistant secretary-treasurer............................do....		130 00
Chief clerk water-works department.............................do....		800 00
Assistant clerk water-works department.........................do....		200 00
Superintendent water-works department..........................do....		450 00
Superintendent on road...do....		300 00
First engineer water-works department..........................do....		†425 00
Second engineer water-works department.........................do....		†375 00
Messenger city-hall..do....		†360 00
Bridge-keeper..do....		†200 00
Keeper of public commons.......................................do....		350 00
Chief of police..do....		600 00
Sergeant...do....		375 00
Policemen..do....		375 00

Wages paid in Three Rivers—Continued.

Occupations.	Lowest.	Highest
Shoe-shop.		
Male..per week..	$125 00	$600 00
Female ....do....	100 00	200 00
Lumbermen.‡		
1883, 1884	8 00	15 00
Boys, half price.		
. Mill hands.§		
Sawers..	1 00	1 25
Assistants..	80	1 00
Filers..	1 50	1 95
Laths and others..	80	1 00

* And lodging.   † And lodging and fuel.   ‡ Wages per winter month, from daylight to dark.
§ Wages paid per day of eleven hours.

PROVINCE OF NEW BRUNSWICK.

SAINT JOHN.

REPORT BY CONSUL WARNER.

RATES OF WAGES.

The rates of wages paid to all classes of labor, as far as can be had, are given in the tabulated forms accompanying this report.

Wages, taking all departments, have changed but little since 1878. In no particular department has there been a change worthy of notice, except in that of the stevedores. They, in 1878, were receiving for loading sailing-vessels, $2.50 a day; in 1879, $2.50; in 1880, $2; in 1881, $2.50; in 1882, $3; in 1883, $3; in 1884, $3.

The same men, for loading steamers, received $4.50 to $5 a day in 1882, 1883, and 1884. The conditions have not changed for the better for the laboring class since 1878.

HABITS OF THE WORKING CLASSES.

To the observant traveler the rural working population of this province seem indolent—lazy. They can raise sufficient crop to keep their families, feed their little stock, and enough to sell or barter for their groceries and their clothing without much labor. When asked, "Why not produce more?" they reply, "What will we do with it? The tariff duties into the United States shuts us out from there, and we have no other market." In this city the greater portion are industrious and trustworthy, another portion about as worthless a class of men as can be found anywhere—working themselves just enough to procure their rum, and depending upon the labor of their wives to procure for them and their children the necessaries of life. The general use of alcoholic drinks is the cause.

ORGANIZED CONDITION OF LABOR.

There is but one labor organization worthy of notice in the province, that of the stevedores of this city. They, in 1865, organized the Laborers' Benevolent Society, which, in 1880, was changed to the Ship Laborers' Union. Its membership was at one time seventeen hundred; now it numbers about seven hundred. The society is organized for the protection of the members. They each pay dues, which constitute the fund for expenses in case of their sick and burial of their dead. Every year there is a contest between the members of the society and the employers. They generally manage to keep the wages in the port high. Vessels generally are loaded by contract, and the disputes are between the stevedores and the contractors; whether the wages are reduced or raised the ship does not feel the change. In 1880, when wages were lowest, the shippers paid the highest for loading their vessels. The proximity to the United States is a great advantage to this class, that market taking up all surplus labor as fast as the natural increase can supply it, there is never trouble on account of too many workingmen.

GENERAL CONDITION OF THE WORKING CLASSES.

The working people of this province, including mechanics and laborers, can, with industry, sobriety, and prudence live very comfortably, and have something to put away at the end of the year. House rent is very low, good quarters, embracing from three to five rooms each, can be had at from $32 to $60 a year. Food of every kind is cheap. Flour for a family of six will cost not to exceed $50 a year. Beef and mutton 7 cents a pound; pork, 10 to 12 cents a pound; veal, 4 to 5 cents a pound. Clothing is cheap, and coals cost here not any more than in the cities of the United States near the mines which produce them. They live well, and usually have meat every day. Few of them occupy less than three rooms to a family, most of them have four to five. Too much strong drink and too much credit are these people's greatest enemies, and do more to demoralize them than anything else. Two-thirds manage to pay their rent, one-third do not, and a portion of the latter are unable on account of misfortune generally; they don't intend paying. Ship carpenters have work about one-half their time, during the idle hours the rum-shops and groceries involve them so largely in debt that with the most honest of them it is a struggle to get on. The absence of reformatories and of a compulsory education law does not tend to improve the situation. Not one-half of the children go to the public schools, and youthful offenders of the laws are imprisoned with the old, and come out with their moral sensibilities blunted and in a worse condition than when sent to prison.

The moral standard is low. Many of these people seem to care but little for their obligations. They obtain credit without intention of paying. They dress well, attend places of amusement, picnics, races, &c., and the shop-keeper who helped them through the cold season waits and seldom gets his money.

Interviews with many workingmen develops the fact that they do not know how their money is spent. They will tell you their flour costs them $45 a year, their meat $35 a year, and so on through all their known expenses. When told they have not accounted for their year's earnings, they say they don't know where it went, and all they do know is that they have nothing left at the end of the year; none of them say they can put anything away for old age. They, none of them, seem to understand how to live simply, prudently, and cheaply.

CAUSES LEADING TO EMIGRATION.

The development of manufactures and other industries not keeping pace with the natural increase of population, and the settlement of the wild lands not having been pushed by the local government, accounts for the large emigration each year.

The influences which locate these emigrants are the letters received from their friends and acquaintances who have gone before them. Their occupations are principally farming and mechanics.

FEMALE LABOR.

Number of women and children employed in industrial pursuits: Manufacturing and mechanical: Women, 3,850; girls under sixteen-922; total, 4,772; commercial, 200; professional and personal, includ, ing government officials and clerks, teachers, artists, hotel and boarding-house keepers, &c., 1,072; grand total, 6,042.

Wages paid female adults: Minimum, $2; maximum, $10; average, $5 per week. Hours of labor, nine to ten per day.

MORAL AND PHYSICAL CONDITION.

The morals of working women are about on a par with women of like occupations in the United States. The physical condition is generally good, seldom showing in their appearance disease, but the reverse.

Employers pay little attention to the improvement of the moral or intellectual condition of their employés, the churches being the only organizations which give the matter attention, and even in them there seems but little zeal in that direction. A free library has been established in this city within the last three years which, it is hoped, will soon furnish reading for all who desire it.

But little care seems to have been taken to avoid disasters in case of fire or other accidents. The general public hospital is free to all who need medical attention on account of sickness. There has been but little increase during the last five years in wages paid women, while there has been a material increase in the price of about all the necessaries of life. The employment of women in this province does not perceptibly affect the wages of men, because they are not employed generally in all departments to the extent they are in many other countries. The education of the working women of the province is very limited, a part, those young in years are better informed, having been sent to the free schools until old enough to earn wages.

D. B. WARNER,

Consul.

UNITED STATES CONSULATE,
  Saint John, June 3, 1884.

I. GENERAL TRADES.

Wages paid per week of sixty hours in Saint John, New Brunswick.

Occupations.	Lowest.	Highest.	Average.
BUILDING TRADES.			
Bricklayers	$18 00	$18 00	$18 00
Hod-carriers	7 50	9 00	8 00
Masons	18 00	18 00	18 00
Tenders	6 00	7 50	7 00
Plasterers	18 00	18 00	18 00
Tenders	6 00	7 50	7 00
Roofers	7 50	10 00	8 00
Tenders	6 00	7 50	7 00
Plumbers	9 00	12 00	9 00
Assistants	1 50	4 00	2 50
Carpenters	7 50	12 00	9 00
Gas-fitters	9 00	12 00	9 00
OTHER TRADES.			
Bakers	2 00	10 00	8 00
Blacksmiths	9 50	15 00	9 50
Book-binders	2 50	12 00	5 00
Brick-makers	7 50	12 00	9 00
Brewers	7 00	9 00	7 00
Butchers	9 00	15 00	12 00
Brass-founders	7 50	12 00	9 00
Confectioners	3 00	9 00	4 50
Cigar-makers	2 00	9 00	5 00
Drivers on street-railways	7 00	10 00	7 00
Engravers (stone)	6 00	30 00	18 00
Furriers (forty-eight hours a week)	3 00	16 00	6 00
Hatters (fifty-four hours a week)	12 00	20 00	14 00
Horseshoers	5 00	9 00	7 00
Jewelers (fifty-four hours a week)	10 00	18 00	12 00
Laborers, porters, &c	5 00	9 00	6 00
Lithographers	10 00	15 00	10 00
Millwrights	9 00	12 00	9 00
Printers	9 00	12 00	9 00
Teachers (public schools) *	*170 00	*1,600 00	*300 00
Saddle and harness makers	7 00	10 00	8 00
Sail-makers	12 00	12 00	12 00
Stevedores	18 00	30 00	20 00
Tanners	7 00	16 00	8 00
Tailors	9 00	15 00	10 00
Telegraph operators	6 00	22 00	10 00
Tinsmiths	6 00	12 00	8 00

* Per year.

II. FACTORIES, MILLS, ETC.

Wages paid per week of sixty hours in factories or mills in New Brunswick.

Occupations.	Lowest.	Highest.	Average.
COTTON MILLS.			
Spinners, mule			$9 00
Spinners, ring			5 50
Spinners	$1 50	$20 00	
Weavers		15 00	
Dyers	6 00	20 00	7 00
SAW-MILLS.			
Filers			14 00
Millwright		12 00	10 50
Gangmen	9 00	10 50	9 00
Pilers	9 50		
SPICE-MILLS.			
Including all departments	3 00	12 00	5 00

II. FACTORIES, MILLS, ETC.—Continued.

Wages paid per week of sixty hours in factories or mills in New Brunswick—Continued.

Occupations.	Lowest.	Highest.	Average.
PAPER-MILLS.			
Manager		$15 00	
Engineer	$12 00	15 00	$13 00
Pulpingmen	6 00	9 00	7 00
Firemen		9 00	
Grinders		7 50	
Laborers		7 50	
Bolt and nut factory	5 00	15 00	6 50
Wood-makers	8 00	12 00	10 00
Trunk-makers	2 00	10 00	8 00

III. FOUNDRIES, MACHINE-SHOPS, AND IRON WORKS.

Wages paid per week of sixty hours in foundries, machine-shops, and iron works in New Brunswick.

Occupations.	Lowest.	Highest.	Average.
Foundrymen	$7 00	$12 00	$7 50
Engine-builders	9 00	18 00	12 00
Edge-tool makers	6 00	18 00	11 00
ROLLING-MILLS.			
Rollers	18 00	22 00	18 00
Heaters	17 00	20 00	17 00
Puddlers	15 00	18 00	15 00
Laborers	6 00	9 00	7 00
Engineers	11 00	16 00	12 00

VI. RAILWAY EMPLOYÉS.

Wages paid per month to railway employés (those engaged about stations as well as those engaged on the engines and cars, linemen, railroad laborers, &c.) in New Brunswick.

Occupations.	Lowest.	Highest.	Average.
Conductors	$52 00	$60 00	
Agents	20 00	70 00	$30 00
Drivers	50 00	60 00	
Firemen		36 00	
Brakemen		36 00	
Trackmen	28 00	35 00	30 00

VII. SHIP-YARDS AND SHIP-BUILDING.

Wages paid per day of ten hours in ship-yards (distinguishing between iron and wood ship-building) in New Brunswick.

Occupations.	Lowest.	Highest.	Average.
Carpenters and teamsters	$1 00	$1 50	$1 30
Ironers, dubbers, hobborors, and blacksmiths	1 00	2 50	1 50

VIII. Seamen's Wages.

Wages paid per month to seamen (officers and men)—distinguishing between ocean, coast, and river navigation, and between sail and steam—in the ports of New Brunswick.

Occupations.	Lowest.	Highest.	Average.
OCEAN, SAIL.			
Masters......	$60 00	$100 00	....
Mate......	28 00	40 00	$35 00
Second mate	22 00	32 00	25 00
Cook and steward	28 00	45 00	35 00
Able seamen	15 00	20 00	18 00
Carpenter	16 00	22 00	20 00
COASTWISE.			
Master	35 00	45 00	40 00
Mate	24 00	27 00	22 00
Cook and steward	25 00	30 00	27 00

NOTE.—By the run to Great Britain, seamen get from $30 to $80, depending upon the demand.

IX. Store and shop wages.

Wages paid per annum in dry goods stores, wholesale or retail, to males and females in Saint John, New Brunswick.

Occupations.	Lowest.	Highest.	Average.
DRY GOODS.			
Wholesale:			
Book-keepers......	$400 00	$900 00	$600 00
Salesmen......	550 00	2,000 00	600 00
Retail:			
Book-keepers......	300 00	1,500 00	600 00
Clerks	300 00	800 00	600 00
Apprentices......	100 00	250 00	200 00
Porters......	....	....	300 00
BOOK STORES.			
Salesmen......	300 00	750 00	450 00

X. Household wages in towns and cities.

Wages paid per month to household servants (towns and cities) in Saint John, New Brunswick.

Occupations.	Lowest.	Highest.	Average.
Cooks	$6 00	$10 00	$8 00
Housemaids......	5 00	8 00	7 00
Chambermaids......	6 00	8 00	7 00
Grooms	25 00	30 00	25 00
Nurses	6 00	8 00	6 00

XI. Agricultural wages.

Wages paid per month to agricultural laborers and household (country) servants in New Brunswick.

Occupations.	Lowest.	Highest.	Average.
Farm hands, with board and lodging......	$10 50	$18 00	$14 00
Farm hands, without board and lodging......	20 00	30 00	25 00

Generally farm work is performed by the farmer himself and his sons, but little hiring of which labor is required.

XII. Corporation Employés.

Wages paid per year to the corporation employés in the city of Saint John, New Brunswick.

Occupations.	Lowest.	Highest.	Average.
Mayor		$1,800 00	
Recorder	$900 00	600 00	
Crown clerk	900 00	2,000 00	
Police magistrate		1,000 00	
Chamberlain		1,800 00	
Harbor-master		1,200 00	
Clerks	200 00	1,000 00	$700 00
Inspector of buildings		400 00	
Censors	400 00	1,800 00	800 00
City engineer		1,080 00	
Chief fire department and salvage corps		1,000 00	
Fire department genius		432 00	
Engineer fire department		540 00	
Firemen		90 00	
Superintendent of ferries		800 00	
Engineers	500 00	672 00	550 00
Chief police		800 00	
Sergeants, police		600 00	
Policemen		530 00	
Laborers	150 00	350 00	250 00

XIII. Government Departments and Offices.

Wages paid per year to employés in Government departments and offices, exclusive of trades men and laborers, in New Brunswick.

Occupations.	Lowest.	Highest.	Average.
Customs department.			
Collectors	$100	$3,000	$675
Surveyors	750	1,500	1,080
Chief clerk		1,500	
Appraisees	600	1,000	740
Landing waiters	250	1,000	700
Tide waiters	60	650	500
Gaugers	750	800	775
Lockers	650	650	650
Clerks	350	1,200	665
Prev officers	100	700	265
Tret revenues.			
Collectors	300	1,400	850
Excesance	400	1,000	700
Inspectors	500	1,800	900
Marine and fisheries department.			
Agent		1,800	
Assistants and book-keeper		800	
Light-house keepers	80	80	80
Fog-whistle and light-house keepers	400	1,000	450
Public works.			
Engineers	1,500	2,000	1,800
Foremen			900
Carpenters			500
Laborers			250
Pay master	750	950	800

XV. Printers and Printing Offices.

Statement showing the wages paid per week of sixty hours to printers (compositors, pressmen, proof-readers) &c., in New Brunswick.

Occupations.	Lowest.	Highest.	Average.
Foremen	$9 00	$12 00	$10 50
Pressmen	6 00	10 50	9 00
Compositors	6 00	10 50	9 00
Apprentices	1 50	4 00	2 50

PROVINCE OF NOVA SCOTIA.

HALIFAX.

REPORT BY CONSUL-GENERAL FRYE.

I beg to submit the following report, containing such information as I have been able to obtain, in relation to the rates of wages and the condition of labor in this consular district, as required by Department circular of February 15, 1884:

I. GENERAL TRADES.

Occupations.	Lowest.	Highest.	Average
BUILDING TRADES.			
Brick-layers ..... per day..	$2 50	$3 00	$3 00
Hod-carriers ..... do....	1 00	1 25	1 20
Masons ..... do....	2 50	3 00	3 00
Tenders ..... do....	1 00	1 25	1 20
Plasterers ..... do....	2 00	2 25	2 00
Slaters ..... do....	2 50	3 00	3 00
Roofers ..... do....	1 75	2 00	1 75
Plumbers ..... do....	1 75	2 25	2 00
Carpenters ..... do....	1 50	2 00	1 80
Gas-fitters ..... do....	1 75	2 00	1 75
OTHER TRADES.			
Bakers.. ..... do....	1 35	2 00	1 60
Blacksmiths ..... do	1 60	2 50	2 00
Brewers ..... do....	1 00	1 25	1 15
Brass-founders ..... do....	1 75	2 00	1 75
Cabinet-makers ..... per week..	8 00	15 00	9 00
Coopers ..... do....	8 00	9 00	9 00
Draymen and teamsters ..... per day..	1 00	1 40	1 25
Gardeners ..... do....	1 00	1 50	1 25
Millwrights ..... do....	2 00	3 00	2 25
Printers ..... do....	1 50	1 50	1 50
Pressmen ..... per week..	7 00	9 00	8 00
Proof-readers ..... do....	8 00	15 00	12 00
Saddle and harness makers ..... per day..	1 25	2 00	1 50
Stevedores ..... per hour..	25	35	35
Telegraph operators ..... per month..	25 00	60 00	40 00
Tailors (cutters) ..... per week..	12 00	25 00	12 00
Tailors (pressmen) ..... do....	6 00	12 00	10 00
Factories, mills, &c.			
Carders ..... per week..	5 00	6 00	5 50
Mule spinners ..... do....	8 00	9 00	8 50
Ring spinners ..... do....	4 00	5 00	4 50
Weavers ..... do....	4 00	7 00	6 00
Slashers ..... per day..	1 50	3 50	2 00
Foremen ..... do....	1 50	3 50	2 00
Foundries, machine-shops and iron-works.			
Foremen ..... per day..	2 00	4 00	2 50
Molders ..... per week..	3 00	12 00	8 00
Machinists ..... do....	3 00	12 00	8 00
Pattern-makers ..... do....	7 00	12 00	9 00
Boiler-makers ..... do....	9 00	15 00	12 00
Assistant boiler-makers ..... do....	6 00	7 50	7 00
Rivet heaters ..... do....	3 00	4 00	3 50
Blacksmiths ..... do....	6 00	12 00	9 00
Gold mining.			
Foremen	1 50	2 25	1 75
Common laborers	1 25	1 50	1 40

*General trades, &c., in Halifax—*Continued.

Occupations.	Lowest.	Highest.	Average.
Coal mining.			
Underground laborers ....per day..	$80	$1 40	$1 25
Underground boys' work..do....	40	85	75
Repairing, &c., (above ground)................................do ...	1 00	1 50	1 25
Pumping...do....	1 20	1 50	1 50
Engineers ....do ...	1 25	2 25	1 75
Firemen ....do ...	85	1 25	1 00
Blacksmiths..do....	80	1 50	1 25
Shipping coal...do....	55	1 25	1 20
Banking ....do ...	75	1 00	1 25
Coal cutting ....per gross ton..	47	50	49
Sail vessels, ocean navigation.			
Masters ....per month..	75 00	100 00	85 00
Mates ....do....	45 00	60 00	50 00
Second mates ....do ...	25 00	30 00	27 00
Able seamen..do...	16 00	20 00	18 00
Ordinary seamen ....do....	14 00	18 09	16 00
Cooks...do....	30 00	40 00	35 06
Sail vessels, coasting.			
Masters ....per month..	25 00	35 00	30 00
Mates ....do....	20 00	25 00	20 00
Able seamen ....do ...	16 00	19 00	17 00
Ordinary seamen ....do....	12 00	16 00	14 00
Cooks ....do....	14 00	22 00	20 00
Steam vessels.			
First engineers...per month..	70 00	100 00	100 00
Second engineers ....do ...	40 00	80 00	65 00
Third engineers...do ..	40 00	60 00	45 00
Firemen ....do....	20 00	25 00	22 00
Trimmers ....do...	18 00	20 00	20 00
Donkeymen...do....	20 00	25 00	24 00
Railway employés.			
Station masters...per annum..	300 00	1,300 00	6 00 00
Telegraph operators.......................................per month..	25 00	50 00	40 00
Checkers ....do ...	*20	50 00	50 00
Porters..per day..	1 25	1 25	1 25
Conductors;			
Passenger ....per month..			70 00
Freight...do....	†2 00	70 00	60 00
Engineers ....do...	†2 00	70 00	70 00
Firemen ....per day..	1 35	1 35	1 35
Baggage-masters:			
Express ....per month..			45 00
Other..do....	†1 35	45 00	†1 35
Brakemen ....per day..	1 35	1 35	1 35
Yard masters ....do....	1 50	2 00	2 00
Switchmen and shunters ....do ...	1 25	1 50	1 35
Track masters...per annum..	1,200 00	1,200 00	1,200 00
Track foremen ....per day..	1 35	1 50	1 50
Trackmen ....do....	1 00	1 25	1 25
Store and shop wages.			
Salesmen...per annum..	300 00	1,400 00	900 00
Book-keepers ....do ...	400 00	1,600 00	1,000 00
Porters ....per week..	6 00	8 00	7 00
Clerks ....do....	5 00	15 00	8 00
Household wages.			
Male servants ....per month..	10 00	20 00	16 00
Cooks (females)..do....	6 50	14 00	8 00
Housemaids ....do ...	5 00	8 00	6 00
Other servants (females) ....do....	5 00	7 00	6 00
Government departments and offices.‡			
Customs officers; at Halifax:			
Collector at Halifax......................................per annum..			3,000 00
Port surveyor ....do ...			1,500 00
Chief clerk ....do....			1,600 00
Chief check clerk......................................do....			850 00
Clerk ....do....			800 00
Cashier ....do....			1,200 00

* Per hour.   † Per day.   ‡ Exclusive of tradesmen and laborers.

*General trades, &c., in Halifax--*Continued.

Occupations.	Lowest.	Highest.	Average.
Government departments and offices—Continued.			
Customs officers; at Halifax—Continued:			
Chief clerk reg. ships ....per annum...			$1,400 00
Chief wharf clerk.....................do...			1,200 00
Statistical clerk ....do ...			800 00
Appraisers, three, each.....................do....	$600 00	$700 00	1,200 00
Gauger and proof officer.....................do....	800 00		1,000 00
Landing waiters (five) ....do....	800 00	1,000 00	900 00
Lockers (thirteen employed).....................do....	500 00	730 00	600 00
Tide surveyers ....do....	600 00		900 00
Other subordinates ....do....	60 00	650 00	550 00
Halifax post-office:			
Postmaster ....do....			2,400 00
Assistant postmaster.....................do....			1,500 00
First-class clerk ....do....			1,200 00
Second-class clerk ....do....			800 00
Other clerks, carriers, messengers ....do....	300 00	800 00	600 00
Post-office inspector ....do			2,200 00
Assistant post-office inspector ....do			1,200 00
Second-class clerk.....................do....			1,100 00
Third-class clerk ....do ...			800 00
Other clerks ....do	400 00	560 00	500 00
Railway mail service:			
Chief clerk ....do....			1,100 00
Second-class clerks	480 00	827 00	650 00
Trades and labor, city employ.			
On streets:			
Foremen.....................per week..	10 00	16 00	10 00
Laborers.....................per day..	80	1 15	1 00
On water works:			
Foremen, pipe layers, &c.....................per week..	10 00	16 00	8 00
Laborers.....................per day..	1 10	1 40	1 20
Sugar refining.			
Foremen of departments.....................per day..	1 50	1 55	1 55
Laborers in departments.....................do ...	1 00	1 20	1 10
Coopers.....................do...	1 50	1 50	1 50
Firemen ....do ...	1 50	1 50	1 50
Ordinary labor.....................do ...	1 00	1 00	1 00

GENERAL WAGE—EXPLANATIONS.

In connection with the subject of seamen's wages it should be mentioned that a large number of men are engaged in the fishing business, and that they are not hired as other seamen, but usually sail on "shares," receiving compensation in proportion to the quantity of fish they catch. With reference to the wages of some other classes of laborers it may be stated that they are often paid according to the amount of labor performed, as when sail makers are paid by the yard, blacksmiths by the piece, printers by the thousand ems, &c.

Farm laborers are most frequently employed for the spring, summer, and fall season at a certain rate per month, though often by the day, during the busy season of haying, &c. They are generally boarded by their employers, receiving per month from $12 to $17, and from $1.25 to $1.75 per day, when employed only during the busy season. As so large a portion of laborers are employed only a part of the time, according to the demand for labor, it is difficult in some cases to estimate the average rates paid them. There are not in Nova Scotia many large factories, mills, or shops employing regularly a great number of men, and consequently there is less system and regularity in the matter of wages than in the greater manufacturing districts.

Under the civil service system prevailing in the Dominion a fee or tax, not exceeding in amount 2 per cent. of the salary, is deducted for the superannuation fund.

About one hundred teachers are employed in the public schools of Halifax, one-fourth of whom are males. The highest salary paid to male teachers is about $1,450 per year. The highest to females is $720. The average to males is about $665, and to females about $260.

COST OF LIVING.

The prices of some of the necessaries of life are lower than in the Eastern States. This is true of such important articles as beef, mutton, fish, potatoes, and some vegetables. The estimated difference is 15 to 20 per cent. Nova Scotia coal is largely used for fuel, except on farms supplied with wood and where the transportation would make it cost higher than wood. It is sold at retail in Halifax at from $5.50 to $6.50 per chaldron of 3,000 pounds. Anthracite coal, which is brought from the United States and is subject to a duty of 50 cents per ton of 2,000 pounds, is not largely used for fuel. Flour is from 50 cents to $1 higher per barrel than in New England. Corn-meal is imported from the United States and is higher than there. Sugar, molasses, tea, and coffee are about the same here as there. House rents vary so much in different localities that it is difficult to state the average rates. Houses rent for good prices in Halifax, but the rates are lower in the smaller towns. Household furniture is higher here than in New England markets and the quality does not appear to be so good.

Shoes and rubbers are from 15 to 20 per cent. higher than in New England, but the prices of most articles of clothing used by laboring men are about the same here as there.

WAGES PAST AND PRESENT.

The rates of wages have increased during the past five or six years, probably from 15 to 20 per cent. on the average. The cost of provisions and the common necessaries of life has continued about the same and the condition of the laboring classes is believed to be slowly improving in respect to the comforts of life.

HABITS OF THE WORKING CLASSES.

The laboring classes appear to be as steady and perhaps as trustworthy and as economical as the same grades of laborers in the United States. Probably intemperance is the cause affecting their habits for evil more than any other, though its effects are not more apparent in Nova Scotia than in some of the States where the laws for the suppression of liquor selling are much more stringent.

FEELING BETWEEN EMPLOYER AND EMPLOYÉ.

Generally the relations are amicable between laborers and their employers, and this condition is of course favorable to the interests of all parties.

ORGANIZED CONDITION OF LABOR.

Labor organizations exist to some extent, but have not been prominent, nor have they affected business or the rates of wages very materially. Of late, however, some of them in the city of Halifax have been more demonstrative, and their members have united in demanding better terms of their employers. One dollar and fifty cents per day is demanded by laborers on the wharves and others, who formerly received $1.25. In some cases the demands have been complied with, though the differences between them and their employers have not yet been fully adjusted. I am not aware of the existence of any counter organizations of capital, nor of any laws bearing specially on such organizations.

STRIKES.

Strikes have not prevailed largely among the laborers of Nova Scotia, though one occurred last year in the coal mines of Cape Breton necessitating the interference of the military authorities. It was finally settled by some compromise, and did not have any very important effect on the interests of the laborers or their employers.

FOOD PURCHASES.

Laborers, as a rule, purchase the necessaries of life as they choose. They are generally paid weekly or monthly in the common currency of the country.

CO-OPERATIVE SOCIETIES.

None exist in this district, nor, so far as I am informed, in Nova Scotia.

GENERAL CONDITION OF THE WORKING PEOPLE.

So far as I am able to judge by observation and inquiry the condition of the laboring people in this province is not very materially different from that of people of similar occupations in the United States; for instance in the State of Maine, between which and Nova Scotia, in respect to climate, the extent of seaboard, and the occupation of the people, there is less contrast than between this province and any other State in the Union. The manner in which the people of both live, their homes, their food, and their clothes, are very similar, though with some odds in favor of the people of that State. With economy, sobriety, and industry, laborers here, with ordinary good fortune, can and do better their condition year by year, and are able to save something against the time of need. The condition of the schools in New England is in advance of it here, though for nearly twenty years the common-school system has been in operation in Nova Scotia, greatly to the advantage, no doubt, of the families of the laboring classes. The province is gradually improving in respect to popular education. The moral and physical condition of the people may in general be said to be fairly good.

SAFETY OF EMPLOYÉS.

Except with reference to the coal-mines it is not of great importance in this report, because there are so few large factories or mills where accidents are liable to occur. In most cases, I am informed, fire-escapes are provided, as well as practical means of extinguishing fires. In the coal-mines great precautions against accidents of all kinds are provided by law, and under competent and careful officials and superintendents casualties have not been of frequent occurrence. In general, I do not understand that employers give *special* consideration to the moral and physical well-being of their workmen and their families, though in some instances they do. In one case under my observation the proprietors of a manufacturing establishment furnish comfortable cottages for their employés at a fair rental, and also a chapel where a Sunday-school or other religious exercises are regularly held under the personal supervision of one of the proprietors. The general relations prevailing between the two classes are agreeable, so far as I can learn.

POLITICAL RIGHTS.

The political rights enjoyed by workingmen in Nova Scotia in respect to suffrage are defined by the following section of the Revised Statutes :

Every male subject of Her Majesty, by birth or naturalization, being of the age of twenty-one years, and not disqualified by law, who shall have been assessed for the year for which the register hereinafter provided is made up, in respect of real estate to the value of $150, or in respect of personal estate, or of real and personal estate together, to the value of $300, shall be qualified to vote at elections of members to serve in the house of assembly for the county in which he shall be so assessed.

The influence of workingmen on legislation is less than it might be if they exercised their political rights with more freedom and took greater interest in politics and the affairs of government. The working people have their full share of taxation according to the property they own. Until 1883 tenants of all houses in Halifax were held to pay the taxes against the premises, there being no lien on the property for the taxes. The law has been amended in this respect, the tax being now assessed to the owner with a lien on the property.

EMIGRATION.

The causes of emigration are a desire on the part of the emigrants to improve their condition, and the belief that it will be improved by emigration to the United States, where better wages than here are paid and more constant employment given. Emigrants are in great part mechanics and laborers, house maids, cooks, and young women who seek employment in the New England factories. They find steadier employment and better wages there than here, and many, though not all, remain permanently in the United States. According to the published report from the Bureau of Statistics (the correctness of which as to emigration from Nova Scotia I have never seen disputed), the number of emigrants to the United States from Nova Scotia in 1883 was 6,435; for the year 1882, it was 12,693; for 1881, 12,425; and for 1880, 17,870. It has been a serious fact for the province that so many of its people have removed to the United States and to the Northwest. Any one acquainted with the resources of the province cannot doubt that they are sufficient to support and employ a much larger population than it now contains.

FEMALE LABOR.

It is impracticable to attempt to ascertain the number of women and children employed in the different industrial pursuits in this consular district, as the number is comparatively small, outside of teachers in the public schools. A limited number is employed in the mills and as clerks, boarding-house keepers, and laundresses, and a still smaller proportion as musicians, government officials, artists, chemists, hotel-keepers, inventors, bankers, brokers, lecturers, and public speakers.

The rate of wages of employés is various, ranging from perhaps $3 per week, as a minimum for clerks, to $750 per year as a maximum for teachers. The estimated average, without board, is $200 per year.

Their moral and physical condition, generally speaking, is fairly good; corresponding very well with the condition of the same classes of laborers in New England. In education, teachers excepted, they are not up to the average of employés of corresponding classes there, but their children generally have the benefit of public schools, and the tendency is toward an improved condition.

ACKNOWLEDGMENTS.

I must acknowledge my indebtedness to the gentlemen named below, among others, for information courteously furnished for this report: Hon. William Ross, collector of customs; H. W. Blackadar, postmaster; R. Borradaile, inspector of internal revenue; S. M. Brookfield, contractor and builder; Roderick McDonald, freight agent Intercolonial Railway; William McKerron, secretary of the Nova Scotia Poultry and Bee-keeping Association; Gordon & Keith, furniture manufacturers and dealers; John P. Mott & Co., spice manufacturers; George Stairs, superintendent of the Dartmouth Rope Works; John Doull, president of the Nova Scotia Cotton Manufacturing Company; J. T. Wylde, secretary of the Starr Manufacturing Company; Mahon Brothers, dry goods merchants; C. & W. Anderson, merchants; J. B. Johnson, clerk of city board of works; E. P. Archibald, treasurer Glace Bay Mining Company; W. L. Lowell, banker; John Patterson, boiler manufacturer; A. B. and H. Bligh, shipping commissioners; Pickford & Black, merchants, all of Halifax; also to the following United States consular agents in this district; D. M. Owen, esq., Lunenburg; J. N. S. Marshall, esq., Liverpool; and Hon. N. W. White, Shelburne.

WAKEFIELD G. FRYE,
Consul-General.

UNITED STATES CONSULATE-GENERAL,
Halifax, May 23, 1884

PRINCE EDWARD ISLAND.

REPORT BY CONSUL WORDEN, OF CHARLOTTETOWN.

I have the honor to transmit herewith my report concerning the condition of labor in the province of Prince Edward Island.

The report has been prepared with a good deal of care, through the assistance of Mr. Hyndman, vice and deputy consul.

COST OF LIVING.

The cost of living in the province is rather below than above the average. Meat can be purchased at from 10 to 14 cents per pound, and by the quarter at a price still less. Fish of various kinds is abundant and cheap. Clothing is as cheap or cheaper than at home, and rents are quite as low. Vegetables are abundant. But little fruit is grown in the province, the soil not seeming adapted to it. Fuel, both wood and coal, is very reasonable, the coal being procured from the neighboring province of Nova Scotia and Cape Breton island. Soft coal, the only coal produced, varies in price from $2.50 to $3.75 per ton.

CONDITION OF THE LABORING CLASSES.

The condition of the laboring class is probably rendered better by the enforcement of what is called the "Scott act." This act prevails throughout the province, and by its adoption prohibits the granting of licenses and sale of malt or spirituous liquors.

There are no trades unions nor organizations for the protection of labor.

The population of the province numbers about 110,000. There is not sufficient consumption of manufactured articles to warrant any extended manufactories, and the greater part are imported from the other provinces, the United States, or Great Britain.

There are in the island two Government hospitals into which seamen are admitted. By a late act of the Dominion Parliament the dues heretofore paid by American vessels are not now received, and in consequence I am advised that seamen of our service are refused admittance.

I trust that the requirements called for by the circular have been in part met, and that the information may be in some degree serviceable.

WARREN A. WORDEN,
Consul.

United States Consulate,
Charlottetown, July 22, 1884.

I. General Trades.

Wages paid per week of sixty hours in Charlottetown.

Occupations.	Lowest.	Highest.	Average.
BUILDING TRADES.			
Bricklayers	$12 00	$12 00	$12 00
Hod-carriers	6 00	6 00	6 00
Masons	12 00	12 00	12 00
Tenders	6 00	6 00	6 00
Plasterers	9 00	12 00	10 50
Tenders	6 00	6 00	6 00
Slaters	15 00	15 00	15 00
Roofers	9 00	12 00	10 50
Tenders	6 00	6 00	6 00
Plumbers	8 00	10 00	9 00
Assistants	6 00	6 00	6 00
Carpenters	6 00	9 00	7 50
Gas-fitters	8 00	9 00	8 50
OTHER TRADES.			
Bakers	4 00	6 00	5 00
Blacksmiths	9 00	10 00	9 50
Strikers	6 00	6 00	6 00
Book-binders	4 00	10 00	7 00
Brick-makers	6 00	9 00	7 50
Brewers	6 00	6 00	6 00
Butchers	4 00	6 00	5 00
Cabinet makers	6 00	10 00	8 00
Confectioners	4 00	6 00	5 00
Coopers	6 00	8 00	7 00
Drivers	5 00	5 00	5 00
Draymen and teamsters	5 00	5 00	5 00
Cab and carriage	5 00	5 00	5 00
Gardeners	4 00	6 00	5 00
Horseshoers	9 00	9 00	9 00
Jewelers	6 00	6 00	6 00
Laborers, porters, &c	5 00	7 00	6 00
Millwrights	7 50	9 00	8 25
Potters	6 00	15 00	10 50
Printers	4 00	7 00	5 50
Teachers, public schools	6 00	20 00	13 00

Wages paid per week of sixty hours in Charlottetown—Continued.

Occupations.	Lowest.	Highest.	Average.
OTHER TRADES—Continued.			
Saddle and harness makers	$7 50	$7 50	$7 50
Sail-makers	9 00	12 00	10 50
Stevedores	12 00	12 00	12 00
Tanners	5 00	6 00	5 50
Tailors	10 00	14 00	12 00
Telegraph operators	5 00	10 00	7 50
Tinsmiths	7 00	9 00	8 00
Boot and shoe makers	6 00	12 00	9 00

II. FACTORIES, MILLS, ETC.

Wages paid per week of sixty hours in factories or mills in Prince Edward Island.

Occupations.	Lowest.	Highest.	Average.
WOOLEN MILLS.*			
Foremen	$12 00	$18 00	$15 00
Weavers	3 00	5 00	4 00
Spinners	7 50	7 50	7 50
Finishers	7 00	12 00	9 50
Carders	3 00	10 00	6 50
Laborers			6 00
STARCH FACTORIES. †			
Managers			20 00
Other hands			6 00

* There are two woolen mills in the island : each employ about forty hands.
† There are ten starch factories in Prince Edward Island, which produce about 250 tons of starch annually, manufactured solely from potatoes. They work only between 25th September and 1st December, and employ about twenty hands each. The starch is exported to United Kingdom principally. Some small shipments go to Upper Canada and the United States.

LOBSTER, MEAT, AND MACKEREL FACTORIES.

In 1883 there were eighty-eight factories on the island, employing about 2,600 men and 1,600 women. The men get on an average $1 per day, and women 50 cents per day when employed. These factories turned out about 56,000 cases of 4-dozen 1-pound cans of lobsters, value about $280,000.

After the lobster season is over in many of the factories the canning of mackerel is carried on. In 1883 there were 4,313 cases of 48 1-pound tins of mackerel preserved, value, $17,622.

After the mackerel season is over some few factories pack meats, mutton and beef principally. In 1883 there were 7,236 cases of 48 1-pound tins put up, value, $32,765.

III. FOUNDRIES, MACHINE-SHOPS, AND IRON WORKS.

Wages paid per week of sixty hours in foundries, machine-shops, and iron works in Prince Edward Island.

Occupations.	Average wages.	Occupations.	Average wages.
Machinists	$9 00	Boiler-makers	$9 00
Moulders and brass founders	9 00	Pattern-makers	8 00
Smiths	8 00	Laborers	6 00

*There are two foundries and machine-shops in Prince Edward Island, and employ on an average forty-five hands.

VI. Railway Employés.

Wages paid to railway employés (those engaged about stations, as well as those engaged on the engines and cars, linemen, railroad laborers, &c.) in Prince Edward Island.

Occupations.	Lowest.	Highest.	Average.
Station-masters..per month..	$30 00	$80 00	$55 00
Clerks .... do ...	30 00	70 00	50 00
Conductors ....do...			55 00
Baggage-masters..per day..	1 35	1 35	1 35
Brakemen ....do ...	1 25	1 25	1 25
Engineers ....do....	2 15	2 40	2 30
Firemen ....do....	1 15	1 35	1 25
Machinists ....do....	1 50	2 20	1 85
Carpenters ....do....	1 40	1 70	1 55
Sectionmen ....do....	1 00	1 50	1·25
Laborers...do....	1 00	1 25	1 12½

There are 200 miles of railway in Prince Edward Island, owned and operated by the Government of Canada.

VII. Ship-Yards and Ship-Building.

Wages paid per week of sixty hours in ship-yards in Prince Edward Island.

Occupations.	Lowest.	Highest.	Average.
Foremen ....♦....................	$12 00	$15 00	$13 50
Carpenters...	5 00	7 00	6 00
Calkers...	9 00	12 00	10 50

VIII. Seamen's Wages.

Wages paid per month to seamen (officers and men), distinguishing between ocean, coast, and river navigation, and between sail and steam, in Prince Edward Island.

Occupations.	Lowest.	Highest.	Average.
Coasting and river navigation:			
Masters	$30 00	$40 00	$35 00
Mates...	20 00	30 00	25 00
Seamen	15 00	20 00	17 50
Ocean-going vessels (sailing):			
Masters	40 00	80 00	60 00
Mates	20 00	35 00	27 50
Seamen	16 00	25 00	20 50
Cooks..	25 00	35 00	30 00

IX. Store and Shop Wages.

Wages paid per week of sixty hours in stores, wholesale or retail, to males and females, in Prince Edward Island.

Occupations.	Lowest.	Highest.	Average.
Salesmen..	$2 00	$12 00	$7 00
Clerks...	2 00	12 00	7 00
Book-keepers..	8 00	20 00	14 00
Shop-boys...	1 00	2 00	1 50

X. Household Wages in Towns and Cities.

Wages paid per month with board to household servants (towns and cities) in Prince Edward Island.

Occupations.	Lowest.	Highest.	Average.
Men servants	$7 00	$20 00	$13 50
Women servants..	4 00	8 00	6 00

XI. AGRICULTURAL WAGES.

Wages paid per month to agricultural laborers and household (country) servants in Prince Edward Island, with board and lodging.

Occupations.	Lowest.	Highest.	Average.
Farm laborers	$10 00	$20 00	$15 00

XII. CORPORATION EMPLOYÉS.

Wages paid per week of sixty hours to the corporation employés in the city of Charlotte-town, Prince Edward Island.

Occupations.	Lowest.	Highest.	Average.
City marshal, chief of police................................			$10 00
Policemen...	$7 00	$8 00	7 50
Laborers...			6 00
City clerk...			16 00
Stipendiary magistrate.....................................		*1,000 00	
Stipendiary clerk		*600 00	

* Per annum.

Mayor and ten councilors: The former is paid $325 per annum : the councilmen are without remuneration.

XIII. GOVERNMENT DEPARTMENTS AND OFFICES.

Wages paid per month of one hundred and fifty hours to employés in government departments and offices—exclusive of tradesmen and laborers—in Prince Edward Island.

Occupations.	Lowest.	Highest.	Average.
Heads of departments, under local government..................			$125 00
Assistants			80 00
Clerks and writers...	$35 00	$65 00	50 00

XIV. TRADES AND LABOR—GOVERNMENT EMPLOY.

Wages paid by the week of sixty hours to the trades and laborers in government employ in Prince Edward Island.

Occupations.	Lowest.	Highest.	Average.
Carpenters..	$12 00	$18 00	$15 00
Masons...	12 00	18 00	15 00
Painters	9 00	15 00	12 00
Laborers	6 00	9 00	7 50

XV. PRINTERS AND PRINTING OFFICES.

Statement showing the wages paid per week of sixty hours to printers (compositors, pressmen, proof-readers, &c.), in Prince Edward Island.

Occupations.	Lowest.	Highest.	Average.
Printers..	$6 00	$12 00	$9 00
Compositors	5 00	8 00	6 50
Pressmen	0 00	10 00	8 00
Foremen	12 00	15 00	13 50

Proof-reading is usually done by the editor or proprietor. There are two daily papers and six weekly papers published in Prince Edward Island.

MEXICO.

REPORT BY CONSUL-GENERAL STROTHER.

MALE LABOR.

The rates of wages paid to laborers of every class, mechanical, mining, factory, public works and railways, domestic, agricultural, and civil
and military employés of the Government, are given in the tables annexed to this report.

COST OF LIVING.

The cost of living to the laboring classes is variable, and it would be
difficult to estimate it with accuracy. On account of the mildness of
the climate the necessary requirements of living here in food, clothing,
fuel, and shelter, are very much less than among people inhabiting the
temperate and more northern latitudes, and among the laboring classes
the average scale of living is lower than among any class we know of
in the United States, not excepting the free negroes in the Southern
States, and decidedly inferior in comfort and neatness to that class when
in a state of slavery. The dwellings of the laboring classes in the cities
are generally wanting in all the requirements of health and comfort—
mostly rooms on the ground floor, without proper light or ventilation,
often with but a single opening (that for entrance), dirt floors, and no
drainage. These rooms rent from $1 to $5 per month, singly or in suits
of two or three together. Of late years, however, proprietors have been
building much better tenements, with wooden floors raised several feet
above the ground, neat, light, and airy, opening on courts ornamented
with trees and shrubbery, supplied with water, paved and drained.
"Viviendas," with two or three rooms and a kitchen in these houses
may be rented for from $5 to $10 per month. In the suburbs and in
the country the dwellings of the cold regions are of adobe and in the
temperate and warm countries mere huts of cane or stakes wattled with
twigs, and sometimes plastered with mud and roofed with plantain
leaves, corn-stalks, or brush. These dwellings are, I believe, generally
the property of the occupants. In the cities, as in the country, the common laborers use neither beds, chairs, nor tables, the only furniture
seen in their dwellings being a variety of earthen vessels to hold their
food and drink and for cooking, a "metate" or flat stone, with a roller
to grind their corn, and some rolls of rush matting, which constitutes
their beds and bedding. Their principal food is of Indian corn ground
by hand on the stone before mentioned and baked in a thin cake called
"tortilla." This is the universal bread of the Indian race and the
laboring classes in Mexico, and is eaten with boiled beans (frijoles), another national dish, with meat boiled or fried and a savory sauce made
of lard, red peppers, onions, cheese, and other strong flavoring ingredients to suit the taste. The national beverage is pulque, the fermented
juice of the maguey plant, a liquor resembling in appearance and flavor
a mixture of hard cider and sharp buttermilk, with an appreciable scent
of putrid flesh from the fresh hides in which it is fermented. This
beverage, taken in moderation, is reputed to be very healthy and no
Mexican laborer or operative considers his meal complete without his
portion of pulque. The average cost of living (food and drink) for a

laboring man in the city is about 25 cents per day; in the country from 12½ to 18 cents. The usual clothing of the male laborer all over the Republic consists of a shirt and pantaloons of "manta," a domestic unbleached cotton cloth, a zerape or blanket of some woolen material, vegetable fiber, or rush matting. Hats of straw or palm-leaf, and if shod at all it is with sandals of raw hide. The women are shod and hatted as the men, but affect gayer colors in their petticoats and rebosas. The average annual cost of a man's dress is probably not over $5; that of a woman double that sum, perhaps, with an undetermined margin for gew-gaws and cheap jewelry. The Indians, who constitute the laboring class of the country both in cities and country, adhere tenaciously to the dress, food, and manner of living inherited from their ancestors; even the women employed as domestic servants in the cities carefully avoiding any imitation of the dress or modes of life pertaining to the upper classes. Among the artisan class and workers in factories, to a greater or less extent of European stock, the ordinary European dress and habits of these classes prevail.

PAST AND PRESENT WAGES.

I have no precise data whereon to base an intelligent answer to the foregoing interrogatory. From 1880 to 1883, while the Mexican Government and various foreign companies were very actively engaged in building railroads and other private and national improvements, there was a general demand for laborers, and consequently wages were increased temporarily in certain localities where the improvements were going on. But since these works have been completed or stopped for lack of funds, and the general prostration of business throughout the country, wages have probably settled down to their level in 1878 and 1879, and in the localities where there has been a temporary inflation the general condition of labor is rather worse than formerly.

HABITS OF THE WORKING CLASSES.

I have heard the agricultural laborers of this country very favorably spoken of as industrious, faithful, and easily managed. Their peculiar attachment to the place of their nativity binds them as closely to their employers and the soil they cultivate as did their former peonage. Enfranchised by law they are still to a great extent the slaves of habit and local attachments, and our road builders in this country have found that they could only rely upon the labor in the immediate neighborhood of their line of construction, and that neither money nor persuasion would induce any number of these people to follow their work any distance from their native fields and villages. They also preserve the same feudal fidelity to the great agricultural, mineral, and manufacturing establishments, where they and their families have been employed, often for successive generations, and a threat of "discharge" will bring the most rebellious and refractory subject to his knees. I have also been very favorably impressed with the orderly behavior, decent manners, and intelligence of the employés in the cotton factories, sugar houses, mines, and other establishments in this district. As a rule, none of the working classes have any idea of present economy or of providing for the future. The lives of most of them seem to be occupied in obtaining food and amusement for the passing hour, without either hope or desire for a better future. As the strongest proof of this improvidence in the city mechanic or laborers is the common demand for money in advance

from the mechanic, under the pretext of getting materials to enable him
to fill your order; from the laborer, to get something to eat before he
begins work. The prevalent vices in Mexico are gambling, drunkenness,
and fighting, the Indian population being especially hasty with their
knives. In the capital the laborer is subject to many demoralizing influences. In summing up the characteristics of the Mexican laborer
it may be said that, with less capacity and intelligence, he is more patient,
docile, and contented than his fellow laborer of the north, and consequently less efficient, but more easily managed.

FEELING BETWEEN EMPLOYER AND EMPLOYÉ.

The laboring classes in Mexico are chiefly Indians of a different race
from their employers—a race once conquered, then enslaved, then liber-
ated by law, but so bound by habit and necessity, that, except in the
cities, there is very little appreciable change in their condition, and while
the laborer remains ignorant, poor, and dependent, he is naturally very
respectful and submissive, but there is very little sympathy or cordiality
in the relations between him and his former master and present employer in the agricultural districts, and still less in cities and manufacturing establishments, where the operatives are better educated and where
the power of habit has not modified the prejudices of race and the jeal-
ousies of caste. Nevertheless, the relations between Mexican families
and their domestic servants in town and country are much more cordial
and intimate than is usual among people of the English race, and the
numerous instances of considerate sympathy and romantic fidelity between employer and employé of this class, are creditable to the manners
and hearts of both.

ORGANIZED CONDITION OF LABOR.

As far as I am informed the only organizations of labor in this country, are mutual aid societies, each member contributing a certain proportion of his earnings to the general fund, for which he is entitled to
assistance when disabled by sickness, expenses of burial in case of
death, and aid to his surviving family to a greater or less extent, according to circumstances. Beyond this limited and temporary pecuniary
assistance, we do not believe these organizations have done anything to
advance the general character and condition of the laborer. The laborer
in this country is too poor and dependent, and his capacity for organization too feeble to provoke counter organization of capital, consequently
nothing of the kind exists here that we are aware of, nor any laws touch-
ing the subject.

THE PREVALENCY OF STRIKES.

Strikes are not infrequent in Mexico, and owing to the uneducated
condition of the laborers they are apt to degenerate into riots and are
promptly suppressed by the authorities. Where conducted on better
principles the poverty and lack of provision of the laborers is so general
that the movement speedily starves out and very rarely terminates advantageously for the strikers. Recently strikes have taken place in
some of the neighboring cities which have continued longer than usual.
They have been conducted in an orderly manner and several attempts
were made to settle the differences by arbitration, some of which failed.
We are not informed as to particulars or whether the difficulties are yet
settled. It may be easily understood, however, that the laborer, who,

without resources, without ideas of economy, and living habitually from hand to mouth, enters into a contest with capital, can scarcely escape defeat and disaster.

FREEDOM OF FOOD PURCHASES.

The laborers of all classes are entirely free to purchase the necessaries of life where they please, although it is common for the employers in large establishments to open furnishing stores for their employés as a matter of mutual convenience. They have also the legal right in all cases to draw their pay in the current silver coin of the country, although in some instances paper checks, receivable for goods and supplies, are accepted by the employés, likewise for the sake of convenience.

SAFETY OF EMPLOYÉS.

Owing to the style of building in Mexico, the factories, mills, &c., being built universally of stone and cement, stone stairways, brick floors and roofs, the climate not requiring stoves or any artificial heating apparatus, and the buildings generally being not over two stories in height, very rarely over three stories, the danger to life and property from fires is very small. Nevertheless, in some of the principal establishments, where the floors are of wood and an accumulation of combustible and inflammable material make some precautions against fire necessary (notably at the "Fabrica of the Hercules," at Queretaro), I have observed the following: steam fire pumps, with hose connected with every room in the building; rows of buckets filled with water in the entries, storerooms, and galleries, with hand-pumps ready to distribute it; spongy blankets hanging along the walls, kept always wet for a sudden emergency. Arrangements of a similar character, more or less efficient, are found in other factories, while some have adopted Babcock's extinguisher and other patented chemical apparatus for fighting fire. Occasional losses of material and machinery occur in the factories, but we very rarely hear of any loss of life by fire.

Many of the principal mines in the country are worked by Englishmen and Americans, and all the railroads that we know of are worked by experts from the United States or Great Britain, and as far as we have been able to observe the same rules and precautions prevail here as in the countries named. We know of no provisions for assisting the sick or wounded miners or railroad men except the mutual aid societies or voluntary subscriptions by their fellow workmen. The character of the relations between employer and employé is treated in the reply to question No. 5, and it may be said further that generally the employer gives but little consideration either to the physical or moral well-being of his workmen, many of the owners of extensive agricultural estates and manufacturing establishments being habitual absentees and knowing nothing of their employés except through their overseers and superintendents. There are doubtless many exceptions to this rule, of several of which we have personal knowledge. These are large landed proprietors and manufacturers who live on their places and who, moved by sentiments of humanity as well as more enlightened views of interest, have given considerable attention to the education and improvement of their employés and families. The working population of Miraflores, an English cotton factory near this city, may be cited as an example of the gratifying success which has attended the efforts of the proprietors to improve the moral and physical condition of their Mexican employés

POLITICAL RIGHTS OF WORKINGMEN.

By the Mexican constitution all adult male citizens of the republic
are invested with full and equal political rights, including the right to
vote at elections, to hold office, &c., but the great majority of the people, including the working classes, take no part whatever in the elections, local or general, nor are they supposed to exercise any influence
on legislation in a legitimate way, although they occasionally manifest
their opinions by tumultuous assemblage and mob violence, thus influencing legislation in a greater or less degree. There is no direct or personal tax imposed on laborers or workingmen of any class. There are,
however, taxes on production and consumption which affect the working classes equally with all other citizens. There are also taxes on incomes and license taxes on trades which affect the artisan directly and
the journeymen indirectly.

EMIGRATION.

As heretofore stated, the native Mexican laborer is remarkable for the
strength of his local attachments, and he never emigrates voluntarily.

FEMALE LABOR.

The proportion of women and children employed in factories, cigar-
making, &c., is estimated at about 50 per cent.

In the city there are shop girls and saleswomen in a few of the fancy
and dry goods stores. Pastry and candy shops, for the most part, are
carried on by foreigners, French and Germans. The proportion of females
employed in commercial houses is, however, very insignificant. In
general transportation I am not aware that females appear at all, but
in the transportation which is done by the Indians on foot the women
do their full part according to their strength.

The ruling opinion in Mexican society would prohibit absolutely any
respectable female from engaging in any professional or personal occupation, including Government officials and clerks, teachers, artists,
chemists, hotel and boarding-house keepers, journalists, laundresses,
musicians, inventors, bankers, brokers, lecturers, and public speakers.
No female name appears on the official lists of the Government in any
capacity whatever, and any occupation or profession that would draw a
woman from the seclusion of her domestic circle would entail upon her
loss of caste and the general reprobation of her sex. An educated lady
may devote herself to teaching the poor from motives of religious zeal, or
exhibit her musical talents in public at a charity concert, but profes-
sionally never. Pressed by poverty a Mexican lady will work in lace,
embroidery, or other artistic labor and sell her productions privately,
or even give private lessons in music, &c., but all the female professional teachers, artists, boarding-house keepers, &c., are foreigners, or
nearly all, for of late years foreign travel, foreign education, and contact with foreigners at home, combined with the liberalizing tendency
of the reform laws, have somewhat modified the strictness of Mexican
society in this regard.

The laundry business is altogether in the hands of the Indian women,
who wash the clothes on the traditional flat rough-grained stone used
in the days of the Montezumas. There was an American steam laundry
here a year ago which failed for lack of encouragement, and the Chinaman has not yet made his appearance.

The Indian women and children work in the fields with the men, like the European peasantry, sharing all the labors of the farm.

Mining is exclusively carried on by male labor. I never saw females engaged about the mines or the smelting and separating works in any other way than in preparing and carrying food to the workmen.

Among the upper classes, as before stated, the dominant social opinion withdraws women, not only from all professions and occupations, but from many of the amusements and social ceremonies where the male sex predominate. Among the Indians and lower classes the women take their part promiscuously in all the labors, occupations, interests, and amusements incident to their condition in life. They are neither oppressed nor secluded, but live on terms of natural equality and companionship with their husbands, sharing their labors and the profits by rules of natural justice.

FEMALE WAGES AND HOURS OF LABOR.

In the same employments the average wages of women are about one-third less than of men :

Cents.

		Cents.
Seamstresses are paid	per day..	37
Weavers at hand looms	do....	50
Washerwomen	do....	37
Ironers	do....	50

Cigar-makers may earn from 50 cents to $1 per day, according to their industry and skill in manipulation, as they work by the job, receiving for cigarettes a tlaco (1½ cents per package) of twenty, or 7½ cents per hundred.

The usual hours of labor are from 6 in the morning until 6 at night, with intervals of an hour each for breakfast and dinner.

MORAL AND PHYSICAL CONDITION.

The moral and physical condition of female employés is apparently good. They are quiet and decent in their behavior and generally look healthy. There are public free schools supported by the Government for the benefit of females as well as males of the working classes. They receive here the elements of literary and technical education, and if they develop any especial talents may be admitted to the higher schools and colleges. There are also mutual aid societies as among the men, as well as some private charities, whose object is to assist and improve the social condition of females of the working classes. Public attention in Mexico is much more occupied with this subject than formerly, but the movement is too recent to have produced as yet any decided or appreciable results.

PAST AND PRESENT WAGES.

Generally there has been no change whatever. In this city the prices of the necessaries of life have gone up during the past two or three years, but are now resuming their former status. As the employment of women in the labor of the country is of ancient date, I have not, in the last five years, observed that it has any especial influence on wages or on the general condition of labor.

FEMALE EDUCATION.

The state of education among the working classes generally is very low, although since the establishment of free schools it is improving, especially in the towns and cities, as also among the employés of some of the larger factories. In a country like Mexico, where the lower classes of the population are sunk in ignorance and poverty, where their ordinary mode of living is on the lowest scale, with its attendant vices and miseries, where low wages and lack of regular employment would seem to forbid the hope of improvement, all regular and reasonably re-munerative labor must be regarded as beneficent in its effects, both on the individual and the family, educating, civilizing, and improving, both morally and physically; and in the cities as in the country I have ob-served that the employés and dependents of the manufacturing, mining, and agricultural establishments, where there was regular and organized labor, were decidedly superior in appearance, intelligence, and civilized appliances to the ordinary population.

DAVID H. STROTHER,
Consul-General.

UNITED STATES CONSULATE,
Mexico, February 15, 1885.

I. GENERAL TRADES.

Wages paid in the city of Mexico.

Occupations.	Lowest.	Highest.	Average.
BUILDING TRADES.			
Bricklayers			
Hod-carriers			
Masons			
Tenders			
Plasterers	(*)	(*)	(*)
Tenders			
Slaters			
Roofers			
Tenders			
Plumbers ....per day..	$1 00	$1 50	$1 00
Assistants ....do....	50	62½	50
Carpenters ....do....	75	1 00	75
Gas-fitters ....do....	1 00	1 50	1 00
OTHER TRADES.			
Bakers:			
Chief bakers ....do....	3 00	5 00	3 00
Attendants ....do....	1 00	1 25	1 00
Blacksmiths ....do....	1 50	2 00	1 50
Strikers ....do....	62½	75	62½
Book-binders ....do....	75	1 25	75
Brick-makers (peons) ....do....	50	75	50
Brewers (peons)† ....do....	50	75	50
Butchers:			
Those who kill the cattle ....do....	3 00	3 50	
Those who deliver or sell ....do....	1 25	1 50	
Brass-founders:			
Head workmen ....do....		2 00	
Assistants and pilers ....do....		75	
Cabinet-makers ....do....	1 00	3 00	1 25
Confectioners ....do....	75	1 00	75
Cigar-makers (by the 100) ....do....	1 00	1 25	
Coopers ....do....	75	1 00	75
Cutlers ....do....	1 00	3 00	1 00
Distillers (peons) ....do....	50	62½	50
Drivers:			
Draymen and teamsters ....do....	50	50	50
Cab and carriage ....do....	25		
Street railways:			
Drivers ....do....	75		
Conductors ....do....	1 00		

* In Mexico all these occupations are under one heading; the mason builds the walls, roofs, floors, stairways, of the same material, with his assistant to carry material, stones, bricks, and mortar; this carrier is a peon or half-grown boy generally. The mason works by the day, earning from 75 cents to $1 per day. The assistant earns from 37½ to 50 cents per day. The boy from 18¾ to 25 cents.

Driver who delivers the beer in the city, $60 per month.

Wages paid in the city of Mexico—Continued.

Occupations.	Lowest.	Highest.	Average.
OTHER TRADES—Continued.			
Dyers:			
Skilled workmen ....do....	$1 50	$2 00	$1 50
Assistants (peons) ....do....	50	75	50
Engravers ....do....	2 50	3 00	2 50
Furriers ....do....	1 50	2 00	1 50
Gardeners:			
Head ....do....	1 00	1 50	....
Peons ....do ..	50		....
Hatters (work by piece) ....do....	75	1 50	1 00
Horseshoers, farriers, and nail-makers ....do....	75	1 00	75
Jewelers:			
Chief workmen...do....	....	3 00	....
Gold and silver smiths....................................do....	75	1 00	75
Laborers, porters, &c....................................do....	41¼	50	....
Lithographers ....do....	1 00	3 00	1 00
Millwrights ....do....	(*)	(*)	(*)
Potters ....do....	75	1 00	75
Printers ....do....	1 00	1 50	1 00
Teachers, public schools ....per month..	30 00	40 00	....
Saddle and harness makers.............................per day..	50	1 00	62½
Sail-makers	(†)	(†)	(†)
Stevedores	(:)	(:)	(:)
Tanners and furriers ....per day..	1 50	2 00	1 50
Tailors .... do....	75	1 00	75
Telegraph operators..................................per month..	....	....	60
Tinsmiths...per day..	75	1 00	75
Weavers:			
Outside of mills (rebosa and scrapo weavers).................do....	75	1 00	75
In factories...do....	75	1 00	....
Lace ....do....	75	75	75
Gilders .... do....	75	1 25	87½
Gold-leaf beaters (work by the piece) ....do ..	50	75	....
Shoemakers ....do....	75	1 25	1 00
Painters, house and sign ....do....	75	1 50	87½

* No separate business; work done by machinists.
† This business not carried on here.
: None in Mexico City or districts.

II. FACTORIES, MILLS, ETC.

Wages paid per week of sixty hours in factories or mills in and near the city of Mexico (Mexicans).

Occupations.	Lowest.	Highest.	Average.
Mill bosses...	$18 00	$35 00	$25 00
Paper mill	12 00	25 00	18 00
Woolen mill	12 00	25 00	18 00
Cotton mill...	9 00	18 00	12 00
Laborers, mill...	3 00	6 00	4 50

III. FOUNDRIES, MACHINE-SHOPS, AND IRON WORKS.

Wages paid per week of sixty hours in foundries, machine-shops, and iron works in the city of Mexico (Mexican mechanics).

Occupations.	Lowest.	Highest.	Average.
Brass foundry...	$9 00	$18 00	$15 00
Iron foundry..	6 00	15 00	12 00
Machinists	12 00	24 00	18 00
Brass turners	12 00	24 00	18 00
Iron turners..	9 00	18 00	15 00
Blacksmiths...	6 00	18 00	12 00
Laborers	4 50	9 00	6 00

IV. Glass Workers.

Wages paid per week to glass-workers in the cities of Puebla, Apizaco, and Apam (Mexicans).

Occupations.	Lowest.	Highest.	Average.
Pane-glass workmen	$17 50	$37 50	$25 00
Pressed-ware workmen	6 00	24 00	18 00
Common blowers	6 00	18 00	12 00
Laborers:			
Men	4 50	9 00	6 00
Boys	1 50	4 50	3 00

V. Mines and Mining.

Wages paid per week of sixty hours in and in connection with mines in the States of Mexico, Hidalgo, Guanahuato, and Zacatecas.

Occupations.	Lowest.	Highest.	Average.
Director	$25 00	$100 00	$50 00
Miner bosses	15 00	25 00	18 00
Underground miners	6 00	12 00	9 00
Outside miners	4 50	9 00	6 00
Underground laborers	3 25	3 75	3 00
Outside laborers	1 87½	3 00	2 25
Pumpmen	12 00	18 00	15 00
Engine-drivers	15 00	25 00	20 00
Firemen	6 00	15 00	9 00
Machinists	18 00	35 00	25 00
Blacksmiths	6 00	18 00	12 00
Carpenters	6 00	18 00	12 00
Teamsters	3 00	6 00	4 50
Assayers	18 00	35 00	25 00
Clerks and like employés	12 00	25 00	18 00

VI. Railway Employés.

Wages paid per week to railway employés (those engaged about stations, as well as those engaged on the engines and cars, linemen, railroad laborers, &c.) on Central and National Railroad.

Occupations.	Lowest.	Highest.	Average.
Station masters	$25 00	$45 00	$35 00
Engine-drivers			35 00
Firemen			12 50
Conductors			35 00
Brakesmen			10 00
Baggage-masters			15 00
Linemen			12 00
Laborers (Mexican)			3 00

IX. Store and Shop Wages.

Wages paid   week of sixty hours in stores, wholesale or retail, to males and females, in Mexico.

Occupations.	Highest.	Lowest.	Average.
Book-keepers	$20 00	$40 00	$25 00
Head clerks (dry goods)	18 00	25 00	20 00
Under clerks (dry goods)	12 00	18 00	15 00
Head clerks (groceries)	12 00	18 00	15 00
Under clerks (groceries)	6 00	12 00	9 00
Head clerks (hardwares)	18 00	25 00	20 00
Under clerks (hardwares)	12 00	18 00	15 00
Tailors	6 00	12 00	9 00
Shoemakers	6 00	18 00	12 00
Hatmakers	6 00	12 00	9 00
Dressmakers (females)	4 50	9 00	6 00
Milliners (females)	6 00	12 00	9 00
Sewing-women	3 00	6 00	4 50
Female clerks	6 00	12 00	9 00
Shop-women	3 00	6 00	4 50

X. HOUSEHOLD WAGES IN TOWNS AND CITIES.

Wages paid per month to household servants (towns and cities) in Mexico City.

Occupations.	Lowest.	Highest.	Average.
Cooks:			
French or Italian	$45 00	$100 00	$50 00
Mexican	10 00	25 00	15 00
Servants:			
Kitchen duties	3 50	10 00	5 00
Chamber duties	3 50	12 00	6 00
Waiters:			
Hotel	10 00	20 00	15 00
Restaurant	5 00	15 00	12 00
Household	3 50	12 00	6 00
Coachmen	10 00	30 00	15 00
Footmen	5 00	15 00	10 00

XI. AGRICULTURAL WAGES.

Wages paid per month to agricultural laborers and household (country) servants in Mexico.

Occupations.	Lowest.	Highest.	Average.
Administrators of sugar estates and other agricultural	$100 00	$500 00	$150 00
Field bosses	25 00	100 00	45 00
Assistants	12 00	30 00	15 00
Field hands:			
Plowmen*	7 50	20 00	10 00
Reapers*	4 50	12 00	8 00

* With rations.

XII. CORPORATION EMPLOYÉS.

Wages paid per week of sixty hours to the corporation employés in the city of Mexico.

Occupations.	Lowest.	Highest.	Average.
Secretary of the municipality	$62 50	....	$62 50
First officer	25 00	....	25 00
Second officer	15 00	....	15 00
Treasurer ($2,000 per year)	38 40	....	38 00
Clerks	15 00	....	15 00
Doorkeepers, pages, &c.	6 00	$18 00	9 00
Chief of the police department			60 00
Captains of the police department			37 50
Lieutenants of the police department			20 00
Policemen			15 00

XIII. GOVERNMENT DEPARTMENTS AND OFFICES.

Wages paid per year to employés in Government departments and officers, exclusive of trades-men and laborers, in the city of Mexico.

Occupations.	Average wages.
President of the Republic	$36,000
Ministers or members of the cabinet	8,000
First officers of each of the departments, such as of finances, war, justice, interior, and public works	4,000
Second officers	2,500
Treasurer-general of the nation	4,000
Assistant treasurer	2,500
Chief officers of the different sections of these departments	1,800
Clerks of the same	800
Porters, pages, &c	360
Chief of the custom-houses of different ports, from $250 to $500 per month, averaging about.	3,600
Under clerks	800
Coast guards	1,200

XIV. TRADES AND LABOR—GOVERNMENT EMPLOY.

Wages paid by the week of sixty hours to the trades and laborers in Government employ at the ciĺidal, city of Mexico.

Occupations.	Lowest.	Highest.	Average.
Carpenters	$6 00	$18 00	$12 00
Blacksmiths	6 00	18 00	12 00
Wheelwrights	6 00	18 00	12 00
Saddlers	4 50	12 00	9 00
Shoemakers	6 00	12 00	9 00
Brass founders	9 00	18 00	15 00
Iron founders	6 00	15 00	12 00
Mettle turners	12 00	24 00	18 00
Machinists and gun-makers	18 00	35 00	25 00
Laborers	4 50	9 00	6 00
Engineers	25 00	50 00	35 00
Engine-drivers	15 00	25 00	18 00

XV. PRINTERS AND PRINTING OFFICES.

Statement showing the wages paid per week of sixty hours to printers (compositors, pressmen, proof-readers, &c.) in the city of Mexico.

Occupations.	Lowest.	Highest.	Average.
Compositors	$8 00	$16 60	$12 00
Pressmen	6 00	12 00	9 00
Proof-readers	7 50	20 00	15 00

Salaries of the civil and military officers and employés of the Federal Government of Mexico, 1884.

Occupations.	Salary.	Occupations.	Salary.
EXECUTIVE DEPARTMENT.		*Section of Europe, Asia, and Africa.*	
President of the Republic	$30,000 00	Chief of section	$3,000 00
		First assistant	2,000 00
OFFICE OF THE PRIVATE SECRETARY.		Second assistant	1,500 00
		First clerk	800 00
Secretary	3,000 00	Second clerk	600 00
Clerk	800 00		
		DEPARTMENT OF COMMERCE.	
STAFF OF THE PRESIDENT.		Chief of department	3,000 00
		First assistant	2,000 00
Adjutant, lieutenant-colonel of infantry	2,466 00	Second assistant	1,500 00
Adjutant, colonel of cavalry	2,714 40	Third assistant	1,200 00
Adjutant, lieutenant-colonel of infantry	1,652 40	First clerk	800 00
		Second clerk	600 00
Adjutant, lieutenant-colonel of cavalry.	1,807 20	Third clerk	600 00
Service.		**DEPARTMENT OF THE SEALS.**	
Doorkeeper of the President's house..	1,000 00	Chief of department	3,000 00
Assistant doorkeeper of the President's house	800 00	General clerk (assistant)	1,500 00
		Penman (calógrafo)	1,000 00
Messenger	370 00	First clerk	800 00
		Second clerk	600 00
STATE DEPARTMENT.		English translator	1,500 00
		German translator	700 00
Secretary of State	8,000 00		
Assistant secretary	4,500 00	**ARCHIVES AND LIBRARIES.**	
DEPARTMENT OF POLITICS.		Keeper of the archives	1,500 00
		First clerk	600 00
Section of America.		Assistant clerk	500 00
Chief of section	3,000 00	*Service.*	
First assistant	2,000 00		
Second assistant	1,500 00	Doorkeeper	600 00
First clerk	800 00	First messenger	300 00
Second clerk	600 00	Second messenger	240 00
Third clerk	600 00	Third messenger	220 00

Salaries of the civil and military officers and employés of Mexico—Continued.

Occupations.	Salary.	Occupations.	Salary.
GENERAL ARCHIVES OF THE NATION.		**Section 7.—Land tax and statistics of the department.**	
Chief of department....................	$2,000 00		
Assistant............................	1,200 00	Chief of section...................	$3,000 00
Clerk...............................	600 00	First assistant	2,500 00
Paleographer	1,200 00	Second assistant.................	2,000 00
Clerk, assistant of above............	600 00	Third assistant..................	1,800 00
Doorkeeper..........................	300 00	Fourth assistant.................	1,500 00
Orderly.............................	60 00	Clerk............................	600 00
TREASURY DEPARTMENT.		**Section 8.—Archives.**	
		Keeper of the archives..............	2,400 00
SECRETARY'S OFFICE.		Assistant.........................	1,200 00
Secretary of the Treasury............	8,000 00	Clerk............................	600 00
Private secretary of above	2,400 00		
Clerk...............................	600 00	**DEPARTMENT OF COMPILATION OF LAWS AND OF THE LIBRARY.**	
CHIEF CLERK'S OFFICE.		Chief of department..............	3,000 00
		Secretary........................	2,100 00
First clerk (chief)...................	4,500 00	Clerk of the librarian...........	1,800 00
Second clerk	3,500 00	Assistant of above...............	1,800 00
Assistant...........................	1,800 00	Clerk............................	600 00
Clerk...............................	600 00		
		OFFICE OF THE DEPARTMENT ATTORNEY.	
Section 1.—Customs.			
Chief of section...........	3,500 00	Attorney	3,000 00
First assistant	2,500 00	Clerk	600 00
Second assistant.....................	2,000 00		
Third assistant......................	1,800 00	**DEPARTMENT OF TECHNICAL CONSULTATION.**	
Fourth assistant.....................	1,500 00		
Clerk	600 00	Consulting attorney..............	3,000 00
Supernumerary.......................	300 00	Civil engineer...................	3,000 00
Keeper of the archives (general clerk).	1,200 00	Clerk............................	600 00
Section 2.—Nationalized estates.		**Service.**	
Chief of section.....................	3,000 00	Doorkeeper.......................	720 00
First assistant......................	2,500 00	Messenger........................	300 00
Second assistant.....................	2,000 00	Janitor..........................	240 00
Third assistant......................	1,800 00	Orderly..........................	60 00
Fourth assistant	1,500 00		
Clerk....	600 00	**GENERAL TREASURY.**	
Supernumerary.......................	300 00		
General clerk, keeper of the archives	1,200 00	Treasurer	6,000 00
		General clerk....................	800 00
Section 3.—Taxes.		Clerk............................	600 00
Chief of section	3,000 00	**Auditor's office.**	
First assistant......................	2,500 00	Auditor..........................	5,000 00
Second assistant.....................	2,000 00	First book-keeper................	4,000 00
Third assistant......................	1,800 00	Second book-keeper	2,500 00
Clerk...............................	600 00	Clerk............................	600 00
General clerk, keeper of the archives..	1,200 00		
		Treasury.	
Section 4.—Accounts of the Treasury.		Treasurer	4,000 00
		Assistant treasurer	2,500 00
Chief of section	3,000 00	Collector and executor...........	900 00
Paymaster	2,400 00	Clerk............................	600 00
Book-keeper	1,500 00		
Assistant book-keeper................	1,200 00	**Section 1.—Collection of taxes.**	
Clerk in charge of the archives.......	1,200 00	Chief of section.................	3,000 00
Clerk...............................	600 00	First assistant..................	2,500 00
		Second assistant.................	1,500 00
Section 5.—Payment of the foreign service.		Third assistant	1,200 00
		Fourth assistant.................	1,000 00
Chief of section	3,000 00	Book-keeper......................	2,000 00
First assistant......................	2,500 00	Assistant book-keeper............	1,200 00
Second assistant.....................	1,200 00	Clerk............................	600 00
Clerk....	600 00		
Supernumerary	300 00	**Section 2.—Pay department.**	
General clerk, keeper of the archives..	1,200 00	Chief of section.................	3,000 00
		First assistant	2,500 00
Section 6.—Public credit.		Second assistant.................	1,500 00
Chief of section.....................	3,000 00	Third assistant..................	1,200 00
First assistant......................	2,500 00	Fourth assistant.................	1,000 00
Second assistant.....................	2,000 00	Book-keeper......................	2,000 00
Clerk..	600 00	Assistant book-keeper............	1,200 00
Book-keeper..........................	1,500 00	Clerk	600 00
General clerk, keeper of the archives..	1,200 00		

Salaries of the civil and military officers and employés of Mexico—Continued.

Occupations.	Salary.	Occupations.	Salary.
Section for revision of the department accounts.		*Store-house for stamps.*	
		Guard of store-house...................	$1,800 00
Chief of section.......................	$3,000 00	Assistant guard of store-house........	800 00
First assistant........................	2,500 00	Clerk	600 00
Second assistant.......................	1,500 00	First messenger......................	400 00
Third assistant........................	1,200 00	Second messenger....................	240 00
Fourth assistant.......................	1,000 00		
Clerk	600 00	*Service.*	
Section of public credit.		Collector and counter of money........	800 00
		Messenger............................	300 00
Chief of section.......................	3,000 00	Watchman	360 00
First assistant........................	2,500 00	Doorkeeper	240 00
Second assistant.......................	1,500 00	Orderly..............................	60 00
Third assistant	1,200 00		
Fourth assistant	1,000 00	POSTAGE STAMP DEPARTMENT.	
Book-keeper...	2,000 00		
Assistant book-keeper..................	1,200 00	*Director's office.*	
Clerk	600 00	Director	4,000 00
Section for liquidation of the public debt.		Sub-director..........................	3,000 00
		Corresponding clerk..................	800 00
Chief of section.......................	3,000 00	Book-keeper.........................	1,800 00
First assistant........................	2,500 00	Assistant book-keeper................	1,000 00
Second assistant.......................	1,500 00	Clerk	600 00
Clerk	600 00	*Store-house for stamps.*	
General messenger.....................	300 00		
		Guard of store-house	1,500 00
Archives.		Assistant guard of store-house........	800 00
		Cutter, folder, and perforator stamps..	240 00
Keeper of the archives.................	2,000 00	Messenger...........................	200 00
Assistan	800 00		
Clerk	600 00	*Engraving office.*	
		First class engineer..................	1,800 00
Service.		Second class engineer	1,200 00
		Third class engineer	1,000 00
Doorkeeper...........................	600 00	Fourth class engineer	800 00
Messenger............................	300 00		
Orderly..............................	60 00	*Machinery department.*	
		Mechanical engineer	1,200 00
Liquidation section.		Black and locksmith	600 00
		Carpenter	420 00
Chief of section.......................	3,000 00	Fireman for steam engine............	240 00
Revising auditor......................	2,400 00		
Assistant............................	1,000 00	*Printing department.*	
Clerk................................	600 00	Chief pressman	1,000 00
Book-keeper..........................	1,500 00	Second pressman	700 00
Assistant book-keeper.................	900 00	Third pressman	500 00
Doorkeeper	480 00	Lithographer	500 00
Messenger	300 00	Assistant lithographer...............	300 00
REVENUE STAMP DEPARTMENT.		*Stamp-gumming department.*	
General office.		Chief stamp-gummer.................	365 00
		Assistant stamp-gummer.............	300 00
Chief of department...................	4,000 00		
First corresponding clerk..............	1,500 00	*Service.*	
Second corresponding clerk............	1,200 00		
Clerk	600 00	Doorkeeper..........................	360 00
Keeper of the archives.................	1,000 00	Messenger...........................	300 00
Inspector............................	2,000 00	Watchman	300 00
Auditor's office.		NATIONAL LOTTERY.	
		Director..............................	3,500 00
Auditor	3,000 00	Secretary of the directive junta, also	
Book-keeper..........................	2,000 00	comptroller.......................	3,000 00
First assistant........................	1,200 00	Clerk of the directive junta...........	600 00
Second assistant......................	1,000 00	First auditor	2,000 00
Treasurer	1,200 00	Second auditor, also book-keeper	1,800 00
Clerk	600 00	Chief clerk of revision and accounts...	1,400 00
Section of revision.		Clerk of revision and remittances......	1,000 00
		Corresponding clerk	600 00
Chief of department...................	3,800 00	Treasurer	2,000 00
First assistant........................	2,000 00	Chief clerk of treasurer..............	1,200 00
Second assistant......................	1,800 00	Clerk who examines the tickets	720 00
Third assistant.......................	1,500 00	Small boy who draws the numbers....	120 00
Fourth assistant	1,200 00	Doorkeeper	300 00
Clerk................................	600 00	Messenger...........................	240 00

Salaries of the civil and military officers and employés of Mexico—Continued.

Occupations.	Salary.	Occupations.	Salary.
CHIEF DIRECTORY OF THE CUSTOMS OF THE FEDERAL DISTRICT.		DIRECTORY OF THE TAXES OF THE FEDERAL DISTRICT.	
Director............................	$4,000 00	*Directory.*	
First assistant, chief of the section of correspondence........................	1,500 00	Director.............................	$4,000 00
Second assistant....................	1,000 00	Corresponding clerk.................	1,200 00
Clerk	600 00	Clerk of the archives	1,000 00
		Assistant clerk.....................	600 00
Auditor's office.			
		Auditor's office.	
Auditor	3,500 00		
Book-keeper	1,500 00	Auditor............................	3,000 00
Clerk of book-keeper..............	1,000 00	First revising clerk................	1,300 00
Clerk.............................	600 00	Second revising clerk	1,100 00
Chief of revisions in charge of statistics...........................	2,000 00	Book-keeper........................	1,200 00
Chief of the comparing section.......	2,000 00	Assistant clerk	600 00
Clerk of the comparing section.......	1,000 00		
Supernumerary......................	300 00	*Section of census and settlements.*	
Chief clerk in charge of revision and copying of miscellaneous documents	1,200 00	Chief of section....................	2,200 00
Keeper of the archives.............	800 00	First assistant....................	1,500 00
Chief of the section for selling foreign and national goods...........	1,200 00	Second assistant...................	1,200 00
		Third assistant	1,000 00
Treasury.		Inspector..........................	300 00
Treasurer..........................	3,000 00	*Collectors' offices in the capital.*	
Money-counter, responsible for missing or counterfeit money..............	1,800 00	Collector of taxes	2,000 00
Clerk.............................	600 00	Clerk	600 00
Inspection department.		*Treasury.*	
		Treasurer responsible for missing or counterfeit money.................	1,400 00
Examiner	3,000 00	Doorkeeper, also money-counter......	500 00
Assistant examiner.................	2,000 00	Supernumerary......................	300 00
Apothecary	2,500 00		
		Service.	
Store-houses and warden ships.			
		Messenger..........................	300 00
Chief store-house guard............	1,500 00	Orderly............................	60 00
Clerk for store-house guard	600 00		
Servant for store-house guard	180 00	DEPARTMENT OF WAR AND MARINE.	
Store-house guard at St. Jerome.....	1,000 00		
Servant for store-house guard at St. Jerome	180 00	SECRETARY'S OFFICE.	
Warden of entrances...............	1,200 00		
Warden of exits...................	1,200 00	Secretary of war and marine.........	8,000 00
Clerk for warden of exits..........	600 00	Chief clerk	4,500 00
Head porter.......................	700 00	First assistant, colonel of cavalry...	2,714 40
		Second assistant, colonel of cavalry..	2,714 40
Buena Vista section.		Third assistant, colonel of infantry....	2,466 00
Treasurer, responsible for missing or counterfeit	1,000 00	Fourth assistant keeper of the archives, lieutenant-colonel of cavalry........	1,807 20
Warden of entrances and exits......	1,000 00	Fifth assistant librarian, lieutenant-colonel of infantry	1,652 40
Clerk.............................	600 00	First captain of cavalry......•.....	1,140 00
		First captain of infantry...........	960 00
General service.		Second captain of cavalry	900 00
		Second captain of infantry..........	840 00
Head doorkeeper of the custom house.	500 00	Lieutenant of cavalry..............	780 00
Assistant doorkeeper of the custom house	300 00	Lieutenant of infantry.............	720 00
Janitor	300 00	Ensign of cavalry..................	720 00
		Sublieutenant of infantry..........	660 00
Corps of customs guards.		Assessor of the army	3,000 00
		First captain of cavalry, clerk of the army	3,140 00
Commander	2,500 00		
Adjutant-commander	2,000 00	*Service.*	
Corporal, mounted and armed.........	1,200 00		
Private, mounted and armed..........	900 00	Doorkeeper.........................	600 00
Private, on foot and armed..........	600 00	Janitor	300 00
Boatman...........................	180 00	Orderly............................	60 00
City gates.		STAFF OF THE ARMY.	
Collector of customs...............	2,000 00	Active general of division	6,000 00
Clerk	1,200 00	Active general of brigade	4,500 00
Assistant clerk....................	600 00	Reserve general of division.........	4,000 00
Gateman...........................	180 00	Reserve general of brigade	3,000 00

Salaries of the civil and military officers and employés of Mexico—Continued.

Occupations.	Salary.	Occupations.	Salary.
MILITARY ASSESSORS.		*Military college.*	
Military assessor	$2,714 00	Director, general or colonel of the staff of artillery or engineers........	(*)
SUPREME COURT OF MILITARY JUSTICE.		Subdirector, colonel or lieutenant-colonel of the staff of artillery or engineers, major	(*)
President of the first hall, general of division	6,000 00	Clerk of the directory	$600 00
Second magistrate, general of brigade	4,500 00	Adjutant, lieutenant of the staff of artillery or engineers	840 00
Third magistrate, by courtesy general of brigade	4,500 00	Surgeon	1,200 00
Secretary, by courtesy colonel of cavalry, who also serves as secretary during the meeting of both halls (tribunal pleno)	2,714 40	Clerk of the subdirectory............	600 00
First clerk, a first adjutant............	1,140 00	Professor of surveying and astronomy.	1,200 00
Second clerk, a second captain of cavalry.................................	960 00	Professor of the art and history of war (director)....................	
First assistant clerk, lieutenant of infantry....	720 00	Professor of staff duty (subdirector).....	
Second assistant clerk, sublieutenant of infantry	660 00	Professor of architecture.............	1,200 00
Orderly, second sergeant of cavalry....	270 00	Professor of analytical machinery	1,200 00
President of the second hall, general of division................................	6,000 00	Professor of applied machinery	1,200 00
Second magistrate, general of brigade	4,500 00	Professor of physics	1,200 00
Third magistrate, by courtesy general of brigade.........................	4,500 00	Professor of chemistry................	1,200 00
Secretary, by courtesy, lieutenant-colonel of cavalry..........................	1,807 20	Professor of mathematics........	1,200 00
First clerk, a first adjutant............	1,140 00	Professor of stereometry, roads, canals, and port improvements	1,200 00
Second clerk, a second captain of cavalry....................................	960 00	Professor of general topography.......	1,200 00
First assistant clerk, lieutenant of infantry	720 00	Professor of military topography, theoretical and practical, also of elementary descriptive geometry...........	1,200 00
Second assistant clerk, sublieutenant of infantry	660 00	Professor of elementary natural history.	1,200 00
Orderly, second sergeant of cavalry....	270 00	Professor of permanent fortification and scientific gunnery....	1,200 00
Supernumerary magistrate, general of brigade	4,500 00	Professor of field fortification and practical gunnery	1,200 00
Supernumerary magistrate, by courtesy general of brigade	4,500 00	Professor of military jurisprudence, laws of war, and elementary logic .	1,200 00
Professional defender, by courtesy colonel of infantry..........	2,466 00	Professor of first course of pilotry and cosmography	1,200 00
Attorney, by courtesy colonel of infantry	2,466 00	Professor of second course of pilotry and naval construction...	1,200 00
Clerk of proceedings, by courtesy lieutenant-colonel of cavalry.............	1,807 20	Professor of nautical nomenclature, terms, and maneuvers, general theories of winds, currents, and movements of ships...................	1,200 00
MILITARY COURTS OF MANDATE.		Professor of machinery applied to navigation...............................	1,200 00
Colonel of cavalry	2,714 40	Professor of naval artillery, torpedoes, and naval law...................	1,200 00
Colonel of infantry	2,466 00	Professor of Spanish......	1,000 00
Secretary, sublieutenant of infantry...	660 00	Professor of geography and elements of history..........................	1,200 00
Secretary, first sergeant of cavalry ...	360 00	Professor of Mexican history	1,200 00
Orderly, second sergeant of cavalry ...	270 00	Professor of topographical, lineal, and geographical drawing...........	840 00
SPECIAL STAFF CORPS.		Assistant professor of topographical, lineal, and geographical drawing	600 00
Commander of the corps...............	4,500 00	Professor of mechanical and architectural drawing.........	1,000 00
Colonel	2,826 00	Professor of French.................	840 00
Lieutenant-colonel.....................	1,807 20	Professor of English	840 00
Major................................	1,560 00	Professor of gymnastics and swimming	840 00
First captain	1,140 00	Professor of fencing......	840 00
Second captain	960 00	Professor of fencing (assistant)......	600 00
Major of cavalry attached	1,560 00	Preparer of apparatus for class of physics	1,200 00
Lieutenant	780 00	Preparer of apparatus for class of chemistry...............................	1,200 00
DEPARTMENT OF ENGINEERS.		Corporal of bugles....................	157 50
General or colonel of the staff..........	(*)	First captain of cadets	1,140 00
First captain, chief of first section.....	1,140 00	Second captain of cadets	960 00
Second captain, chief of the staff	960 00	Lieutenant of cadets..................	780 00
Sublieutenant, clerk	720 00	First sergeant of cadets...............	276 00
		Second sergeant of cadets.............	264 00
Staff.		Corporal of cadets....................	252 00
Colonel of the staff	2,826 00	Private of cadets	240 00
Lieutenant-colonel of the staff.........	1,807 20	Musician	180 00
Major of the staff..............	1,560 00		
First captain of the staff...............	1,140 00	*Service.*	
Second captain of the staff........	960 00	Superintendent (third in command) ...	1,080 00
Lieutenant of the staff.................	780 00	Nurse for each hospital..............	192 00
Guard	600 00	Riding master, also veterinary........	300 00
		Cook.................................	300 40
		* Pay of his rank.	

Salaries of the civil and military officers and employés of Mexico—Continued.

Occupations.	Salary.	Occupations.	Salary.
Service—Continued.		*School of artillery.*	
Artificer	$158 40	Colonel. director	$2,826 00
Scullion	120 00	Lieutenant-colonel or major, subdirect-	
Janitor	144 00	or	(*)
Keeper of the forest	360 00	First or second captain or lieutenant,	
Gardiner	140 00	secretary	(*)
		First sergeant, clerk	360 00
Battalion of sappers.		Second sergeant, head doorkeeper	313 20
		Assistant doorkeeper	180 00
Colonel of the staff	2,826 00		
Lieutenant-colonel of the staff	1,807 20	*Battalion of artillery.*	
Major of the staff	1,560 00		
Adjutant, first captain of the staff	1,140 00	Colonel	2,826 00
Subadjutant, lieutenant of the staff	840 00	Lieutenant-colonel	1,807 20
First captain of the staff	1,140 00	Major	1,560 00
Second captain of the staff	960 00	Adjutant, first captain	1,140 00
Lieutenant of the staff	780 00	Subadjutant, lieutenant	780 00
First sergeant	360 00	First captain	1,140 00
Second sergeant	313 20	Second captain	960 00
Corporal	157 50	Lieutenant	780 00
Private and musicians	135 00	First sergeant	360 00
Teamster	180 00	Second sergeant	313 20
		Corporal	157 50
CORPS OF ARTILLERY.		Private and musician	135 00
		Veterinary	360 00
General or colonel of the staff, chief of		Riding-master	360 00
department, pay of his rank	*)	Saddler	360 00
Lieutenant-colonel of the staff, chief of		Corporal of teamsters	270 00
first section	1,807 20	First class teamster	225 00
Chief of the section of material and ex-		Artificer	180 00
penses	2,826 00		
First captain of the staff, translator, also		*Squadron of train guards.*	
in charge of the archives	1,140 00		
Powder-guard clerk	720 00	Major	1,560 00
		First captain, chief of detachment	1,140 00
General ammunition department.		Lieutenant, adjutant	840 00
		Second captain	960 00
Colonel of the staff, chief of the depart-		Lieutenant	780 60
ment	2,826 00	First sergeant	360 00
First captain of the staff	1,140 00	Second sergeant	313 20
Lieutenant of the staff, adjutant	780 00	Bugler	135 00
Storehouse-keeper (considered as third		Corporal of teamsters	270 00
in command)	1,140 00	First-class teamsters	225 00
Paymaster (considered as third in com-		Riding-master	360 00
mand)	960 00	Veterinary	300 00
Powder-guard	720 00	Saddler	360 00
Third-class artificer	225 00	Artificer	180 00
Doorkeeper	300 00		
Trustworthy laborer(Peon de confianza)	360 00	MILITARY POLICE.	
Work-shops.		Colonel or lieutenant-colonel of cav-	
		alry	(*)
Colonel or lieutenant-colonel of the staff,		Major, chief of detachment	1,560 00
director	(*)	Subadjutant, ensign	780 00
First captain of the staff	1,140 00	First captain	1,200 00
Lieutenant of the staff, adjutant	780 00	Second captain	1,020 00
Storehouse keeper (considered as third		Lieutenant	840 00
in command)	1,140 00	Ensign	780 00
Paymaster (considered as third in com-		First sergeant	540 00
mand)	960 00	Second sergeant	480 00
Powder-guard	720 00	Corporal	420 00
Doorkeeper	360 00	Private and musician	360 00
Trustworthy laborer (Peon de con-		Veterinary	340 00
fianza)	360 00	Saddler	360 00
		Artificer	180 00
Company of workmen.			
		DEPARTMENT OF INFANTRY.	
Second captain of the staff	960 00		
Lieutenant of the staff	780 00	General or colonel, chief of the depart-	
First-class machinist	1,140 00	ment of infantry and cavalry	(*)
Second-class machinist	1,080 00	Colonel of infantry, subinspector	2,466 00
Head workman	900 00	Lieutenant-colonel of infantry	1,652 40
Sergeant of workmen	670 00	Major of infantry	1,468 80
Corporal of workmen	540 00	First captain of infantry	960 00
First-class workman	450 00	Second captain of infantry	840 00
Second-class workman	360 00	Lieutenant of infantry	720 00
Third-class workman	225 00		
Apprentice	135 00	* Pay of his rank.	

Salaries of the civil and military officers and employés of Mexico—Continued.

Occupations.	Salary.	Occupations.	Salary.
Battalion of infantry.		**DEPARTMENT OF THE INTERIOR.**	
Colonel	$2,466 00		
Lieutenant-colonel....................	1,652 40	**SECRETARY'S OFFICE.**	
Major.........	1,468 80		
First captain, adjutant...............	1,140 00	Secretary of the Interior..............	$4,500 00
Sublieutenant, subadjutant	660 00	Chief clerk	4,500 00
First captain	960 00		
Second captain	840 00	***First section.***	
Lieutenant	720 00		
Sublieutenant	660 00	Chief of first section, inspector of the	
First sergeant	360 00	other five......................	3,000 00
Second sergeant.....................	234 00	First assistant.....................	1,200 00
Corporal	135 00	Second assistant	800 00
Private and musician.................	112 50	Clerk.........................	600 00
Teamster.......................	180 00	Supernumerary...................	180 00
		Second section.	
DEPARTMENT OF CAVALRY.			
		Chief of section....................	3,000 00
Colonel, subinspector....., ...	2,714 40	First assistant......................	1,200 00
Lieutenant-colonel	1,807 20	Second assistant..................	800 00
Major	1,560 00	Clerk..........................	600 00
First captain	1,140 00	Supernumerary...................	180 00
Second captain	960 00		
Lieutenant	780 00	***Third section.***	
		Chief of section, inspector of rural po-	
Regiment of cavalry.		lice	3,000 00
		First assistant	1,800 00
Colonel............................	2,714 40	Second assistant.................	1,000 00
Lieutenant-colonel	1,807 20	Clerk..........................	600 00
Major	1,560 90		
First captain, adjutant...............	1,140 00	***Fourth section.***	
Second subadjutant, ensign...........	720 00		
First captain	1,140 00	Chief of section, inspector of public im-	
Second captain	960 00	provements	3,000 00
Lieutenant	780 00	First assistant.....................	1,800 00
Ensign.........................	720 00	Second assistant.................	800 00
First sergeant	360 00	Treasurer	2,000 00
Second sergeant	270 00	Inspector (visitador)	1,800 00
Corporal..........................	157 50	Clerk (auditor of the Treasury)........	800 00
Private and musician.................	135 00	Clerk..........................	600 00
Saddler	360 00		
Veterinary	360 00	***Fifth section.***	
Artificer..........................	180 00		
Teamster..........................	180 00	Chief of section....................	3,000 00
		Assistant.........................	1,200 00
DEPARTMENT OF MARINE.		Clerk	600 00
		Supernumerary...................	180 00
Chief of department..................	3,000 00		
Assistant.........................	1,200 00	***Section of the archives.***	
Clerk	600 00		
		Chief of section, general clerk	1,500 00
NAVY.		First assistant......................	1,200 00
		Second assistant.................	800 00
Chief of squadron....................	3,000 00	Clerk....	600 00
Captain or commander	2,100 00	Supe. numerary........	180 00
Second lieutenant..................	1,440 00		
First boatswain	510 00	***Service.***	
Second boatswain..................	360 00		
Gunner..........................	540 00	Doorkeeper......................	600 00
Carpenter.....	420 00	Janitor.........................	240 00
Cook	240 00		
Steward	300 00	**SCHOOL FOR THE BLIND.**	
Surgeon	300 00		
First corporal of sailors	300 00	Director	1,200 00
Second corporal of sailors.............	240 00	Administrator	360 00
First-class sailor	180 00	Professor of primary instruction	900 00
Second-class sailor.................	120 00	Professor of secondary instruction .	480 00
First-class gun-corporal	300 00	Lady in charge of the interior of the	
Second-class gun-corporal	240 00	house..........................	480 00
Bugler or drummer..................	180 00	Lady professor for girls	600 00
Engineer, inspector..................	2,100 00	Keeper of children..................	300 00
First-class engineer	1,800 00	Professor on brass instruments, leader	
Second-class engineer................	1,410 00	of the orchestra................	480 00
Third-class engineer	1,200 00	Professor of gymnastics	240 00
Apprentice engineer	300 00	Professor (lady) of piano for girls	240 00
First-class fireman.................	480 00	Professor of stringed instruments	240 00
Second-class fireman................	240 00	Professor of the clarionet.............	240 00

* Pay of his rank.

Salaries of the civil and military employés of Mexico—Continued.

Occupations.	Salary.	Occupations.	Salary.
SCHOOL FOR THE BLIND—Continued.		*Foot police.*	
Professor of the flute	$240 00	Chief of battalion attached to central	
Professor of the hautboy and fagot	240 00	station	$1,600 00
Professor of printing	240 00	Paymaster attached to central station	1,600 00
Professor of the bass guitar	120 00	Company commandant	1,000 00
Professor of the piano, also instructor		Clerk	840 00
in singing for children	240 00	Private	365 00
Professor of cane-weaving	240 00	Auxiliary	182 50
Professor of lace making	240 00		
Professor of book-binding	240 00	**POSTAL SERVICE.**	
Professor of chain-making	120 00		
Lady instructor in cigaretto making	84 00	*Central office.*	
Doorkeeper	108 00		
Chamberlain	108 00	Postmaster-general	4,500 00
Janitor	108 00	General clerk	1,200 00
Cook	108 00	Ordinary clerk	600 00
Scullion	72 00		
Chambermaid	96 00	*First section.*	
Gardener	120 00		
Doctor	192 00	Chief of section	3,000 00
Washerwoman	384 00	Clerks, speaking English and French	1,200 00
		Keeper of the archives	1,200 00
		Clerk	600 00
SCHOOL OF ARTS AND PROFESSIONS FOR WOMEN.		Printer	500 00
		Assistant printer	300 00
Director	1,200 00		
Subdirectress	1,000 00	*Second section.*	
First monitor	360 00		
Second monitor	360 00	Chief of section	2,400 00
Third monitor	360 00	First assistant	1,200 00
Fourth monitor	360 00	Second assistant	600 00
Lady in charge of expenditures	300 00		
Clerk	180 00	*Third section.*	
Pupil in charge of the wardrobe	96 00		
Book-keeper and paymaster	360 00	Chief of section	2,400 00
		First assistant	1,200 00
		First assistant in charge of stamps	1,800 00
BOARD OF HEALTH.		Second assistant	600 00
Voter (vocal)	1,400 00	*Fourth section.*	
Secretary	800 00		
Clerk of statistics	800 00	Chief of section	3,000 00
Clerk	500 00	Examining clerk	1,500 00
First general messenger	240 00	First book-keeper	2,400 00
Second general messenger	180 00	Second book-keeper	1,000 00
Preserver of vacuna	1,000 00	Cashier	1,800 00
Collector (agente) of vacuna	460 00	Clerk	600 00
Keeper of vacuna	460 00		
Vaccinator for the federal district	600 00	*Service.*	
Inspector of drinks and eatables	2,400 00		
Auxiliary of above	600 00	Doorkeeper	400 00
		Messenger	300 00
RURAL POLICE.			
		Special agents.	
Corps of cavalry.			
		District inspector	3,200 00
Commandant	2,520 00	Supernumerary inspector (visitador)	1,800 00
Chief of detachment	1,800 00		
Paymaster	1,440 00	**DEPARTMENT OF PUBLIC**	
First corporal	1,260 00	**WORKS, COLONIZATION, IN-**	
Second corporal	720 00	**DUSTRY, AND COMMERCE.**	
Private	405 00		
		SECRETARY'S OFFICE.	
MUNICIPAL POLICE.			
		Secretary of public works, coloniza-	
Mounted police.		tion, industry, and commerce	8,000 00
		Chief clerk	4,500 00
Commandant	2,000 00		
Chief of battalion	1,600 00	*Section 1.—Geography, statistics, coloni-*	
Paymaster	1,600 00	*zation, and public lands.*	
Company commandant	1,000 00		
Second adjutant	800 00	Chief of section	3,000 00
Clerks	600 00	First assistant	2,000 00
Detachment commander	365 00	Second assistant	1,800 00
Private	273 75	Third assistant	1,500 00
Farrier	540 00	Fourth assistant	1,200 00
Saddler	365 00	Fifth assistant	960 00
Armorer	365 00	Clerk	600 00

Salaries of the civil and military officers and employés of Mexico—Continued.

Occupations.	Salary.	Occupations.	Salary.
Section 2.—Industry, mints, telegraphs, weights, and measures.		**CENTRAL METEOROLOGICAL OBSERVATORY.**	
Chief of section	$3,000 00	Director	$4,000 00
First assistant	2,000 00	First observer (subdirector)	2,500 00
Second assistant	1,800 00	Second observer	1,200 00
Third assistant	1,500 00	Auxiliary	720 00
Clerk	600 00	Telegraph operator	600 00
		General messenger	300 00
Section 3.—Roads, bridges, canals, railroads, drainage of the Valley of Mexico, harbor and general improvement.		**DEPARTMENT OF JUSTICE AND PUBLIC INSTRUCTION.**	
Chief of section	3,000 00	**SECRETARY'S OFFICE.**	
First assistant	2,000 00	Secretary of justice and public instruction	8,000 00
Second assistant	1,800 00		
Third assistant	1,500 00	Chief clerk	4,500 00
Fourth assistant	1,200 00		
Fifth assistant	960 00	*Section of justice.*	
Clerk	600 00	Chief of section	3,000 00
Section 4.—Agriculture, commerce, and mining.		First assistant	1,200 00
		Second assistant	1,000 00
Chief of section	3,000 00	Clerk	600 00
First assistant	2,400 00		
Second assistant	2,000 00	*Section of public instruction.*	
Third assistant	1,800 00	Chief of section	3,000 00
Fourth assistant	1,500 00	First assistant	1,200 00
Clerk	600 00	Second assistant	1,000 00
Section 5.—Pay department, revision, and auditing of the accounts of all branches of the Department, including telegraphy.		Clerk	600 00
		Section of the archives.	
		Keeper of the archives	1,500 00
Chief of section	3,000 00	Clerk in charge of the department's statistics	1,200 00
First assistant	2,000 00	Clerk	600 00
Second assistant	1,800 00		
Third assistant	1,200 00	*Service.*	
Fourth assistant	1,200 00	Doorkeeper	600 00
Fifth assistant	1,000 00	Chief messenger	400 00
Sixth assistant	960 00	General messenger	300 00
Seventh assistant (examiner)	900 00		
Clerk	600 00	**PALACE OF JUSTICE.**	
Section 6.—Maps of the department.		Doorkeeper	800 00
Engineer director	2,000 00	Messenger	360 00
Draftsman	1,200 00	**TRIBUNALS OF THE FEDERAL DISTRICT.**	
Aspirant (aspirante)	600 00	*Supreme court of the district.*	
Section of the archives.		Property-holding judge	4,000 00
Keeper of the archives	1,800 00	Property-holding judge (supernumerary)	4,000 00
General clerk	1,600 00	Secretary	3,000 00
Clerk	600 00	Chief clerk	2,000 00
		Book-keeper of the first hall	1,000 00
Service.		Clerk of proceedings	1,200 00
Doorkeeper	600 00	Clerk	600 00
Messenger	300 00	Librarian	720 00
Orderly	60 00	Solicitor	500 00
		Executor	800 00
GENERAL DIRECTORY OF STATISTICS AND SOCIETY OF GEOGRAPHY AND STATISTICS.		Janitor	250 00
		Doorkeeper	400 00
General directory of statistics.		*Civil courts.*	
		Judge of civil courts	1,000 00
Director	3,000 00	Secretary	2,000 00
First assistant	2,000 00	Chief clerk	1,500 00
Second assistant	1,500 00	Clerk of proceedings	1,200 00
Clerk of the archives	1,200 00	Clerk	600 00
Clerk	600 00	Commissary	200 00
General messenger	300 00		
Society of geography and statistics.		*Criminal courts.*	
		Judge of criminal courts	4,000 00
		Secretary	2,000 00
Clerk	600 00	Clerk	600 00
Messenger	300 00	Commissary	300 00

Salaries of the civil and military officers and employés of Mexico—Continued.

Occupations.	Salary.	Occupations.	Salary.
Public office.		**Secondary school for girls—Continued.**	
Solicitor of justice	$5,000 00	Professor of teaching	$1,200 00
Deputy	3,000 00	Professor of operatic singing	700 00
Book-keeper	1,200 00	Professor of piano music	700 00
Clerk	600 00	Assistant for the two foregoing	500 00
General messenger	300 00	Professor of horticulture and garden-	
Clerk hired sessions	600 00	ing, and the elements of practical	
Commissary of Belem prison, assistant		and natural sciences, with their ap-	
of above	600 00	plication to the ordinary usages of	
Attorney for the poor	2,400 00	life	1,200 00
Petty courts.		Instructress in the higher branches of manual labor and in the art of ar-	
Judge	2,400 00	ranging mosses	1,200 00
Secretary (attorney)	1,200 00	Instructor in fancy-box making and	
Chief clerk	720 00	wood-carving	600 00
Clerk	360 00	Professor of gymnastics for the school	
Commissary	300 00	and also for the finishing annex	300 00
DEPARTMENT OF PUBLIC INSTRUCTION.		Doorkeeper	500 00
		Assistant doorkeeper	300 00
Directive committee of public instruc-		A servant for the departments of phys-	
tion.		ics, chemistry, natural history, tele-	
Secretary	1,200 00	graphy, and galvano-plastic, who as-	
Clerk	800 00	sists in making preparations for ex-	
Doorkeeper of the Ex-Hospital de Tar-		periments	300 00
ceros and of the School of Commerce.	600 00	Maid servant	144 00
Doorkeeper	240 00	Man servant	144 00
Messenger	192 00	Watchman	180 00
Dustman	60 00	A servant who attends to the pumps and waters the flowers of the estab-	
Secondary school for girls.		lishment	144 00
Directress	1,500 00	**Preparatory school for boys.**	
Subdirectress; also chief prefect	1,000 00	Director	2,000 00
Secretary of this school and the annex		Chief prefect and secretary	1,300 00
of the finishing school, also in charge		Clerk of the directory and secretary's	
of the library	1,200 00	office	600 00
Prefect	600 00	Prefect	760 00
Professor of mathematics, first and sec-		Superintendent	1,000 00
ond years	1,200 00	Clerk of superintendent	300 00
Professor of mathematics, third and		Librarian	700 00
fourth years	1,200 00	Assistant librarian	600 00
Professor of mathematics, fifth and		Professor of mathematics, first course	1,200 00
sixth years; also inspector of the		Assistant professor of mathematics,	
classes of the two foregoing	1,200 00	first course	1,000 00
Professor of physics and elements of		Professor of mathematics, second	
chemistry, fifth and sixth years	1,200 00	course	1,200 00
Assistant of above	600 00	Professor of cosmography and geogra-	
Professor of theoretical telegraphy	720 00	phy	1,200 00
Professor of practical telegraphy	720 00	Assistant in charge of the apparatus	
Professor of galvano-plastic	600 00	of the foregoing classes, of the astro-	
Professor of Spanish grammar, first		nomical observatory, and of the col-	
and second years	1,200 00	lection of mineralogy, and geology	480 00
Professor of Spanish grammar, third		Professor of physics	1,200 00
and fourth years	1,200 00	Assistant, who performs experiments	1,000 00
Professor of Spanish grammar, fifth		Assistant of above	300 00
and sixth years; also inspector of		Professor of practical mechanics	1,000 00
the classes of the two foregoing	1,200 00	Professor of mineralogy and geology	1,200 00
Professor of chronology and geography,		Professor of chemistry	1,200 00
first and second years	1,200 00	Assistant, who prepares the experi-	
Professor of history, third and fourth		mental apparatus	1,200 00
years	1,200 00	Allowance for above when he performs	
Professor of history, fifth and sixth		experiments	300 00
years; also inspector preceding		Professor of natural history	1,200 00
years' classes	1,200 00	Assistant in charge of the geological	
Professor of penmanship	600 00	department and the botanical mu-	
Professor of book-keeping	1,200 00	seum	1,200 00
Professor of medicine, domestic econ-		Assistant of above, in charge of the	
omy, and duties of women	1,200 00	garden and green-house	480 00
Professor of hygiene and physiology;		Professor of logic and morals	1,200 00
also physician of the school	1,200 00	Professor of general chronology and	
Professor of natural and ornamental		Mexican history	1,200 00
drawing and painting in water colors.	800 00	Professor of music	400 00
Assistant of above	600 00	Professor of shorthand writing	800 00
Professor of French	700 00	Professor of gymnastics	500 00
Professor of English	700 00	Professor of literature	1,200 00
Professor of Italian	700 00	Allowance to one of the foregoing who	
Professor of manual labor	600 00	teaches mathematics	600 00
		Professor of Latin	800 00
		Professor of Spanish	1,200 00

Salaries of the civil and military officers and employés of Mexico—Continued.

Occupations.	Salary.	Occupations.	Salary.
Preparatory school for boys—Continued.		*Preparatory school for boys—Continued.*	
Professor of Mexican or Nahuatl	$600 00	Professor of practical and theoretical	
Professor of Greek	1,000 00	pharmacy	$1,400 00
Professor of French	700 00	Professor of physiology	1,200 00
Professor of English	700 00	Professor of general and topographical	
Professor of German	700 00	anatomy	1,200 00
Professor of Italian	700 00	Professor of external pathology for second year	
Professor of lineal drawing	700 00	ond year	1,200 00
Professor of galvano-plastic and electro-		Professor of external pathology for	
gilding	720 00	third year	1,200 00
Assistant of foregoing	300 00	Professor of external clinic for second	
Professor of practical telegraphy	720 00	year	1,400 00
Professor of theoretical telegraphy	720 00	Professor of internal clinic for third	
Professor of natural and ornamental		year	1,400 00
drawing	700 00	Professor of external clinic for fourth	
		year	1,400 00
Service.		Professor of internal clinic for fifth year	1,400 00
		Professor of internal pathology for sec-	
Head doorkeeper	600 00	ond year	1,200 00
Doorkeeper of the big side of the school		Professor of internal pathology for	
building	360 00	third year	1,200 00
Doorkeeper of the little side of the		Professor of history of drugs	1,200 00
school building	300 00	Professor of chemical analysis	1,400 00
Chief of servants	240 00	Assistant preparer of apparatus for	
Janitor and servant of the telegraphy		above	800 00
class	192 00	Professor of obstetrics	1,200 00
Master's doorkeeper	240 00	Professor of clinic of obstetrics	1,400 00
Servant of the physics class	192 00	Professor of legal medicine	1,200 00
Servant of the chemical class	192 00	Assistant preparer of mixtures for	
Servant of the natural history class,		above	600 00
who also collects plants	300 00	Professor of normal histology (general	
Servant of the galvano-plastic class	192 00	and special)	1,200 00
Servant (general)	192 00	Professor of public and private hy-	
Gardener	300 00	giene and medicinal meteorology	1,200 00
Assistant gardener	141 00	Assistant (preparer for above)	600 00
		Professor of operative medicine	1,200 00
SCHOOL OF JURISPRUDENCE.		Professor of general pathology	1,200 00
		Professor of therapeutics	1,200 00
Director	2,000 00	Assistant (preparer of apparatus for	
Secretary	1,000 00	the classes of pharmacy and history	
Prefect	760 00	of drugs	800 00
Superintendent	1,000 00	Assistant for classes of physiology and	
Librarian	460 00	pharmacology	600 00
Professor of literature and eloquence	1,200 00	Dissector for professor of descriptive	
Professor of natural law	1,200 00	anatomy	800 00
Clerk of the secretary	300 00	Dissector for professor of topographi-	
Professor of first course of Roman law	1,200 00	cal anatomy	800 00
Professor of second course of Roman		Assistant for professor of normal his-	
law	1,200 00	tology	600 00
Professor of first course of national		Assistant for professor of topographi-	
law	1,200 00	cal anatomy	200 00
Professor of second course of national		Assistant explainer (repetidor) of the	
law	1,200 00	practical working of operative medi-	
Professor of constitutional and admin-		cine	800 00
istrative law	1,200 00	Assistant for internal clinic, third year.	800 00
Professor of international and maritime		Assistant for internal clinic, fifth year..	800 00
law	1,200 00	Assistant for external clinic, fourth	
Professor of elements of penal legisla-		year	800 00
tion	1,200 00	Assistant for external clinic, second	
Professor of civil proceedings	1,200 00	year	800 00
Professor of criminal proceedings	1,200 00	Assistant for clinic of obstetrics	800 00
Professor of comparative legislation	1,200 00	Repairer and keeper of anatomical mu-	
Professor of legal medicine	1,200 00	seum	560 00
Professor of political economy	1,200 00	Secretary for offices of director, secre-	
		tary, and treasurer	500 00
Service.		*Service.*	
Doorkeeper	300 00	Head doorkeeper, chief of servants	400 00
Assistant doorkeeper	240 00	Assistant doorkeeper	300 00
Servant	240 00	Servant of the pharmacy and chemical	
		classes	240 00
SCHOOL OF MEDICINE.		Assistant of the pharmacy and chem-	
		ical classes	240 00
Directors	2,000 00	Servant of the anatomy and practical	
Secretary	800 00	classes	240 00
Superintendent	1,000 00	Assistant of the anatomy and practical	
Prefect	760 00	classes	240 00
Librarian, also clerk	600 00	Servant of the histology, hygiene, and	
Assistant of librarian	300 00	physiology classes	210 00
Professor of descriptive anatomy	1,400 00	Janitor	240 00

Salaries of the civil and military officers and employés of Mexico—Continued.

Occupations.	Salary.	Occupations.	Salary.
SCHOOL OF COMMERCE.		**SCHOOL OF ARTS AND TRADES.**	
Director	$1,500 00	Director	$2,000 00
Secretary	600 00	Secretary, chief prefect, and librarian.	1,500 00
Maintainer of order, and assistant secretary	400 00	Superintendent and treasurer	1,000 00
Librarian and keeper of the museum	300 00	Tool and store house keeper	1,200 00
Professor of arithmetic and mercantile correspondence	800 00	Prefect	760 00
Professor of Government book-keeping.	1,000 00	Professor of French	700 00
Professor of commercial book-keeping.	800 00	Professor of English	700 00
Professor of geography, statistics, and history of commerce	1,200 00	Professor of mathematics	1,200 00
Professor of mercantile, consular, and maritime law	1,200 00	Professor of natural and ornamental drawing	600 00
Professor of administrative and constitutional law	1,200 00	Professor of molding and wood carving	600 00
Professor of practical knowledge of home and foreign products	600 00	Professor of lineal and mechanical drawing	800 00
Professor of chemistry applied to commerce	800 00	Professor of Spanish grammar, arithmetic, geography, and penmanship..	600 00
Assistant who prepares mixtures for above	300 00	Professor of physics and elementary mechanics	1,200 00
Professor of French (morning classes).	650 00	Professor of general and industrial chemistry	1,200 00
Professor of French (evening classes)	650 00	Assistant preparer of apparatus for above	800 00
Professor of English (morning classes).	650 00	Assistant preparer of apparatus for physics class	800 00
Professor of English (evening classes).	650 00	Director of work-rooms	600 00
Professor of German	700 00	Assistant director of work-rooms	240 00
Professor of political economy, theory of credit, rights of the people, diplomatic usages, and correspondence ...	1,200 00	Servant of work-rooms	180 00
Professor of Mexican history	1,200 00	Professor of music	480 00
Janitor	240 00	Professor of gymnastics	300 00
Servant of the chemical class	100 00	*Service.*	
		Doorkeeper	300 00
SCHOOL OF FINE ARTS.		Watchman	180 00
Director	1,200 00	Janitor	240 00
Subdirector and secretary	1,200 00		
Superintendent, treasurer, and prefect	1,200 00	**SCHOOL FOR THE DEAF AND DUMB.**	
Watcher (celador) over the students..	500 00	Director	1,500 00
Librarian, also clerk	720 00	General professor	1,200 00
Professor of painting	1,200 00	Assistant professor	600 00
Professor of sculpture and ornamental molding	1,200 00	Treasurer-secretary	1,000 00
Professor of embossing	1,200 00	Physician for this school, also for the "preparatory" "jurisprudential" and "arts and trades" schools	1,000 00
Professor of engraving on plates	1,200 00	Professor of horticulture	360 00
Professor of drawing from nature	1,500 00	Professor of drawing	360 00
Professor of drawing from copies (day classes)	800 00	Professor of book-keeping	360 00
Professor of drawing from copies (night classes)	800 00	Professor of penmanship	360 00
Professor of drawing with crayon	800 00	Professor of gymnastics	400 00
Professor of decorative and ornamental drawing	1,500 00	Prefect	480 00
Professor of anatomy of figures	600 00	First girl aspirant (aspirante) to a professorship	360 00
Professor of lineal drawing	600 00	Second girl aspirant (aspirante) to a professorship	300 00
Professor of composition architectural, classic orders, and copy of monuments	1,200 00	First boy aspirant (aspirante) to a professorship	360 00
Professor of descriptive geometry and stereotypography	1,200 00	Second boy aspirant (aspirante) to a professorship	300 00
Professor of legal architecture, estimates, valuations, and topography..	1,200 00	Third boy aspirant (aspirante) to a professorship	240 00
Professor of rational (racional) and applied mechanics	1,200 00	Chief workman in book-binding and gilding rooms	240 00
Professor of elementary minerology and geology, who will also make a chemical analysis of the building materials used in this city	1,000 00	Teacher of lithography	360 00
Professor of practical construction, architecture, and carpentry	1,200 00	Lady prefect	400 00
Keeper of the galleries of painting and sculpture	360 00	*Service.*	
Keeper of the galleries of engraving..	240 00	Doorkeeper	180 00
Restorer of paintings	900 00	Cook	108 00
		Scullion	72 00
Service.		Washerwoman	84 00
Doorkeeper	300 00	Seamstress and ironer	120 00
Servant	240 00	Servant	141 00
		Gardener	150 00
		NATIONAL MUSEUM.	
		Director	1,500 00
		Professor of mineralogy	1,200 00
		Professor of paleontology	1,200 00
		Professor of zoology	1,200 00

Salaries of the civil and military officers and employés of Mexico —Continued.

Occupations.	Salary.	Occupations.	Salary.
NATIONAL MUSEUM—Continued.		*Auxiliary primary school for boys.*	
Professor of botany	$1,200 00	Director	$1,000 00
Professor of taxidermy	800 00	Assistant	600 00
Draftsman	600 00	Auxiliary	480 00
Secretary, clerk, treasurer, and keeper		Professor of English	300 00
of the collections	1,200 00	Professor of English	300 00
		Professor of gymnastics	300 00
Service.		Servant	150 00
Servant	300 00		
Doorkeeper	240 00	*Elementary school, No. 1, for girls.*	
Orderly	60 00		
		Directress	600 00
NATIONAL LIBRARY.		Assistant	360 00
Director	2,500 00	Servant	150 00
Clerk	1,000 00		
Librarian	480 00	*Conservatory of music.*	
Clerk in charge of artisans' department.	700 00		
Decipherer of ancient documents	1,200 00	Director	2,000 00
Clerk	600 00	Clerk of director	600 00
		Librarian in charge of music and in-	
Service.		struments	800 00
Doorkeeper	500 00	Superintendent	1,000 00
Assistant doorkeeper	240 00	Clerk of superintendent	360 00
Gardener	295 00	Prefect of the boys	300 00
Messenger	200 00	Watchman	260 00
		Inspectress of girls	900 00
National primary school for boys (Nos.		Lady watcher (celadora) over the girls.	720 00
1, 2, 3, and 7).		Assistant of foregoing	360 00
		Copyist of music	240 00
Director, also professor	1,200 00	Tuner of instruments	180 00
Second professor, who uses objective		Doorkeeper and gardener	300 00
method	900 00	Janitor	120 00
Assistant professor	480 00	Street-sweeper	36 00
Auxiliary professor	360 00	Professor of elements of theoretical	
Professor of English	600 00	music and preliminary ideas of har-	
Professor of music	600 00	mony	600 00
Assistant of above	360 00	Professor of music for children	600 00
Servant	150 00	Professor of music for adults	600 00
Gardener for No. 7	150 00	Professor of music for girls and young	
Pupil who assists in teaching	300 00	ladies	600 00
		Professor of chorus-singing (solo)	600 00
National primary school for girls (Nos.		Professor of popular glee-singing	600 00
4, 5, 6, 8, and 9).		Professor of chorus-singing, with ac-	
		companiment	600 00
Lady professor (directress)	1,200 00	Professor of high artistic singing and	
Assistant lady professor, who uses ob-		elementary anatomy, physiology, and	
jective method	900 00	hygiene of the vocal organs	1,200 00
Assistant professor	480 00	Professor of the piano	600 00
Professor of English	600 00	Lady professor of the piano	600 00
Professor of English (No. 9)	300 00	Professor of piano accompaniments	600 00
Professor of music	600 00	Professor of repeating piano	500 00
Professor of music (No. 6)	300 00	Professor of violin and viol	600 00
Professor of gymnastics	300 00	Professor of violin	600 00
Servant	150 00	Professor of repeating violin	500 00
Pupil who assists in teaching	300 00	Professor of violoncello	600 00
Paymaster	360 00	Professor of bass viol	600 00
		Professor of harp	600 00
Night school for men.		Professor of flute	600 00
Director	800 00	Professor of hautboy and fagot	600 00
Second professor	600 00	Professor of clarionet	600 00
Assistant professor	300 00	Professor of trumpet	600 00
Servant	120 00	Professor of brass instruments	600 00
		Professor of harmony, counterpoint,	
Night school for women.		and composition	1,200 00
Directress	800 00	Professor of theoretical and practical	
Second lady professor	600 00	æsthetics, history of music, and bio-	
Assistant lady professor	300 00	graphy of celebrated musicians	1,200 00
Servant	120 00	Professor of acoustics and phonography.	350 00
		Professor of music and zithern playing.	350 00
Finishing school for girls.		Professor of writing music	350 00
		Professor of French	600 00
Directress in charge of reading class,		Professor of Italian	600 00
also of second year's course of study		Player of accompaniments	240 00
and English class	1,200 00		
Assistant lady professor in charge of		*Academy of professors of primary in-*	
first year's course of studies	480 00	*struction.*	
Lady prefect in charge of first section.	480 00		
Lady prefect in charge of second section	480 00	Professor of teaching, whose classes	
Lady prefect in charge of third section.	480 00	are attended by the assistants of the	
Lady professor of manual labor	600 00	primary schools	1,200 00
Lady professor of music	600 00	Secretary	600 00
Lady professor of drawing	480 00		
Auxiliary	576 00		
Servant	144 00		

Salaries of the civil and military officers and employés of Mexico—Continued.

Occupations.	Salary.	Occupations.	Salary.
Academy of medicine.		*Administration of the "journal of debates" of the Senate.*	
Clerk (medical student)	$600 00	Director	$600 00
Servant	300 00	Editor	1, 200 00
		Folder	300 00
LEGISLATIVE DEPARTMENT.		Messenger....................	240 00
CHAMBER OF DEPUTIES.		*Section of the archives.*	
Deputy	3, 000 00	Chief of the section	1, 000 00
		Clerk	600 00
CHAMBER OF SENATORS.		*Service.*	
Senator	3, 000 00	Doorkeeper.........................	800 00
		Messenger......................	410 00
OFFICE OF THE CHAMBER OF CONGRESS.		DEPARTMENT OF THE CHIEF AUDITOR OF THE TREASURY AND PUBLIC CREDIT.	
Chief clerk	3, 000 00		
First assistant.....................	1, 800 00	Chief auditor	4, 000 00
Second assistant	1, 200 00	First-class auditor.............. .	2, 500 00
Third assistant	1, 000 00	Second-class auditor	2, 000 00
Fourth assistant....................	900 00	Examining clerk	1, 000 00
Fifth assistant	800 00	Book-keeper	1, 500 00
General clerk auxiliary of the first section	1, 000 00	Corresponding clerk	1, 000 00
Chief editor	1, 400 00	Clerk	600 00
Assistant editor	800 00	Chief of the archives.........	1, 000 00
Clerk.... -	600 00	Clerk of the archives..............	600 00
Clerk (telegraph operator)...........	800 00	Doorkeeper....	500 00
		Messenger......................	360 00
Section of stenography.		Orderly......................	60 00
Chief stenographer.................	1, 800 00	*Special section for the revision of retarded accounts, commencing on July 1, 1865.*	
Second stenographer	1, 200 00		
Ordinary stenographer	720 00	Chief auditor	2, 500 00
Supernumerary stenographer.........	200 00	Second auditor	2, 000 00
		First examining clerk..............	1, 500 00
Section of the archives.		Second examining clerk	1, 200 00
		Third examining clerk	1, 000 00
Chief of section	1, 200 00	Fourth examining clerk	800 00
Assistant chief of section.............	800 00	Fifth examining clerk	700 00
Clerk	600 00	Clerk	600 00
Administration of the "journal of debates."		DEPARTMENT OF JUSTICE.	
		Supreme court.	
Director of the "journal"	600 00	Judge of the supreme court	4, 000 00
Editor of the "journal "	1, 200 00	Supernumerary judge of the supreme court	4, 000 00
Proof-reader	300 00	Solicitor-general of the nation........	4, 000 00
Folder	340 00	Clerk of above	600 00
Messenger	200 00	Attorney-general	4, 000 00
		Clerk of above	600 00
Treasury of Congress.		Agent advocate, who is prohibited from practicing law within the federal jurisdiction, assistant of solicitor and attorney generals	2, 000 00
Treasurer	4, 000 00		
Messenger	240 00	Attorney for the defense who practices exclusively in the federal tribunals and the courts of the federal district.	2, 400 00
Service.		*Secretaryships.*	
Doorkeeper....	1, 200 00	Secretary of mandates of the first court	3, 000 00
Doorkeeper for chief clerk's department	600 00	Secretary of mandates of the second court	3, 000 00
Messenger	410 00	Chief clerk	2, 500 00
House guard	400 00	Assistant of above	2, 000 00
Watchman	300 00	Book-keeper	1, 800 00
Dustman	72 00	Clerk	600 00
		Auxiliary clerk....................	360 00
OFFICE OF THE CHAMBER OF SENATE.		Executor	600 00
Chief clerk.......................	3, 000 00	Second assistant in charge of the archives	2, 500 00
First assistant	1, 800 00	Clerk of proceedings	1, 200 00
Second assistant...................	1, 200 00	Solicitor	600 00
Third assistant	1, 000 00		
Acting general clerk	800 00	*Service.*	
Clerk	600 00	Doorkeeper,.....................	500 00
Section of stenography.		Janitor	300 00
Stenographer........................	1, 200 00	Orderly..........................	60 00
Clerk.....:	600 00		

LOWER CALIFORNIA.

REPORT BY CONSUL LAMBERT, FOR SAN BLAS, GUADALAJARA, AND TEQUILA

SAN BLAS.

DIFFICULTY IN SECURING LABOR STATISTICS.

Pursuant to the Labor Circular issued by the Department of State at the solicitation of the leading trade and industrial associations of the United States, with a view of obtaining through consular officers the fullest attainable information concerning the condition of labor throughout the world, I have the honor to submit the following results of an imperfect and unsatisfactory investigation made in this consular district. I say unsatisfactory, because it is a difficult task to examine the labor question in this vicinity from the American standpoint on account of there being neither racial, climatic, nor industrial similarities. It is equally difficult to deduce useful comparison, for the reason that a study of the subject here results in presenting to the student a complete economic paradox, namely: Labor in this portion of Mexico, with its knowledge and requirements, is more satisfied, contented, and independent than labor at home, yet a transfer of the Mexican laborer and his conditions into the United States would be at once revolting to our ideas of manhood and civilization.

HABITS AND CONDITION OF THE LABORERS.

As an abstract proposition, labor in this consular district is polite, honest, and faithful, and these qualities are mainly attributable to the almost wholly natural and untutored condition of the laboring class.

Nearly, if not quite all, of the trials and troubles Mexico has undergone politically may be attributed to the discontent and ambitions of men, begotten by a promiscuous system of education, aided no doubt by their racial antecedents.

On the other hand, the comforts required by the laborer of the United States, the food and attention, the demands of society and appearance, the laudable ambition to lead, the dissatisfaction which prevails to a greater or less extent in the breasts of our workmen at the misfortune of their lot in life, the temptation of social and political preferment—these and other considerations frequently culminate in politics, laziness, or crime. It absolutely disqualifies a great many of our best laborers for usefulness in the broader and nobler fields of production.

Notwithstanding the social friction produced by these antagonistic and conflicting forces agitating the majority class, the Anglo-Saxon race (so called) in America and Australia have gradually advanced in material and political prosperity.

By these acts of orderly progress they have unveiled to the world a colossal monument unconsciously erected and dedicated to the inherent power of that great race for self-government, and it has no contemporary on earth.

Those Anglo-Saxons who settled in the United States of America are even prospering to-day, with universal education among the masses, regardless of race or color; unlimited emigration from Europe, and an unrestricted system of naturalization.

With these enormous economic gaps existing between the twin sister republics of the western hemisphere, Mexico is not behind by any means; in fact, she leads all others, except, perhaps, Chili.

One must visit this country and observe its undeveloped commercial, agricultural, and mineral resources in order to fully comprehend the magnitude of the calamity which befell Mexico when Cortez escaped from the battle of Otumba.

GUADALAJARA.

INDUSTRIES.

In size and commercial importance Guadalajara stands next to the national capital. It has 15 tanneries, 1 glass manufactory, 5 sugar factories, while nearly every hacienda has its *panoche* pans ; 5 wax-match factories, 6 cigarette factories, 10 shoe factories, 11 flour mills, 4 cotton factories, 7 soap factories, 5 breweries, 21 places where mescal is distilled, 4 hotels, and a plaza de torros where bull-fights are regularly held every Sunday afternoon, and which I am constrained to include among its prosperous industries from the attendance noticed last Sunday.

The manufacture of leather is eminently successful; the same may be said of pottery and all agricultural industries. On account of the altitude, flour of a very good quality is made and sent to all the coast districts, the nearest competitor being the State of Sonora.

The large industry of Mexican pottery occupies a great many Indian laborers, but has no organized form, every hut making its own wares. Iron, tin, and copper cooking utensils, as well as water-coolers, bottles, &c., are almost entirely unknown in domestic life. The Indian manufacturer packs his pottery into wicker crates, about 2 feet square and from 5 to 6 feet long, and starts to different portions of the country on foot with the crate on his back. I have seen one arrive at the port of San Blas, a distance of over 230 miles, dispose of his articles at prices varying from 1½ cents to 12½, and in cases of large pieces as high as 18 cents per piece. The aggregate sales of his cargo will not exceed $12 or $15, but it is nearly all clear gain, there being very little expense except the wear and tear of sandals.

The image-makers are generally of a more elevated grade, although their products find distribution in nearly the same manner.

All the skilled labor employed in the industries before referred to receive generally 25, 31, and 37½ cents per day, Mexican money, when they work. The wax-match factories employ only boys and girls, who average 12½ and 15 cents per day. The large cigarette factory of Lucas Barron employs 600 women and 95 men. I happened to be there when they were being paid off, and found that it was all piece work, the average wage per day being about 30 cents.

RATES OF WAGES.

The prices paid laborers here are from 33½ to 50 per cent. cheaper than at San Blas or any other seaport. This is owing to the tropical climate of the coast, its unhealthy rainy seasons, and expensive traveling into the interior every time that season returns. The altitude and latitude of this city makes it the perfection of climatic excellence.

FOOD PRICES.

Notwithstanding the difference in wages between the sea coast and the table lands, they are substantially equal in effect, for the reason that the purchasing power of a dollar here is equal to about a dollar and a half on the coast. For example, at San Blas beef and pork is worth from 18 to 20 cents per pound; sugar, 20 cents; coffee, 25 cents; corn, from 2 to 3 cents; beans, from 2 to 3 cents; flour is little used among the working classes, and is worth from 10 to 12 cents per pound, while in this locality beef is worth from 12 to 15 cents; sugar, 15 cents; coffee, 16 cents; corn and beans, about 1¼ cents per pound, and flour 5½ cents.

The clothing used by the laboring classes exclusively is heavy unbleached muslin, and a serape, while sandals and a broad-brimmed straw hat complete the outfit, at an aggregate outlay of $3.

TEQUILA.

This place is noted for its celebrated distillations from a peculiar branch of the *Aloe americana*, which grows much smaller than that branch of the same family producing *pulque.*

As these plants are only ready to yield their valuable saccharine product once, and that at the exceedingly tardy period of seven years after planting, the area devoted to its cultivation must necessarily be large. The product of this local distillation having become so popular, the beverage is called after the name of the town where it is made, and not *vino de mezcal,* which is the correct name.

The price of labor here is the same, but, like nearly every industry located outside of city limits, there are hacienda stores everywhere, and it is rarely that the laboring class ever get out of debt.

LABOR IN LOWER CALIFORNIA AND IN THE UNITED STATES.

This country is beyond question the Utopian paradise of the capitalist, there being no known "intelligent masses" here to menace or abridge the "reasonable demands" of corporations.

However imperfect this report may be in the direction of furnishing comparative statistical data, it will nevertheless tend to show to my fellow-countrymen, the laboring and mechanical classes of the United States, that they do not half realize the exalted position they hold to-day as compared with the laboring classes of their near neighbors.

The average laborer and mechanic of this country scarcely ever has a bed or pillow to sleep on; he may have a mat and serape, and that is really all he wants. He rarely knows the toilet uses of wash-bowl, towel, or soap, and is equally unmindful of his head. He may be fortunate enough, if luck be not too uncharitable towards him, to get a suit of tanned goat skin, costing about $6, which will last him as many years with proper care. His daily food consists of tortillas, beans, and fruit. He has by law every civil, political, and charitable right belonging to the best citizen of this Republic, but his conditions are incompatible with the exercise thereof. His comparative relation to the employer is about equal to the relations enjoyed between the New York bootblack and the Wall street banker.

Strikes are comparatively unknown; poverty and redundancy of population render these institutions entirely impracticable. Therefore, every laborer or mechanic who can squeeze out a living in the United States, even in this age of commerce and competition, should never permit the ephemeral spirit of venture nor the fictitious legends of the Aztecs to turn his head, unless he be a natural faster and trained to feats of endurance on foot.

RATES OF WAGES.

Following are the daily wages paid laborers, reduced to American money, at $7.5 for the Mexican dollar.

RICHARD LAMBERT,

Consul.

UNITED STATES CONSULATE,

   San Blas, May 26, 1884.

I. GENERAL TRADES.

Wages paid per day of ten hours in the San Blas consular district.

Occupations.	Lowest.	Highest.	Average.
BUILDING TRADES.			
Bricklayers	$0 43	$1 30	$0 75
Hod carriers	33	43	33
Masons	43	1 30	75
Tenders	33	43	33
Plasterers...	43	1 30	75
Tenders...	33	43	33
Roofers...	43	1 30	75
Tenders...	33	33	33
Carpenters..	43	1 30	75
OTHER TRADES.			
Bakers..	43	1 30	75
Blacksmiths...	43	1 30	75
Strikers	33	43	33
Bookbinders	43	1 30	75
Brickmakers (tile)	43	43	43
Butchers	50	1 00	50
Cabinet makers	43	1 30	75
Confectioners	43	43	43
Cigar makers (piece-work entirely)...	....	....	43
Coopers	43	1 30	75
Distillers	43	30	30
Drivers: Draymen and teamsters, cab, carriage, and street railways.. {	18	25	18
	16	20	1s
Dyers.....	30	20	20
Engravers...	43	62	43
Gardeners...	16	20	16
Hatters	43	33	33
Horseshoers..	43	81	65
Jewelers	43	81	65
Laborers, porters, &c	30	37	30
Potters...	20	43	30
Printers.....	33	43	33
Teachers, public schools	1 75	1 75	1 75
Saddle and harness makers	43	65	43
Tanners	33	43	33
Tailors	33	43	33
Telegraph operators	87	1 30	87
Tinsmiths..	33	43	33

The foregoing are the prices paid when work is done. It is well enough to state that there are thirteen church feast days in this country every year to be celebrated. During that time these day laborers, from religious devotion, cannot be made to work. The feast days are exclusive of Sundays, and sometimes their observance occupies more than a single day. In addition to this, every individual in this country has his own patron saint's day, which he feels called upon to celebrate, as well as those of his family and friends, when the employer will stand it.

II. FACTORIES, MILLS, ETC.

Wages paid per week of seventy-two hours in factories or mills in Tepic and Santiago.

Occupations.	Lowest.	Highest.	Average.
Weavers	$3 00	$5 25	$4 00
Spinners (men and boys)	1 95	4 00	3 00
Carders	2 62	8 75	4 00
Packers	2 87	4 00	3 00
Mill hands generally	1 50	2 75	2 50
Machinists	1 00	1 25	1 00
Foundrymen	3 62	3 75	3 62
Blacksmiths	4 00	5 00	4 00
Sugar-mill feeders	1 75	1 75	1 75

The superintendents and foremen of all manufactories are either Englishmen or Americans, and they receive a yearly salary, by contract entered into before coming here. In these establishments they will not permit this promiscuous system of absence on feast days. Three national holidays, patron-saints' days, and Christmas week are allowed, but none other. Sunday is always observed as a day of rest, as in other countries.

V. MINES AND MINING.

Wages paid per day of ten hours in and in connection with silver mines near Tepic and Guadalajara.

Occupations.	Lowest.	Highest.	Average.
Foreign foremen	$2 65	$4 37	$2 87
Native foremen	50	87	65
Native miners	33	65	43
Native laborers	25	33	33

The superintendents and skilled miners are paid fair salaries by contract. Americans have been here who were skilled in mining in the Western States, but having no prior contract, were unable to obtain labor at all, unless accepting the native prices.

VIII. SEAMEN'S WAGES.

Wages paid per month to seamen (officers and men) in the port of San Blas.

Occupations.	Lowest.	Highest.	Average.
Captains	$25 00	$50 00	$25 00
Mates	10 00	20 00	12 00
Seamen	6 00	12 00	10 00

Captains also get a percentage on the delivery of their cargoes and collection of freight equal to about 2½ per cent. All local traffic is coasting. There is no foreign service nor deep-water navigation on the coast, so far as I can ascertain.

IX. STORE AND SHOP WAGES.

Wages paid per week of seventy-two hours in stores, wholesale or retail, to males in the San Blas consular district.

Occupations.	Lowest.	Highest.	Average.
Clerks	$3 40	$9 00	$5 00
Salesmen	3 40	9 00	5 00
Bookkeepers	11 00	15 00	12 00

X. HOUSEHOLD WAGES IN TOWNS AND CITIES.

Wages paid per month to household servants in the district of San Blas, with board and lodging.

Occupations.	Lowest.	Highest.	Average.
Waiters	$6 00	$15 00	$8 00
Cooks (female)	4 00	8 00	6 00
Hotel cooks (female)	8 00	15 00	12 00
Chambermaids	4 00	4 00	4 00
Porters	0 00	8 00	6 00

XI. AGRICULTURAL WAGES.

Wages paid per day to agricultural laborers in the district of San Blas.

Occupations.	Lowest.	Highest.	Average.
Farm hands*	$0 12½	$0 30	$0 19

* With 16 pounds of corn per week.

XII. CORPORATION EMPLOYÉS.

Wages paid per month to the corporation employés in the city Guadalajara.

Occupations.	Highest.	Occupations.	Highest.
Chief of police	$216 33	Secretary board of aldermen	$100 00
Inspector police	100 00	Assistant treasurer	60 00
Second inspector police	60 00	Clerks in treasurer's office	40 00
Chief mounted police	80 00	Secretary to municipal judges	30 00
Secretary to chief police	100 00	Policeman (day)	11 37
Assistant secretary to chief police	60 00	Policeman (night)	15 00
General clerks	40 00	Mounted policeman	22 50

This city is the capital of the State of Jalisco and the civil power is supreme.
The towns of San Blas, Acaponeta, Santiago, Navarrette, Compostella, and the city of Tepic, together with the adjoining territory, constitute the military district of Tepic, although belonging to the State of Jalisco. This is the only method which insures peace in those localities, so remote from the seat of state goverument, and which even defied the General Government for twenty years, under the leadorship of Lozado.

In the ports of San Blas and Santiago.

Occupations.	Highest.	Occupations.	Highest.
Sub-director politico	$66 66	1 porter	$15 60
2 chiefs of police (each)	35 00	Clerk to municipal council	30 00
1 captain of day police	20 00	Hospital steward	40 00
1 captain of night police	18 00	Physician	150 00
5 day police (each)	15 00	Porter to hospital	8 00
4 night police (each)	18 00	Cook to hospital	5 00
Municipal treasurer	50 00	2 public school teachers (each)	50 00
Municipal clerk	30 00	1 health officer	30 00
3 guards at city custom-house (each)	25 00	2 street cleaners (each)	15 00
Clerk to municipal judge	30 00		

The sub-director politico is appointed by the military commander at Tepic, and is superior to the civil authority.
The municipal council and judges are purely honorary and receive no salary.
The foregoing salaries are given in Mexican money.

XIII. GOVERNMENT DEPARTMENTS AND OFFICES.

Wages paid per month of two hundred and ten hours to employés in Government departments and offices—exclusive of tradesmen and laborers in the custom-house at San Blas.

Occupations.	Highest.	Occupations.	Highest.
1 collector of customs	$291 66	10 harbor police (each)	$65 62
1 cashier	218 75	2 captains of boat (each)	29 16
1 treasurer	145 83	8 boatmen (each)	20 41
1 appraiser	175 00	1 porter to cashier	35 00
4 clerks (each)	51 04	1 porter in custom-house	17 50
1 commandant	182 29	1 captain of the port	70 00
1 keeper of warehouse	131 25	1 captain of boat	29 16
1 assistant	109 37	4 boatmen	20 14
2 chiefs of harbor police (each)	109 37		

The captain of the port also receives $3.50 from every vessel entering the harbor. There is also a pilot, who is not required to go aboard, but receives $1.75 per foot for every foreign vessel arriving also $4 for every time a vessel changes her anchorage. These salaries are reduced to American money.

XV. PRINTERS AND PRINTING OFFICES.

Statement showing the wages paid per day of twelve hours to printers (compositors, pressmen, proof-readers, &c.,) in Guadalajara and Tepic.

Occupations.	Lowest.	Highest.	Average.
Printers	$0 25	$0 37½	$0 33
Pressmen	33	43	33
Apprentices	12	15	12

Compositors receive from 33 to 43 cents per thousand proof-readers about $8 per week, when employed. The styles of printing are crude and unartistic.

LA PAZ.

REPORT BY CONSUL VIOSCA.

I have the honor to inform the Department that with all the diligence within my power, my investigations with certain class of laborers and also about the general wages paid to laborers in the different trades and industries of this peninsula, became effective ; the result could not be attained as desired or expected, on account of the exceptional condition, practices, habits, customs, and the entirely primitive state of every industry and of its people ; as to the practicability to give an answer on each of the subjects, it is beyond the reach of any human being, at present, because the instability of every leading trade, as well the irregularities by which the enterprises are managed, the depopulated condition of this country, and the long and slow way of communicating with the interior towns, leave no way or chance for a more extensive or correct report on the subject.

I have simply filled the forms alluded to in the circular and which are here inclosed, knowing that it is not conforming with the manner explained by the Department, but have arbitrarily filled them as the circumstances permit it, leaving the *average column* to be taken as the standard of wages prevailing in this country.

JAS. VIOSCA,
Consul.

UNITED STATES CONSULATE,
La Paz June 7, 1884.

I. General Trades.

Wages paid per week of ten hours in La Paz, Lower California.

Occupations.	Lowest.	Highest.	Average.
BUILDING TRADES.			
Bricklayers	$1 00	$1 50	$1 25
Hod-carriers	63	75	69
Masons	2 00	2 50	2 25
Tenders	50	62	56
Carpenters	2 00	2 50	2 25
OTHER TRADES.			
Bakers	75	1 33	1 09
Blacksmiths	50	1 75	1 12
Strikers	75	1 00	87
Bookbinders			
Brick-makers	75	75	75
Brewers			
Butchers	1 00	1 50	1 25
Drivers, draymen, and teamsters	1 00	1 33	1 16½
Gardeners	50	80	65
Laborers, porters, &c.	50	67	58½
Printers	80	1 00	90
Teachers, public schools	2 00	3 33	2 66½
Sailmakers	1 00	1 25	1 12½
Stevedores	1 50	1 50	1 50
Tailors	1 00	1 50	1 25
Tinsmiths	1 75	2 00	1 87½

Food and food prices.—The working people of this country are free to purchase the necessaries of life to suit their own convenience. Their daily food consisting of corn, beans, jerked beef, and meat: Cost of corn, 3 cents per pound; beans, 2½ cents per pound; jerked beef, 20 cents per pound: meat (fresh), 10 cents per pound.

V. Mines and Mining.

Wages paid in and in connection with the Progreso Company, Valle Perdido Company, and San José Island Mines in Lower California.

Occupations.		Lowest.	Highest.	Average.
Superintendents	per year..	$4, 000 00	$5, 000 00	
Assayers	do....	2, 000 00	2, 500 00	
Assayers' assistants	do....	900 00	900 00	
Foremen	do....	900 00	900 00	
Ore millers	per day..	1 50	1 50	$1 50
Engineers	per month..	80 00	100 00	90 00
Machinists	do ...	60 00	80 00	70 00
Drillers	per day..	1 75	2 50	2 12½
Miners inside of mine	do....	1 75	2 50	2 12½
Operators in the furnaces	do....	1 75	2 00	1 87½
Boys employed in the separation and cleansing of the ores	do....	50	75	62½
Common laborers	do....	1 00	1 00	1 00

VII. Ship-Yards and Ship-Building.

Wages paid per day of ten hours in ship-yards in La Paz, Lower California.

Occupations.	Lowest.	Highest.	Average.
Wood ship-building	$2 50	$3 00	$2 75
First assistants	1 00	1 50	1 25
Second assistants	50	75	62½

Note.—Computation for average wages cannot be rated here, as per form suggested in circular, for it would not be exact with the rules for labor; rates for wages customary in this country, as wages are generally paid by month or day in isolated works.

VIII. Seamen's Wages.

Wages paid per month to seamen (officers and men)—distinguishing between ocean, coast, and river navigation, and between sail and steam, in La Paz, Lower California.

Occupations.	Lowest.	Highest.	Average.
OCEAN SAIL NAVIGATION.			
Masters	$60 00	$100 00	$80 00
Mates	30 00	50 00	40 00
Seamen	16 00	22 00	19 00
Cooks	25 00	25 00	25 00
COAST SAILING NAVIATION.			
Masters	40 00	75 00	57 50
Mates	20 00	30 00	25 00
Seamen	14 00	18 00	16 00
Cooks	18 00	20 00	19 00
STEAM COAST NAVIGATION.			
Captains	100 00	100 00	100 00
First mates	60 00	70 00	65 00
Second mates	30 00	35 00	32 50
Seamen	20 00	20 00	20 00
Chief engineers	100 00	100 00	100 00
First assistant engineer	60 00	80 00	70 00
Second assistant engineer	40 00	60 00	50 00
Third assistant engineer	40 00	60 00	50 00
Firemen	30 00	30 00	30 00

It is beyond possibility to give an idea of the wages for oil and pearl fisheries, around the bay and adjacent islands; but men employed in that line of business generally work under contract; a common rule taken for an average rate makes it at $6.31 per week.

IX. Store and shop wages.

Wages paid per month in stores, wholesale or retail, to males and females, in La Paz.

Occupations.	Lowest.	Highest.	Average.
Bookkeepers	$75 00	$125 00	$100 00
Clerks, first class	40 00	60 00	50 00
Clerks, second class	30 00	50 00	40 00
Clerks, assistants	20 00	30 00	25 00

X. Household wages in towns and cities.

Wages paid per month, with board and lodging, to household servants (towns and cities) in La Paz, Lower California.

Occupations.	Lowest.	Highest.	Average.
Female cooks	$9 00	$10 00	$9 00
Male cooks	12 00	15 00	13 50
Chambermaids	10 00	10 00	10 00
Male servants	6 00	10 00	8 00
Female servants	4 00	6 00	5 00
Washwomen	8 00	10 00	9 00

XI. AGRICULTURAL WAGES.

Wages paid to agricultural laborers and household (country) servants in Lower California.

Occupations.	Lowest.	Highest.	Average.
Male servants* ....per month..	$10 00	$14 00	$12 00
Servants employed in the sugar mills........................per day..	50	75	62½
Household male servants*...................................per month..	5 00	8 00	6 50
Household female servants*.......................................do....	4 00	8 00	6 00

* With board and lodging.

XIII. GOVERNMENT DEPARTMENTS AND OFFICES.

Wages paid per month to employés in Government departments and offices, exclusive of tradesmen and laborers, in La Paz, Lower California.

Occupations.	Lowest.	Highest.	Average.
Governor	$333 33½	$333 33½	$333 33½
Secretary	150 00	150 00	150 00
First assistant	80 00	80 00	80 00
Second assistant	50 00	50 00	50 00
Third assistant	50 00	50 00	50 00
Marshal..	20 00	20 00	20 00
Superintendent public schools	100 00	100 00	100 00
Male teachers..	100 00	100 00	100 00
Female teachers..	80 00	80 00	80 00
Male teachers in the interior..................................	60 00	60 00	60 00

XV. PRINTERS AND PRINTING OFFICES.

Statement showing the wages paid per month to printers (compositors, pressmen, proof-readers, &c.) in La Paz, Lower California.

Occupations.	Lowest.	Highest.	Average.
Printers...	$25 00	$30 00	$27 50
Type-setters	16 00	20 00	18 00

NUEVO LEON.

REPORT BY CONSUL CAMPBELL, OF MONTEREY.

I have the honor to submit the following notes on the industries and labor of the State of Nuevo Leon :

PRINCIPAL INDUSTRIES.

The principal industries of this State are cotton factories, flouring mills, tanneries, distilleries, manufactories of hats, shoes, blankets, saddles, harness, soap, matches, candles, carriages, wagons and ice; also such industries as tin and coppersmiths, bookbinderies, printing, &c. The above manufactories and industries furnish employment to a very large number of laborers, both male and female. There is very little machinery used in the different shops, and that of the most antique style ; nearly all the work being done by hand.

RATES OF WAGES.

The rates of wages paid to laborers of every class, mechanical, mining, factories, public works and railways, domestic, agricultural, &c., are exhibited in the inclosed tabular statement.

COST OF LIVING AND FOOD.

The cost of living to the laboring classes is about the same as that in the United States, though their food is of a different kind. The laborer here lives principally on beans and tortillos (a flat cake made of a coarse corn-meal ground on a stone with the hands) and a small quantity of fresh beef, goat, or mutton. They could not afford to eat bacon, as it is 50 cents a pound, and other articles commonly used by laborers are very expensive here.

HABITS OF THE WORKING CLASSES.

They are steady workers, but are generally eye-servants. They make it a rule to spend all they make, chiefly for good clothing. They are very proud about their dress, and will stint themselves of food in order to buy a $10 sombrero and a good suit of clothes. They are generally temperate in their habits. The feeling existing between employé and employer is good.

STRIKES.

Such things as strikes are not known among this people.

FOOD PURCHASES.

No restrictions are imposed on the laborers by the employers as to where they shall purchase the necessaries of life. They are paid altogether in silver, as they are afraid of any other kind of currency.

GENERAL CONDITION OF THE WORKING CLASSES.

The general condition of the working people is good, though at present they may be compelled to live unusually economically on account of a long-continued drought and the unsettled condition of the country. Their houses are built of adobe (sun-dried brick), covered with a thatched roof, neatly whitewashed on the inside, and are generally quite neatly kept, however sparse their furniture. They are not of large frame, but of great endurance physically. While a large number are fond of mescal, a spirituous liquor, yet very few comparatively are addicted to intoxication. The wages of both male and female laborers have been considerably increased in the last five years, caused by the introduction of railroads and other American enterprises. The wages of men and women do not conflict with each other except perhaps in cotton factories, which of course tends to maintain harmonious and kindly relation among all concerned. A majority of the women can read and write, and the children are being educated in the public schools; the education of the children is, however, limited to reading, writing, arithmetic, and geography. There is desire on their part to increase the facilities offered by the public schools.

ROBT. C. CAMPBELL,
Consul.

UNITED STATES CONSULATE,
Monterey, Mexico, May 1, 1884.

I. GENERAL TRADES.

Wages paid per week in Monterey.

Occupations.	Lowest.	Highest.	Average.
BUILDING TRADES.			
Bricklayers	$6 00	$12 00	$10 00
Hod-carriers	2 25	4 50	3 00
Masons	4 50	12 00	10 00
Tenders	1 50	4 50	3 00
Plasterers	4 50	12 00	10 00
Tenders	1 50	4 50	2 50
Roofers	4 50	12 00	10 00
Tenders	1 50	4 50	2 50
Carpenters	4 50	12 50	10 00
OTHER TRADES.			
Bakers	3 00	9 00	6 00
Blacksmiths	9 00	12 50	10 00
Strikers	4 50	9 00	7 50
Bookbinders	3 00	4 50	3 50
Brick-makers	6 00	9 00	8 00
Butchers	4 50	6 00	5 00
Brass-founders	9 00	12 50	10 00
Cabinet-makers	9 00	15 00	12 00
Confectioners	3 00	6 00	4 00
Cigar-makers	3 00	4 50	3 50
Coopers	4 50	12 00	10 00
Distillers	3 00	4 50	3 50
Drivers:			
Draymen and teamsters	3 50	5 00	4 50
Cab and carriage	3 50	5 00	4 50
Street railways	5 00	5 00	5 00
Gardeners	2 00	3 00	2 50
Hatters	6 00	7 50	6 50
Horseshoers	9 00	12 50	10 00
Laborers, porters, &c	2 00	4 00	3 00
Lithographers	7 00	10 00	8 00
Millwrights	6 00	9 00	7 50
Nailmakers (hand)	3 00	4 50	3 50
Potters	3 00	4 50	3 50
Printers	5 00	8 00	7 00
Teachers public schools	10 00	15 00	12 50
Saddle and harness makers	10 00	12 00	10 00
Tanners	2 50	3 50	3 00
Tailors	7 00	10 00	8 00
Telegraph operators	12 50	25 00	18 50
Tinsmiths	3 00	4 00	3 50
Weavers (outside of mills)	3 00	6 00	5 00

MONTEREY STREET RAILWAY.

Wages paid, without board.

Occupations.	Lowest.	Highest.	Average.
Bookkeeper .... per month..	$100 00	$100 00	$100 00
Yard foreman ....do....	50 00	50 00	50 00
Blacksmith ....do....	75 00	75 00	75 00
Conductors ....do....	20 00	20 00	20 00
Drivers ....do....	20 00	20 00	20 00
Watchman ....do....	25 00	25 00	25 00
Ordinary stable hands ....do....	20 00	20 00	20 00
Relay boys ....do....	10 00	10 00	10 00
CONSTRUCTION.			
Foreman of track ....do....	100 00	100 00	100 00
Track hands ....per day..	50	50	50
Spikers ....do....	75	75	75

II. FACTORIES, MILLS, ETC.

Wages paid per week in factories or mills in and near Monterey.

Occupations.	Lowest.	Highest.	Average.
Foreman	$8 00	$10 00	$9 00
Spinners	4 00	6 00	5 00
Weavers	6 00	8 00	7 00
Servants	4 00	6 00	5 00
Females:			
Spinners	4 00	6 00	5 00
Weavers	6 00	8 00	7 00
Servants	2 00	3 00	2 50
Others	6 00	8 00	7 00

Board in factories, $2.50 per week.

V. MINES AND MINING.

Wages paid per day in mines in the State of Nuevo Leon.

Occupations.	Lowest.	Highest.	Average.
Miners	$0 50	$1 00	$0 75
Smelters	75	1 25	1 00
Ordinary hands	50	75	62½

IX. STORE AND SHOP WAGES.

Wages paid per week of seventy-eight hours in stores, wholesale and retail, to males, in Monterey.

Occupations.	Lowest.	Highest.	Average.
Clerks in retail stores	$5 00	$15 00	$10 00
Clerks in wholesale stores	10 00	20 00	15 00
Bookkeepers	12 50	25 00	18 50
Porters	2 00	3 00	2 50

X. HOUSEHOLD WAGES IN TOWNS AND CITIES.

Wages paid per month to household servants (towns and cities) in Monterey.

Occupations.	Lowest.	Highest.	Average.
Male servants	$8 00	$20 00	$12 00
Male cooks	10 00	20 00	12 00
Female cooks	10 00	20 00	12 00
Female nurses, &c	5 00	8 00	6 00
Villages:			
Male servants	4 00	10 00	8 00
Female servants	3 00	5 00	6 00

XV. PRINTERS AND PRINTING OFFICES.

Statement showing the wages paid per week to printers in Monterey.

Occupations.	Lowest.	Highest.	Average.
Job printers	$5 00	$20 00	15 00
Compositors	5 00	8 00	7 00
Pressmen	4 00	7 00	6 00

XI. AGRICULTURAL WAGES.

Wages paid to agricultural laborers and household (country) servants in State of Nuevo Leon.

Occupations.	Lowest.	Highest.	Average.
Laborers: *			
Field..per day..	$0 37	$0 50	$0 37
During harvest...do....	50	1 00	75
Field laborers †.................................per month..	5 00	8 00	7 00
Shepherds...do....	8 00	10 00	9 00
Household servants.....................................do....	4 00	8 00	6 00

         * Without board.   † With two bushels of corn.

SONORA.

REPORT BY CONSUL WILLARD, OF GUAYMAS.

SONORA, ITS PEOPLE AND INDUSTRIES.

I beg leave to acknowledge the receipt of "Labor Circular" from the Department, date of February 15 last, and in reply would state:

That in this consular district of Guaymas, which embraces the State of Sonora, Mexico, the largest city, Hermosillo, contains not more than 12,000 people, and the port of Guaymas 6,000 people. Three other towns, Alamos, Magdalena, and Altao, containing from 2,000 to 3,000 population each; also a number of small villages and pueblos of from 100 to 500 inhabitants.

The entire consular district, which is estimated to contain an area of 35,000 square miles, contains less than 120,000 people, which includes the civilized Indian tribes, estimated to be one-fifth of the entire population. There are no manufacturing establishments in the State, excepting a small cotton mill, near Hermosillo, for the manufacture of unbleached muslin, which is idle for six months of the year, the pursuits of the people being confined to merchandising, stock-raising, and mining. The status of this consular district is such that it is difficult to meet the requirements of the circular as to the information sought for.

I beg leave, also, to state that the rates given are more applicable to, at or near, what is called our large towns or cities. In the small towns in the interior of the country there is proportionately a cheaper rate paid for all classes of labor than mentioned in the following tables.

RATES OF WAGES AND COST OF LIVING.

I herewith inclose rates of labor, which will be found in tables annexed. The cost of living of the laboring classes varies in the large towns and cities, where the cost is full 30 per cent. higher than in the interior of the country, and varies according to condition from 20 to 60 cents per day, while skilled labor, clerks, and employés vary from 30 cents to $1 per day. The articles of food consist of meat, bread, coffee, sugar, vegetables, &c., a list of which is hereto annexed, with the retail prices in our towns.

In making a comparison of the rates of labor from 1878 to 1884, as regards prices paid for work, it can be estimated at 30 per cent. higher and the price of food, &c., 10 per cent. more than the year 1878.

HABITS OF THE WORKING CLASSES.

The working classes as a rule spend what they acquire almost as soon as earned, rarely saving money. Their wants are few and simple, and they appear to act on the adage of "sufficient unto the day are the wants thereof."

FEELING BETWEEN EMPLOYER AND EMPLOYÉ.

The feeling between employé and employer is not marked by the antagonism which exists in other countries more populous and prosperous. There are no labor unions or organizations, no strikes of employés on any organized scale, and, generally speaking, all disputes are settled amicably, without reference to law.

HOURS OF LABOR.

A day's work is generally considered from sunrise to sunset, with two hours' intermission at noon. This applies to out-door employment. In the mines they usually receive task-work, which is, as a rule, estimated at about ten hours per day. The laboring classes that work by the day or week are paid in silver (coin). Those that are employed by the month are paid according to contract entered into. In some cases one-half or one-third is paid in cash, and the rest in provisions and merchandise. In the agricultural districts men are generally employed at the rate of $8 per month, receiving in addition an almud (about a peck) of corn or wheat each week. Beef, sugar, and other articles of food or clothing, if said laborer needs them, he must purchase. The peon system in this part of Mexico, which formerly existed, is practically null and void.

POLITICAL RIGHTS.

The laboring classes, as a general rule, have few political rights or do not care to exercise them, and they do not enter into the political contest. Their votes always, as a rule, go with that of their employer.

EMIGRATION.

There has been from this consular district before the commencement and completion of work on the Sonora Railroad a considerable emigration to Arizona and California, as wages there were higher and the disordered condition of the country was such that more chances of bettering their condition and obtaining personal security was presented. Since the completion of the railroad some few have returned as price of wages have increased and a more prosperous condition of affairs throughout the country exists.

RAILROADS AND REVOLUTION.

With the advent of the railroad have ceased revolution and civil disturbances, and the laborer to-day is not liable to be compelled to do forced military duty, as was the case formerly in the constantly recurring civil disturbances which appeared at one time to be the normal condition of this part of Mexico.

WOMEN LABORERS.

The employment of women who labor in this consular district is almost entirely confined to household duties, such as housekeepers, laundresses, seamstresses, teachers, musical instructresses, cigarette-makers (small cigars), cooks, shop-keepers, &c. The average rate paid per day for such employment, including board and lodging, ranges from 20 cents to $1 per day.

FOREIGN LABORERS IN SONORA.

The foreign labor, as it exists in this consular district to-day, is confined almost exclusively to skilled artisans in different branches of trade. In Sonora there are 56 Chinamen, 50 of whom are engaged exclusively in the manufacture of shoes and boots and the others as cooks at hotels or mining establishments.

I hope that this incomplete report may serve to give an idea of labor as it exists to-day in this part of the northwestern portion of Mexico.

A. WILLARD
Consul.

UNITED STATES CONSULATE,
Guaymas, June 12, 1884.

I. GENERAL TRADES.

Wages paid per week of sixty hours in Guaymas.

Occupations.	Lowest.	Highest.	Average.
GENERAL TRADES.			
Bricklayers	$15 00	$18 00	$16 25
Hod-carriers	6 00	7 50	6 60
Masons	12 00	18 00	14 40
Tenders	4 50	6 00	5 10
Plasterers	12 00	18 00	14 40
Tenders	4 50	6 00	5 10
Carpenters	13 50	27 00	18 90
OTHER TRADES.			
Bakers	10 50	15 00	12 30
Blacksmiths	9 00	13 50	10 80
Strikers	4 50	6 00	5 10
Bookbinders	6 00	8 00	6 80
Brickmakers	7 50	15 00	
Butchers	6 00	8 00	6 80
Cabinet-maker	12 00	15 00	13 20
Confectioners	6 00	9 00	7 20
Cigar-makers	4 50	8 00	5 80
Drivers	12 00	16 00	13 00
Draymen and teamsters	15 00	20 00	17 00
Cab, carriage, and street railway	18 00	30 00	22 80
Gardeners	4 50	6 00	5 10
Hatters	6 00	7 50	6 60
Jewelers	6 00	10 00	7 00
Laborers, porters, &c	3 50	6 00	4 50
Printers	6 00	7 50	6 60
Teachers, public schools	12 00	20 00	15 20
Saddle and harness makers	7 50	10 00	8 50
Sail makers	6 00	8 00	6 80
Tailors	7 50	12 00	9 30
Telegraph operators	16 00	18 00	16 80
Tinsmiths	6 00	8 00	6 80

VI. Railway Employés.

Wages paid per day to railway employés (those engaged about stations, as well as those engaged on the engines and cars, linemen, railroad laborers, &c.) in Sonora, 1884.

Occupations.	Lowest.	Highest.	Average.
Conductors	$4 25	$4 25	$4 25
Brakemen	3 00	3 00	3 00
Engineers, locomotive	6 00	6 00	6 00
Engineers, stationary	3 50	4 00	3 70
Firemen	4 00	4 00	4 00
Machinists	2 50	4 50	3 10
Station agents	2 50	5 00	3 50
Telegraph operators	2 00	4 25	2 90
Clerks	2 50	5 00	3 50
Section foremen	3 00	3 00	3 00
Laborers	1 00	2 00	1 40
Track-walkers	1 50	1 75	1 60
Baggage-masters	2 50	3 00	2 70
Engine-cleaners	1 75	2 00	1 85
Car-builders	3 75	4 25	3 95
Carpenters	3 00	4 00	3 40
Blacksmiths	2 50	3 50	2 90
Civil engineers	3 00	5 00	3 80
Line men	1 00	1 50	1 20
Painters	2 50	3 00	2 70

VII. Mines and Mining.

Wages paid per day of ten hours in and in connection with gold, silver, and copper mines in Sonora, Mexico, 1884.

Occupations.	Lowest.	Highest.	Average.
Foreman	$1 50	$2 00	$1 70
Assayer	1 50	2 00	1 70
Bookkeeper	1 00	1 50	1 20
Miners	2 00	4 00	2 80
Engineers	3 50	4 00	3 70
Mill hands	2 50	4 00	3 10
Blacksmiths	2 00	6 00	3 60
Carpenters	2 50	6 00	3 00
Storekeepers	75	1 25	95

VIII. Seamen's Wages.

Wages paid per month to seamen (officers and men) in the port of Guaymas, Mexico, 1884.

Occupations.	Lowest.	Highest.	Average.
Captains	$30 00	$60 00	$42 00
Mates	20 00	35 00	26 00
Seamen	12 00	18 00	14 40
Cooks	10 00	16 00	12 40

IX. Store and Shop Wages.

Wages paid per month, Guaymas, Mexico, stores, wholesale and retail, to males and females' 1884.

Occupations.	Lowest.	Highest.	Average.
Bookkeepers	$40 00	$150 00	$84 00
Clerks	15 00	45 00	27 00
Porters	16 00	20 00	17 60
Female clerks in shops	8 00	12 00	9 60

X. HOUSEHOLD WAGES IN TOWNS AND CITIES.

Wages paid per month to household servants, towns and cities, in Sonora, Mexico, 1884.

Occupations.	Lowest.	Highest.	Average.
Cooks	$6 00	$15 00	$9 60
Washers and ironers	4 00	16 00	8 80
Servants	3 00	8 00	5 00
Porters	8 00	12 00	9 60
Nurses	5 00	8 00	6 20

XI. AGRICULTURAL WAGES.

Wages paid per month to agricultural laborers and household (country) servants in Sonora, Mexico.

Occupations.	Lowest.	Highest.	Average.
Foreman of ranch work	$20 00	$40 00	$28 00
Laborers	6 00	8 00	6 80
Herders (vaqueros)	10 00	15 00	12 00
Cooks	6 00	8 00	6 80

XII. CORPORATION EMPLOYÉS.

Wages paid per week of sixty hours to the corporation employés in the city of Guaymas, Sonora.

Occupations.	Lowest.	Highest.	Average.
City secretary	$15 00	$25 00	$19 00
Clerks	5 00	7 50	6 00
Surveyor	12 50	15 00	13 50
Assessor	25 00	31 25	27 50
Collector	6 25	7 50	6 75
Jailer	5 00	6 25	5 60
Assistant jailer	2 50	3 75	3 00
Treasurer	20 00	25 00	22 00
Captain police	12 50	15 00	13 50
Policemen	6 25	7 50	6 75
Cartmen	2 00	3 00	2 40
Indian governors	2 00	2 00	2 00
School teachers, male	10 00	25 00	16 00
School teachers, female	10 00	15 00	12 00
City physician	15 00	15 00	15 00

XV. PRINTERS AND PRINTING OFFICES.

Statement showing the wages paid per week of sixty hours to printers (compositors, pressmen, proof-readers, &c.) in Sonora, Mexico.

Occupations.	Lowest.	Highest.	Average.
Foremen	$10 50	$15 00	$12 50
Pressmen	9 00	12 00	10 20
Type setters	9 00	13 50	10 80
Assistants	4 50	7 50	5 70

A general average of values at retail of provisions, rent, clothing, &c., in Sonora, Mexico, 1884.

Articles.	Value.	Articles.	Value.
Flour........................ per pound..	5½	Vinegar ....per gallon..	60
Sugar :		Milk.................................do....	70
White ....do....	16	Bread.......................per pound..	5
Brown. ....do....	4½	Fish...............................do....	3
Coffee................................do....	21	Oysters ....per gallon..	2½
Tea...................................do....	89	Vegetable....................per pound..	3½
Beans.................................do....	9½	Water.......................per gallon..	¾
Corn..................................do....	2¼	Potatoes.....................per pound..	6
Lard..................................do....	25	Rent ....per month..	4 00
Meat:		Calico........................per yard..	20
Fresh...............................do....	11	Mantu cotton cloth ....do....	18
Dried...............................do....	18	Shoes.......................... per pair..	1 75
Dried peas..........................do....	3		

MATAMOROS.

REPORT BY CONSUL-GENERAL SUTTON.

I. GENERAL TRADES.

Wages paid per week of sixty hours in Matamoros.

Occupations.	Lowest.	Highest.	Average.
BUILDING TRADES.			
Bricklayers...	$9 00	$15 00	$12 00
Hod-carriers..	3 00	3 00	3 00
Masons	9 00	18 00	12 00
Tenders......................................	3 00	6 00	4 00
Plasterers..	6 00	12 00	9 00
Tenders...	3 00	4 50	4 00
Roofers	9 00	12 00	10 00
Tenders...	3 00	4 50	4 00
Carpenters...	9 00	18 00	12 00
OTHER TRADES.			
Bakers..	6 00	15 00	9 00
Blacksmiths...	6 00	9 00	8 00
Strikers...	4 50	4 50	4 50
Bookbinders	6 00	9 00	7 00
Brick makers	4 50	9 00	6 00
Brewers..	4 50	9 00	6 00
Butchers..	4 00	5 00	4 50
Confectioners	4 00	10 00	6 00
Cigar-makers	4 50	6 00	5 00
Drivers:			
Draymen and teamsters........................	2 50	5 00	3 00
Cab and carriage......................................	2 50	5 00	3 00
Street railways	3 00	3 00	3 00
Gardeners	3 00	4 50	4 00
Horseshoers	9 00	12 00	10 00
Jewelers	6 00	12 00	8 00
Laborers, porters, &c...	6 00	9 00	7 50
Printers	6 00	12 00	9 00
Teachers public schools..	6 00	25 00	10 00
Saddle and harness makers..	6 00	9 00	7 00
Tailors	7 50	18 00	9 00
Tinsmiths..	7 50	9 00	8 00

VI. RAILWAY EMPLOYÉS.

Wages paid per month to railway employés (those engaged about stations, as well as those engaged on the engines and cars, linemen, railroad laborers, &c.) in Matamoros.

Occupations.	Lowest.	Highest.	Average.
Engineers..	$60 00	$85 00	$60 00
Firemen..			50 00
Conductors..			75 00
Brakemen...			40 00
Road-master			75 00
Section foremen..			40 00
Section men..			20 00
Watchmen..	25 00	30 00	27 50
Station agents...	75 00	83 00	80 00
Warehousemen			30 00

IX. STORE AND SHOP WAGES.

Wages paid per week of eighty hours in stores, wholesale or retail, to males and females, in Matamoros.

Occupations.	Lowest.	Highest.	Average.
Bookkeepers	$7 50	$25 00	$15 00
Cashiers..	12 50	30 00	25 00
Salesmen:			
Better sort..	10 00	20 00	15 00
Small shops	3 00	7 00	5 00
Boys	1 25	7 50	5 00

X. HOUSEHOLD WAGES IN TOWNS AND CITIES.

Wages paid per month to household servants (towns and cities) in Matamoros.

Occupations.	Lowest.	Highest.	Average.
Cooks:			
Men	$6 00	$25 00	$10 00
Women..	4 00	10 00	7 00
House servants:			
Men	6 00	30 00	12 00
Women..	3 00	15 00	8 00
Nurses...	3 00	15 00	8 00

XI. AGRICULTURAL WAGES.*

Wages paid per month to agricultural laborers and household (country) servants in Matamoros, Mexico, with or without board and lodging.

Occupations.	Lowest.	Highest.	Average.
Farm laborers..	$5 00	$15 00	$12 00

*An allowance of corn, and occasionally other supplies, and houses, are generally added.

XII. Corporation Employés.

Wages paid per week of sixty hours, more or less, to the corporation employés in the city of Matamoros, Mexico.

Occupations.	Lowest.	Highest.	Average.
Secretary			$20 00
Writers	$7 50	$12 00	10 00
Porter			5 00
Keeper of the clock			5 00
Treasurer	20 00	30 00	25 00
Bookkeeper			15 00
Weigher	12 00	25 00	20 00
Guards at gates	8 00	12 00	10 00
Alcalde			7 50
Director of hospital			15 00
Administrator			8 00
Druggist			6 00
Chief nurse*			6 00
Nurses*			3 50
Cook*			4 00
Grinder*			2 75
Chief of police			15 00
First assistant			7 50
Mounted police			7 50
Foot police	4 00	6 00	5 00
Night police	5 00	7 50	6 00
Scavengers	5 00	8 00	6 00
Hide and cattle Inspector			6 00

* And food.

XIII. Government Departments and Offices.

Wages paid per month of two hundred hours, more or less, to employés in government departments and offices, exclusive of tradesmen and laborers, in Matamoros, Mexico.

Occupations.	Lowest.	Highest.	Average.
Collector of customs			$300 00
Auditor			200 00
Chief clerk			125 00
Second clerk			100 00
Vista			125 00
Writers			60 00
Chief of guards			150 00
Second chief of guards			125 00
Guards	$40 00	$60 00	50 00
Federal district judge			300 00
Secretary to court			120 00
Public prosecutor			200 00
Postmaster			80 00
Federal fiscal agent			200 00
Auditor			125 00
TELEGRAPH.			
Division superintendent			125 00
Manager			108 00
Operators	66 00	91 00	70 00
Bookkeeper			60 00
Clerk			50 00
Translator			25 00
Governor			300 00
Secretary			200 00
Private secretary			100 00
Clerks and writers	30 00	75 00	50 00
Deputies			100 00
Chief clerks			100 00
Writers, &c	20 00	45 00	30 00
SUPREME COURT.			
Magistrates			150 00
Treasurer			150 00
Secretary			100 00
Writers, &c	30 00	60 00	50 00
Defender of poor			80 00
Judges of the first instance			125 00
Defender of poor			30 00
Writers			30 00
Treasurer			200 00
Auditor			100 00
Bookkeepers, writers, &c	30 00	70 00	50 00
Public printer			100 00
Director			40 00

XV. PRINTERS AND PRINTING OFFICES.

Statement showing the wages paid per week of sixty hours to printers (compositors, pressmen, proof-readers, &c.) in Matamoros, Mexico.

Occupations.	Lowest.	Highest.	Average.
Compositors...	$20 00	$55 00	$30 00
Pressmen (thirty hours)	10 00	24 00	20 00

BRITISH HONDURAS.

REPORT BY CONSUL MORLAN, OF BELIZE.

RATES OF WAGES.

I have the honor to inclose herewith a statement of the condition of the laborers of the colony of British Honduras.

The report is as exact as is possible when the large extent of the colony is considered, and the fact that the greater part of the population is employed in wood cutting—mahogany and logwood—and various agricultural pursuits.

The position of the laborers in general may be said to be a happy one, their wants being few and easily and cheaply supplied. There are no beggars among the natives of the colony, and, unless caused by sickness, there is no want. No general value can be placed on the cost of living here, as the average laborer can live on next to nothing; most of them live on the rations furnished by their employers, and have no additional expense, except for clothing, which is of the cheapest and most primitive kind. These people could always manage to save something, but they seldom do so. They are generally a happy-go-lucky set, and when they are paid off at the end of the year the money soon vanishes—often for some very trifling thing. They are not, as a rule, given to drunkenness, although most of them drink more or less rum during the year. The statements are prepared in the order of the interrogatories.

COST OF LIVING.

A large proportion of the laborers live in their own houses and upon their own lands or lots. There is a portion, however, who have to pay rent. Buildings or rooms to let have become more and more scarce of late years, and prices are on the rise, as there is an actual lack of as many as are wanted. Strangers coming to Belize find no abiding places, except at hotels or in private families; and the latter who care to entertain are also few.

People can live here in almost any kind of a house when driven to it by circumstances, as there is no cold weather the year round, and no pressing need of warm or protected rooms. Small houses of from three to four rooms no ground floors cost from $4 to $7 per month, although some cheap affairs rent as low as $2.50 and $3 per month.

The sanitary condition of habitable dwellings generally is good, and tolerable ones, when procurable at all, rent at from $10 to $25 per month. Working people rarely pay more than $5 to $7 per month. Most of the tenements are built on large lots which have a yard in common with a number of small houses, varying in price from $2 to $6 per month each.

Prices paid for clothing are about the same as in the United States, the material being usually a little cheaper, but the making quality considered higher. In the way of ready-made clothing, boots, shoes, &c., prices are a little higher. It must be remembered, however, that very little clothing is needed by the laboring classes, one or two garments being all that is needed by the common laborers the year round. Their children are generally fully dressed with a hat and a cheap cotton slip reaching to the knees. The tradesmen and mechanics dress pretty much the same as those of the United States, with the difference that their clothing is not so heavy.

Fires are necessary only for cooking, and wood is pretty expensive, a stick of wood a yard long and about the thickness of 3 to 4 inches costing one-half to three-fourths of a cent.

Plantains, yams, and coco (a kind of potato) form a large part of the food of the laborers; fish also are very cheap and abundant and form a part of the daily fare to laborers in the country, either on plantations or wood cuttings. Rations of 4 pounds of pork and 7 quarts of flour are given each man per week.

There is an abundance of all kinds of English and American canned goods, such as biscuits, pickles, fruits, vegetables, &c. In the following list is given the average general retail prices of food and some necessary household articles procurable at the markets and provision shops. The values given are American money, the standard here being the Mexican dollar, which is at a discount of 10 to 15 per cent.

FOOD PRICES.

Prices of provisions are as follows:

Articles.	Lowest price.	Highest price.	Articles.	Lowest price.	Highest price.
Fresh:			Cheese, American per pound.	$0 27	$0 33
Beef........per pound..	$0 11	$0 16½	Dried apples, plums, currants, &c.... per pound..	22	....
Pork ....do ..	....	16½	Sago, tapioca, &c ......do....|	16½	33
Mutton ....do....	22	˙33	Starch:		
Veal........ ....do....	....	22	Native ....do....	10	....
Sea fish ....do....	03	05½	American........do....	11	....
Sea turtle........do....	09	11	Soap, English and American, per pound.................	10	....
River turtle ......do ..	16½	22	Candles, English and American......per pound..	16½	....
Shell fish ....do....	03	05½	Wheat flour .... do....	04	07
Salted sea fish ....do....	03	04	Corn-meal ....do....	02	03
American mess pork ..do....	11	15	Oatmeal, Scotch ......do....|	11	....
American bacon......do....	16½	29½	Corn shelled......per quart..|	02	05
American hams ......do....|	22	33	Rice, native and imported, per quart	10	....
American salted beef..do....	16½	22	Beans:		
Fresh eggs......per dozen.	33	44	Native........per quart..|	11	....
Chickens............each.	33	55	American............do....	16½	....
Venison and game meats, per pound......	11	22	String ......per pound..	11	$0 18½
Ducks........each.	44	66	Peas, American......do	10	....
Pigeons ....per pair.	33	44	Barley, pearl .... do....|	16½	....
Geese........per pound..	....	22	Tomatoes, fresh ....do....'	07	11
Turkeys............each.	75	1 50	Potatoes:		
Lard:			American............do....	11	....
Native......per pound..	16½	22	Native, sweet......do....	02	05
American .... do ..	....	22	Onions:		
Condensed milk, pound tins..	16½	27	Native............do....	11	16½
Chocolate......per pound..	33	50	American .... do....|	16½	22
Cacao:			Garlic:		
Imported ....do....	22	27	American .... do ....|	22	....
Native........do....	33	45		16½	....
Tea........do....	75	1 25	Cabbages ....do....|	05½	....
Coffee, Guatemala ....do	16½	22	Tamarinds............do....|	03	05½
Sugar:					
Native............do....	5½	˙09			
Imported cut loaf .do....	16½	....			

Food prices—Continued.

Articles.	Lowest price.	Highest price.	Articles.	Lowest price.	Highest price.
Bread:			Vinegar..........per quart..	$0 11	$0 22
Bakers'......per pound..	$0 05¼	....	Beer:		
Pilot.........do ..	05¼	....	American.........do....	33	....
Codfish, American .. do....	11	....	English............do....	22	....
Oranges.........per dozen..	12½	$0 16½	Rum, native.........do....	22	44
Aguacates (alligator pears),			Matches, German and Ameri-		
per dozen..........	33	55	can............per dozen..	11	....
Onions and radishes, spring,			Cigars, native and imported,		
per dozen......	05½	....	each	02	08
Plantains........ per dozen..	11	15	Tobacco ....per pound..	22	....
Bananas..............do...	05	10	Gunpowder.......... do....;	44	87
Cocoanuts, fresh. .....do ...	16½	22	Firewood.... per 100 sticks..	50	75
Melons and pumpkins each..	11	50	Charcoal........per barrel..	75	....
Fruits *	....	....	Shoes:		
Dates,figs,nuts,&c.per pound	25	37½	Men's..........per pair..	1 00	4 00
Kerosene oil.....per gallon..	22	30	Women's ....do....	1 25	3 50
Honey, native fresh.per quart	33	45	Moccasins.............do....	1 00	2 50

* Wild are cheap and abundant.

Crockery, glass and table ware are rather cheaper than in the United States. Household furniture stoves, and kitchen utensils are dearer.

WAGES PAST AND PRESENT.

As I have not seen the circular or the reports that were made at that time, I cannot make an exact statement of the difference in prices paid for labor between then and now, but there has been a general advance of wages of all kinds of labor, more particularly the agricultural department, caused principally by the increased demand for fruit-planting purposes. The general increase has been about 30 per cent.

HABITS OF THE WORKING CLASSES.

The working classes here are usually steady, but they are not, as a rule, given to saving. Most of them go out of town to work and are hired by contract, part of their wages being paid in advance and the remainder at the end of the time contracted for. Their money soon disappears, being used in buying clothing, luxuries in the way of eating, drinking, carriage-riding, &c., and they then hire for another year.

FEELING BETWEEN EMPLOYER AND EMPLOYÉ.

The feeling which prevails between employer and employé is generally kindly, and I think has a beneficial effect on the prosperity of the colony.

LABOR ORGANIZATIONS AND STRIKES.

The laborers of this colony have no trade or other organizations, and consequently no strikes.

FOOD PURCHASES AND CO-OPERATIVE SOCIETIES.

The laws of the colony provide that no contract can be made to pay the laborer otherwise than with the legal coin of the country, which may be said to have the Mexican or Spanish dollar (silver) as the standard. They are usually paid off and their accounts settled at the end of the year.

There are no co-operative societies.

GENERAL CONDITION OF THE WORKING CLASSES.

The general condition of the working people of this colony is pretty fair, as their wants are few. The climate being mild they are not under the necessity of buying heavy clothing, strong food, or having their houses warmed by fires. Some of them live in old sheds that in the United States would not be considered fit for stables. A large share of them in jail, who only spend a few days or weeks in town during the winter, do not trouble themselves about houses, but sleep under the market sheds, awnings of business houses, trees, &c. Those who are indus- trious and saving have every facility for saving (the Government pro- viding a savings bank and paying interest on their deposits) and provid- ing themselves with homes for their old age. The morals of most of them—having been slaves—are not good from the American stand- point, but are improving. Previous to the year 1880 the larger part of the births were illegitimate, but they are now all taken with the idea for getting married. It is a common sight to see people who have lived together for years, and have grown-up families, getting married and having a grand time at the wedding.

The larger part of the population is composed of negroes and their descendants intermixed with all nationalities, and they very much re- semble their brethren in the Southern States of our own Union.

SAFETY OF EMPLOYÉS.

There are no factories, mines, railroads, &c., in the colony, and there- fore no provisions need be made for accidents such as are common in the manufacturing countries. The Government, however, provides a public hospital, in which charges are made for those who are able to pay, while those who are indigent receive treatment and medicine gratis. There are also asylums for the insane, blind, &c.

POLITICAL RIGHTS.

This being a Crown colony, the people are governed by officers ap- pointed by the colonial office in England, and have no voice in the mat- ter. They are not directly taxed, as the revenue on the goods imported into the colony, together with the tax on spirits, licenses, and a light tax on property, pay the expenses of the colony. The tariff on im- portations is for revenue only, and averages about 10 per cent. ad valorem.

The Government is paternal in its management, and several laws have been lately passed protecting the laborers.

EMIGRATION.

There is no regular emigration from the colony.

PART II.—FEMALE LABOR.

WOMEN AND CHILDREN EMPLOYED.

There is no means of ascertaining the exact number of women em- ployed as teachers, dressmakers, or saleswomen, which occupations, with the exception of domestic servants, laundresses, &c., are the only employments offered to women in the colony. The number of domes- tic servants in the colony in the year 1881 was 813.

FEMALE WAGES.

The minimum, maximum, and average wages paid to female adults approximate as follows, viz:

Occupations.	Minimum.	Maximum.	Average.	Hours per week.
Teachers...........................per week..	$3 00	$6 50	$5 40	30
Saleswomen...........................do....	3 00	7 00	5 00	54
Cooks...........................do....	85	1 62	1 06	42
House-servants ....do....	50	1 80	1 06	72
Nurses...........................do ...	60	1 52	1 25	72
Plantation hands...........................do....	1 62	2 10	1 80	60

Dressmakers and laundresses usually work piece-work and make about the same wages as saleswomen. Cooks, house-servants, and nurses get their food in addition to the above wages, but are not usually provided with lodgings. Almost all of the house servants come to the house in the morning, and, after attending to the morning work (cooking and serving breakfast, house-cleaning, washing, &c.), go home until time to prepare the dinner, about 2 to 3 o'clock, after which time (6 to 8 o'clock) they are free.

MORAL AND PHYSICAL CONDITION OF FEMALE EMPLOYÉS.

The morals of the domestic servants of the colony are not of a high order, very few of them being married, but almost all of them having one or more children. Their physical condition is pretty good, although they are much given to complaining of their health, strength, &c.

SAFETY AND CARE OF FEMALE EMPLOYÉS.

No provisions are made by employers for the improvement, safety, or sickness of their female employés in the colony, the Government providing schools, asylums, and hospitals.

FEMALE WAGES, PAST AND PRESENT.

There has been an increase in the wages of female labor of all kinds, amounting to about 15 to 20 per cent. House rents have also increased, but provisions and other articles usually kept by the stores and shops have slightly decreased in price.

FEMALE EDUCATION.

The education of the women of the colony is pretty fair, most of them being able to read and write, which is about all they ever have use for. Almost all the children attend the schools, which are sectarian and receive Government aid according to the number of pupils they have.

PROPOSED IMMIGRATION FROM THE UNITED STATES.

In conclusion, I will add that, owing to the scarcity of labor in general in the colony, a project is on foot for the introduction of plantation labor from the United States, it having been stated by a labor agent of New Orleans that although laborers from the United States would have to be paid more per diem, it would be cheaper to the employers, as the laborer from the United States, being more intelligent and industrious, would accomplish two or three times as much work as the native laborer used at the present time.

Almost all labor in the way of wood-cutting and plantation work is done by tasks, and the laborer, if industrious, usually completes his task in from five to seven hours, having the remainder of the time to rest and amuse himself.

ALBERT E. MORLAN,
Consul.

UNITED STATES CONSULATE,
Belize, May 30, 1884.

I. GENERAL TRADES.

Wages paid per week of fifty-four hours in Belize, British Honduras.

Occupations.	Lowest.	Highest.	Average.
Bricklayers	$4 80	$10 20	$7 20
Hod carriers		5 40	5 40
Masons	4 80	10 20	7 20
Tenders	5 40	5 40	5 40
Slaters	4 50	9 60	6 90
Roofers	4 50	9 60	6 90
Carpenters	4 50	9 60	6 90
Bakers	5 10	8 40	6 60
Blacksmiths	4 50	9 60	6 90
Strikers	5 40	5 40	5 40
Butchers	5 10	8 40	6 60
Assistants	3 90	4 10	3 90
Cabinet-makers	3 80	10 20	6 40
Cigar-makers	2 25	6 30	4 20
Coopers	4 50	9 60	6 90
Draymen	4 10	6 90	5 10
Carriage drivers	4 90	8 40	6 40
Gardeners	5 80	12 60	9 10
Laborers, porters, &c	2 55	6 30	3 40
Millwrights		9 60	9 50
Printers	5 95	14 85	8 50
Teachers of public schools:			
Male	6 00	16 00	9 00
Female	3 00	6 80	5 40
Sail-makers	6 40	10 20	9 00
Stevedores		12 00	10 00
Lightermen	6 50	8 60	7 65
Tailors	3 80	10 65	6 40
Tinsmiths	3 80	8 40	5 90
Agricultural laborers	2 55	3 65	2 85
Female adults work	2 05	4 20	3 60
Painters	3 80	9 60	7 20
Fishermen	2 55	6 50	4 00
MISCELLANEOUS.*			
Teachers:			
Male	24 00	44 50	38 00
Female	12 00	25 00	22 50
Editors	80 00		80 00
Book-keepers	40 00	120 00	85 00
Chemists (dispensing)			60 00
Collectors			45 00

* Per month.

VII. SHIP-YARDS AND SHIP-BUILDING.

Wages paid per week of fifty-four hours in ship-yards—wood ship-building—in Belize, British Honduras.

Occupations.	Lowest.	Highest.	Average.
Carpenters	$4 50	$9 60	$6 90
Iron workers	4 50	9 60	6 90
Painters	3 80	9 60	7 20
Sail makers	6 40	10 20	9 00

VIII. SEAMEN'S WAGES.

Wages paid per month with board to seamen (officers and men)—distinguishing between ocean, coast, and river navigation, and between sail and steam—in Belize, British Honduras.

Occupations.	Lowest.	Highest.	Average.
Coast captains (sail)	$26 00	$35 50	$38 80
Coast mates (sail)	18 50	26 50	20 50
First-class coast seamen (sail)	11 90	13 50	12 75
Second-class coast seamen (sail)	9 52	10 80	10 00
Ocean seamen	20 10	30 80	23 00
Fishermen (with rations):			
Captains	15 40	24 00	22 50
Men	8 90	14 48	12 80

IX. STORE AND SHOP WAGES.

Wages paid per week of fifty-four hours in dry goods and grocery stores, wholesale or retail, to males and females, in Belize, British Honduras.

Occupations.	Lowest.	Highest.	Average.
Commercial clerks:			
Male	$7 00	$25 00	$16 00
Female	3 00	7 C0	5 00
Shop salesmen	3 50	9 40	5 00
Saleswomen	3 00	7 00	5 00

X. HOUSEHOLD WAGES IN TOWNS AND CITIES.

Wages paid per month with board to household servants (towns and cities) in Belize, British Honduras.

Occupations.	Lowest.	Highest.	Average.
Females:			
Cooks	$3 40	$5 10	$4 25
Domestics	2 00	7 10	4 25
Nurses	2 40	6 10	5 60
Males:			
(Carib) errands	1 90	7 10	4 25
Porters	8 40	10 90	8 40
Footmen		12 00	10 00
Coachmen	15 00	20 00	20 00

XI. AGRICULTURAL AND WOOD-CUTTING WAGES.

Wages paid per month to agricultural laborers and household (country) servants in British Honduras, without board and lodging.

Occupations.	Lowest.	Highest.	Average.
Fruit plantations:			
Males	$13 20	$14 60	$14 40
Females	6 50	8 40	7 20
Sugar plantations:			
Males	14 50	16 20	15 20
Females	6 50	8 40	7 20
Other farm laborers (male)	10 00	15 00	11 70
Mahogany cutters	15 10	16 50	15 65
Mahogany raftmen	9 40	12 60	10 00
Logwood cutters	14 50	16 50	15 65
Logwood boatmen	8 90	10 80	9 60
Wood cutters:			
Foremen			16 50
Clerks			18 40

XIII. GOVERNMENT DEPARTMENTS AND OFFICES.

*Wages paid per month to employés in Government departments and offices, exclusive of trades-
men and laborers, in British Honduras.*

Occupations.	Hours per day.	Lowest.	Highest.	Average.
Lieutenant governors	6		$675 00	$675 00
Private secretaries to above	6			88 00
Colonial secretaries	6			212 00
First clerk to same	6			80 00
Second clerk to same	6			70 00
Colonial treasurers	6			206 00
First clerk to same	6			112 00
Second clerk to same	6			70 00
Surveyor-general	6			140 00
Clerk to same	6			30 00
Colonel engineer	6			200 00
Clerk to same	6			46 00
Chief justice	6			375 00
Chief police (inspector)	6			128 00
Sergeants (inspector)	12			36 00
Corporals (inspector)	12			32 00
Constables:				
First class	12			27 00
Second class	12			23 00
Third class	12			18 00
Revenue officers	12			45 00
Prison superintendent	12			85 00
Turnkeys	12			39 00
Matrons	12			20 00
Overseers	10			20 00
Lighthouse keepers	10	$7 00	44 00	30 00
District magistrates	10	20 00	200 00	120 00
Interpreters and clerks	10	24 00	50 00	38 00
Attendants and messengers	10	15 00	24 00	19 00

XIV. TRADES AND LABOR—GOVERNMENT EMPLOY.

*Wages paid by the week of fifty-four hours to the trades and laborers in Government employ
in British Honduras.*

Occupations.	Lowest.	Highest.	Average.
Masons		$10 20	$10 20
Bricklayers		10 20	10 20
Hod-carriers		5 40	5 40
Other tenders		5 40	5 40
Roofers		9 60	9 60
Carpenters		9 60	9 60
Blacksmiths		9 60	9 60
Coopers		9 60	9 60
Draymen		6 90	6 90
Gardeners		12 60	12 60
Printers	$5 95	14 85	9 50
Agricultural laborers	2 55	3 05	3 05
Female laborers	3 05	4 20	3 60
Male porters, &c.	3 10	4 60	4 20
Painters	6 90	9 60	9 60

XV. PRINTERS AND PRINTING OFFICES.

*Statement showing the wages paid per week of fifty-four hours to printers (compositors'
pressmen, proof-readers, &c.), in British Honduras.*

Occupations.	Lowest.	Highest.	Average.
News compositors	$6 30	$10 00	$9 00
Pressmen (hand)			6 00
Book work (law)		14 85	12 00
Job work (plain)	9 00	14 85	12 00

UNITED STATES OF COLOMBIA.

BARRANQUILLA.

REPORT BY CONSUL DAWSON.

DIFFICULTY OF SECURING STATISTICS.

I have the honor to acknowledge the receipt of Labor Circular of February 15, 1884, and in reply to the same I beg respectfully to call your attention to the difficulty of obtaining such information accurately in this country, where there are no statistics or organizations to aid one. Consequently the facts presented have been obtained after many personal applications to those in authority, who finally consented to their use. This has naturally consumed much time in the preparation. I will now consider your questions in their order.

I. GENERAL TRADES.

Wages paid per week of sixty hours in the consular district of Barranquilla, United States of Colombia.

Occupations.	Lowest.	Highest.	Average.
BUILDING TRADES.			
Bricklayers	$3 34	$9 66	$7 74
Hod-carriers	1 92	4 84	3 90
Masons	3 84	9 66	7 74
Tenders	1 92	4 84	3 90
Plasterers	3 84	9 66	7 74
Tenders	1 92	4 84	3 90
Slaters	5 62	12 06	7 74
Roofers	5 62	12 06	7 74
Tenders	1 92	4 86	3 90
Plumbers	12 06	24 18	14 52
Assistants	4 84	9 72	7 74
Carpenters	5 92	12 06	7 74
Gas-fitters	12 06	24 18	14 52
OTHER TRADES.			
Bakers	3 84	7 74	4 84
Blacksmiths	3 84	12 06	9 60
Strikers	1 92	4 84	4 84
Book-binders	4 84	5 92	4 84
Brickmakers	1 92	9 66	4 84
Butchers	1 92	3 84	3 84
Cabinet-makers	5 92	14 52	7 74
Confectioners	1 92	7 74	4 84
Cigar-makers	1 92	4 84	4 84
Distillers	1 92	4 84	3 84
Drivers:			
General	1 92	7 74	3 84
Draymen and teamsters	1 92	4 84	3 84
Cab, carriage, &c	1 92	7 74	4 84

Wages paid per week in the consular district of Barranquilla—Continued.

Occupations.	Lowest.	Highest.	Average.
OTHER TRADES—Continued.			
Gardeners	$1 92	$7 74	$3 84
Hatters	1 92	7 74	3 84
Horse-shoers	3 84	12 06	9 66
Jewelers	5 92	12 06	9 66
Laborers, porters, &c	1 92	4 84	3 84
Nail-makers (hand)	3 84	12 06	9 66
Potters	1 92	9 66	4 84
Printers	3 84	5 92	4 84
Teachers (public schools)	7 74	30 22	12 09
Saddle and harness makers	4 84	7 74	5 92
Stevedores	4 84	7 74	5 92
Tanners	4 84	9 66	5 92
Tailors	3 84	9 66	4 84
Telegraph operators	3 84	20 15	12 09
Tinsmiths (outside of mills)	3 84	9 66	5 92

II. FACTORIES, MILLS, ETC.

Wages paid per week of sixty hours in factories or mills in the United States of Colombia, Barranquilla consular district.

Occupations.	Lowest.	Highest.	Average.
Soap and candle factory :			
Foreman	$4 03	$12 09	$7 74
Engineer	12 09	20 15	12 09
Mixer	3 22	4 03	3 22
Laborer	1 92	5 92	3 84
Saw-mills :			
Sawyer	4 03	9 66	7 74
Engineer	12 09	20 15	12 09
Fireman	1 92	3 84	2 90
Cotton ginning :			
Foreman	4 03	12 09	7 74
Engineer	12 09	20 15	12 09
Fireman	1 92	3 84	2 90
Sugar-mills :			
Foreman	4 03	12 09	7 74
Engineer	12 09	20 15	12 09
Laborer	1 92	3 84	2 90
Tannery :			
Foreman	4 03	24 18	12 09
Laborer	3 84	7 74	4 84
Match factory : *			
Foreman	12 09	12 09	12 09
Engineer and sawyer	20 15	20 15	20 15
Mixer	7 74	7 74	7 74
Errand boy	1 92	1 92	1 92

* Only one of these.

III. FOUNDRIES, MACHINE-SHOPS, AND IRON WORKS.

Wages paid per week of sixty hours in foundries, machine-shops, and iron works, in Barranquilla consular district.

Occupations.	Lowest.	Highest.
Railroad shops :		
Master mechanic	$30 22	$30 22
Shop foreman	16 12	16 12
Mechanic	12 09	12 09
Blacksmiths	12 09	12 09
Helpers	6 04	6 04

IV. GLASS-WORKERS.

There are no glass workers in the country. A glass manufactory was started near Bogota, but did not succeed.

V. MINES AND MINING.

Wages paid per day or week of sixty hours in and in connection with the gold placer mines in Barranquilla consular district, United States of Colombia.

Occupations.	Lowest.	Highest.
Foreman	$30 22	$30 22
Engineers	24 18	24 18
Laborers, washers	4 84	7 74
Clerks	16 12	16 12

There are a few mines working in this consular district. These are gold placer, and are worked very simply. They are exploring for copper, coal, petroleum, and asphaltum.

VI. RAILWAY EMPLOYÉS.

Wages paid per month to railway employés in Barranquilla consular district.

Occupations.	Average wages.	Occupations.	Average wages.
Managers	$201 50	Foreman of shop	$64 48
Cashier	80 60	Master carpenter	64 48
Assistant cashier	40 30	Road foreman	32 24
Clerks	32 24	Linemen	32 24
Ticket agents	56 42	Switchmen	24 18
Telegraph operators	36 27	Track boss	32 24
Storekeeper	80 60	Captain of tugboats	80 60
Assistant storekeeper	48 36	Engineer of tug boats*	80 60
Check clerks	40 30	Seamen*	20 95
Master mechanic	120 90	Pilots*	32 24
Conductor	64 48	Bargemen*	25 79
Engine driver	48 36	Porter	16 12

* Put with railway employés, as they work under the control of the railway company.

VII. SHIP-YARDS AND SHIP-BUILDING.

There are no ship-yards established here.

The river steamers are built abroad and erected here under the management of foreigners sent out with the material. Flat-boats, canoes, and bungoes are built and all classes of vessels are repaired by house carpenters. If any modeling is to be done, plans must come from abroad.

VIII. SEAMEN'S WAGES.

Wages paid per month to seamen in Barranquilla consular district.

Occupations.	Lowest.	Highest.	Average.
Steamers, river :			
Captains	$48 36	$241 80	$120 90
Pilots	64 48	120 90	80 60
Pursers	32 24	48 36	48 36
Engineers...	72 54	120 90	120 90
Second engineers...	48 36	64 48	48 36
Mates..	16 12	40 30	24 18
Firemen	12 09	16 12	12 09
Stewards...	16 12	32 24	24 18
Superintendents	161 20	403 00	....
Agents*..			
Steamers, ocean :			
Captain		80 60	....
Engineer		80 60	....
Seamen	8 06	20 95	....
Pilots		32 24	....
Bargemen		25 79	....
Canoe-men and bargemen:			
Pilots	24 18	80 60	32 24
Canoe-men...	7 68	24 18	....

* Five per cent. commission of the freight receipts.

IX. STORE AND SHOP WAGES.

Wages paid per month of three hundred hours in stores, wholesale and retail, to males and females, in Barranquilla consular district.

Occupations.	Lowest.	Highest.	Average.
Corresponding clerk	$24 18	$120 90	$80 60
Bookkeepers	24 18	120 90	40 30
Salesmen...	6 48	32 24	16 12
Apprentices	4 03	8 06	4 03
Errand boy	4 03	8 06	8 06
Storage *			

* One-half per cent. commission.

Many of the retail stores are attended by the members of the family, and consequently no salaries are paid.

X. HOUSEHOLD WAGES IN TOWNS AND CITIES.

Wages paid per month to household servants (towns and cities) in Barranquilla consular district.

Occupations.	Lowest.	Highest.	Average.
Cooks..	$7 24	$16 12	$12 09
Water-carriers..	2 42	9 67	4 84
Nurses...	7 24	16 12	12 09
Waiters..	4 84	16 12	8 06
Washerwomen	12 09	16 12	12 09
Seamstresses...	8 06	24 18	16 12

XI. AGRICULTURAL WAGES.

Wages paid per week to agricultural laborers and household (country) servants in Barranquilla consular district, with board.

Occupations.	Lowest.	Highest.
Farm hands..	$4 84	$20 15
Woodmen...	4 84	20 15
Cattle men	4 84	20 15
Women servants...	(*)	8 06

* Board.

XII. Corporation Employés.

Wages paid per month to the corporation employés in the city of Barranquilla, United States of Colombia.

Occupations.	Wages.	Occupations.	Wages.
Governor	$120 00	Policemen	$12 09
Mayor	120 90	Servants	4 84
Secretaries	56 42	Judges	161 20
Chief of police	80 60	Interpreter	48 36

XIII. Government Departments and Offices.

Wages paid per month of three hundred hours to employés in Government departments and offices, exclusive of tradesmen and laborers, in Barranquilla consular district.

Occupations.	Pay.	Occupations.	Pay.
ARMY.*		CUSTOM-HOUSE.	
General (army*)	$201 50	Collector	$201 50
Colonel	141 05	Assistant	120 90
Lieutenant-colonel	100 75	Storekeeper	48 36
Major	80 60	Weighmaster	72 54
Captain	65 49	Clerks	32 24
Lieutenant	50 37	Captain of the port	80 60
Ensign	40 30	Interpreter	48 36
Private	12 09	Guardsmen	20 15
		Inspectors	120 90
		Laborers	24 18

* In time of war all officers receive three times this amount of pay.

XV. Printers and Printing Offices.

Statement showing the wages paid per week of sixty hours to printers (compositors, pressmen, proof-readers, &c.) in Barranquilla consular district.

Occupations.	Lowest.	Highest.
Editors	$8 06	$40 30
Printers	6 45	16 12
Apprentices	81	2 42

COST OF LIVING.

The cost of living to the laboring classes varies greatly in this consular district; and it may be well to refer to my report on " Labor in Colombia," printed in the United States Consular Reports, No. 34, October, 1883. It is perfectly safe to say the cost of living to the work-people here is equal to their wages.

WAGES PAST AND PRESENT.

The rates of wages have not changed since 1878.

HABITS OF THE WORKING CLASSES.

The working classes are steady and trustworthy for a time, but owing to the facility with which their necessities are supplied, they are not as much disposed to laborious industry as they might be. Their vices are those attendant upon drinking. They do not save.

FEELING BETWEEN EMPLOYÉ AND EMPLOYER.

As this is a free country, employer and employé affiliate freely, and the effect is a general interest in any subject affecting the community, and the educational standing is thereby increased. Much can be accomplished by appealing to their citizenship which would otherwise remain undone.

ORGANIZED CONDITION OF LABOR.

There is no organized condition of labor or capital. All business is conducted in accordance with the local conditions which surround capital or labor, and vary in detail as the localities vary. While the laws authorize the governor to bind men to work as per any agreement which may be made before him, yet few, if any, of the authorities would aid in compelling men to carry out their contract should they see fit to break it.

PREVALENCY OF STRIKES.

Strikes are unknown here. Most disagreements are settled by arbitration.

FOOD PURCHASES.

The working people are free to purchase what and where they please. They would resent any other treatment. They are paid every Saturday night in silver or bank bills. It is sometimes customary to give each workman 20 cents per day to buy the day's provisions.

CO-OPERATIVE SOCIETIES.

These societies are unknown here.

GENERAL CONDITION OF THE WORKING PEOPLE.

The homes of the working classes do not vary greatly, excepting those in the larger cities who may belong to a better class than those in the small towns or country. In the country a man can locate his house in the woods without fear of disturbance, erect the same in one day from the wild growth surrounding him, and soon have a clearing made upon which he can grow three crops of corn in a year. He must not plant more than his children can protect, however, from the wild parrots and animals, which like cultivated food. The plantain and banana produce within eight months from the seed, and thereafter, without much care, yield a continual harvest. The yam and yuca, a species of potato, yield quickly and are very hardy. Sugar-cane once planted is always present. With these productions growing around him, and the river near to supply him with fish, the native is happy, depending for his meat upon the wild animals he can kill with spears made from the lance-wood of the country, or which he can entrap with the variety of contrivances he has the faculty of making. His only necessity for money is to provide salt, rum, tobacco, clothes, and the machete, a long knife which he uses for every purpose, from picking his teeth to cultivating his lands. The money is gained by work for some richer neighbor; by cutting wood for the river steamers; by catching and drying fish for the city markets, or by cultivating the ground in excess of his own requirements. Fruits grow very abundantly. By planting the necessary trees the native secures his marketing very easily, if living near a large city.

The number of articles which he obtains, the purchase of which requires money, depends in a great measure on the facility for securing remunerative work and the energy of the man. The salt for the food of the family amounts to very little, and becomes an important factor only, when fishing or hunting, to make the results of his labor available for the market. The rum of the country varies from the Chicha, which is merely fermented cane-juice, to the distilled liquor. As taken by the poorer people, the liquor is colorless and cheap. The tax imposed by the municipal authorities varies from $1 to $3 per demijohn. Tobacco is grown in certain sections of the country, and as men, women, and children generally use it, this article has become a necessity, and money goes for this as long as any remains. The clothing of these families amounts to very little, as the children usually go without any until they attain an age at which they are self-sustaining; and as neither hat, shoes, nor stockings are required, this expense is saved. If any wish these articles, they make them from the fibers of the trees and plants near them. The men wear hats, shirts, pantaloons, and shoes; the hat is plaited from the reeds of the swamps; the shoes are cut from the tanned hide of any animal they may kill, domestic or wild, pig or alligator. This shoe is simply a piece of the leather cut more or less according to the shape of the sole of the foot, and fastened on by strings. The clothes are made of coarse cotton or linen goods. Two suits will last a man a year. The actual cash required to supply this family one year would be about as follows: Actual necessities, $8; rum and tobacco, $10.40. There are many of this class in the country. In Barranquilla a laboring man can get board for $6.20 per month.

Laborers in the city and on cattle ranches eat the most meat. They will have meat daily, if possible, or at least three times a week, and house servants expect it twice a day. Salt fish is, however, the main support, and as the city laborer must purchase everything, he is better paid, as will be seen from the following statement:

A BARRANQUILLA MASON'S STATEMENT.

I am thirty years old. I am a mason. I have a wife and six children, the oldest ten years and the youngest one month old. I receive $1.61 per day. The average wages paid to masons is $1.29 per day. I have work about two-thirds of the time. I begin work at 6 o'clock in the morning and quit at 5 o'clock in the afternoon, and have one hour for breakfast at 10 o'clock in the forenoon. Supper comes after the day's work is done. My wife does not earn anything in addition to my earnings. With general good health I can earn about $380 per year. I pay per annum as follows:

Items.	Cost.	Items.	Cost.
For rent of house and grounds	$72 00	For religious purposes	$8 60
For water, brought on donkeys' backs, at 10 cents a load	29 82	For repair to tools, &c.	15 00
		For tobacco, rum, sweets, &c.	36 50
For clothing for self and family	77 40	For sundries	9 37
For food, about	116 80		
For residence tax	3 22	Total	380 00
For doctor's bills, as per last year	12 09		

My family and myself have coffee and corn bread. The latter is made out of corn pounded fine, mixed with water and salt, wrapped in a corn husk, and boiled. For breakfast we have dried fish, plantain and yam, yuca and beans boiled together into a "sancoche" (a soup); for dessert, melons, mangoes, bananas, or other fruits. For dinner we have a meat "sancoche." Sometimes we have bread; always coffee, or a drink made by dissolving the native sugar in water, called guarapo. It is difficult to save anything with my family, and the very little that is saved is by my wife from her chickens, pigs, and goats.

The standard of the laboring class is improving slowly. Their natural physical condition is one of strength; but the climate does not promote longevity, and consequently there are but few old men.

RELATIONS BETWEEN EMPLOYER AND EMPLOYÉ.

The relations between employer and employé are those of amity and good-will, as the laboring man will not work for money only, but requires to be treated as a freeman.

POLITICAL RIGHTS.

Every man, under the law, has the right to vote, but comparatively few exercise that right; consequently the workingman has little or no influence on legislation.

The revenues of the General and State governments are raised by impost duties; the local tax by imposts on rum, rents, and licenses; also by a direct tax of two days' labor annually or its equivalent in cash.

The tendency of legislation is to extend railways and open water communication by subsidizing various projects, and thus benefit the laboring classes and give greater facilities to actual settlers on Government lands.

PART II.—FEMALE LABOR.

Any statement of the number of women and children employed in this consular district in industrial pursuits, not including ordinary household duties, or domestic servants, would be mere guess-work, as there are no statistics to aid one, and no returns by the manufacturer to the Government. Therefore I can give but a general idea.

In the manufacturing and mechanical pursuits women make hats, mats, and pottery. They do not work by the day, but sell their own wares. Their number is small. Commercial, including transportation, number small.

Very few women in this country fill any of the professional and personal occupations, excepting those of teachers, hotel and boarding-house keepers, laundresses, and musicians. The last two classes abound.

In the pursuit of agriculture the women and children often take the place of the men, and cultivate the ground and market the produce, while the head of the house is fishing or attending to other matters. Where gold is washed out of running streams, it is not unusual to see husband and wife washing the dirt side by side, but women never work in the mines for wages.

It is supposed there is a surplus of females in the country, and that a majority of them are workers; but it is impossible to classify or number them. It may, perhaps, be safely said they do the heaviest part of the work, and yet are in complete subjection to their lords.

The average wages paid to female adults do not vary from those paid to males, when they perform the same work. The hours of labor are the same, and in general the same remarks may be applied to both sexes.

THE COLOMBIAN WORKINGMAN.

The laboring man is willing to work, docile in his nature, apt in learning, and, when treated with the kindness and consideration due to human nature, will accomplish any reasonable task assigned him. His wages are low, but on a scale with his requirements. Without any great incentive to improve his condition, the innate desire of gain and comfort causes his exertions, and the inbred principle of barter makes merchants of all of them, and Colombia has the bone and sinew and natural resources to raise her into a great producing country.

THOMAS M. DAWSON,
Consul.

UNITED STATES CONSULATE,
  Barranquilla, August 23, 1884.

MEDELLIN.

REPORT BY CONSUL ESMOND.

In accordance with the "Labor Circular" from the Department of State of February 15, 1884, I have the honor to submit the following in response thereto:

RATES OF WAGES.

The rates for every class of labor in this State vary only in the expertness of one laborer over another, independent of the vocation, whether mining, mechanical, or agricultural. Price per day, from 4 rials to 1 peso (32 to 80 cents), and if away from their homes board included.

COST OF LIVING.

The cost of living is greatly dependent upon the man's disposition to work extra hours or not, as the natural fertility and cheapness of the ground renders it easy for each laborer to possess a garden spot sufficient to produce the necessaries of life, with but little taken from his wages to accomplish the same. Nearly all grow their own corn, platinos (species of banana), and yucas, and in addition to these their food is simple, and costs, according to the locality, whether mining or agricultural, as follows:

Mining districts.—Panela,* 2 to 6 pounds for 2 rials (16 cents); beans per almud (17½ pounds), 8 to 20 rials (64 to 160 cents); beef is used very sparingly, 15 to 25 cents per pound.

Agricultural districts.—Panela, 7 to 15 pounds, 2 rials (16 cents); beans per almud, 5 to 12 rials (40 to 96 cents); beef, 7½ to 12½ cents per pound.

The few who do not raise corn, platanes, and yucas need to pay for the same in mining districts. Corn per almud (17½ pounds), 6 to 10 rials (48 to 80 cents); platinos and yucas, 5 to 10 rials (40 to 80 cents) per 100.

Corn per almud, 2½ to 6 rials (20 to 48 cents); platinos and yucas, 2 to 4 rials (16 to 32 cents) per 100. Rice, cheese, and butter are luxuries, and bread from flour of wheat is a rarity. The "representative man" is generally in debt, keeps no account of his income or expenditures, and any definite idea of the costs per capita of his family living per month or year would be quite troublesome even for him to obtain.

The clothing consists of trousers of coarse cotton cloth, costing from 9 to 13 rials (72 to 104 cents), and a shirt of white cotton or a fancy-

---

* Crude sugar in 1-pound cakes. The "staff of life" of the laboring class of this State.

checked calico, costing 4 to 10 rials (32 to 80 cents). Needing neither boots nor coats, the cost of clothing is inconsiderable.

The majority have small houses of their own. Those not having them live with relatives and escape rents.

WAGES PAST AND PRESENT.

Am not aware whether report upon Labor Circular was made for this district in 1878 or not.

By inquiry I find that the wages of all classes have advanced 20 per cent. since that date without any change in the conditions then prevailing other than the present increased and increasing currency of bank bills in lieu of the silver coin, concerning which bills the laboring class, possibly without reason, are very suspicious.

HABITS OF THE WORKING CLASSES.

The majority steady, but not trustworthy; faithful, but as a man knowing that he has to work and is watched. Many are trustworthy and receive from their employers confidences that if misplaced would cause losses of thousands of dollars.

They have small chance of "saving," as their families are large, and until such time as a man has a family expense of his own he is called upon and generally does assist that of his parents.

The principal cause of evil is the extreme laxity in enforcing good laws, and the rank poison, aguardiente (new white rum), sold at nearly every house on the road or in towns at less than 2 cents per glass.

FEELING BETWEEN EMPLOYER AND EMPLOYÉ.

The employer pays the least he can, taking advantage of every circumstance of the man, and demands all the work the man is capable of executing; the man working for the best price he can get, for such time as his convenience permits, and leaves without notice, no matter how great inconvenience or loss the employer may suffer thereby. A contract to labor a specified time at a specified price is of no account.

A feeling of distrust exists between employer and employé to the extent of preventing the carrying to success any considerable work of importance depending upon the services of the laboring classes.* This distrust I believe hinders in a great degree the prosperity of the community.

There are laws upon the statutes that would correct the cause of this distrust, but they are not enforced.

There are no labor organizations within this State, and strikes are unknown.

FOOD PURCHASES.

They are free to purchase where they choose. Some mines have stores of their own, but neither ask or expect the men to purchase there if they do not wish to.

Establishments in or near cities pay weekly in coin and bank bills. Mines distant from cities pay every month and during the month if requested—all in silver coin.

CO-OPERATIVE SOCIETIES, ETC.

There are none here.

* Since writing the above, in speaking with several prominent capitalists and merchants, they tell me that such is the fact.

GENERAL CONDITION OF THE WORKING CLASSES.

From the fact that they can save but a very small sum, if anything at all, for old age, accident or sickness, their general condition is bad.

In that it is true that to all who care to work opportunity is never lacking at wages that will secure the necessaries of life (with which their ambitions are satisfied), one might say their condition was good, for no severe seasons or failure of employers to pay ever distresses them.

They live harmoniously, each man securing a habitation for his family by themselves, it being very rare indeed for two families to live under the same roof.

Their homes are in small houses of two or three rooms, beside the cook room (generally a small "lintern" unconnected with the other rooms), neither having a floor other than the earth, and without chairs or furniture, and generally lacking a table; a rude bench upon one side of the main room serving for a "settee" during the day and bed at night for those of the family who cannot "pack in" in the bedroom proper. These rooms are kept clean and tidy. Every family keeps a few hens and a pig to fatten, the pig being their only savings bank, the receipts from the sale of which are not used for living expenses, but in reducing the little store debt or re enforcing the clothing of the family.

Food.—At 5 to 6 a. m. agua dulce (sugar and water) and one arepa (cake of corn bread); at 9 to 10 a. m. breakfast brought to the work, consisting of sancocho (a mixed soup of yucas, bananas, and a small piece of meat), one-fourth pound of panila (crude sugar in cake), and one arepa, the meal occupying 20 or 30 minutes. Dinner brought into the works at 3 p. m., occupying 30 minutes, and consisting of sancocho, a large dish of boiled beans, a pint of masamora (similar to the American farmer's "hulled corn"), and one-fourth pound of panila. After work at night, the agua dulce and arepa, same as in the morning.

Clothing.—Working suit of pants and shirt so skillfully patched as to completely hide the original material. Hat of straw, cheap affair. For Sundays and feast days, clean and tidy trousers and shirt of fancy-colored design, surmounted by the cloth ruana (poncho). A fine hat of home manufacture costs from $2 to $6.

With the exceedingly strongly marked line that exists between the employer and employé, and the reciprocal distrust between them, with the money in the hands of a few, it seems evident that the chances for bettering the condition of the laboring classes here are very slight. Their moral condition is generally good; the physical more than good, and the majority take a pride in performing long and arduous tasks when directed what to do, or working at tasks that they understand how to perform.

The influences that surround them for good or evil are, upon the one hand, the church and family; the other, lax administration of the law and free rum shops.

STATEMENT OF A WORKINGMAN.

A representative man of the working class answers as follows:

Question. How old are you?—Answer. Forty-two.
Q. What is your trade?—A. Rough carpenter and experienced miner.
Q. How much of a family have you?—A. Wife and six children.
Q. What wages do you receive per day?—A. Four to eight reals (32 to 65 cents) for twelve hours' work.
Q. How much time out of the twelve hours do you have for meals?—A. One half hour for breakfast and one half hour for dinner.

Q. Can you lay up any money upon those wages?—A. No, not a cent.

Q. What do you do, then, in case of sickness or you suffer an accident?—A. Oh, get along some way; what ever God wills (*lo que Dios quiera*); run in debt maybe, or if the wife has the pig fattened, we sell it.

Q. Can you tell me how much it costs you for your living per month or year?—A. No; only that it is all I earn, whether I work every day or not.

Q. Are you contented with this?—A. (with a shrug of the shoulders and raising of eyebrows). Why not? I might be worse off. I only worry when the wife or children are sick.

SAFETY OF EMPLOYÉS.

No means furnished for safety nor provision for care of laborers in case of accident; no thought given by employer to the moral or physical condition of his laborers.

The relations between the two are civil, polite, and with outward kindness, the laborer taking offense at any seeming "bull-dozing" or severe criticism, and may stop work, however urgent it may be.

POLITICAL RIGHTS.

They have all the political rights of others. Without ambition or organization, they have no influence upon legislation whatever. There having been no taxes collected upon real estate or personal property, the laboring class pay nearly all the taxes, in the way of high prices (comparatively) for all things purchased, as *all taxes are levied upon the importations of goods and merchandise into the State.* Recently there has been passed a law to tax real estate, and is now being put into effect.

Present legislation is upon questions that would not appear to effect labor or the working people.

CAUSES OF EMIGRATION.

The laboring classes do not emigrate. They vegetate, work, and die in or near the State in which they were born.

I deem it but just to say that from a personal experience of two years in employing a large number of these laborers, they are more *faithful* and *better workers* than the railroad and canal building laborers of our own country, and although the native employer is indifferent to the moral and physical condition of his laborers, he is very charitable to the infirm, aged, or crippled.

FEMALE LABOR.

In this State the female industrial labor of any number congregated is confined to the one hundred or more in the Zancudo gold and silver mines, and the seventy-five to one hundred carrying coal for the evaporization of salt water at Heliconia.

In the mines they are paid according to the amount of labor performed, consisting of wheeling or carrying mineral from the mines to the mill, earning from 3 to 6 reals per day (24 to 48 cents.) There is but very little, if any, difference between the work and the pay of the men and the women.

In the salt works at Heliconia the works pay a stipulated price per 84 arrobas (2,100 pounds) of coal delivered, the coal mines being located from 300 to 1,000 yards distant; the women purchasing from the mines and "backing" or carrying the same in bags (100 to 200 pounds each) upon their heads to the works. They gain for this from 4 to 10 reals (32 to 80 cents) per day.

Neither of the above descriptions of work of women has produced any effect upon the wages of the men. Like the men, they are uneducated beyond the forms of the church (Catholic).

Apart from the above are numerous women working in the tobacco districts as "selecters" and "strippers," realizing from 4 to 5 rials (32 to 40 cents) per day.

Many women throughout the State employ their spare time in making so-called Panama hats, thousands of which are annually sold at the capital and for exportation. The labor is performed at their homes, and this scattered product is so great that it would be a hazardous venture to erect a factory for this class of work.

E. RICHARD ESMOND,

Consul.

United States Consulate,

Medellin, May 28, 1884.

I. GENERAL TRADES.

Wages paid per day of twelve hours in Medellin.

Occupations.	Lowest.	Highest.	Average.
BUILDING TRADES.			
Bricklayers	$0 40	$0 60	$0 50
Plasterers	40	60	50
Tenders	20	30	25
Plumbers	40	70	50
Assistants	20	40	25
Carpenters	1 00	1 50	1 00
OTHER TRADES.			
Blacksmiths	80	1 20	1 00
Strikers (apprentices)	20	30	20
Bookbinders	50	80	70
Brick-makers	40	80	50
Brewers	30	50	40
Distillers	1 20	3 00	2 50
Drivers (boys)	20	60	25
Cab and carriage drivers	20	60	25
Laborers, porters, &c	20	50	40
Potters	40	1 00	60
Printers	40	80	50
Teachers public schools *	30 00	60 00	40 00
Saddle and harness makers	50	1 20	60
Tailors	50	1 50	75

* Per month.

NOTE.—All wages marked in American values, the peso or dollar of Colombia being the equivalent (less the premium of exchange) of the American gold dollar. Premium deducted at present rates of exchange (25 per cent.) to procure the prices above.

II. FACTORIES, MILLS, ETC.

Wages paid per day of twelve hours in factories or mills in Medellin, Antioquia, United States of Colombia.

Occupations.	Lowest.	Highest.	Average.
MILLS.*			
Foreman or superintendent	$0 60	$0 80	$0 60
Fireman	50	60	50
Laborers	40	60	40
FACTORY.†			
Superintendent and director	3 00	3 00	3 00
Laborers	25	40	35
Foreman	1 20	1 20	1 20
Assistant foreman	90	90	90

* Ten or twelve small mills, making sugar and sirup, all of which are equipped with English machinery.
† One factory for pottery, constructed by Germans, and producing poor work.

III. FOUNDRIES, MACHINE-SHOPS, AND IRON WORKS.

Wages paid per day of twelve hours in foundries, machine-shops, and iron works in Medellin, Antioquia, United States of Colombia.

Occupations.	Lowest.	Highest.	Average.
BLAST-FURNACE.			
Superintendent and general foreman.....●	$2 00	....	$2 00
Helpers	40	$0 60	50
MACHINE-SHOP.*			
Superintendent of woodwork	2 50	....	2 50
Superintendent of machine-shop	2 50	....	2 50
Assistant superintendents	1 00	2 00	1 25

* Under the name of "School of Arts and Sciences," conducted by the State, in educating machinists and artisans.

V. MINES AND MINING.

Wages paid per day of twelve hours in and in connection with the majority of hydraulic and quartz mines in the State of Antioquia, United States of Colombia.

Occupations.	Lowest.	Highest.	Average.
Mines in a good climate and near a town of any size:			
Boys and helpers*	$0 15	$0 40	$0 25
Ordinary laborers *	25	60	40
Experienced native miners*	40	80	50
Mining boss, American, English, or Frenchman †	4 50	7 50	5 00
Superintendent and director*	5 00	10 00	7 00
Mines in a bad climate:			
Boys and helpers †	25	50	30
Ordinary laborers †	40	80	60
Experienced native miners †	60	1 50	80
Mining boss †	5 00	10 00	7 00
Superintendent and director †	8 00	12 50	10 00

* Without board and lodging.   † With board and lodging.

The board and lodging of men costs from 20 cents to $35 cents per man per day, according to the remoteness of the works from the base of supplies.

IX. STORE AND SHOP WAGES.

Wages paid per month in the generality of stores, wholesale and retail, to males in the district of Medellin, United States of Colombia.*

Occupations.	Lowest.	Highest.	Average.
Salesmen and first-class bookkeepers	$20 00	$150 00	$50 00
Clerks	8 00	50 00	30 00

* Have not seen any female employés in any store of the State up to date.

X. HOUSEHOLD WAGES IN TOWNS AND CITIES.

Wages paid per month to household servants (towns and cities) in the district of Medellin United States of Colombia.

Occupations.	Lowest.	Highest.	Average.
Female cooks	$1 50	$5 00	$2 40
Female general housework	80	3 00	2 00
Male servants, general work	2 00	6 00	3 50

XI. AGRICULTURAL WAGES.

Wages paid per month to agricultural laborers and household (country) servants in the di; trict of Medellin, with board and lodging.

Occupations.	Lowest.	Highest.	Average.
General out-door work	$3 00	$10 00	$8 00
Plowman, and men that can work oxen	6 00	20 00	12 00
Household servants of "general utility"	80	3 00	2 00

VENEZUELA.

LA GUAYRA.

REPORT BY CONSUL WINFIELD S. BIRD.

In reply to the questions contained in "Labor Circular" from the Department of State of date February 15 ultimo, the following observations are respectfully submitted:

MALE LABOR.

The rates of wages paid to all classes of laborers, as near as can be ascertained, are indicated in the tables hereto attached.

COST OF LIVING.

In general terms it may be stated that the cost of all provisions, except sugar, rice, and coffee, is nearly, if not quite, one hundred per cent. dearer than in the United States. This is made so by the enormous import duties paid on flour, lard, meats, &c. The cost of living increases, therefore, in the same ratio; or, to be practically accurate, board that

may be obtained in the United States for $16 per month costs in La
Guayra the sum of $28 per month. The prices of dry goods are from
33 to 40 per cent. dearer than in the United States. Rents in the city
are fully as dear as in cities of the same size in the United States, dwelling houses ranging from $5 to $40 per month, and business houses from
$20 to $60 per month.

WAGES PAST AND PRESENT.

No comparison, from personal knowledge, can be made between the
present rate of wages and that of 1878, nor between the conditions
prevalent then and those obtaining now; but from information, it is
presumed that the circumstances are not materially changed.

HABITS OF THE WORKING CLASSES.

As to the habits of the working classes, it may be said that they are
good enough in every respect except as to steady and faithful labor.
By nature and habit they are not industrious, nor, unless with intelligent direction, can they be trusted to accurately and promptly perform
any particular service. They are really shiftless and time-serving, and,
lacking the persistent energy and patience that characterize our farmer
and laborer. They delight in the oft-recurring feast days peculiar to
all Catholic countries, and lose no opportunity to let off rockets in honor
of patron saints, to have a dance at a baptism, and grand masquerades
at the carnival season. While they have not the proper appreciation
of the institution of marriage, it is also true that they are faithful in
their attachments and happy at home. They live in the to-day and
take no thought of the duties and responsibilities of to-morrow. The
poorer classes live on plantains, bananas, cassava, and vegetables, with
a small modicum of beef or fish daily, and are thus in their poverty enabled to defy famine. Their clothing, consonant with the climate, is always of coarse cotton goods, with native straw hats and leather sandals
for the feet. With all this, however, they are generally of remarkably
temperate habits, and are quite exempt from crime, in this respect comparing most favorably with any community in our own country. In
searching for the causes that affect their habits, as above generally
stated, it is naturally concluded that the delicious climate and spontaneous fruits of the soil combine to enervate them and that their filial respect and reverence for the priest and the church exercise a powerful
influence and restraint over them.

FEELING BETWEEN EMPLOYER AND EMPLOYÉ.

The feeling between employé and employer is one of mutual trust and
confidence, rarely betrayed on the part of either, as is too often the case
in some of our own communities.

LABOR ORGANIZATIONS AND STRIKES.

There are no organizations of either capital or labor.
As a consequence of the lack of labor unions strikes are unknown.

PAY AND FOOD PURCHASES.

The laborer receives his stipulated wages by the day, week, or month,
as the case may be, in silver currency, and is at liberty to purchase the
necessaries of life wherever he chooses.
There are no co-operative societies existing here.

GENERAL CONDITION OF THE LABORING CLASSES.

The question asked has already been answered in a general manner. As to the general condition of the common people, it may be added that, although poor, their wants are few and simple. Their houses are rude structures of adobe with thatched roofs and without window, chimney, or door shutter, to which the cats, dogs, pigs, and chickens have free access. A wick in a pan of grease serves for a lamp, an iron pot with some charcoal is a fair kitchen outfit, a flour-barrel inverted serves for a table, and some boards overlaid with straw suffice for a bed.

There are no mills or manufactories, properly so called, in this district.

POLITICAL RIGHTS.

The political rights enjoyed by workingmen in this Republic are fairly presumed to be the same as those pertaining to other classes, yet it may reasonably be doubted whether or not they generally exercise these rights, and if they are, in any degree, able to thereby influence legislation. They pay no local or general taxes; and, in legislation, their civil and political rights, although fully recognized, are not a matter of disturbance or agitation.

There is no emigration from, and but little immigration to Venezuela.

FEMALE LABOR.

After proper inquiry it is found impracticable to furnish any facts in reference to female labor, simply because the women do not work. It should be said that education is making fair progress amongst the lower classes, owing to the system of free schools established throughout the country, and, if there is any good future to be hoped for from the rising generation, it must come through this channel.

WINFIELD S. BIRD,
Consul.

UNITED STATES CONSULATE,
La Guayra, May 5, 1884.

I. GENERAL TRADES.

Wages paid per week of sixty hours in La Guayra.

Occupations.	Lowest.	Highest.	Average.
BUILDING TRADES.			
Bricklayers			
Hod-carriers			
Masons			
Tenders	$3 47	$11 58	$6 95
Plasterers			
Tenders			
Carpenters	3 47	11 58	6 95
Foreign gas-fitters	23 16	30 11	27 79
OTHER TRADES.			
Bakers	26 94	34 63	30 00
Blacksmiths	10 27	16 42	12 00
Strikers	4 11	5 36	4 50
Bookbinders	6 15	9 24	7 50
Brick-makers	7 00	8 40	7 75

Wages paid per week of sixty hours in La Guayra—Continued.

Occupations.	Lowest.	Highest.	Average.
OTHER TRADES—Continued.			
Butchers	$8 76	$10 15	$9 00
Cabinet-makers	6 95	13 90	9 26
Confectioners	4 81	8 65	6 73
Cigar-makers	9 24	11 55	10 00
Coopers *			
Drivers on street railways	6 12	8 43	7 00
Dyers *			
Engravers *			
Gardeners	4 63	9 26	5 79
Hatters	11 58	16 21	13 90
Horseshoers *			
Laborers, porters, &c	7 00	8 40	7 75
Lithographers	14 42	28 84	19 23
Printers	7 70	8 24	8 00
Teachers, public schools	7 20	11 54	7 70
Saddle and harness makers	11 58	17 37	14 00
Stevedores	† 1 93	† 1 93	† 1 93
Tanners	9 24	11 55	10 00
Tailors	9 60	11 50	10 00
Telegraph operators	4 81	7 69	5 77
Tinsmiths	5 75	6 90	6 00
Weavers (outside of mills)			
Chocolate factory	4 81	4 81	4 81
Shoemakers	6 95	17 37	10 00

* Per job.   † Per day.

II. FACTORIES, MILLS, ETC.

Wages paid per month in factories or mills in La Guayra.

[Week of 54 hours.]

Occupations.	Average wages.
Superintendent	$110 00
Engineer	50 00
Laborers	30 00

VI. RAILWAY EMPLOYÉS.

Wages paid per month to railway employés (those engaged about stations, as well as those engaged on the engines and cars, linemen, railroad laborers, &c.) in La Guayra Station, Veneznela.

Occupations.	Fixed wages.	Occupations.	Fixed wages.
Station master	$121 25	Foreman porters	$50 00
Chief clerk and cashier	76 92	Porters	24 62
Booking clerk	46 15	Telegraph clerk	76 92
Goods clerks	50 00	Engine drivers	87 30
Checkers	29 23	Firemen	58 20
Foreman of goods-shed	50 00	Cleaners	34 62
Shunter, foreman	50 00	Plate layers	87 30
Shunters, under	29 23	Laborers, permanent way	24 62
Pointsmen	29 23	Conductors:	
Night watchmen	34 62	Passenger	76 92
Messengers	29 23	Freight	61 54

VIII. SEAMEN'S WAGES.

Wages paid per month to seamen (officers and men) distinguishing between ocean, coast, and river navigation, and between sail and steam, in La Guayra.

Occupations.	Lowest.	Highest.	Average.
SAIL VESSEL, COAST.			
Captain	$19 23	$34 62	$28 95
Second official	15 39	23 08	23 16
Sailor	7 70	9 25	8 08
STEAM VESSELS.			
Captain	46 15	57 69	50 97
Second officer	38 46	46 15	41 36
Sailor	11 55	11 55	11 55
Fireman	15 39	19 23	17 32
First engineer	76 96	96 15	86 57
Second engineer	57 69	61 54	59 62
Purser	38 46	46 15	43 28

Wages paid for ocean, coast, and river navigation alike.

IX. STORE AND SHOP WAGES.

Wages paid per month in dry goods, &c., stores, wholesale and retail, to males, in La Guayra.

Occupations.	Lowest.	Highest.	Average.
WHOLESALE.			
Bookkeeper	$61 54	$76 92	$65 62
Chief clerk	92 31	115 38	101 32
Cashier	76 92	92 31	81 06
Clerks	30 77	61 54	38 60
Porters	38 46	46 15	40 53
RETAIL.			
Clerks	38 46	46 15	40 53

X. HOUSEHOLD WAGES IN TOWNS AND CITIES.

Wages paid per month with board to household servants (towns and cities) in La Guayra, with board.

Occupations.	Lowest.	Highest.
Servants	$6 15	$11 55
Maid servants	3 08	7 70
Cooks	3 08	7 70
Stable boys	3 08	6 15

XI. AGRICULTURAL WAGES.

Wages paid per day to agricultural laborers and household (country) servants in district of La Guayra, with board and lodging.

Occupations.	Lowest.	Highest.
Agricultural laborers	$0 50	$0 80
Other laborers	40	50
Boys and girls	15	25

XII. CORPORATION EMPLOYÉS.

Wages paid per month to the corporation employés in the city of La Guayra.

[Week of 60 hours.]

Occupations.	Salary.*	Occupations.	Salary.*
Mayor	$123 52	Jailer	$27 02
Secretary	69 48	Inspector of market	30 88
Secretary of council	69 48	City physician	30 88
Collector	123 52	Inspector of woods	23 16
Bookkeeper and cashier	54 04	Lamp-lighter	18 13
Chief of police	46 32	Porters	19 30
Policeman	23 55	Municipal porter	23 16

* These are fixed wages.

XIV. TRADES AND LABOR—GOVERNMENT EMPLOY.

Wages paid by the month to the trades and laborers in Government employ in La Guayra

Occupations.	Fixed wages.*	Occupations.	Fixed wages.*
Collector of customs	$205 86	Customs officer	$30 88
Deputy collector	154 40	Captain of launch	30 88
Cashier	92 64	Interpreter	40 45
Bookkeeper	92 64	Copyists	44 20
Liquidator	123 52	Boatmen	42 46
Assistant liquidator	77 20	Physicians (no salary)	
Assistant cashier	43 23	Harbor clerk	30 88
Assistant bookkeeper	43 23	Director coast trade	61 76
Store guard	92 64	Judge	92 64
Weighmaster	92 64	Porters	45 03
First captain coast guard	92 64	Laborers	12 35
Second captain coast guard	92 64	Ship police	30 88

* These wages do not vary.

XV. PRINTERS AND PRINTING OFFICES.

Statement showing the wages paid per week of fifty-four hours to printers (compositors, press-men, proof-readers, &c.) in Caracas and La Guayra.

Occupations.	Lowest.	Highest.	Average.
Compositor	$8 00	$24 00	$12 00
Pressman	9 00	16 00	10 00
Proof-reader	12 00		
Typesetter	6 00	10 00	8 00
Newsboy	4 00	7 00	5 00

MARACAIBO.

REPORT BY CONSUL PLUMACHER.

Referring to the Labor Circular issued by the Department, and bearing date of February 15 last, I have the honor to inclose the forms there-with sent, which I have filled out to the best of my ability.

In Part I of the circular, relating to "male labor," there are many questions to which answers can hardly be given, as far as this country is concerned.

COST OF LIVING.

The necessary cost of living among the laboring classes, as referred to in question 2, may be estimated at about 30 cents per day for each individual, and the rent of a small house to accommodate, say, a family of five persons will amount to perhaps $5 per month.

The chief food consumed is fresh and salt meat, fish, and plantains, meat commanding a price of from 10 to 15 cents per pound, and plantains being sold at an average rate of 20 cents per hundred.

The clothing worn costs but little, consisting, as is natural in this hot climate, of cotton fabrics. It may be said in this connection that neatness is the rule among this class.

WAGES PAST AND PRESENT.

In reply to question 3, wages, since 1878, have somewhat lowered and the prices of the necessaries of life are higher.

HABITS OF THE WORKING CLASSES.

As to question 4, the working classes are improvident and by no means steady, though it can scarcely be said that as a rule they are untrustworthy.

LABOR ORGANIZATIONS.

Referring to the remaining questions under the head of "male labor," it may be briefly stated, as will be readily understood when the condition of this country is taken into consideration, that there can be no labor organizations nor strikes.

FOOD PURCHASES.

A negative answer may be returned to all the inquiries except No. 8.

The working people purchase where they please, and are paid in silver, which, in Venezuela, comprises coins of all countries.

FEMALE LABOR.

Regarding female labor, there is still less to be said.

Female employés, as we understand the term, are unknown, the occupations of women being confined to domestic service, washing and ironing and sewing.

The undeveloped condition of this section renders it exceedingly difficult to reply satisfactorily to questions regarding labor, but the inclosed returns, which I have collected with much exertion and some difficulty, will, I hope, give a fair general idea.

E. M. PLUMACHER,
Consul.

UNITED STATES CONSULATE,
Maracaibo, May 19, 1884.

I. General Trades.

Wages paid per week in Maracaibo.

Occupations.	Lowest.	Highest.	Average.
BUILDING TRADES.			
Bricklayers	$9 60	$15 00	$12 30
Hod-carriers	3 60	4 80	4 20
Masons	9 60	18 00	13 80
Tenders	3 00	4 80	4 20
Plasterers	12 00	14 40	13 20
Tenders	3 60	4 80	4 20
Slaters	12 00	14 40	13 20
Roofers	6 60	13 20	9 90
Tenders	3 60	4 80	4 20
Plumbers	15 00	17 50	16 25
Assistants	7 20	12 00	9 60
Carpenters	7 20	15 00	16 10
Gasfitters	15 00	21 00	18 00
OTHER TRADES.			
Bakers	10 00	14 00	12 00
Blacksmiths	18 00	22 00	15 00
Strikers	4 80	7 20	6 00
Bookbinders	12 00	16 00	14 00
Brick-makers	12 00	15 00	13 50
Butchers	12 00	15 00	13 50
Brass-founders	18 00	34 00	21 00
Cabinet-makers	12 00	16 00	14 00
Confectioners	12 00	18 00	15 00
Cigar-makers	8 00	14 00	11 00
Coopers	24 00	30 00	27 00
Cutlers	16 00	20 00	18 00
Distillers	12 00	15 00	13 50
Drivers	8 00	12 00	10 00
Draymen and teamsters	12 00	15 00	13 50
Cab and carriage	8 00	12 00	10 00
Street railways	8 00	12 00	10 00
Dyers	8 00	12 00	10 00
Engravers	18 00	24 00	21 00
Furriers	12 00	15 00	13 50
Gardeners	8 00	12 00	10 00
Hatters	16 00	22 00	20 00
Horse-shoers	18 00	24 00	21 00
Jewelers	20 00	26 00	23 00
Laborers, porters, &c	6 00	10 00	8 00
Lithographers	18 00	24 00	21 00
Millwrights	28 00	28 00	28 00
Nail-makers (hand)	14 00	18 00	16 00
Printers	3 50	12 50	8 00
Teachers, public schools	12 00	16 00	14 00
Saddle and harness makers	18 00	24 00	21 00
Sailmakers	12 00	16 00	14 00
Stevedores	12 00	24 00	18 00
Tanners	12 00	16 00	14 00
Tailors	12 00	18 00	15 00
Telegraph operators	14 00	20 00	17 00
Tinsmiths	14 00	24 00	19 00
Weavers (outside of mills)	8 00	20 00	14 00

II. Factories, Mills, Etc.

Wages paid per week of sixty hours in factories or mills in Maracaibo, Venezuela.

Occupations.	Lowest.	Highest.	Average.
Superintendent	$24 00	$32 00	$28 00
Overseers	18 00	20 00	19 00
Laborers	8 00	12 00	10 00

We have only a few factories here; one cocoa-oil factory, one ice-factory, and a few soap and candle factories. All manufactories are yet in their infancy. In the interior, on the border of the lake, we have some sugar-mills; some driven by steam, others by water-power, but most by animal power.

III. FOUNDRIES, MACHINE-SHOPS, AND IRON WORKS.

Wages paid per week of sixty hours in foundries, machine-shops, and iron works in Maracaibo, Venezuela.

Occupations.	Lowest.	Highest.	Average.
Superintendent	$30 00	$45 00	$37 50
Chiefs of different machines	24 00	30 00	27 00
Workmen	16 00	18 00	17 00
Common laborers	8 00	12 00	10 00

We have yet hardly any such establishments which could be honored with the name of machine-shops, &c.

IV. GLASS-WORKERS.

Glass works do not exist in this part of Venezuela, so far as known. Lately a concession was given to a foreign house by the Government to erect glass works in the country. Up to this date everything is imported from Europe.

V. MINES AND MINING.

Wages paid per week of sixty hours in and in connection with mines.

Occupations.	Lowest.	Highest.	Average.
Superintendent	$25 00	$35 00	$30 00
Assistant superintendent	15 00	20 00	17 50
Laborers of higher class	12 00	16 00	14 00
Laborers of lower class	8 00	12 00	10 00

The above prices have been taken from small works established in the interior.

VI. RAILWAY EMPLOYÉS.

Wages paid per month to railway employés (those engaged about stations as well as those engaged on the engines and cars, linemen, railroad laborers, &c.) in the Cúcuta district, with board.

Occupations.	Lowest.	Highest.	Average.
First engineers of locomotive	$150 00	$200 00	$175 00
Second engineers of locomotive	75 00	100 80	87 50
Firemen	25 00	30 00	27 50
Tracklayers	60 00	100 00	80 00
Laborers	25 00	30 00	27 50
Station master	50 00	70 00	60 00
Section master	60 00	80 00	70 00

We have as yet no railroads in this consular district. The above figures are taken from the Cúcuta Railroad, leading from Cúcuta to Villamizar, in the State of Tachira, from whence the railroad will be continued through a part of this consular district to Santa Cruz, on the Zulia River.

As the railroads here have to be built through uninhabited countries, where no communications exist, it is natural that the company has to feed and attend to all the wants of the employés.

VII. SHIP-YARDS AND SHIP-BUILDING.

Wages paid per week of sixty hours in ship-yards (distinguishing between iron and wood ship-building) in Maracaibo.

Occupations.	Lowest.	Highest.	Average.
Boss carpenter	$18 00	$24 00	$21 00
Carpenters	12 00	16 00	14 00
Laborers:			
First class	18 00	24 00	21 00
Second class	8 00	10 00	9 00
Iron workers:			
Boiler-makers	20 00	30 00	25 00
Riveters	16 00	20 00	18 00
Assistants	6 00	10 00	8 00
Ship blacksmiths:			
First class	18 00	24 00	21 00
Second class	12 00	16 00	14 00
Laborers	8 00	12 00	10 00

We have no regular ship-yards here; only small repairing is done, but it is understood that in a short time we will have a ship-yard here for the repair of the vessels of the Venezuelan navy and for other ships, sail and steam, up to 1,000 tons register.

VIII. SEAMEN'S WAGES.

Wages paid per month to seamen (officers and men)—distinguishing between ocean, coast, and river navigation, and between sail and steam—in Maracaibo, Venezuela.

Occupations.	Lowest.	Highest.	Average.
OCEAN NAVIGATION.			
Steamers.			
Captain	$100 00	$150 00	$125 00
First mate	40 00	70 00	55 00
Second mate	30 00	45 00	37 50
Boatsmen	30 00	40 00	35 00
Sailors:			
First class	16 00	24 00	20 00
Second class	10 00	16 00	13 00
Engineers:			
First class	100 00	200 00	150 00
Second class	40 00	80 00	60 00
Oilers	10 00	18 00	15 00
Firemen	18 00	24 00	21 00
Stokers	10 00	14 00	12 00
Sailing ships.			
Captain	60 00	80 00	70 00
First mate	30 00	40 00	35 00
Second mate	25 00	30 00	27 50
First boatsman	25 00	30 00	27 50
Sail-makers	20 00	25 00	22 50
Sailors:			
First class	15 00	20 00	17 50
Second class	10 00	12 00	11 00
Sailor boys	5 00	8 00	6 50
COAST.			
Steamers.			
Captain	60 00	100 00	80 00
First mate	40 00	60 00	50 00
Second mate	30 00	40 00	35 00
First boatsman	20 00	30 00	25 00
Sailors:			
First class	16 00	20 00	18 00
Second class	10 00	10 00	13 00
Engineers:			
First class	70 00	100 00	85 00
Second class	40 00	70 00	55 00
Oiler	10 00	15 00	12 50
Firemen	16 00	20 00	18 00
Stokers	10 00	14 00	12 00
Sailing ships.			
Captain	40 00	50 00	45 00
First officer	20 00	25 00	22 50
Second officer	15 00	20 00	17 50
Boatsman	15 00	20 00	17 50

Wages paid per month to seamen (officers and men), &c.—Continued.

Occupations.	Lowest.	Highest.	Average.
COAST—Continued.			
Sailing ships.			
Seamen :			
First class..	$10 00	$12 00	$11 00
Second class..	6 00	10 00	8 00
Sailor boy	2 00	5 00	3 50
RIVER STEAMERS.			
Captain	50 00	100 00	75 00
First officer	46 00	60 00	50 00
Second officer	30 00	40 00	35 00
First boatsman	20 00	30 00	25 00
Seamen :			
First class...	16 00	20 00	18 00
Second class...	12 00	16 00	14 00
Engineers :			
First class...	75 00	150 00	112 50
Second class...	40 00	70 00	55 00
Oilers	10 00	15 00	12 50
Firemen..	16 00	20 00	18 00
Stokers	10 00	12 00	11 00
*Bongos.**			
Master of bongos	40 00	60 00	50 00
Bongomen	20 00	30 00	25 00

* Name of vessels used in the rivers.

IX. STORE AND SHOP WAGES.

Wages paid per month in stores to males, in Maracaibo, Venezuela.

Occupations.	Lowest.	Highest.	Average.
WHOLESALE.			
Foreigners :			
Bookkeepers, &c..	$150 00	$250 00	$200 00
Salesmen...	150 00	250 00	200 00
RETAIL.			
Foreigners..	50 00	100 00	75 00
Natives	10 00	80 00	45 00

It is not customary to employ females in stores and shops. All the labor in stores, wholesale and retail, is done by men. The foreign houses import their young employés from Germany, and give them, if they turn out well, and after they have served a number of years, an interest in the business. The native houses take natives or creoles from the Dutch island of Curaçao. Many of the clerks of the foreign houses keep house, and the younger ones board with them or with their chiefs. The foreigners, with their many wants and necessities, of course have great expenses, so that their salary is hardly adequate to cover them.

X. HOUSEHOLD WAGES IN TOWNS AND CITIES.

Wages paid per month to household servants (towns and cities) in Maracaibo, Venezuela.

Occupations.	Lowest.	Highest.	Average.
MALES.			
Coachmen*...	$10 00	$20 00	$15 00
Cook	15 00	40 00	22 50
Steward..	20 00	40 00	30 00
Male servants...	5 00	12 00	8 50
Boys, for errands and housework	3 00	6 00	4 50
FEMALES.			
Cook	4 00	8 00	6 00
House servant	4 00	8 00	6 00
Washerwomen (help)	3 00	5 00	4 00
Ironing	5 00	8 00	6 50
Seamstress	5 00	10 00	7 50
Nurse, for children	3 00	6 00	4 50

* Including food and lodging.

XI. AGRICULTURAL WAGES.

Wages paid per month to agricultural laborers and household (country) servants in Maracaibo, with or without board.

Occupations.	Lowest.	Highest.	Average.
Field laborers*	$8 00	$12 00	$10 00
Teamsters*	12 00	18 00	15 00
House laborers and for stables	12 00	15 00	13 50
Laborers to clear fields and to cut timber†	20 00	30 00	25 00
Cowboys*	5 00	8 00	6 50
Herders*	5 00	8 00	6 50

* With food.   † One meal a day.

XII. CORPORATION EMPLOYÉS.

Wages paid per month to the corporation employés in the city of Maracaibo, Venezuela.

Occupations.	Average.	Occupations.	Average.
Mayor (civil chief)	$144 00	Sanitary inspector	$24 00
Secretary	60 00	City physicians	64 00
Clerk	40 00	City council:	
Porter	16 00	Secretary	60 00
Police department:		First clerk	40 00
Inspector	80 00	Second clerk	24 00
Sub-inspector	24 00	Porter	20 00
Captains	48 00	Collector of city taxes	32 00
Lieutenants	27 00	Cashier	64 00
Roundsmen	24 00	Clerk in tax office	32 00
Patrolmen	20 00	Porter in tax office	20 00

XIII. GOVERNMENT DEPARTMENTS AND OFFICES.

Wages paid per month to employés in Government departments and offices, exclusive of tradesmen and laborers.

Occupations.	Average wages.	Occupations.	Average wages.
Custom-house collector	$192 00	Interpreter	$25 00
Comptroller of customs	128 00	Porter	23 33
Chief guardian of custom-house depots.	80 00	Commandant of the coast guard	80 00
Cashier of the custom-house	80 00	Inspector of the coast guard	32 00
Custom-house liquidator	80 00	Custom-house officers	26 66
Bookkeeper of the custom-house	80 00	Boatsmen of custom-house boats	26 60
Chief of the coast-trade	56 00	Oarsmen	13 33
Chief of goods in transitu	53 33		

XIV. TRADES AND LABOR IN GOVERNMENT EMPLOY.

Wages paid by the month to the trades and laborers in Government employ in Maracaibo, Venezuela.

Occupations.	Lowest.	Highest.	Average.
Bandmaster			$100 00
Musicians			12 00
Director of workshops in penitentiary			40 00
School-teachers in night schools			10 00
Postmen	$12 00	$20 00	16 00
Draymen			40 50
Gardeners			40 00
Laborers			28 00
Masons			56 00
Carpenters			64 00
Department of primary instruction.			
Preceptors of municipal schools	20 00	34 00	25 00
Subdirectors	12 00	18 00	15 00
Auxiliary subdirectors			10 00
Preceptors of federal schools			30 00

XV. PRINTERS AND PRINTING OFFICES.

Statement showing the wages paid per week of sixty hours to printers (compositors, pressmen, proof-readers, &c.) in Maracaibo, Venezuela.

Occupations.	Lowest.	Highest.	Average.
Printers	$3 50	$12 50	$8 00
Pressmen	5 00	6 00	5 50
Proof-readers	6 00	8 00	7 00
Bookbinders	8 50	10 50	9 50
Printer devils	4 00	7 00	5 50
Boys for distribution of newspapers	4 00	4 00	4 00

Monthly wages in the government of section Zulia.

Occupations.	Average wages.	Occupations.	Average wages.
Governor	$280 00	Bookkeeper	$56 00
Secretary of state	120 00	Collector of taxes	36 00
Clerks	53 00	Porter of treasurer's office	16 00
Members of sectional council	80 00	Inspector of wharves	60 00
Secretary of council	86 00	Subinspector of wharves	30 00
Porter of council	20 00	Bandmaster	100 00
Treasurer of section	140 00	Assistant bandmaster	30 00
Cashier of section	100 00	Musicians	12 00
Liquidator of section	56 00	Warden of penitentiary	64 00

Monthly wages in judicial department of Zulia.

Occupations.	Wages.	Occupations.	Wages.
Supreme court:		Secretary	$40 50
President	$96 33	Criminal judge	64 00
Secretary	40 50	Secretary	40 50
Clerk	20 00	Clerk	9 24
Porter	16 40	District judge	56 00
Superior judge	64 00	Secretary	32 00
Secretary	40 50	Municipal judges	24 00
Civil judge	64 00	Secretaries to above	16 00

Wages paid monthly to the employés of the various corporations and societies existing in Maracaibo.

Occupations.	Wages.	Occupations.	Wages.
Society Mutuo Auxilio:		Hospital of Chiquinquira:	
Treasurer	$24 00	Overseer	$20 00
Porter	32 00	Physicians*	
Physicians	32 00	Apothecary	20 00
Bank of Maracaibo:		Nurses	8 00
Manager	80 00	Servants	4 80
Cashier	80 00	Hospital of the Casade Beneficencia:	
Clerk	16 00	Resident inspector	20 30
Lazaretto:		Chaplain	15 00
Warden	64 00	Physician	40 00
Chaplain	36 00	Hospital assistants	9 30
Physician	32 00	Apothecary	16 00
Apothecary	24 00		
Policemen	20 00		
Cooks	20 00		

* Gratis.

PUERTO CABELLO.

REPORT BY CONSUL WHITE.

HOW THE WORKING CLASSES LIVE.

The wants of the laboring classes in this country are few. Exempt by the tropical climate from any care or preparation for winter, the laborer needs no fuel to promote warmth, nor a habitation to keep out the cold. A roof and walls to exclude the sun and rain are all he needs for a house ; a shirt of coarse cotton cloth with pantaloons of the same material, and a hat, suffice for clothing; shoes are not required.

The working people live largely upon soup made from a little meat and vegetables ; they also eat bananas and plantains, beans, Indian corn or maize, raised in the country, rice, and salt fish. Bananas and plantains cost from 1 to 2 cents each, as they are plentiful or otherwise ; beef is from 14 to 19 cents a pound ; salt fish, 9½ to 14 cents ; beans, when plentiful, 5 cents a pound ; maize, from 1 to 2½ cents ; rice, 5 cents a pound.

WAGES PAST AND PRESENT.

As far as I am able to learn, the rate of wages at present paid in this country is about the same in the cities and towns as it was in 1878, but in the country, on the estates, wages are lower now than in 1878.

HABITS OF THE WORKING CLASSES.

The working classes here are for the most part trustworthy. All the testimony on that branch of the subject is the same. In illustration it is stated that postmen who for years have traveled on horseback over lonely roads, and who often carry large sums of money with them for merchants or others, have never been robbed. The muleteers who drive the donkeys or carts with merchandise between different points, are often intrusted with sums of money to carry by parties to whom they are strangers and to whom their names are not even known; the simple fact that they are muleteers and going to any given point is enough, and they faithfully deliver at its destination the money which they have had in charge.

The working classes in this country are not saving. On the contrary they are exceedingly improvident. Many are addicted to drinking and gambling. As has been stated, their wants are few and easily supplied, and they spend their money quickly after earning it. On this point, too, the testimony all agrees. Said one employer to me, " If they are paid on Saturday night their money is gone on Monday morning."

FEELING BETWEEN EMPLOYER AND EMPLOYÉ.

The feeling is kind on the part of the employer, and independent on the part of the employé.

No organization of labor exists here.

Strikes are unknown in this country.

The laborer buys wherever he chooses. No conditions are imposed by the employers. The laborers are paid by the week—every Saturday night. They are generally paid in silver—Venezuelan and other dollars and fractional parts of dollars.

There are no co operative societies in this country.

GENERAL CONDITION OF THE WORKING PEOPLE.

The climate is such they do not need the same shelter or clothing as those who live in colder climes. Their food is healthful and generally abundant. As a whole, the working classes in this country are a simple people, of kind disposition, and trustworthy; but they are ignorant, and their life generally is on a very low plane in the scale of humanity.

PART II.—FEMALE LABOR.

NUMBER OF FEMALE EMPLOYÉS.

There are not many women or children in this district employed in industrial pursuits.

Cotton mill in Valencia.—In the city of Valencia there is a cotton factory, or weaving establishment as it is called, where quite a number of women are employed. Valencia is a city of from 25,000 to 30,000 inhabitants, and is the capital of the State of Carabobo, in which State is Puerto Cabello. This factory was started by Señor Domingo A. Olavarria, manager of the Bank of Carabobo; but at first it was not successful, owing to the cost of the machinery and expense of putting it up, &c. It was subsequently sold at a reduced price to a company, and when I visited the establishment recently it was said to be running on a paying basis. The cotton used in this factory is grown in the vicinity. From this cotton is manufactured a coarse but strong and durable cotton cloth, which is used by the people of the country for shirting, sheets, &c. They also manufacture a coarser cloth, which is used for making into cheap shoes, or sandals—shoes that retail for 38 cents a pair. As many as one hundred hands, chiefly women and children, have been employed at one time at this establishment. At the time of my visit the force was about seventy hands. All the operatives at the looms are women and boys, the boys being for the most part tenders, or assistants, to the women. The women who have become skilled at the work are paid 38 cents a day, United States currency, for their work; the boys, when they commence to work at the factory, are paid only 9½ cents a day, and are paid more as they become more skilled. The time for the operatives to be at the factory is from 6 o'clock in the morning until 6 in the afternoon, with one hour allowed for meals. The engineer and foreman are paid from $15.38 to $30.77 per month.

The establishment can turn out 20 pieces of 40 yards each in a day.

MORAL AND PHYSICAL CONDITION OF FEMALE EMPLOYÉS.

To the interrogatories in regard to the moral and physical condition of such employés, the means provided for their improvement, the means provided in case of fire or other dangers, and what provisions are made by the employers in regard to sanitary measures, and for the care of the sick and disabled, I reply: The women and children seemed in good health, and appeared bright and cheerful. They compared favorably in appearance in these respects with operatives of a similar class in the United States. No children, however, should be allowed to work in any factory. The factory is all on the ground floor, so that, of course, the same necessity does not exist for providing means of exit in case of fire as for factories of several stories. There are no means of improvement provided for these operatives, and there are no provisions made in regard to sanitary measures or for the care of the sick and disabled.

Women in hat factory.—The firm of Sandoval & Co., in Valencia, hatters, who manufacture felt hats, out of a force of from sixty to seventy hands—men, women, and boys—in April last, employed fourteen women. These women were paid 48 cents a day. The working hours at this establishment are from 6½ o'clock in the morning until 12 at noon, and from 1 to 5½ o'clock in the afternoon.

Women cigar-makers.—Quite a number of women in Puerto Cabello gain their livelihood by making cigars and cigarettes. Some of them purchase the tobacco and manufacture the cigars and cigarettes, others work for cigar manufacturers.

ACKNOWLEDGMENTS.

In obtaining information for this report I am indebted to General Joaquin Berrió, president of the State of Carabobo, and to Señor Domingo A. Olavarria, of Valencia, manager of the Bank of Carabobo. I have also received valuable assistance in obtaining rates of wages, &c., from William Von der Brelje, esq., of Puerto Cabello, who has been for thirty years a resident of this country.

EDWARD E. WHITE,
Consul.

UNITED STATES CONSULATE,
Puerto Cabello, June 10, 1884.

I. GENERAL TRADES.

[In converting Venezuelan into American values in the following tables, the Venezuelan dollar was estimated at 76.92 cents, and the Venezuelan real at 9.6 cents United States currency.]

Wages paid per week in Puerto Cabello.

Occupations.	Lowest.	Highest.	Average.
BUILDING TRADES.			
Bricklayers	$6 90	$11 52	$8 04
Hod-carriers	4 62	5 76	5 04
Masons	6 90	11 52	8 46
Tenders	2 28	4 62	3 42
Plasterers	6 90	11 52	8 04
Tenders	4 62	5 76	5 04
Roofers	6 90	9 24	7 50
Tenders	4 62	5 76	5 04
Carpenters	4 62	11 52	6 48
OTHER TRADES.			
Bakers	1 79	* 3 59	* 2 42
Blacksmiths	8 04	13 86	9 66
Strikers	6 90	6 90	6 90
Brickmakers	4 62	6 90	6 24
Butchers	13 86	13 86	13 86
Cabinet-makers	4 62	11 52	6 48
Cigar-makers	† 1 15	‡ 77	

* And found.   † Per thousand cigars.   ‡ Per hundred cigars.

II. FACTORIES, MILLS, ETC.

There is in Valencia, in this consular district, a cotton factory concerning which details are given in the body of this report.

In the Puerto Cabello there is a soap and candle factory where a small number of hands are employed. The average rate of wages paid is 96 cents per day.

III. FOUNDRIES, MACHINE-SHOPS, AND IRON WORKS.

The firm of Winckelmann Brothers, a German firm in Valencia, in this consular district, have a machine-shop, an iron-foundry, and wheel-wright establishment in one. They employ 44 men in the shops, but have about 100 men altogether employed, including those employed in cutting wood, driving mules, &c. The 44 men employed in the shops are paid as follows: Lowest wages, $1.15 a day; highest wages, $1.92 a day; average wages, $1.35 a day.

This firm is allowed by the Venezuelan Government to import a certain amount of raw iron each year free of duty.

Messrs. Wittstein & Co. have a machine-shop and foundry in Puerto Cabello. At present they have employed only about 10 or 15 hands. The lowest wages are 96 cents a day; highest wages, $1.54 a day; average wages, $1.15 a day.

VIII. SEAMEN'S WAGES.

Wages paid per month to seamen (officers and men) engaged in navigation on the coast of Venezuela.

Occupations.	Lowest.	Highest.
STEAMERS.		
Captain		$61 54
Mate		30 77
Sailors		11 55
Do		9 23
Engineer		92 31
First fireman		38 46
Other firemen		23 08
Do		19 23
SAILING VESSELS.		
Captain	$23 08	46 15
Mate	13 85	19 23
Sailors	7 69	10 77

X. STORE AND SHOP WAGES.

Wages paid per month in stores, wholesale and retail, to males, in Puerto Cabello.

Occupations.	Lowest.	Highest.	Average.
Wholesale stores	$76 92	$192 30	$115 38
Retail stores or shops	7 69	30 77	12 69

X. HOUSEHOLD WAGES IN TOWNS AND CITIES.

Wages paid per month to household servants (towns and cities) in the consular district of Puerto Cabello.

Occupations.	Lowest.	Highest.	Average.
Household servants	$3 08	$7 69	$6 12

XI. AGRICULTURAL WAGES.

Agricultural laborers are paid by the piece. A certain amount of work is allotted them, for which they are each paid 58 cents. In the vicinity of Puerto Cabello this is generally a day's work, though some laborers perform more work and consequently receive more pay. In the interior, on more elevated land, where it is cooler, the laborers can perform more work, and some do. It may be stated in general terms that the wages of agricultural laborers are from 58 cents to 96 cents per day, without board, in the vicinity of cities and towns. In the interior a less rate by the piece is paid.

XII. CORPORATION EMPLOYÉS.

Salaries paid per month to corporation employés in the municipality of Puerto Cabello.

Occupations.	Salary.	Occupations.	Salary.
1 civil chief	$115 38	1 warden of the market place	$30 77
1 secretary	46 15	1 warden of the cemetery	26 92
1 clerk of council	30 77	1 warden of the prison	23 08
1 porter	26 92	1 warden of the aqueduct	23 08
1 secrotary of council	76 92	1 first master of public works	19 23
1 administrator of municipal taxes	123 08	1 warden of plaza "Guzman Blanco"	34 62
1 bookkeeper	46 15	1 warden of plaza "Concordia"	23 08
1 clerk	23 08	3 school teachers (male), each	61 54
1 chief of the police guard	46 15	3 school teachers (female), each	38 46
18 members of the police guard, each	30 77	6 school teachers (male), ea h	23 08
8 chiefs of municipalities (lesser municipalities all comprising the municipality of Puerto Cabello), each	15 38	6 school teachers (female), each	23 08
		1 superintendent of schools	50 00
		1 city physician	23 08
1 prefect of the market place	30 77	1 physician for hospital	15 38

Monthly salaries of custom-house officials and wages of laborers in the consular district of Puerto Cabello, Venezuela, per month.

Occupations.	Salary.	Occupations.	Salary.
MARITIME CUSTOM-HOUSE.		MARITIME CUSTOM-HOUSE—Continued.	
Collector of customs	$184 62	36 wardens of the guard in Puerto Cabello, each	$30 77
Second collector of customs	123 08	12 wardens of the guard in Yaracuy and Tucacas, each	23 08
Clerk of liquidation	115 39		
Second clerk of liquidation	76 92	25 boatmen in Yaracuy and Tucacas, each	23 08
Cashier	92 31		
Bookkeeper	92 31	2 chiefs of laborers of custom-house, each	76 92
Clerk of coasting trade	76 92		
Clerk of weights	76 92	2 overseers of laborers of custom-house, each	46 16
Storekeeper	76 92		
Clerk of correspondence and archives	43 08	100 laborers of custom-house, each	38 47
Interpreter	43 01	Judge of the public treasure	92 35
Physician of public health	23 08	Secretary	46 16
Porter	25 64	Porter	19 23
First commander of coast guard	92 31		
Second commander of coast guard	76 92	ADUANA TERRESTRE INLAND CUSTOM-HOUSE.	
Commander of coast guard in Tucacas	51 28		
Commander of coast guard in Yaracuy	51 28	Collector of customs	123 08
5 corporals of the guard in Puerto Cabello, each	38 47	Bookkeeper	61 54
2 corporals of the guard in Yaracuy	26 92	Clerk	38 47
1 corporal of the guard in Tucacas	26 92	Porter	19 23

XIII. Government Departments and Offices.

Yearly salaries paid to members of the State legislature, Government officials, &c., in the State of Carabobo, in the consular district of Puerto Cabello, Venezuela.

Occupations.	Salary.	Occupations.	Salary.
STATE LEGISLATURE.		**JUDICIAL AUTHORITIES—Continued.**	
14 deputies from the 7 districts of the State paid for a session of 40 days (19.3 cents each per day) ......each..	$2,810 08	1 secretary	741 12
		1 judge of the first instance of the second district	1,389 60
EXECUTIVE BRANCH.		1 secretary	694 80
President of the State.................	3,242 40	1 judge of the first instance of the third district	1,019 04
Secretary general.........	2,316 00	1 secretary	579 00
First official....................	1,158 00	Judge of the district of Valencia......	1,019 04
3 officials ....each..	1,667 52	Judge of the district of Puerto Cabello	926 40
Official in charge of statistics..........,	555 84	2 secretaries......	1,111 68
3 counselors of administration ..each..	3,800 88	5 judges of the districts of Nirgua,	
Amanuensis.................	370 56	Bejuma, Monsalban, Guacare, and Ocumare	2,779 20
		5 secretaries	1,621 20
CIVIL AUTHORITIES.		Attorney general:	
7 civil chiefs of districts	4,215 12	First district.........	1,158 00
7 secretaries................	1,945 44	Second district	926 40
		PUBLIC INSTRUCTION.	
JUDICIAL AUTHORITIES.		6 teachers (male) of the schools Cathedral, Sta. Rosa, Candelaria, Los	
6 ministers (judges) of the supreme court	7,781 76	Gayos, Puerto Cabello, Nirgua	2,223 36
2 first officials.....................	1,296 96	4 teachers (male) of the schools Belen, Cuyagua, Aguirre, Cedeño	1,111 68
1 judge of the first instance, criminal cases	1,422 24	1 teacher (male) of the school El Olivo.	231 60
1 secretary	741 12	Night school for artisans in Puerto Cabello.........	185 28
1 judge of the first instance of the first district..................	1,389 60		

XIV. Trades and Labor—Government Employ.

Wages paid by the month to laborers in Government employ in the consular district of Puerto Cabello.

Occupations.	Average wages.	Occupations.	Average wages.
Porter employed at the capitol in Valencia.............................	$23 16	1 porter at court of first instance, second district	$19 30
Porter employed in charge of the gardens at the capitol	30 88	1 porter at court of first instance, third district.	15 44
2 porters at supreme court .....each..	19 30	2 porters at district courts of Valencia and Puerto Cabello............each..	15 44
1 porter at court of first instance	19 30	5 porters at other district courts.each..	7 72
1 porter at court of first instance, first district............................	19 30		

BRITISH GUIANA.

REPORT BY CONSUL FIGYELMESY.

The rates of wages paid to laborers in this colony are contained in the tabular forms.

COST OF LIVING.

The cost of living to the agricultural laboring class is as follows:

Coolie laborers.—The coolie laborer indentured for five years spends from 50 cents to 60 cents per week for the necessaries of life, say for food, consisting of rice, curry, tumeric, and ghee or native butter, and drinking cocoanut toddy, saving most of their earnings, consequently living niggardly, their clothing being only a muslin or calico turban for the head, and a simple cloth folded round the loins, commonly called "baba," the other parts of their body being nude; they are comfortably lodged, and have medical attendance and medicine supplied to them free of expense by the plantation on which they work. These laborers, after five years' service, and being employed for five years more as free immigrants, are entitled to return passages to India; they often remit or take with them from $50,000 to $60,000 in money and jewelry—each batch of 300 to 400—which they accumulate during that time; some 2,000 to 3,000 immigrants arrive annually, and about 1,500 to 1,800 depart. The free or unindentured coolie laborer lives on the same food as the indentured coolie, is clothed in the same manner, but chooses to lodge wherever he likes in town or country, renting a small room at $1.50 to $2 per month, in which three to four dwell.

Chinese and Portuguese laborers.—The Chinese and Portuguese laborers spend from 32 to 48 cents per day for food, consisting of both fresh and salt meat, poultry, and fish; for vegetables they use pumpkins, cabbages, rice, onions, garlic, and potatoes; tea and coffee being their principal beverage. They clothe and house better than the former, and save money.

Native laborers.—The creole or native laborer spends from 24 to 32 cents per day for food, consisting of salted codfish, pickled mackerel, herrings, beef, pork; and for vegetables, plantains, yams, potatoes, rice, corn, and cornmeal; wheat flour, butter, oil, lard, and sugar are used for culinary purposes. These laborers are very much addicted to drinking strong spirits. Their clothing is made of cotton and woolen cloth, from 8 cents to 20 cents per yard; house rent from $2 to $4 per month for one tenement built to hold two persons, but in which are crowded together some six to eight, including children—hence all kinds of sickness.

Tradesmen and clerks.—Tradesmen, operatives, and clerks, earning more money, live very well at from $1 to $3 per day for the necessaries of life in food and clothing, and for house rent from $10 to $30 per month.

WAGES PAST AND PRESENT.

The same rates of wages prevail here now as in 1878.

HABITS OF THE WORKING CLASSES.

The coolies, Chinese, and Portuguese are industrious and save money, but the creoles, or natives, and immigrants from the West India islands, are indolent to a great extent, which affects their habits for evil.

FEELING BETWEEN EMPLOYER AND EMPLOYÉ.

The feeling which prevails between employé and employer: If the employer is kind, generous, and liberal, it affects the employé to energy, honesty, and general good feeling throughout the community; but if the employer is unkind, strict in rules, and exacting, it affects the employé to negligence and ill feeling.

ORGANIZED CONDITION OF LABOR.

There is no organized condition of labor in this colony. Strikes do not prevail.

FOOD PURCHASES.

The working people are free to purchase wherever they choose. The laborer is paid weekly in dollars and cents.

CO OPERATIVE SOCIETIES.

The societies formed in this colony are as follows: The Portuguese Benevolent Society, which is the largest and most prosperous; entrance fee, $4.80; one-half to be paid on admission and the other half to be paid in five months after in monthly installments of 48 cents per month, and 24 cents contribution, besides, to be paid regularly every week. A member of one year's standing falling ill is entitled to medical attendance, medicines, and, in case of death, a decent burial; a member of two years' standing falling ill is entitled to medical attendance, medicines, and $10 per month pecuniary relief, and, in case of death, a decent burial; a member of three years' standing is entitled to medical attendance when ill, medicines, and $15 per month pecuniary relief, and, in case of death, a decent burial; members of four years' standing are each entitled to medical attendance when ill, medicines, and $18 per month pecuniary relief, and, in case of death, a decent burial. Widows of members are each entitled to $10 per month pecuniary relief, and where a widow has more than one child, $15 per month pecuniary relief is allowed for five years.

Children of members who have lost both parents are entitled to receive $5 per month, each, until they attain the age of twelve years.

The other societies are: The Friendly; the Guild; the Mechanics; the Hand of Justice; the St. Vincent de Paul; the Foresters No. 1; and the Foresters No. 2.

These last seven societies are in connection with the Anglican, the Scotch, Roman Catholic, and Methodist churches, and though less prosperous than the Portuguese Benevolent Society, are founded on the same basis, and guaranteeing similar relief.

GENERAL CONDITION OF THE WORKING CLASSES.

The general condition of the working people is with the coolies, Chinese, and Portuguese laborers, better than the creoles, or natives, and laborers from the neighboring islands, as the former three manage to save money with the prospect of returning to their countries to enjoy it, while the two latter spend all their earnings, and never have a thought of laying by one cent for sickness, old age, distress, or death; their ultimate resort, when incapable of working, being the public hospital or almshouse.

SAFETY OF EMPLOYÉS.

There are no means furnished for the safety of employés. In case of accident the working people are taken to the public hospitals on the plantations or in the city of Georgetown, where every care is taken of them at the expense of the Government.

MORAL AND PHYSICAL WELL-BEING.

The moral and physical well being of the employés have no consideration with the employers. In some instances confidence is placed in the employé, in others not.

POLITICAL RIGHTS.

Workmen possess no political rights here, and have no influence on legislation; they bear their portion of the duty levied on imports of provisions, clothing, &c., but no direct tax. The tendency of legislation in regard to labor is chiefly to encourage immigration from other countries.

CAUSES OF IMMIGRATION.

The causes which lead to the immigration of the working people to this colony are their poverty, starvation, and not being able to obtain work in their native countries, and the scarcity of creole laborers in this colony; also the high rate of wages offered here, which induce coolies, Chinese, and Portuguese to emigrate.

The principal occupations of the laborers here are working on the plantations—sugar-cane and others—and many, after their time of service have expired, and have saved money, either return to their native countries or settle here and open business of all kinds.

NUMBER OF FEMALE EMPLOYÉS.

Children, none: women in mechanical and manufacturing pursuits, none; in commercial pursuits, none; in personal, see Table No. X; as clerks, see Table No. IX; as teachers, see Table No. I; as artists, none; as chemists, none; as hotel and boarding-house keepers, 6; as journalists, none; as laundresses, cannot be accurately ascertained, as nearly every female of the laboring class is a laundress; as musicians, 6; as inventors, none; as bankers, none; as brokers, none; as lecturers, none; as public speakers, none; as agriculturists, cannot be accurately ascertained: in mining pursuits, none.

FEMALE WAGES.

There are from three to four domestic servants generally employed in every large house, working from 10 to 11 hours daily. For their wages, see Table No. X, accompanying.

MORAL AND PHYSICAL CONDITION OF FEMALE EMPLOYÉS.

Moral condition bad; physical condition of some is good, and of robust and healthy constitutions, of great endurance and efficiency as servants, while others are indifferent and inefficient. Domestic servants as a class are fair, and generally answer the requirements.

MEANS FOR IMPROVEMENT.

No means provided other than there are upwards of forty churches, school-houses, meeting-houses, &c., of all denominations, in this colony, but which have little or no effect in counteracting the immorality which prevails to the greatest extent. I may here state that on this account the prisons are crowded.

SAFETY OF EMPLOYÉS.

There is a very efficient fire-brigade here under the superintendence of the inspector general of the police force, which works admirably and answers every emergency.

CARE OF SICK AND DISABLED.

There are no provisions made by the employer in regard to these measures, but the colony is under the control of a board of health and sanitary superintendents; the latter visit all over the colony periodically and cause it to be cleansed from all impurities and infectious matter. Public hospitals and almshouses are provided for the sick and disabled, which are kept up at the expense of the Government.

FEMALE WAGES PAST AND PRESENT.

There has been no increase during the past five years in the wages paid to women. The employment of women has no effect on the wages of men, as women are generally allotted to lighter tasks in agriculture than men; therefore the effects, if any, are rather beneficial, causing both male and female to obtain labor.

FEMALE EDUCATION.

Some of the women are entirely uneducated, others partly educated, but the children by a compulsory law of this colony, which enforces very strict measures on the parents if the children are not put to school, are being educated.

This system of education is entirely new to the laboring class, being only established about four years. It may have a good effect in the future, but at present I could not offer an opinion on it.

PH. FIGYELMESY,
Consul.

UNITED STATES CONSULATE,
Demerara, June 16, 1884.

I. GENERAL TRADES.

Wages paid per week in British Guiana.

Occupations.	Hours per day.	Lowest.	Highest.	Average.
BUILDING TRADES.				
Bricklayers	9	$4 80	$7 20	$6 00
Hod-carriers	9	1 92	3 36	2 64
Masons	9	6 00	7 92	6 96
Tenders	9	1 92	3 36	2 64
Plasterers	9	6 00	7 92	6 96
Tenders	9	1 92	3 36	2 64
Slaters	9	4 80	7 20	6 00
Roofers	9	4 80	7 20	6 00
Tenders	9	2 88	3 84	3 36
Plumbers	9	7 20	10 08	8 64
Assistants	9	1 20	4 16	2 70
Carpenters	9	4 80	6 48	5 76
Gas-fitters	9	6 00	8 40	7 32
OTHER TRADES.				
Bakers	12	4 00	15 00	6 08
Blacksmiths	9	4 00	10 00	7 00
Strikers	9	1 92	2 88	2 40
Bookbinders	9	4 00	20 00	9 50
Butchers	10	4 00	7 00	5 00
Brass-founders	9½	3 24	40 00	11 50
Cabinet-makers	9	5 00	12 00	6 40
Coopers	11	1 92	10 00	4 09
Drivers:				
Draymen and teamsters	10	1 92	2 88	2 30
Cab	12	3 36	6 00	4 80
Carriage	12	2 40	6 00	4 12
Tram-car	16½	3 00	3 00	3 00
Gardeners:				
Women	9½	1 44	1 44	1 44
Men	9½	1 92	4 80	3 30
Horseshoers	9	8 00	8 00	8 00
Jewelers	9	2 40	12 00	8 20
Laborers, porters, &c	10	3 84	3 84	3 84
Teachers public schools	5	75	12 50	6 62
Saddle and harness makers	9	4 00	10 00	7 24
Sailmakers	9	9 50	12 00	10 18
Stevedores*				
Tailors	10	3 00	10 00	5 00
Telegraph operators	11	3 84	38 46	8 40
Tinsmiths	10	3 84	9 00	7 80

* These are not paid per week, but have special charges, viz: For sugar hogsheads, 20 cents each; tierces, 16; barrels, 8; bags, 6. Rum buns, 16; hogsheads, 12; barrels, 8.

II. FACTORIES, MILLS, ETC.

Wages paid per week of fifty-eight hours in factories or mills in British Guiana.

Occupations.	Lowest.	Highest.	Average.
Match-making	$2 88	$25 00	$4 72
Box-making	1 00	4 32	1 26

III. FOUNDRIES, MACHINE-SHOPS, AND IRON WORKS.

Wages paid per week of fifty-four and one-half hours in foundries, machine-shops, and iron works in British Guiana.

Occupations.	Lowest.	Highest.	Average.
Brass and iron founders	$3 24	$10 00	$9 50
Smiths	4 50	10 00	6 80

VI. RAILWAY EMPLOYÉS.

Wages paid per week to railway employés (those engaged about stations, as well as those engaged on the engines and cars, linemen, railroad laborers, &c.) in British Guiana.

Occupations.	Lowest.	Highest.	Average.
Station masters	$7 50	$12 50	$9 43
Engineers	10 00	15 00	12 50
Carmen	7 50	8 00	7 75
Linemen	4 40	5 00	4 77
Laborers	3 64	3 64	3 84

VII. SHIP-YARDS AND SHIP-BUILDING.

Wages paid per week of fifty-four and one-half hours in ship-yards (wood ship-building) in British Guiana.

Occupations.	Lowest.	Highest.	Average.
Ship-carpenters	$7 56	$15 00	$12 40
Apprentices	60	3 12	1 98

There are no iron ships built here.

VIII. SEAMEN'S WAGES.

Wages paid per month to seamen (officers and men)—distinguishing between ocean, coast, and river navigation, and between sail and steam—in British Guiana.

Occupations.	Lowest.	Highest.	Average.
Ocean:			
Sailing	$9 60	$100 00	$35 00
Steaming	11 20	120 00	45 60
Coast:			
Sailing	10 00	40 00	14 00
Steaming	15 00	50 00	24 50
River steaming	15 00	50 00	24 50

IX. STORE AND SHOP WAGES.

Wages paid per month in stores, wholesale or retail, to males and females, in British Guiana.

Occupations.	Lowest.	Highest.	Average.
Wholesale:			
Males	$25 00	$150 00	$45 00
Retail:			
Males	10 00	50 00	22 50
Females	3 00	7 50	4 50

X. HOUSEHOLD WAGES IN TOWNS AND CITIES.

Wages paid per month to household servants (towns and cities) in British Guiana.

Occupations.	Lowest.	Highest.	Average.
Butlers	$6 00	$15 00	$10 00
Cooks	6 00	10 00	7 20
Housemaids	3 00	5 00	4 32
Nurses	3 00	6 00	5 00

XI. AGRICULTURAL WAGES.

Wages paid per day to agricultural laborers and household (country) servants in British Guiana, with lodging.

Occupations.	Lowest.	Highest.	Average.
Predial : *			
Cane-cutters	$0 24	$0 80	$0 64
Shovelmen	40	60	56
Weeders	24	32	29
Suppliers	32	60	54
Puntmen	36	60	56
Manufacture:			
Cane throwers	32	40	37
Boilermen	48	56	50
Firemen	48	80	72
Sugar curers	40	54	48
Boxmen	32	40	35
Megass carriers	20	24	22
Clarifiers:			
Headmen	48	48	48
Other than headmen	20	24	23
Distillers	32	48	44
Others about the buildings	24	32	28
Tradesmen:			
Engineers	96	2 00	1 50
Carpenters	80	1 20	96
Masons	80	1 20	88
Coopers	1 20	1 52	1 24
Managers †	2,400 00	3,000 00	2,700 00
Overseers †	200 00	600 00	450 00
Domestics †	36 00	144 00	87 60

* This work is ordinarily done by *task*, and industrious coolies and blacks can earn more by working beyond the seven hours defined by law as a day's work.
† These are annual wages, with board and lodging.
There is really no fluctuation in the rate of the foregoing wages. A careful inquiry into the matter has shown that the total amount of money paid away for wages per annum is about $5,000,000. The falling off in the supply of immigrants has interfered with the progress of the extension of cultivation, and until there is a considerably larger importation of immigrant laborers the area under canes is likely to decrease.

XII. CORPORATION EMPLOYÉS.

Wages paid per week of forty-nine and one-half hours to the corporation employés in the city of Georgetown, Demerara, British Guiana.

Occupations.	Lowest.	Highest.	Average.
Mechanics	$5 28	$9 50	$7 39
Engine-drivers	4 40	5 28	4 84
Firemen (stoking)	2 64	3 74	3 19
Masons and bricklayers	5 50	6 38	5 94
Carpenters	4 40	6 00	5 20
Foremen of tradesmen	9 00	12 00	10 50
Foremen of laborers	4 00	4 00	4 00
Street labor:			
Men	2 64	2 64	2 64
Women	88	1 76	1 32
Boys	88	1 32	1 10
Task gang labor:			
Digging canals, &c	2 20	5 50	3 85
Mowing grass	2 64	3 28	2 96
Cart hire:			
Mule, cart, and driver	9 90	11 00	10 45
Stone breakers:			
Men and women	84	3 20	2 02

XIII. GOVERNMENT DEPARTMENTS AND OFFICES.

Wages paid per month of one hundred and eighty hours to employés in Government departments and offices (exclusive of tradesmen and laborers) in British Guiana.

Occupations.	Lowest.	Highest.	Average.
Governor			*$2,960 00
Private secretary			120 00
Administrators-general	$50 00	$600 00	152 50
Analytical chemist			250 00
Auditor-generals	60 00	400 00	140 00
Civil engineers	30 00	400 00	122 09
Commissaries	50 00	320 00	141 00
Crown agent..			40 00
Customs...	30 00	400 00	91 19
Harbor-master..			200 00
Health officer..			125 00
Immigration agent at Calcutta			640 00
Immigration	12 00	600 00	123 08
Inspector of villages			250 00
Judicial	15 00	1,000 00	207 74
Magistrates:			
Special	200 00	200 00	200 00
Stipendiary	280 00	320 00	286 66
Magistrates' clerks..	80 00	120 00	83 62
Police magistrates	40 00	400 00	132 50
Postal	7 75	250 00	21 57
Provost marshals	25 00	333 34	82 42
Registrars (births and deaths)..................................	50 00	160 00	82 85
Secretaries	40 00	600 00	180 00
Secretary to central board of health...........................			240 00
Surveyors	41 67	240 00	123 12
Treasury..	20 00	400 00	106 54

* $2,000 salary, and for contingencies $960.

GOVERNMENT INSTITUTIONS.

Wages paid per month of one hundred and eighty hours to employés in Government institutions in British Guiana.

Occupations.	Lowest.	Highest.	Average.
Ecclesiastical:			
Church of England...................................	$120 00	$800 00	$177 62
Church of Scotland	166 67	280 00	204 67
Missionaries	120 00	160 00	136 00
Roman Catholics *....................................			12,000 00
Wesleyans*			7,000 00
Dissenters*			1,000 00
Educational board	30 00	400 00	125 72
Hospital	70 00	201 68	149 50
Leper asylum...	30 00	80 00	39 00
Lunatic asylum	25 00	320 00	50 88
Militia..	9 00	80 00	17 50
Orphan asylum	10 33	100 00	22 51
Police force...	10 00	400 00	23 25
Poor-law board	32 00	160 00	38 40
Prisons..	10 00	320 00	34 12

* This amount is an annual grant.

XIV. TRADES AND LABOR—GOVERNMENT EMPLOY.

Wages paid by the week of forty-nine and one-half hours to the trades and laborers in Government employ in British Guiana.

Occupations.	Lowest.	Highest.	Average.
Blacksmiths	$5 28	$12 00	$6 62
Carpenters	6 00	8 64	6 29
Laborers	3 84	3 84	3 84
Masons	6 48	9 00	6 90
Watchman...			3 84

XV. PRINTERS AND PRINTING OFFICES.

Statement showing the wages paid per week of sixty hours to printers (compositors, pressmen, proof-readers, &c.) in British Guiana.

Occupations.	Lowest.	Highest.	Average.
Compositors..	$3 25	$7 00	$6 12
Pressmen	2 88	3 12	2 96
Proof-readers	2 00	2 40	2 18
Apprentices	48	72	64

BRAZIL.

RIO DE JANEIRO.

REPORT BY CONSUL-GENERAL ANDREWS.

The following is a report on the rate of wages, cost of living, &c., of the laboring classes in the city of Rio de Janeiro, in answer to the questions contained in the " Labor Circular" of the Department of State of February 15, 1884 :

RATES OF WAGES.

The answer to this question is contained in the tables numbered from I to XV.

COST OF LIVING.

In the following list is given the lowest and highest price of goods :

Article.	Lowest price.	Highest price.	Article.	Lowest price.	Highest price.
Fresh beef* .....per pound..	$0 07	$0 10	Cognac......... per bottle..	$0 63	$1 72
Pork ....do....	16	24	Rum (national).......do....	13	16
Mutton ....do....	14	19	Milk ....per quart..	12	14
Dried salt meat ....do....	12	13	Fowls.................each..	86	1 08
Dried codfish ....do....	12	13	Chickens .... do....	26	51
Coffee:			Eggs...........per dozen..	32	51
Ground ....do....	16	26	Felt hats ....each..	2 58	5 16
Grain ....do....	11	14	Beaver hats ....do....	4 30	4 73
Tea:			Straw hats ....do....	1 29	2 58
Black ....do....	95	1 06	Suits:		
Green ....do....	95	2 15	Black cloth	25 80	38 70
Butter ....do....	36	59	Diagonal	21 50	30 10
Cheese .... do....	16	59	Kerseymere	21 50	30 10
Bread ....do....	08	....	Coats:		
Lard :			Alpaca	2 58	5 16
American ....do....	22	26	Black cloth	2 15	4 30
National ....do....	17	22	Trousers:		
Black beans.......per pint..	03	04	Black cloth.............	4 30	8 60
White beans ....do....	05	....	Kerseymere	3 44	7 44
Indian corn ....do....	02	....	Drill, linen	1 72	2 58
Rice ....do....	04	07	Boots............ per pair..	1 72	7 44
Mandioca flour.......do....	03	04	Shoes................do....	2 15	6 00
Sugar.........per pound ..	07	09	Slippers.............do....	43	2 15
Potatoes ....do....	03	06	Wooden shoes........do....	16	75
Bacon ....do....	16	22	Cotton socks....per dozen..	2 58	3 97
Starch ....do....	13	16	Cotton stockings.....do....	2 58	5 16
Soap ....do....	04	13	Shirts ....do....	15 50	25 80
Indian-corn meal......do....	06	....	Collars ....do....	3 44	4 30
Rice-meal ....do....	10	....	Cuffs ....do....	3 44	4 30
Macaroni ....do....	22	25	Drawers...............do....	15 50	25 80
Tobacco ....do....	26	43	Umbrellas ....each..	1 29	8 60
Salad oil........per bottle..	32	51	Shirting..........per yard..	08	16
Lamp oil ....do....	22	26	Print ....do....	10	26
Kerosene...........per can..	1 72	2 15	Satinet ....do....	25	50
Vinegar ....per bottle..	10	16	Merino ....do....	86	1 50
Beer...................do....	08	43	Silk ....do....	86	6 45
Wine..................do....	22	4 30	Velvet ....do....	2 15	4 30

* Considerable waste meat is sold with the parts that can be consumed. For example, a long strip of flank accompanies a piece of sirloin, and the round is cut lengthwise. Actually, therefore, beef is not much cheaper at Rio than in the United States.

As a rule, laborers who have no family take their meals in cheap and very plain eating-houses, termed "pasture-houses" (*casa de pasto*). There with 10 to 16 cents they get a breakfast or a dinner, having for breakfast a hash or a stew with rice, mandioca flour, bread, and maté (a kind of te t grown in the south of Brazil) or coffee; for dinner they can have a soup, black beans with dried salt meat, and mandioca flour, a hash with rice, and bananas. The married laborers bring their breakfast from home, and only dine after the day's work is over, at home. Usually at 4.30 o'clock the day's work is finished. The chief support of the workpeople is black beans, dried beef, dried codfish, small fish (such as sardines, which can be got four for 1 cent), mandioca flour, rice, sweet potatoes, bread, and coffee or maté. Instead of beer or wine they take rum at their dinner, and consider it very good for helping the digestion.

As regards clothing, the women wear usually print dresses, or else a coarse national drill, both of which, comparatively, may be got cheap. The men generally get their clothes in second-hand shops, where they may obtain—

Articles.	Lowest price.	Highest price.
Coat, woolen or kerseymere	$0 86	$2 15
Waistcoat, woolen or kerseymere	59	86
Trousers, drill or kerseymere	1 08	1 29
Shirts, cotton or linen	59	1 29
Vests, cotton	22	51
Drawers, cotton or linen	22	51
Hats, straw or felt	86	2 15
Boots, new	1 51	3 00

The laboring class usually live either in "estalagens" or in "corticos." "Estalagen" is the name given to a number of small houses built together, forming a square, rectangle, or sometimes even occupying the ground floor of a respectable dwelling-house. A "cortico" is where these houses are almost limited to one room each, and have to be reached by a common staircase and veranda. A house in an estalagen may be rented for from $5.16 to $8.60 a month, whilst a dwelling in a cortico does not exceed $4.30 and may be had even for $3.44 a month. Single men who hire only one room pay from $2.58 to $3.44 per month.

WAGES, PAST AND PRESENT.

The answer to this can only be given in general terms, namely, that no marked change has taken place between the present rates and those which prevailed in 1878. The times, however, were more flush in Rio then than now.

HABITS OF THE WORKING CLASSES.

The working people may be divided principally into two parts—the native and the Portuguese elements, and the Italian element. The working people are chiefly composed of these three nationalities. The latter are rather disorderly; living close together in the corticos, they have ample opportunity of quarreling, and they avail themselves of it. The former are more quiet. As a rule the working classes are perhaps steady, but there are too many who are not trustworthy. and who think very little of living in a house two, three, or more months without paying a cent for it, until the owner turns them out. Buying on credit at the shops and paying the seller with " have patience" is too common.

FEELING BETWEEN EMPLOYER AND EMPLOYÉ.

The general feeling prevailing between employé and employer is that of fear on the part of the employé, especially as regards those serving corporations. There is certainly no marked sympathy on either side.

LABOR ORGANIZATIONS.

Both labor and capital appear to be devoid of organizations in respect of their relations to each other.

STRIKES.

Strikes are not common and their effects have been of no importance. The last strike on record, if such it may be called, was amongst the laborers of the custom-house; Government having enforced the use of a uniform, the laborers refused to go to work, but were put down by military force and obliged to wear the uniform, the cost thereof being deducted from their salaries.

FOOD PURCHASES.

The working people are free to purchase wherever they choose. They are paid as a rule every fifteen days in paper money. Servants, clerks of shops, and the higher officers are paid every month in the same currency.

CO-OPERATIVE SOCIETIES.

There are no co-operative societies in Rio. There did exist one once, but it was unsuccessful.

GENERAL CONDITION OF THE WORKING CLASSES.

The lower working class live as described before. The best of their houses never have more than three rooms, a sitting-room, a bedroom, and a kitchen. The sitting-room and the bedroom are generally each about 10 feet square, the kitchen much smaller. Some houses have no kitchen, in which case they cook out in the common yard. In the sitting-room are generally found a pine-wood table, wooden or sometimes cane-seated chairs, and more rarely a sofa, which would be cane-seated. In the bedroom stand a bedstead, an iron washstand, and perhaps a chest of drawers, and on the walls may be seen some cheap picture of a saint. In the kitchen there are an iron stove belonging to the house, a water-jar, and shelves. As a rule the bedroom is without a window, but there is some opening at the top of the wall for ventilation. These quarters are generally crowded and their sanitary condition poor. The workman leaves his home for his work, and the wife passes the whole day washing and ironing. On visiting these dwellings one will see, stretched across the common yard in all directions, lines upheld by bamboos, with linen hung thereon to dry, and the women either at the washing-tub or in their sitting-rooms over the ironing-table. The moral condition of these people is of rather a low grade. As regards their physical condition, the men are as a rule strong and enjoy health, but among the women it is otherwise ; the continual going and coming from the wash-tub to the ironing-board and back again to the washing soon tells upon them, and often results in pulmonary consumption. Their chance of laying up for old age or sickness is small; however, one does see men, particularly the unmarried, put themselves to all kinds of privation and lay by their money in the savings bank, and sometimes even acquire a fortune and afterwards a title of nobility. A short time ago there died here a baron owning nearly a whole row of houses in one of the best streets of the city, which brought him in monthly the revenue of $1,720, and who began his life as a peddler of liver, tripe, &c.

After the day's work is over, time is frequently passed in card-playing or in a game at quoits, or in singing. Especially the Italian part of the work people are very fond of singing, and they amuse themselves by singing to the accordion or the banjo.

A LABORER'S STATEMENT.

The following questions were put to a laborer, aged 25 years, in compliance with the circular, and his answers are given :

Question. Are you married or single ?—Answer. I have a wife and a daughter.
Q. What is your employment ?—A. I work in the custom-house, where I get 66 cents a day.
Q. Is that sufficient for you to support your family ?—A. No; my wife has to help me ; she washes and irons, by which means she gains an average of 43 cents a day.
Q. In what way, more or less, do you spend your money ?—A. We pay for a house of three rooms, nicely situated in a by-street, monthly, $5.16; for food we manage with $10.75, eating what poor people generally eat; and the rest of our earnings is for clothing, &c., $13.49 ; total, $29.40.

This man is unable to read or write, and states that he does not lay up anything.

At many wholesale and retail stores and manufactories in Rio the employés receive their breakfast and dinner at the establishment.

SAFETY OF EMPLOYÉS.

As a rule employers furnish no means at all for the safety of the workmen, neither provide for them in any way in case of accidents. There are nevertheless some establishments provided with an arrangement in case of fire; and some corporations provide in some measure for accidents amongst their employés ; in cases of death through an accident in the service of the corporation they help towards the burial and set a small pension on the widow ; in cases of sickness, they provide for a doctor and the medicines ; but for the latter they are generally made to pay a small percentage of their income. The general relation between employer and employés is merely that of courtesy.

POLITICAL RIGHTS.

There is no especial application of the law in regard to the working people; they enjoy the same rights as any other class. To have the right of voting the citizen must have an income of $86 yearly, which may consist of wages or salary as well as income on capital. A person wishing to vote must draw up a petition to the judge of the court of his district, inclosing documentary evidence of his qualification, which may cost him some dollars. This has to be done in September before the election. If the judge finds the documents satisfactory, after forty days (time allowed for opposite parties to protest against his qualifications) he goes to an official recorder, who gives him his permanent "diploma" of voter. Having done that, he has only to wait for the election day. The voting takes place in a church or other public building in his parish, where he must appear, within the time appointed, to answer his name, presenting his diploma when his name is called. The list is called by the judge of the judicial district in presence of two other delegates appointed by law.

They are subject to the same direct and indirect taxes as the other classes, according to their income, expenses, and property. There are no laws which regulate labor, apart from the existence of slavery, in any especial way. The tendency of legislation is favorable to labor. As yet, however, the employment of minors in manufactures has not been the subject of legislation.

CAUSES OF EMIGRATION.

There is no emigration from Brazil. The immigrants to Brazil are principally from Portugal and Italy, and mostly engaged in agricultural work in the interior. The farmers, especially in the provinces of Saõ Paulo, Paraná, and Rio Grande do Sul, enter into contracts with them as is most convenient to both parties. Immigrants who have any special qualifications find employment in the public works, on railways, in private enterprises, &c.

NUMBER OF FEMALE EMPLOYÉS.

Up to the present time the employment of women in industrial pursuits has been very limited. There are no authentic statistics published on this subject, nor, indeed, any statistics.

a. I have ascertained that one cotton and woolen factory in this city employs 60 women and 47 children, boys and girls, as operatives. Other such factories employ some female operatives. Six boot and shoe manufactories that have been visited employ 108 women, the most of whom work at home. They are not employed in bookbinderies. In two of the principal dress-making establishments 57 women are employed at sewing. Estimated number employed in manufacturing, 1,500.

b. Are employed only in a few French and German shops; estimated number employed, 100.

c. Public teachers paid by Government, 90 ; in private schools, 100; teachers of music, drawing, and languages, 40 ; in telephone stations, 20; laundresses, nearly every poor woman.

d. Agriculture, generally only slaves.

FEMALE WAGE RATES.

Wages paid to females, where there are any, will be found specified in the tables of wages paid to men. Public teachers are paid the same as the men. Hours of labor are the same as for the men.

MORAL AND PHYSICAL CONDITION.

The same as the men, with the exceptions that have been stated.

MEANS OF IMPROVEMENT.

There are 94 public schools belonging to Government, 47 for each sex, besides other schools belonging to private beneficent societies, where they can receive any education they wish, free of any expense whatever beyond that of books. Besides this there is nothing else provided for their improvement.

SAFETY OF FEMALE EMPLOYÉS.

None whatever. Fires, however, are very rare in Rio, owing partly to the style of building, and partly to the infrequent use of fires for heating purposes.

PROVISIONS FOR SICK AND DISABLED.

The provisions made by the employers in regard to sanitary measures and for the care of the sick and disabled are very scanty, if any.

EFFECTS OF WOMEN'S EMPLOYMENT.

There has been some little increase in the wages of women in the past five years, but the necessaries of life five years ago were exceptionally high on account of the famine in the north part of the Empire. However, there is liability of an increase in the prices of necessaries henceforth, on account of the probability of increase of duties on articles of importation. The employment of women does not appear to have affected the wages of men.

STATE OF FEMALE EDUCATION.

The women employed as operatives possess, as a rule, very little education, and are mostly single. Their occupation in this regard has not apparently produced injurious effects on the family circle. As applying generally to the working classes, the habits of thrift are not so well developed here as in some other countries. Although, as has been said, the tendency of legislation is favorable to labor, yet the fact that Government supports lotteries for the purpose of revenue, notwithstanding their acknowledged injurious effects on the economical condition of this class, illustrates the situation tolerably well. The bone and sinew of this large city are replenished every year by some thousands of temperate, industrious, and hardy people from the Azore Islands and the mountain districts of Portugal. The lot of the laborer here is not necessarily a hard one. With reasonable skill in his calling; with attention and application, and of course thrifty habits, he can lay up money. It is my opinion that the condition of the working class has much improved in the past thirty years. In my annual report published in the April, 1884, number of Consular Reports are some observations on slavery in Brazil, and upon agricultural and other labor.

Attention is called to explanatory statements, also remarks in regard to pensions in the civil service, in the accompanying Tables I to XV.

C. C. ANDREWS,
Consul-General.

UNITED STATES CONSULATE-GENERAL,
Rio de Janeiro, August 4, 1884.

I. General Trades.

Wages paid per week of sixty hours in Rio de Janeiro

Occupations.	Lowest	Highest.	Average.
BUILDING TRADES.			
Bricklayers	$6 48	$10 30	$8 25
Hod-carriers	3 87	5 67	4 64
Masons	7 74	11 61	6 45
Tenders	3 87	5 67	4 64
Plasterers	9 03	15 48	12 90
Tenders	3 87	5 67	4 64
Slaters	6 45	10 32	8 25
Roofers	4 64	9 03	8 25
Tenders	3 87	5 67	4 64
Plumbers	7 22	9 03	8 25
Assistants	3 87	5 67	4 64
Carpenters	7 74	10 32	9 03
Gas-fitters	7 74	10 32	9 03
OTHER TRADES.			
Bakers	5 16	9 00	7 74
Blacksmiths	15 48	25 80	16 77
Strikers	5 70	7 74	6 45
Bookbinders	5 16	12 90	9 03
Brick-makers	8 25	10 32	4 64
Brewers	10 75	21 50	16 00
Butchers	3 09	5 16	3 87
Brass-founders	10 32	25 80	12 90
Cabinet-makers	9 03	12 90	11 61
Confectioners	4 30	12 90	7 50
Cigar-makers	7 74	15 48	12 90
Coopers	3 80	8 60	6 45
Distillers	15 92	21 50	15 92
Drivers:			
Draymen and teamsters	2 58	4 30	2 58
Cab, carriage, &c	2 58	4 30	2 58
Street railways	8 60	9 50	9 56
Dyers	2 58	15 37	5 37
Engravers	12 90	25 80	12 90
Gardeners	4 30	6 45	4 30
Hatters	2 58	12 90	10 32
Horseshoers	7 74	9 80	9 00
Jewelers	7 74	20 64	12 90
Laborers, porters, &c	3 87	5 67	4 64
Lithographers	12 90	51 60	12 90
Millwrights	3 52	25 80	15 48
Potters	3 00	5 16	3 87
Printers	5 16	25 80	12 90
Teachers, public schools	10 75	21 50	16 00
Saddle and harness makers	3 87	6 45	5 16
Sail-makers	10 32	20 64	10 32
Stevedores:			
Day (12 hours)	7 74	9 03	7 74
Night (11 hours)	11 61	12 90	11 61
Tanners (besides 2 meals per day *)	2 60	4 87	4 30
Tailors	3 87	13 00	5 16
Telegraph operators	6 45	15 70	10 75
Tinsmiths	5 67	11 61	9 03
Watchmakers	10 75	32 25	21 50
Painters	5 16	25 80	7 74

* Some other classes of workmen, such as drivers, saddle-makers, and tailors, get two meals a day besides the wages stated in the columns.

II. FACTORIES, MILLS, ETC.

Wages paid in factories, mills, &c., in Rio de Janeiro.

Occupations.	Lowest.	Highest.	Average
GLOVE FACTORY.			
Men in cutting out gloves...........................per month..	$12 00	$19 35	$17 20
Men in scraping the skins..................................do...	10 75	12 90	11 00
Dyers..do....	10 75	15 05	12 90
Sewing women ....do....	6 45	10 75	8 60
Apprentices:			
Men...do....			3 20
Women..do....			4 30
FURNITURE MAKERS.			
Cabinet-makers ....per week..	6 45	15 48	11 61
Sculptors ....do....	6 45	15 48	11 61
Cane-seat makers...do....	3 87	6 45	5 16
Varnishers...do....	5 16	10 32	7 74
Turners..do....	6 45	15 48	11 61
Ironsmiths..do....	6 45	14 20	10 32
CLOTH MANUFACTORY.			
Masters..per week..	19 35	43 00	34 40
Overseers...do....	7 74	11 61	7 74
Engineer...do....	12 90	25 80	17 20
Firemen..do....	6 45	7 74	6 45
Weavers:			
Men...do....	5 16	6 45	5 16
Women..do....	2 06	3 35	2 60
Children...do....	77	2 06	1 30
Packers...do....	5 16	6 45	5 16
WALL-PAPER PRINTING FACTORY.			
Master...per week..	8 60	21 50	16 00
Workmen...do ...	3 22	5 37	4 30

III. FOUNDRIES, MACHINE-SHOPS, AND IRON WORKS.

Wages paid per day of ten and a half hours in foundries, machine-shops, and iron works in Rio de Janeiro.

Occupations.	Lowest.	Highest.	Average.
Machine department:			
Turner......	$0 52	$2 15	$1 72
Fitters	1 50	2 58	1 72
Engineers	2 15	3 00	2 50
Assistants			1 07
Apprentices.....		64	21
Copper-boiler makers:			
Master			3 44
Workmen			2 15
Assistants			1 07
Iron-boiler makers:			
Master.....	3 00	4 30	4 30
Workmen	1 29	3 00	1 93
Riveters.....	77	1 03	86
Assistants and apprentices (boys).....	21	64	21
Foundry:			
Master	3 00	4 30	4 30
Workmen	1 72	2 58	2 15
Assistants.....	77	1 03	86
Blacksmiths:			
Master	3 44	4 30	4 30
Workmen	2 58	3 00	2 79
Strikers.....	1 03	1 29	1 07
Modellers:			
Master	3 00	3 21	3 00
Workmen	1 29	2 15	1 72

IV. GLASS-WORKERS.

Wages paid per week of fifty-six hours to glass-workers in Rio de Janeiro, Brazil.

Occupations.	Lowest.	Highest.	Average.
Apprentices	$1 29	$2 58	$1 29
Workmen, blowers, &c	3 87	7 74	5 16

Not much can be said of glass-workers in Rio, since there exists only one manufactory, and that very insignificant. The working room is perhaps not larger than 15 square yards; it is on the first floor of a wooden-built edifice, staircase, floor, &c., all being of wood. In the center of the room stands the furnace with the molten glass; on one side of the room stand the annealing ovens, whilst the other three sides of the room are of glass. Lamp chimneys, common tumblers, jars, &c., are about the only articles manufactured.

V. MINES AND MINING.*

Wages paid in connection with the gold mine in Goyaz, Brazil.

Occupations.	Lowest.	Highest.	Average.
The following is all that could be ascertained of the above mine:			
Manager ....per year.		$5,160 00	
Chief engineer.....................................do.		5,160 00	
Carter ....per month.		8 60	
Workmen on the hydraulics ....per week.			
Carpenters ....do.			
Blacksmiths ....do.	$2 06	12 90	$2 58
Fitters ....do.			
Miners ....do.			

* No details can be given in this line, since there are no mines in Rio de Janeiro.

There is a total of 108 employés receiving monthly the amount of $1,075.

VI. RAILWAY EMPLOYÉS.

Wages paid per week to railway employés (those engaged about stations, as well as those on the engines and cars, linemen, railroad laborers, &c.), in Rio de Janeiro, Brazil.

Occupations.	Lowest.	Highest.	Average.
Engineers, locomotive	$10 32	$25 80	$15 48
Firemen	5 16	9 03	6 45
Train-guard	8 60	15 91	12 90
Brakeman	3 87	5 67	5 16
Man who oils the wheels	5 16	7 74	6 45
Assistant			5 16
Luggage-keeper	5 16	6 45	5 16
Linemen	4 64	5 16	4 64
Overlooker	5 67	7 74	6 45
Station-guard			5 16
Station master	10 75	21 50	19 35
Telegraph operators	6 45	15 70	10 75
Quarriers	7 74	9 03	7 74
Masons	10 32	12 90	11 61
Bricklayers	9 03	10 32	9 80
Carpenters	9 03	11 61	10 32
Ironsmiths, adjusters	10 32	15 48	12 90
Strikers	5 16	6 45	6 45
Solderingman			10 32
Assistant			6 45
Pavers	6 45	8 24	7 74

VII. Ship-yards and Ship-building.

Wages paid per week of sixty hours in ship-yards—distinguished between iron and wood building—in Rio de Janeiro, Brazil.

Occupations.	Lowest.	Highest.	Average.
Iron-boiler makers...	$5 16	$25 80	$14 19
In iron :			
Turners...................................	5 16	25 80	14 19
Molders..................................	5 16	25 80	14 19
Fitters...................................	5 16	25 80	14 19
Riveters..................................	5 16	25 80	14 19
Copper-boiler makers	5 16	25 80	14 19
Blacksmiths...................................	5 16	20 64	14 16
Carpenters....................................	5 16	20 64	14 19
Calkers	5 16	20 64	14 19
In wood :			
Riveters..................................	5 16	20 64	14 19
Pulley-makers.............................	5 16	20 64	10 32
Turners...................................	5 16	20 64	10 32
Fitters...................................	9 03	25 80	14 19
Sail-makers...................................	10 32	20 64	15 48
Apprentices...................................	2 00	3 87	2 58

VIII. Seamen's Wages.

Wages paid per month to seamen (officers and men)—distinguishing between sail and steam—in Rio de Janeiro, Brazil.

Occupations.	Lowest.	Highest.	Average.
Sailing vessel:			
Captain	$43 00	$107 50	$64 50
Able seamen	15 05	15 05	15 05
Ordinary seamen	10 75	10 75	10 75
Steamers:			
Captain	143 00	258 00	215 00
Able seamen	15 05	17 00	15 05
Ordinary seamen	10 75	12 90	10 75
Stewards...............................	17 00	25 80	21 50

IX. Store and Shop Wages.

Wages paid per week of ninety-six hours in connection with stores, wholesale or retail, to males and females in Rio de Janeiro, Brazil.

Occupations.	Lowest.	Highest.	Average.
Accountants	$32 25	$86 00	$53 75
Cashiers	21 50	53 75	32 25
Salesmen	5 37	21 48	10 74
Apprentices.......................................	1 29	2 58	1 29

Employés in stores are paid according, first, to the wealth of the establishment; secondly, according to the training of the individual; it makes no difference whether it be in a wholesale or retail store, or whatever kind it may be.

X. Agricultural Wages.

Unfortunately, up to the present time most of the agricultural labor has been done by slaves. To the south of Rio, however, they are beginning to employ free hands, and these generally get 43 cents a day, besides their food. Government, however, favors emancipation, and slavery has already been abolished in two provinces—Amazons and Ceará.

XI. HOUSEHOLD WAGES IN TOWNS AND CITIES.

Wages paid per month to household servants (towns and cities) in Rio de Janeiro, Brazil.

Occupations.	Lowest.	Highest.	Average.
Man cook	$12 00	$25 80	$17 20
Female cook	8 60	19 35	12 90
Wet nurse	21 50	38 70	25 80
Dry nurse	6 45	12 90	8 60
Laundress	6 45	17 20	12 90
Ironing woman	6 45	17 40	12 90
Sewing woman	8 60	17 20	12 90
Housekeeper	8 60	12 90	10 75
Gardener	8 60	25 80	17 20

XII. CORPORATION EMPLOYÉS.

Wages paid to the corporation employés in the city of Rio de Janeiro.

[Per week of sixty-six hours.]

Occupations.		Lowest.	Highest.	Average.
Street-railway company:				
Pavers	per week	$6 45	$8 24	$7 74
Master of the line	do			10 32
Conductor of the cars	do			9 50
Drivers of the cars	do			9 50
Sweepers of the line	do			5 16
Changer of animals	do			5 16
Stablemen	do			5 16
Workmen on the line	do	5 16	7 74	5 16
Car-cleaners	do	4 66	5 16	4 66
Despatchers	do	10 75	12 90	10 75
Signal-men	do	4 66	5 16	4 66
Banks:				
Managers	per month	430 00	1,290 00	
Sub-managers	do	142 00	387 00	
Accountant	do	129 00	258 00	
Clerks	do	43 00	150 00	86 00
Cashiers	do	129 00	215 00	

XIII. GOVERNMENT DEPARTMENTS AND OFFICES.

*Annual salaries paid to employés in Government departments and offices, exclusive of trades-
men and laborers, in Rio de Janeiro, Brazil.*

Occupations.	Salary.	Gratifica-tion.*
Ministers (each)	$5,160 00	
Senators	3,225 00	
Deputies	2,580 00	
Professors (medicine)	1,376 00	$688 00
Substitutes (medicine)	688 00	344 00
Polytechnic Enginering School:		
Director	1,720 00	860 00
Professors	1,376 00	688 00
Substitutes	860 00	430 00
Public teachers (primary schools)	516 00	258 00
Observatory:		
Director	1,980 00	1,030 00
First astronomer	1,720 00	860 00
Second astronomer	1,420 00	730 00
Third astronomer	1,120 00	600 00
Calculator	1,032 00	516 00
Hospitals:		
Director	3,096 00	
Physicians	2,580 00	
Chemists	774 00	
Supreme court of justice:		
Presiding judge	2,580 00	1,290 00
Secretary	1,290 00	645 00

* Gratification only paid, or a proportionate part when full time is devoted.

Annual salaries of employés in Government departments, &c.—Continued.

Occupations.	Salary.	Gratifica-tion.*
Hospitals—Continued.		
Judges	$1,032 00	$516 00
Chief of police	1,032 00	516 00
Department of finance:		
1 minister	5,160 00	....
4 directors general (each).....	2,580 00	1,290 00
2 sub-directors (each)	2,064 00	1,032 00
1 assistant attorney-general.....	2,064 00	1,032 00
1 secretary in chief	2,064 00	1,032 00
5 counters (each)	2,064 00	1,032 00
4 secretaries or clerks (each)	1,118 00	602 00
2 secretaries (each).....	1,118 00	602 00
31 first clerks (each).....	1,118 00	602 00
32 second clerks (each)	903 00	473 00
30 third clerks (each(.....	645 00	344 00
4 second secretaries (each)	903 00	473 00
4 copyists (each)	645 00	344 00
14 supernumeraries (each)	301 00	129 00
1 treasurer-general.....	2,150 00	946 00
To cover losses.....	344 00	....
2 curators (each).....	1,290 00	645 00
1 teller.....	1,290 00	688 00
To cover losses.....	258 00	....
4 curators (each).....	688 00	344 00
1 archivist	860 00	430 00
1 assistant	430 00	215 00
1 doorkeeper	688 00	344 00
1 assistant	430 00	258 00
Department of finance:		
9 messengers (each)	344 00	172 00
4 mounted orderlies	516 00	215 00
32 officers and clerks of the mint (aggregate).....	35,368 00	....
38 officers and clerks of bureau of currency (aggregate) ...	48,934 00	....
90 officers and clerks office of receipt of public money (aggregate).......	55,900 00	....
196 officers and clerks of custom house of Rio (aggregate)	166,625 00	....

*Gratification only paid, or a proportionate part when full time is devoted.

Pensions.—All public civil employés after thirty years service receive a pension equal to their full salary. If they retire before the thirty years have expired they receive a part of their salary proportionate to the time they served. As to professors their term of service is 25 years, receiving full pay ; and if they continue beyond that time and then retire they receive a certain part of their gratification additional.

XIV. Trades and Labor in Government Employ.

Wages paid by the week of sixty hours to trades and laborers in Government employ in Rio de Janeiro.

Occupations.	Lowest.	Highest.	Average.
Custom-house :			
Overlooker....	....	....	$25 80
Assistant.....	....	....	10 32
Workmen at the cranes.....	....	....	6 45
Laborer, effective.....	....	....	5 16
Laborer, additional.....	....	....	3 87
Public works :			
Foreman	$0 03	$12 90	10 32
Assistant	6 45	7 74	6 45
Clerk	6 45	10 32	7 74
Time keeper.....	6 45	9 03	7 74
Chain-man.....	6 45	7 74	6 45
Foreman :			
Bricklayer.....	10 32	15 48	12 90
Carpenter.....	10 32	15 48	12 90
Stone mason.....	10 32	15 48	12 90
Blacksmith.....	10 32	15 48	12 90
Bricklayer	6 45	10 32	7 74
Carpenter.....	6 45	10 32	7 74
Stone mason	7 74	10 32	9 03
Pavers	6 45	9 60	7 74
Blacksmith.....	6 45	10 32	9 03
Fitter.....	7 74	10 32	9 03
Turner (in iron).....	7 74	9 03	7 74
Molder	8 80	10 32	9 50
Vice men.....	7 74	10 32	9 03
Plumber.....	6 45	10 32	9 03

Wages paid by the week of sixty hours to trades and laborers, &c.—Continued.

Occupations.	Lowest.	Highest.	Average.
Public works—Continued.			
Common painter	$7 74	$10 32	$9 30
Miner	6 45	9 80	9 50
Striker...	5 16	5 67	5 16
Laborer	3 87	6 45	5 16
Gardener..	5 16	6 45	5 16
Carter..	5 16	5 67	5 16
Marine and war departments:			
Iron and copper boiler-makers, turners, molders, fitters, riveters:			
Master	16 77	25 80	....
Undermaster	14 19	20 64	....
Workmen:			
First class....................................	9 00	14 19	....
Second class..................................	7 74	12 90	....
Third class...................................	6 45	11 61	....
Fourth class..................................	5 67	10 32	....
Fifth class	5 16	9 03	....
Sixth class	3 87	7 74	....
Apprentices......................................	2 06	3 87	....
Blacksmiths:			
Master	14 19	20 64	....
Workmen:			
First class....................................	9 00	14 19	....
Second class..................................	7 74	12 90	....
Third class...................................	6 45	11 61	....
Fourth class..................................	5 66	10 32	....
Fifth class	5 16	9 03	....
Sixth class	3 90	7 74	....
Apprentices......................................	2 06	3 87	....
Carpenters, calkers, and riveters:			
Master	11 61	20 64	....
Undermaster	9 03	18 06	....
Workmen:			
First class....................................	7 74	14 19	....
Second class..................................	6 50	11 61	....
Third class...................................	5 16	9 03	....
Fourth class..................................	3 90	7 74	....
Fifth class	3 12	6 45	....
Sixth class	2 58	5 16	....
Apprentices......................................	2 00	2 58	....
Pulley-makers and turners:			
Master	11 61	18 06	....
Undermaster	9 03	14 19	....
Workmen:			
First class....................................	6 45	10 32	....
Second class..................................	5 67	9 03	....
Third class...................................	5 16	7 74	....
Fourth class	3 90	6 45	....
Fifth class	3 09	5 16	....
Apprentices......................................	2 00	2 58	....
Sailmakers:			
Master	11 61	20 64	....
Workmen:			
First class....................................	6 45	11 61	....
Second class..................................	5 16	10 32	....

XV. Printers and printing offices.

Statement showing the wages paid per week of forty-eight hours to printers (compositors, pressmen, and proof-readers) in Rio Janeiro.

Occupations.	Lowest.	Highest.	Average.
Compositors...			*$0 43
Pressmen:			
Large Liberty press	$10 32	$12 90	11 64
Small Liberty press	5 16	10 32	9 06
Job-work	5 16	10 32	9 06
Bookbinders	5 16	12 90	9 06
Men to damp paper			6 48
Men to fold paper			†43
Men to fold inferior work			†22
Proof-readers......................................	16 12	21 50	16 12
Gilders..	12 90	15 48	12 90
Men to rule paper.................................	9 06	12 90	10 32
Men to page books			6 48

* For every 1,000 ems.　　　　　† For every 1,000 sheets.

PERNAMBUCO.

REPORT BY CONSUL ATHERTON.

COST OF LIVING.

The work-people live in the most primitive way, not any of them paying over $42 a year for rent. Codfish from Newfoundland is a great article of consumption—it costs 2 to 3 cents a pound; mandioca flour also is their principal article of consumption in the way of flour. Imported flour is too dear for them, costing at retail about 10 cents per pound and $9 by the barrel, while the mandioca flour costs 16 cents a peck. Potatoes are dear; fruits are cheap, and in the way they are eaten by the working-class do more harm than good. Beef is worth from 16 cents a pound to 30 cents. Jerked beef, of which a great deal is consumed here, is worth about 11½ cents a pound.

Comparison of present price of labor (1878) about the same.

HABITS OF THE WORKING CLASS.

Work as little as they can to live. It is to be hoped that as the children of these people have a chance for common-school training that there will be an improvement in the next generation (the children are bright and, I understand, learn quickly). They do not save any money; many of them have been slaves and have not the habit of saving. The slaves on the plantations, many of them, are degraded and stupid, but that depends greatly on the kind of masters they have or have had.

PREVALENCY OF STRIKES.

There has been one since I have been here, done by a sort of impulse; no organization about it. There are no organizations of labor that I know of. The working people are free to purchase, as a rule. Most of the employés are backwards in paying; only well-to-do people and tradesmen pay promptly. They are paid in paper money and in copper coin. No other money is in circulation here.

GENERAL CONDITION OF THE WORKING CLASSES.

The general condition of the working people, as a rule, is that they are poorly paid, fed, and clothed; but they are satisfied with their life so long as they have enough to eat and a place to live in.

POLITICAL RIGHTS.

Some few are voters; they have no influence on legislation except, perhaps, by their talk when excited. They do not pay any taxes unless they are voters; then it is a small sum.

The whole may be summed up in this: They are changing from slave to free labor, and the present generation of laborers as a body do not know how to read or write; they have no hope of improving their condition, and therefore live from hand to mouth; but I think there will be a decided improvement in the next generation, as they will have (the most of them) a fair common-school education, and will learn quickly any trade or calling they may be put at, and with the knowledge they have will probably be anxious to live better.

There is no female labor except as servants ; they are paid from $4 to $12 per month with board.

The same state exists in the consular agencies, so that one report will answer for all.

HENRY L. ATHERTON,
Consul.

UNITED STATES CONSULATE,
Pernambuco, June 2, 1884.

I. GENERAL TRADES.

Wages paid per week in Pernambuco.

Occupations.	Lowest.	Highest.	Average.
BUILDING TRADES.			
Bricklayers	$2 54	$19 20	$7 56
Hod-carriers	5 04	10 08	5 25
Masons	5 04	7 56	5 25
Tenders	1 92	1 92	1 92
Plasterers	2 52	5 04	3 72
Tenders	1 92	1 92	1 92
Roofers	1 98	2 52	2 42
Tenders	1 92	1 92	1 92
Plumbers	5 04	10 08	7 59
Assistants	2 52	2 52	2 52
Carpenters	3 78	15 02	5 25
Gas-fitters	2 52	10 08	5 04
OTHER TRADES.			
Bakers	2 52	5 04	3 72
Blacksmiths	5 04	15 02	10 08
Strikers	2 52	5 04	3 72
Bookbinders		6 30	6 30
Brickmakers	1 92	2 52	2 42
Brewers	2 52	6 30	5 04
Butchers	5 04	7 56	5 25
Brass-founders	2 52	4 56	5 04
Cabinet-makers	5 04	14 32	5 25
Confectioners	1 26	5 04	2 52
Cigar-makers	1 50	3 72	2 52
Coopers	2 52	5 04	2 52
Distillers	2 52	7 56	5 04
Drivers	5 04	14 32	7 50
Draymen and teamsters	2 52	5 04	4 50
Cab and carriage	3 78	7 56	5 14
Street railway	3 75	5 25	4 28
Horseshoers	3 04	10 08	5 04
Laborers, porters, &c	1 94	3 78	2 00
Printers		12 00	12 00
Teachers (public schools)	5 04	12 60	7 56
Saddle and harness makers		7 56	
Tailors	5 04	12 60	7 56
Telegraph operators*	2 52	6 30	5 04
Tinsmiths	3 72	6 30	5 04

* The operators of the English submarine cable are paid about $3.50 per day.

II. FACTORIES, MILLS, ETC.

Wages paid per week of forty-eight hours in factories or mills in Pernambuco.

Occupations.	Lowest.	Highest.	Average.
Cotton factories:			
Workmen	$2 52	$10 08	$5 04
Clerks	3 78	12 60	5 04
Directors, superintendents, &c	12 60	35 28	25 20

Only one factory here of cotton; they have the right for this province; they only make cotton bagging ; all the other cotton goods are imported; the lowest sort of white or unbleached cotton sells for about 12 cents per yard.

III. FOUNDRIES, MACHINE-SHOPS, AND IRON WORKS.

Wages paid per month of two hundred and eighty-eight hours in foundries, machine-shops, and iron works.

Occupations.	Lowest.	Highest.	Average.
Directors	$168 00	$246 00	$147 00
Molders	24 60	49 20	31 50
Carpenters	24 60	49 20	33 60
Carpenters, new beginners	3 36	6 30	4 20

VI. RAILWAY EMPLOYÉS.

Wages paid per month to railway employés (those engaged about stations as well as those engaged on the engines and cars, linemen, railroad laborers, &c.) in Pernambuco.

Occupations.	Lowest.	Highest.	Average.
Station masters	$10 50	$24 20	$9 60
Ordinary workmen	13 00	16 80	....
Engine drivers*	37 80	75 00	63 00
Firemen*	12 60	16 80	14 70
Linemen	10 50	31 50	14 70

* Engine drivers and firemen have one day off in every week.

VIII. SEAMEN'S WAGES.

Wages paid per month to seamen in Pernambuco.

Occupations.	Lowest.	Highest.	Average.
Seamen	$16 00	$17 00	$16 75

X. HOUSEHOLD WAGES IN TOWNS AND CITIES.

Wages paid per month with board to household servants (towns and cities) in Pernambuco.

Occupations.	Lowest.	Highest.	Average.
Butler	$8 40	$16 80	$12 60
Tutor	14 70	16 80	15 54
Cook	8 40	21 00	14 70
House servants	4 20	8 40	6 30
Footmen	8 40	12 60	10 50
Washer women	8 40	12 60	10 50

XI. AGRICULTURAL WAGES.

Wages paid to agricultural laborers and household (country) servants in Pernambuco.

Occupations.	Lowest.	Highest.	Average.
Overseers on plantations * .... per month..	$16 80	$42 00	$30 00
Cane-cutters * .... per day..	53	63	48
Laborers † .... do....	33	63	....
Sugar boilers † .... do....	1 26	1 68	1 47
Gardeners * .... per month..	12 60	21 00	16 80

*With board.   † Without board.

XIII. GOVERNMENT DEPARTMENTS AND OFFICES.

Wages paid to employés in Government departments and offices in Pernambuco.

Occupations.	Lowest.	Highest.
Collector .... per month..	....	$3 36
Surveyor .... do....	....	2 10
Chief of section .... do....	....	2 10
First clerk or writer .... do....	....	139 86
Second clerk or writer .... do....	....	105 00
Third clerk or writer .... do....	....	63 00
Examiner to see that the rates are properly charged .... do....	....	176 40
Laborers .... per week..	$5 46	7 35
Watchmen and assistants .... do....	....	7 35
Governor of the laborers .... per month..	....	210 00
Inspectors for receiving and delivering cargo .... do....	....	37 80
Chief inspector of the above .... do	....	67 20
Watchmen for the harbor .... per week..	....	8 59

The custom-house does not open on Sundays or holidays, of which there are quite a number in a year, including church holidays and imperial holidays.

XIV. TRADES AND LABOR—GOVERNMENT EMPLOY.

Wages paid by the month of two hundred and eighty-eight hours to the trades and laborers in Government employ in Pernambuco.

Occupations.	Lowest.	Highest.	Average.
Blacksmiths	$37 80	$63 00	$53 60
Shoemakers	8 82	25 60	12 60

FALKLAND ISLANDS.

REPORT BY CONSUL LASAR, OF PORT STANLEY.

I. GENERAL TRADES.

Wages paid in Port Stanley.

Occupations.	Lowest.	Highest.
Building trades ....per hour..	$0 24	$0 24
Bricklayers ....do....	24	24
Masons ....do ...	24	24
Tenders...do....	15	15
Plasterers..do....	24	24
Tenders ....do....	15	15
Carpenters ....do....	24	48
Blacksmiths...do....	....	4 00
Strikers...do....	....	1 95
Butchers ....per month..	26 73	36 45
Coopers..per hour..	24	24
Gardeners...per month..	29 16	38 88
Laborers, porters, &c...per hour..	15	15
Printers ....do....	24	24
Sail-makers ....per day..	3 00	4 00
Stevedores ....do....	2 00	2 00

VII. SHIP-YARDS AND SHIP-BUILDING.

Wages paid per day in ship-yards distinguishing between iron and wood ship-building—in Port Stanley.

Occupations.	Average wages.
Ship-builders in wood...	$3 00

VIII. SEAMEN'S WAGES.

Wages paid per month to seamen (officers and men)—distinguishing between ocean, coast, and river navigation, and between sail and steam—in Port Stanley.

Occupations.	Lowest.	Highest.
Coasting:		
Seamen	$19 44	$24 30
Officer's mate	29 16	29 16
Ocean navigation:		
Seamen	19 44	38 88
Officers	34 02	48 60

Seamen are shipped here only for steamers coasting.

IX. STORE AND SHOP WAGES.

Wages paid per month in stores, wholesale or retail, to males and females in Port Stanley.

Occupations.	Lowest.	Highest.
Storekeepers, retail...	$29 16	$60 75
Assistants	29 16	29 16

X. HOUSEHOLD WAGES IN TOWNS AND CITIES.

Wages paid per month to household servants (towns and cities) in Port Stanley.

Occupations.	Lowest.	Highest.
Male servants	$24 30	$24 30
Female servants	6 07	9 72

Their whole time is given to their masters or mistresses. The moral and physical condition is good. The climate here, although boisterous, promotes their health considerably. The advantages are a Sunday school and a tolerable library, to which, for a small fee, they may have access, and books are loaned to them.

XIII. GOVERNMENT DEPARTMENTS AND OFFICES.

Wages paid to employés in Government departments and offices, exclusive of tradesmen and laborers, in the Falkland Islands.

Occupations.	Salary.	Occupations.	Salary.
Governor ....per month..	$405 00	Government pilot.........per annum..	$486 00
Colonial secretary ....per annum..	1,458 00	Chief constable..................do....	729 00
Government clerk..................do....	972 00	Constables ....per month..	24 30
Colonial surgeon................ do....	1,458 00	Government messenger ....do....	34 02
Colonial chaplain ....do....	1,458 00	Government printer.............do....	29 16
Police magistrate ....do....	729 00		

XIV. TRADES AND LABOR—GOVERNMENT EMPLOY.

Wages paid to the trades and laborers in Government employ in the Falkland Islands.

Occupations.	Average wages.
Carpenter.........per day..	$2 00
Day laborers........per hour..	15

PERU.

REPORT BY ACTING CONSUL BRENT, OF CALLAO.

UNSATISFACTORY CONDITION OF AFFAIRS.

In reply to the labor circular of the Department of State, dated the 15th of February, and received at this consulate on the 19th of April, I have the honor of transmitting herewith the respective blanks, filled in as instructed.

From the exceptional condition of this republic, emerging from a long and disastrous war, the data given should not be regarded as that obtaining in normal times. Enterprise and business activity are still paralyzed; fortunes represented five years ago, by the government paper money on which all transactions were then based, and their having an exchangeable value of from 18 to 20 pence sterling for the sol, have disappeared with the fall of that same paper currency to a value of 2½ pence sterling for the sol, and consequently the necessary capital for the development of industrial undertakings is not attainable. Therefore it is, that the demand is proportionately limited, and laborers obliged to accept such wages as they can secure in the few openings for work afforded to them. A skilled mechanic, for instance, who in 1877 or 1878, could easily have commanded from four to six silver sols or its equivalent, per day, must now, from the slack opportunity, content himself with half or a third of that amount.

So it is in every branch of industry from the counting-house, or the great importing establishments, to the petty tradesmen or artisans. The first cannot find a market for their goods, and the last named suffer from the general stagnation of business, the lack of capital, and the disinclination to grant credit or accommodation. The banks crippled in their resources can do nothing to assist their clients.

The balance of trade formerly in favor of Peru, from her large exports of guano and nitrates, is now against her, since Chili has taken possession of those sources of such enormous wealth; owing to the war and heavy customs duties the output of sugar has fallen from 100,000 to 40,000 or 45,000 tons yearly, and the drain of men for military service left the mines and agricultural districts in the interior, if not quite deserted, at least in such a state as to render work uncertain and unprofitable.

The Government in Peru, formerly the distributer of wealth and resources, now finds a scanty income in the customs revenue and in the taxes on lands and property, which are maintained at nearly the same high price as before, notwithstanding the almost general poverty and even penury. This burden naturally contributes in great measure towards depressing and restricting financial advancement.

HOPEFUL OUTLOOK.

But nearly all classes of persons have well-founded hopes in the elasticity of Peru, and that with the consolidation of internal tranquillity and the establishment of peace abroad, the immense resources of the country will be developed; foreign capital is looked for and, indeed, promised, to open up again the wonderfully rich silver-mining district of the Cerro de Pasco, which, in itself, would be a guarantee for progress.

And the Government, when once relieved from the pressing cares incident on such a thorough reconstruction as that now called for, will doubtless reduce the almost prohibitory duties imposed on the exportation of sugar and ores, and then the laboring classes in Peru will have the opportunity given to them for regaining their former advantageous positions and emoluments.

WAGES AND COST OF LIVING.

The question of the cost of living to the laboring classes in Peru can, at present, be answered by referring to the sums they gain by their work.

Rice, beans, fish, potatoes, and sometimes a little pork or beef, form their usual food. If a man earns say $9 per week, and few do, the surplus remaining after paying for the week's supply of provisions is infinitesimal.

Lodgings are not so expensive, for this class of people generally live in long "callejones" or alley-ways, where two rooms may be obtained for a monthly rent of from $2 to $4.

Among the better class of mechanics and skilled workmen the condition of affairs is about the same, for their pay is proportionately small, and their position entails a greater expenditure in the way of clothing, house-rent, &c. So that I may conclude on this point by stating as my firm conviction that, at this moment in Peru, ninety-nine out of a hundred of the classes alluded to live literally from hand to mouth, and this is emphatically proven by a ramble through the streets of Lima, and the spectacle of the countless pawnbrokers' shops and places for the purchase of old furniture and household goods that have come into existence since the war, and that are crowded to the roofs by the accumulation of such objects sold at a ruinous sacrifice by the people to whom I refer.

Were it within the scope of this paper, I might even extend my remarks to other and higher classes who have been reduced to almost mendicity by the terrible calamities afflicting the republic politically and socially.

HABITS OF THE WORKING CLASSES.

The habits of the working classes are not so satisfactory as might be desired. There are three obstacles, principal ones, standing in their way:

First, the laxative influence of the climate, combined with the peculiar character of the Spanish-American people in the tropics.

Second, the extraordinary and wholly unnecessary number of feast-days, religious, political, and social, observed during the year, it being computed that, exclusive of Sundays, there are fifty days of the three hundred and sixty-five that are given over to the celebration of religious anniversaries, some political or martial reminiscence, or birth-days or saints' days. A peculiar custom obtains amongst almost all Peruvian workmen of the laboring class, of knocking off work on Mondays, which they popularly term "San Lunes," or Saint Monday; and,

Third, the unfortunate circumstance existing of the abundance and cheapness of the native brandy, made from the Italia grape, and termed aguardiente, pisco blanco, &c., and of the chicha, an intoxicating compound produced from the fermentation of grain and copiously seasoned with strong liquor.

The Peruvians of the lower class, male and female, are passionately addicted to these beverages, and the result is painfully and frequently noticeable in deficient pay-rolls and crowded calabooses. In the interior the Indians, possessing land that is extraordinarily fertile, need only till their ground for three or four months of the year; the harvesting of their crops of maize, potatoes, and "garbanzos," similar to our lentiles, requires but little labor, and for the rest of the twelve months they are busily engaged in feasting, and spend their easily-acquired subsistence.

On the plantations, estates, and mines it is different, for there the overseers so manage to keep them bound as regards salary, that it becomes essential to labor more regularly.

I am referring now to the Peruvians who hold small farms or "chacaras." It will be readily understood that these habits are, in a measure, transmitted to and adopted by the Peruvian workmen on the coast, ↩ without being what might be precisely designated as indolent or lazy; a few days of hard labor are always rewarded by a spell of idleness and frequently of debauch.

Of course there are many exceptions to this rule.

With regard to their stability of character, I may safely say that no contractor in Peru would guarantee to terminate his undertaking on a fixed day, had he to wholly depend on the assistance of the lower classes of Peruvian laborers.

Artisans, skilled mechanics, small tradesmen, and the like, observe better habits from a sense of respectability and of necessity. But in my opinion nothing could be more harmful to the laborers than the incessant recurrence of these feast-days, or holidays, and, notwithstanding the efforts made by the Government and Church authorities to curtail them, the custom still holds.

Therefore, as a class, the Peruvian workman cannot be considered as steady or, as a general thing, trustworthy, in so far as a persevering application to labor is concerned.

FEELING BETWEEN EMPLOYER AND EMPLOYÉ.

As to the feeling between employé and employer, I would pronounce it in the main as friendly and considerate. There is a good deal of that old patriarchal spirit of intercourse yet existing that was general in the time of Spanish domination, on the coast, and the employés in many cases regard their employers as a sort of feudal lords.

Socialism has not yet taken root in this republic, and when an isolated attempt at general robbery and spoliation was made by the worst classes of Lima, after its fall in 1881, it was so effectually stamped out by the good people of that city, Peruvian and foreign, that a recurrence of the danger is not dreaded.

The relations between the different classes of the community are, I think, eminently satisfactory. I except, of course, the transitory excitement and feelings brought into existence by some political or revolutionary disturbance.

ORGANIZATION OF LABOR.

Trades unions are unknown in Peru. The artisans and some classes of laborers have guilds established, but the object of these is to secure uniformity of action when engaged on questions of paying duties or trade licenses to the Government, and sometimes to dismiss some unruly or unworthy member.

Neither are there any organizations of capital, since the reason does not exist.

STRIKES.

During my long residence in Peru, extending over twenty years, only two strikes have come within my notice, and those within the past few months. In both cases the matters were promptly and amicably arranged, both of the interested parties making concessions.

FOOD PURCHASE.

I have never learned of an instance where the liberty of food purchase was restricted. With the exception of the mines in the interior, and the nitrate works at Tarapacá, there are no general provision depots connected with industrial establishments, excepting, of course, on the large sugar-producing plantations that are remote from towns or villages.

The laborers are paid according to contract by week, day, or month, and in silver, or its equivalent in paper money, which is more convenient for ordinary daily transactions.

CO-OPERATIVE SOCIETIES.

These are as yet unknown in Peru. The general condition of the working people has already been described in this report.

SAFETY OF EMPLOYÉS.

Ordinary precautions are taken for the safety of employés in factories, mines, on railways, &c. The character of the buildings in Peru, spa'cious and low, does away with the necessity of fire-escapes, there not being one of these appliances in this republic. I know of no provision made for the workman in case of accident. Such cases are so extremely rare that no standard has been established, but I am clear on the point that as a general thing the employers are liberal to a degree with those who may become incapacitated in their service.

COOLIE LABOR IN PERU

In this relation I must, however, except the cases of the Chinese laborers on the sugar and agricultural properties.

Now that the supply of labor from China has wholly disappeared the planters are of necessity obliged to treat the few coolies they have under contract with consideration and care, but in former years the lot of a Chinese laborer on a plantation was a miserably unhappy one. As soon as their contracted terms expire, the Chinese seek new occupations, generally in the cities where they become domestic servants, or open small cheap condas or eating houses. Many of them remain on the plantations, but as free laborers, receiving fair wages, and released from the absolute control exercised over them during the term of their obligatory servitude. The number of Chinese to-day in Peru is calculated at forty thousand, scattered throughout the republic as far south as Mollendo.

POLITICAL RIGHTS.

The working men, Peruvians, have the same political rights that are granted to all the citizens of Peru under the constitution.

They possess the right to vote at all elections but their innate influence is insignificant, as in the very great majority of instances they obey the orders and follow the views of some personal favorite.

There is no poll-tax in Peru. The heavy contributions are laid on landed property, and on the privilege of doing business. Therefore the workmen are almost wholly exempt from the burden of aiding financially in the support of the government.

EMIGRATION.

There is no emigration from Peru. With the exception of a few hundred people who left this country for California in the days of the gold excitement, I can hear of no further instances of emigration.

FEMALE LABOR IN PERU.

With regard to female labor and the labor of children in this republic, outside of purely domestic products, there is nothing to be said, for the reason that such labor is not employed.

At the cotton-cloth factory of Santa Clara, 20 miles from Lima up the Oroya Railway, there are a few, probably twenty-five or thirty, women engaged in the more delicate portions of the manufacture, but, so far as I can learn, this is the solitary exception. In the far interior the women sometimes labor together with their husbands or brothers on their little farms, but I scarcely think that this instance is comprised in the interrogatory made by the Department.

In conclusion I hope it will be remembered, when taking this report into consideration, that the existing state of affairs and labor in Peru is particularly referred to, and were we again in normal and prosperous times, the condition of the laborer, the prospects of emolument and advantage, and the sphere of his action might certainly be portrayed in a highly favorable and even inviting light.

H. M. BRENT,
Acting Consul.

CONSULATE OF THE UNITED STATES,
Callao, May 5, 1884.

I. GENERAL TRADES.

Wages paid in Lima and Callao.

Occupations.	Lowest.	Highest.
BUILDING TRADES.		
Bricklayers ....per day..	$1 64	$2 46
Hod-carriers..do....	82	1 00
Masons ....do....	2 46	2 46
Tenders ....do....	82	82
Plasterers ....do....	1 64	2 46
Tenders ....do....	82	1 00
Carpenters...do....	1 48	1 64
Gas-fitters ....do....	(*)	....
OTHER TRADES.		
Bakers ....per day..	40	82
Blacksmiths ....do....	2 05	3 29
Strikers ....do....	1 00	1 50
Book-binders..do....	1 34	3 29
Brick-makers ....do....	1 64	2 46
Brewers ....per month..	82 30	82 30
Butchers ....per day..	1 64	2 46
Cabinet-makers ....do....	2 46	2 46
Confectioners ....do....	60	82.3
Cigar-makers ....do....	....	†1 20
Coopers ....do....	1 00	1 50
Drivers:		
Draymen and teamsters..per month..	12 00	16 00
Street railways...do....	28 75	28 75
Engravers..per day..	3 29	3 29
Gardeners..per month..	20 00	20 00
Hatters ....per day..	1 50	1 50
Jewelers ....do....	1 64	3 00
Laborers, porters, &c..do....	33	82
Lithographers...do....	3 29	3 29
Printers...do....	1 34	1 80
Teachers (public schools)..per month..	41 15	60 00
Saddle and harness makers...per day..	2 46	2 46
Stevedores...do....	82	82
Tanners...do....	82	82
Tailors ....do....	1 64	1 64
Telegraph operators ....per month..	49 38	49 38
Tinsmiths...per day..	1 00	1 50

* Per job.   † Average.

II. FACTORIES, MILLS, ETC.

Wages paid in ice factory and brewery of Backus & Johnston, Lima.

[Hours of labor, nine per day.]

Occupations.		Lowest.	Highest.
Business manager	per month..		$246 00
Assistant manager	do....		205 00
Brewer	.. do....		82 30
Master machanic	do....		125 75
Engineers	per day..	$1 25	1 64
Assistant engineers	do....	82	1 25
Firemen:			
First class	do....	1 25	1 64
Second class	do....	82	1 25
Carpenter	per month..	82 30	....
Assistant carpenter	per day..	82	1 25
Cartmen	do....	82	1 04
Factory hands	do....	33	82

NOTE.—There is one cotton cloth-factory near Lima, where the wages paid are about 25 per cent. under those given above. The wages paid at the woolen-cloth factory at Cuzco are not known in Lima.

III. FOUNDRIES, MACHINE-SHOPS, AND IRON WORKS.

*Wages paid in shops of the Oroya Railway.**

[Hours of labor, nine per day.]

Occupations.		Lowest.	Highest.
Foreman of shop	per month..	....	$123 45
Foreman blacksmith	do....	$102 82	102 82
Foreman founder	do....	102 82	102 82
Foreman of carpenter shop	do....	74 07	74 07
Foreman of paint shop	do....	74 07	74 07
Machinists	per day..	1 90	2 63
Assistants	do....	65	1 66
Blacksmiths	do....	2 05	3 20
Assistants	do....	98	1 31
Molders in foundry	do....	1 81	2 05
Laborers	do....	82	1 23
Carpenters	do....	1 48	1 64
Assistants	do....	82	1 31
Car repairers	do....	82	1 64
Car cleaners	do....	82	82
Painters	do....	82	1 66

* The foundry and machine-shops of the Oroya Railway may be taken as a representative of the class.

V. MINES AND MINING.

Wages paid in and in connection with silver-producing mines in the central departments of Peru.

Occupations.		Lowest.	Highest.
Chief of the mine	per month..	$32 02	$41 15
Chief of the lead	do ...	19 57	24 60
Pickmen	per day..	50	50
Ore carriers (hide buckets)	do....	40	40
Assistants	do....	20	20
Ore pickers and selectors	do....	50	50

NOTE.—Wages are generally paid every fortnight. The majority of mines have provision depots attached. Some of the peons or workmen do double duty, working at night, and gain double pay. Many workmen labor on contract agreements, receiving so much per running meter or so much per quintal (hundred-weight), according to the nature of the ground.

The "cajon" of metal-bearing ore, the standard, is 50 quintals or hundred-weight. The marco or mark of silver is eight ounces, and the technical phraseology is "so many marcos to the cajon."

VI. RAILWAY EMPLOYÉS.

Wages paid to railway employés (those engaged about stations, as well as those engaged on the engines and cars, linemen, railroad laborers, &c.) in Peru.

Occupations.	Lowest.	Highest.
Station agents ....per month..	$49 38	$102 87
Telegraph operators* ....do....	49 38	49 38
Ticket sellers*	....	49 38
Locomotive engineers ....do....	82 30	123 45
Firemen ....per day..	1 45	1 45
Coal passers....................................do....	98	98
Wipers...do....	82	82
Wipers ....per night..	1 25	1 25
Conductors...................................per month..	61 72	102 00
Brakemen ....per day..	82	98
Baggagemen ....do....	82	1 31
Baggage-masters ....per month..	41 15	41 15
Porters and laborers ....per day..	82	1 23
Linemen ....do....	49	82
Watchmen ....do....	82	98
Freight agents .... per month..	82 30	82 30
Freight assistants..............................do....	24 69	65 74
Yard masters....................................do....	74 07	74 07

* Telegraph operators and ticket sellers are generally combined.

NOTE.—These are the salaries and wages paid on the Lima, Callao and Oroya Railway, which may be taken as a representative.

VIII. SEAMEN'S WAGES.

Wages paid per month to seamen in Peru.

Occupations.	Lowest.	Highest.
General run of seamen...	$8 20	$20 00

NOTE.—It must be taken into consideration when giving this general answer, that Peru has no steam marine, and her merchant marine is composed of a few dozen of coasting schooners and smacks, carrying fruit and fire-wood from one port to the other. Now that peace is declared with Chili, the Peruvian flag will probably resume its place on many vessels that for safety's sake, changed nationality during the war. The Peruvians as a general thing do not make good sailors. From Sechura, a point near Payta, however, good men may be obtained, and it is a notable circumstance that the officers of the Peruvian navy who most distinguished themselves in the recent war were from the north of the Republic.

IX. STORE AND SHOP WAGES.

Wages paid per week of seventy hours in warehouses, and stores, wholesale or retail, to males in Lima, Peru.

Occupations.	Lowest.	Highest.	Average.
Salesmen..	$37 00	$74 00	$50 00
Book-keepers	28 00	56 00	35 00
Cashiers	28 00	56 00	35 00
General clerks and shopmen.....................	28 00	43 00	30 00
Junior clerks	18 00	28 00	20 00
Shop boys	4 00	12 00	6 00
Messengers and porters.........................	4 00	12 00	6 00

NOTE.—Female labor in Peru is almost unknown save as domestics and in millinery establishments.

X. HOUSEHOLD WAGES IN TOWNS AND CITIES.

Wages paid per month to household servants (towns and cities) in Lima and Callao.

Occupations.	Lowest.	Highest.	Average.
Mayordomo (butler)	$8 20	$16 40	$12 00
Second major domo (butler)	6 00	10 00	6 00
Boy of all work	4 00	6 00	5 00
Cooks:			
Chinese	8 20	12 00	8 20
Native	8 20	12 00	8 20
Amas de llave (houskeepers)	12 00	16 40	14 00
Seamstresses	*1 25	*2 00	*1 25
Nurses	16 40	16 40	16 40
Wet nurses	20 00	20 00	20 00
Porters	6 00	6 00	6 00
Coachmen	20 00	20 00	20 00

* Per day.

NOTE.—In hotels and on board the passenger steamers male servants are exclusively employed. Seventy-five per cent. of the cooks in Lima and Callao are Chinese, originally coolies, but who have worked out their contracts, and have settled in Peru.

There are probably few cities in the world where domestic services are so indifferently performed as in Lima, and for the first time, a few weeks since, a police regulation was established, obliging servants and masters to give "warning," a custom heretofore unknown.

XI. AGRICULTURAL WAGES.

Wages paid to agricultural laborers and household·(country) servants in Peru (sugar estates and others).

Occupations.	Average wages.	Occupations.	Average wages.
Cashier ....per month..	*$28 80	Stable-keeper ....per month..	†$9 00
First engineer machinist.........do....	*200 00	Native and Chinese laborers, in manufactory ....per day..	‡30
Second engineer machinist ....do....	*60 00	Sugar-packer.....................do ...	1 00
Collector ....do....	†20 00	Field hands ....do....	‡40
Field overseer.............. ......do....	*15 00	Manager, assistant ....do ...	†20 00
Apothecary ....do ...	†17 00	Plowmen..........................do....	§40
Warehouseman ....do...	†17 00	Irrigators ....do....	§35
Storekeeper ....do....	†17 00	Mud fence makers ....do....	§40
Sugar-boiler.....................do....	†17 00	Sowers ....do....	§35
Distiller ....do....	†15 00	Gardener.........................do....	§40
Caporales (foreman)..............do....	†10 00	Cook ....per month..	†10 00
Black and copper smith..........do....	†20 00	Donkey drivers, muleteers...per day..	30
Turner ....do....	†8 00		to 40
Cattle driver or herdser ....do....	†17 00		

* With board for self and family.   ‡ Two pounds rice each daily.
† With rations for self.   § Rice ration.

XII. CORPORATION EMPLOYÉS.

The mayor (alcalde) and common councilors ("municipales" and "sindicos") of Lima, have no salary.

The different branches of the public servive, such as street cleaning, the slaughter-house, the contracts for lighting the streets, and for police duty, &c., are farmed out at auction to the highest bidder, who collects from the citizens the taxes or contributions imposed for such service, conducts the same, and the municipality simply deputes one of its members to act as an inspector over the contractor. The few employés in the municipality are the secretaries, comptroller of statistics, treasurer, amanuenses, and clerks. Their yearly salaries range from $2,050 to $493.

XIII. GOVERNMENT DEPARTMENTS AND OFFICES.

Wages paid to employés in Government departments and offices, exclusive of tradesmen and laborers, in Peru.

I find it impossible to answer this interrogatory. The whole staff of Government employés is now on half pay, and what with the sum placed on one side for pension fund, war discount, &c., it would be almost out of the question to arrive at any exact figures. In normal times the salaries are more or less as follows, per annum:

Occupations.	Salary.	Occupations.	Salary.
Minister of state	$4,938 00	Chiefs of bureaus	1,650 00
Chief clerk of department	2,469 00	Ordinary clerks	1,000 00
Cashier	1,340 00	Porters	400 00
Interpreter	1,340 00		

XV. PRINTERS AND PRINTING OFFICES.

Statement showing the wages paid to printers (compositors, pressmen, proof-readers &c.) in Lima and Callao, Peru.

Occupations.	Lowest.	Highest.	Average.
Foremen ...... per month..			$57 61
Pressmen ...... per day..	$1 34	$2 46	2 00
Compositors ...... do....	1 34	2 05	1 75
Proof-readers ...... do....	1 34	3 00	2 00
Book-binders ...... do....	1 34	3 29	2 00
Rulers ...... do....	1 34	3 29	2 00
Lithographers ...... do....		3 29	3 29
Engravers ...... do,...		3 29	3 29

. NOTE.—There is no no Government printing office on a large scale in Peru. That now existing, which was probably the finest in South America before the recent war with Chili, was despoiled of its most valuable plant during the recent war.

ECUADOR.

REPORT BY CONSUL BEACH, OF GUAYAQUIL.

CONDITIONS IN LOWER AND UPPER ECUADOR.

In presenting the information requested by Department of State circular of February 15, 1884, it is essential at the outset that the explanation be made that as relating both to wages and cost of living in Ecuador, that the country embraces two distinct sections—sections having a greater contrast of prices than exists in almost any other country, and with a broader difference than often exists between any two countries. Geographically these two sections are Guayaquil and the lower provinces, and Quito and the upper provinces. The chief cause of the differences in prices prevailing in the two sections is the cost of transportation from one to the other, which has to be done on the backs of mules and donkeys, occupying from six to nine days, and costing $4 per 100 pounds. This large cost of transportation works as a prohibition against an exchange of commodities, and against the sale for cash of commodities produced in one section in the other. Hides and a few other articles, except hides of little value or importance, are taken from Quito to Guayaquil; and from Guayaquil there is sent to Quito dry goods, crockery, cutlery, and drugs and medicines. These articles are more expensive at Quito and in the upper provinces than at Guayaquil and in the lower provinces. But the general articles of food do not cost more than one-half as much in the upper provinces as in the lower, rents are correspondingly low, and wages likewise. The tabular statement of wages herewith presented is for the lower provinces, except in one or two instances as otherwise noted, and to form a correct estimate of the wages of the whole country, the wages of the upper half of the country, including Quito and the upper provinces, should be rated at one-half of those given in the tables. This will be very accurate. Quito is not only the highest city in the world in point of altitude, but the lowest in the world, as regards the expense of living. At the best hotels, and very good ones they are, meals cost but $15 a month, meals for one day can be obtained at good restaurants at from 25 to 30 cents, and at common restaurants for a very insignificant sum. Servants of either sex can be employed at from 10 to 20 cents a day.

For general convenience all prices have been reduced to and are rendered in United States currency.

COST OF LIVING.

The men performing manual labor, who have families, pay from $1 to $2 a week for house rent. Their main living is soups and bread. Wholesome and nutritious soups are made by combining coarse pieces of meat costing from 5 to 8 cents a pound, with plantain and native vegetables, which are not very expensive. The food of a family of from four to six persons will cost from 30 to 50 cents per day. The climate is so uniformly warm that but little clothing or bedding is required, and no fuel is necessary except for use in cooking. A family outfit is often comprised in a few low-priced hammocks, and a few iron dishes for cooking the food.

Single laboring men sleep almost anywhere at from no cost to $1 a week, and obtain their meals at low-priced restaurants at from 15 to 30 cents a day. Clerks and book-keepers, if single, hire lodging rooms at from $2 to $5 a week, and obtain their meals at from $15 to $30 a month. Those who have families and keep house pay monthly rents ranging from $20 to $50. The cost of living for families of the better grade is according to the style, and may be quite small or large. To live in "good style" is more expensive than living in the same style in the United States.

The prices of articles that go to make up the expense of living in Guayaquil may thus be enumerated: Meats by the pound, 10 to 15 cents; fish by the pound, 5 cents; sugar by the pound, 4 to 15 cents; rice by the pound, 4 to 5 cents; wheat flour by the pound, 7 to 10 cents; corn meal by the pound, 4 to 5 cents; beans by the pound, 3 to 6 cents; ice by the pound, 10 cents; sweet and Irish potatoes by the pound, 2 to 3 cents; plantains and bananas, by the hundred, 15 to 20 cents; charcoal by the bushel, 30 to 40 cents; eggs by the dozen, 30 cents; milk by the quart, 10 to 20 cents; water by the 18 gallon, 10 to 20 cents. Clothing, dry goods, crockery, hardware, drugs and medicines, furniture, and all other imported articles, cost from one-half more to twice their cost at the places from which they are imported. The imported articles are used only to a very restricted extent by the manual labor class.

HABITS OF THE WORKING CLASSES.

Wages have not changed within the recollection of old residents. The working class in the main lives for to-day, letting to-morrow care for itself. This class works sufficient to earn a subsistence, but exhausts no energies in efforts at accumulation. The cause is an example handed down from age to age and generation. The tendency is to follow in a beaten track, to do things now as they were done last year, or ten or fifty years ago. They are not hostile to innovations and new things; but they do not seek them, and only accept them when it is easier to accept than to cast aside. The people are docile, especially the largely predominating Indian element. A good feeling usually exists between employés and employers, but without any discernible effect on general prosperity. There are no organizations among laborers nor among employers. There are no disagreements, no strikes, no arbitrations, and no riots. The laborers are free to purchase their supplies where they choose; but for convenience, and perhaps profit, the owners of large estates provide supplies for those employed. In the villages and cities all payments for labor are made in money, and without any restriction as to how or where it should be used. Common laborers are paid every week. Clerks, book-keepers, and others employed in stores or the public service are paid monthly. All are paid in the currency of the country.

LABOR ORGANIZATIONS.

All secret societies are prohibited, and there are no labor organizations or co-operative associations. The laboring class has a great field for improvement in method of living and in education. Morally and physically this class here appears to compare favorably with the same class elsewhere. The working class without property pays no tax. The workingmen are entitled to vote if citizens of the country. They do not exert any political influence, that is divided between the church and military leaders. There is no mentionable emigration or immigration, and the births and deaths being very equal, the total population is maintained year after year with great uniformity.

FEMALE LABOR.

The females so far as employed for wages are mostly servants, teachers, and laundresses. None of them are clerks, artists, chemists, hotel and boarding-house keepers, journalists, professional musicians, inventors, bankers, brokers, lecturers, preachers, public speakers, or compositors. They are not employed to work in the fields or factories. From the best information obtainable it does not appear that their wages, compensation, or general condition has changed during the last fifty years.

CONTENTMENT OF THE LABORING CLASSES.

The great uniformity of wages paid for skilled labor in the different vocations is a noteworthy fact. There are an abundance of laboring people in Ecuador. There is no important development of new enterprises, and there are no signs that either the rate of wages or the general condition of the working class will be changed for many years to come. When there is a great change it must result from external influences. The working class appears to be much more contented with its condition here than the same class in those countries where a greater degree of intelligence and a higher order of civilization abounds.

HORATIO N. BEACH,
Consul.

UNITED STATES CONSULATE,
Guayaquil, May 27, 1884.

I. GENERAL TRADES.

Wages paid per week of sixty hours in Guayaquil.

Occupations.	Lowest.	Highest.	Average.
BUILDING TRADES.			
Bricklayers	$6 00	$9 00	$7 50
Hod-carriers	3 00	6 00	4 50
Masons	6 00	9 00	7 50
Tenders	3 00	6 00	4 50
Plasterers	6 00	9 00	7 50
Tenders	3 00	6 00	4 50
Roofers, tile	6 00	9 00	7 50
Tenders	3 00	6 00	4 50
Plumbers	7 00	12 00	10 00
Assistants	5 00	7 00	6 00
Carpenters	9 00	12 00	10 00
Gas-fitters	6 00	12 00	8 00
OTHER TRADES.			
Bakers	6 00	12 00	10 00
Blacksmiths	6 00	12 00	9 00
Strikers	3 60	6 00	5 00
Book-binders	6 00	9 00	7 50
Brick-makers	6 00	9 00	7 50
Butchers	8 00	10 00	9 00
Brass-founders	9 00	12 00	10 00
Cabinet-makers	9 00	12 00	10 30
Confectioners	6 00	12 00	9 00
Cigar-makers	4 00	10 00	8 00
Coopers	9 00	12 00	10 00
Distillers	12 00	12 00	12 00
Drivers	8 00	10 00	9 00
Draymen and teamsters	8 00	10 00	9 00
Cab and carriage	8 00	10 00	9 00
Street railway	7 00	9 00	8 00
Engravers	9 00	12 00	9 00
Hatters	7 00	9 00	8 00
Horseshoers	10 00	14 00	12 00
Jewelers	10 00	13 00	12 00
Laborers, porters, &c	3 60	12 00	8 00
Millwrights,	18 00	25 00	20 00
Potters	2 50	3 00	2 75
Printers	6 00	12 00	10 00
Teachers, public schools	8 00	10 00	9 00
Saddle and harness makers	6 00	12 00	10 00
Stevedores	9 00	9 00	9 00
Tanners	7 00	9 00	8 00
Tailors	6 00	12 00	10 00
Telegraph operators	27 00	27 00	27 00
Tinsmiths	6 00	12 00	10 00
Quito—weavers (in mills)	1 50	2 10	1 80
Shoemakers	6 00	12 00	9 00
Barbers	8 00	12 00	10 00
Street-pavers	3 60	12 00	6 50

NOTE.—The butchers are employed on Sundays the same as other days; likewise the coach-drivers. The barber-shops are open Sunday forenoons. The telegraph offices are open every Sunday at stated hours.

II. FACTORIES, MILLS, ETC.

Wages paid per week of sixty hours in factories or mills in Guayaquil, Ecuador.

Occupations.	Lowest.	Highest.	Average.
Planing mills	$4 20	$12 00	$8 00
Ice factories	12 00	12 00	12 00
Chocolate factories	6 00	12 00	8 00
Bottlers of mineral waters	6 00	10 00	8 00

NOTE.—The ice factories are operated on Sundays the same as other days.

III. FOUNDRIES, MACHINE-SHOPS, AND IRON WORKS.

Wages paid per week of sixty hours in foundries, machine-shops, and iron works in Guayaquil, Ecuador.

Occupations.	Lowest.	Highest.	Average.
Common laborers	$3 00	$6 00	$1 50
Mechanics	7 50	12 00	10 00
Foremen	20 00	25 00	22 00
Engineers	25 00	50 00	35 00

V. MINES AND MINING.

Wages paid per week of forty-eight hours in and in connection with Zaruma mines in Ecuador.

Occupations.	Lowest.	Highest.	Average.
General work	$4 20	$6 00	$4 50
Foremen	10 00	25 00	18 00

VI. RAILWAY EMPLOYÉS.

Wages paid per month to railway employés (those engaged about stations, as well as those engaged on the engines and cars, linemen, railroad laborers, &c.) in Ecuador.

Occupations.	Lowest.	Highest.	Average.
Conductors:			
Railway	$28 00	$45 00	$40 00
Street	36 00	46 00	40 00
Drivers, street	28 00	36 00	30 00
Brakemen, railway	32 00	32 00	32 00
Track repairers, railway	20 00	20 00	20 00
Switchmen, railway	20 00	20 00	20 00
Engineers, railway	100 00	100 00	100 00

NOTE.—All street-car employés work on Sundays the same as other days.

VII. Ship-yards and Ship-building.

Wages paid per week of sixty hours in ship-yards (all wood shipbuilding) in Guayaquil, Ecuador.

Occupations.	Lowest.	Highest.	Average.
Common labor	$3 00	$6 00	$4 50
Skilled workmen	6 00	12 00	10 00
Foremen	12 00	18 00	15 00

VIII. Seamen's Wages.

Wages paid per month to seamen (officers and men) in Ecuador.

Occupations.	Lowest.	Highest.	Average.
Small sailing vessels	$8 00	$15 00	$12 00
Small local steamers	10 00	20 00	16 00
Engineers, local steamers	40 00	40 00	40 00
Captains, local steamers	70 00	70 00	70 00
Pursers, local steamers	40 00	40 00	40 00
Stewards, local steamers	30 00	30 00	30 00

NOTE.—All classes of vessels are operated on Sundays as other days.

IX. Store and Shop Wages.

Wages paid per week, of forty-eight hours in wholesale, seventy-eight hours in retail, stores, to males, in Guayaquil.

Occupations.	Lowest.	Highest.	Average.
Book-keeper	$14 00	$26 00	$20 00
Cashier	26 00	26 00	26 00
Clerk	10 00	15 00	12 00
Correspondent	26 00	26 00	26 00
Porter	3 00	4 00	3 50

NOTE.—Many of the retail stores are kept open all day Sunday, and all of them during the forenoon.

X. Household Wages in Towns and Cities.

Wages paid per month to household servants (towns and cities) in lower provinces of Ecuador.

Occupations.	Lowest.	Highest.	Average.
Cooks	$8 00	$12 00	$10 00
Men servants	8 00	12 00	10 00
Female servants	5 00	10 00	6 00

XI. Agricultural Wages.

Wages paid per day to agricultural laborers and household (country) servants in Ecuador.

Occupations.	Lowest.	Highest.	Average.
Men laborers, boarded	$0 30	$0 50	$0 40
Men laborers, without board	50	70	60
Women servants, with board	10	20	15

XII. CORPORATION EMPLOYÉS.

Wages paid per month to the corporation employés in the city of Guayaquil.

Occupations.	Lowest.	Highest.	Average.
Chief of police	$200 00	$200 00	$200 00
Assistant chief of police	140 00	140 00	140 00
Police sergeants	50 00	50 00	50 00
Policemen	40 00	40 00	40 00
Common laborers	36 00	36 00	36 00
Street cleaners	36 00	36 00	36 00

XIII. GOVERNMENT DEPARTMENTS AND OFFICES.

Wages paid per month to employés in Government departments and offices—exclusive of tradesmen and laborers—in Guayaquil.

Occupations.	Lowest.	Highest.	Average
Governor of province			$200
Guayaquil collector of customs	$175 00	$175 00	175
Guayaquil postmaster	175 00	175 00	175
Clerks and book-keepers	35 00	70 00	60
Customs stevedores	36 00	36 00	36
General of army			200
Colonel of army			127
Captain of army			47
Major of army			66
Corporal of army			16
Common soldier			

NOTE.—On "ship days" the custom-house and post-office are open for the discharge of cargo, ta on of cargo, clearance of vessels, and the receipt and making up of the mails. The other work is pended for the day.

XIV. TRADES AND LABOR—GOVERNMENT EMPLOY.

Wages paid by the week of sixty hours' to the trades and laborers in Government emp Guayaquil.

Occupations.	Lowest.	Highest.	Avera
Stevedores	$9 00	$9 00	$9 00
Lightermen	9 00	9 00	9 00

NOTE.—The lightermen work the same on Sundays as other days.

XV. PRINTERS AND PRINTING OFFICES.

Statement showing the wages paid per week of sixty hours to printers (compositors, pressmen, proof-readers, &c.,) in Guayaquil.

Occupations.	Lowest.	Highest.	Average.
Printers	$6 00	$12 00	$10 00
Pressmen	10 00	14 00	12 00
Proof-readers	12 00	17 00	15 00
Foremen	15 00	15 00	15 00

WEST INDIA ISLANDS.

BRITISH WEST INDIES.

THE BAHAMAS.

REPORT BY CONSUL M'LAIN.

In response to the labor circular issued by the Department of State, under date of February 15, 1884, I beg to submit the following report:

The character of labor and the conditions which surround it in this colony are so peculiar and so different from those which prevail in Europe, for which continent the circular before me was prepared, that I have deemed it advisable to discard to a great extent the printed interrogatories and schedules furnished, and to submit, as far as possible, in a different method, the information sought for.

THE CHARACTER OF OUR LABOR.

There are no mills, foundries, iron works, glass works, mines, or railways in this colony. The only industries in that line are the Marine Railway at Nassau and one or two factories for the canning of pine-apples. The labor of the people is confined substantially to agriculture, simple mechanical pursuits, trading, fishing, sponging, wrecking, cutting woods, salt-making, and ship-building.

RATES OF WAGES.

Agricultural laborers.—I presume there are 5,000 or 6,000 men, women, and children engaged in agriculture and in the rough out-door work of the plantation. Wages paid to adult male laborers are from 30 to 50 cents per day of nine hours; average, about 42 cents, without maintenance. Females receive from 20 to 40 cents per day, average 33 cents, without board. Youths of both sexes, from 10 to 15 cents per day. Most of the agricultural laborers own their own small piece of land, which they also cultivate.

Mechanics.—In the towns and settlements many of the ordinary mechanical pursuits are followed, the rates of wages being as follows, viz:

Occupations.		Lowest.	Highest.	Average.
Bricklayers	per day	$0 84	$1 25	$1 00
Masons	do	84	1 25	1 00
Carpenters	do	72	1 25	1 00
Bakers	do	72	1 12	96
Blacksmiths	do	60	1 00	90
Butchers	do	80	1 20	1 00
Cabinet-makers	do	72	1 00	90
Cigar-makers	do	75	1 25	1 00
Coopers	do	75	1 00	80
Drivers	do	40	60	50
Printers	per week	4 75	6 00	5 50
Sail-makers	per day	75	1 00	80
Stevedores	do	50	72	60
Tailors	do	60	80	72
Tinners	do	60	80	72
Painters	do	84	1 25	1 00
Wagon-makers	do	72	1 00	90
Plasterers	do	84	1 25	1 00
Shoemakers	do	72	1 00	90
Seamstresses	do	60	72	62
Shell-workers	do	30	60	50
Stone-cutters	do	50	84	72
Upholsterers	do	72	1 00	84
Salt-rakers	do	40	60	50
Sponge-packers	do	75	1 00	90

TRADING.

There are numerous traders, mostly in a small retail way, with a few wholesale houses. Hundreds of women are venders of confectioneries, nuts, and fruits, hawking them about the streets in baskets and wooden trays, in the settlements and towns, earning a livelihood in this way. The hours for employés in stores and shops are nine or ten per day, most of the places closing at dark. Very few females are employed in stores, but when they are used their wages are the same as those paid to males, viz: from $3 to $5 per week, average $3.75, without maintenance.

Fishing, sponging, and wrecking.—Probably one half the population of the Bahamas is engaged in these three industries; but no rate of wages can be given for these people for the reason that the entire business is carried on under the "system of shares." The owners of the vessels fit them for the voyage : out of the proceeds of the "catch" are taken the expenses, and the balance is divided by shares amongst all concerned. The most that can be said is that, taking one voyage with another, these laborers make a comfortable living, though they seldom accumulate property. The fish caught are not exported, but, fresh and cured, are used for food in the colony.

Those engaged in wrecking occasionally secure a large reward for salving some valuable ship or cargo : but these prizes are not so frequent as in the days which preceded the erection of light-houses and the introduction of steam vessels. Besides, the wreckers are proverbially extravagant fellows, and the end of the season finds them no better off than they were at its beginning.

The landing of the sponges furnishes employment to many other people in washing, bleaching, and clipping them, and in packing them for shipment. There are a dozen sponge-yards in Nassau, where the laborers employed receive wages as follows : Packers, from 75 cents to $1 per day—average 90 cents. All other hands, from 60 to 84 cents per day—average 75 cents, without board.

Salt making and wood-cutting.—A large quantity of salt is made, and much dye and cabinet wood is cut in the colony. The labor, however, employed in these industries is of the ordinary kind, muscle, rather than skill, being the desideratum. The wages earned by wood-cutters and salt-rakers are from 40 to 50 cents per day—average, say, 45 cents per day, without board.

Ship-building.—The ship-building of the colony is confined mostly to the making of small boats, fishing-smacks, and sponging schooners, with an occasional vessel of from 100 to 150 tons burden. The largest vessel ever built here, and she was exceptionally large, measures 233 tons. There are perhaps from fifteen to twenty small ship-yards in the colony. There is also at Nassau a marine railway, where ships less than, say, 800 tons can be repaired. The vessels built are all of wood. The day's work at the yards and at the railway consists of nine hours, and the wages paid (very little difference being made between the different kinds of workmen) are from $4.50 per week to $7.50—the average being $6.25, without maintenance.

Preserving of fruit.—There are three or four establishments in the colony, where ripe fruit is put up in cans—principally pine-apples, of which the islands produce from 5,000,000 to 6,000,000 every year. The crop is partly exported and partly canned here. These factories give employment, during May, June, and July, to perhaps 600 persons, men, women, and children, who are engaged in handling, paring, slicing. putting fruit in cans, beating, soldering, and packing cans in cases. At another factory the fruit is "candied" especially for confectioners' use. The wages paid employés in these factories are as follows: Men, from 36 to 60 cents per day—average, 50 cents; women, from 24 to 50 cents—average, 30 cents; youths, from 10 to 12 cents per day; tinners, by the job, soldering, earn from 90 cents to $1.50—average, $1 per day; boys, soldering by job, average 25 cents per day.

Seamen.—A number of vessels belonging to the colony are engaged in regular trade among the islands, to the West Indies, and to the United States, giving employment to several hundred persons. The wages paid to this class of men are as follows: For foreign voyages: Masters, $35 to $50 per month—average, $45; mates, $24 to $30 per month—average, $25; cooks, $17 to $20—average, $18 per month; seamen, $13 to $18 per month—average, $15. For interinsular voyages: Masters, $22 to $28—average, $26; mates, $14 to $16—average, $15 per month; cooks, $10 to $13 per month—average, $11; seamen, $7 to $11 per month—average, $8.50. These wages are for sail vessels, no steam vessels belonging to the colony. Foreign vessels shipping crews here are generally obliged to pay wages from 30 to 40 per cent. above these prices.

Household servants.—The wages paid to household help does not differ much in town or country. House servants, as a rule, do not lodge with their employers. Their wages, with board, are as follows: Cooks, from $2.50 to $4 per month—average, $3; house maids, $2 to $3.50—average, $2.50 per month; men-servants, $3 to $4—average, $3.25; butlers, $5 to $8—average, $6.50; laundresses, $5 to $8—average, $6 per month; youths, from ten to fifteen years old, $1 to $1.50 per month—average, $1; grooms and coachmen, average, $5 a month.

Government and corporation employés.—There are no incorporated cities, towns or villages in the Bahamas. The capital, Nassau, containing 12,000 inhabitants, is governed directly by the colonial authorities, without the intervention or assistance of any municipal officers or boards whatsoever; hence there are no wages of corporation employés to be reported. The following wages are paid to employés in Government offices, exclusive of heads of departments, viz: chief clerks, $725 per annum; assistant clerks, $144 to $360—average, $275; tide waiters, $384, or when temporary ones are employed, at 75 cents per day; overseers of prison, $194; turnkeys of prison, $280; overseers of roads, $600; sergeants of police, $388; corporals of police, $291; policemen, $220 to $250—average, $240. The fire department is principally volunteer, under charge of the police. Care of the streets and public works and property and general improvements are attended to by overseers with convict labor; and if extra help is needed laborers are employed at about 50 cents per day, and mechanics at their customary wages, as already reported.

THE COST OF LIVING.

The food of the poorer classes of working people is simple and by no means expensive. It consists largely of corn-bread, hominy, or as it is properly called "grits," rice, conchs, fish, yams, and fruits. The corn meal, rice, and hominy are imported, yams and fruits grow luxuriantly everywhere, and the sea supplies the fish and conchs. Corn-meal costs 4 cents per quart; rice, 8 cents per quart; grits, 6 cents per quart. For 3 or 6 cents a man can buy all the fruit he can eat at one time, and for a few pennies more fish and yams enough for an ordinary family. The better class of laborers often add to the foregoing list ; but grits, fish, and fruits are found upon the tables of rich and poor alike. Articles of quite common consumption cost at retail as follows :

Articles.	Cost.	Articles.	Cost.
	Cents.		Cents.
Flour:		Salt pork..............per pound..	15 to 20
Wheat..............per pound..	3 to 6	Salt fish..............do....	10 12
Corn ....per quart..	4 5	Fresh fish..............do ...	3 5
Butter..............per pound,.	30 50	Bread..............do....	6 7
Rice..............per quart..	6 8	Cheese..............do ...	20 30
Coffee..............per pound..	18 24	Fresh meat..............do....	18 30
Tea ....do....	40 100	Milk ....per quart..	16 20
Sugar:		Chickens..............per pair..	40 60
Brown..............do....	7 10	Eggs..............per dozen..	24 50
Refined..............do....	15 20	Candles ....per pound..	18 30
Grits..............per quart..	6 7	Kerosene oil..............per quart..	9 12
Bacon ....per pound..	18 20	Lard ....per pound..	12 18

In the matter of clothing it is very evident that much more money is spent by many of the poorer classes than there is any necessity for. A desire to dress well and to wear personal adornments is prevalent among these people. In a climate where the thermometer never falls to 50°, and where it seldom drops to even 60°, but little clothing is required to protect from the cold, and yet competent judges assert that not less than 75 per cent. of the earnings of a majority of the laboring people are spent for wearing apparel and adornments. The working clothes of the poor are largely of cottons, prints, or calicoes, and jeans or drills, straw or palmetto hats. Many wear no shoes at all. Good cottons can be bought for 9 cents per yard; prints for 8 cents; jeans and drills for 20 cents; lawns for 25 cents; shoes for $1.25 to $1.50 per pair, and other goods in proportion. But these qualities do not suit for Sundays, holidays, and festive occasions, when many really expensive articles are worn. Bright colors and showy goods are the favorites regardless of cost, and the appearance presented by an assemblage of the laboring classes of the Bahamas, upon some public occasion, in the matter of dress, would be suggestive of anything but poverty or hard lines in earning a livelihood. With the same economy in clothing that their fellows exercise in America or in England, the laboring classes here could easily put by something in store for a rainy day.

GENERAL CONDITION OF WORKING PEOPLE.

The working classes are in a reasonably comfortable condition, that is, there is a fair amount of work to be done at fair prices, so that while there is not much accumulation of property amongst them, there is on the other hand comparatively little of actual want or suffering. Thrifty ones generally own their own plot of land and cabin, whilst comfortable houses can be rented at from $2 to $3 per month. Their houses are either of stone or wood, with wooden or thatched roof, containing from one to four rooms, mostly one story in height, with many openings, as is needed in a tropical climate. No fuel is required except a little wood for cooking purposes. These cabins or dwellings are generally surrounded by fruit trees, which give shade and contribute to the support of the family.

It is very customary for the women to take in washing or sewing to help the husband when it can be procured. The laborers begin their daily work at 6 o'clock in the morning, stopping from 8 to 9 for breakfast, and continue from 9 till 5 p. m., with an hour's intermission at noon for a meal. They have their supper about 6 o'clock. I have made reference to their food, and will only add that fresh meat, and indeed any kind of meat, is seldom used by the poorer classes.

There is considerable intemperance among the poorer classes, quantities of Holland gin being drunk, and much Jamaica rum, the latter being sold very cheaply. There are, on the other hand, a number of temperance societies which are exercising a good reformatory influence upon the drinking classes.

MISCELLANEOUS INFORMATION.

There has been no change for many years in the rate of wages paid in the colony, and the conditions which surround the labor question here continue the same from year to year.

There are no organizations of either capital or labor, and strikes may be said to be unknown in the islands, a kind and friendly feeling almost always prevailing between employer and employé, which has a beneficial effect upon the prosperity of the community.

Co-operative societies are not known. The working people are paid each day or each week in British gold and silver, and are at perfect liberty to make all purchases wherever they may choose, employers imposing no conditions in this regard.

Political rights.—The political rights possessed by the workingmen are few. The colony is a dependency of Great Britain, and officials are not elected by the people. Once in seven years a lower house of assembly is elected by popular vote, every male citizen over twenty-one who owns any real estate, keeps a house, or pays taxes, being a voter. As, however, the upper house is appointed by the Imperial Government, and as the governor, also, is a crown official, and possesses an absolute veto power, the authority of the popular house is much curtailed. And even in the lower house, owing to crown and official influences, an independent majority is seldom obtained at an election. This septennial election is the only opportunity the workingman has to exercise any political influence. It is but just to say, however, that the crown and colonial authorities have usually a most kindly feeling towards the laboring classes, and that the tendency of legislation is in the direction of the improvement and welfare of these people.

Taxation.—The proportion of taxation borne by the laboring classes is not easily determined. There is very little of direct or local taxation in the colony; indeed, nothing in the way of municipal rates, or of levies upon assessed valuations of real or personal property. Probably seven-eighths of the entire revenue of the colony arises from duties on imports and from licenses. The laboring classes, therefore, pay taxes in proportion to the quantity of imports they consume, which, being an unknown quantity, prevents me from giving a satisfactory answer upon this point. There is no discrimination against them in the matter of taxes. Duties on imports are about 20 per cent. ad valorem.

Emigration.—There is very little emigration from the colony. The working classes are generally contented with their condition. The climate is semi-tropical; they are certain of a living here; but little toil is necessary to earn a livelihood; they are not ambitious to improve their condition, but as a rule are content to let well enough alone; and are attached to their homes with the indolent, free-from-care life of these quiet islands, which are not inaptly termed the "negroes' paradise."

Population.—The population of the entire group of the Bahamas will not exceed 45,000 souls, and of these it is safe to assert that not to exceed

5,000 or 6,000 are whites, the rest being made up of all shades of color, from the pure octoroon to the coal-black native African set free from slave ships captured in the adjacent waters by British cruisers. Slavery was abolished in these islands in 1838. The physical condition of the whites and blacks is good; but the mixed race seem deficient in good constitutions, yielding easily to the attacks of disease. The moral condition of the better class of working people is not different from that which obtains among such people in the world generally; but among the lower orders vice and immorality abound to a shocking extent. Population increases slowly, about 1 per cent. per annum being the rate during the past decade.

Women employés.—Women are employed in agricultural work, in the preserving of fruit, and in household services generally, but I do not know that this fact has any appreciable effect upon the wages of men or on social and industrial conditions. Their wages, as appears elsewhere, are lower than those paid to males. There are no female artists, chemists, journalists, inventors, bankers, lecturers, or public speakers. There are perhaps twenty clerks, twenty-five teachers of schools and in music, six boarding-house keepers, and one hundred workers in shell manufacture. Outside of the services mentioned in this paragraph there is little employment for women in this colony. I do not know that any special consideration is given by employers to the moral or physical well-being of their employés; in fact, I think they are quite indifferent to the same. And as their employments are not dangerous no provisions are made for the safety of employés or for their care in case of accidents.

Education.—The majority of the laboring classes are ignorant, but among the better classes of the working people there is considerable intelligence. There are public schools throughout the colony, supplemented by many schools under the auspices of the Church of England. There are also in existence strict compulsory education laws, which are fairly well enforced, so that many children are receiving a common-school education in this colony, a condition of affairs that cannot but produce beneficial results in the near future.

Labor organizations.—There are in the colony, among the working people, a number of organizations called " friendly " and "burial" societies, the object of which is to encourage habits of industry, and economy among the members, and to provide relief in case of illness or to secure proper burial at time of death. These societies are prudently managed and are largely united with by the laboring classes, and are unquestionably exerting a wholesome and desirable influence amongst the people for whose benefit they were created.

CONCLUSION.

In conclusion I would say that labor in this colony is in such a primitive condition (very little of what can properly be termed "skilled" labor existing, and scarcely any that finds employment in the operating of machinery or of any complicated mechanical appliances) that it has been difficult to treat the subject in a way that would enable the Department to institute a satisfactory comparison between our rude forms and the advanced and highly-developed condition in which labor exists in the United States. I have, however, done the best I could in the premises and trust the report, which embraces all my agencies and the entire Bahamas, will be acceptable to the Department.

THOS. J. McLAIN, Jr.,
Consul.

UNITED STATES CONSULATE,
Nassau, New Providence, Bahamas, May 7, 1884.

TURK'S ISLAND.

REPORT BY CONSUL SAWYER.

In response to Department circular under date of February 15, I have the honor to make the following brief statement in regard to labor on this island and the dependency thereof.

There are but few daily laborers, and these are engaged in the manufacture of salt in some of its branches, or in the manufacture or gathering of guano at two points.

There are but few mechanics and these of the most ordinary kind. These command $1.25 per day, supposed to work ten hours for the day.

Common laborers at the salt business receive 75 cents per day of ten hours. The local authorities regulate the time when to commence work and when to quit.

The men are supposed to commence work at 6 o'clock a. m.; they work until 10 o'clock when they have an hour for breakfast. At 11 they commence work, and some crews quit for the day at 2 o'clock; these receive 50 cents for the day, while those who continue until 5 o'clock receive 75 cents.

The Government interferes for the laborers and says the men shall be paid weekly and in cash, but as many of them have to anticipate their wages, when Saturday night comes they have taken up a good share of the week's wages at the shop, as most of the manufacturers keep a supply shop.

The cost of living is what provisions cost in New York, freight, the local tax here, and the profit of the dealer added.

Good feeling exists between the employers and the employed. The workmen are mostly black or colored. They are, as a general rule, industrious and frugal.

N. K. SAWYER,
Consul.

UNITED STATES CONSULATE,
Turk's Island, August 26, 1884.

SPANISH WEST INDIES.

CUBA.

CIENFUEGOS.

REPORT BY CONSUL PIERCE.

Referring to your circular letter of February last, I beg to say that almost all the unskilled labor of this consular district, as well as a very considerable proportion of the skilled labor, is employed on sugar plantations in cultivating sugar cane and converting the same into sugar and molasses.

WAGES ON SUGAR PLANTATIONS.

The following table will show the monthly cost and arrangement of labor upon a sugar plantation of 1,500 acres, well supplied with modern machinery, in full operation during the late grinding season and during the present dull season:

LATE GRINDING SEASON.

Occupations.	Number of employés.	Hours of actual work.	Monthly wages in addition to food
Administrator's services	1	12	$100 00
Cutting cane	50	11	1,050 00
Lifting cane	30	11	630 00
Driving cars and wagons	12	11	252 00
Leading stock-cattle (boys)	16	11	168 00
Laying portable railroad	10	11	210 00
Attending furnaces	25	8	750 00
Attending boilers	2	12	44 00
Carting the megass	10	10	220 00
Drying the megass (women)	18	10	250 00
Attending engines	5	12	206 00
Attending mills	12	13	168 00
Carpentering	4	10	115 00
Blacksmithing	1	10	45 00
Hauling " cogollo "	2	6	34 00
Mayordomo's services	1	12	34 00
Work at cane conductor	12	12	268 00
Work at megass conductor	6	12	102 00
Mayoral's services	1	12	34 00
Services of stablemen	2	8	30 00
Coopering *	5	9	225 00
Attending to working cattle†	5	12	64 00
Attending dam and water wheel	2	12	40 00
Attending vacuum pan and tripple effect	5	12	331 00
Attending centrifugals	4	14	100 00
Attending defecation	4	13	88 00
Mixing sugar	4	14	112 00
Work at the packing-house	3	13	72 00
Distributing juice in kettles	1	10	28 00
Washing tanks	2	9	38 00
Weighing cane	1	14	25 00
Watchman's services	1	10	24 00
Dumping ashes	2	8	36 00
Carrying water for hands (boys)	5	12	53 00

PRESENT DULL SEASON.

Cultivating cane‡	150	13	1,500 00
Attending stock and miscellaneous work *	5	13	53 00
Carrying water for hands (boys)	5	13	25 00
For services of administrator	1	12	100 00
For services of mayordomo	1	12	17 00
For services of engineer	1	10	68 00
Assistant to engineer	1	10	12 00
Coopering	5	9	225 00
For services of mayoral	1	13	25 00

* The coopers have an organization, whereby they each secure at least $45.
† Four boys and one man.
‡ This will be sufficient force to clean the cane and do a reasonable amount of replanting (but not primitive planting) with the hoe exclusively. On new wood-land soil the plow is not used.

The foregoing tables are on the most economical basis, and an up-ward margin of as much as 25 per cent. should be allowed in order to include the higher prices, and even this margin will not include the highest prices paid on some plantations.

CONDITION OF AGRICULTURAL LABOR.

The agricultural labor of this district is in a serious state of derange-ment and uncertainty. It is surrounded with a variety of complica-tions, more or less varying, in each neighborhood. The various causes existing here calculated to reduce the price of labor would in the United States unquestionably reduce labor to a state of desperation. But for reasons hereinafter given the price of agricultural labor this summer, on an average, in the Cienfuegos jurisdiction, is reduced only about 30 or 35 per cent. of what it was last summer, and I am of the opinion that the unemployed labor of this consular district will never manifest itself in the way of bread riots. Whatever turbulence it may manifest will be the outgrowth of over-leisure aggravated more by other causes than by an insufficiency of food. My reasons will appear further on.

The causes which tend to cheapen the agricultural labor of the dis-trict are:

First. A serious degree of ignorance and want of concert and organi-zation among the laborers.

Second. The low price of sugar.

Third. The fact that many plantations have suspended or lessened their labor operations from inability to obtain the necessary capital.

It is estimated that three-fourths of the plantations of the Cienfuegos jurisdiction have reduced the number of their laborers since a year ago, some of them to such an extent as to now permit the cane to grow up without cultivating it, and it is believed that unless the price of sugar increases that quite a number of planters will not even attempt to grind their cane the coming season.

It is also understood here (but I am unable to verify the rumor) that one or two planters in the island have freed their slaves, being unable to successfully employ them, and also that thirty sugar-mills have been sent from the island to Mexico.

Fourth. The conversion of Spanish soldiers into agricultural laborers. Soldiers are allowed to work for wages on plantations when they so desire.

Fifth. An increase in the number of native white laborers. While negro slavery was in full force on the island, manual labor of every kind was recoiled from more than it ever was in our Southern States. The commanding position of Cuban sugar surrounded the wealthier classes with a flood of extravagance, on which the thriftless whites lived in comparative idleness. But now Cuban sugar has lost its power, wealth is crumbling into bankruptcy, the price of provisions has under-gone little or no reduction, and the poor whites, like the blacks, are driven to the choice of working for meat and bread or living on less costly food. As a rule, however, this class of labor is not as constant as the free negro labor. It is estimated that 25 per cent. of the native white agricultural laborers under employment at this season of the year remain at work not more than two months at a time, while not more than 8 per cent. of the free negro laborers actually employed fluc-tuate to this extent.

Sixth. An increased immigration of laboring people within the last year or two. I am, however, unable to estimate this increase.

Turning now to the causes which tend to decrease the supply and enhance the value of agricultural labor, I beg to say that in Cuba, as in the United States, the negro women on being freed are disposed to withdraw from field labor and devote themselves to household work. Following the results of emancipation, in this direction, I cannot do better than to quote from my report of last August on the credit system of the district, with the remark that subsequent developments tend to sustain what was therein predicted; although the serious decline in the price of sugar has made labor of less importance in agriculture than I then anticipated: "But the labor question is the great problem for the future. Labor is now passing from slavery to freedom, and the future results of the change are wrapped in fear and doubt. We cannot with full safety estimate the future of the negro population here by the commendable bearing of the negro population of our Southern States under the license of freedom. There they ceased to cultivate the land at the command of the landlord only to cultivate it at the command of their own necessities. Here not so. The nutritious fruits and herbs which grow in abundance with little or no cultivation, the fishes of the surrounding sea and inland streams, the warm climate and ample shelter of the bark and leaf of the palm tree, all combine to relieve them from such necessities. There, too, the freedmen were constrained by their very humanities to be worthy citizens of the Republic when the novelty of the change had passed and they realized themselves clothed with legal and political equality, their children being educated and the pathways to honorable distinction opened before them; their own manhood recognized and their occupation respected, they were constrained to place confidence in the future, and to be animated to industry and laudable ambition. Here such bids fair not to be the case. Freedom to the Cuban negro, while a step in the right direction, will hold out no such incentive to personal wealth and patriotism. The freedman will remain an insignificant factor in the political world; motives to subserve the public good of his progeny will not be inspired by the situation; and without such motives and without the necessity of gaining his livelihood by labor he will be apt to become a very unreliable and indifferent tiller of the soil."

THE COLONIAL SYSTEM.

Within the last few years what is called here the "colonial" system has been inaugurated and meets with considerable favor. This consists in farming out land for cultivation or in making such arrangements with small land owners as to enable them to cultivate their land in sugar cane. These conditions somewhat vary. They are, however, in the main, about as follows: The planter allows a certain quantity of land to the "colono," who is to pay for it at $1 per acre, and duly cultivate it in sugar cane, and cut and deliver the cane at the "central" place where the planter grinds it. The planter on the other hand pays to the "colono" $3.50 for each 2,500 pounds of canes so delivered; and the planter also furnishes sufficient cane for the first two plantings, and sufficient live stock and utensils.

HOW THE LABORERS LIVE.

The daily habits and mode of life of the working classes in the country are in no wise elevated. Nearly, if not quite all, live in thatched houses without flooring; they look forward to the necessities of old age with little concern, and are much more content to live from "hand to mouth" than any class of laborers in the United States.

During the busy or crop season (about five months) they work during the entire Sunday on some estates and part of the Sunday on all of them. They are, however, fed as well or better than the corresponding class of laborers in our Southern States, who, in Georgia at least, formerly received 2½ pounds of bacon (uncooked) and a peck of meal per week, together with such vegetables as they themselves might raise around their cabins. Here their daily rations are usually taken in sufficient quantities from the following list: jerked beef, sweet potatoes, rice, bread, beans, plantain, pork, aguardiente, codfish, olive oil, lard, fresh beef, and salt beef; and they usually get a daily allowance of coffee and sugar. The skilled laborers (machinist, carpenters, &c.) are allowed to eat at a table and the food of the unskilled laborers usually given to them on plates. The owner of one of the largest plantations in the island, which during the crop season employs about five hundred persons, tells me that by cooking for them, which he does by steam, he is enabled to feed the skilled laborers at 33 cents a day, the unskilled white laborers at 22 cents a day, and to feed the unskilled negro laborers at 16 cents a day. A distinction is usually though not always drawn between white and negro laborers of the same class.

SLAVE LABOR.

The slaves here are allowed by law $3 [per month?] (equal to $2.796 in United States money), and it has long been customary to allow plantation slaves to have a piece of land on which to cultivate vegetables, raise poultry, and also raise one or two pigs. This custom, it is said, was intended to create an inducement for the slave not to run away from the plantation. It is noticed here, as it was in the United States, that the negroes on becoming free usually leave the plantation on which they have been held as slaves, but show a disposition to return to it after an absence of a year or two.

WAGES IN THE CITY OF CIENFUEGOS.

The following table will give an approximate idea of the price of labor in the city of Cienfuegos, a place of about 21,000 inhabitants. I beg to state, however, in advance that the prices are unsettled, employment uncertain and irregular, and the sources of information on the subject more or less unsatisfactory. I have attempted to show the monthly compensation each occupation gives, when employment is obtained, though in some cases payment is made according to the work performed, and in other cases by the day. All classes of laborers in the city usually work from 6 to 5, stopping one hour for breakfast, and most of them work an hour less on Saturday. Shops and stores are kept open and retail business transacted on Sunday, but artisans are not required to work on Sunday when employed by the month. When paid by the day twenty-six days are accounted a month. Prices are so irregular that it is extremely difficult to approximate an average. Owing to the fact that the supply of the city labor is greatly in excess of the demand, it would seem not unreasonable to assume that the average wages will not exceed 10 per cent. over the lowest throughout the table.

The tables of this report and all amounts of money mentioned are in Spanish coin; a dollar in Spanish is equal to $0.932 in United States coin.

Wages paid per month.

Occupations.	Lowest.	Highest.	Occupations.	Lowest.	Highest.
Brick-layers	$38 00	$52 00	Teachers, public school	$50 00	$100 00
Rod-carriers	21 00	30 00	Saddlers and harness-mak-	30 00	50 00
Stone-masons	65 00	78 00	ers		
Plasterers	65 00	78 00	Sail-makers	60 00	105 00
Plumbers	52 00	65 00	Stevedores	52 00	104 00
Carpenters	65 00	78 00	Tanners	25 00	40 00
Rough carpenters	39 00	52 00	Tailors	25 00	45 00
Gas-fitters	25 00	31 00	Tinsmiths	32 00	49 00
Bakers	30 00	60 00	Shoemakers	34 00	55 00
Blacksmiths	52 00	65 00	Barbers	30 00	54 00
Strikers	26 00	32 00	Household servants, with		
Book-binders	25 00	34 00	board:		
Brick-makers	30 00	34 00	Cooks	10 00	25 00
Butchers	17 00	25 00	Chambermaids	4 00	9 00
Cabinet-makers	78 00	91 00	Dress-makers	12 00	15 00
Confectioners	60 00	80 00	Railroad employés:		
Cigar-makers	37 00	60 00	Road-masters	40 00	102 00
Coopers	45 00	60 00	Switchmen	30 00	30 00
Draymen and teamsters	25 00	34 00	Breakmen	30 00	30 00
Cab and carriage	30 00	37 00	Firemen	30 00	30 00
Gardeners	17 00	34 00	Blacksmiths	65 00	187 00
Hatters	34 00	62 00	Boiler-makers	65 00	130 00
Horse-shoers	27 00	40 00	Carpenters	32 00	154 00
Jewelers	50 00	80 00	Brick-layers	45 00	58 00
Laborers and porters	21 00	34 00	Engineers	120 00	130 00
Printers	30 00	60 00			

COST OF LIVING TO CITY LABORERS.

The laborers of Cienfuegos are more intelligent than those of the country, and command better wages, though the general depression of business has thrown a large number of them out of employment. Living, of course, is more expensive than in the country, and is probably more expensive in this particular city than any other of its size on the island. Plantains (which, according to my liking, are a better substitute for meal and bread than either sweet or Irish potatoes) are as a rule brought here from other localities, and so are yams (another substantial food of the island), in considerable quantities, in order to supply this market.

The usual cost of living per month in this city of a family consisting of husband (under employment at $3.50 per day), wife, and three children under twelve years of age, may be estimated as follows:

Wages		$91 00
House rent	$17 00	
Provisions	30 00	
Clothing	11 50	
Education (two children)	8 50	
Washing, fuel, lights, and other necessaries	16 00	
		83 00
Leaving for cigars and diversions only		8 00

If, however, the husband should lose his employment, and he should wish to curtail his expenses while looking for work, and at the same time keep up appearances, he could maintain his family without much discomfort on $40, and, if the worst should come, he could manage to maintain them all with wholesome food and dry shelter, but without coffee, bread, and meat, on from $10 to $15 per month.

FEMALE LABOR.

Female labor is very much more restricted than in the United States. Female slaves work in the plantations reasonably well. Emancipation from slavery, however, decreases the efficiency and amount of their labor much more than it does that of men. In the cities female occupations, outside of private domestic employment, is exceedingly limited. There is probably not a single chambermaid or other female employed in the management of any hotel in this city. The females, however, are generally industrious in their respective homes. Their sphere of usefulness is greatly restricted by the customs of the country, but within their allotted sphere they are faithful, cheerful, and industrious.

WM. P. PIERCE,
Consul.

UNITED STATES CONSULATE,
Cienfuegos, July 31, 1884.

SANTIAGO DE CUBA.

REPORT BY CONSUL LANDREAU.

In regard to the laboring classes it is impossible to give an exact average, as the so-called slaves are paid three different rates of wages; the free ones have adopted an arbitrary rule, and the sugar planters have found themselves compelled to agree to their demand, that is to say, that at present and for the last four months they have been obtaining $30 and food monthly, and some of them up to $45, and the consequences are that the planters find themselves compelled to abandon the sugar cultivation. Concerning the prices paid by said laborers for necessaries of life, this remains a complete mystery, owing to their different ways of living.

Generally speaking they are neither steady nor saving, being too fond of pleasures.

Strikes are never heard of here.

They are free to purchase necessaries of life wherever they choose, and no conditions imposed by employers, and they are paid in Spanish gold. Rents are very high here, and living very costly to people who have to do so decently.

Owing to the planters stopping work, it is feared that the result will be a bread war, due to so many people out of employment.

JOHN C. LANDREAU,
Consul.

UNITED STATES CONSULATE,
Santiago de Cuba, June 30, 1884.

I. GENERAL TRADES.

Wages paid per day in Santiago de Cuba.

Occupations.	Lowest.	Highest.	Average.
BUILDING TRADES.			
Bricklayers	$2 00	$5 00	
Hod-carriers	1 00	2 00	
Masons	1 00	2 00	
Tenders	1 00	2 00	
Plasterers	1 00	2 00	
Tenders	1 00	2 00	
Roofers	1 00	1 50	
Plumbers	1 50	3 00	
Assistants	1 00	3 00	
Carpenters	2 50	4 00	
Gas-fitters	1 50	2 00	

Wages paid per day in Santiago de Cuba—Continued.

Occupations.	Lowest.	Highest.	Average.
OTHER TRADES.			
Bakers	$1 50	$2 00	
Blacksmiths	2 50	3 00	
Strikers	1 00	3 00	
Book-binders	1 00	2 00	
Brick-makers	1 50	2 50	
Butchers			$1 50
Brass-founders			1 50
Cabinet-makers			1 00
Confectioners			1 50
Cigar-makers			2 00
Coopers			1 00
Cutlers			1 00
Distillers			1 00
Drivers			1 00
Draymen and teamsters			1 00
Cab and carriage			1 00
Street railway			1 00
Gardeners			1 00
Hatters			1 00
Jewelers			1 50
Laborers, porters, &c			1 00
Teachers, public schools	*30 00	*80 00	
Saddle and harness makers	1 50	2 00	
Sail-makers	1 50	2 00	
Stevedores			1 00
Tailors	1 00	1 50	
Telegraph operators	1 50	2 50	
Tinsmiths			1 00

* Per month.

II. FACTORIES, MILLS, ETC.

Wages paid per day of ten hours in factories or mills in Santiago de Cuba.

Occupations.	Lowest.	Highest.
General labor	$1 00	$1 25

III. FOUNDRIES, MACHINE-SHOPS, AND IRON WORKS.

Wages paid per day in foundries, machine-shops, and iron works in Santiago de Cuba.

Occupations.	Lowest.	Highest.
General labor	$1 50	$3 50

V. MINES AND MINING.

Wages paid in and in connection with Iron Mines Company in Santiago de Cuba.

Occupations.	Lowest.	Highest.	Average.
Chiefs of camps	per month			$100 00
Storekeepers	do			35 00
Doctors' assistants	do			30 00
Overseers	do			30 00
Carpenters	per day			1 25
Laborers	do			80
Railroad men	do	$1 15	$1 90	
Locomotive engineers	per month	225 00	300 00	
Bridge carpenters	per day	2 50	3 00	
Firemen	do	1 25	1 75	
Track-layers	do	75	90	
Miners	do			1 50
Drill runners	do			2 00
Clerks	per month	50 00	100 00	

VI. RAILWAY EMPLOYÉS.

Wages paid per annum to railway employés (those engaged about stations as well as those engaged on the engines and cars, linemen, railroad laborers, &c.) in Santiago de Cuba.

Occupations.	Average wages.	Occupations.	Average wages.
Administrator of railroad.............	$2,400 00	Conductors............................	$720 00
Computer.............................	1,200 00	Station clerks........................	720 00
Treasurer.............................	1,200 00	Telegraphists........................	720 00
Secretary.............................	1,000 00	Machinists...........................	1,200 00
Cashier..........................,.....	1,000 00	Chief of foundry.....................	2,400 00
Office clerks..........................	500 00	Laborers.........	*1 00

* Per day.

VII. SHIP-YARDS AND SHIP-BUILDING.

Wages paid per day of ten hours in ship-yards—distinguishing between iron and wood ship-building—in Santiago de Cuba.

Occupations.	Lowest.	Highest.
Ship carpenters	$2 00	$5 00

VIII. SEAMEN'S WAGES.

Wages paid per month to seamen (officers and men) in Santiago de Cuba.

Occupations.	Lowest.	Highest.
Seamen (officers and men)	$15 00	$25 00

IX. STORE AND SHOP WAGES.

Wages paid per month in stores, wholesale or retail, to males and females, in Santiago de Cuba.

Occupations.	Lowest.	Highest.
Book-keepers..	$70 00	$85 00
Cashiers...	60 00	75 00
Salesmen..	25 00	30 00
Grocery clerks	10 00	17 00

X. HOUSEHOLD WAGES IN TOWNS AND CITIES.

Wages paid per month to household servants (towns and cities) in Santiago de Cuba, Island of Cuba.

Occupations.	Lowest.	Highest.
Coachmen...	$17 00	$20 00
Cooks...	8 50	17 00
Servants..	6 00	10 00
Washer and ironers...	8 00	9 00

XI. AGRICULTURAL WAGES.

Wages paid per month to agricultural laborers and household (country) servants in Santiago de Cuba.

Occupations.	Lowest.	Highest.
Free laborers..	$17 00	$20 00
Patrocinados, or conditonally freed................................	2 00	4 00

XII. Corporation Employés.

Wages paid, per year, to the corporation employés in the city of Santiago de Cuba.

Occupations.	Lowest.	Highest.	Average.
Mayor of the city			$2,000
Secretary			1,200
Clerks			500
Computer of board of aldermen			1,600
Secretary of board of aldermen			1,600
Officers			840
Clerks			4,000
Municipal school teachers	*$40 00	*$90 00	

* Per month.

XIII. Government Departments and Offices.

Wages paid per year to employés in Government departments and offices, exclusive of tradesmen and laborers, in Santiago de Cuba.

[Five hours a day.]

Occupations.	Average Wages.	Occupations.	Average Wages.
Civil governor	$7,000	POST-OFFICE.	
Secretary of government	3,000		
Assistant secretary	1,800	Postmaster	1,800
Fire officers, 1st, 2d and 5th	1,260	Interventor	1,300
Civil judges	4,500	Officer	1,000
Attorneys	2,700	Assistants	400
		International officer	1,000
SUBINTENDENCY.		Mail-carrier, steamers' officer	330
Subintendent	6,000	Clerk	400
Secretary	1,800	INSPECTION OF CIVIL ENGINEERS.	
First officer	1,600		
Clerks	1,400	Chief engineer	3,700
Collector of taxes	2,800	Assistant	1,300
Chief of section	1,600		
Third officer	1,400	INSPECTION OF MINES.	
Fifth officer	1,070		
Counselor at law	1,400	Chief inspector	3,700
Computer	2,050	Assistant	1,750
Second officer	1,400	Clerk	400
Fourth officer	1,200		
Sixth officer	1,000	PUBLIC WORKS.	
Treasurer	1,600		
		Chief inspector	4,000
CUSTOM-HOUSE.		Assistants	1,800
		Overseers	700
Collector	2,500	Drawer	500
Computer	1,850		
Fifth officer	1,000	TELEGRAPH.	
Third officer	1,400		
Fourth officer	1,000	Station chief	1,500
Interpreter	1,000	Officers	600
Druggist	500	Officer of station	690
Weighers	1,200	Do	900
Captain of port	4,200	Clerks	400
Assistant captain of port	1,125	Telegram carriers	240
Clerks	720	Clergy:	
Paymaster	480	Archbishop	18,000
		Vicar-general	4,000
POLICE.		Attorney-general	2,700
		Clerk	480
Chief of police	3,000	Dean of the cathedral	4,500
Officers	1,200	Prebendaries	3,000
		Do	2,500
BOARD OF HEALTH.		Do	2,000
		Cathedral orchestra	5,200
Doctor-secretary	1,200	Parish priests	600

XV. PRINTERS AND PRINTING OFFICES.

Statement showing the wages paid, per annum, to printers (compositors, pressmen, proof-readers, &c.) in Santiago de Cuba.

Occupations.	Lowest.	Highest.
Manager of printing office	$480 00	$500 00
Type composers	300 00	400 00
Pressmen	340 00	400 00
Proof-readers	204 00	250 00

SAN DOMINGO.

PUERTO PLATA.

REPORT BY CONSUL SIMPSON.

In answer to labor circular of February 15, 1884, I have the honor to return herewith the blanks which refer to the classes of labor in this district, filled to the best of my knowledge correctly, and to submit the following in answer to the interrogatories.

COST OF LIVING.

The cost of living to the laboring classes here is but little, as with a loaf of bread, a few plantains, and occasionally some fresh beef or pork, they have all they want to eat.

Of clothing but little also is required, and that of the commonest kind. Rents are from $5 to $10 per month for one or two rooms. Flour sells for $14 per barrel, but is seldom bought in a crude state, as they have neither ovens nor stoves in which to cook it. Fresh beef costs from 12 to 15 cents per pound, and pork from 20 to 25. Common cod and hake (of which considerable is consumed) sells for 10 cents per pound; salt pork, 20 cents.

HABITS OF THE WORKING CLASSES.

The habits of the working classes are not very steady, especially in the country, as when they have worked hard and accumulated a few dollars they are apt to want a rest, and generally at the time when their services are most needed.

Within a year or two, however, there has been a marked improvement in this respect, and it is believed it will continue. As for laying by anything for a rainy day, few do it.

MISCELLANEOUS.

Good feeling prevails between employé and employer.

There are no labor organizations and no strikes occur.

They are free to purchase where they please, and are paid weekly, generally, in Mexican dollars or their equivalent.

There are no co-operative societies.

WORKING PEOPLE.

Their wants are few, as the climate is always warm. A roof to cover them, a few chairs, a table, cot or hammock, are sufficient for the hour.

One or two suits a year of blue denim, with the same number of shirts, of coarse cloth, are enough to clothe them.

As for bettering their condition, few think or care; neither do they think of laying by anything for old age or sickness. They are quite temperate, but somewhat addicted to gambling in the form of lotteries, cock-fighting, &c.

POLITICAL RIGHTS.

All males over twenty-one years of age are entitled to vote, and may vote for whom they please; but they generally follow the lead of some official or prominent man in their district. Their votes have, however, very little influence on legislation. There are no direct taxes on the workingman, the revenue of the country being derived from duties on imports and exports.

THOMAS SIMPSON,
Consul.

UNITED STATES CONSULATE,
Puerto Plata, May 28, 1884.

I. GENERAL TRADES.

Wages paid per week of sixty hours in Puerto Plata.

Occupations.	Lowest.	Highest.	Average.
Carpenters	$6 00	$12 00	$7 50
Bakers	6 00	11 50	7 25
Cigar-makers	6 00	11 25	7 10
Coopers	6 00	11 50	7 25
Laborers, porters, &c	6 00	6 00	6 00
Printers	6 00	7 50	6 75
Teachers, public schools	*40 00	*100 00	*80 00
Stevedores	9 00	12 00	10 75
Tailors	4 75	9 00	7 25

* Per month.

II. FACTORIES, MILLS, ETC.

Wages paid per week of sixty hours in sugar mills in Puerto Plata.

Occupations.	Lowest.	Highest.	Average.
Engineers	$12 50	$25 00	$20 00
Sugar-makers	12 50	25 00	20 00
Cane-cutters, helpers, &c	3 00	3 60	3 30

VIII. SEAMEN'S WAGES.

Wages paid per month to seamen (officers and men) in Puerto Plata.

Occupations.	Lowest.	Highest.	Average.
Ordinary seamen (coast)	$12 00	$12 00	$12 00
Masters	25 00	25 00	25 00

IX. Store and Shop Wages.

Wages paid per month in stores, wholesale or retail, in Puerto Plata.

Occupations.	Lowest.	Highest.	Average.
Clerks (with board)	$20 00	$50 00	$30 00
Bookkeepers (without board)	100 00	200 00	125 00

X. Household Wages in Towns and Cities.

Wages paid per month to household servants (towns and cities) in Puerto Plata.

Occupations.	Lowest.	Highest.	Average.
Cooks	$3 00	$5 00	$4 00
Chambermaids	3 00	4 00	3 50
Nurses	2 50	4 00	3 00

XI. Agricultural Wages.

Wages paid per week to agricultural laborers and household (country) servants in Puerto Plata.

Occupations.	Lowest.	Highest.	Average.
Cane-cutters*	$3 00	$3 60	$3 30
Cooks†	4 09	5 00	4 50
General laborers*	3 00	3 60	3 30

* Without board.   † With board.

XIII. Government Departments and Offices.

Wages paid per month of two hundred and eighty-eight hours to employés in Government departments and offices (exclusive of tradesmen and laborers) in Puerto Plata.

Occupations.	Lowest.	Highest.	Average.
Collector customs		$120 00	$120 00
Collector, deputy		90 00	90 00
Appraiser		150 00	150 00
Appraiser, deputy		90 00	90 00
Registrar		60 00	60 00
Interpreter		60 00	60 00
Clerks	$45 00	60 00	50 00
Tidi waiters	10 00	15 00	11 00
Laborers	15 00	20 00	17 50

XV. Printers and Printing Offices.

Statement showing the wages paid per week of sixty hours to printers (compositors, pressmen, proof-readers, &c.) in Puerto Plata.

Occupations.	Lowest.	Highest.	Average.
Compositors	$6 00	$7 50	$6 75
Pressmen	6 00	7 50	6 75

CONTINENT OF ASIA.

—

TURKEY IN ASIA.

ASIA MINOR.

SMYRNA.

REPORT BY CONSUL STEVENS.

WANT OF STATISTICS.

Soon after receiving the Labor Circular bearing date February 15, 1884, Department of State, I began the collection of facts and figures required in the preparation of a truthful statement of the present condition of labor within my consular jurisdiction, which extends over the pashalic of Aidin and includes the chief commercial city of the Turkish Empire.

The work has been attended with difficulties from the outset, hindering expedition and calling into exercise all the skill, patience, and tact at my command. The natives are suspicious of all foreigners who question them concerning their social and economic relations. Moreover, the methods of imposing and collecting taxes are such that they conduce to habits of reticence, concealment, and evasion. These and other qualities peculiar to Mohammedans and to rayahs, render them unpromising subjects for the interviewer.

Nevertheless, I have succeeded in getting full and nearly accurate information on all essential points. The industrial conditions here are, however, so exceptional when contrasted with those of Christian countries that I have been compelled to deviate somewhat from some of the printed forms and to omit others altogether.

I cannot learn that statistics covering the subjects named in the circular have ever before been collected in this country. In 1854 the American consul here sent a partial report on the then rate of wages and cost of living, but if any later statement of a kindred nature has been made, the records in this office fail to show it.

EXPLANATORY.

In striking averages the instructions of the Department have been closely followed. Hence the average column represents the amount of wages paid to the larger number of the workmen in the various occupations enumerated.

Many of the occupations given are followed for only a part of the year, being dependent upon agricultural or horticultural production, and the wages fluctuate accordingly as this is large or small, or as it is affected in price by the markets. Then, again, workmen engage successively in two or more different kinds of employment, and in this way fill out the year.

Formerly nearly all the skilled workmen on the two lines of railway which connect Smyrna with the interior came from England. Latterly, however, their places have been taken by young men of the country, who have been trained in the workshops of the two companies.

The rates of wages were all collected in the Turkish unit of values— the piaster—and then reduced to our currency, careful consideration being given to fractional equivalents.

ACKNOWLEDGMENTS.

For valuable assistance in the procurement of information, I take pleasure in acknowledging indebtedness to the following-named parties: Mr. Thomas Hall, firm of Hall & Mingardo, ship chandlers; Mr. Stab, a local statistician of merit and correspondent of various learned societies; Mr. Edward Purser, general manager of the Ottoman Railway; Mr. H. Kemp, general manager Smyrna and Cassaba Railway; Mr. Papps, proprietor machine-shop; Mr. Carmanyolo, proprietor machine-shop; Mr. Issigonis, proprietor machine shop; Mr. D. Uffley, an American merchant and farmer residing in Smyrna. I come now to the specific inquiries.

RATES OF WAGES.

The hours of labor vary somewhat, but in no branch or department are the hours so many or the labor so continuous as in Europe or America. Mechanics frequently work from sun to sun, but they take two hours for dinner, with long "rests" in the intervals of work. Railway workmen average about the same number of hours and perform pretty much the same amount of labor as their prototypes in the west. Agricultural laborers work about six hours per day. They begin at 8 a. m. and finish at 4 p. m., with two hours suspension at noon. When, as sometimes happens, there is work which requires haste, such as digging the vineyards (in the month of February), and similar work, more hours are improved, usually with a corresponding increase of pay. At such times an able-bodied farm laborer gets 20 piasters (81 cents) per day. There are certain kinds of labor, such as packing figs, sorting valonia, gathering grapes, &c., the demand for which is confined mainly to the harvest season. If the demand is pressing, wages are increased; if lax, wages fall correspondingly.

COST OF LIVING, ETC.

If the wages of the laboring man are small, so are his necessities. He is content with the cheapest and simplest food, an abode having little or no furniture but such as he has himself fashioned, and clothing of common material, made up in the family. The climate is so mild that for nine months in the year shoes or other covering for the feet, and heavy clothing as well, are dispensed with. The daily meals consist of coffee and bread for breakfast, olives, onions, and bread for dinner, soup (made of peas, beans, or rice), vegetables, and bread for supper. This bill of fare is varied occasionally by the addition of eggs, meat, and fish. The cost of living to an average family in the country does not exceed 4 piasters, say 16 cents, per day, and the clothing can hardly aggregate $15 per year, except for the better class of mechanics and laborers residing in Smyrna or along the railway lines, where there is a disposition among the female members of the family to wear showy dresses. It is noticeable that the hardest working laborers in the cities, viz, the porters or "hamals," live the most frugally. Their daily fare consists of bread and onions, with now and then an olive, and yet they carry enormous loads upon their bent backs, loads such as few European porters could stand under, much less carry, over uneven pavements, and through streets too narrow and crooked for the passage of any four-footed beast of burden. The material of their clothing, which is always scanty, is thin canvas, and a suit costs about $2. One suit will last a year or more.

COMPARISON OF WAGES, ETC.

As I have no data at hand from which to draw a comparison with the wages which prevailed here in 1878, I am compelled to go back to a report made in 1854 by the gentleman in charge of this consulate at that time, from which I have been able to construct the following statement covering some of the leading occupations:

Occupations.		1854.	1884.
Bakers	per week..	$0 80	$1 46
Blacksmiths	do....	4 80	6 11
Butchers	do....	3 00	3 67
Carpenters	do....	3 84	4 89
Coopers	do....	5 40	6 11
Dyers	do....	4 32	3 67
Laborers	do....	1 44	2 69
Masons	do ..	3 36	4 16
Millers	do....	2 88	2 93
		29 84	35 69
Increase			* 5 85

* Nearly 20 per cent.

HABITS OF THE WORKING CLASSES.

Unobjectionable in the main. If regularly employed and paid, they are trustworthy and steady, although inclined to be indolent. An average American laborer will do as much work in one day as an Asiatic workman in two. This is due, in part at least, to climatic influences. They are not, as a rule, frugal or saving, being content to live in the sphere in which they were born. In the cities, however, they display more ambition, and some of them have acquired considerable property. Nearly all own the houses in which they live, miserable structures, to be sure, but rent free. Even the poorest laborer seldom marries until he has a roof to cover him, although it may not be worth, land included, $25, and consists of only one small apartment. In the rural districts he is a very poor laborer indeed who does not possess a cabin and a goat or two.

One of the chief causes operating against the advancement of the laboring classes in Asia Minor is the insecurity of property, arising from lawlessness on the one hand, and the rapacity of dishonest officials on the other. The peasant sees his rich neighbor and employer despoiled, and is content to remain an object too pitiful to tempt the cupidity of the despoiler. Then there is a strong tendency, in the rural districts, to keep to the old ways, using tools identical in pattern with those of the dark ages, and to look with disfavor upon the march of improvement.

THE FEELING BETWEEN EMPLOYÉ AND EMPLOYER.

There is no feeling of antagonism between employé and employer. On the contrary very kind relations exist between them, and they not unfrequently share and share alike. With a prosperous season the employer shares his good fortune with his faithful workmen; in a bad season, the burdens are proportionately borne. As a result of this state of affairs, employers do not make large fortunes, as in some other countries, nor are the laboring classes ever reduced to absolute want, a condition of things often brought about in more favored (?) lands.

ORGANIZED LABOR, STRIKES, ETC.

In answer to paragraphs six and seven of the circular, I may say that there is no organized condition of labor or of capital, hence no local laws bearing upon the subject, no strikes, and few cases for arbitration.

Concerning the eighth paragraph it can be said that the working people are free to purchase the necessaries of life wherever they choose, and that they are paid weekly as a rule, in the current coin of the country. Paper money is not current anywhere in Turkey.

CO-OPERATIVE SOCIETIES.

There are but two such in this country, and they are of English origin, having been established for the convenience of the English employés on the two lines of railway heretofore mentioned. The shares are mostly owned by workmen. They are understood to be in a prosperous condition, enabling the workmen to purchase the ordinary necessaries of life at a low figure, and also to get from England some of those articles of food and apparel to which they were formerly accustomed.

GENERAL CONDITION OF THE WORKING PEOPLE, ETC.

The condition of the working people in Asia Minor is not one of hardship or destitution. There is no suffering from poverty, and employment of some kind can almost always be had. Their homes are not attractive, but for eight months of the year they pass most of their time out of doors. Their food is wholesome, but simple; their clothes scant and cheap; they have no wish apparently to better their condition or to make provision for old age or sickness. There are exceptions, of course, in the cities and among the artisans, especially those of foreign birth, but the great mass of the laboring population in the rural districts is content if present needs are supplied, and it takes little heed of the morrow. Physically, they will compare favorably with workingmen of other countries; but their moral standard is not high. They are ignorant and superstitious. Few of them know how to read. I refer to all the races and sects, Moslem, Greek, Jew, and Armenian. The influences by which they are surrounded are not calculated to elevate them in the scale of humanity or of happiness, unless it be true that " ignorance is bliss." Until a government of organized oppression and robbery is succeeded by one having the welfare of all its subjects at heart, there is little hope of the moral and material improvement of the working classes of this country at all commensurate with its natural advantages. Here I submit a statement made by the owner of a large farm :

The united earnings of a husband and wife having two children dependent upon them for one year amounts to, say, 3,000 piasters or $122.25.

They spend as follows:

For rent of two rooms and a kitchen	$26 89
For clothing	24 45
For food	45 64
Saving	25 27

In addition, they generally cultivate, after regular work hours, a small piece of land, purchased of the Government, and raise grapes for the market, realizing quite a little sum.

No special provision is made for the safety of employés in factories, mills, or railroads. The working people enjoy no political rights whatever, but bear their full share of the burdens of taxation.

FEMALE LABOR.

Women are found in almost every department of labor, but children are only employed at farm work and in the cities in fruit packing and valonia cleaning. Women labor in the fields as continuously as the men. In the towns they cultivate the gardens, pack fruit, and do white-washing in addition to their usual avocations. The whitewashers are stout Jewesses. Why they have taken up this branch of work, so coarse and laborious, I do not know; but it is true that they have a monopoly of whitewashing. The average wages paid to females are given in the accompanying tables. Their hours of labor are from seven to eight per day, with rest for meals. In the country they frequently work from nine to ten hours. They are physically strong and healthy, and morally not lower than the same class in other countries where women are regarded as inferior beings and treated as beasts of burden.

The effect of the employment of women on the wages of men is not perceptible, but taking the former from the care of the household and placing them in the fields and at other masculine employments is in every way injurious. There is absolutely no education among the employed women and their children; but while the home circle is necessarily much broken family ties seem to be very strong.

CONCLUDING REMARKS.

I ought to have stated in the introductory part of this report that this consulate does not possess a copy of the Department publication "Showing the state of labor in Europe in 1878." I have not been able therefore to institute any comparisons based upon that work.

It should be stated also that there are no public institutions in this country for the support of the poor or the unfortunate, and no public schools. There are no workhouses, no asylums for the insane, the blind, the deaf and dumb, or the idiotic. There are hospitals in the larger places, and also schools, but they are wholly supported by private sub-scriptions.

The result of this state of affairs is swarms of beggars of hideous mien upon all the streets and thoroughfares, and universal illiteracy among the poorer classes of the laboring people.

Well-informed people remark a change for the better among laborers, especially in Smyrna, where the wages of both sexes have increased during the past six years from 10 to 20 per cent. Among the more re-munerative trades a desire to educate their children is shown.

I cannot close this report without giving credit to my faithful clerk, Mr. E. G. Corbetti, for his share in its preparation. The labor of pre-paring the tables, a tithe of the amount of which and the necessary painstaking does not show to the casual examiner, was performed by him. I have incurred no extra expense in gathering the facts embodied in this report; but in view of his very inadequate compensation, his fidelity and loyalty, I venture to suggest that a gratuity be allowed to Mr. Corbetti.

Regretting the unavoidable delay which has attended the preparation of this report.

W. E. STEVENS,
Consul.

UNITED STATES CONSULATE,
Smyrna, July 11, 1884.

I. GENERAL TRADES.

Wages paid per week of sixty-six hours in Smyrna.

Occupations.	Lowest.	Highest.	Average.
BUILDING TRADES.			
Bricklayers	$3 67	$4 89	$4 16
Hod-carriers	1 22	2 44	1 71
Masons	3 67	4 89	4 16
Tenders	1 22	2 44	1 71
Plasterers	3 67	4 89	4 16
Tenders	1 22	2 44	1 71
Slaters	3 67	4 89	4 16
Roofers	3 67	4 89	4 16
Tenders	1 22	2 44	1 71
Plumbers	3 67	9 78	4 89
Assistants	2 44	3 67	2 93
Carpenters	2 44	6 11	4 89
Gas-fitters	3 67	12 22	6 11
OTHER TRADES.			
Bakers	1 22	2 44	1 46
Blacksmiths	2 44	12 22	6 11
Strikers	1 22	4 89	2 44
Book-binders	1 22	7 33	3 67
Brick-makers	1 22	4 89	2 44
Butchers	2 93	4 39	3 67
Brass-founders	4 07	12 22	6 11
Cabinet-makers	3 67	12 22	4 89
Confectioners	2 44	4 89	3 67
Cigarette-makers (girls)	1 22	1 95	1 46
Coopers	4 89	7 33	6 11
Cutlers	1 22	2 44	1 71
Distillers	1 46	2 20	1 71
Drivers:			
Draymen and teamsters	2 44	4 89	3 67
Cab and carriage	2 44	4 89	3 67
Street railway	2 44	4 89	3 67
Dyers	2 44	4 89	3 67
Engravers	4 89	9 78	7 33
Furriers	2 44	7 33	4 89
Gardeners	2 44	3 67	2 93
Hatters	2 44	6 11	3 67
Horseshoers	1 22	3 67	2 44
Jewelers	4 89	9 78	6 11
Laborers, porters, &c	2 44	2 93	2 60
Lithographers	4 89	9 78	7 33
Millwrights	2 44	6 11	4 89
Nail-makers (hand)	1 95	3 67	2 44
Potters	1 22	4 89	2 44
Printers	2 44	4 89	3 67
Teachers, public schools	4 07	12 22	6 11
Saddle and harness makers	1 95	3 67	2 44
Sail-makers	4 39	6 11	4 89
Stevedores	4 39	6 11	5 37
Tanners	1 95	2 93	2 44
Tailors	2 44	4 89	3 67
Telegraph operators	2 44	6 11	2 93
Tinsmiths	2 44	4 89	3 67
Weavers (outside of mills)	1 95	2 93	2 44

NOTE.—The above wages are given in United States gold dollars at the rate of $0.04075 per Turkish silver piaster.

II. FACTORIES, MILLS, ETC.

Wages paid per week of sixty-six hours in factories or mills in Smyrna.

Occupations.	Lowest.	Highest.	Average.
Engineer (native)	$11 00	$16 50	$13 20
Foremen	9 78	12 22	10 76
Stone dressers	5 38	9 78	6 60
Firemen	3 42	4 16	3 67
Millers	2 69	3 91	2 93
Assistant millers	2 44	2 93	2 69
Laborers	2 44	3 42	2 69

III. FOUNDRIES, MACHINE-SHOPS, AND IRON WORKS.

Wages paid per week of sixty-six hours in foundries, machine-shops, and iron works in Smyrna.

Occupations.	Lowest.	Highest.	Average.
Foremen	$12 22	$18 34	$14 67
Smiths	5 62	11 49	7 82
Boiler-makers	6 11	9 78	7 33
Coppersmiths	6 11	9 78	7 33
Fitters	5 38	9 78	6 85
Turners	5 38	9 78	6 85
Pattern-makers	4 89	7 82	6 11
Molders	4 89	6 85	5 62
Assistant boiler-makers	3 42	4 16	3 67
Firemen	3 42	4 16	3 67
Boiler cleaners	2 69	3 42	2 93
Strikers	2 44	4 16	2 93
Assistant molders	2 44	3 42	2 69
Laborers	2 44	3 42	2 69
Boys	1 22	2 44	1 71

V. MINES AND MINING.

Wages paid per day of eleven hours in and in connection with chrome, emery, and manganese mines in Asia Minor.

Occupations.	Lowest.	Highest.	Average.
Foremen	$1 22	$2 44	$1 63
Drillers	61	2 04	1 02
Diggers	41	1 02	61
Sorters	41	1 02	61

VI. RAILWAY EMPLOYÉS.

Wages paid to railway employés (those engaged about stations, as well as those engaged on the engines and cars, linemen, railroad laborers, &c.) in Smyrna.

Occupations.	Lowest.	Highest.	Average.
Way inspectors ..... per month..	$35 86	$44 82	$39 12
Station masters ..... do....	20 37	81 50	36 67
Guards of trains ..... do....	23 63	36 67	27 71
Gaugers of parties of workmen ..... do....	21 19	30 97	25 26
Clerks and telegraphists ..... do....	8 96	30 97	19 56
Ticket collectors ..... do....	15 48	25 26	17 93
Underguards of trains ..... do....	13 04	18 74	15 48
Guards of stations ..... do....	9 78	17 11	11 41
Drivers of engines ..... per day..	1 02	2 04	1 43
Boiler-makers, fitters, turners, and smiths ..... do....	61	1 83	1 14
Masons ..... do....	81	1 43	1 02
Carpenters ..... do....	65	1 83	94
Firemen ..... do....	49	1 02	65
Laborers ..... do....	41	61	49
Porters, pointsmen, pumpers, &c ..... do ...	41	61	49
Roadmen ..... do....	41	49	45

VII. Ship-yards and ship-building.

Wages paid per week of sixty-six hours in ship-yards in Smyrna.

Occupations.	Lowest.	Highest.	Average.
Overseers	$9 78	$14 67	$12 22
Shipwrights	3 67	7 33	4 89
Calkers	3 67	7 33	4 89
Boys	1 22	2 44	1 71

IX. Store and shop wages.

Wages paid per week of sixty-six hours in hardware, millinery, grocery, and dry goods stores, wholesale or retail, to males and females in Smyrna.

Occupations.	Lowest.	Highest.	Average.
Cashiers	$12 22	$24 45	$14 67
Book-keepers	7 33	12 22	8 56
Salesmen	6 11	9 78	7 33
Money collectors*	6 11	9 78	7 33
Saleswomen	2 44	4 89	3 67
Errand-boys	1 22	2 44	1 71

* Money collectors employed by the job get from 5 to 10 per cent. on amount collected ; sometimes 25 to 50 per cent. for bad debts.

XI. Agricultural wages.

Wages paid per day of ten hours to agricultural laborers in Smyrna, without board or lodging.

Occupations.	Lowest.	Highest.	Average.
Boss husbandmen	$0 81	$1 22	$1 02
Grafters	61	1 02	81
Tillers	41	81	61
Sowers	41	81	61
Mowers	41	81	61
Thrashers	41	81	61
Vine tarrers	41	81	61
Vintagers*	20	41	29
Fruit gatherers*	20	41	29
Weeders *	20	41	29
Vine sulphurers *	20	29	24

*Mostly women and boys.

XV. Printers and printing offices.

Statement showing the wages paid per week of sixty-six hours to printers (compositors, pressmen, proof-readers, &c.) in Smyrna.

Occupations.	Lowest.	Highest.	Average.
Compositors	$4 89	$6 11	$5 38
Proof-readers	4 89	6 11	5 38
Pressmen	2 44	3 42	2 69
Inkers (boys)	1 22	1 71	1 47

XVI. FEMALE LABOR.

Wages paid per day of ten hours to female laborers in Smyrna.

Occupations.	Lowest.	Highest.	Average.
Laundresses	$0 61	$0 81	$0 73
Teachers	41	81	61
Dressmakers	41	81	61
Seamstresses	20	41	29
Fig-packers	20	41	29
Valonia cleaners	20	41	29
Gum-tragacanth sorters	20	41	29
Farm laborers	20	41	29
Cigarette-makers	20	33	24
Rag-sorters	16	33	20
Bone-sorters	16	33	20
Cotton-pickers	12	20	16
Carpet-weavers	12	20	16
Servants*	08	16	12

*In addition to board and lodging servants get three pair of shoes and two dresses per year.

MYTILENE.

REPORT BY CONSULAR AGENT FOTTION.

Conformably to the instructions contained in the Department's circular of February 15, 1884, I have the honor to submit the following report concerning the condition of labor at Mytilene. The result of my examination revealed that the average weekly wages paid to each common laborer amounts to $3.50.

The hours of labor are from 6 to 6, with one hour for breakfast and one hour for dinner, or per week sixty hours, except Sunday, and in winter till dusk.

Farm laborer, from 6 a. m. to 6 p. m., with eating time.

A workingman can live on from $1.75 to $2.10 per week, with wife and three or four children.

I give the following table showing the average weekly expenses for the support of a common laborer, with wife and three or four children:

Taxes $0 01

House-hire.—Everybody here has his own house, and a bit of land, with olive trees or vines, upon which he raises what vegetables he uses.

Clothing and washing...30

Eating and drinking:

Liquor	17
Bread	80
Meats	32
Vegetables	10
Fishes	10
Rice	10
Cheese	20

Total 2 10

FOOD PRICES.

I give also the market prices of articles of food as sold there.

Articles.	Cost.	Articles.	Cost.
Ox meat .... per 3½ pounds..	$0 19	Butter .... per 3½ pounds..	$0 55
Mutton .... do....	16	Fish .... do....	20
Veal .... do....	20	Bread .... do....	06
Cheese .... do....	30	Onions .... do....	02
Fowls .... each..	40	Rice .... do....	05
Ducks .... do....	35	Sugar .... do....	20
Flour .... per 3½ pounds..	06	Coffee .... do....	40
Potatoes .... do....	06	Cabbages .... per dozen...	04
Eggs, fresh .... per dozen..	12		

Classes and position.	Compen-sation.	Annual cost of liv-ing.
Civil.		
Governor...per year..	$6, 500 00	....
Secretaries...do....	1, 500 00	$1, 200 00
Chief of police...do....	750 00	900 00
Policemen...do....	120 00	120 00
Legal.		
Judges...do....	180 00	800 00
Notaries...	(*)	....
Medical.		
Doctors and surgeons..	(†)	....
Literary.		
Director of school.............................per year..	1, 000 00	800 00
Professors..do....	500 00	500 00
Teachers...do....	150 00	150 00
Clerical.		
Archbishops...do....	5, 000 00	3, 000 00
Priests..	(‡)	....
Commercial.		
Agents...per year..	500 00	400 00
Clerks and book-keepers.......................................do....	200 00	200 00
Salesmen...do....	170 00	140 00
Errand boy	90	....
Washerwomen.......................................per day..	20	....
Customs.		
Director...per year..	840 00	700 00
Assistants...do....	240 00	500 00
Interpreters...do....	420 00	500 00
Inspectors...do....	1, 200 00	....
Telegraph operators.......................................do....	360 00	....
Artisans.		
Shoemakers...per day..	50	....
Iron-workers...do....	40	....
Carpenters...do....	70	....
Masons...do....	80	....
Tailors ....do....	40	....
Brick-makers...do....	18	....
Cigar-makers...per M..	1 00	....
Producers.		....
Farm hands ....per day..	35	....
Woodmen ....do....	18	....
Fishermen ....do....	20	....
Servants.		
Family servants...per year..	§25 00	....
Water-carriers...per day..	20	
Cookwomen...per year..	§28 00	
Nurses ....do....	§50 00	....

* Per cent. † Fifty, sixty, and seventy cents per visit. ‡ Fees. § Two dresses.

M. M. FOTTION, ·
Consular Agent.

UNITED STATES CONSULAR AGENCY,
Mytilene, May 22, 1884.

SYRIA.

REPORT BY CONSUL ROBESON, OF BEIRUT.

In reply to the Department circular, dated February 15, 1884, asking for full information concerning the condition of labor, I have the honor to state that I have carefully examined the subject and beg to submit the following report, with tables :

PRESENT CONDITION OF THE LABORING CLASSES.

The general condition of the laboring classes in this consular district is neither satisfactory nor prosperous. The state of commerce is depressed on account of the trouble in Egypt. That country being the principal market for Syrian and Aleppo goods, the demand for the same has fallen off very much during the last three years, and wages have consequently lowered in proportion. Most of the native weavers of silk and cotton goods receive from 20 to 40 cents a day, a sum which hardly suffices to secure for them the daily necessaries of life. Not over 5 per cent. are able to save anything from their wages, and in many cases weavers work for wages received in advance. The condition of agricultural laborers is not any better throughout the country. The fellaheen (peasants) for many years have been subjected to heavy taxes, and pay exorbitant interest upon money borrowed, while the prices of cereals and other crops are below the average. They have, in fact, been struggling for their own maintenance and that of their families, although the climate is good and the soil rich and productive in most parts of the country. The wages paid for an adult plowman with a team of oxen are from 40 to 50 cents a day. The plowman, as a rule, feeds himself and team. The only classes of laborers whose wages have increased for the last few years are masons and carpenters. This increase is due to the fact that many of the capitalists of the country, being unable to use their capital advantageously in commercial transactions, owing to the dullness of trade prevailing in this part of Turkey, have turned their attention to buying and improving real estate both in town and country. The number of masons and carpenters not being sufficient for the demand, their wages have increased considerably. The silk factories, which number ninety-five in Syria, provide work for about eight thousand laborers. The average wages paid to spinners of both sexes is $1 a week. Although the said amount seems to be very small when compared to the wages for similar work in America, it is considered very satisfactory by the working class of people in this country. The industry of the country is gradually improving, and would improve very materially were it not for the prejudice of the Government against foreign capitalists and foreigners coming into the country. · The number of laborers is few in comparison to the population. Foreign industrial and agricultural machinery has not yet found its way to the Syrian market, field, or workshop to any extent. The looms on which the native stuffs are made are of a primitive character, and the tools are the same as have been used for centuries.

SOCIAL CONDITION OF WOMEN.

The social condition of women has greatly improved in this country within the last twenty-three years. Female education was for a long time considered as one of the most degrading innovations introduced into the East by European civilization. Since 1860 a new era has opened for woman, and the new generation considers woman as the companion of man. This change has taken place in the cities and villages where schools have been opened by missionaries, but in many parts of the country woman still remains in a degraded state of ignorance, and is compelled to perform work which she is unfitted for. On farms women plant, sow, and reap. They have also to do the dairy-work and feed the animals of the farm. A large majority of the mountain girls are engaged either as spinners in the silk factories of the country or as servants, maids, or nurses with the better classes.

SYSTEM OF HIRING LABORERS.

There is no regular or public system adopted for hiring laborers. When a person wants to hire laborers he speaks with some leading person of the class he wishes to employ, who will bring the number wanted, and for this service he will receive a small compensation from the employer.

RATES OF WAGES.

The rates of wages are dependent in this country on the supply and demand. During the winter season wages, as a rule, decrease, as a great number of peasants collect in the towns, from their agricultural districts, where they try to find work till spring. The wages of the laborers who permanently reside in cities do not change very much. It is common to see a man working one day as a mason and another as camel or mule driver or in some other capacity wherever he can get the highest wages.

COST OF LIVING.

There have been no statistics compiled on labor in this country, but the cost of living has been for the last twenty years gradually increasing. The opening of the Suez Canal, the increase in population of the country, and the extension of commercial relations between Europe and this part of Turkey have facilitated the exportation of various articles of food, and an increase in price of about 15 per cent. has been the result.

House rent is one of the burdens under which almost every workman labors here. A small room can be hired for $1.25 per month. The mildness of the climate in this country, especially on the coast and plains, makes clothing and fuel a light charge on the laborer when compared with other expenses. The cost of living for a family of five persons (husband, wife, and three children, on an average), with an income of $2.50 per week, is as follows:

Income, $2.50 per week, or $130 per year.

Rent expenses ....per year..		$15 60
Taxes, gas, fuel, &c...do....		9 00
Clothing ....do....		13 50
		38 10
Bread ....per day..	$0 12	
Meat ....do....	03	
Olives, cheese, and oil...............................do....	07	
Vegetables ....do....	07	
	29 =	90 48
		128 58
Balance saved.....		1 42

Turkish coin has different rates in every city throughout the Ottoman Empire, and even in the same place it often has two or three rates. The gold lira, which is the standard currency, is worth 100 piasters at the Imperial Ottoman Bank, the Government and customs departments, while at the market its rate is 123 piasters.* However, the money used generally for paying all working classes in this country is the silver currency, the standard coin of which is the medjidi, the value of which is 22 piasters and 30 paras, equal to 82 cents.

PAST AND PRESENT WAGES.

The difference between the present rates of wages and those that prevailed in 1878 is about 15 per cent. As to the conditions of the same they have been gradually improving.

HABITS OF THE WORKING CLASSES.

Native workmen are generally steady but not very trustworthy; they are generally improvident, while some of them are given to drink. Oppressive laws, heavy taxation, the want of education and moral instruction, as well as the entire absence of sympathy shown on the part of the Government for the working classes, have a demoralizing effect on their habits.

FEELING BETWEEN EMPLOYER AND EMPLOYÉ.

The feeling which prevails between employé and employer in this country is, as a rule, good, and has a satisfactory influence on the prosperity of the country.

LABOR ORGANIZATIONS, STRIKES, ETC.

The laboring population in this part of Turkey have neither trade unions nor organized societies.

Strikes among the laboring classes of this country are of rare occurrence, and when they take place they seldom if ever succeed for want of organization and capital. Further, as a rule, the supply of laborers is greater than the demand.

FOOD PURCHASES.

Working people here are free to purchase the necessaries of life wherever they choose, no conditions being imposed upon them in this respect. Laborers in this country are generally paid once a week, i. e., on Saturday evenings. The wages are given in Turkish coin, according to the market rate of silver currency.

CO-OPERATIVE SOCIETIES.

There are no co-operative societies in existence in Turkey in Asia..

GENERAL CONDITION OF THE WORKING CLASSES.

The working people here are generally uneducated, poor, superstitious, and attached to old customs, principles, and traditions. With regard to the manner of life they lead, they generally seem to be satisfied with what they possess and live up to their incomes. They live in

---

* Twenty-seven and a half piasters make $1.

small huts poorly furnished. Frequently four or five persons live together in one room. The food which most, if not all, laborers eat consists of bread, olives, onions, cheese, and oil. Potatoes are expensive
and not indulged in by the laboring classes. The price of meat varies,
in the course of the year, from 10 to 20 cents per pound, as well as coffee,
rice, sugar, milk, &c., which are only used as a treat on Sundays and
special holidays or feast days. The usual dress worn by the working
people is made of Manchester cotton goods or native stuffs. As long as
they are left without instruction, burdened with heavy taxes, and oppressed by the wealthy they can have no chances for bettering their
condition. The wages of the working classes in this country being generally low, very few laborers are able to lay up anything for old age or
sickness. The moral condition of the working people of the country
and Bedouins will compare in some respects very favorably with more
civilized countries. Their physical condition is, on the whole, good.

The influences for evil surrounding workmen in this country are grog-
shops, where "arak," native spirits, and other bad, intoxicating liquors
are sold. There are no libraries, museums, gymnasiums, or other moral
entertainments to amuse or instruct the working people here. In many
of the towns and villages there are missionary schools, where services
are held on Sundays and Sunday-schools taught in the afternoon, which
are attended by a considerable number of the Christian working people,
but not by the Mussulmans.

SAFETY OF EMPLOYÉS.

No special means are furnished for the safety of employés in factories,
&c., in this country, nor are any provisions made for them in case of
accident. Little, if any, consideration is given by the employers to the
moral and physical well-being of the employés. As to the relations
prevailing between the employer and the employed they are generally
amicable and satisfactory.

POLITICAL RIGHTS.

Workmen neither vote nor exercise any political rights in this country. The wealthy classes elect the few officers that are not appointed
by the Porte or the governor of the province. The working people pay
about 20 per cent. of the taxes. The tendency of the law as carried out
in this country is to oppress the working people. There seems to be
little hope of relief for them from any source.

EMIGRATION.

The causes that lead to emigration are the want of more liberty and
heavy taxation.

NUMBER OF FEMALE EMPLOYÉS.

The number of women and children employed in this district in industrial pursuits may be estimated as follows:
Manufacturing, 12,000; teachers, 2,000; laundresses, 900; professional
musicians, 800; agricultural, 3,000; all other pursuits, 3,000.
Women are not engaged in this country in any public profession except in the above mentioned.

FEMALE WAGES.

Female adults are paid as follows, per week, from seven to eleven
hours a day:
Minimum, 48 cents; maximum, $8; average, $2.

Wherever women are engaged with men in the same work they work the same number of hours, i. e., from seven to eleven hours a day.

MORAL AND PHYSICAL CONDITION.

The moral condition of women here will compare favorably with those of other countries. From best information, the number of illegitimate children born in this country will not amount to more than 2 per cent. of the whole population; but in an educational point there is much to be desired. With regard to the physical condition of the working classes of women it is unsatisfactory, as little, if any, attention is given to their physical welfare; further, many of the girls employed in factories fall victims to long hours and bad ventilation of the factories.

IMPROVEMENT OF FEMALE LABORERS.

No means are provided by the manufacturers for the improvement of their employés. The moral and educational improvement of the country is provided almost entirely by foreign missionaries.

SAFETY OF FEMALE EMPLOYES.

No special means are provided in case of fire or other dangers for their safety, but fires are here of rare occurrence.

There are no provisions made by the employers regarding the sanitary condition of their employés. In case of sickness the employés have to return to their huts; in many instances sick girls and women are sent to the missionary or charitable hospitals in town.

During the past five years an increase of about 10 per cent. has taken place in the wages paid to women, as well as in the price of the necessaries of life. The effect is insignificant.

The women employed in the factories are not educated, and there is little attempt to educate the children of women so employed; but in some seasons of the year some of these children employed in factories attend mission schools.

In collecting reliable statistics for this report I found the same difficulty as when trying to get reliable information on the commercial and manufacturing resources of the country. In each class of labor I have had to make personal inquiry, as no statistics can be obtained. In many instances the people would not answer questions regarding the wages received or cost of living. The answer they give is, why do you want such information, and what do you want to make such report, for?

JOHN T. ROBESON,
Consul.

UNITED STATES CONSULATE,
Beirut, July 8, 1884.

I. General Trades.

Wages paid per day of eleven hours in Beirut.

Occupations.	Lowest.	Highest.	Average.
BUILDING TRADES.			
Bricklayers	$2 30	$4 70	$4 00
Masons	2 88	6 00	4 80
Tenders	1 20	1 92	1 68
Plasterers	2 88	4 80	3 12
Tenders	1 20	1 92	1 68
Decorators	3 60	10 00	5 50
Roofers	1 70	2 50	2 00
Pavers	3 84	6 00	4 32
Plumbers	2 50	3 50	3 00
Carpenters	2 40	4 80	4 08
OTHER TRADES.			
Bakers	96	1 92	1 44
Blacksmiths	48	3 36	1 20
Book-binders	5 00	9 00	6 50
Butchers	96	1 92	1 44
Cabinet-makers	2 40	6 00	4 80
Confectioners	72	1 44	1 20
Cigar-makers	2 20	3 30	2 30
Distillers	76	1 92	1 44
Drivers, cab and carriage	1 20	1 92	1 44
Dyers	24	1 92	1 20
Engravers	4 80	7 00	5 70
Furriers	3 60	4 80	4 20
Gardeners	1 20	2 40	1 92
Horseshoers	48	2 40	1 44
Jewelers	48	2 64	1 68
Laborers, porters, &c	1 20	2 40	1 68
Nail-makers (hand)	48	1 44	96
Potters	48	4 32	2 16
Male teachers	1 00	3 50	2 00
Female teachers (with board)	50	2 50	1 50
Saddle and harness makers	1 20	4 80	3 36
Tanners	1 92	4 80	2 88
Tailors	72	2 40	1 92
Tinsmiths	24	2 64	1 30
Weavers (outside of mills)	1 20	2 40	1 75
Camel drivers	3 80	5 00	4 40
Muleteers (man and mule)	3 40	4 80	
Muleteers (man and donkey)	1 92	2 68	2 40

II. Factories, Mills, etc.

Wages paid per week of seventy-seven hours in factories or mills in the United States consular district of Beirut, Asia, Turkey.

Occupations.	Lowest.	Highest.	Average.
SILK FACTORIES.			
Inspector	$3 70	$4 60	$4 10
Fireman	1 50	4 60	3 00
Cocoons-mover	95	1 90	1 40
Spinner (boy or girl)	48	1 56	1 00
Cocoons-cleaner	24	74	49
PAPER-MILL.			
Machinist	3 50	9 00	6 00
Fireman	1 00	4 20	2 60
Cylinder inspector	1 00	3 20	2 00
Paper cutter	1 30	2 50	1 85
Bleacher	1 20	2 50	1 80
Rags and rope cutter	1 50	1 90	1 66
Cylinder workman	1 50	1 80	1 60
Assistant machinist	50	1 90	1 20

VI. Carriage Roads.

Wages paid per month to employés on Ottoman Carriage Road Company between Beirut and Damascus in the Beirut consular district.

Occupations.	Lowest.	Highest.	Average.
Director	$172 00	$206 00	$183 00
Comptroller	75 00	103 00	89 00
Head saddler	25 00	56 00	40 00
Clerk	20 06	41 33	25 00
Head coachman (conductor)*	18 58		
Station officer	16 00	24 83	20 06
Coachman	12 80	18 58	15 50
Farrier	12 80	14 40	13 40
Saddler	10 33	20 66	15 50
Toll-collector	10 33	12 80	12 00
Carman	10 00	12 80	11 15

* Fixed.

NOTE.—The Ottoman Road Company own and control the wagon road from Beirut to Damascus, crossing the Lebanon and Anti-Lebanon Mountains, 112 kilometers in length. By this road 65 per cent. of the goods transported between the said cities are carried and the foregoing table shows the wages paid to the employés of said Ottoman Road Company. The said company is owned and controlled by Frenchmen.

VIII. Native Seamen's Wages.

Wages paid per month to seamen, coast and river navigation, in the ports of Beirut, Haifa, and other Syrian ports.

Occupations.	Lowest.	Highest.	Average.
Captain of sailing (coast) vessels	$13 00	$25 50	$19 00
Seamen	9 00	15 00	11 50
Lightermen	5 50	7 00	6 00
Boatmen	5 00	6 80	5 50

IX. Store and Shop Wages.

Wages paid per week of fifty-four hours in banks and retail dry-goods stores to males in the consular district of Beirut.

Occupations.	Lowest.	Highest.	Average.
Bank comptroller and cashier	$24 00	$42 00	$33 00
Bank clerk	4 00	19 00	12 00
Book-keepers	3 00	12 00	6 50
Salesmen	2 50	6 00	4 15
Helpers	1 00	3 20	2 00

X. Household Wages in Towns and Cities.

Wages paid per month to household servants (towns and cities) in the Beirut consular district.

Occupations.	Lowest.	Highest.	Average.
Cook	$4 50	$12 00	$8 00
Nurse	4 50	6 00	5 00
Man or maid servant	1 00	4 30	2 55

XI. AGRICULTURAL WAGES.

Wages paid per day to agricultural laborers and household (country) servants in the Beirut consular district, without board.

Occupations.	Lowest.	Highest.	Average.
Farmer	$0 32	$0 60	$0 40
Grafter	25	50	35
Reaper	18	38	23
Plowman	30	45	33
Shepherd	12	25	15

XII. CORPORATION EMPLOYÉS.

Wages paid per week to the corporation employés in the city of Beirut.

Occupations.	Average wages.	Occupations.	Average wages.
President of municipality	$36 00	Treasurer of municipality	$6 20
Engineer of municipality	19 60	Contract notary of municipality	6 20
Doctor of municipality	18 57	Chief police of municipality	6 20
Chief clerk of municipality	18 57	Policemen of municipality	3 25

XIII. GOVERNMENT DEPARTMENTS AND OFFICES.

Wages paid per month, seven hours a day, to employés in Government departments and offices—exclusive of tradesmen and laborers—in the provinces of Syria, Aleppo, and Adana.

Occupations.	Class I.	Class II.	Class III.
Wali (governor-general)	$1,118 00	$800 00	$559 00
Mutasarrif (governor)	447 00	330 00	266 00
Judge (cadi)	225 00	120 00	35 00
Attorney-general	179 00	130 00	100 00
Comptroller	112 00	90 00	67 00
President of court	156 00	88 00	22 00
Kaimmakam (deputy governor)	100 00	80 00	56 00
Assistant attorney	76 00	70 00	62 00
Chief clerk	78 00	46 00	13 00
Chief of police	67 00	44 00	22 00
Mudir (director)	33 00	27 00	18 00
Member of court	67 00	39 00	11 00
Clerk	65 00	35 00	10 50
Inquirer	44 00	30 00	13 50
Officer of police	18 00	14 00	10 00
Policeman	15 00		
Jailer	11 00	8 00	4 50

Turkish military service—pay of officers, non-commissioned officers, and privates, per month, independent of rations, in the Beirut consular district.

Occupations.	Average wages.	Occupations.	Average wages.
Marshal (mushir)	$637 00	Color-bearer	$14 00
Full general	255 00	Adjutant	10 70
Lieutenant-general	170 00	Quartermaster	10 00
Major-general	85 00	Sergeant-major	8 00
Brigadier-general	54 00	First sergeant	2 50
Military doctor	51 00	Second sergeant	2 00
Colonel (binbashi)	42 00	Chief farrier	2 50
Lieutenant-colonel (kol aghasi)	32 00	Assistant farrier	1 80
Chaplain (imam)	32 00	Saddler	1 80
Apothecary	17 00	Corporal	1 42
Arms repairer	17 00	Chief fifer	1 23
Major	14 00	Fifer	1 00

Wages paid to the Beirut custom-house employés, per week, for seven hours work a day.

Occupations.	Lowest.	Highest.	Average.
Chief collector (nazer)..			$61 00
Director (mudir)..			20 00
Assessor			12 00
Chief clerk..			12 00
Cashier and treasurer			9 00
Weighter	$2 50	$5 00	3 00
Clerks	2 80	4 60	3 00
Searchers	2 80	4 60	3 00
Chief guardian..			1 00
Guardian..			1 40

XIV. GOVERNMENT TELEGRAPH OFFICES.

Wages paid paid by the week, of seventy-two hours, to the telegraph employés in Government employ in the consular district of Beirut.

Occupations.	Lowest.	Highest.	Average.
Chief director..	$12 50	$23 00	$17 50
Inspector	12 00	18 50	15 15
Assistant director...	8 00	10 00	8 75
Assistant inspector	7 80	9 80	8 50
Chief operator, employé	6 43	7 50	6 96
Operator, employé	3 21	4 75	4 00
Wire repairer	2 00	3 00	2 50
Janitor and message boy	1 00	1 50	1 25

XV. PRINTERS AND PRINTING OFFICES.

Statement showing the wages paid per week of fifty-four hours to printers (compositors, press-men, proof-readers, &c.) in the consular district of Beirut.

Occupations.	Lowest.	Highest.	Average.
Proof-readers and revisers......................................	$3 00	$8 00	$5 00
Compositors..	2 50	6 00	4 22
Engineer...	3 00	5 00	3 70
Printers..	2 73	3 45	3 00
Book-collectors..	1 00	2 00	1 30
Book-seamstresses...	80	1 90	1 30

PALESTINE.

REPORT BY CONSUL MERRILL, OF JERUSALEM.

In answer to the circular from the Department of State, dated February 15, 1884, I have the honor to make the following report on the condition of labor and the laboring classes in Palestine:

DIFFICULTIES UNDER WHICH THE REPORT IS MADE.

It is hardly possible to exaggerate the difficulties under which such a report as that required by the Department of State in its labor circular of February 15, 1884, is made in Palestine.

The Turkish Government takes almost no interest in anything which might concern the welfare of its subjects. Instead of a happy and prosperous people, one sees on every hand oppression and suffering, ignorance and degradation.

No statistics of any kind are kept, hence the consul must first collect and collate his facts, which in a more advanced country would exist ready to his hand, before a report on any subject can be made. After all the trouble and time that I have expended in getting materials for this report, I feel that I have only the most meager results to offer to the Department. In reality it seems to me that any results and facts which I am able to present will serve much more as a matter of curiosity than for any purposes of comparison with anything that exists in America.

NO BASIS OF COMPARISON BETWEEN PALESTINE AND THE UNITED STATES.

There is between the two countries no common basis of comparison, as will readily be seen by such facts as the following:

1. Everything here is of the most primitive character and on the smallest scale, while in the United States everything is modern and costly and on the grandest scale.

2. No one here works by the week. In fact, so far as the Mohammedan portion of the inhabitants is concerned, there is no distinction of weeks in the matter of labor. The Mohammedan laborer observes no day of rest unless he is employed by a Jew or a Christian. Most labor here is done by the day or by the job.

3. There is no rule about the number of hours which constitute a day's work. The apparent rule is from sunrise to sunset, yet the laborer often begins his work long before sunrise and leaves off before sunset, or continues working after sunset, as the particular circumstances demand.

4. There is no very marked distinction between employers as a class and laborers as a class, because of the fact that nine tenths of all laborers are in some way for themselves. A man may be absolutely for himself, he may combine with others and each have a certain share in the profits, or he may give his labor as an offset to that of another man who does an entirely different kind of work.

5. Hardly any kind of labor continues throughout the year; this affects the living and the habits of the people in a very marked manner.

6. Large numbers of trades and kinds of occupation that are well known in America do not exist here, and, on the other hand, there are a few trades and kinds of occupations common in Palestine that are not known in America.

7. There are here no settled rules about paid labor. Every workman asks at first a very high price and in the end takes what he can get, it may be only a fraction of what he at first demanded.

8. Furthermore, there are here no fixed values either of anything that is sold in the shops or of any article of produce that is raised in the country and brought to the towns for sale. (There are two or three shops kept by Europeans to which the first part of this remark does not apply, but these are the only exceptions.) Every person asks about double what he actually gets at last for his goods, provided he makes a sale. The people of the country do not seem to have any well-defined ideas about values; they know in a general way that 20 cents will buy more than 10 cents, but of intrinsic values they know nothing.

The population of Jerusalem is remarkable as being composed of Mohammedans, Jews, native Christians, and Europeans. Of the 40,000 inhabitants of the city, one-fourth are Christians (including the Europeans), one-fourth are Mohammedans, and one-half are Jews, who number not far from 20,000 souls. The houses are built of stone, the rooms in them are small and poorly lighted, the streets are narrow and filthy, and the people crowd together in stifled apartments where all sanitary laws are set at defiance.

The present city is built upon the ruins of ancient Jerusalem, or rather upon the ruins of many ancient cities, since the city has undergone no less than twenty-six sieges, in several of which it has been reduced to a heap of ruins. The Jerusalem of two thousand or three thousand years ago, lies in some places at a depth of 10 feet, in other places at not less than 90 feet, below the present surface of the ground. The Jerusalem of to-day is poorly built, and the inhabitants are for the most part poor and wretched. Formerly there were among the natives a large number of wealthy families, while to-day there are very few, their wealth having been dissipated by the peculiar social and political circumstances of modern times.

<h2>PEOPLE SUPPORTED BY CHARITY.</h2>

Nearly all the Jews of Jerusalem receive charity, while two-thirds of them depend mainly upon these funds, which come mostly from Europe, for their support. With many of the Jews the struggle for life—for a daily pittance of bread—is a hard one. In spite of the large sums that are annually distributed among the Jews of Jerusalem, it cannot be shown that their condition is thereby materially bettered year by year. On the other hand, it would be easy to show how this so-called charity is a curse rather than a blessing, chiefly because it puts self-reliance at a discount and fosters idleness.

Among the Greeks (meaning those who are of the Greek religion) we find some wealth but a great deal of poverty, and the same is true of the Latins or Roman Catholics. The Greek and Latin convents are large owners of property in the shape of gems, jewels, and treasures stored away in the churches and convents, and also in houses and lands in and around Jerusalem. Both the Greek and Latin convents give to every family in their special communions a house free of rent. It is a common practice for a Greek, if he owns a house, to rent it to a Mohammedan, a Jew, or a Protestant, and get for himself a house free of rent from the convent. Each convent has likewise a large flouring mill and a bread-making establishment, and they furnish bread gratis to every family twice a week. It is not probable, from all the data that I am able to collect, that there are fifty Christian families (and this number, of course, includes the native Protestants, but does not include the Europeans) in Jerusalem, who pay house rent.

It will be seen that neither Greeks, Latins, nor Jews are self-supporting. Were the aid which they receive from outside to be cut off suddenly they would perish from starvation. Greeks, Latins, and Jews are here for religious purposes. They wish to devote themselves to religion and meantime to lean on some one beside themselves for support. This state of things is just the opposite of what it should be. The current now indicated is so strong that the native Arabs or Mohammedans have been largely affected by it, and they likewise find idleness more pleasurable than labor, consequently they are consuming whatever they may have inherited from their fathers, and they lack both the enterprise and the disposition to accumulate anything either for themselves in their old age or for their posterity.

OBSERVATIONS ON THE DEPARTMENT BLANK FORMS.

With regard to the blank forms furnished by the Department, I have retained those from II to XV, since under only four of those fourteen different heads could I make any entries, and the scanty information which I might give under those four heads is incorporated in my general report or in the list of "general trades," which accompanies it.

OBSERVATIONS ON THE DEPARTMENT'S LIST OF GENERAL TRADES.

Some miscellaneous observations are necessary with regard to the list of "general trades" that has been furnished by the Department.

Although there is no absolute rule in the matter, I consider that twelve hours in twenty-four is about the time that a laborer is expected to devote every day to his work.

I have taken the liberty to draw a line through such of the trade mentioned in the list as do not exist in Palestine. Among these, for example, I have thus marked out "cabinet-makers" for the reason that no such class is known here in distinction from "carpenters."

In like manner there is no distinction between "tenders" of masons, "tenders" of plasterers, and "hod-carriers," who in America have to do chiefly or exclusively with brick-layers.

Under the head of "drivers" only one class is known here, namely, those who drive the so-called "carriages" corresponding to our lumber or farm wagons, which pass between Jerusalem and Jaffa.

I have been obliged to make a distinction between the wages received by the natives of the country and those received by Jews. It is interesting to notice that of thirty-three different trades mentioned, the Jews engage in twenty-two, that is, in two-thirds only, and of these twenty-two trades they receive wages equal to the Arabs in thirteen, while in the remaining nine they receive less than the Arabs.

VERY FEW STEADY EMPLOYMENTS.

While all the trades are uncertain as to the income to be derived from them, some are far more precarious in this respect than others. For instance, "porters" I have put down as earning $2.40 per week. This means, of course, if they have continuous work. There is a large number of this class and the work is hard. One of these men will carry a heavy box half across the city, take it upstairs beside, if need be, for 6 cents, and be occupied in doing this thirty minutes or one hour. If he is fortunate he may pick up five or six such jobs during the day. One day he will earn half a dollar, perhaps, and then for one, two, or three days he may not earn a cent.

Similar remarks apply to the boatmen at Jaffa. Their life is one of danger and hardship, and their income is very uncertain.

Again, barbers, in order to eke out their precarious livelihood, take up dentistry as a branch of their business. There being no proper dentists in the city, the barbers are the dentists, or rather, since they never fill teeth, they are the teeth-pullers (literally jaw-breakers) of Jerusalem. Barbers also keep leeches for sale, and bleed people when they imagine they need it.

DIFFICULTY OF ARRIVING AT "AVERAGE WAGES."

In four only of the trades mentioned have I been able to obtain a middle rate of wages, consequently it is much more difficult to arrive at what may be called the "average wages" of a working-man. But I arrive at it approximately in this manner: Considering that the majority of laborers receive the lowest rate of wages mentioned in the schedule, while only a very few receive the higher, it is sufficiently correct to say that where one man receives 60 cents a day, or $3.60 per week, four others will receive each 40 cents a day, or $2.40 per week; hence—

Four men at $2.40 per week	$9 60
One man at $3.60 per week	3 60
	13 20

This amount divided by five gives $2.64 as the average per week. The above computation is in the case of blacksmiths.

In the case of Jew blacksmiths—	
Four men receive $1.92 per week	$7 68
One man receives $2.40 per week	2 40
	10 08

This amount divided by 5 give $2.01¾ per week.

It may be put down as a rule that where one man receives the larger wages mentioned in the schedule four men will receive the smaller wages. To this there are important exceptions, for in some cases where one man receives the larger wages nineteen others will receive the smaller wages.

COST OF LIVING.

Daily expense of living of a laboring man who receives 40 cents a day, or $2.40 per week : Bread, 10 cents ; olive oil, 2 cents ; vegetables, 2 cents ; olives or cheese, 2 cents; total, 16 cents.

Daily expense of living for a family of five persons—a man, his wife, and three children—where the man earns 40 cents a day, or $2.40 per week: Bread, 16 cents: oil, 4 cents; lentils, 8 cents; vegetables, 8 cents; charcoal, 4 cents; total, 40 cents.

Daily expense of living for a common farm laborer who receives 24 cents a day, or $1.44 per week : Bread, 8 cents ; oil or olives, 4 cents; onions, 2 cents; total, 14 cents.

Daily expense of living for the family of a common farm laborer, consisting of himself, his wife, and two children, who receives 24 cents a day, or $1.44 per week : Bread, 16 cents; oil or olives, 8 cents: onions, 4 cents; total, 28 cents.

Daily expense of living of a laboring man, if he is a Jew, who receives 40 cents a day, or $2.40 per week : Bread, 5 cents ; vegetables, 6 cents ; coffee, sugar, tea, salt, and pepper, 6 cents; total, 17 cents.

The daily expense of living for a Jewish family of five persons—a man, his wife, and three children—where the man receives 40 cents a day, or $2.40 per week, would be 40 cents a day, or $2.80 per week solely for food: and for their yearly expenses they would require: For food, $145.60; for rent, $22 ; for clothing, $25; total, $192.60.

In case of a common farm laborer, his wife and children, if the latter are old enough, labor in the field as well as himself.

While the figures show what a common Jewish family requires yearly for their support, it should be said that very few families have that amount to spend. Probably they do not have even $100 for their entire expenses, per annum.

In regard to all these classes, so far as food is concerned, they must live on less than they earn, else they could not pay for rent and clothing in the towns, or provide farm implements and clothing for themselves on a farm.

As to the laborer who receives 40 cents a day and spends, according to our reckoning, 16 cents a day for food, it will be asked if he does not lay up something; it is almost certain that he lays up nothing or at best but very little. We must remember that he has work but about half or two-thirds of the time. This reduces the surplus to nothing, especially where they have no habits of economy and never think of laying up anything for the future.

These people have the habit of spending all they get whether it be little or much. If they receive large wages they consume them all, and if they receive next to nothing they manage to live on that.

Those who receive larger wages than those indicated above are able to live slightly better, but only slightly after all. They are able to add rice to the variety of their food, and also meat once a week, or it may be three times in a fortnight. The staple articles of food of all the laboring classes, and of the large majority of the inhabitants of the country, are bread, oil or olives, leben or cheese, rice, and vegetables. Under the head of vegetables they have onions, garlic, watermelons, two kinds of cucumbers, kusa, egg-plant, and grapes.

HOURS OF DAILY LABOR ON A FARM.

With regard to the number of hours which constitute a day's work it may be said that farm laborers start before it is light so as to reach the field by daybreak. In the harvest fields women and children labor equally with the men. They start thus early because the wheat or barley must be cut while the dew is upon it. After about 10 o'clock the grain becomes so dry that it falls from the head if an attempt is made to cut it. The laborers lie off until near sunset when they commence again.

HOUSE SERVANTS AND NURSES.

As to house servants it must be remembered that there is a considerable class here who have been held as slaves. They are black people from Nubia, and having been brought up as slaves and knowing no other kind of life, they, in many cases, remain with their old masters. Practically, some of them are still slaves, although they are not bought and sold; such persons get nothing besides their clothing, shelter, and food. There are likewise numbers of native servants who in a sense belong to the families with whom they live, who get little besides their clothing, shelter, and food, but are free to go when they choose. A good native servant will receive 50 cents a week and her food. A good European servant-girl—this class are mostly Germans—receives 75 cents or $1 a week and her food, while a German man-servant will receive $1.50 per week and his food. Germans are employed, it need hardly be said, only in hotels and in European families. A native woman who is employed as a nurse receives $1.50 per week.

LARGE CLASSES DEPENDENT UPON TRAVELERS.

People who are not familiar with this country can hardly realize to what an extent the laboring classes and trades-people are dependent upon travelers for a large part of their support; among these are boat-men, carriage owners and drivers, hotel-keepers, waiters, cooks, and servants in hotels, waiters, cooks, servants, muleteers, and others who go with travelers through the country; donkey drivers, owners of horses and mules, guides, errand-boys, porters, makers and venders of olive wood work, beads, mother of pearl, and Jerusalem curiosities in gen-eral, shopkeepers, dealers in incense, wax candles, pictures of saints, and other articles of "piety and devotion," as they are called, and still other classes.

It is no exaggeration to say that thousands of people in Jerusalem and Palestine look to the traveling season as their harvest time, as almost the only time during the year when they can receive any con-siderable amount of money; consequently, when this business is inter-fered with, as it was seriously in 1882, because of the war in Egypt, and again in 1883, by the quarantine, great hardship and suffering ensue.

WAGES PAID BY TOURIST COMPANIES.

In general, the wages paid by the large tourist companies are several times greater than what laboring men ordinarily receive in Palestine. Consideration must be had for the fact that the traveling season is short, lasting but about three months, namely, during February, March, and April. A trip through the country occupies twenty, or it may occupy thirty, days, and those who are employed in this business cannot expect to make more than two trips during a single season. For this and for other reasons the wages paid must be correspondingly high. See "cooks," "dragomans," and "waiters," in the schedule. In the traveling season a horse is worth $1 a day, and frequently one cannot be obtained for less than $2 a day. Mules also are worth during the season $1 or $1.50 per day, while donkeys are worth 60 cents a day, in-cluding a boy. A camel is worth $1 a day. As a rule the owner of the animals feeds both himself and them unless a special arrangement otherwise is made. If a man owns two or three mules and they are hired for a certain journey, he goes with them himself.

EMPLOYMENT OF DRAGOMANS.

There are two kinds of dragomans here, those employed at the con-sulates and convents, who act as interpreters, clerks, agents, &c., and those whose business it is to conduct parties of tourists and travelers through the country. It is only the latter that are included in the schedule of "general trades." They must know two or more languages well, and be familiar with all parts of the country. As a class they are superior men and their wages are high, but they do not have work for a longer period than one-third of the year. It is doubtless well known that travelers do not visit this country during the summer and autumn on account of the great heat.

GUARDS AT THE CONSULATES.

The class called in the general list "kawasses" are the guards at the consulates and convents. They are all Mohammedans, and are loaned to the different foreign governments by the Turkish Government. Were they not thus employed they would be in the Turkish army, since they are really soldiers, or at least persons liable to military duty. Count-ing all the consulates and their agencies, together with the large convents, there are a large number of this class, and it may interest the statisticians, merchants, and others in America to know that the United States Government pays the guards of its consulate in Jerusalem less than any other Government, the lowest sum paid by any other Government being $3 per week, while the highest sum paid by the United States is $2 per week.

WINES AND LIQUORS.

In the list of "general trades" distillers are mentioned, and I have drawn a mark through the word. There is one brewery in Jerusalem where beer of an inferior quality is made by a German. Most of the beer consumed here is brought from Europe. Large quantities of wine are made, since this is a land of grapes and vineyards. While there are here no public distilleries large quantities of liquor are made, nevertheless, and drank by the inhabitants. After the grapes have been pressed for wine the pomace is subjected to a certain process by which an inferior quality of liquor is obtained which can be sold at a very low price. The poor here do not abstain from drinking, but manage to provide a liquor which is adapted to their limited means. Almost every Jewish family makes this poor liquor for its own use, and they consume a great deal of it. It is called *arak*, and if indulged in is very injurious to the system.

SALARIES OF TEACHERS.

The wages paid to teachers in the schools, including the Mohammedan, the Jewish, and the Christian, will no doubt attract attention. The teachers provide for themselves food, clothing, and lodging. Those who receive the highest sum, namely, $4.80 per week, are the rare exceptions. Probably where one receives this amount per week, nineteen receive the lower sum, or $1.20 per week.

TELEGRAPH OPERATORS.

As to telegraph operators there are but four in the city and much of the time there are only three persons connected with the office, including the director. When the staff is full their wages are, per week, respectively, $1.50, $3, $4.50, and (for the director) $15. The management of the telegraph is in a bad way, although it corresponds to everything else in Turkey. Sometimes it takes three days to send a telegram to Beirut and get an answer, although the distance is only 120 miles. It takes from three to five days to send a message to Egypt and to receive an answer. The Turks have never yet learned to associate promptness and speed with their idea of the telegraph.

POST-OFFICE EMPLOYÉS.

In the Turkish post-office there are two persons. The post-office and the telegraph are so united that the employés of the latter sometimes assist in distributing the mail. Turkey is in the postal union, and in Europe and America it is supposed that she is sufficiently civilized to deserve to be thus admitted, but those Europeans and Americans who reside here realize, to their sorrow often, that letters in the Turkish post are common property when they see them scattered promiscuously about the single room of the post-office on window ledges, tables, and the tops of boxes, on divans, and on the floor.

As to shop hands or clerks in stores, it is not probable that one in a hundred receives the larger wages, and it is next to impossible to fix an average. *

FEMALE LABOR.

In its circular the Department asks with regard to female labor. On this subject very little is to be said in addition to what has been reported when speaking of house servants and nurses. In the capacity of house servants many women are employed at very moderate wages. Peasant women labor in the fields with the men, and most of the small produce and merchandise is brought to market by women. They carry their burdens on their heads, and many of them come from a distance of ten or more miles. The rule is that any work that is considered menial or degrading is put upon the women, while everything in the way of labor that is at all honorable or respectable is monopolized by the men.

CONDITIONS WHICH CONTROL THE TRADE OF PALESTINE.

This being, as I have indicated, a poor city, and the inhabitants likewise poor, all the business that is done here is on a very small scale. There are no large mercantile establishments of any kind. On the contrary, there is a multitude of very small shops 6 by 8 feet or 8 by 10 feet in size. A shop or store in Jerusalem that measures 10 by 15 feet is considered large. The ceiling is low, and an upstairs apartment is not known. In general the customer stands in the street while he trades, since the merchant who stands or sits inside needs all the available space for manipulating his yard-stick or his scales.

The wants of a half-civilized people like the natives of this country, especially if they are poor, are few and simple. Nor are the Jews on any higher level than the natives themselves. In their own estimation they are the noblest people on earth and deserve special consideration from all other races; but in the eyes of others who are competent to judge they are very low in all that pertains to refined life. This is not saying what they might be under favorable circumstances, but they are suffering from generations of oppression, ignorance, and poverty. They come here from Europe, where their condition is most wretched, bringing with them their peculiar habits, and they are unable to add anything to Jerusalem except bigotry and filth. Very many of the small shops are kept by Jews, and some of the more fortunate ones are able to accumulate a little property.

Whatever goods are brought here must be adapted to the means of the purchaser; hence, as a rule one can expect to buy at these shops only inferior articles, second-hand goods, goods purchased in Europe at auction, bankrupt stocks, prints and clothing that are out of style in European cities, damaged and shop-worn articles; also adulterated wines, oils, liquors, drugs, and whatever else can be adulterated. It is this class and quality of goods that are brought to Jerusalem and which one must expect to find in the shops. The Jews outnumber so largely all the rest of the population of the city that their methods—purchasing, selling, having cheap, inferior, and adulterated goods, &c.—affect all the native shopkeepers in Jerusalem. The entire trade of the city is, as I have said, adapted to the ideas and means of the purchaser. There are, fortunately, two or three European stores in the city where good articles can be bought at a fixed price. With regard to the Jews it should be said that if they have property they put it into jewels, with which, on special occasions they load their persons. In this form property can easily be hoarded and secreted, and whenever it is necessary to do so money can be raised on it. They lose the interest, of course, but they have the satisfaction of being able to display their wealth, which they frequently do upon their necks and arms.

RATE OF INTEREST AND AN INDIFFERENT GOVERNMENT.

One great obstacle to the prosperity of this country (especially is this true of the farmers), is the scarcity of money. Everybody wants to spend more than he earns. Everybody wants to use a little more money than he can legitimately command. Hence borrowing money has become a vice and a curse, and many people in Palestine and Syria are irrevocably in debt. The rate of interest here is something frightful. Twelve per cent. per annum is a low rate of interest. Money will easily command 30 per cent. per annum. Of course here, as elsewhere, the higher the rates the greater the risk. People understand that. The peasants or farmers, who are often obliged to raise money in some way, even if they are ruined by it, not infrequently pay 50 or 100 per cent. for it. It is only a question of time how long any man's capital and substance will last under such wealth-annihilating circumstances. So long as this extortion is allowed there are always plenty of men ready to take advantage of others, to furnish money on their own terms, which of course are always ruinous. The Government might help its subjects by establishing a fixed rate of interest. But the Government itself is only an organized system of tyranny, oppression, and robbery. It does nothing for internal improvements. It does not desire that the resources of the country should be developed, and prohibits the introduction of any foreign capital that otherwise would be brought here for that purpose. It is opposed to the passing of any portion of the land of the Empire into the hands of Christians from Europe. In every way in its power, short of actual hostilities it opposes the establishing of Christian missions and schools. In a word it stands in the way of all progress. It is then no wonder that its subjects, at least all the Arab portion of them, hate their own Government, and secretly, but most earnestly, desire and look for a change. Under the circumstances it is not surprising that the wealth of the old families of the empire is being dissipated; that the mass of the people are poor and ignorant, and that the finances of Turkey are in a ruinous condition.

POOR PROSPECT FOR AMERICAN LABORERS IN PALESTINE.

There is a class of persons in America who desire to come to this country to settle. They are for the most part laboring people of little education, and of very limited means. They have very crude notions of Palestine, and do not consult those books or persons in America that could give them the best information. Occasionally they write to the consul making inquiries, but, as a rule, they are pretty sure not to follow his advice, especially when it is adverse to their coming. In their minds their coming here is connected with some crude religious notions which they expect will be realized the moment they have planted their feet upon the soil of the Holy Land. The ignorant leaders of these people inflame their minds in many ways, but especially by articles in the small journals, which are the only papers that are read by or that circulate among these obscure sects. Misrepresentations are made to the effect that the climate here is delightful; that the earth yields grain, fruits, and vegetables with very little labor being expended upon it, and that workmen of all kinds are needed who, it is asserted, would command here excellent wages. The names of such papers and quotations from them could be given, were it necessary, to justify the above remarks. Last year one such family arrived, and last January eight other individuals came expecting to find here the workingman's paradise and the fanatic's heaven. The result is disappointment, suffering, and sickness for the deluded people themselves, and embarrassment, annoyance, and trouble for the consul. I do not know that the Government can prevent their coming here, as it prevents the pauper classes of Europe from entering the United States. The head of the family referred to as coming last year had only $4 in his pocket when he arrived in this city, and he had not a dollar in the world besides. that he could draw upon for his support. The family were soon reduced to terrible straits, and a few charitable persons assisted the consul in sending him back to America. One of those who came last January was in our war with the Federal troops, and was in forty battles. He has been twice to my office and cried like a child while begging me to send him home to Massachusetts.

If some of the facts which I have reported, with regard to labor in this country, could be placed before such people, they might be deterred from coming here. The trouble is, however, that they would believe their own religious leaders sooner than they would believe the Government. Palestine is one of the poorest countries in the world to which a laboring man can go with the hope of earning a living. He cannot compete with native laborers, who work for 15 cents a day and find their own food. It is very doubtful if he would be able to stand the climate. Even if one has some means, this is not a country where business can be created easily as it can be in America. No one should think of coming here unless he has ample means to live upon for a period of years, or until he can establish himself in some business or employment that will yield him a living income.

SELAH MERRILL,
Consul.

UNITED STATES CONSULATE,
Jerusalem, July 5, 1884.

I. GENERAL TRADES.

Wages paid per week of seventy-two hours.

Occupations.	Lowest.	Highest.
BUILDING TRADES.		
Hod-carriers :		
Jews	$0 72	$0 96
Natives	72	1 20
Masons :		
Jews	2 40	3 60
Natives	2 88	7 20
Tenders, natives	72	1 20
Plasterers :		
Jews	2 40	3 60
Natives	2 88	5 52
Tenders, natives	72	1 20
Carpenters :		
Jews	1 92	3 60
Natives	1 92	7 20

Wages paid per week of seventy-two hours—Continued.

Occupations.	Lowest.	Highest.
OTHER TRADES.		
Bakers:		
Jews	$1 20	$2 40
Natives	1 20	2 40
Blacksmiths:		
Jews	1 92	2 40
Natives	2 40	3 60
Book-binders:		
Jews	1 92	4 80
Natives	2 40	7 20
Butchers:		
Jews		2 88
Natives		2 88
Drivers of carriages:		
Jews	2 40	3 60
Natives	2 40	3 60
Dyers:		
Jews		2 88
Natives		2 88
Horseshoers, native	2 40	3 60
Jewelers:		
Jews	2 40	4 80
Natives	2 40	4 80
Porters:		
Jews	2 40	3 60
Natives	2 40	3 60
Potters:		
Jews	1 92	3 60
Natives	1 92	3 60
Printers:		
Jews	1 44	2 40
Natives	1 92	3 60
Teachers public schools:		
Jews	1 20	4 80
Natives	1 20	4 80
Saddle-makers:		
Jews	1 92	3 60
Natives	1 92	3 60
Tanners, native	2 40	3 60
Tailors, native	1 44	4 80
Telegraph operators, native	1 50	15 00
Tinsmiths:		
Jews	1 44	4 80
Natives	1 44	4 80
Weavers (outside of mills), native	1 92	2 88
Barbers:		
Jews	1 20	1 92
Natives	1 20	2 40
Boatmen, native	1 20	4 80
Cooks, native	9 00	30 00
Dragomans, native	12 00	20 00
Kawasses, native	2 00	4 50
Oil-makers:		
Jews	1 92	3 60
Natives	1 92	3 60
Pearl-workers, native	1 20	3 60
Shoemakers:		
Jews	1 20	3 60
Natives	1 92	3 60
Stone-cutters:		
Jews	1 44	1 92
Natives	2 40	4 32
Waiters, native	6 00	12 00
Whitewashers:		
Jews	2 40	3 60
Natives	2 40	3 60
Farm laborers:		
Jews	1 20	2 40
Natives	1 44	4 80
Post-office clerks, native	1 50	7 40
Police, natives	75	10 00
Shop hands or clerks:		
Jews	50	5 00
Natives	50	10 00

PERSIA.

REPORT BY CONSUL-GENERAL BENJAMIN, OF TEHERAN.

I have the honor to inclose to you to-day a report on the statistics of labor or the laboring classes in Persia.

Illness has prevented an earlier response to the circular of the Department. Mr. A. B. Keün, our dragoman, and Mirza Ali Asker-khan, our moonchee, have aided me in collecting the facts embodied in this report, which have been obtained from every possible source in this vicinity.

It will be seen that it includes a variety of trades and pursuits peculiar to this part of the Orient. Observations in the margin convey additional facts. I may say here, however, that there are no strikes in Persia, and little evidence that there has been much change among the laboring classes for ages.

They are not more discontented than the same classes elsewhere, all things in life being relative, and discontent generally arising from two causes—a knowledge of a better condition of things and a hope or ambition of reaching it.

The ignorance existing here regarding the conditions of society elsewhere, the fact that all, high and low, are equally slaves of the King, and that the great, being more prominent, are more liable to the outbursts of royal caprice, rage, or injustice, tends to produce content.

I know of no laboring classes in other countries who appear more cheerful and satisfied with their lot. The climate, also, in most parts of Persia, is of such a nature as to reduce the actual wants of the people. One hears occasionally of riots or attacks on tax collectors, guilty of more than ordinary rapacity, but I cannot learn that these are more frequent than formerly.

The peasant class are, man for man, actually better off and happier than the peasantry of Turkey or India. Of course, as foreign ideas creep in and foreign labor-saving inventions gradually take root in Persia, displacing methods in use for thousands of years, discontent in larger measure may be looked for.

Discontent among all classes is the penalty the nineteenth century pays for the privilege of being foremost among the progressive ages, so-called.

But material progress will a long time be so gradual in this country that the laboring classes will be able to adapt themselves to the changes without the violence which attended the introduction of steam in the mills of England early in the century.

S. G. W. BENJAMIN,
Consul-General.

TEHERAN, *September 6, 1884.*

I. General trades.

Wages paid per day to workmen in Persia. a

Occupations. Persian name.	Occupations. English name.	Fixed. b	Lowest.	Highest.
Benā seft kar	Wall maker or bricklayer		$0 32 8/31	$0 48 12/31
Chaggird	Assistant c		16 4/31	24 6/31
Benā gueteh kar	Plasterer		32 8/31	48 12/31
Chaggird	Assistant		16 4/31	24 6/31
Benā gool kar	Fine plasterer		56 14/31	80 20/31
Chaggird	Assistant		24 6/31	32 8/31
Amaleh	Tender d		12 3/31	20 5/31
Naveh kesch	Hod carriers		24 6/31	48 12/31
Benā	Roofer, mason, &c		20 5/31	40 10/31
Kooreh pez	Brick-maker		48 12/31	80 20/31
Chaggird	Assistant		24 6/31	32 8/31
Khecht mäll	Sun-burnt brick-maker e		32 8/31	48 12/31
Nadjar	Carpenter f		32 8/31	48 12/31
Chaggird	Assistant	$0 20 5/31		
Nadjar uazook kar	Joiner		56 14/31	80 20/31
Chaggird	Assistant	32 8/31		
Messguér	Copper-smiths g			
Four assistants:				
Calemzenn	Engraver on copper		32 8/31	80 20/31
Tcharkoshzen	Beater		24 6/31	32 8/31
Chaggird	Tender	24 6/31		
Messgodass	Founder		18 2/31	12 3/31
Sefidguerr	Copper whitener h	32 8/31		
Chaggird	Assistant		12 3/31	16 4/31
Kânod	Confectioner	48 12/31		
Chaggird	Assistant	32 8/31		
Reng rez	Dyer	40 10/31		
Chaggird	Assistant		16 4/31	24 6/31
Ha kak	Engraver (seals) i		48 12/31	1 61 9/31
Chaggird	Assistant		16 4/31	24 6/31
Noon za	Baker j			
Six assistants: k				
Chatirr noon za	Handler of loaves at the oven		64 16/31	1 29 1/31
Khamirguirr	Kneader		24 6/31	48 12/31
Sararondārr	Weigher of bread		24 6/31	32 8/31
Attechendaz	Oven tender	32 8/31		
Nanguirr	Distributer of loaves	24 6/31		
Chaggird	Tender to all	08 2/31		
Khar dooz	Fur sewer	80 20/31		
Chaggird	Assistant	32 8/31		
Kulah dooz	Persian hats-maker l	64 16/31		
Chaggird	Assistant	32 8/31		
Serkesh dooz	Saddle sewer	64 16/31		
Chaggird	Assistant	32 8/31		
Sarradj	Bridle and saddle-bag maker	64 16/31		
Chaggird	Assistant	32 8/31		
Dah bagh	Tanner	64 16/31		
Three assistants:				
Chaggird	Tender	24 6/31		
Pucht tarrach	Hide splitter	32 8/31		
Moo kenn	Hide cleaner	12 3/31		
Oroo ssi dooz	Shoemaker	64 16/31		
Chaggird	Assistant		24 6/31	32 8/31
Halaby saz	Tinsmith	32 8/31		
Chaggird	Assistant	16 4/31		

a Work from sunrise to sunset. In winter about one hour's leave at noon for breakfast. In summer workmen leave twice in a day; first, at about 11 o'clock for breakfast, and then in the afternoon for lunch. Generally there is no work on Fridays.

b These might also be considered as average wages.

c Chaggird is an assistant and at the same time a pupil.

d Amaleh is a general tender or assistant used in any gross work.

e Generally paid 48 12/31 cents for a thousand bricks.

f Armenian carpenters are paid at higher rates: .80 20/31 cents to $1.61 9/31 to the carpenter, and .24 6/31 to .64 16/31 cents for his assistant.

g Owner of the shop or foundry.

h Also paid according to weight of copper to whiten.

i Also paid according to number of letters engraved on the seals. A very important pursuit in Persia.

j Owner of the shop.

k These assistants receive also, each of them, about half a maün or 3 pounds of bread.

l Important industry. Hats being of same form and made of lambskin, or imitation lambskin.

| Occupations. | | Fixed. | Lowest. | Highest. |
Persian name.	English name.			
Hasseer baff	Mat-maker a	$0 40¹⁰₃₁		
Chaggird	Assistant	20₃₁		
Alagh bend	Ribbon-maker		$0 48¹⁷₃₁	$0 80³⁹₃₁
Chaggird	Assistant		24⁸₃₁	32⁵₃₁
Nemad mall	Felt-maker		48¹⁷₃₁	64¹⁵₃₁
Two assistants:				
Chaggird	Tender		24⁸₃₁	32⁵₃₁
Nabehreez	Painter of designs of felt carpets		4⁸⁵₃₁	64¹⁵₃₁
Chichehguerr	Glass-worker		48¹⁷₃₁	80⁵₃₁
Chaggird	Assistant	24⁸₃₁		
Attes endar	Fire-tender	32⁵₃₁		
Abenguerr	Blacksmith	64¹⁵₃₁		
Chaggird	Assistant	32⁵₃₁		
Koorch dam	Tender	16⁵₃₁		
Khaviatt	Tailor	48¹⁷₃₁		
Chaggird	Assistant		16⁴₃₁	40¹⁰₃₁
Khayiatt armeny	Armenian tailor		64¹⁵₃₁	4 83³⁷₃₁
Chaggird	Assistant		32⁵₃₁	80³⁹₃₁
Tebitt sazi:	Cotton printing: b			
Kaloop trach	Wooden patterns maker c		43¹⁶₃₁	80³⁹₃₁
Siah saz	Printer in black dyes		48¹⁷₃₁	64¹⁵₃₁
Zagh saz	Printer in red dyes	32⁵₃₁		
Tabz saz	Printer in green dyes	24⁸₃₁		
Nill saz	Finisher of work of the above		16⁴₃₁	48¹⁷₃₁
Chaggird	Assistant	12⁸₃₁		
Poteel reng koon	Dyer and fixer		64¹⁵₃₁	80³⁹₃₁
Chaggird	Assistant		24⁸₃₁	32⁵₃₁
Sahra karr	Washer of prints d	24⁸₃₁		
Teguer saz	Applier of gold designs		32⁵₃₁	48¹⁷₃₁
Moorch kech	Print sizer		40¹⁷₃₁	48¹⁷₃₁
Nakach	Painter		48¹⁷₃₁	to 61⁵₃₁
Chaggird	Assistant		16⁴₃₁	24⁸₃₁
Salem kar moomy:	Prints for export: e			
Siah saz	Printer in black dyes f		32⁵₃₁	48¹⁷₃₁
Zaghvaz	Printer in red dyes g		16⁴₃₁	24⁸₃₁
Moom saz	Wax applier		12⁸₃₁	16⁴₃₁
Moom pessguir	Finisher to above		16⁴₃₁	24⁸₃₁
Davatt guerr	Metal repairer	40¹⁷₃₁		
Chaggird	Assistant	20₃₁		
Samovar saz	Brazier	80³⁹₃₁		
Chaggird	Assistant	32⁵₃₁		
Kharratt	Turner	48¹⁷₃₁		
Chaggird	Assistant		20₃₁	24⁸₃₁
Fooladguerry:	Steel foundry: h			
Foolad saz	Founder		1 12³⁸₃₁	161⁵₃₁
Perdakhgnir	Polisher		16⁴₃₁	24⁸₃₁
Tela koo	Damascening i		1 61⁵₃₁	3 22¹⁶₃₁
Kalemsen monabettkarr	Engraver in steel		48¹⁷₃₁	80⁵₃₁
Chaggird	Assistant		24⁸₃₁	32⁵₃₁
Rooh saz	Turner in stone	40¹⁷₃₁		
Chaggird	Assistant	16⁴₃₁		
Chemchir saz	Sword maker j		40¹⁷₃₁	80³⁹₃₁
Chaggird	Assistant		16⁴₃₁	24⁸₃₁
Tchakou saz	Penknife maker j	40¹⁷₃₁		
Chaggird	Assistant	16⁴₃₁		
Kaetchee saz	Scissors-maker j		40¹⁷₃₁	80³⁹₃₁
Chaggird	Assistant		12⁸₃₁	16⁴₃₁
Zerguer	Jeweler		48¹⁷₃₁	1 61⁵₃₁
Chaggird	Assistant	24⁸₃₁		

a Generally paid 4³₃₁ to 5³⁹₃₁ cents per square yard.

b Very important industry though European imports are daily ruining it. Principal factories at Tepahan, Broudjird, &c.

c One hundred and forty-two of these patterns are employed to complete the designs on one curtain.

d The poteel reng koon or dyer and fixer of designs dyes the cotton cloth after it passed through the printing process, then it goes to the washers, who, spreading the cloth on the ground near the stream, throw water on it during forty days, after which the paint applied by the dyer disappears, leaving the cloth white, with only the designs printed and fixed by this process.

e These are for Turkestan.

f Afghanistan.

g Kurds, &c. They are not so good in quality as the first, but are more showy. A coat of wax is applied to the cloth, and the surplus taken off by the finisher after absorption.

h Chief foundries are in Tspahan, where they form an important industry.

i The tela koo generally gets paid by taking half the gold or silver given to him to inlay in steel; that is, if one wants to have five grains of gold inlaid ten grains must be given to the tela koo.

j These are three separate industries, every man working in his own shop generally.

Wages paid per day to workmen in Persia—Continued.

Occupations.		Fixed.	Lowest.	Highest.
Persian name.	English name.			
Shall baff	Shawl-maker *a*	....	$0 48 12/31	$0 80 20/31
Chaggird	Assistant	$0 40 6/12	....	....
Haladj	Cotton beater	....	32 8/31	48 12/31
Chaggird	Assistant, boy	8 2/31	....	....
Ossar	Oil merchant	....	32 8/31	48 12/31
Chaggird	Assistant	....	16 4/31	24 6/31
Kachee saz	Potter in faience	....	24 6/31	80 20/31
Chaggird	Assistant	24 6/31	....	....
Sā-āff	Book-binder *b*	....	....	....
Chaggird	Assistant	....	12 26/31	16 4/31
Rah saz	Rice and butter-merchant *c*	48 12/31	....	....
Chaggird	Assistant	20 5/31	....	....
Achpez bazaree	Cook at the market place *c*	48 12/31	....	....
Chaggird	Assistant	24 6/31	....	....
Baghban	Gardeners	....	24 6/31	32 8/31
Amaleh	Assistants, each	....	12 3/31	16 4/31
Mokanee	Sanaught digger *d*	....	32 8/31	64 16/31
Chaggird	Assistant	16 4/31	....	....
Kenaz	Sewerer	48 12/31	....	....
Amalehs	Assistants, each	24 6/31	....	....
Iabah Keeb	Tray carrier	....	24 6/31	64 16/31
Icharkochzen	Hammerer *e*	....	24 6/31	40 10/31
Kassap	Butcher	....	16 4/31	40 10/31
	Cigar-makers	....	24 6/31	32 8/31
Chireh kesh, or arak frooch	Distiller and wine merchant *f*	....	16 4/31	24 6/31
Naöl bend	Horseshoer	....	24 6/31	32 8/31
Naël boor	Horseshoe-maker	....	48 12/31	64 16/31
Mich saz	Nail-maker	....	24 6/31	32 8/31
Koozehguerr	Potters	....	24 6/31	40 10/31
Semsar	Broker *g*	....	1 61 9/31	96 77 13/31
Chaggird	Assistant	....	32 8/31	40 10/31
Basmatchee	Lithographers	....	40 10/31	64 16/31
Tchaptchee	Printers	....	25 25/31	48 12/31
	Musical instrument makers	....	32 8/31	40 10/31
Zinn saz	Saddle-maker	....	32 8/31	48 12/31
Sarradj	Harness-maker	....	32 8/31	48 12/31
Hayam	Tent-maker	....	48 12/31	64 16/31
Chaggird	Assistant	....	24 6/31	32 8/31
Lah baff	Rope-maker	....	16 4/31	32 8/31
Gaali baff	Carpet-weaver *h*	....	....	....
Zen	Woman assistant	....	40 10/31	48 12/31
Merd	Man assistant	....	24 6/31	32 8/31
Tharer baff	Weaver *i*	....	40 10/31	48 12/31
Dellac	Barber *j*	....	16 4/31	32 8/31
	Gunsmith	....	16 4/31	40 10/31
Khamal	Porters	....	08 2/31	24 6/31
Gordjeh dooz	Shoemaker for women	....	32 8/31	40 10/31
	Women:			
	Gross work	....	16 4/31	80 20/31
	Pearl embroidery; silk, silver, and gold work, &c.	....	53 15/31	1 61 8/31

a Factories in Meched, Yezd, and Kachan.
b Sometimes paid at the rate of 12 3/31 cents for each book when there are many.
c This is an important industry, as the pillo or pilloff, the national dish in the Orient, is made only of rice and butter, and accompanied by the khorecht, or ragout of some sort or other, both sold at the market-place.
d Sanaught is the subterranean aqueduct common in Persia.
e Special industry. Total stock in trade, a hammer applied wherever required.
f These are the wages paid to the assistants by the owner of the shop, who is always a Jew or Armenian.
g This is an important business; a semsar being a broker, pawnbroker; and a semsar in Persia has never been known to fail; and the corporation of Teheran pays a tax of $967.74 6/31 to the King.
h Owner of factory.
i Principal factories of weavers at Kachan, Yezd, and Rescht.
j The barber works from morning to noon in the hot baths, then goes to his shop; he cannot make more than 40 10/31 cents a day, except in exceptional cases. But the work is steady, for the prophet ordained the shaving of the crown of all true believers of the male persuasion.

X. GENERAL HOUSEHOLD WAGES IN PERSIA.

Wages paid per month to Persian servants.

Occupations.		Lowest.	Highest.	Average.
Persian name.	English name.			
Nazeer	Steward	$\$8\ 06\frac{14}{31}$	$\$16\ 12\frac{28}{31}$	
Pichkhedmatt bachee	Head waiter	$8\ 06\frac{14}{31}$	$21\ 19\frac{11}{31}$	
Pishkhedmatt	Waiter *a*	$4\ 83\frac{27}{31}$	$8\ 06\frac{14}{31}$	
Sherbettdār	Preparer of refreshments	$3\ 22\frac{18}{31}$	$8\ 06\frac{14}{31}$	
Chaggird	Assistant	$1\ 61\frac{9}{31}$	$2\ 41\frac{29}{31}$	
Kaochtchee	Coffee-maker	$3\ 22\frac{18}{31}$	$4\ 83\frac{27}{31}$	
Chaggird	Assistant			$\$2\ 41\frac{29}{31}$
Achper	Cook	$3\ 22\frac{18}{31}$	$8\ 06\frac{14}{31}$	
Chaggird	Assistant *b*			$2\ 41\frac{29}{31}$
Ayaktchee	Scullion	$3\ 22\frac{18}{31}$	$4\ 03\frac{7}{31}$	
Chaggird	Assistant			$1\ 61\frac{9}{31}$
Ferrach	Footman, tent-pitcher, &c. *c*	$3\ 22\frac{18}{31}$	$4\ 03\frac{7}{31}$	
Ferrach khelvatt	Valet de chambre	$4\ 83\frac{27}{31}$	$6\ 45\frac{5}{31}$	
Nayeb (second)	Second	$4\ 03\frac{7}{31}$	$5\ 64\frac{16}{31}$	
Ferrach bachee	Head footman			$8\ 06\frac{14}{31}$
Khardjbe-arr	Errand-boy			$3\ 22\frac{18}{31}$
Sendook darr	Chest-keeper *d*	$4\ 83\frac{27}{31}$	$6\ 45\frac{5}{31}$	
Mirr-akhor	Equerry	$\$4\ 83\frac{27}{31}$	$6\ 45\frac{5}{31}$	
Djélćodarr	Avant courier	$3\ 22\frac{18}{31}$	$4\ 83\frac{27}{31}$	
Méh-ter	Hostler *e*	$2\ 41\frac{29}{31}$	$3\ 22\frac{18}{31}$	
Ichabook Savar	Groom *f*			$1\ 61^{9}$
Kaleskedjee	Coachman	$4\ 83\frac{27}{31}$	$8\ 06\frac{14}{31}$	
Abdarr	Mounted attendant *g*	$3\ 22\frac{18}{31}$	$4\ 83\frac{27}{31}$	
Chaggird	Assistant			$2\ 41\frac{29}{31}$
Hadjeh	Eunuch *h*	$8\ 06\frac{14}{31}$	$16\ 12\frac{28}{31}$	
Leleh	Old household servant *i*	$3\ 22\frac{18}{31}$	$6\ 45\frac{5}{31}$	
Soreïdarr	Keeper of house in family's absence.			$3\ 22\frac{18}{31}$
Kapootchee	Doorkeeper	$3\ 22\frac{18}{31}$	$4\ 03\frac{7}{31}$	
Baghban	Gardener	$2\ 41\frac{29}{31}$	$4\ 83\frac{27}{31}$	
Iayeh	Wet-nurse *j*	$3\ 22\frac{18}{31}$	$4\ 83\frac{27}{31}$	
Sendookdar	Chest-keeper	$1\ 61\frac{9}{31}$	$3\ 22\frac{18}{31}$	
Khayatt	Seamstress	$4\ 03\frac{7}{31}$	$4\ 83\frac{27}{31}$	
Pishkhedmatt	Maid			$4\ 83\frac{27}{31}$
Pahdō	Maid of all work			$80\frac{20}{31}$
Zerdooz	Embroiderer *k*	$16\ 12\frac{28}{31}$	$48\ 38\frac{22}{31}$	
Achpez	Cook *l*			$1\ 61\frac{9}{31}$
First moonchee Second moonchee Third moonchee Fourth moonchee	Persian scribes for legations *m*			$32\ 25\frac{25}{31}$ to $80\ 64\frac{16}{31}$
Gholam	Mounted servants *n*; sort of body-guard.			$5\ 64\frac{16}{31}$
Jerrach	Footman *o*			$5\ 64\frac{16}{31}$
Pishkhedmatt	Waiter *p*			$8\ 06\frac{14}{31}$

a There are sometimes six waiters in a house.

b Receives also his board.

c A house may have from one or two to fifty footmen; ferraches of the Government act as guards, policemen, &c., together with the gholams or cavalrymen, who are in reality mounted ferraches, though not considered to be so; the usage is that the ferrach must be armed with a long dagger, and the gholam with the gun and curved poignard; the gholam wages vary from 35.48\frac{12}{31}$ to 96.77\frac{13}{31}$ for man and horse yearly.

d Clothing and precious articles are usually kept in trunks, and the office of chest-keeper in some rich houses is very important.

e There is always *one* hostler for every *four* horses.

f One groom to every *two* horses; he receives also his house and clothing.

g *The abdar* is a special servant, carrying in saddle-bags materials for preparing smoking-pipes and tea and coffee on the road.

h To be a hadjeh or eunuch is also a special Oriental pursuit in Persia, more followed there by white men than by Ethiopians. Care must be taken not to confound hadjeh with hadji, pilgrim—the eunuch receives also board and clothing.

i The leleh is an old servant of the house who has charge of the children, who are usually numerous in wealthy Persian households.

j These are all servants to the enderoun or harem, and they receive board and clothing.

k In pearl, gold, silver, silk work, not a regular servant.

l Female cook, only for the enderoon or women's apartment.

m See note at the end of this list about moonchees.

n These servants are couriers, avant-couriers, body-guards; they accompany members of the legations on official business and form a body-guard to the minister; they are paid by the Government of the legation employing them.

o Two of these are paid by the Government, the others are personal servants.

p These—also the nazeer or steward, who receives higher wages but is considered as a waiter or head waiter—these are personal servants.

Wages paid per month to Persian servants—Continued.

Occupations.		Lowest.	Highest.	Average.
Persian name.	English name.			
Ferrach defter	Office servants *a*			$4 $83\frac{27}{31}$
Ferrach khelvatt	Valet *b*			5 $64\frac{16}{31}$
Mirr a khor	Equerry			8 $06\frac{14}{31}$
Mehter	Hostlers			4 $03\frac{7}{31}$
Achpez	Cook			14 $51\frac{19}{31}$
Sherbette dar	Refreshments preparer			6 $45\frac{5}{31}$
Kavehtchee	Coffee and tea maker *c*			5 $64\frac{16}{31}$
Three chaggird	Assistants			4 $03\frac{7}{31}$
	Common servants for all work *d*			4 $83\frac{27}{31}$
Kapootchee	Doorkeeper *e*			4 $03\frac{7}{31}$
Soreidar	Keepers of house *e*			4 $83\frac{27}{31}$
Baghban	Gardeners *e*			4 $83\frac{27}{31}$
Baghban bachee	Head gardener *e*			16 $12\frac{28}{31}$
Sakka	Water-bearers *e*			4 $83\frac{27}{31}$
Karal-ol	Soldiers *e*			1 $20\frac{30}{31}$
Vakeel	Sergeant *e*			1 $61\frac{9}{31}$

a The ferrach defter are men paid by the Government, whose business is to take care of the office of the legation, keep the keys, clean the rooms, bear letters, and be employed as messengers for official errands.

b The valet or ferrach belvatt is a personal servant, the equerry and three of the hostlers are paid by the Government.

c The kavetchee is paid by the Government, as well as his assistant.

d These are personal servants.

e These are paid by the Government.

NOTE.—All these servants receive twice yearly cloth for a coat and the amount of one month's wages on an average as a present.

NOTE.—The moonchee; the only moonchee employed at the United States legation receives only 10 tomans (16.12\frac{28}{31}$) a month, with some of the usual presents, and no allowance in summer, and owing to insufficiency of appropriation no gholams or ferraches can be employed at this legation at present; the same is true of several other classes of servants. The moonchee is an employé of legation, Persian as a rule, their monthly wages vary according to qualifications, rank, and term of service, from 32.25\frac{25}{31}$ and 24.19\frac{11}{31}$ to 80.64\frac{16}{31}$; they receive a present on the new year's day, and in the summer when the legation is transferred to the country place, they receive a certain sum a day for the surplus of expenses; their work is to take verbal messages to the foreign office or officers of the Government, to write and copy Persian letters, to attend to the small business of the legation, to be sent to witness punishments demanded by the legation, to bring information, to attend to complaints from legation servants, and under instructions from their superiors to see to justice being done to such claims; their duties, in a word, are peculiar to a legation in Oriental countries. Every legation employs one to four, but when a legation has only one moonchee his wages must not be less than 24.19\frac{11}{31}$, and go to 48.38\frac{22}{31}$ a month. They are very useful. They have no rank among Europeans and are not considered as officers of the Government by the foreign office. The office is considered to amount to something more than a steward and less than a private secretary. The minister of foreign affairs receives them sometimes on official business, but as a rule they are directed to address themselves to the under-secretaries of the foreign office.

COST OF LIVING TO THE LABORING CLASS.

Though the following may be considered as a fair average of cost of living in all Persia, it is special to Teheran:

The cost of living of the laboring class or of any class in Persia is difficult to find out; there are people who earn 1 kran = 16$\frac{4}{31}$ cents a day and live on that; others earn 6.45\frac{5}{31}$, or 40 krans, a month, and spend 10 tomans, or 16.12\frac{28}{31}$.

On an average one might say that a married man with three children, and having a house of his own, may live on 2 krans = 32$\frac{8}{31}$ cents a day; if obliged to pay rent, on 3 krans, or 48$\frac{12}{31}$ cents a day. But this is poor and miserable living even in Persia. To live in comparative comfort a workman who has to support a wife and three children needs 7 krans, = 1.12\frac{28}{31}$ a day. A man might even live on 8$\frac{2}{31}$ and 16$\frac{4}{31}$ cents by eating anything and sleeping anywhere.

The rate of expenses for such a family is as follows:

Daily:

One maun = 6¼ pounds of bread, 10 shahis	$0 $08\frac{2}{31}$
One-quarter of a maun of meat, 8 shahis	0 $06\frac{14}{31}$
Light, coal, wood, tobacco, &c., 20 shahis	0 $16\frac{4}{31}$

Weekly :
A dish of pillau or rice, butter, and meat, 3 krans .... $0 48$\frac{17}{31}$
Hot bath for five persons, 3 krans .... 0 4$\frac{51}{31}$
Monthly :
Rent of house, 20 krans .... 3 22$\frac{18}{31}$
Yearly :
Man's clothing, 100 krans....................................... 16 12$\frac{28}{31}$
Woman's clothing, 100 krans .... 16 12$\frac{28}{31}$
Three children's clothing, 150 krans............................ 24 19$\frac{14}{31}$

One kran at actual rate of exchange equals 16$\frac{4}{31}$ cents ; one shahi (20 shahis making 1 kran) equals $\frac{25}{31}$ cents ; the toman is worth 10 krans. The currency has depreciated recently slightly over 2 shahis to a dollar.

This would make 1,595$\frac{1}{2}$ krans of annual expenses (equaling 257.33\frac{23}{31}$) or 4 krans, 7 and $\frac{31}{73}$ shahis a day (= 70$\frac{17}{31}$ cents), and is still a very low average, not enabling the workman to save anything for old age or in case of illness or accident.

INCREASE IN LIVING EXPENSES.

It is said that the cost of living has increased since 1878 25 per cent., the chief reasons being the depreciation in the value of money, the European imports crushing Persian industry and somewhat the increase of European population.

THE MODAKHEEL OR COMMISSION SYSTEM.

The servants generally earn 3 to 5 tomans a month (equaling 4.83\frac{17}{31}$ to 8.06\frac{14}{31}$), this not being sufficient for their expenses, especially if they have a family to support. The difference is made up by what is called the "modakheel." This is a Persian word meaning *profit*, but specially applied to the 10 per cent. (or more) commission persons in service are accustomed to add to cost of purchases ; many do not attempt to gain more than this ; but on the other hand, as it is easy to see, advantage is taken by multitudes to appropriate far more than the 10 per cent. winked at by custom. It is scarcely too strong a statement to affirm that the modakheel is accepted by all, in every grade of Persian society.

TAXES.

There are no regular taxes bearing on the working class. Brokers, traders, artisans, farmers, land-owners, and miners pay duties to the Government. Villagers, after having cultivated their land and disposed of the crop, come to the cities and engage themselves as workmen. Out of the money they earn during their stay in the cities they pay their taxes.

HABITS OF THE WORKING CLASSES.

The habits of the working classes are generally steady and saving. They attend to their religious duties; they like to have their houses in good condition and properly furnished. When their means allow it they dress well, and are comparatively clean in their dress and habits. On an average one might say there are 10 per cent. of unprincipled men, most of them to be found among camel and mule-drivers and ferraches. These are rather given to gambling, drinking, and quarreling, but the working class is otherwise less affected by these vices. Most of them try to save money, no matter what their wages may be. Those who come for a certain time from their villages would even save on seven cents a day. They are also more careful now about their expenses than they were a few years ago. Formerly it was customary for a well-to-do workman to give twice a year an entertainment to his friends, costing each time from 15 to 30 tomans (about $24 to $50). This is not done any more, or rarely, as, seeing the cost of living rising every day, they prudently try to save more.

An average of 50 per cent. can be said to be honest among them; but honest in their way. They would not steal openly the smallest sum of money, but would make any amount of "modakheel."

Their general condition is good when compared to that of the working classes of other oriental countries.

FEELING BETWEEN EMPLOYER AND EMPLOYÉ.

The feeling that prevails between employés and employer is usually good; strikes are exceptional occurrences, necessarily never general, and do not succeed. Workmen are paid in copper or silver currency every day or week; they are free to buy the necessaries of life wherever they choose. As a rule, the employer is solicitous of the safety and health of the workmen. The custom exists that when a workman is wounded or gets ill while in service the employer will provide for his and the family's expenses until the man is cured. In case of death by accident in building, &c., the employer offers a certain sum of money to the family of the deceased (from $160 to $320), and in case they refuse to accept it the employer, according to usage, provides for their daily expenses until the children are old enough to work for the family.

EMIGRATION.

Emigration does not exist. In case a workman goes out of Persia he goes with the intention of returning, and only goes when sent. In such case he does not leave unless a good sum of money is first given to his family to pay expenses until his return.

CO-OPERATIVE SOCIETIES, POLITICAL RIGHTS, ETC.

Regular corporations and societies do not exist in Persia, as they would not be approved by the authorities, and no co-operative associations are found.

The working class does not enjoy any political rights.

WOMEN WORKERS.

Education among men, women, and children of the working classes is not worth mentioning. A great many of them can keep their accounts and read the Koran, but that is all they get in the way of education. Women have no education whatever, generally speaking.

CAUSES OF REDUCTION OF WAGES.

The employment of women does not seem to affect workmen's wages, their respective work being quite distinct and different. What has contributed to reduce wages were and are the imports from Europe, which, having been a cause of ruin to a great number of small factories all over Persia, have thrown out of work since the time of Fath Ali Shah thousands of workmen and lessened the demand for labor. Paper, ink, lamp oil, leather, cotton prints, cloth, and nearly all the necessaries of life were manufactured in Persia, but the custom duty of 5 per cent. not protecting enough the Persian trade and industries, the European imports got possession of the market.

MINES AND MINING.*

This industry is not thoroughly developed in Persia, though the country is rich in mining districts. Turquoise mines are worked to a great extent; gold and silver mines could not be made to pay until now. Copper, alum, sulphur, coal, and lead mines are worked to a certain degree, and pay, the only working materials being gunpowder, hammer, pickaxe, and crow-bar.

Sometimes people farm a mine and work it for themselves. When the Government or a farmer of mines employs miners their wages vary from 10 to 15 and 20 shahes for boys ($8\frac{2}{3T}$ and $12\frac{3}{3T}$ to $16\frac{4}{3T}$ cents), and 20 to 50 shahes for men ($16\frac{4}{3T}$ to $40\frac{10}{3T}$ cents) a day. The work begins at sunrise and ends at about sunset, meals (bread and cheese) being taken in the mine. The chief workman is sometimes paid 3 krans ($48\frac{12}{3T}$ cents) to 4 krans ($64\frac{16}{3T}$ cents), and some, whose chief business is to build props, and who are known to be experienced, receive up to 5 krans or $80\frac{20}{3T}$ cents a day, this being considered very high pay. The overseer receives from 35 to 50 krans a month ($5.64\frac{16}{3T}$ to $8.06\frac{4}{3T}$). Mining is not a special pursuit (except turquoise mining), as the workmen are generally peasants who go to the mines when not required, or getting as high wages, in the fields.

• ## FEMALE LABOR.

Women are often employed in weaving factories, cotton work, carpet work. They are also employed for cutting down wheat, fruits, &c., for light work at mines but not *in* mines, and for farm work. In some wandering tribes they herd sheep, bake bread, make cheese and butter. People are wont to say that in some tribes in the south women do men's work to the extent of even putting on male clothes, only covering their faces with the yachmak, and ride off to attack caravans and commit robberies on the highways. Women do nearly all the embroidery work. They are employed as servants only in the harems or enderouns, and sometimes in European families. They do not suffer from impertinence in going about their work, being generally respected. Their wages vary a great deal. As servants they receive from 5 to 35 and 40 krans ($80\frac{20}{3T}$ cents to $5.64\frac{16}{3T}$ and $6.45\frac{5}{3T}$) a month, with board and clothing, in Persian houses; they only board in European families. Thirty-five and 40 krans ($5.64\frac{16}{3T}$ and $6.45\frac{5}{3T}$) a month are high wages, paid only by Europeans; the Persians, as a rule, do not give them more than 30 krans ($4.83\frac{37}{3T}$).

Embroiderers can earn a great deal either working at their houses or going out in families; they can get from 10 to 30 tomans a month ($16.12\frac{48}{3T}$ to $48.38\frac{23}{3T}$); exceptionally, more than that. For other work their wages vary from 16 shahis and 1 kran to $2\frac{1}{2}$ krans and 5 krans, in exceptional cases, a day ($12\frac{3}{3T}$ and $16\frac{4}{3T}$ to $40\frac{10}{3T}$ and $80\frac{20}{3T}$ cents). In many cases their work amounts to the time they can save from their household duties, as they must be at home one or two hours before sunset to prepare supper. Sometimes they employ a maid at home so that they may be able to go out to work themselves out-doors.

---

* Report prepared by Mr. A. B. Keun for Consul-General Benjamin.

It is impossible at present to find out the number of women employed. As for the means afforded for their improvement, safety, &c., there is no rule. Much depends on the good-will of the employer. In general, so far as safety is concerned, the employer is solicitous of not appearing too hard.

PERSIAN VS. UNITED STATES CURRENCY.

1 shahee (copper) equal	$0 00¾₄
1 abbassee, 4 shahees, equal..	03₄₇
1 kran, 20 shahees (silver) equal..	16₄₇
1 re-äll, 25 shahees, equal	20₄₇
1 tomänn, 10 krans (gold) equal	1 61₉₇
1 kooroor (or kroor) is a term used for 500,000.	
1 cent, equal shahee..	1₂₈₅
$1, equal krans	6₇₂₀

HAMADAN.

REPORT PREPARED FOR CONSUL-GENERAL BENJAMIN, BY THE REV. R. Y. HAWKES, OF HAMADAN.

In reply to your request to fill out answers to the questions contained in the labor circular received a few days ago, I have collected the following facts, which I hope you will find serviceable:

MALE LABOR.

The following is a list of classes of laborers who receive the wages mentioned opposite their names and are engaged in this city:

Occupations.	Lowest.	Highest.	Average.
	Krs. Sh.	*Krs. Sh.*	*Krs. Sh.*
Masons ....per day..	1 10	2 10	2 00
Hod-carriers..do....	1 10	2 00	1 15
Carpenters ....do....	1 00	1 15	1 10
Blacksmiths ....do....	0 12	1 10	1 00
Wood-choppers..do....	1 5	1 18	1 10
Muleteers ....do....	1 00	1 10	1 00
Shoemakers..do....	0 16	1 10	1 00
Pack-saddle sewers..do....	1 00	1 10	1 00
Silversmiths..do....	1 5	2 00	1 10
Coppersmiths..do....	1 5	2 00	1 10
Rock-cutters ....do....	2 00	2 10	2 00
Well-diggers ....do....	2 00	2 10	2 00
Laborers:			
Common (or amaleh) ....do....	0 12½	0 18	0 15
In tannery ....do....,	1 10	2 10	1 15
In flour mill..do....	0 12	1 00	0 15
On telegraph line ....do....	1 00	1 10	1 5

Servants receive per month from 8 krans to 10 tomans, with food and clothes, one suit per year. A very common agreement is to pay them 12 tomans a year and 2 kharvars of wheat.

PERSIAN MONEY AND WEIGHT.

The money in use here is the same as that of Teheran.* There are two "mauns" or "battmans" in use here, the first, like that of Teheran,

---

* See Currency of Persia and the United States.

has 40 "seers," and the second 50 "seers." One maun of 40 seers equals 6½ pounds. Imported articles are weighed by the first, while the second is the more common and is always used in heavy weights.

PRICES OF THE NECESSARIES OF LIFE.

The prices of the necessaries of life are about as follows :

Articles.	Lowest.		Highest.		Average.	
	Krs.	*Sh.*	*Krs.*	*Sh.*	*Krs.*	*Sh.*
Bread..per maun..	......	....	......	....	....	7
Meat...do....	1	12	2	4	2	00
Cheese..do....	0	15	1	10	1	00
Rice ....do....	1	12	2	00	1	15
Fruits ....do....	0	2	0	10	0	7
Melons ....do....	0	20	0	10	0	7
Milk..do ..	....		....		0	15
Flour ....do....	0	5	0	14	0	5
Oil, lard..do ...	4	00	6	00	5	00
Sour milk...do....	0	5	0	12	0	5
Cracked wheat.....................................do....	0	5	0	14	0	10
Chickens ....do....	0	6	0	10	0	8
Wheat..per harvar..	25	00	40	00	30	00
Hens...	0	15	1	00	0	18

NOTES. One to two "mauns" consumed per day in a family of six. One-quarter of "maun" consumed per day in family of six.

Bread, meat, fruit, melons, cheese, together with sour milk, are staples of diet. Cracked wheat is also eaten, one-quarter of "maun" making a meal for five persons; one-half "maun" rice makes a meal for five.

COST OF CLOTHING.

The rule for clothing is two suits a year, costing from 3 to 6 tomans per suit. An average suit costs 3 tomans. A suit for a woman costs from 3 to 5 tomans, an average suit costing about 3 tomans.

The cost of separate articles ranges as follows :

Articles.	Lowest.		Highest.	
	Krs.	*Sh.*	*Krs.*	*Sh.*
Hat..	0	12	4	00
Shirt...	2	00	0	00
Socks..	0	10	0	15
Shoes..	2	10	4	00
Pantaloons	4	10	7	00
Coat..	12	00	20	00
Cloak..	12	00	30	00
Dress..	4	00	10	00

COST OF FUEL.

For fuel these people use fine charcoal, which costs about 4 shahees a "man," and it takes about 50 mans to keep a fire during the winter months. Rent for one room with cellar ranges from 6 to 8 tomans a year.

HABITS OF THE WORKING CLASSES.

Their habits are good under certain limitations. Intemperance among them is rare. They work well under an overseer, otherwise not well. They are good-natured. Lying and stealing are not considered sinful, but are habitually practiced. They are steady so long as they are in need of the necessaries of life, but when these become satisfied they

become lazy. Very few of them are saving, since they cannot more
than supply their wants; and, again, if they could save anything it
would be liable to be taken from them by some "ferrach," who lives
on what he can pick up legally or otherwise. But for all this they are
more peaceable and their habits better than the higher classes.

FEELING BETWEEN EMPLOYER AND EMPLOYÉ.

The employés feel well toward most employers, except sayyids (descendants of the prophet), who have a reputation of being poor pay-
masters.

LABOR ORGANIZATIONS.

There are no regular organizations of laborers, except as the members
of a single trade unite, employés and employers, to resist the Government in the imposition of excessive taxes. On such occasions they
sometimes close their shops and stop work until a settlement is made.
On the other hand the local authorities sometimes close a certain branch
of trade when it is making good or extra profits, in order to obtain a
tribute, to allow them to go on with their work. The general effect of
all this is demoralizing to trade and checks prosperity, though in individual cases the laborer gets the benefit of carrying his point.

FOOD PURCHASE AND MODE OF PAYMENT.

If there are any restrictions on the laborer in respect to the purchasing of the necessaries of life, they are of minor importance.

Day laborers are generally paid off in the evening in the currency of
this part of Persia; others, according to agreements, in the same currency. I hear of no co-operative societies.

STATEMENT OF A HAMADAN PORTER.

A "hammal" (or porter) came into my yard to-day on business, and
upon inquiry I obtained the following facts in regard to his life:

He is about thirty-seven years of age; has a wife and three children,
the oldest being a girl of eight years. He makes from 15 to 30 shahees
per day, averaging about 1 kran. His work is hard, and he has about
twenty holidays a year, but no Sunday. He owns one-half a house,
which is worth about 20 tomans. He just about makes ends meet, take
the year round. The food for himself and family is as follows:

Bread per day, 1 kran; fruit and melons in their season, 1 kran;
meat, 0.3 shahee worth; oil, 1 "man"* per year; rice, 1 "man" per
year; cracked wheat, 15 "mauns" per year; sour milk, 2 "mauns" per
month.

He spends on clothes for himself about 1 toman per year, and for his
wife and children 3 tomans per year. Fire costs him about 2 tomans a
year. Bathing at public bath with soap costs him about 16 krans a
year. His case is representative.

R. J. HAWKES.

HAMADAN, PERSIA, *August* 20, 1884.

*A mann of 40 seers amounts to about 6½ pounds; the harvar equals 100 manns.

CEYLON.

REPORT BY CONSUL MOREY, OF COLOMBO.

LABOR CONDITIONS IN CEYLON VS. THE UNITED STATES.

Department circular of February 15, 1884, requiring "labor statistics," reached me somewhat late, say May 17, 1884, and I have been ever since to some extent engaged collecting materials for a reply. The result, I suspect, in regard to a bearing upon industrial problems in the United States will prove insignificant, as the conditions of labor throughout the Orient are so different from those prevailing in the United States as to be inconceivable to people who have not observed and carefully studied them. Here labor is a degradation imposed upon certain classes by ancient customs and unwritten laws, as immutable as the "edicts of the Medes and Persians." Here the producers of wealth, they who, delving in mines, abstract from the bowels of the earth valuable minerals, or toiling as handicraftsmen and manufacturers, fashion crude materials into forms of utility; those who, to a great extent, plow the fields, sow the seed, and reap the harvest, all in fact who "earn their bread by the sweat of their brows" and contribute a fraction to the world's utilized wealth, are, and have been from time immemorial, the most inconsiderable beneficiaries from the results of their own toil, and mere ministers to the idle, greedy, luxurious drones forming the so-called superior castes and classes.

Poverty in consequence, paucity of intellect, want of ambition, and an incapacity to comprehend more than the littlest things in life, are therefore so bred and ingrained in the very natures of the coolie people at least, that even the miserable pittances allowed them are ordinarily quite as much as they know how to use properly, and any enhancement of their pay generally results in demoralizing them altogether.

It will be difficult for an American blacksmith to comprehend that $2.50 per week (scarcely one day's pay for himself) is not only the average of his Ceylon fellow-craftsman's earnings, but as much as the latter knows how to expend properly. Yet such is the case.

This is the natural result of the degradation of labor; though it must be said the picture applies more to the people of continental India, who come here in large numbers and do most of the coolie work, than to the inhabitants proper of Ceylon, who seldom hire out as common laborers, but exchange work in agriculture and cultivate the ground on shares; also in the capacities of clerks, handicraftsmen, and domestic servants, monopolizing most of those pursuits.

With them (the Singhalese) caste restrictions have never been so burdensome as in India, owing mostly to their being Buddhists, which religion, in its purity, excludes all idea of caste; nevertheless, even these regard labor as a degradation, and avoid it by all available means, always considering that the smallest compensation possible is enough for those who work with their hands.

SCHEDULED PARTICULARS.

Schedule forms Nos. I to XV, minus Nos. IV–VII and XIV, have been filled up from the most reliable sources; the latter numbers being omitted on account of there being no such occupations here as glass-working and ship-building; nor is there any material difference in the wages paid to tradesmen and laborers in Government employ to what they get privately.

HOW THE GENERAL TRADES-PEOPLE LIVE.

It appears per schedule I, that amongst handicraftsmen, gas-fitters earning an average of $4.50 per week, jewelers $2 per week, blacksmiths, plumbers, and brass-founders $2.50 per week, are as a rule the highest paid of that class of people, though occasionally a head mason gets as much as $3.42 per week.

The lowest paid are the hatters, mostly women, who work at home in their villages, and earn from 30 cents to 50 cents per week, average 40 cents; just enough, in fact, to pay for their simple clothing and a few cheap ornaments, these being their only incentives to such labor, as they belong to families possessing small patrimonies yielding a plain livelihood to all the members thereof who remain content to abide by it.

The lowest average wage per week for adult men* is $1, the recipient of which would generally be a bachelor, whose frugal subsistence on rice and curry costs 50 cents per week, lodging 12¼ cents, making a total of 62½ cents per week, and leaving a balance of 27½ cents for clothes, washing, and a little arrack, &c.

If the same man happens to have a wife she will earn half or two-thirds as much as himself in various occupations, such as grass-cutting, tending on masons, coffee-sorting, &c., besides keeping house for her husband; and thus between them the pair might save 75 cents per week for purposes exclusive of bare food and shelter. Some of the artisans, earning from $1.60 to 4.50 per week, take advantage of their enhanced emoluments, to inhabit better houses, consume better food, wear better clothes, and occasionally drink gin or sour beer in preference to arrack or toddy. A good many, however, neglect to improve their mode of life, and instead patronize the gin and cheap beer aforesaid to such an extent that they soon are unfit to earn even $1 per week or anything at all. Then they take to begging, and great numbers of such characters are now to be seen in our cities, who, having discarded the degradation of work, beg with an effrontery only to be accounted for on the principle that they have abandoned the mean habit of earning a living and adopted something more honorable, labor, in the Asiatic mind at least, being counted meaner than begging.

FOUNDERS AND MACHINISTS.

Schedule No. II. applying to a Government iron foundry and machine-shop, was filled up authoritatively, and denotes that artisans are not more highly paid by Government than by private employers. My foregoing remarks therefore apply exactly to their condition. In fact, it appears from No. III, which refers to the principal private foundry here, that native employés there are paid quite as high an average as those employed in corresponding situations by Government, and it will be seen throughout the whole ensuing roll, from miners to printers, that, wherever natives are concerned, their pay is perhaps a twelfth of what people correspondingly employed in America receive.

---

* Handicraftsmen.

SINGHALESE AGRICULTURAL LABOR.

Respecting agriculture, as I have before intimated, the Singhalese seldom employ labor for fixed pay, or hire themselves out in that manner, the custom rather being with them to exchange work in husbanding their crops, or to labor for a share of same; and I believe it has been carefully computed that the absolute earnings of an ordinary farm laborer in Ceylon do not amount to over 10 cents per diem; though, as most of them are small owners, the spontaneous productions of their little patrimonies enable them to live in comparative comfort and save up some wealth.

COOLIE LABOR IN CEYLON.

There is, however, a branch of agriculture under European patronage, viz, estate planting, in which the laborers, mostly emigrants from Southern India, are paid, or supposed to be paid, by the day. I alluded to those in both my annual reports for the years 1883 and 1884, respectively, and therefore have less to write on this occasion. There have been in the past probably as many as 500,000 of these coolie people in the island at one time, but that number will be considerably reduced now, owing to many having gone away on account of the partial failure of the coffee enterprise.

The pay these coolies were popularly supposed to get was 12 cents per diem, and throughout the year they probably were given work five days per week, upon an average. At this rate their earnings would amount to 60 cents per week, and in prosperous times that was about the amount they were paid.

After 1878, however, as the coffee crops diminished so likewise did the payments to these people fall off, until, in 1883, the fact that they could scarcely be said to be paid at all became so notorious that near the close of that year the local government interfered and early in 1884 the labor laws were so amended that those poor people were enabled to go into the courts for their earnings with some chance of obtaining the money.

The passing of these new ordinances raised a terrible storm in planting circles, and the parties responsible for their enactment got so well abused for their interference that much which was purposed to be done in this direction was abandoned by the executive. Enough was accomplished, however, to give the poor coolies some juridical status, and a sufficient sentiment of public shame was engendered to cause in some measure an alleviation of the hardships of a much suffering laboring population.

During the discussion of this burning question of "coolies' pay," the newspapers were full of correspondence, pro and con, upon the subject; and I interpolate herewith one of the most characteristic of the letters, appearing in the Ceylon Observer, during that period, together with the editor's very proper retort upon his correspondent, merely adding, en passant, that the luxuries of life the writer prates about would be, if they were forthcoming, just so much as 32 cents per diem would pay for, and the equivalent of 32 Ceylon cents is 12 cents in United States currency.

As a matter of fact, however, many estate coolies have been getting less than half that sum as daily pay for years. The "clean and watertight shelter," so feelingly alluded to by the same writer, is, alas, generally a vile hut, into which the planter would not like to put a favorite horse. The bushel of rice, sometimes supplied as almost the sole sustenance for a month, costs about $1.20; and the "cumblie" is an indescribable blanket, furnished once a year, costing 27 cents, and charged for perhaps at 50 cents.

The privilege of going to court for their pay, which is so strongly objected to, was simply a new provision by which all the laborers on an estate might sue *en masse*, it actually being the case that it required the combined earnings for several months of the whole gang to make up a sum sufficiently large to go to court for; and the "three isolated cases," so naively referred to, were, properly speaking, near three hundred.

[Extract from the Ceylon Observer of November 24, 1883.]

COOLIES' WAGES—AND NO WAGES.

Dear Sir: In your editorial of the 19th instant you say the "few inclined to cheat and by the much larger number who put off payment hoping for better times and ability to pay." Not denying that there are some inclined (to cheat I emphatically decline to believe) to put off payment, I ask you, is the native who never came to Ceylon, and *who has no money due him by the estate* better off than he who has? Not he. The estate laborer receives regular rice, cumblies, and small advances in money, has a clean and water-tight shelter over his head, with medical officers to attend him when ill, and lives here contented and happy with wife and children'; does he who "stays at home" get these advantages? What is his life at his "*cheemie*?" A dog's life! Ask any cooly you like—and "wages" or "no wages" we shall always have a supply of labor quite sufficient for all our wants. Seeing, thus, how much better off the Ceylon brother is to his Indian brother, I cannot agree with you in wishing for further legislation on his behalf. That for the sake of three isolated cases facilities are to be given to a kangani or his gang (with a few months' pay due) of going to law is, in my opinion, absurd; and by this, the power in the event of any disagreement with the proprietor, of retaliating by putting him (the proprietor) into court and placing him in a most undesirable position both as regards his agents and estate.

I do not take up my position, as you see, on moral grounds, I say that he (the proprietor and planter) who supports and helps to supply so many human beings with the necessities, and, but for providential visitation, with the luxuries of life, should have some consideration shown him. With this, I remain, yours truly.

[We insert this as a mental curiosity, for the writer candidly states he does not go on moral grounds. Truly not. He agreed to give his coolies so much per diem for every day they worked. He gives them only part in the shape of rice, and then says to the coolies, "True you have not got what I promised to give you and what you ought to get, but then consider how much better off you are than your brethren who never came to Ceylon!" The poor devils could not dispute such wonderful logic, but they could say: "If we do not get our money balances we can never go back to see how it is with the old folks at home; whether they are worse off or better. Granting, what we fear, that they are badly off, we should like to have our cash balances to help them. It was in the hope of being able to do so we came to Ceylon." Wages or no wages, this wonderful reasoner says, the planters will have plenty of labor! If our correspondent can get men to agree to serve him merely for rice advances, good and well; an agreement is an agreement. But so is an agreement to pay 32 cents per diem, and the agreement ought to be kept or enforced, otherwise coolies will cease to come to Ceylon.—Editor C. O.]

Further comment upon this subject is almost unnecessary; nevertheless the fact should be stated that, notwithstanding all the ventilation such matters have received during the last twelve months, the systematic robbing of coolies out of their miserable pittances for years is even now regarded here as so mild an offense that insolvents, whose indulgence in the practice was notorious, and who, during their passage through the courts, were able to live luxuriously, and go rolling about in gay equipages, finally emerged from their bankruptcy proceedings, with clean No. 1 certificates, and apparently were none the worse thought of for their heartless behavior.

Non-resident and absentee proprietors are the greatest offenders in these matters, for they neither know the coolies who cultivate their estates nor have they any sympathy with them, whereas resident proprietors and superintendents generally, I believe, become tolerably familiar with their people and too solicitous of their welfare to mulct them willingly of any part of their small earnings. Most of the latter class, however, are in the hands of their agents, who, having advanced them funds, want their "pound of flesh" back, and, as planting has not been profitable lately, financial embarrassment is common; consequently many people have failed to pay their laborers who fain would have done otherwise.

Referring again to the "Observer" article, it is a significant fact that the people in Southern India, from whom the estate laborers in Ceylon are drawn, and who that writer states are in worse plight than their miserably paid brethren here, are likewise under British rule, though not in European employ.

W. MOREY,
Consul.

UNITED STATES CONSULATE,
Colombo, Ceylon, December 5, 1884.

I. GENERAL TRADES.

Wages paid per week of fifty-three hours in Ceylon.

Occupations.	Lowest.	Highest.	Average.
BUILDING TRADES.			
Bricklayers	$2 04	$2 31	$2 25
Hod-carriers	85	85	85
Head masons	3 42	3 42	3 42
Tenders	54	85	75
Plasterers	2 31	2 31	2 31
Tenders*	60	75	68
Roofers	1 50	1 50	1 50
Tenders*	54	85	75
Plumbers	2 40	2 60	2 50
Assistants	1 45	1 45	1 45
Carpenters	1 50	3 42	1 60
Gas-fitters	3 75	6 00	4 50
OTHER TRADES.			
Bakers	1 80	2 40	1 95
Blacksmiths	2 30	3 42	2 50
Strikers	85	1 20	1 00
Book-binders	75	3 37	1 00
Brick-makers	85	1 50	1 25
Butchers	1 50	3 42	2 00
Brass-founders	1 75	3 50	2 50
Cabinet-makers	1 75	3 50	2 25
Coopers	1 70	2 30	2 00
Distillers	3 75	5 00	4 00
Drivers	1 00	1 50	1 25
Draymen and teamsters	1 00	1 50	1 25
Cab and carriage drivers	1 00	1 50	1 25
Gardeners	1 00	1 50	1 25
Hatters (women)	30	50	40
Horse-shoers	2 00	3 00	2 25
Jewelers	2 50	3 50	3 00
Laborers, porters, &c.	2 00	2 00	1 75
Potters	1 25	2 50	1 75
Printers	40	6 50	3 50
Teachers public schools	2 50	9 00	5 00
Saddle and harness makers	2 50	3 50	2 75
Sailmakers	2 00	3 00	2 25
Stevedores	2 00	2 50	2 25
Tanners	1 00	2 00	1 75
Tailors	1 20	2 40	1 50
Telegraph operators	3 85	12 50	5 87
Tinsmiths	1 00	1 50	1 25

* Boys, old men, and women.

II. Factories, Mills, etc.

Wages paid per week of sixty hours in the Government factory, Colombo.

Occupations.	Highest.	Lowest.	Average.
Fitters	$5 62	$0 84	$1 69
Carpenters	6 75	84	1 69
Smiths	5 62	1 24	1 69
Molders	5 62	1 13	1 40
Tinkers	5 62	1 13	1 69
Pattern-makers	3 38	1 69	2 25
Cabinet-makers	4 50	1 13	1 69

III. Foundries, Machine-shops, and Iron Works.

Wages paid per week of fifty-eight hours in foundries, machine-shops, and iron works in Colombo.

Occupations.	Lowest.	Highest.	Average.
Native:			
Iron workers	$1 20	$7 20	$2 50
Carpenters	1 20	4 80	2 00
Assistants	60	70	75
European:			
Foremen engineers	15 00	30 00	23 00
Carpenters	11 50	25 00	20 00
Molders	11 50	25 00	20 00

V. Mines and Mining.

Wages paid per week of sixty hours in and in connection with plumbago mines.

Occupations.	Lowest.	Highest.	Average.
Foremen	$2 40	$2 40	$2 40
Tunnelers	1 20	2 40	2 00
Pitmen	90	1 80	1 50
Carriers	60	1 40	1 00

VI. Railway Employés.

Wages paid to railway employés (those engaged about stations, as well as those engaged on the engines and cars, linemen, railroad laborers, &c.).

Occupations.		Lowest.	Highest.	Average.
European locomotive foremen	per annum	$1,200 00	$1,600 00	$1,400 00
European engine-drivers	do	575 00	960 00	750 00
European firemen	do	288 00	384 00	335 00
European foremen plate-layers	do			864 00
European plate-laying overseers	do	214 00	384 00	250 00
Native shunting engine-drivers	do			360 00
Native firemen	do	60 00	130 00	120 00
Native patrols	do			74 00
Native plate-layers	do	50 00	60 00	55 00
Native fitters	do	90 00	420 00	200 00
Head carpenters	do	240 00	420 00	300 00
Carpenters	do	74 00	240 00	120 00
Time-keepers	do	192 00	384 00	250 00
Storemen	do	108 00	261 00	175 00
Engine-turners	per day	60	60	60
Engine-lighters	do	28	50	39
Engine-cleaners	do	17	40	20

Occupations.	Lowest.	Highest.	Average.
Pumping engine-men ....per day..	$0 40	$0 40	$0 40
Pumpers...do....	17	40	20
Coppersmiths ....do....	1 30	1 30	1 30
Head blacksmiths ....do....	1 20	1 20	1 20
Blacksmiths ....do....	30	1 00	60
Painters..do....	34	60	35
Pattern-makers...do....	50	70	60
Apprentices...do....	20	40	23
Machinists ....do....	20	30	25
Boiler washers ....do....	60	60	60
Molders...do....	35	50	41
Stationary engine-men.......................................do....	30	30	30
Stokers ....do....	25	25	25
Saddlers..do....	50	50	50
Trimmers ....do....	35	60	47
Carriage examiners ....do....	40	140	80
Masons ....do....	25	60	35
Canganies(gang overseers) ....do....	30	60	40
Laborers ....do....	07	20	14
Carriage cleaners ....do....	17	20	18
Carriage greasers...do....	20	20	20
Gate men ....per annum..	60 00	60 00	60 00
Watchmen ....per day..	20	20	20

ED. STRONG,
Resident Engineer.

CEYLON GOVERNMENT RAILWAY,
ENGINEER'S DEPARTMENT,
Colombo, 2d *July,* 1884.

VIII. SEAMEN'S WAGES.

Wages paid per month to seamen (officers and men), distinguishing between ocean, coast, and river navigation, and between sail and steam.

Occupations.	Lowest.	Highest.	Average.
European sailing vessels and steamers.			
Mates...	$60 00	$80 00	$70 00
Second mates...	30 00	55 00	40 00
Third mates..	20 00	40 00	30 00
Boatswains	12 00	16 00	15 00
Cooks	12 00	20 00	16 00
Stewards...	12 00	20 00	16 00
Seamen	6 00	12 00	10 00
Native boatmen...	6 00	12 00	10 00
Native sailors..	6 00	10 00	8 00
Native cooks...	6 00	12 00	10 00
Native coasters, sailing.			
Masters..	10 00	12 00	11 00
Mates..	6 00	8 00	7 00
Sailors...	4 00	6 00	5 00
Cooks	3 00	4 00	3 50

IX. STORE AND SHOP WAGES.

Wages paid per month in stores, wholesale and retail, to males in Colombo.

Occupations.	Lowest.	Highest.	Average.
European general assistants	$57 75	$192 50	$115 87
Burgher general clerks.....................................	3 85	38 50	19 25
Native general clerks.......................................	3 85	19 25	9 77
Coolies for store work......................................	3 85	5 27	4 82

X. Household wages in towns and cities.

Wages paid per month to household servants (towns and cities).

Occupations.	Lowest.	Highest.	Average.
Butlers	$4 10	$8 20	$5 00
Cooks	3 50	5 00	4 10
Nurses	3 50	6 50	4 50
General helps	2 50	4 10	3 50
Coachmen	4 10	10 00	5 00
Grooms	3 50	4 10	3 80
Gardeners	3 00	6 00	4 00

XI. Agricultural wages.

Wages paid per day to agricultural laborers in the Central Province (Ceylon), without board.

Occupation.	Lowest.	Highest.	Average.
Estate laborers*	$0 05	$0 15	$0 12

* This is what they are popularly supposed to get, but during the last five years they probably have not received half of even so small an amount.

XII. Corporation employés.

Wages paid to the corporation employés in the municipal city of Colombo.

Occupations.		Lowest.	Highest.	Average.
Secretary of the council	per year..			$2, 240 00
Clerks	do....	$96 00	$800 00	300 00
Sanitary officer	do....			1, 200 00
Gas inspector	do....			1, 200 00
Superintendent of roads	do....			3, 000 00
Head overseer	do....			150 00
Minor overseer	per day..	30	60	35
Coolies	do....	10	20	15
Cartmen	do	14	20	17
Masons	do....	30	60	40

XIII. Government departments and offices.

Wages paid per annum to employés in Government departments and offices, exclusive of tradesmen and laborers, in surveyor-general's department.

Occupations.	Lowest.	Highest.	Average.
Chief surveyor*	$2, 000	$3, 200	$2, 600
District surveyors*	1, 300	2, 000	1, 650
Assistant surveyors*	438	1, 277	858
Extra assistant surveyors*	146	920	350
Clerks and draughtsmen †	219	1, 277	500

* European. † Burghers and natives.

XV. PRINTERS AND PRINTING OFFICES.

Statement showing the wages paid per day to printers (compositors, pressmen, proof-readers, &c.) on the Ceylon Observer, Colombo.

Occupations.	Lowest.	Highest.	Average.
Proof-readers	$0 60	$3 00	$2 00
Piece-work compositors (first class)	2 50	4 50	3 50
Piece-work compositors (second class)	1 80	2 50	2 25
Fixed compositors	2 00	4 20	3 00
Volunteer compositors (apprentices)	40	1 00	65
Pressmen	60	2 00	1 12
Foremen	5 00	6 50	5 85

THE PHILIPPINE ISLANDS.

REPORT BY CONSUL VOIGHT, OF MANILA.

In reply to the labor circular issued by your Department, dated 15th February last, I have the honor to address the following preliminary remarks:

The Philippines, with a population of about 6,500,000, are still in a very primitive state, there being, counting Spaniards and their descendants, less than 20,000 white foreigners to be met with.

The natives, a Malay race, peaceful and frugal enough, are yet decidedly below the average, both in their physical and intellectual endowment, and do not begin to compare in that respect with the Chinese, who, to the number of perhaps 35,000, form the only element of real laboring industry in these regions. Owing to the tropical climate, added to a wonderful fertility of the soil, the simple wants of the native race are easily satisfied, who, moreover, shun exertion and disclaim ambition.

The hardly-concealed contempt of all foreigners, Spaniards particularly, towards these people does not tend to render them more willing laborers, and, although actual servitude does not exist, yet the condition often resembles enforced obedience. It is a singular fact that hereabouts the female intellect is so much above that of the male population, that in matters of business the women are conceded the lead, and acquit themselves with credit; but they never perform hard or any unbecoming labor, such as other Indian or even more advanced nations exact.

Under the above circumstances it will serve but little purpose to furnish data for laborer and wages in comparison with those obtaining in civilized countries or even regulated communities. For what is not in its crude state here is but slightly and artificially removed therefrom. For instance, should the few foreigners and the industrious Chinese quit these islands nothing would prevent their speedily retrograding into dullness and stupid stagnation.

I therefore have, in the accompanying schedules, confined myself to an approximate outline of current wages in Manilla and vicinity, disclaiming all intention to be able thereby to contribute towards the labor statistics invited by the circular of 15th February.

JULIUS G. VOIGHT.

UNITED STATES CONSULATE,
Manila, September 1, 1884.

I. GENERAL TRADES.

Wages paid per week of fifty-four to seventy-two hours in Manila.

Occupations.	Lowest.	Highest.	Average.
BUILDING TRADES.			
Bricklayers	$3 62	$6 00	$4 00
Hod-carriers	2 25	3 00	2 50
Masons	3 75	6 00	5 00
Tenders	2 25	3 00	2 50
Plasterers	3 75	6 00	5 00
Tenders	2 25	3 00	2 50
Slaters	3 75	6 00	5 00
Roofers	3 75	6 00	5 00
Tenders	2 25	3 00	2 50
Plumbers	3 75	6 00	5 00
Assistants	2 25	3 00	2 50
Carpenters	4 50	6 00	5 00
OTHER TRADES.			
Bakers	3 00	4 00	3 50
Blacksmiths	4 50	18 00	9 00
Strikers	4 50	6 00	5 00
Book binders	6 00	9 00	7 50
Brick-makers	2 25	3 75	3 00
Butchers	4 50	6 00	5 00
Brass-founders	9 00	15 00	12 00
Cabinet-makers	4 50	9 00	7 00
Confectioners	3 00	4 50	4 00
Cigar-makers	4 50	6 00	5 00
Coopers	6 00	10 00	7 00
Distillers	4 50	6 00	5 00
Drivers	2 25	3 50	3 00
Draymen and teamsters	4 50	6 00	5 00
Cab and carriage	2 25	4 50	3 50
Street railways	3 00	6 00	5 00
Dyers	4 50	6 00	5 00
Engravers	9 00	18 00	12 00
Gardeners	1 90	3 00	2 50
Hatters	4 50	6 00	5 00
Horse-shoers	4 50	9 00	7 00
Jewelers	5 00	12 00	10 00
Laborers, porters, &c	3 00	4 00	3 50
Lithographers	4 00	7 00	6 00
Nail-makers (hand)	3 00	6 00	5 00
Potters	3 00	6 00	5 00
Printers	4 50	8 00	6 00
Teachers (public schools)	3 00	5 00	4 50
Saddle and harness makers	3 00	6 00	5 00
Sail-makers	3 00	6 00	5 00
Stevedores	4 50	9 00	7 00
Tanners	4 50	9 00	7 00
Tailors	6 00	9 00	7 00
Telegraph operators	4 50	9 00	7 00
Tinsmiths	4 50	9 00	7 00
Weavers (outside of mills)	4 50	9 00	7 00

NOTES.—Consul Voight has computed his wage-rates in Spanish dollars = 96 cents American. Average wages for common laborers are 5 reales = 62½ cents per diem, and all the skilled labor here is foreign, excepting Chinese mechanics. No female labor, except seamstresses and cigar-makers. The average cost of living for native ordinary laborers amounts to about $200 per annum for one family.

II. FACTORIES, MILLS, ETC.

Wages paid per week of seventy-two hours in factories or mills in Manila.

Occupations.	Lowest.	Highest.	Average.
Rope-makers	$3 00	$6 00	$4 00
Sugar refiners	3 50	5 00	4 00

III. FOUNDRIES, MACHINE-SHOPS, AND IRON WORKS.

Wages paid per week of seventy-two hours in foundries, machine shops, and iron works in Manilla.

Occupations.	Lowest.	Highest.	Average.
General workers..	$9 00	$18 00	$10 00

V. MINES AND MINING.

Wages paid per week of seventy-two hours in and in connection with gold mines in the Philippines.

Occupations.	Lowest.	Highest.
Miners	$2 25	$6 00

NOTE.—There is but one gold mine in the Philippines. No silver mining and very little coal, which being of poor quality is neglected.

VII. SHIP-YARDS AND SHIP-BUILDING.

Wages paid per week of seventy-two hours in ship-yards (wood ship-building) in Manilla.

Occupations.	Lowest.	Highest.
Various grades	$4 50	$6 00

VIII. SEAMEN'S WAGES.

Wages paid per month to seamen (officers and men) distinguishing between ocean, coast, and river navigation, and between sail and steam, in Manilla.

Occupations.	Lowest.	Highest.	Average.
Native boatmen..	$18 50	$22 50	$20 00
Native coasting sailors	7 00	15 00	10 00
Foreign sailors..	15 00	50 00	16 00

IX. STORE AND SHOP WAGES.

Wages paid in retail and wholesale stores to males in Manilla.

[Per week of seventy-two hours.]

Occupations.	Lowest.	Highest.	Average.
Male employment in retail stores....................per week..	$3 00	$7 50	$4 00
Clerks in wholesale stores......................per annum..	1,500 00	5,000 00	2,500 00

X. HOUSEHOLD WAGES IN TOWNS AND CITIES.

Wages paid per month, and found, to household servants (towns and cities) in Manilla.

Occupations.	Lowest.	Highest.	Average.
House servants	$4 00	$10 00	$5 00
Cooks (Chinese)	30 00	40 00	30 00
Cooks (native)	4 00	6 00	5 00
Coachmen	4 00	10 00	5 00
Gardeners	4 00	10 00	5 00

XI. AGRICULTURAL WAGES.

Wages paid per day to agricultural laborers and household (country) servants in the Philippines.

Occupations.	Lowest.	Highest.	Average.
Laborers	$0 50	$1 50	$0 50

XII. CORPORATION EMPLOYÉS.

Wages paid per annum to the corporation employés in the city of Manilla, 1884.

[Office hours from 8 a. m. to 1 p. m.]

Occupations.	Lowest.	Highest.
Various grades	$600 00	$2,500 00

XIII. GOVERNMENT DEPARTMENTS AND OFFICES.

Wages paid per annum to employés in Government departments and offices, exclusive of tradesmen and laborers, in Manilla.

[Office hours from 8 a. m. to 1 p. m.]

Occupations.	Lowest.	Highest.
Various grades	$600 00	$5,000 00

XV. PRINTERS AND PRINTING OFFICES.

Statement showing the wages paid per week of sixty hours to printers (compositors, pressmen, proof-readers, &c.) in Manilla, 1884.

Occupations.	Lowest.	Highest.	Average.
Printers, various	$5 00	$12 50	$6 00

JAPAN.

REPORT BY CONSUL-GENERAL VAN BUREN.

Referring to the Department's "Labor Circular" of the 15th of February last, addressed to all the consuls of the United States, I beg respectfully to refer to my report upon the subject, dated October 6, 1880, and published in the Department's Consular Reports, No. 2, of November, 1880, which is exhaustive, and which I beg may be included in any general publication the Department may contemplate making up from the reports from other consulates when received.

THOS. B. VAN BUREN,
Consul-General.

UNITED STATES CONSULATE GENERAL.
Kanagawa, Japan, April 25, 1885.

LABOR IN JAPAN.*

[Republished from Consular Reports, No. 2, for November, 1880.]

In all historic times the subject of labor and the condition of the laborer have been of the first importance. In later ages, since trade and commerce have multiplied, population increased, wealth and accumulated capital in a few hands, the question has been complicated by that of the relations which should exist between capital and labor, and now that steam and electricity are bringing all nationalities and races into close and active competition, the subject has received added importance.

In all the countries of the civilized world this topic is agitating the public mind, and is being discussed in the halls of legislation, in the busy marts of trade, on the great money changes, in the homes of the artisans, and in the huts and hovels of the humblest toilers. All systems of government and all organizations of society on every continent and on the far-off islands of the ocean are disturbed by this question and its portending conflict.

In view of this a full, accurate, and comprehensive account of the condition of the laborers of any race or country is of more than passing importance. The following statement of the status of labor in a new and comparatively unknown land cannot fail, therefore, to be of interest:

It is now nearly a quarter of a century since Perry opened the sealed gateways of Japan to the commerce and travel of the world. The unique civilization of an island empire, with an area of 150,000 square miles and more than 35,000,000 of people, was then first presented to modern times for study and investigation. Since that time libraries of books and pamphlets and volumes of letters have been written upon every phase of that civilization, except the status and condition of the laborer. Of the importance and power of 35,000,000 of people as added factors in the products of the world there can be no question.

In this paper I shall refer briefly to all facts that seem to me to affect

---

* Consul-General Van Buren acknowledges the valuable assistance of Dr. H. Latham, formerly vice-consul-general at Shanghai, in the preparation of this report.

to any appreciable extent the condition of the laboring population of Japan, believing that such information will be found valuable to the economist, statesman, or philanthropist, who shall make the happiness of mankind his study. The topography, soil, climate, laws, religion, government, education, morals, finances, and means of transportation, as well as the prices of labor and living, all have an influence, directly or indirectly, upon the condition of the laborer, and are all, therefore, legitimate subjects of study in this connection.

LATITUDE AND LONGITUDE OF JAPAN.

The islands of Japan extend along the eastern coast of Asia, from the 31st to the 46th parallels of north latitude, and from the 130th to the 145th degrees of east longitude. It is estimated that these islands contain from 150,000 to 160,000 square miles, or once and a half the area of the British Isles.

TOPOGRAPHY.

Through the center of this island chain is one long mountain range, with spurs of lesser elevation running at right angles. Interspersed through all these mountain masses are innumerable fertile valleys, through which the drainage of the whole area finds its way to the sea. Along either coast are extensive alluvial plains, the weatherings and washings of the mountains during untold centuries. The crests of the higher mountains are rocky and precipitous, but as the spurs slope away toward the sea they present gentler hill-sides susceptible of tillage. It is on these alluvial plains along the sea, through these fertile valleys and on the gentle mountain slopes, that the laborer is to be found. Both the eastern and western coasts present deep indentations of gulfs and bays extending far into the mainland.

SOIL.

For all the purposes of this paper, it is sufficient to say that the soil, with which the laborer of Japan has to deal, is a black, vegetable mold, from 2 to 10 feet in depth, superimposed upon a deep clay subsoil. This mold is a mass of decomposed vegetation, grown luxuriantly in a warm summer climate, combined with a great rain-fall. It is a true humus, with an excess of humic acid, which renders its fertile elements more or less insoluble. Even in its virgin state this black, rich-looking soil, without some chemical solvent, will not produce a paying crop, but with lime or potash every product of the latitude grows luxuriantly.

WATER.

Draining the great mountain range and its spurs is a system of rivers and canals, furnishing abundance of clear, pure water. Excellent wells can be had almost everywhere on the lower levels for the digging.

CLIMATE.

I shall not attempt to give the full meteorology of this country, as the temperature and rain-fall will be sufficient for our purposes.

Temperature.—In Yokohama, in latitude 35° 46', observations have been made for nine years. The following are the monthly and annual means of temperature:

Fahr.

January	39.2
February	42.2
March	46.0
April	54.7
May	64.6
June	71.6
July	78.7
August	79.4
September	70.2
October	59.8
November	49.5
December	47.5
Annual mean	57.7

The highest temperature for these nine years was 93°, and the lowest, 21°. The absolute range of mercury was, therefore, 72°.

Rain-fall.—The average precipitation, as observed at the same place and about the same time, was as follows:

Inches.

January	4.23
February	4.22
March	3.19
April	5.84
May	4.33
June	10.17
July	3.15
August	6.62
September	12.05
October	6.14
November	8.67
December	2.56
Annual rain-fall	71.17

The greatest amount of snow which has fallen at Yokohama for one year is 15 inches. The highest annual precipitation since foreign trade with this country was in 1868, being 122 inches, and the smallest amount in 1867, being 42 inches.

The following table shows the average number of rainy days for each month in the year:

January	4.42
February	6.28
March	8.42
April	9.72
May	8.42
June	11.23
July	10.00
August	9.23
September	11.85
October	7.00
November	6.57
December	4.28
Average rainy days per year	97.52

POPULATION.

The population of Japan, as shown by the census of 1878, is between 35,000,000 and 36,000,000, but as full tables of that census are not as yet available, I have been compelled to resort to those of the census of two years earlier. The population at that time was 33,300,675.

Number of the higher and lower nobility..	1,894,784
Common people..	31,405,891
Number of males of whole population	16,891,729
Number of females of whole population	16,408,946

Number of farmers, males......................................	8,004,014	
Number of farmers, females....................................	6,866,412	
		14,870,426
Number of mechanics, males..................................	521,295	
Number of mechanics, females................................	180,121	
		701,416
Number of merchants, males..................................	819,782	
Number of merchants, females................................	489,409	
		1,309,191
Mixed occupations, males......................................	1,218,266	
Mixed occupations, females...................................	911,256	
		2,129,522
Total producing population		19,010,555
Of children under fourteen years of age there were.......		9,056,309

GOVERNMENT.

The Government of Japan up to 1868 was absolute and irresponsible, with an emperor at its head, who held all authority by divine right, and who ruled through a number of feudal princes, at whose head stood the Shogun (Tycoon).

The laborer had no privileges, except such as his immediate prince conceded. He was absolutely under the control and in the power of his feudal lord and that lord's retainers.

There were no courts for the trial of causes which might arise between him and his superiors. The position of the laborer was so immeasurably below that of the ruling class that it was as much as his life and liberty were worth to even petition his prince or appeal to the Shogun or Emperor against any act of the upper classes. The common people were bound to the soil, and could not leave it without permission. Their lives even were in the hands of their immediate superiors, and fancied insolence or insubordination was sufficient justification for taking them. The Government divided the people into five general classes, as follows:

1. Military and official: this class included the Emperor and his blue-blooded nobility, the Tycoon and the Daimios, and their retainers.
2. Farmers who held land under lease.
3. Artisans.
4. Merchants and bankers.
5. Laborers, or the cooly class.

There was the widest gulf between the first class and all the others. The latter had no rights which the first class were bound to respect.

In 1868 the Government was essentially remodeled. The feudal system was abolished; the feudal lords were pensioned, and their power taken from them and assumed by the central government.

Although the laborer had no voice in the making and execution of the laws he has been materially benefited by the change. A system of courts has been established, wherein he can be heard against even the highest classes. He can claim the intervention of these courts to insure the payment of his wages, which he could not do under the old organization.

A vast, burdensome system of men-at-arms, with absolute authority, has been set aside, the old division of the people abolished, and all, in the eyes of the law, made of the same class. Of course, the power and influence of the old class system is still felt, and will be for years; but it must gradually die out, and thus the laborer will be on equal ground with all. One peculiar feature of the old absolutism, however, still exists. I refer to the police surveillance of all the people. The Empire is divided into districts, called ken and fu, over each of which is placed an officer, known as the "ken-rei" or "fuchiji," rendered in English, "governor." At the office of this official every native resident must be registered, and he or she cannot remove to another ken without written permission first obtained; and upon arrival at destination, he or she must be immediately registered there. And so strict is this supervision that a Japanese cannot travel, or even sleep, out of his district without permission of the authorities. A block of every ten houses has its supervising officer, and each hundred a superior official, keeping watch and ward over the movements of the occupants, so that any change or movement, even for a day, is immediately known. And this interference by the Government is not confined to the movements of the people, but extends to all their trades and industries. Monopolies are granted to certain parties, either of trade or transportation, and the Government itself often becomes a purchaser and seller in the market.

LAND TENURE.

All the land of the Empire was the Emperor's. Through the Shogun (Tycoon) it was granted to the military favorites for the maintenance of the military power. These favorites leased it in small divisions to farmers, who held it at the pleasure of the lessors. So long as the lessee paid the stipulated price, in produce, he was left undisturbed. Such was the land tenure up to 1868. Since that time the feudal institutions have been abolished, the land tenure has been changed, and the land has been sold, and is held in fee simple. This great reform has infinitely bettered the condition of the farmer. About three-tenths of all tilled land is now in the possession of small proprietors, the balance being held in larger divisions.

ORGANIZATION OF DOMESTIC SOCIETY.

Society was here, as elsewhere in Asia, essentially patriarchal. The *pater familias* had almost unlimited control over all the members of the family. The whole course of life of a child was marked out, shaped, and controlled by the father. Marriages were entirely within his authority. No son or daughter, no matter of what age, could leave the paternal roof and go out into the world without the parental consent. Among the lower classes, daughters were sold by their parents to be concubines, or to be trained as singing or dancing girls, or for immoral purposes, or they were mortgaged for a term of years to labor.

When a girl left the house of her parents and entered another as a wife or concubine, all the allegiance due to her parents was transferred to her husband or master and his parents. She could be divorced and sent away from her children at the will of the husband and his family.

Much of this power of the *pater familias* has been done away with, but his authority is still incomparably greater than in any Western society.

RELIGION.

The religion of the imperial families is Shintoism, or the worship of the country or Empire through its heroes or great men. That of the great mass of people is Buddhism; not that of India, but a system

grafted upon the original Pagan worship, and retaining much of the
gross superstitions of the latter.

The common people not only believe in the Buddhistic deities, but
also in the demons and evil spirits of Paganism. These religious beliefs
and superstitions affect directly the condition of the laboring classes.
The belief in *shrine cure* prevails everywhere with them. The result is
a large number of blind and diseased persons, who, if they had been
properly medicated in time, would be healthy producers instead of burdens upon society. Large numbers of children, when sick, are carried
to the favorite shrine instead of to the doctor, and thus mortality and
the number of physically weak and diseased people are largely increased.

The priesthood, although less than formerly, is still a mighty power
with the lower classes, and the income of shrines and temples, although
materially reduced, is still immense and a most oppressive burden to the
people.

EDUCATION.

The education of the higher classes was in former times Chinese.
The literature, philosophy, and science (if it can be said that there was
any true science) were all Chinese. It is safe to say that among these
higher classes there was no illiteracy; all could read and write. Nearly
all of the other classes, although not learned, could also read and write
enough for their business purposes. There were, of course, exceptions,
but of the male farmers and artisans not 10 per cent. were illiterate.
Schools were to be found in the larger towns of the provinces and in
many of the smaller villages. Where schools were not available, reading and writing were, in some measure, taught in the household.

It must be understood that what is denominated as education here
is not education in the sense the term is used in Europe and America,
and especially in recent times. The most highly educated man in Japan
knew some thousands of Chinese characters, a few books of the Chinese
classics, the books of ceremonies, and some of the truisms and proverbs
of the Chinese sages, and could write impromptu poetry in Chinese characters. He need not know the history even of his own country, much
less that of any other. He had absolutely no knowledge of anything
worthy the name of science. In art, he might paint and draw.

The lower classes, in place of this Chinese culture, knew just enough
arithmetic to serve their daily use and could read and write in the
Japanese characters. There was some knowledge of Japanese history,
mixed up with the marvellous, gleaned from books or the traveling
story-teller, who, by the roadside, recited to gaping crowds the stories
of the wars and amours of the olden times.

The whole system of education has been remodeled since 1868. Public schools have been established and scientific text-books from Europe
and America have been translated and brought into use. Probably the
percentage of illiteracy has not been much reduced by these reforms,
but the scientific learning of the West has largely taken the place of the
useless proverbs and superstitions of the East. It is safe to say that, at
the present rate of educational progress, another decade will see a useful education within reach of every Japanese laborer.

The report of the minister of education for the year 1879 shows:

Number of elementary schools	25,459
Number of teachers	59,825
School population	5,251,807
Scholars	2,066,566

The per cent. of scholars to school population, therefore, seems to be about 39.3. There are 389 schools of a higher grade with 910 teachers and 20,522 scholars. There are 96 normal schools with 766 teachers and 7,949 scholars. There exist also two so-called universities.

The whole amount of school expenditure, as shown in said report, was 5,364,870 yen,* of which 2,640,629 yen were paid in salaries, the salary of each teacher being an average of 44.72 yen per year.

Public libraries have been opened, one of which, at Tokio, has about 70,000 volumes.

Medical science and education.—The health and welfare of the laborer and his family everywhere are largely affected by the system of medicine prevailing, and by the intelligence of the members of the profession. An intelligent system of medicine, a high standard of admission to its practice, with low fees, give a lower percentage of mortality, a higher physique, and fewer lame, blind, and deaf.

The first system of medicine that, in any degree, took the place of *shrine cure* was the Chinese, which had no claims to be a science, and was full of ignorance, superstitions, and absurdities. The system had no knowledge of anatomy, physiology, pathology, chemistry, or the properties or actions of medicines. This was, and is the old school of medicine in Japan. Upon it was built a new system by the introduction of Dutch medical text-books, in the seventeenth century, which struggled for supremacy with the Chinese school for two hundred years.

Although this was an improvement upon the old practice, the latter continued to embrace the most numerous followers and to receive the confidence of the laboring classes, whenever they emancipated themselves from the superstitions of the shrine cures of the priesthood.

When the country was opened to foreign intercourse, modern medicine was introduced. Within the past ten years a medical college has been established in Tokio, and all the local or ken governments have opened hospitals, with a foreign surgeon for each and a class of medical students.

These local schools were necessarily inefficient, as no one man is fitted or has the time to teach all the branches of medicine and surgery, but with the text-books and the clinics of the hospital, a better class of practitioners than the country has ever had before has been sent out. I know of no means of arriving at the number of practitioners of these several schools in the whole Empire.

In this ken or province of Kanagawa, in which this consulate-general at Yokohama is situated, there are 659 practicing physicians; of these, 41 are students of the new schools and hospitals, 106 of the old Dutch school, and 512 of the Chinese school.

The population of this ken is now (1880) about 500,000. This gives one physician to 760 people. It must be borne in mind that this ken contains the principal foreign port and has had a hospital for years, with a foreign surgeon, and is within 20 miles of the medical college in Tokio. In the interior I do not think there is more than one physician to every 1,500 people, and the old, ignorant Chinese method preponderates more largely than here.

MORALS.

It is difficult to write of the morals of the Japanese people in such manner as to make the subject entirely intelligible to the Western reader. The habits and customs of centuries in which the relations of

* The Japanese yen = $0 99.7.

the sexes in this country have been looked upon so differently to those to which we have been accustomed, have created a code of morals, if the term be permissible, from which morality, in this connection, has been excluded. The relation of master and concubine is here considered perfectly proper, and neither party loses caste or respectability.

After marriage the wife is expected to be true to her husband, and it seldom happens that she fails in this duty. As mothers, Japanese women are models. None can be kinder or more affectionate to their children than they. They will spare no pains to amuse or instruct them, and seldom use force to compel obedience or punish faults. As wives, these women are simply slaves to the humors and caprices of their husbands and the families of their husbands. They have absolutely no rights, and are often subjected to seeing the attention of their lords transferred to some favorite concubine, to whom they are obliged to be considerate and respectful.

Bathing together, by both sexes, in public bath-houses, in a state of nudity, is practiced everywhere, but rudeness, vulgar language, or indecent gestures, in these places, are never indulged in.

As has been seen in the statistics of population, the males in Japan greatly exceed in number the females, and, in consequence of this fact, and the additional one of concubinage, so largely practiced, the number of unmarried men among the laboring class is very large. These persons frequent houses of prostitution, and spend much of their earnings also in gambling and drinking. It must be said, however, that drunkenness is exceptional, especially among the better class of laborers.

The strong drink is "sake," a distilled spirit made mostly from rice, of about the strength of ordinary table sherry.

The Japanese, like all Eastern peoples, are somewhat given to exaggeration in their speech, and their intense suavity and politeness to each other is proverbial.

MEANS OF TRANSPORTATION.

The islands of Japan are long and narrow. There is no point in the center of the larger islands more than 100 miles from navigable water. Cheap ocean transportation, is, therefore, everywhere easily available. On the alluvial plans of the eastern and western coast, besides the tidal rivers, there exists an extensive system of canals. In the interior, in former times, there was no general system of roads worthy of the name. It is true, the Tokugawa Tycoons, and some of the Daimios had built a few roads, but they were illy adapted to carriage traffic, and, in places, were entirely impassable except for footmen and pack-horses. Aside from these roads, built for war purposes, the only means of travel were mere footpaths.

Now two short lines of railway have been built, in all less than 100 miles. Some of the footpaths have been made wide enough for carriages, but, in the whole of Japan, it is safe to say that there are not more than 1,000 miles of carriage roads. From and to the interior districts all the products and all articles of trade are carried on the backs of men or horses. Such carriage is slow and costly and ruinous to both producer and consumer. As a tax, it bears heavily on the shoulders of labor, and will do so until better roads are built by the Government. So much man-packing is not only laborious, but degrading. It prevents production, consumption, and trade.

The building of good roads and the providing of cheap transportation must be a condition precedent to the settlement and development of the wild lands of the country.

By sea, river, and canal the means of transportation are reasonably good and cheap. Lines of steamers and sailing vessels, of foreign construction, have been established to all the principal ports of the country. The fleet of vessels owned by one company, the Mitsu-Bishi, represents, in round numbers, a gross tonnage of 50,000 tons. This company has had the countenance and support of the Government; its fleet is being constantly increased and the service rendered more effective.

In addition, there are many smaller companies in Tokio, Osaka, and Nagasaki, which run steamers and sailing vessels, of foreign style, to some of the smaller ports. Some of these smaller steamers are Japanese built, and although not of the best construction, give promise that in time Japan will be independent of foreign countries in ship building.

There are no means available for giving accurate data as to the number and tonnage of the old style of native sailing vessels, known as "junks." The gross tonnage must be very large. They run along the coast to and from all the ports, and give cheap service, much cheaper than steam or foreign sailing vessels.

Latterly loud complaints have been made of the interference by the Government with these vessels in the interests of the steam monopolies. Experience will certainly compel an abandonment of such attempts, which, if persisted in, must disastrously affect both the Government and people.

As bearing upon the question of inland transportation of the products of labor, the statistics of the number of cattle and horses of both Japan and the United States may be properly inserted here, so that the contrast may be seen.

In Japan, her 35,000,000 people have 900,274 horses and 814,324 cattle. In the United States, in 1870, the 38,000,000 people had, in round numbers, 10,000,000 horses and mules and 26,000,000 cattle. This will show what burdens the laborer here has to carry on his back, and what unnecessary calls are made upon his earnings in the way of carrying his products.

Mails.—The mail transportation that has been established within the last ten years, both coastwise and inland, is cheap and excellent. The number of miles of mail routes aggregates 36,052. The number of post-offices is 3,927. The number of letters carried for the year ending June 30, 1880, was 55,775,206, and that of newspapers 11,203,731. These figures throw great light upon the volume of business of the country and the amount of reading and writing done by the people.

Connected with the postal department is a well organized postal money-order service and postal savings-bank system. The number of these banks is 595.

TENEMENTS.

In forming an opinion of the tenements of the laborer, the climate of the country must be borne in mind. Although there are unlimited quantities of good, durable building-stone everywhere in the mountain ranges, and vast deposits of firm clay for making brick, no stone or brick houses are built. The frequency and severity of earthquakes make the use any but wooden structures impracticable. Timber is scarce, and there is nothing worthy the name of forests except in a portion of Yesso, in the far north.

All buildings, or nearly all, are one story, and, compared to those of America and Europe, small. But the reader must bear in mind that the requirements of this oriental civilization are less than with us. A laborer's house here will, at most, have no more than four little rooms. Generally there is one main room, which serves as a sitting, dining, and sleeping room, and, in addition, a small nook for cooking and another for bathing. That the uses of one room for the purposes of eating, sitting, and sleeping may be understood, it should be explained that the rooms are covered with clean soft mats, upon which no boot or shoe ever treads. When meals are served, small tables, not more than one foot high, are used, and the family sit on the floor like tailors on their benches. When the meal is finished the table is removed and the room is ready for a sitting-room, the mats serving as seats. At night cotton comforters are brought from a small clothes-press and spread on the mats, and lo! a sleeping chamber. Thus, much of the room required by a laborer of our Western civilization is saved. A Japanese laborer's house with three rooms can be built for from 25 to 200 yen. And the furniture, including matting and sliding partitions, will not exceed 50 yen.

The house, by reason of non-use by the people of boots and shoes, is neat and clean. The bath, found in almost every laborer's house, is in daily use, and, cheap and small as the house is, it is comfortable.

None of the houses are built with a view to ventilation or warmth, the partitions and sides being of paper, protected in cold weather or storms by strong wooden shutters. The vast majority of the houses are thatched, and therefore stove-pipes and chimneys are impossible. In fact, there are no stoves or grates in Japan. In villages and towns the house is warmed, if at all, by a small fire-box filled with charcoal, but more generally by a square zinc or copper lined fire-place, sunk in the middle of the floor, in which wood is burned, the smoke from which rises and escapes through a hole in the roof. But little heat is generated in this way, and much discomfort from the smoke is experienced, and diseases of the eye are prevalent.

As a rule the principal protection from cold is by additional padded clothing. The laborer, however, suffers in the three winter months, when, although in many parts of the Empire the thermometer does not mark very low, the cold storms of snow and rain are exceedingly uncomfortable.

The drainage from sinks and cess pools in the vicinity of tenements is, as a rule, extremely defective, and is, doubtless, a powerful agent in producing epidemic diseases.

In 1875, when the population was 33,300,675, there were 7,389,371 houses or tenements, the average number of occupants to each being, therefore, less than 5. In Tokio the number is 4; in Kanagawa ken, 4.5; Nagasaki ken, 4.7; Fukushima ken, 5.5; Miyaga ken, 5.9; Awamori ken, 5.8; Osaka City, 3.7.

The houses of cities seem to be less crowded than those of the poorer rural districts.

FUEL.

The fuel, which is used chiefly for cooking and heating baths, is charcoal, cut and split wood, brush and dried grass.

Charcoal is made in the wooded regions, burned in small clay pits, and carried to the settlements on the backs of men and horses in straw sacks. The selling price varies according to the distance from which it is brought, from 25 to 50 cents per 100 pounds. Cut wood is sold in small bundles of six sticks, each stick being about 18 inches in length, and 2 inches in diameter; 80 to 100 bundles are sold for $1. I am quoting the rates of districts remote from the foreign settlements.

Brush and dried grass are gathered from the wild lands, to which certain rights of commons attach, as in England in early times. The value of the fuel bought and sold in 1875 was as follows: Wood, $6,107,974; charcoal, $2,219,986.

As the farmer and country laborer gets his fuel from his own land or from the commons, this must have been mostly used in the larger villages and cities, showing how little is consumed for house warming even by the richer classes.

FARMERS.

As has been said, the farmer, under the old system of classes, ranked next to the samurai or governing class. In the new order he holds the same position in public opinion and general estimation. He is now owner of the soil he tills, and is taxed according to its producing capacity.

The kocho, or village officer, in all agricultural villages, has always been a leading farmer, and some villages had and still have the right to choose this officer. He had little more than a general supervision of village affairs. He settled petty disputes, maintained the peace, kept the register of the inhabitants, granted traveling permits, arrested thieves, and was a general advisor of the village.

Within the past two years the Government has taken a step which has greatly enhanced the position and influence of the landholder. A decree has been promulgated by which local election assemblies have been created. the electors of which are confined to such of the landholders as pay at least $10 land tax.

At present the power of these assemblies is only deliberative and advisory. The governor of the province submits his fiscal estimates for local expenditures and they examine and pass upon them. If they disagree with him the whole matter goes to the General Government for its decision.

Although these assemblies possess no legislative power, they contain the germ of representative local self-government. The system needs to be extended so as to include, among the representatives, intelligent people of all classes, and to have the powers now exercised materially increased. That this consummation will be achieved is almost certain. Nor will reform in this direction stop here.

The agitation pervading all classes in Japan in favor of a national representative assembly is manifested daily in petitions to the Emperor and his ministers, in conferences and lectures, and in newspaper communications and editorials. The question is so prominent and the determination to achieve success so universal, that the genro-in, the deliberative and advisory council of the Empire, is now said to be taking it into serious consideration, and probably the country, before the lapse of many years, possibly months, will find itself in possession of some such chamber, wherein the views of all the people may be presented and discussed, and laws for their welfare enacted. That it will be entirely free to act as its members may be inclined is not probable, and it may be a matter of doubt if such freedom would at present be wise.

Farmers in Japan have no seasons of rest as in colder climates, the climate in nearly all portions of the country being so mild in winter as to admit of raising the hardier crops.

A considerable percentage of the landowners are not workers, large numbers of the tea, silk, rice, tobacco, and sugar raisers being able to employ laborers for that purpose.

Almost every farmer can read, write, and keep his farm accounts. He sends his sons to some school to learn the same, and has his daughters taught music and needle-work at home.

All labor on a farm is, to the present time, mere hand work. A plow is seldom seen. Sometimes in the lowland rice fields an implement 5 feet in length with a wooden cross piece and depending iron teeth 20 inches in length, set 4 or 5 inches apart, is used with a horse as a pulverizer of the soil, after the latter has been thoroughly dug up and worked over with a mattock. Ninety-nine per cent., however, of all labor is still manual. In 1878 the number of farmers, out of a population of 35,000,000, was something over 15,500,000, of which over 7,000,000 were women ; but as a large number of these latter, including the old and young, are engaged in household duties, spinning, weaving, making clothing, &c., there were probably not more than two or three million women employed in field work.

The area of land in actual cultivation in the whole Empire in 1875 was about 12,000,000 acres, so that to the actual farming population there were only three-quarters of an acre per head. The tillage is of the most thorough order. Two crops are invariably raised each year, so that the producing capacity of the area cultivated is double that of the number of acres named.

The wages of an able-bodied farm-hand are about $35 per year with board, and without board, $50. Per day, with board, it will not average more than 15 or 20 cents. Female labor is much cheaper. To do work in a house or on a farm stout healthy women are engaged at from $8 to $10 per year with food, and without food from $25 to $30, and by the day at from 10 to 15 cents. The number of hours of labor will not average more than 9 and probably not more than 8.

The Japanese farmer is an easy task-master, and treats his hired laborer with great kindness. In ordinary farming there is little skilled labor, but in tea, silk, and sugar cultivation and preparation, skill and experience are required, and are paid higher prices. A good tea-firer on a tea plantation, or a silk-winder, receives double the wages of the unskilled laborer.

Food.—The food of a farm laborer is almost entirely vegetable. It consists of rice, barley, or wheat, millet, beans, peas, turnips, potatoes, onions, carrots, and a few other vegetable products. In some districts rice is too high in price, and only barley, turnips, and millet, with some few additions, are used. On rare occasions the laborer may eat an egg or chicken and some cheap fish, but he is essentially a vegetarian. Religion, custom, popular prejudice, and price forbid the use of animal flesh.

Clothing.—The clothing of the farm-laborer in summer is little more than nature sent him into the world with; in winter, a cotton garment or two is worn, with straw sandals or wooden clogs. The whole clothing of a year will not cost more than $4 or $5.

Holidays.—Several holidays are allowed each year, such as religious festivals and family celebrations. When a man and his wife work for yearly wages they will receive, without board, about $75. From this he has to pay from $8 to $10 for a two or three small-roomed house, and buy clothing for a family of four or five, amounting, perhaps, to $20. He will have a small garden with his house, from which one-half of his living is produced; a few chickens and ducks, tended by the children, will buy many articles of necessity or of ornament for holiday use; a child of six or seven years, perhaps with a babe of six months strapped on its back, will gather brush or dried grass on the commons for fuel; and by great frugality in eating, and scrupulous care of clothing, at the end of a year he finds he has supported his family, had several enjoyable holidays, and has a few dollars hidden away in some secret place.

Taxes.*—The average government tax of low irrigable rice-land is $5 per acre. The average value of such lands is $200 per acre. The land tax is therefore 2½ per cent.; this is the government assessment; that for local purposes is ½ per cent., making 3 per cent. in all.

Rice culture.—The average value of the product of rice-land is about $40 per acre. Four or five acres of lowland rice fields form quite a respectable holding for one person. This, with another acre or so of upland where vegetables are raised, and a little bluff land for timber, fuel, and grass to feed the pack-horse, supports his family, pays for hired help, and gives a little surplus at the annual settling day.

The homes of the rice, silk, and tea farmers are the best of all the agricultural laborers in Japan. The house is often as large as 30 or 40 feet square, universally one story, thatched roof, strongly built, with veranda in front, and five or six rooms, one being kept as a spare or reception room. If built with a view to light and warmth, they would compare in comfort with the average New England farm-house.

Rice is grown in all of the sixty provinces of Japan. The whole area in cultivation in 1878 was about 6,500,000 acres, and the product was 180,000,000 bushels. This includes upland as well as lowland rice, the average yield of all being about 30 bushels per acre. On low land the yield will average 40 bushels.

The total value of the rice product, as returned to the home department in 1878, was $202,521,750.

Wheat.—Wheat is grown in all parts of the empire. The product in 1878 was 38,000,000 bushels, valued at $19,000,000.

Barley.—The climate and soil are everywhere favorable to the growth of barley. The product in 1878 was 60,000,000 bushels, valued at $36,000,000.

Millet, beans, peas, &c.—The value of these products for the same year was returned as $16,007,360.

The value of all other vegetables was $10,849,623, and of seeds and fruits, $8,217,798.

Tobacco.—The product of tobacco was about 90,000,000 pounds, valued at $7,500,000. A considerable quantity was exported to England and Germany. The quality is inferior and the price low, but much higher than ten years ago, averaging about 8⅜ cents per pound.

Tea.—The tea-culture is one of the most important and lucrative of all Japanese industries, the leaf being one of the chief articles of export. The product in 1878 was about 60,000,000 pounds. The export trade has increased wonderfully. In 1869 the amount exported was 4,890,430 pounds; in 1875, 22,384,893 pounds; in 1879, 33,692,391 pounds; and that of 1880 is estimated to reach 38,000,000 pounds.

As has been remarked, the tea farmer lives in a comparatively good house, has servants, keeps a horse to do his packing, and has a balance to his credit at the end of a good year.

The best tea grows on the hillsides, sheltered from the sea winds, which latter make the leaf tough and of bad flavor.

The ordinary labor wages are paid for the tillage of the soil, but the man who trims the plant must be skilled, and will get as high as 30 to 35 cents per day. The tea-picking is done by women and girls and requires care. When they work by the day they get from 10 to 12½ cents. Tea rollers and firers in the country must be skilled, and they command from 15 to 30 cents per day. In the open ports tea-firing is done entirely by women, who are paid about 15 cents per day.

*As to general taxation, see Table B, Appendix.

In the export of tea there is employment for a large number of carpenters in making boxes, printers and lithographers in the manufacture of labels, &c., who are paid as skilled mechanics.

The area of tea-growing is rapidly increasing, and as there are plenty of hillsides and plains well adapted for the culture available, and still unoccupied, it will increase as long as there is a foreign demand. It seems to be one of the great fields for the spread and use of an increasing labor population. The habit of adulterating tea, however, with leaves of the wisteria plant seems to be on the increase in this country, and if not arrested may materially affect the demand. The wisteria leaf is not poisonous, but cannot be said to improve the flavor of the cup that "cheers, but not inebriates."

Silk.—The area of land in mulberry trees is not stated in any of the late census product returns. In 1875 the total value of silk product is given at $31,250,000. The export of silk and silk-worm eggs for the year ending June 30, 1878, was $11,640,976.64.

The trade is steadily growing and giving increased employment to labor, and as better processes of preparing silk are introduced and a better article is produced, more and more skilled labor will be required and higher wages be paid.

Mulberry plantations are found in fifty of the sixty-six provinces of Japan. The soil nowhere is exclusively devoted to this tree. Universally between the rows of trees, other crops, both summer and winter, are grown. The business of silk production is carried on in the house where the family lives. The mulberry leaves are either picked off by women and children and carried into the house, or the young limbs with the leaves on are cut off and taken there, where the leaves are picked off, washed, cut up, and fed to the worms. Little skill is required.

When the cocoons are ready for winding, that, as well as all the other work thus far referred to, is done by women and girls. To make an even thread requires experience, care, and skill, and such labor commands wages accordingly. Spinning, warping, dyeing, and weaving are all more or less skilled branches and require skilled labor.

There are some establishments that buy the cocoons, wind them, spin the thread, and weave the cloth ; but nine-tenths of the silk, raw and manufactured, of the country is family made. The machinery of manufacture, whether in the factory or private house, is crude, and still remains as though Jacquard and Arkwright never lived. The beautiful stuffs made by such crude means testify to their skill and ingenuity.

The man who tends the trees commands ordinary farm wages, while the leaf-pickers and feeders, winders, spinners, and weavers of plain cloth will get from 20 to 40 cents per day. Weavers of fancy-patterned goods get much more, even as high as $1 per day ; but this is very exceptional.

Cotton.—Reliable statistics cannot be obtained by which to estimate the amount of this staple raised in the country. The returns of 1875 show cotton goods manufactured to the value of $10,564,578, and that it formed part of textures valued at $12,915,586. The cotton itself is coarse, and in consequence the manufactured cloth is of an inferior quality, and the labor employed is not skilled and commands small wages. It is generally believed that these manufacturers have increased within the past few years from 30 to 50 per cent.

ARTISANS.

The Japanese artisan, like the farmer, has always held a respectable position. He was in a class above the merchant and banker, but in reality his position, pay, and privileges were no greater.

For a thousand years a very high mechanical art has existed. The Japanese articles and implements of steel were of the best. Some of the old swords are worthy to be classed with the Toledo and Damascus blades. Their lacquered wares have been and still are unrivaled, and they made beautiful porcelain long before Palissy and Boettcher were born. Their silk cloth, embroideries, and silk tapestries were exquisitely beautiful at a time when some Western peoples wore the coarsest stuffs. Their oldest bronze compares with the finest products of Europe. Their paintings on silk and paper, porcelain and lacquer excite the warmest admiration. Their ivory and wood carvings are wonders of skill, ingenuity, and patient labor.

There is hardly a house in Japan where some mechanical trade is not carried on. Even in the households of the higher classes, silk, cotton, and other goods are made by the servants, and the members of the family have some knowledge of the art. Every farmer's house has its wheel and loom. Many of the smaller merchants make more or less of their goods.

In this view there are many more artisans in the country than are shown by the census of 1875. The number, as I have previously stated, is placed between 700,000 and 800,000. I believe that there are more than double that number who devote the greatest share of their time to manufacture, and five or six millions who work more or less at mechanical trades.

Many of the wares used for home consumption require no special skill in their production, and therefore the labor wage is low. In the manufacture of silk, lacquer, porcelain, enamels, bronzes, embroideries, and in their paintings, skilled labor must enter, and is paid proportionately.

What has been said of agricultural labor as to the use of machinery can be repeated of mechanical work. It is, in the main, hand labor. Labor-saving machinery does not enter as a factor, to any appreciable extent, into the industries of Japan. I doubt if there are more than two saw-mills in the whole Empire. All such labor is by hand in every branch of mechanical art.

Porcelain and earthenware.—Porcelain and earthenware are manufactured in every province. By the last census returns available (1875) the value of all porcelain produced was about $3,000,000. With one exception, that of the home department in the province of Hizen, there is no foreign machinery or mode of manufacture in use. The clay is manipulated as it was in the earliest days. The same wheel is used for turning that is pictured on the walls of the tombs and temples of Egypt. All decorations are by hand. There is a marked improvement of late years in designs and decorations of all kinds of articles of ornament. No more beautiful or exquisite ceramic articles are made than come from the hands of the Japanese artisan. Love of beautiful pottery has been a national passion for a thousand years, and skilled labor has commanded relatively high wages.

Much of the cruder work can be done by apprentices and common journeymen, but a good turner at the wheel gets from 50 to 70 cents per day, and the best painters from 75 cents to $1.15. The average is, however, much less.

Makers of flowers and figures of birds, &c., for ornamenting the larger vases and jars in bas-relief receive from 50 to 70 cents per day. A safe person skilled in baking the ware can be had for from 40 to 60 cents per diem, and clay washers and mixers at from 20 to 30 cents.

Enamels.—Makers of enameled copper and porcelain receive much the same wages. The enameled copper or cloisonné of the present time commands higher prices in the market than any now made elsewhere. There has been the greatest improvement within the last three or four years. When machinery takes the place of the hand in shaping the copper base and in polishing the enamel the ware can be produced for much less than at present, and probably of a superior quality. As it is, Japan has no close competitor in the finer articles of this manufacture.

Bronze.—Bronze workers get about the same wages as workers in porcelain. The highest skill in inlaid bronze manufacture commands from $1 to $1.50 per day, but ordinary skill can be had from 30 to 70 cents per day.

Ivory carvers get from $10 to $20 per month; carpenters from 25 to 50 cents per day; blacksmiths are cheaper, and can be had from 18 to 40 cents per diem.

Lacquer.—Modern lacquer workers, in the best product of that art, rank with porcelain and bronze artisans. Wages range from 20 cents to $1.25 per day, according to the skill of the individual and the grade of the article made.

It has been thought the art of making fine lacquer was on the decline, but I think this is a mistake, and that as fine, if not finer, articles than ever graced the Tycoon's castle can be made if the same prices are offered.

Ship-builders work mostly near the open ports, where wages are much higher than in the interior. A good ship carpenter gets 40 to 50 cents per day, and a foreman from $50 to $60 per month.

PROFESSIONAL LABOR.

As was seen in giving the statistics of education, the average yearly salary of all the school teachers in Japan was 44.72 yen.

Physicians, as a rule, do not charge for the visit to the patient, but for the medicine which they give; but, as one who has reputation charges more for the same medicine than the less known practitioner, it amounts to the same thing. An ordinary physician will receive a call in office hours and give medicine for from 12½ to 20 cents. As to charges for surgical cases, the knife was unknown to the old school. The fees of the new foreign school cannot be much higher, for if they were the physicians would not get patronage.

Lawyers.—Until lately there were no native lawyers. Now several are practicing before the courts in Tokio and Yokohama. It can hardly be said that they have established a footing yet, or that the profession has a well-defined existence. As no civil code has been adopted, and as the criminal code has been little modified, it may be a long time before they reach a position of much importance.

Writers, translators, and *interpreters* can be had at all prices, from $10 to $50 per month; *clerks, salesmen,* and *book-keepers* command from $18 to $20 per month, including board.

COOLIE OR COMMON LABOR.

This is the lowest class of labor in Japan. As has been stated, these people were the serfs of the soil. Although the whole class system has been done away with, yet the effect of a thousand years of degradation remains. The year 1868 found this class in utter poverty. Probably not one in a hundred of them owned a foot of land or the rude roof which illy sheltered their heads from the storms. Twelve years have done much to improve their condition. Many now own their own houses

and tools. Some have bought land and are now farmers, on their own
account. Wages have been raised, and schools, in many instances, are
available for their children.

Carriers.—Probably the hardest worked laborers in Japan are the
carriers. This class includes the jinrickisha men, car-men, and packers. Jinrickishas, or man-wagons, introduced into Japan by a foreigner,
in 1870, are now in use in all parts of the country, and it is estimated
that they number between 300,000 and 400,000. A man is expected to
go from 30 to 40 miles per day, pull this carriage, of some 50 pounds in
weight, with a man weighing 150 more, over all kinds of roads, and he
gets from 35 to 60 cents for it. Some own their own jinrickishas, but
in most cases a company or guild is the owner, and for rental of a ve-
hicle the coolie must pay from 6 to 10 cents per day. The cost of these
carriages is from $12 to $16 each. One of these men will carry you 6
miles in an hour, and when you stop to make a call, the poor fellow,
bathed in perspiration, waits, perhaps, in a cold winter wind or storm,
with no protection but his cotton garments. The result is necessarily
rheumatism, consumption, and a short life.

Car-men.—There are two kinds of cart carriage—one where the cart
is drawn by men and the other by a bull or cow. Where man-drawn,
usually there are four men—two in front and two behind. They draw
heavy loads, and go slowly, indulging in a sort of measured shout, to
mark time. In the south, smaller carts are in use—some for two and
others for one man. I have seen an old man and a young woman, the
latter with a small child strapped on her back, pulling a cart load of
wood or coal up steep hills and over sandy plains. Ten to twelve miles
a day with a loaded cart is a day's work, and 600 to 700 pounds an average load for two persons. For this heavy work from 10 to 20 cents
each per diem is considered good pay.

However dark this picture, these people know how to enjoy it. They
go in a train of several carts, taking their food, rain-coats of plaited
straw, and sun-hats, and at intervals stop by some stream where there
is clear water and cool shade, where, with the laughter and light-heart-
edness of children, they indulge in their simple meals.

Bull-carts are drawn by only one animal. The driver walks by the
latter's side and guides him by a small cord fastened to his nose by an
iron ring. The bull is stout, quiet, and gentle; he will go about 12 to
15 miles per day, and draw 600 to 700 pounds. The earnings of such a
cart and man are about 50 cents per day.

Packers.—These are of two kinds, men and women who carry loads of
produce and goods on their backs over the mountain paths and along the
highways, down to the rivers and sea-coast, and those who use horses for
the same purpose. Men and women carry from 80 to 120 pounds each,
and go from 12 to 15 miles a day, earning from 10 to 16 cents. The
horse, in summer, gets little but grass, with, perhaps, a little rice or
barley bran. There are no iron or steel shoes worn by pack horses.
They are shod with straw, and, in the interior, these straw shoes cost
2 cents per set. On some of the stony roads two sets are required per
day.

The other coolie labor has been referred to when treating of farming
and mechanical industries, where they are used to do the heavy and
coarse work.

FISHERMEN.

Surrounded on all sides by the ocean, indented everywhere by broad
gulfs and bays, all the alluvial portions cut up by tidal streams and

canals, the waters swarming with a great variety of food-fishes, it is only natural that there should be a numerous fishing population in Japan. There are no separate returns of this class, but it is very large.

Every shore has its fishing villages. All the bays and inlets, on fair days, are white with the sails of fishing boats. I am inclined to think that this is the lowest class in the country. Their houses are the poorest and dirtiest, and they are the least intelligent. There are fewer schools in these isolated villages than elsewhere and the percentage of illiteracy is greater. Physically they are the equals of the other people, which is owing to a plentiful supply of fish-food. There is no religious or other prejudice against eating fish, and all kinds are cheap.

A good fishing boat for two men costs about $70. On fair days an average catch is from 60 to 90 cents' worth. The wages of an able-bodied fisherman, working by the day, are 15 to 20 cents. Women and children work along the shores at low tide, gathering oysters, clams, &c.

The preparation of salted fish gives employment to large numbers of the cheaper class of laborers. This numerous fishing population, the island location of the country, the numbers and variety of fish in all the waters, the cheapness of transportation from the fisheries to the centers of population on the sea-shores and river banks, all have an important bearing upon the welfare of the laboring class.

In the larger towns the fish-markets are all under the control of guilds, and in some places the boats are owned and the men employed by these guilds. In the city of Nagoya, in the province of Owari, the fish guild four years ago owned 1,200 boats and employed 4,000 men. Some of these boats were large and carried 8 and 10 men. Their sales of fish were $1,500,000 per year.

Fish can be had at all prices, from 2 to 12½ cents per pound, according to the quality and the locality where sold. The product of the fisheries in 1878 was about $10,000,000.

MINERS.

The mines of Japan, in the value of the product, do not take high rank. The total value from all mines and quarries in 1878 did not exceed $5,000,000.

Labor is cheap, and for poverty and ignorance the miner takes a position side by side with the fisherman. His lot is harder and his pleasures are less. Common mine labor can be had for from 8 to 20 cents day, and by the month for less.

Exactly what the mine wealth of Japan is cannot be ascertained at present, and probably will never be known until the country and its hidden resources are opened to foreign skill and enterprise; and this may be said with equal truth as to the cultivable lands. If worked in large tracts by skilled labor and modern foreign implements, the taxable wealth of the country would be vastly increased.

SPORTS AND PASTIMES.

The national sports and games of Japan were less active and athletic in character than those of Europe and America. The samurai were fond of horseback riding, but the laboring classes were not allowed to ride on the public roads. Even now, when the pack-horses are returning unloaded from market and the drivers ride a portion of the way, they make sure to dismount in the presence of any of the old, higher class. The absence of roads also discouraged the practice of equestrianism. Foot races or walking matches were not in vogue. So of boat racing. Exclusively warlike games and practices were indulged in by the higher classes. They practiced archery and fencing, and, on eating and drinking occasions, had trials of strength and skill within doors.

The lower classes had a more active class of sports. Under the harvest moon you may see a whole village collected to witness wrestling, racing, and fencing. Theatrical performances are popular, and traveling troupes of actors go from village to village, erect bamboo and mat shelters, and give entertainments for a week at a time. On such occasions the laboring classes turn out in great numbers, with all their holiday finery on, and enjoy every incident of the performance. Laboring men in the evening go to tea houses, drink a light wine made from rice, sing songs, play games of skill, and recite in dramatic style from the old historians and poets. Women and girls gossip in groups at some neighbor's house, or at the public baths. Women play a simple game of checkers, while men are skilled in chess. The children have battledore and kite-flying.

In addition to this the Japanese are great travelers. In certain months when farm labor is not pressing, 20 or 30 friends and neighbors will arrange a pilgrimage to some of the noted shrines and temples in the mountains, going on foot as far as 150 or 200 miles. They walk leisurely along the roads and paths, talking, laughing, and singing. In the middle of the day, when tired, they sleep in the shade of the groves, eat rice and drink tea, and are as happy as the day is long.

These pilgrimages are an important feature in the social life of the laborer. They afford mental and physical relaxation, give extended observation of wide regions of country, of new, varied and better industries, and an insight into the life and habits of their far-off countrymen.

There is another amusement to be met with on festival days, which, in the smaller villages of the interior, still exerts an influence upon the lower classes. I allude to the wayside story-telling. This afforded the only means which certain classes had of knowing the history of their country. The story-tellers have rude booths, and for a mere pittance recite by the hour the civil and military history of the different dynasties which have ruled the country. They speak the pure old Japanese unmixed with Chinese words, which the learned affected, and thus are perfectly understood by their hearers.

LABOR ORGANIZATIONS.

Every branch of labor and trade has its guild, although not, like those of western countries, originally formed to protect labor from the exactions of capital. The Government, for purposes of revenue, farmed out to favorites exclusive privileges of trade or of labor, and these persons formed guilds and levied taxes upon all engaged in such occupations. These organizations, in time, fell more and more under the influence and control of those taxed. They gradually grew to be used for the protection of the interests of the trades. They could petition the local authorities, and, from their numbers and unity, had no inconsiderable influence.

Although the Government has abolished this practice of farming these guilds and substituted therefor individual licenses, the guilds still exist and zealously guard the interests of their members.

As has been said, there are no manufactories employing large capital and great numbers of operatives, but the manufactures of Japan are distinctively household. In some cases a few outside laborers are employed, but in many, perhaps a majority, of these household workshops, the laborer is interested in the capital and profits of the manufacture.

If labor-saving machinery, large capital, and great establishments employing hundreds of people shall ever be introduced, these guilds now operating partially in the interest of labor may assume the importance and influence of the labor organizations in the United States.

FINANCES.

While the finances of a country have an important bearing upon the condition of the laborer, it is not within the province of this paper to enter into an elaborate review of the financial system of this country. Briefly, the estimates of the revenues of the General Government are, for the years 1880-'81, $54,558,304. The principal sources of this revenue are as follows:

1st. Land tax	$41,901,441
2d. Imports and exports	2,369,462
3d. Taxes on spirits, tobacco, stamp taxes, licenses, &c	9,000,000
4th. Income from Government property, such as sales and rents from public lands, yield of mines, &c	1,400,000

The burdens of taxation are light upon all industries except agriculture, where the tax is a uniform one of 3 per cent. of its value, as has been shown, estimated from its products. The estimated expenditures are the same for the year 1880-'81 as the revenue, the principal items of which are for—

Reduction of national debt	$5,817,538
Interest on national debt	15,631,369
Pensions	1,059,403
Expenses of the ten departments of the Government	23,051,409
Expenses of local or provincial governments	4,539,280
Police	1,261,500
Miscellaneous: home and foreign industrial exhibitions, libraries, museums, &c	1,331,559

Currency.—The currency of the country is—

1st. Treasury notes	$108,683,203
2d. National bank notes, about	32,000,000
Making the total paper circulation about	140,683,203

The treasury notes are irredeemable, but are interchangeable for 6 per cent. Government bonds. There is an annual drawing for a certain amount of these bonds, which are paid at par in gold.

The national bank issues are secured by a deposit of Government bonds of 80 per cent. of the amount so issued, but are redeemable only in treasury notes.

Both the treasury and bank notes are much depreciated and are now, September, 1880, worth from 60 to 70 cents only, in silver.

The debt has been reduced during the past year nearly $11,000,000, and the estimated reduction for the present year is about $6,000,000. The interest on public debt for the present year, 1880-'81, is $15,631,369.

PAUPERISM.

In all time Japan had her beggar class, who were permitted to solicit alms by the roadside, and to live in huts on the waste lands. The origin of this class is unknown. Whether they are descended from the lepers or from pardoned criminals, and thus outcasts, or from the conquered aborigines, is uncertain. Although they may still be seen here and there by the roadsides, the Government discourages these proceedings, and in many cases they are arrested and subjected to punishment. There was an attempt some years since, by the various local authorities, to reduce the number of these beggars by furnishing them with labor, food, and clothing, but without marked success. With this exception, the Government has never made any provision for the extremely poor. Farms for the poor, pauper asylums, systems of out-door relief, were and are unknown. In fact, there was little need for them. So little food and clothing will supply the wants of the poor that the near and distant relatives of which the family and class are formed were enabled to provide that little. As the influence of the family organizations grows weaker and their responsibility less, the necessity of some public provision begins to be felt.

There is another feature of society here which makes numbers of aged, indigent people less dependent upon public charity. The family never becomes extinct, the line of descent never ceases. If there are no male children to bear the name, a younger son of another family is adopted, who takes the family name, and upon whom the aged and decrepit lean for support.

THE BLIND.

The number of blind persons in Japan, owing to causes already enumerated, is very large. In every city or village of any size they are organized into associations or guilds, controlled by a president or head man. This officer, although 'chosen by the members, was formally commissioned by the Government authorities. Unless otherwise disabled, the blind are not idle. They go about the streets making their presence known at night by blowing, every few steps, upon a shrill whistle, and are employed as shampooers by any one in pain or suffering from fatigue. Their districts of labor, prices, and general behavior are regulated by the head officer. They live by themselves, do their own cooking, and are, in general, a peaceable and worthy class, and not a burden upon the community.

SCENERY.

The remarkable beauty of Japanese scenery has won the admiration of every visitor. Her grand mountain ranges, covered with trees and shrubs, clothed in perpetual green, towered by the world-renowned Fujiyama, rearing its shining summit above the clouds, reverenced by millions of her people as the reflection of Deity itself, and the holy shrine to which thousands of pilgrims yearly bend their steps; the charming and picturesque valleys, carpeted with richest verdure and blossoming with flowers of a thousand hues, including the lotus, queen of lilies, which fills the atmosphere with its rich perfume; the rushing torrents and winding rivers, sparkling with clearest water; her numerous and varied islands; her indented coasts, bays, and harbors; her varieties of shrubs and trees, and her skies of purest blue—all combine to make their impress on the character of her people.

Cheerfulness of disposition and love of the beautiful are striking characteristics of the natives of Niphon. Born and reared amidst such charms of nature, forms of beauty become to them every day familiar objects, and it is no matter of wonder that they bring into existence some of the lovliest works of art that human hands have ever formed, or that the smiles of sky and earth, air and sea, should be reflected on their faces and in their lives.

The laborer sings at his toil, goes cheerfully to his simple meal, and engages with the enthusiasm of boyhood in his holiday sports.

ETHNOLOGY.

It is perhaps too early to state with certainty to which of the families of the human race the Japanese belong.

Morton, long since, after examining a number of Japanese crania, decided that they are not of Chinese origin. Their language, which is always considered the strongest evidence of race, makes it certain that they are neither Chinese, Polynesian, or of that aboriginal race to which the inhabitants of Northeastern Asia belong. Whitney and Müller are inclined to place them in the great Indo-European family. If so, the conquerers of these islands must have started from the central regions of Asia, and instead of traveling west, as the other migratory hordes did, came east, crossed to Japan, and wrested the country from the Ainos, the then possessors of the soil.

ORIENTAL CIVILIZATION.

The distinctive characteristic of Oriental civilization, as compared to ours of the west, is its extreme simplicity of food, dress, houses, household appurtenances, and general style of living. The precepts of religion, the maxims of government, and the fashions of the times inculcate and command the practice of frugality and rigid economy, while the whole influence of western civilization tends to lead the laborer to habits of show and luxury beyond his means. Our styles of architecture, of food, and of clothing are incomparably more costly than those of the Orient.

If a Japanese laborer had to live in our style of house, eat our animal flesh and pastries, and wear our clothing, to say nothing of the social demands upon his time and means, the cost of his living would be more than quadrupled, and the price of his products enhanced accordingly. This question of the comparative simplicity and cost of living and of production of the two civilizations will grow in importance as the two systems are brought more and more into contact and competition.

There are seven or eight hundred million people dwelling on the southern and eastern shores of Asia, the majority of them workers, living up to the requirements of this Oriental simplicity, who are all ready to compete with our people in every branch of human industry. And it may be worth our while to inquire if the demands of our social system do not handicap our laborer too heavily in the contest. Of course it is not to be contemplated that our laborers are to be put upon the rice, fish, or vegetable diet of these eastern workers. Our climate alone utterly forbids such a consummation, if, in any view, it were desirable. The labor-saving machinery, created from the active brains of our inventors, so often looked upon by laboring men as destructive of employment and ruinous to their interests, constitutes for the present the barrier which protects them and their interests against the rapid and perhaps lowering competition of the vast masses of laborers to which I have alluded. But this is not all that is needed. The reduction of taxation and equalization of the burdens of government, as far as possible, the multiplication of cheap means of transportation, the building of economical and comfortable houses in cities, the positive prevention of swindling in food and clothing, the rigid scrutiny of all beverages sold, and the prohibition, under the severest penalties, of the sale of impure drinks, and the encouragement of proper co-operative associations for the purchase and sale of good and cheap provisions, are all necessary for the welfare of our great laboring population, the producers of our wealth and prosperity.

THOS. B. VAN BUREN,
Consul-General.

UNITED STATES CONSULATE-GENERAL,
Kanagawa, October 6, 1880.

TABLE A.—*Showing prices of food in Japan, according to quality.*

		Cents.
Rice	per pound..	2 to 3
Barley	do....	1¼ to 2
Wheat	do....	1 to 1¾
Millet	do....	¾ to 1
Wheat flour	do....	2 to 3
Salt	do....	½ to ¾
Sugar, common brown	do....	4 to 5
Sugar, white brown	do....	8 to 10
Peas	do....	1½ to 2
Beans	do....	1½ to 2
Potatoes, Irish	per 100 pounds..	20 to 40
Potatoes, sweet	do....	12 to 25
Onions	do....	20 to 40
Carrots	do....	20 to 30
Cabbages	do....	15 to 20
Egg plants	per pound..	1 to 1½
Parsnips	per 100 pounds..	20 to 30
Turnips	do....	10 to 20
Squashes	do....	11 to 15
Watermelons	each..	2 to 5
Muskmelons	do....	1 to 1½
Peaches	per pound..	2 to 3
Pears	do....	1 to 2
Plums	do....	2 to 3
Grapes	do....	2 to 2½
Ducks, tame	each..	20 to 35
Ducks, wild	do....	15 to 30
Geese, tame	do....	40 to 80
Geese, wild	do....	30 to 50
Pigeons	do....	10 to 12
Pheasants	do....	10 to 20
Fresh fish	per pound..	2 to 20
Oysters	per quart..	6 to 10
Clams	do....	6 to 10
Salt fish	per pound..	3 to 10
Beef	do....	12 to 18
Pork	do....	10 to 15

As I have remarked, little animal flesh is eaten by the laborer. It is only in the open ports that it is at all used.

Milk, butter, and cheese are also unknown articles of food.

TABLE B.—*Japanese taxation.*

Land tax (local and General Government), 3 per cent. on valuation.

Corporations: On sales amounting to—	Yen.	Sen.
10,000 yen and over	15	00
7,000 to 10,000 yen	13	00
5,000 to 7,000 yen	10	00
3,000 to 5,000 yen	7	00
1,000 to 3,000 yen	5	00
700 to 1,000 yen	3	00
Under 700 yen	1	50

Merchants, wholesale: On sales amounting to—

	Yen.	Sen.
10,000 yen and over	15	00
7,000 to 10,000 yen	13	00
5,000 to 7,000 yen	10	00
3,000 to 5,000 yen	7	00
1,000 to 3,000 yen	5	00
700 to 1,000 yen	3	00
500 to 700 yen	2	00
300 to 500 yen	1	00
100 to 300 yen		50
Under 100 yen		25

Merchants, retail, and goods brokers: On sales amounting to—

	Yen.	Sen.
10,000 yen and over	15	00
7,000 to 10,000 yen	13	00
5,000 to 7,000 yen	10	00
3,000 to 5,000 yen	7	00
1,000 to 3,000 yen	5	00
700 to 1,000 yen	3	00
500 to 700 yen	2	00
300 to 500 yen	1	00
100 to 300 yen		5
30 to 100 yen		2.5

Public and private libraries, lenders of furniture and articles of clothing, &c.: On gross income .... 1 per cent.
Commission merchants: On gross commissions received .... 1½ per cent.
Contractors: On gross receipts .... 1½ per cent.

Manufactures, corporations: On sales amounting to—

	Yen.	Sen.
10,000 yen and over	15	00
7,000 to 10,000 yen	13	00
5,000 to 7,000 yen	10	00
3,000 to 5,000 yen	5	00
1,000 to 3,000 yen	3	00
700 to 1,000 yen	2	00
500 to 700 yen	1	00
300 to 500 yen		50
Under 300 yen		25

Mechanics: House-painters, clock, paper, and lacquer-ware makers, carvers, image-makers, photographers, pen-makers, picture-painters, match manufacturers, makers and mixers of colors, embroiderers, tailors, washmen, gold, silver, and tin smiths, pot and kettle workers, blacksmiths, carpenters, locksmiths, porcelain and bronze workers, same as above.

Carriers: Carriages—

	Yen.
2-horse carts per annum	3
1-horse cart per annum	2
Jinrickishas to carry two persons	2
Jinrickishas to carry one person	1
Wheelbarrows	1
Pack-horses	1
Man-carts, two men	1
Man carts, four men	2

Auctioneers: On gross sales .... 3 to 5 per cent.
Theatrical, acrobatic, and other exhibitions: In houses, on gross receipts.. 5 per cent.

	Yen.	Sen.
Billiard-rooms, bowling-alleys, archery galleries: Per month	1	00

Eating-houses: On gross receipts of—

	Yen.	Sen.
800 yen and over	12	00
From 500 to 800 yen	10	00
From 300 to 500 yen	6	00
From 200 to 300 yen	3	00
200 and under	1	50

Hotels, with stables attached: On receipts of—

	Yen.	Sen.
800 yen and over, per annum	10	00
500 to 800 yen per annum	9	00
300 to 500 yen per annum	7	00
200 to 300 yen per annum	2	50
100 to 200 yen per annum	1	00
Under 100 yen per annum		50

Eating-houses where only one kind of food is permitted to be served: On gross receipts of—

	Yen.	Sen.
800 yen and over, per annum	10	00
500 to 800 yen per annum	7	50
300 to 500 yen per annum	5	00
200 to 300 yen per annum	2	50
100 to 200 yen per annum	1	00
Under 100 yen per annum		50

Pawn-shops: On gross receipts of—

10,000 yen and over	15	00
7,000 to 10,000 yen	13	00
5,000 to 7,000 yen	10	00
3,000 to 5,000 yen	7	00
1,000 to 3,000 yen	5	00
700 to 1,000 yen	3	00
500 to 700 yen	2	00
300 to 500 yen	1	00
100 to 300 yen		50
Under 100 yen		25

Exchange brokers: On income, same as above.
Transportation companies: On gross earnings of, same as above.

Junk-shops: On transactions of—

	Yen.	Sen.
5,000 yen and over	10	00
3,000 to 5,000 yen	9	00
1,000 to 3,000 yen	7	00
700 to 1,000 yen	5	00
500 to 700 yen	3	00
300 to 500 yen	2	00
Under 300 yen	1	00

Booths (for tea drinking): Per month, each | 50
Places for sale of ice-water: Per month each | 80
Bath-houses: On gross receipts | 1 per cent.
Barbers' license: Two yen per year, and 1 per cent. of gross receipts.
Intelligence offices: License of 5 yen per year.
Dancing-masters, music-teachers, street story-tellers, and actors: License, 1 yen per month.
Wrestlers: License of 50 sen per month.
Regular singing and dancing girls: License from 1.50 to 3.50 yen per month.
Licensed attendants upon dancing and singing entertainments: Seventy-five sen to 2 yen per month.

Water-power mills for hulling rice:

	Yen.	Sen.
20 stamps and over, per annum	5	00
10 to 20 stamps per annum	3	00
5 to 10 stamps per annum	1	50
3 to 5 stamps per annum		50
Less than 3 stamps per annum		30

Live stock:

Horses, each, per annum	1	00
Grown cattle, each, per annum		20
Young cattle, each, per annum		10
Sheep and hogs, each, per annum		05

Marine licenses:

Junks or native vessels, with a capacity to carry 500 bushels and under, per annum	1	00
Every 500 bushels additional, per annum	1	00
Steamers, each 100 tons measurement, per annum	15	00
Sailing vessels, foreign model, each 100 tons, per annum	10	00
Small boats, 20 sen to 1 yen per annum, according to size.		

Shooting licenses:

Professional hunters, per annum	1	20
Others, per annum	10	00

Horse and cattle dealers:

Licenses, per annum	2	00
For every animal sold, additional, per annum	1	00

Manufacturers of weights and measures: Twenty-five per cent. ad valorem.
Druggists: License, 2 yen per annum. All patent medicines, 25 per cent. ad valorem.
Manufacturers of alcoholic drinks: The tax is levied upon the quantity of rice used in brewing. Common saké (a species of wine), from 2 to 4 yen, according to quality, upon each koku (about 5 bushels) of rice used.

Tobacco:

	Yen.
License, wholesale dealers, per annum	10
License, retail dealers, per annum	5

There is also a stamp tax of 2 per cent. on all sales.

Stamped paper: All written transactions of 10 yen and above pay a tax of 3 sen. No agreement in writing can be enforced without a stamp.

Copyright: The price of 6 copies of the work is charged.

Stock-brokers: Ten per cent. of commissions.

Bankers: On every 1,000 yen loaned, 7 yen.

Passengers on foreign vessels, 10 sen per head.

Houses of prostitution, 1 to 7 yen per month.

Every inmate, 1 to 4 yen per month.

Taxes are collected in the different fu and ken (provinces of the Empire), and the expenditures for local purposes must first be approved by the General Government.

CHINA.

AMOY.

REPORT BY CONSUL GOLDSBOROUGH.

MALE LABORERS.

1. The rates of wages, &c.: The same as stated in tables.

2. The cost of living, &c.: About $3 per month.

3. Comparison between 1884 and 1878 in wages, &c.: The same; no difference.

4. The habits of the working classes, &c.: Steady.

5. The feeling between employé and employer, &c.: Generally good.

6. The organized condition of labor, &c.: There is none.

7. The prevalency of strikes, &c.: Of very rare occurrence, and then always settled by arbitration.

8. Are the working people free to purchase the necessaries of life wherever they choose, or do the employers impose any conditions in this regard? Those who get the pay but no provisions are free to deal wherever they choose; but those who are furnished with provisions are subject to the conditions imposed by the employers in this regard.

9. Co-operative societies, &c.: Good.

10. The general condition of working people, &c., how they live: Cheaply. Their homes: Cheap. Their food: Common. Their clothes: Common. Their chances for bettering their condition: They may expect. Their ability to lay up something for old age or sickness: Rather hard to do so on account of small wages. Their moral and physical condition: Rather bad, because most of them are opium smokers. The influence for good or evil, by which they are surrounded: The opium-smoking is the chief evil.

11. The means for their safety in factories, &c.: No factories, &c., here.

12. The political rights enjoyed by working-men: They know little of law, but still usually enjoy the political rights as others do. Their influences on legislation: They have none. The share borne by them in local and general taxation: Very little. The tendency of legislation in regard to labor and the working people: No change during centuries.

13. The causes leading to the emigration of the working people and influencing their selection of their new homes: To better their condition.

The principal occupations of the emigrants, &c.: Mining and general labor.

1. The number of women and children, or the closest possible approximation thereto, employed here in industrial pursuits, not including ordinary household duties or domestic servants, classifying as follows: Impossible for one to say.

a. Manufacturing and mechanical: None.

b. Commercial, including transportation: None.

c. Professional and personal, including Government officials, and clerks, teachers, artists, chemists, hotel and boarding-house keepers, journalists, laundresses, musicians, inventors, bankers, brokers, lecturers, public speakers, &c.: None.

d. Agriculture: Some help their husbands and parents, but get no pay.

e. Mining: None.

f. All other pursuits: Impossible to answer.

2. The minimum, maximum, and average wages paid to female adults: None.

3. Their hours of labor: No certain hours.

4. The moral and physical condition of such employés: Rather good.

5. The means provided for the improvement of these employés and by whom: No such means provided.

6. The means provided, in case of fire or other dangers, for their safety: No such means provided.

7. The provisions made by the employers in regard to sanitary measures, and for the care of the sick and disabled: No such means provided.

8. Has there been any increase during the past five years in the wages paid women and in the prices of the necessaries of life, or otherwise? None.

What are the effects of employment of women on the wages of men, and on general social and industrial conditions? An unknown quantity.

9. The state of education among the women employed, and among their children: The women and children know very little of—or rather have no education at all.

W. E. GOLDSBOROUGH,
Consul.

UNITED STATES CONSULATE,
Amoy, ——, 1884.

I. GENERAL TRADES.

Wages paid per month of ten hours per day in Amoy.

Occupations.	Lowest.	Highest.	Occupations.	Lowest.	Highest.
BUILDING TRADES.			BUILDING TRADES—continued.		
Bricklayers	$7 00	$9 00	Plumbers	$5 00	$6 00
Assistants	(*)	(*)	Assistants	4 00	5 00
Masons	9 00	18 00	Carpenters	8 00	10 00
Assistants	6 00	9 00	Assistants	(*)	(*)
Plasterers	7 00	9 00			
Assistants	(*)	(*)	OTHER TRADES.		
Roofers	7 00	9 00			
Assistants	(*)	(*)	Bakers	8 00	9 00

* Provisions only.

Occupations.	Lowest.	Highest.	Occupations.	Lowest.	Highest.
OTHER TRADES—continued.			**OTHER TRADES—continued.**		
Blacksmiths	†$4 00	‡$6 00	Jewelers	†$14 00	‡$16 00
Strikers	†2 90	‡3 00	Assistants	(*)	(*)
Book-binders	†4 00	†6 00	Laborers, porters, &c.	5 00	6 00
Brick-makers	6 00	8 00	Nail-makers (hand)	†4 00	†6 00
Assistants	(*)	(*)	Assistants	(*)	(*)
Brewers	7 00	8 00	Potters	4 00	5 00
Assistants	(*)	(*)	Assistants	(*)	(*)
Butchers	8 00	10 00	Printers	5 00	6 00
Assistants	(*)	(*)	Assistants	(*)	(*)
Brass-founders	6 00	8 00	Sail-makers	8 00	10 00
Assistants	(*)	(*)	Assistants	(*)	(*)
Cabinet-makers	6 00	8 00	Tanners	†9 00	†10 00
Assistants	(*)	(*)	Assistants	(*)	(*)
Confectioners		3 00	Tailors	†6 00	†9 00
Coopers	†1 50	†1 70	Assistants	(*)	(*)
Cutlers	4 00	8 00	Tinsmiths	†9 00	†10 00
Distillers	†7 00	†8 00	Assistants	(*)	(*)
Dyers	†10 00	†20 00	Weavers (outside of mills):		
Assistants	(*)	(*)	Of cloth	†7 00	†8 00
Engravers	8 00	10 00	Of silk	†22 00	†24 00
Gardeners	5 00	7 00	Assistants	(*)	(*)
Assistants	(*)	(*)			
Hatters	†5 00	†6 00			
Assistants	(*)	(*)			

* Provisions only.   † With provisions.

VII. Ship-yards and Ship-building.

Wages paid per month of ten hours per day in ship-yards (Chinese junks, cargo boats, and small sampans) in Amoy.

Occupations.	Lowest.	Highest.
Carpenters	*$10 00	*$12 00
Assistants	(†)	(†)

* With provisions supplied by employer.   † Provisions only.

VIII. Seamen's Wages.

Wages paid per month to seamen (officers and men) distinguishing between ocean, coast, and river navigation, and between sail and steam, in Amoy.

Occupations.	Lowest.	Highest.
Seamen (foreign ships)	$17 00	$20 00
Seamen (Chinese junks)	6 00	8 00

IX. Store and Shop Wages.

Wages paid per month of twelve hours per day in stores, wholesale or retail, to males and females, in Amoy.

Occupations.	Lowest.	Highest.
Shop-keepers	*$2 00	*$3 00

* With provisions, and very small percentage on sales.

X. HOUSEHOLD WAGES IN TOWNS AND CITIES.

Wages paid per month to household servants (towns and cities) in Amoy.

Occupations.	Lowest.	Highest.
Household servants (in native employment).................................	*$1 00	*$3 00

* With provisions.

NOTE.—Those employed by foreigners usually receive about three times as much as are paid by natives. No provisions.

XII. CORPORATION EMPLOYÉS

Wages paid per month of twelve hours per day to the corporation employés in the city of Amoy.

Occupations.	Lowest.	Highest.
Managers..	*$10 00	*$15 00
Accountants...	*6 00	*8 00
Assistants.	(†)	(†)

* With provisions. † Provisions only.

HANKOW.

REPORT BY CONSUL SHEPARD.

In answer to "Labor Circular" of February 15, I have the honor to submit the following statistics and remarks:

The forms given have little pertinency to the state of affairs in this locality, from facts which will appear, and any attempt to follow them would afford little information that would be valuable. In this jurisdiction there are no laborers in Classes II, III, IV, VI, XII, XII, XIV, and no establishment of the kind in which to labor.

GENERAL TRADES.

The rate of wages for journeymen mechanics differs little in the various trades, 13 or 14 cents per day being a fair average, with food furnished by employers. Apprentices receive from 3¾ to 4 cents per day with food. The cost of food in such cases will average 5 cents daily per man. All trades have nearly the same standard of wages, with perhaps a slight advance on the above rates for blacksmiths, founders, and brass-workers.

The income of a sampan-man or boatman is 5,000 cash per month, as near as may be, equivalent to $4.80, Mexicans, varying slightly according to rates of exchange or the scarcity of silver. This sum includes his boat as well as his own labor and his cost of living.

A cook, when employed by native households, can average 1,500 cash per month, $1.40; but he has besides certain allowable "squeezes" or percentages paid by those of whom he purchases the family provisions as well as advances of prices, which is invariably the practice with his employer. In foreign employ, the same man gets from $7 to $10 per month wages, and probably his "squeezes" net him as much more.

Ordinary coolie labor in this locality is 120 cash per day, say 10½ cents, the laborer finding himself. This statement will hold true of the pay of Classes V, VII, VIII, IX, X, XI, and XV.

FOOD AND FOOD PRICES.

The common food for all laboring people is fish, pork, rice, vegetables, oil, and salt. Rice costs about 1½ cents per pound; fish, 3 cents; pork, 8 cents; vegetables, 1½ cents; oil, 6½ cents; salt, 5 cents.

RENTS.

As to rents, it is not easy to give a reliable estimate of the cost. Most agriculturists own their dwellings, which are rude and primitive at the best. The laboring classes generally live in frail structures of bamboo matting, or of reeds plastered with mud. In the cities the crowded apartments cost each occupant about 10 cents per month, as nearly as I can ascertain, but the data is not reliable. I fail to learn anything I can absolutely state as the fact.

HARACTERISTICS OF HANKOW LABORERS.

The Chinese are a patient, hard-working people, steady at employment, but very slow workers. They accomplish little as compared with American laborers, probaly not one-fourth as much, but they have no intermittent seventh day of rest.

LABOR ORGANIZATIONS.

I can learn of no organizations of labor to control wages, nor any attempt to associate for influence upon prices. The laborer is as free as his employer, and slight social distinction exists between them. They work when they please, spend their wages as they please, and for what they please. It is rare, however, to see a person intoxicated, though strong drinks are common. As a rule they are used with extreme moderation.

CLOTHING.

The clothing of male laborers is very simple and inexpensive. Two garments, generally, are only worn, trousers and a sort of loose blouse, both of ordinary cotton cloth, either white or blue. In cold weather these are padded with cotton batting. The better classes vary the upper garment by elongation, when the blouse becomes a robe, which is often covered by a third garment, a sleeveless tunic of cloth. Materials are varied as means allow, and silks and satins supplant the cotton cloth. The cost, of course, depends on material, but the essential cotton garments of laborers cost about $3, and two suits last at least a year.

POLITICAL RIGHTS.

Common people have no political rights, and seem not to care for them. They live in abject fear of rulers, but appear not to discuss possibility of change. One would judge they never thought, and were contented with their abject condition. No emigration has ever occurred from this region. Education, even in the Chinese sense, is very limited, but most men can read a few characters and write them as well, and can keep accounts.

FEMALE LABOR.

Female labor is only known as within domestic seclusion, as a rule. In agricultural districts women are seen at field labor, but not commonly. No statistics can be given on this point. Very few females are taught to read.

ISAAC F. SHEPARD,
Consul.

SOUTHERN CHINA.

REPORT BY CONSUL SEYMOUR.

I have the honor, in compliance with the "Labor Circular," to make the following statements showing the value of labor in Canton and vicinity, or Southern China.

The rates of wages paid to laborers of various classes are as follows, and the compensation stated generally requires their services from daylight to dark, with half-pay allowance for holidays, and an understanding that every laborer provides his own sustenance; an hour of time being allowed for mid-day meal and a few minutes, forenoon and afternoon, for tea and refreshments.

CLASS $4.50 TO $5.50 PER MONTH.

Bakers, book-binders, brick-makers, wine-makers, butchers, confectioners, cigar-makers, distillers of essences, boatmen, dyers, gardeners, hat and cap makers, shoemakers, nail-makers, potters, printers, leatherware makers, saddle and harness makers, tailors, tinsmiths, porters, and city laborers.

CLASS $4.50 TO $8.00 PER MONTH.

Brick-layers, masons, plasterers, roofers, plumbers, carpenters, blacksmiths, brass-founders, cabinet-makers, coopers, cutlers, engravers, jewelers, lithographers, sail-makers, weavers (outside of mills, there are few worthy of the name of mills), glass-makers, and ship-yard laborers.

OTHER CLASSES.

Employés in shops and stores in cities get from $3.50 to $4.50 per month

Sailors on Chinese junks and native boats get from $3.50 to $5.50 per month, and on river and coast steamers, from $6 to $14 per month, according to experience and responsibility. Stevedores range from $9 to $13.50 per month; soldiers $4.50 per month; teachers, with from twenty-five to forty pupils, receive from $3 to $4.50 per year for each pupil, with "holiday presents" according to circumstances.

Telegraph operators (Chinese ex-students in United States) get from $20 to $30 per month.

In mines and for mining men receive 20 cents per day, and women and boys, for pumping and scouring, 15 cents per day.

Household wages, to indoor servants and for country land laborers in the service of native employers, are usually about $1.50 per month, with food, and feast-day gifts which last item is fairly and equitably respected, and so applied as to be an incentive to industry.

Foreigners usually get good cooks and male house-servants at from $7 to $10 per month; the servants generally arrange with the cook for "chow," or food, at $2 to $2.50 per month.

The staple article of food is rice, and the ordinary cost of nourishment for laborers and the industrial classes of Chinese is from $2 to $2.50 per month, according to fluctuations in the value of rice and the native ground-nut oil (in lieu of butter), and morsels of pork, fish, &c. In fact, the cost of living has been reduced to the minimum standard, and all seem to be healthy and contented; and as for industry, every ounce of muscle in men, women (and children above three years of age) is utilized until indolence is scarcely visible.

The currency of the common people is a small copper coin called "cash," equivalent to about 1 mill, or one-tenth of a cent, and that of the business classes in silver, for weighing which nearly every one is supplied with coin-scales or small wooden substitutes for "steel-yards."

There is very little chance for any one to get out of the groove of life in which his lot is cast.

Although the severities of "caste," as known in some countries of Asia are not in force in China, the boundaries and spheres of the various classes are clearly defined and practically recognized and enforced.

If the working people of the United States were compelled subsist on the dirt, and conform to the economies of Asia, which holds half of the population of the globe, and realized the miserable scale or standard of human existence prevalent in these cheap-labor countries, between which and the well-requited industry of the United States the adoption of international agrarianism would establish an average; there would be less clamor in favor of a pernicious policy which contemplates competition between two systems of labor, with the certainty of leveling down American labor to the point at which it is proposed to elevate the value of Asiatic labor, which is satisfied with from 20 to 50 cents per day, and garbage for food.

CHARLES SEYMOUR,
Consul.

UNITED STATES CONSULATE,
Canton, China, June 9, 1884.

CONTINENT OF AFRICA.

MOROCCO.

REPORT BY CONSUL MATHEWS.

In compliance with your labor circular, dated February 15 (which I only received last month from California, where it was sent with my mail from here), I have the honor to transmit herewith the statistics of labor wages in this country.

The cost of living varies in accordance with the position and character of the workmen, as, where town-people are in the habit of buying meat, fish, and wheaten bread, the countrymen can live on oaten cakes or bread made of dari seed, which does not cost above 3 cents per person per day, where in the town the average would be from 7 to 10 cents for a laborer's food.

The working classes are generally of abstemious habits; though not generally trustworthy, they are steady and hard working when well looked after; otherwise they are neglectful; as a rule they are not saving and only live from day to day.

The feeling between employers and employés is only indifferent; neither of them takes interest in the other's welfare; hence their lack of prosperity.

There is no organization in the condition of labor nor of capital; all is conventional, and labor and capital are simply relative to demand and supply.

Strikes are unknown in the country, workmen being always to be found to replace those who may refuse work.

No conditions are imposed to laborers with regard to the purchase of their necessaries of life. The wages are paid in native currency or Spanish coins at current rate of exchange.

There are no co-operative societies, not sufficient interest being taken by the people to better the condition of each other.

The general condition of the working people is not of the most enviable, being themselves careless of the future, they spend all they gain, and when sickness or old age comes they have recourse to charity.

There are neither mines, factories, nor other enterprises where a number of workmen are employed. The great mineral resources of the country are not permitted to be developed.

Workmen have no political rights, nor seek any; they have no influence and no special legislation is established with regard to them. Few, if any, working people ever emigrate.

FEMALE LABOR.

It is impossible to get at anything like a fair estimate of what number of women and children are employed in any district of Morocco. All depends upon the condition of the country and the abundance of

349

crops or otherwise, as when crops are plentiful field labor is preferred, and the number of hands working in the town gets reduced by nearly 75 per cent. over other times when scarcity compels them to seek work in towns.

Women and children as a rule work at minimum rate of wages, and no distinction of any sort is made between them and men as to the treatment or provisions, &c.

There has been an increase of wages generally within the last five years, something like 25 to 35 per cent., for as much as workmen and women generally ask higher pay as they recover from the effects of the famine which compelled them to abandon the fields and seek work at any price.

The average here is calculated on one-half of highest and lowest wages, the greater portion of workmen, women, and children being paid at the medium rates, more especially as the improved condition of the fields and country keeps away from town most of the cheaper hands.

The hours of labor for working people hired by the day in Morocco are from 8 o'clock in the morning to half past 3 in the afternoon, and from 6 in the morning to 4 o'clock in the afternoon, occupying one hour at noon for rest.

The education among the Moors, such as it is, belongs exclusively to the male sex.

FELIX A. MATHEWS,
Consul.

UNITED STATES CONSULATE,
Tangier, November 6, 1884.

I. GENERAL TRADES.

Wages paid per day of ten to twelve hours in Tangier.

Occupations.	Lowest.	Highest.	Average.
BUILDING TRADES.			
Bricklayers	$0 50	$1 50	$0 75
Hod-carriers	10	25	17½
Masons	50	2 00	1 25
Tenders	25	75	50
Plasterers	1 00	2 00	1 50
Tenders	25	75	50
Slaters	50	1 00	75
Roofers	50	1 00	75
Tenders	25	75	50
Plumbers	50	2 00	1 25
Assistants	25	75	50
Carpenters	50	1 50	1 00
OTHER TRADES.			
Bakers	40	1 00	70
Blacksmiths	20	1 50	85
Strikers	10	50	30
Book-binders	20	1 00	60
Brick-makers	10	50	30
Butchers	10	80	45
Brass-founders	50	1 50	1 00
Cabinet-makers	50	2 00	1 25
Confectioners	40	1 00	70
Coopers	40	2 00	1 20
Cutlers	40	1 50	95
Distillers	10	50	30
Drivers	10	50	30
Draymen and teamsters	10	20	15

Wages paid per day of ten to twelve hours in Tangier—Continued.

Occupations.	Lowest.	Highest.	Average.
OTHER TRADES—Continued.			
Dyers	$0 30	$1 00	$0 65
Engravers...	40	1 00	70
Furriers...,..	20	80	50
Gardeners...	20	40	30
Horseshoers...	20	40	30
Jewelers..	30	80	50
Laborers, porters, &c................................	10	40	25
Potters	25	75	50
Printers..	50	2 00	1 25
Teachers, public schools..............................	40	1 00	75
Saddle and harness makers.............................	40	2 00	1 20
Stevedores..	50	2 00	1 25
Tanners...	20	1 00	60
Tailors...	40	2 00	1 20
Tinsmiths...	20	1 00	60
Weavers (outside of mills)	40	1 00	70

IX. STORE AND SHOP WAGES.

Wages paid per week of sixty hours of six days in stores, wholesale and retail, to males and females in Tangier and other parts of Morocco.

Occupations.	Lowest.	Highest.	Average.
Shop men and women...................................	$1 20	$6 00	$3 60
Clerks	2 40	7 50	4 95
Errand boys and girls.................................	1 00	3 00	2 00

X. HOUSEHOLD WAGES IN TOWNS AND CITIES.

Wages paid per month to household servants (towns and cities) in Morocco, with board.

Occupations.	Lowest.	Highest.	Average.
General servants.....................................	$2 00	$10 00	$6 00
Waiters...	5 00	15 00	10 00
Grooms..	5 00	15 00	10 00
Stablemen...	3 00	10 00	6 50
Stewards and butlers	5 00	15 00	10 00
Cooks	5 00	15 00	10 00

XIII. GOVERNMENT DEPARTMENTS AND OFFICES.

Wages paid per month to employés in Government departments and offices—exclusive of tradesmen and laborers—in Tangier and neighborhood.

Occupations.	Lowest.	Highest.	Average.
Governors of towns	$30 00	$60 00	$45 00
Deputy governors.....................................	10 00	20 00	15 00
Lower functionaries	5 00	15 00	10 00
Custom-house:			
Administrators	60 00	90 00	75 00
Clerks	15 00	45 00	25 00
Under employés	10 00	30 00	20 00

CAPE COLONY.

REPORT BY CONSUL SILER, OF CAPE TOWN.

To report upon the labor question in South Africa is a matter of much difficulty, inasmuch as the scattered nature of the population, the varying conditions of the different districts, and the peculiarity of its industrial pursuits render generalization almost impossible; and details, if possible, are yet more difficult to obtain. In the outlying hamlets, at a distance from easy communication, wages depend almost entirely upon the demand for any special kind of labor, particularly mechanical. A carpenter who in Cape Town may earn 6s. a day, would, probably, under certain circumstances, treble that amount in an interior country town; this advance of wages would be due to the circumstance that a sudden demand for that class of labor had arisen, and so with all other hands.

A steady mechanic may generally rely on constant work at remunerative rates, but the prices of provisions varying considerably in different localities, the ratio between the cost of living and the rate of wages is hard to determine. At the present time depression is wide-spread, and as the mechanic is generally the first to feel the falling off of trade, it is not surprising that many skilled laborers have recently emigrated to more favorable lands. The Government railways have for some years employed a considerable number of skilled laborers, and at the present time a mechanic considers himself uncommonly fortunate when he obtains employment under Government.

Perhaps, next to railways, the greatest demand for skilled labor is at the diamond fields. The whole of the unskilled labor employed there is native. Engine drivers, fitters, carpenters, blacksmiths, and some other classes of tradesmen receive comparatively high wages, but the cost of living there is more than proportionately heavy. In the copper mines most of the heavy work is performed by native labor at low wages.

Manufactures in Cape Colony may be fairly stated as non-existent. A few boots and shoes are made, but nine-tenths of the finished leather is imported.

With regard to wood-work there is little done beyond actual immediate local requirements; even staves for the barrels and casks required in the wine trade are imported. Wagons and carts for rough country work are made to a limited extent, but the better class of vehicles come from foreign sources.

The wine industry is entirely in the hands of the Dutch and Huguenot settlers in the vicinity of Capetown, whose employés and laborers still live in the old patriarchal style, either in the homestead or on the property of their employers. Nearly every process necessary for the manufacture of wine is performed by native labor under the immediate direction of the viticultural farmer or his relatives. Of late there have been established several breweries, doing a good business in the lighter brews; but this is a matter more of experience and capital than labor.

Up to the time of the present business depression, which has now extended over two years, the artisan was the most independent man in the country, and frequently commanded his own price and dictated his own hours of labor; particularly was this so in the remote districts.

Any man may enjoy the privilege of the elective franchise here by taking the oath of allegiance to the Crown, and registering his name at the voting precinct. But with the possible exception of Cape Town and Kimberley, the workingmen as a body have no distinct political influence.

I know of no effort having been made here for the moral improvement and elevation of the laborer. However, the Europeans and those of European extraction will probably compare favorably with men of their class in most countries; but the condition of the native laborer is wretched and degraded beyond conception. He is regarded by his white brother as no better than a beast of the field, and it is doubtful if his own opinion of himself differs very materially; drink is his bane, a supply is always near at hand, and he will eagerly barter his food and clothes in exchange for it.

There are no societies or trades union among the workingmen of this colony; indeed between them there seems to be no common object or interest. It is true that a somewhat serious strike, terminating in a riot in which some lives were lost, occurred among the mining laborers at Kimberley some months since, but that had no relation to wages or hours of labor, but was simply a protest against a law recently enacted which required every employé to be stripped and searched on ascending from the mines. This seemed, and was, a humiliating ordeal for white men to submit to, but they did eventually submit to it.

In the following schedule of wages and prices of food and clothing I have taken the rates obtaining in different districts and localities, and endeavored to reduce the same to a general average; and the result arrived at I believe to be reliable.

JAS. W. SILER,
Consul.

UNITED STATES CONSULATE,
Cape Town, July 22, 1884.

I. GENERAL TRADES.

Wages paid per week of sixty hours in Cape Town.

Occupations.	Lowest.	Highest.	Average.
BUILDING TRADES.			
Bricklayers	$7 00	$12 00	$10 00
Hod-carriers	3 60	6 00	4 75
Masons	7 00	12 00	10 00
Tenders	2 50	4 75	3 60
Plasterers	6 00	8 00	7 00
Tenders	2 50	4 75	3 60
Slaters	9 00	12 00	10 50
Roofers	9 00	12 00	10 50
Tenders	2 50	4 75	3 60
Plumbers	8 00	10 00	9 00
Assistants	2 50	5 00	3 00
Carpenters	7 00	12 00	10 00
Gas-fitters	6 00	8 00	7 00
OTHER TRADES.			
Bakers	7 29	10 94	7 47
Blacksmiths	8 00	11 00	9 00
Strikers	6 00	7 50	6 50
Book-binders	5 00	9 00	7 20
Brick-makers	5 00	9 00	7 20

Wages paid per week of sixty hours in Cape Town—Continued.

Occupations.	Lowest.	Highest.	Average.
OTHER TRADES—Continued.			
Brewers	$7 00	$11 00	$9 00
Butchers	10 00	12 00	11 00
Brass-founders	8 00	12 00	10 00
Cabinet-makers	8 00	12 00	10 00
Confectioners	5 00	8 00	7 00
Cigar-makers	8 00	12 00	10 00
Coopers	8 00	12 00	10 00
Cutlers	7 00	11 00	8 00
Distillers	10 00	14 00	12 00
Drivers	5 00	6 00	5 50
Draymen and teamsters	5 00	6 00	5 50
Cab and carriage	5 00	7 00	6 00
Street railways	6 00	8 00	7 00
Dyers	5 00	8 00	6 50
Engravers	8 00	11 00	9 00
Gardeners	5 00	12 00	8 00
Hatters	8 00	13 00	11 00
Horse-shoers	8 00	11 00	9 00
Jewelers	8 00	12 00	10 00
Laborers, porters, &c	3 00	5 00	4 00
Lithographers	10 00	16 00	12 00
Mill-wrights	8 00	12 00	7 50
Printers	7 00	15 00	11 00
Teachers, public schools	8 00	15 00	12 00
Saddle and harness makers	5 00	8 00	7 00
Sail-makers	5 00	10 00	8 00
Stevedores	8 00	14 00	11 00
Tanners	5 00	12 00	9 00
Tailors	7 00	10 00	8 50
Telegraph operators	8 00	12 00	10 00
Tinsmiths	7 00	13 00	11 00

VI. RAILWAY EMPLOYÉS.

Wages paid per day to railway employés (those engaged about stations, as well as those engaged on the engines and cars, linemen, railroad laborers, &c.) in Cape Colony.

Occupations.	Lowest.	Highest.	Average.
Maintenance department.			
General inspectors	$3 58	$4 00	$3 75
Inspectors	2 43	2 90	2 50
Subinspectors	2 10	2 20	2 14
Timekeepers	1 92	2 25	2 00
Scale examiner	1 84	2 10	1 90
Detectives	1 60	1 60	1 60
Yard foremen	2 43	2 75	2 50
Foremen carpenters	2 43	2 45	2 44
Carpenters	1 58	2 20	1 75
Blacksmiths	1 56	2 60	1 90
Gaugers	1 46	1 95	1 60
Plate-layers	81	97	85
Masons	1 82	2 43	1 95
Painters	1 33	2 20	1 50
Plumbers	1 20	2 20	1 60
Strikers	48	1 40	80
Fitters	2 55	2 55	2 55
Sawyers	1 33	2 45	1 50
Sail-makers	1 46	1 46	1 46
Watchmen	1 20	1 20	1 20
Laborers	36	1 20	50
Office attendants	97	1 10	1 00
Traffic department.			
Foremen	1 20	1 78	1 30
Guards	1 40	2 00	1 60
Foremen ticket collectors	1 58	1 58	1 58
Ticket collectors	1 48	1 48	1 48
Shunters	1 46	1 78	1 55
Porters	73	1 45	90

Occupations.	Lowest.	Highest.	Average.
Traffic department—Continued.			
Watchmen	$1 20	$1 20	$1 20
Signalmen	85	1 40	95
Signalwomen	10	75	20
Locomotive department.			
Timekeepers	1 21	1 94	1 60
Office boys	48	60	50
Foremen:			
Locomotive works	2 67	3 05	2 50
Running shed	3 24	3 68	3 35
Carriage	3 04	3 04	3 04
Smiths	3 44	3 46	3 45
Pattern-makers	2 69	2 73	2 70
Boiler-makers	2 69	2 83	2 72
Helpers	1 07	1 88	1 45
Fitters	1 88	2 98	2 65
Tinsmiths	2 16	2 16	2 16
Coppersmiths	2 43	2 43	2 43
Spring-makers	2 73	2 73	2 73
Blacksmiths	1 88	3 04	2 10
Strikers	1 21	1 82	1 40
Turners	1 76	2 98	2 60
Brass-finishers	2 73	2 73	2 73
Machinists	1 21	2 73	2 20
Molders:			
Iron	1 48	2 98	2 10
Brass	2 98	2 98	2 98
Assistants	54	1 21	80
Drillers	1 29	1 62	1 40
Carriage makers and joiners	1 62	2 73	1 50
Painters:			
Engine	1 21	2 73	2 20
Carriage	66	2 43	1 50
Trimmers	1 21	2 02	1 65
Sawyers	1 35	1 76	1 40
Sail-makers	1 76	2 09	1 90
Laborers (European and native)	95	1 62	1 25
Engine-drivers	1 70	2 43	1 95
Engine firemen	1 09	1 70	1 30
Cleaners (European and native)	24	1 46	75
Stationary-engine drivers	40	1 88	1 70
Shedmen	1 35	1 82	1 40
Watchmen	54	1 58	1 10
Pumpers (European and native)	54	1 58	1 00
Carriage and wagon examiners	2 29	2 43	2 35
Wagon-lifters	1 21	2 06	1 85
Apprentices	40	1 48	70
Boys	48	48	48
Gatemen	1 46	1 46	1 46
Wheelmen	1 21	1 62	1 30
Brick-archmen	1 03	1 03	1 03
Carriage-fitters	2 29	2 43	2 30

VIII. SEAMEN'S WAGES.

Wages paid per month to seamen (officers and men) in Cape Town, Cape of Good Hope.

Occupations.	Lowest.	Highest.	Average.
First mates	$30 00	$50 00	$35 00
Second mates	20 00	30 00	25 00
Seamen:			
Able	10 00	15 00	12 00
Ordinary	8 00	10 00	9 00
Boys	4 00	7 00	5 00
Cabin stewards	18 00	30 00	20 00
Cabin cooks	25 00	40 00	30 00
Ships' cooks	20 00	30 00	25 00

NOTE.—The above figures give a fair average of the wages out of this port, whether by steam or sailing vessels, ocean-going or coastwise. There are no river-going craft in the colony and no really navigable streams. However, shipping of men at this port is mostly confined to sailing vessels: the mail steamers shipping their crews in England for the entire voyage—outward and return.

IX. STORE AND SHOP WAGES.

Wages paid per week of fifty hours in stores, wholesale or retail, to males and females, in Cape Town, Cape of Good Hope.

Occupations.	Lowest.	Highest.	Average.
Book-keepers	$10 00	$30 00	$20 00
Assistant book-keepers	5 00	10 00	7 00
Salesmen, dry goods	8 00	15 00	10 00
Saleswomen, dry goods	5 00	7 00	6 00
Shop-walkers	8 00	15 00	10 00
Salesmen, hardware	10 00	20 00	15 00
Porters	5 00	6 00	5 50
Boys	2 50	4 00	3 00
Chemists' assistants	10 00	20 00	12 00
Grocery clerks	5 00	12 00	8 00
Barmen	5 00	10 00	8 00
Barmaids	6 00	12 00	9 00
Shipping clerks	8 00	16 00	10 00

XII. CORPORATION EMPLOYÉS.

Wages paid per week of fifty-four hours to the corporation employés in the city of Cape Town.

Occupations.	Lowest.	Highest.	Average.
Laborers	$6 00	$6 00	$6 00
Policemen	8 00	12 00	10 00
Engineers, steam fire-engines	20 00	20 00	20 00
Blacksmiths	10 00	10 00	10 00
Turncocks	7 50	7 50	7 50
Plumbers	12 00	12 00	12 00
Assistants	8 00	8 00	8 00
Messenger	7 50	7 50	7 50
Assistant	4 50	4 50	4 50
Overseer water supply	12 00	12 00	12 00

XIII. GOVERNMENT DEPARTMENTS AND OFFICES.

Wages paid per annum to employés of Government, exclusive of tradesmen and laborers, in Cape Town, Cape Colony.

Occupations.	Lowest.	Highest.	Average.
Ministerial departments, civil establishment.			
Chief clerks	$15 00	$20 00	$18 00
Clerks	5 00	12 00	9 00
Messengers	3 00	5 00	3 50
Storekeepers	12 00	17 50	13 00
Jailers	4 00	4 00	4 00
Office-keepers	4 00	5 00	4 50
Interpreters	5 00	7 50	6 00

Articles.	Price.	Articles.	Price.
Oatmeal..................per pound..	$0 12	Wine (ordinary)............per gallon...	$1 25
Flour ....do....	07	Brandy (colonial).................do...	1 96
Bread .... do...	07	Milk.................. per bottle..	0 08
Mutton.........................do...	14	Candles ....per pound..	28
Beef.........................do...	13	Lamp-oil ....per gallon .	76
Pork ....do...	20	Kerosene.........................do....	60
Bacon.........................do...	30	Shirts........................ each...	1 50
Butter:		Shoes........................per pair..	2 50
Fresh ....do....	54	Jackets .... each..	3 25
Salt........ .. ..do ...	44	Waistcoats...................... do ...	1 50
Herrings ....per tin..	54	Trowsers .... per pair..	3 00
Cheese ....per pound..	34	Hats.......................... each..	1 50
Tea ....do....	80	Bonnets... ....do ...	75
Coffee.........................do....	24	Boots (women's)............per pair..	2 20
Sugar ....do....	11	Calico ....per yard..	12
Rice.........................do....	07	Flannels ....do....	55
Tobacco:		Coats .... each..	5 00
Colonial ....do....	36	Prints.......................per yard..	14
Manufactured ....do....	1 00	Shawls .... each..	2 90
Raisins and dried fruits ....do....	13	Sheetings ....per yard..	48
Salt (colonial).............per bushel..	94	Shirts (flannel)	1 86
Pepper.....................per pound..	28	Socks........................per pair..	26
Beer:		Blankets ....do ...	5 00
English.............per bottle..	34	Counterpanes ....each..	2 60
Colonial ....do....	15	Mattresses ....do ..	7 25

SENEGAL.

REPORT BY CONSUL STRICKLAND. OF GOREE-DAKAR.

As Senegal is merely a colony with but comparatively few European inhabitants, a detailed report from it based on statistics is, of course, not to be expected, and yet there are phases of life among tradesmen here which cannot but prove interesting to many of our people, and for their sake I can give something of the general result of my observations for the last twenty years.

DIVISION OF LABOR.

Among Europeans here the lines drawn between the different trades and professions, of course, correspond with those drawn between the same trades and professions in the mother country—France, but among the natives the most varied habits prevail, all, however, being strongly pervaded by the spell of that eastern institution, caste. A carpenter would lose half a day rather than degrade his occupation to that of a laborer by carrying a board he wanted to use a block. A sailor would see any quantity of merchandise spoil by rain on a wharf rather than risk being called a land-lubber should he assist in removing it. A man among the natives would almost sooner suffer martyrdom than do work which is accounted as belonging to a woman to do, and for the most part the native women seem to have no inclination to intermeddle in what are deemed proper employments for men.

This caste feeling among the natives of both sexes no doubt contributes to retard their advancement; but it cannot be denied that, considering their disadvantages, some of the native trades-people perform their work surprisingly well. We have now in Goree native carpenters, joiners, blacksmiths, and masons who habitually turn out perhaps better work than can be had from the average of our tradesmen in the same lines of industry. This, however, is doubtless owing to the thoroughness of their seven-year apprenticeships.

WAGES.

The wages of carpenters, masons, and other tradesmen of Senegal average about the same, being 75 cents per day for males just out of their apprenticeship and $1.15 for experienced hands. Sailors get about $7.50 per month, and male servants, including cooks, from $8 to $20 per month, according to their proficiency. Female servants and cooks get from $6 to $10 a month; they are seldom liked as well as their male competitors, either as servants or cooks. Even the European ladies resident here usually prefer male attendants. This is largely due to the more prevalent disposition among the females to shirk their duties. They are not near so reliable and painstaking as the males, though as common laborers, where much care and fidelity are not requisite, they appear to do more in proportion to their strength and the wages they receive than the men. The average price of male labor is at present about 50 cents a day, and for female 25 cents.

Further south, however, women only get 12½ cents per day. Women are largely employed in transporting light articles which can be carried on the head. They carry their babies at the same time, tied by a strip of cloth astride their hips, and it is no uncommon thing to see women in the last stages of pregnancy trudging along all day, under their various burdens, for the last-named miserable pittance. They appear quite joyous, however, smoke their pipes constantly when they can get tobacco, and literally "take no thought for the morrow."

COST OF LIVING.

The cost of living in Senegal is on the whole much dearer than might be expected, due to causes, however, which might be prevented, and of which I shall say something hereafter. Corn ranges from 80 cents to $1.30 per bushel; beef, whether shin pieces or sirloin, is 10 cents a pound; eggs are 2 cents apiece, and average very small; rice and fish are the cheapest articles of food, the former retailing for 4 or 5 cents a pound, and the latter selling sometimes for less than 1 cent a pound. Rice, with a condiment of meat, fish, tomatoes, or palm oil, is the orthodox dish, and constitutes the main article of food for the natives. The better class of natives, however, when observed by Europeans, copy after them, but when alone with the rest they also love to squat cross-legged around their immense calabashes of rice, fish, and palm oil, bailing with both fists into the greasy mass until they are filled to repletion and no more can be swallowed. In doing this they usually litter the ground as badly as parrots would in feeding. Most of them appear to have no idea of economy, and when liberally supplied, even at their own expense, will waste by carelessness and inattention almost as much as they eat. If the people of Senegal were all civilized in their habits, and more industrious, the cost of living here would be much less than in the United States.

This is undoubtedly a rich country, and, as things are, its almost wild natural products suffice to support in comparative idleness and vice quite a large population. Under cultivation Senegambia would be one of the most productive countries in the world.

COMMUNISM.

Communism is not a theory among the inhabitants of Senegal, but an institution which has existed "from eternity," and it bids fair to be as permanent as the barbarism of the race. All earnings in effect are engrossed in a common stock, so that when it comes to eating and drinking, all are on terms of the most perfect equality. This explains the apparent hospitality of most eastern peoples, for where it is a universal custom to have everything in common, the matter of giving freely to strangers, from whom as much in like circumstances would invariably be expected, is hardly as meritorious as might at first sight be supposed. When seated around their calabash of rice and palm oil all distinctions appear to be forgotten, and not a word is said or gesture given to create a sense of unworthiness in any of the recipients, be they in public estimation good or bad, provident or improvident, deserving or undeserving, industrious or lazy.

Thus in certain moral aspects the system seems an admirable one, but in reality it is all in the seeming; there are no positive upbuilding virtues in communism. As an illustration of its evil effects, I know of a bright, industrious young carpenter, of good moral character in every respect, who for the last five years has averaged in earnings at least $25 per month, and but for this wretched system might to-day have a cottage of his own with all pleasant surroundings. Not more than one-third of his earnings are spent on himself, the rest all being appropriated by a parcel of lazy, improvident, and oftentimes vicious leeches, not one of whom would work like him for a day unless driven to it by pinching hunger or some other dire necessity. Communism is thus largely responsible for the almost utter indifference of the mass of natives toward having their condition improved; but in its "struggle for existence" with European civilization it must either eventually perish or those who hold to it will become a burden to the colony. As yet but little has been accomplished towards weaning the natives from their communistic habits and sentiments, and as a result there are but few instances of thrift and prosperity among them. Unless the whole barren mountain mass can be moved bodily no diamonds are to be had. This is communism, and its tendency, especially when it must compete with a high civilization, is toward poverty, extinction, and death. There is hope, however, that with the division of the country into small farms, and a more extensive development of the present school system, a better state of things will prevail.

INTEMPERANCE.

Drunkenness to a greater or lesser extent seems to be the general condition of the vast majority of the trades and other people of Senegal who are not Mohammedans. Drunkenness to an extent which stupefies all the faculties is not perhaps so prevalent here as in Europe; the difficulty is, drinking, with the vices and miseries which attend it, are here almost universal, and outside the settlements there are no restraints of law to protect the innocent from the murderous disposition which drunkenness often engenders. It is my deliberate conviction that it costs the native trades-people in Senegambia more for rum than it does for food, and what makes it very annoying for their employers, is the fact that their services cannot be depended on so long as they have the means in hand to buy rum. House servants are as bad as the rest, and unless European families are lucky enough to secure Mohammedans for their cooks they can never know when a fast will be intruded upon' them. The women in the matter of drinking are if anything worse than the men, and if employed for waiters are sure to smash all the crockery within their reach in an incredibly short space of time. It is a custom among them also to form themselves into "drinking

clubs" of a dozen or so each, and whenever their accumulated means
are sufficient to purchase three or four gallons of liquor, they will, after
excusing themselves from work on some frivolous pretext, meet at a
house selected for the purpose, and indulge in orgies too terrible to be
described. It is sometimes a week before they recover from these de-
bauches, and the interests of those who are, after all, obliged to employ
them, suffer accordingly.

Added to the annoyance from their drinking habits is also the fact
that most of these intemperate women are of such easy virtue in other
respects that their husbands seldom trust them, but leave them for
others on the slightest pretexts. The women also change partners as
often as chance follows occasion, so that society, as we recognize the
term, scarcely has an existence. It is one of the most common of things
among the so-called Christian natives of Senegambia to see children,
brothers and sisters through their mother, but all having different
fathers, thus completely reversing the Mormon custom, where children
are often brothers and sisters through their father but not through their
mothers. Scores of children also die through neglect, exposure, and
vile diseases, for which the drunken habits of their mothers are directly
responsible. That drunkenness is the principal cause of these irregularities and miseries is proven by the fact that among the Mohammedan
part of the population things go on a great deal better. In a fair comparison between what is called the native Christian population of Senegambia and the Mohammedan population the advantage without doubt is
in favor of the latter, all owing, however, to their aversion to rum. And
it does seem as though our Government must be culpable in granting
drawbacks on rum and alcohol, which is exported by the ship-load, to
debauch and destroy the unreflecting inhabitants of uncivilized countries. It is my deliberate conviction that rum in Africa is at present
doing *as much mischief as the slave trade ever did*, and that it is a shame
for a civilized country like the United States to aid any of its merchants
in exterminating these Northern Zulus of Africa.

FUTURE PROSPECTS.

What the future of labor is to be in Senegal, with the present blight-
ing influences to retard its higher development, it is, of course, difficult
to determine. Most of the races which now inhabit the country are
superior in physique as compared with other Africans, and if they could
be subjected to good upbuilding influences instead of being poisoned
physically and having their moral faculties blotted out by New England
rum, they would undoubtedly make rapid advances in all the great departments of industry. There is no lack of capacity among the Faulahs,
Jaloffs, and Mandingoes, but worthy objects which challenge admiration
and impel men to better their condition are not sufficiently held up to
their sight. A little is perhaps being accomplished by teaching some
of their children in the parochial schools, but what is most needed is
something to convince the native mind that to be truly prosperous men
should be temperate, frugal, and industrious. As things are now most
of the boys who have learned to write their names in school and can
place figures in row or column expect to be merchants like the Europeans they see, and think it beneath them to perform any manual labor.
They are quick to observe and imitate, and if a dozen European mechanics with their families were settled among them for a spell, and
they could see and realize how well things can go on among the thrifty,
moral, and industrious who labor at home, they would receive more

benefit than from all the missionaries, who, in the absence of any such examples to which they can call attention, have recourse only to dry precept and dogma, which, to minds unaccustomed to reason away from the animal, accomplish very little in the way of enlightenment. European mechanics do not emigrate here because the climate is considered unhealthy, but European capital is seeking investment in railroads, plantations, and other enterprises, which must very soon compel skilled labor in the country. Sugar, oil, and rice mills are already in course of construction. Coastwise navigation has received considerable development, new roads are being built, and I presume the time is close at hand in which all branches of industry must be developed and flourish in Senegal. Whether this will have to be done mostly by imported labor, or whether a small remnant of the descendants of the present natives will grow out of their prejudices and survive in spite of rum and the other poisons used to kill them, remains for some future observer to chronicle.

PETER STRICKLAND,
Consul.

UNITED STATES CONSULATE,
Goree-Dakar, July 9, 1884.

SIERRA LEONE.

REPORT BY CONSUL LEWIS.

COST OF LIVING.

Rice from $3.60 to $4.80 per 100 pounds : cotton goods for the clothing of poor people, very low rates; rent of a small house, $2 per month.

This is without doubt a good country for the very poor or laboring class ; being warm the year round, very little clothing or shelter is needed, and rice and fish are always to be had at moderate prices.

There is really no distress here for the want of something to eat, as seen in Europe or the United States.

I don't think there is any change in the present rate of wages and those prevailing in 1878, and conditions are about the same.

The habits of the working class are not very trustworthy, not saving, and they spend all they make, be it much or little.

No strikes.

Working people are perfectly free to purchase the necessaries of life where they choose. The laborer is paid by the day, week, or month, in English coin.

No co-operative societies.

General condition of the working people ? Some pretty good, others very bad. The common laborer only receives enough to keep soul and body together, and can never lay up anything for sickness or old age : but many might if they were not so fond of fine dress and of following in all European customs of extravagance.

Moral and physical conditions ? Can't say much in favor of the former, but physically they are very hardy, and endure great hardships.

Workingmen have all the rights of any citizens, but their influence on legislation is very limited.

There is no direct taxation on rich or poor. All revenue is raised by customs duties on imports and exports.

Women and children are employed largely in trading on their own
account, and few if any are hired at employment for wages.

No means provided in case of fire.

Good hospitals for the sick, and since the epidemic of yellow fever of
this May and June, sanitary measures are enforced rigidly.

JUDSON A. LEWIS,

Consul.

UNITED STATES CONSULATE,
  Sierra Leone, November 10, 1884.

I. GENERAL TRADES.

Wages paid per week of forty-eight hours in Sierra Leone.

Occupations.	Lowest.	Highest.	Occupations.	Lowest.	Highest.
BUILDING TRADES.			**OTHER TRADES**—continued.		
Bricklayers	$2 88	$5 04	Butchers	*$0 72	*$1 00
Hod-carriers	1 44	1 80	Cabinet-makers	3 24	5 04
Masons	2 88	5 04	Coopers	2 88	3 60
Tenders	1 44		Gardeners	2 16	
Plasterers	2 88	5 04	Jewelers	(†)	(†)
Slaters	2 88	3 60	Laborers, porters, &c	1 44	1 80
Carpenters	2 52	5 04	Mill-wrights	4 32	10 80
			Printers	2 16	4 32
OTHER TRADES.			Teachers, public schools	2 40	9 60
			Sail-makers	2 88	4 32
Bakers	2 16	2 88	Stevedores	2 16	2 88
Backsmiths	2 88	4 32	Tailors	2 16	4 32

* Per bullock.　　　† Job working: Gold, 50 per cent.; silver, 100 per cent.

VII. SHIP-YARDS AND SHIP-BUILDING.

Wages paid per week of forty-eight hours in ship-yards in Sierra Leone.

Occupations.	Lowest.	Highest.
Boat building or repairing wooden ships	$5 04	* $10 80

* The highest price is that paid to the boss workmen; all others receive the low price named.

VIII. SEAMEN'S WAGES.

*Wages paid per month to seamen (officers and men)—distinguishing between ocean, coast, and
river navigation, and between sail and steam—in Sierra Leone.*

Occupations.	Lowest.	Highest.
Masters of small steamers plying about the coast and up the rivers (white)	$50 00	$100 00
Mates for same (black)	7 20	15 00
Stokers (black)	4 80	7 20
Engineers (black)	10 00	18 00
Sailors	5 00	12 00
Sailors and small sailing crafts	5 00	10 00

IX. Store and Shop Wages.

Wages paid per week of forty-eight hours in stores, wholesale or retail, to males, in Sierra Leone.

Occupations.	Lowest.	Highest.
European clerks........	$5 00	$25 00
Native clerks...	5 00	12 00

Note.—Head book-keepers and confidential clerks—European—get as high as $3,000 per year in some of the large European houses.

X. Household Wages in Towns and Cities.

Wages paid per month with board to household servants (towns and cities) in Sierra Leone.

Occupations.	Lowest.	Highest.	Average.
Male cooks..	$4 80	$16 80	$7 20
House boys	2 40	7 20	4 80

Note.—Nearly all cooking is done by males.

XI. Agricultural Wages.

Wages paid per day, to agricultural laborers and household (country) servants in Sierra Leone and rice.

Occupations.	Lowest.	Highest.	Average.
Managing man for farm	$0 48	$1 00	$0 72
Laborers	24	36	....

XII. Corporation Employés.

Wages paid per week of forty-eight hours to the corporation employés in the city of Sierra Leone.

Occupations.	Lowest.	Highest.	Average.
Superintendent of roads and buildings			$14 00
Artisans in wood, iron, and stone....................................	$2 16	$5 76	3 00

XIII. Government Departments and Offices.

Wages paid per month of one hundred and ninety-two hours to employés in Government departments and offices, exclusive of tradesmen and laborers in Sierra Leone.

Occupations.	Lowest.	Highest.	Average.
Foremen	$15 00	$48 00	$25 00
Clerks..	8 00	40 00	30 00

XIV. Trades and Labor—Government Employ.

Wages paid by the week of forty-eight hours to the trades and laborers in Government employ in Sierra Leone.

Occupations.	Lowest.	Highest.	Occupations.	Lowest.	Highest.
Painters....................	$2 88	$5 76	Iron workers	$2 88	$5 76
Carpenters	2 88	5 04	Coopers....................	2 88	5 04
Masons....................	2 88	5 04 .			

XV. Printers and Printing Offices.

Statement showing the wages paid per week of forty-eight hours to printers (compositors, pressmen, proof-readers, &c.) in Sierra Leone.

Occupations.	Lowest.	Highest.	Occupations.	Lowest.	Highest.
Foreman	$2 88	$5 04	Pressmen	$1 44	$2 16
Compositors...............	1 44	4 85	Proof-readers...............	2 88	5 04

MADEIRA.

REPORT BY VICE-CONSUL HUTCHISON.

The following brief notes on this subject are respectfully submitted, in compliance with the instructions of July 15 last. The field is so limited and the remuneration of labor so uniform that there are no materials for a report under all the heads stated in the circular.

The cost of living to the laboring classes is small, their food consisting chiefly of Indian corn, price 2½ cents per pound, and sweet potatoes, price 1 to 1½ cents per pound, and occasionally bread and fish. Their clothing consists of coarse cotton or linen material, the climate enabling them for the greater part of the year to work in shirt and trousers only. In some cases the laborers have houses of their own, rudely constructed of rough stone, and thatched, the floor being of earth or paved with round stones from the beach. Those who pay rent usually pay from $15 to $18 per annum.

Their habits are generally good, the laborers being temperate and steady. They are disposed to be saving, but with their wages that is impossible.

Good feeling prevails between employer and employed.

There is no organization of labor nor of capital, nor are there any strikes.

The working people can buy where they choose. They are paid weekly, in the current coin of the country.

There is one co operative society in Funchal, but it is not prosperous.

The general condition of the working class is not good, and the only chance of improving their condition is by emigration. In sickness they usually go to the public hospital in Funchal.

Workingmen have the right of voting in the election of deputies for the Cortes, or Portuguese Parliament, and they pay a very small tax on their industrial income, varying from 20 to 50 cents per annum.

The causes of emigration are low wages, and they eagerly emigrate to whatever country requires their services. Latterly, agricultural laborers have been emigrating in large numbers to the Hawaiian Islands, and emigration to that country is now actively going on.

FEMALE LABOR.

The average wages earned by female adults in agricultural labor is 20 cents a day. The hours of labor average 7 to 11 hours daily, according to the season of the year. There are no means provided for their improvement. The employers make no provision for the sick and disabled.

The state of education is very low, very few of either sex being able to read.

Lists of wages of the principal occupations accompany this report.

J. HUTCHISON,
Vice-Consul.

UNITED STATES CONSULATE,
Funchal, May 26, 1884.

I. GENERAL TRADES.

Wages paid per day of 9 hours.

Occupations.	Lowest.	Highest.	Average.
BUILDING TRADES.			
Hod-carriers			$0 37
Masons			75
Tenders			37
Plasterers			75
Tenders			37
Roofers			75
Tenders			37
Plumbers			1 00
Assistants			40
Carpenters			75
OTHER TRADES.			
Bakers	$0 45	$0 65	55
Blacksmiths			65
Bookbinders			55
Brassfounders			65
Cabinet-makers			65
Confectioners			55
Cigar-makers			65
Coopers			1 00
Gardeners			65
Hatters			85
Laborers, porters, &c			37
Printers			90
Stevedores			65
Tailors			65
Tinsmiths			40

IX. STORE AND SHOP WAGES.

Wages paid per month in stores, wholesale or retail, to males.

Occupations.	Average wages.
Salesmen or clerks	$15 00

No females employed in the above-named capacities.

X. Household Wages in Towns and Cities.

Wages paid per month, with board, to household servants (towns and cities).

Occupations.	Average wages.	Occupations.	Average wages.
Cooks (men)	$8 00	Cooks (women)	$6 00
Waiters	10 00	Grooms	5 00
Chambermaids	5 00	Boys	3 00

XI. Agricultural Wages.

Wages paid to agricultural laborers and household (country) servants.

Occupations.	Average wages.
Laborers ....per day..	*$0 37
Servants (female) ....per month..	†2 00

* Without food.　　† With food.

AUSTRALASIA.

VICTORIA.

REPORT BY CONSUL-GENERAL SPENCER, OF MELBOURNE.

MALE LABOR.

Doubtless one of the most perplexing of modern social problems is the peaceable readjustment of the unfriendly relations which at present exist between capital and labor. It is exceedingly unfortunate for both that they should assume an attitude of antagonism to each other, for their interests are identical. Capital and labor, in fact, are but different forms of the same thing. Labor is undeveloped capital, and capital is crystallized labor. According to the opinion of not a few of the leading thinkers of the day, co-operation is the only practicable solution of this great problem; co-operation instead of competition. Competition makes all men Ishmaelites—every man's hand against that of his fellow. Co-operation would apply the golden rule to business affairs, and make of all mankind a common brotherhood.

That the relations of employers and employed are everywhere strained and unsatisfactory will hardly be denied. Labor contends that it does not receive its legitimate share of the profits arising from its union with capital. It utters its protests in the form of strikes, but hitherto with only partial success. Having thus signally failed to obtain a redress of its grievances, it has learned the value of combination and is becoming aggressive and defiant. Happy will it be for capital if it takes timely warning and averts the threatened conflict. First there comes the muttering of the distant thunder; after that the thunderbolt.

RATES OF WAGES.

Victoria has been styled the "workingman's paradise," and not without reason, if it is compared in this respect either with Great Britain or any other country in Europe. Much interesting information relating to the general condition of the laboring and artisan classes in the colony has been elicited by the royal commission on the tariff and the employés in shops commission, which goes to show that the hours of labor are shorter and the rates of remuneration, on the average, higher in Victoria than they are in England or any other country of the Old World. With a propitious climate and a fruitful soil, with eight hours as the recognized working day, and with high wages for almost every description of labor, there is probably no country in the world, if we except the United States, that offers greater attractions to the working-man than Victoria.

COST OF LIVING.

According to the evidence taken before the royal commission, the cost of living to the laboring classes is, on the whole, less in Victoria than it was ten years ago. During the past six months, however, there has been a sensible increase in the prices of some of the necessaries of life, owing to the severe and long-continued drought and the large export of frozen meat to the old country. House rent is higher than in England. The rent of cottages in the suburbs of the city suitable for clerks and shopmen range from $250 to $500 per annum, and those for artisans and laborers from $2 to $4 per week. As for clothing, it would be difficult to estimate, even approximately, the expense for any particular class, involving, as it does, a question of taste as well as the purchasing ability of the consumer.

WAGES PAST AND PRESENT.

With a few exceptions the present rate of wages and the conditions of labor are about the same as those which prevailed in 1878. There has been a sensible reduction in the wages paid to journeymen shoemakers and tailors, owing in part to the keen competition, and in part to the introduction of machines and female labor. On the other hand, there has been a slight advance in the wages paid to agricultural laborers and domestic servants.

HABITS OF THE WORKING CLASSES.

That habits of economy and thrift prevail to a great extent is evident from the fact that in a population of 900,000 persons, of whom 330,000 are under fifteen years of age, there are 122,584 who are depositors in savings-banks, with an aggregate amount of $15,600,000 standing to their credit. The various friendly societies have an income, in round numbers, of $1,000,000, and $2,000,000 invested; the building societies have an income of $7,000,000, beside $5,000,000 on deposit. Of the $83,000,000 of deposits bearing interest in the various banks of the colony, a certain proportion—although there are no means of ascertaining the exact amount—is deposited by the working classes.

On the other hand, there is a considerable amount of poverty, occasioned for the most part by intemperance or other misconduct. The fact that a community of less than a million of inhabitants expends not less than $15,000,000 per annum upon intoxicating liquors is quite sufficient to explain why a certain amount of destitution and misery exists.

FEELING BETWEEN EMPLOYER AND EMPLOYÉ.

The feeling which prevails between employers and employés in the colony of Victoria is, generally speaking, of a friendly character. Owing to the fact that the legislature has not, for a considerable number of years past, appropriated any portion of the public revenue for immigration purposes, as well as to the great distance of Australia from Europe, which operates as a bar to voluntary emigration from the Old World, the increase of population from without, is comparatively insignificant. Consequently the labor market is rarely or never overstocked; wages are high, and skilled workmen of every description are able to dictate their own terms. Hence it is to the interest of employers to cultivate friendly relations with their workmen; for the independent position of the latter and the trades combinations which exist among them enable them to resist and resent any harsh or arbitrary act of authority on the part of the former, while it is only due to these to state that their conduct, as a general rule, is courteous and considerate towards the wage-earning classes.

Eight hours, as a rule, constitute a day's labor, the remuneration of which is so liberal that a frugal, sober, and enterprising operative will often succeed, after a few years of patient and persevering toil, in raising himself to the position of a foreman, overseer, contractor, or employer of labor himself. As such he feels a certain amount of sympathy for those out of whose ranks he has raised himself, and he shapes his actions towards them accordingly. In most large establishments it is customary for principals to give an annual picnic, to which the whole of the men, together with their wives and families, are invited; the entire expense being defrayed by the firm. This has the effect of cementing the good feeling which exists between employers and employed, and, as a natural consequence, the peace and prosperity of the community are promoted by these harmonious relations.

ORGANIZED CONDITION OF LABOR.

Not only have all the branches of handicraft their trades unions, but the day laborers also have a similar organization. Each has its committee of management; and a trades hall, erected on a block of land granted for that purpose by the government, furnishes them with a place of rendezvous. Meetings are held in it once a fortnight, or oftener, as may be required by the committee of each trade. There are something like twenty different industries thus represented. Questions of policy involving trade usages or matters in dispute between employers and employed are discussed at such periodical meetings with fairness, intelligence, and impartiality; and each of these bodies may be regarded as a separate committee of what constitutes in the aggregate a congress or parliament of labor.

The effect of such organizations is to increase the power and also the self-respect of their individual members. Bound together by a community of sentiment and interest, and ready to support each other in case of emergency, the United Trades are an important factor in political and social dynamics. They succeeded some years ago, by a combined effort, in establishing the principle of eight hours labor, eight hours rest, and eight hours refreshment and recreation; and the anniversary of its institution is observed as a public holiday by the wage-earning classes in Melbourne, when all the trades march in procession through the streets, with their respective banners and the emblems of their daily occupations.

There are no counter-organizations of capitalists. The chamber of manufacturers occupies itself with the general concerns of trade and manufactures. Some minor associations have been formed by the producers of, or dealers in, particular articles, chiefly with the object of procuring steadiness of price, discountenancing illegitimate competition and dishonest trading, as well as of protecting themselves against fraud and embezzlement. But otherwise, capital has not resorted to any unions, either for aggressive or defensive purposes.

STRIKES AND COURTS OF ARBITRATION.

As each of the trades has been organized in the manner previously described, and has a standing committee to watch over its interests, strikes are not often had recourse to as a means of adjusting the current rate of wages, and determining the market value of skilled or of unskilled labor. More often than otherwise any reasonable demand for increased remuneration is acceded to by employers in preference to encountering the loss, annoyance, and anxiety which would be entailed by the suspension of industrial operations in consequence of a lock-out.

On the other hand, occasions have arisen in which advantage has been taken by employés of their knowledge of the fact that a certain public or private contract must be completed within a given time and under a heavy penalty, to exact an advance in wages, without due justification, and not unfrequently to the serious detriment or actual loss of the contractor. The knowledge that such strikes are possible, and even probable, is of course a disturbing element in all calculations affecting important works, involving a considerable outlay of capital and extending over a lengthened period of time. There can be very little doubt but that great public undertakings are rendered much more costly to the community than they otherwise would be by contractors feeling themselves compelled to guard against a contingency of this kind in preparing their schedules of prices.

Among employers of labor, and among the more intelligent of the skilled artisans, there is a general desire for councils of conciliation such as exist upon the continent of Europe, to be composed of employers and employés in equal numbers, with a president unconnected with either class; and it is understood that a measure to give legal effect to this desire and legal authority to its decisions will shortly be submitted to the parliament of Victoria, with the strong probability that it will be enrolled upon the statute-book.

In the final report of the royal commission on employés in shops the commissioners say:

In the opinion of your commissioners the most effective mode of bringing about industrial co-operation and mutual sympathy between employers and employed, and thus obviating labor conflicts in the future, is by the establishment of courts of conciliation in Victoria whose procedure and awards shall have the sanction and authority of law.

Your commissioners therefore recommend that, during the ensuing session of Parliament, the Government introduce a measure having for its object the establishment and maintenance of courts of conciliation in Victoria.

Of the proposed act, the following are the principal provisions:

I. A central council to be established in Melbourne which shall be permanent.

II. The central council to consist of fourteen members, seven of whom shall represent employers and seven employés.

III. The central council to be elective.

IV. The qualification of those entitled to vote for representatives on the central council to consist of electors being on the one part employers and on the other part employés, none of whom shall be less than twenty-one years of age.

V. Qualified electors to be eligible for membership of the central council and local courts of conciliation.

VI. The method of recording the votes of electors to be determined by the various trade organizations. Failing the existence of such in any particular locality at the time, then through some kindred association which may accept the responsibility of collecting and recording such votes.

VII. Candidates for the central council to be nominated fourteen days at least prior to the day of election.

VIII. The government to be requested to make the necessary arrangements for the election of members of the first central council.

IX. The central council to be a court of appeal from local courts of conciliation.

X. The position of members of the central council and of local courts to be honorary.

XI. Vacancies occurring in the central council through disqualification to be filled up by the remaining members representing the interest for which the person disqualified had been elected.

XII. The question of disqualification to be decided by a majority of those members of the council identified with the interest which the person affected had been elected to represent.

XIII. Two members of the central council to retire annually, one being a representative of employers and the other of employés. At the end of the first year after election the representative on each side who obtained the smallest number of votes shall retire, when two others shall be elected to fill their places, and so on in rotation. Retiring members to be eligible for re-election.

XIV. Local courts of conciliation may be appointed in any municipality or district in the colony.

XV. Local courts to be temporary and their duties specific, except in cases where it may be considered desirable by the trade organization in any district to elect a local court to represent them for a period not exceeding twelve months; the members of such court to consist of an equal number of employers and employés.

XVI. The mayor of any city, town, or borough, and the president of any shire, to receive applications for the establishment of a local court, on receipt of which he shall within twenty-four hours make the necessary arrangement for the election of the members of such court, and shall act as returning officer of the same, or appoint a deputy to act on his behalf.

XVII. There shall be a president and vice president of the central council, elected by the members from each side respectively.

XVIII. The president, vice president, or whoever in the absence of those shall preside during the adjudication of any cause, shall not be entitled to a casting vote.

XIX. Rules XVII and XVIII to apply to local courts.

XX. When the necessary authority has been obtained by the parties interested for the establishment of a local court, they shall proceed to the election of representatives under the act.

XXI Expenses to be limited to the actual outlay incurred in hearing the dispute, for which the plaintiff may be required to give security in the first instance.

XXII. Any local court failing to arrive at an amicable settlement regarding the matter in dispute, an appeal may be made to the central council.

XXIII. A permanent secretary to the central council, to be appointed by the government.

XXIV. The central council to frame its own rules and regulations and mode of procedure under the act.

XXV. The president, vice president, and members of the central council, to be *ex officio* magistrates of the central bailiwick.

XXVI. Decrees made by the central council to be enforced under provisions to be embodied in the act.

XXVII. President of central council to have power to inflict a penalty—either a fine not exceeding £—— or a term of imprisonment not exceeding — days—for contempt of court.

Employés are usually paid weekly in English sterling. They are perfectly free to make their purchases, of whatever kind, wherever they choose.

CO-OPERATIVE SOCIETIES.

"Co-operation," says the Earl of Roseberry, "is the obvious and only remedy for all troubles arising out of the conflict between capital and labor." And yet, although the conditions here are more favorable than in England, co-operation among the wage-earning classes of Victoria has hitherto met with only indifferent success. One of the largest iron foundries in the colony has been conducted upon this principle for a period of something like twenty years, but, as I understand, it has never paid a dividend. Whether the members of the co-partnery have been drawing the same wages as they would have done had they been working for private employers, I have no means of ascertaining. Neither has co-operation for distributive purposes been any more successful among the operative classes. Experiments have been made, but hitherto they have almost invariably ended in failure. There are at the present time two large associations of this kind in Melbourne, but they have been founded and carried on by the middle and upper classes of society almost exclusively. One of them, the mutual store, in the city of Melbourne, has paid 8 per cent. per annum, besides occasional bonuses, for many years past. The other, the Equitable Co-operative Society, has been established too recently to justify me in speaking with confidence of its position and prospects. The secretary of this society, however, in his paper on co-operation, read recently before the Intercolonial Trades Union Congress, says:

This society has only been in business two months, yet it employs nearly two hundred work-people, males and females, of whom about fifty are employed as tailors, upholsterers, mantle-makers and milliners, and the remainder as distributors. Other trades will quickly follow. It has a buyer located in London, who buys direct from manufacturers; a banking account there which means bringing capital for use here, and which the colonies so much need, and without which progress is impossible. This society could easily establish branches all over Melbourne, and give the management to local committees, consisting of the trusted members of the working class, supplemented by one or more of its own committee. This society has an influential shareholding body, and is adding about twenty-five members per week. It is established upon the most democratic principles, for only one vote is allowed for each head, whatever capital its owner may have invested, and all the profits are divided among the purchasers in proportion to their individual support, after paying capital not more than a fair rate of dividend, viz, 8 per cent. per annum. All the profits of the working-class societies at home are divided in this manner, with the exception that 8 per cent. is the rule as regards interest.

There is one form of co-operation in Victoria, however, which is very popular and highly beneficial. I refer to that of building societies; by means of which, workingmen, small shopkeepers, mercantile clerks, and others, are enabled to acquire houses of their own by means of a small monthly subscription spread over a period of time ranging from four to ten years. Some millions of pounds sterling have been accumulated and invested in this way during the last thirty years with this result, that in the suburbs of Melbourne and in the country districts the great bulk of the thrifty and industrial population are their own landlords. There are about fifty building societies in Victoria which send in their returns to the Government statistician. These have an income of $7.500,000 and have made advances, secured on real property, to the extent of $16,000,000, exclusive of loans granted in previous years and subsequently redeemed.

GENERAL CONDITION OF THE WORKING CLASSES.

Probably there is no country in the world in which the condition of the working man is more favorable than it is in the colony of Victoria. The climate is such that those who pursue out-of-door occupations do not probably, on an average, lose more than ten days in the year, and then it is owing to heavy rains. In the winter months the thermometer rarely falls below 32° Fahrenheit; when it does it is after night-fall, and it will probably register 70° in the sun at noon. The heat of the summer months is a dry and stimulating, and not an enervating and oppressive heat. The eight-hour system, with the Saturday half-holiday, is the prevalent one. For eight months in the year a householder requires no fuel except to cook with, and his outlay for clothing is of course very much less than it is in countries subject to a severer climate.

Numbers of the artisan classes occupy neat suburban cottages, containing from four to six rooms, each surrounded by a small garden plat where the laboring man may sit, in no figurative sense, under his own vine and fig tree.

The skilled laborer lives generously, and has a substantial meal, with meat, three times a day. The state supplies his children with education gratuitously; public libraries and free reading-rooms furnish him with the means of instruction and intellectual improvement; public parks are provided for his recreation, while a large annual expenditure by the government on railways and other public works maintains wages at an unnaturally high level, and as manhood is the sole qualification for the suffrage, and he belongs to a class which has a numerical majority, he and his fellow-workmen are masters of the political situation.

A skilled artisan earning $15 a week for forty-eight hours' labor can save $10 a week out of it without denying himself any of the necessaries of life. This is assuming that he is a single man. And it may be said of those who are married to good domestic managers, and are sober and thrifty themselves, that they can lay up at least $100 a year. All the necessaries of life are comparatively cheap, with the exception of those articles of wearing apparel, furniture, working implements, &c., the cost of which is enhanced by protective duties.

On the whole, the moral and physical condition of the people is sound and healthy. In a bright and exhilarating climate, with free access to libraries and museums, and with a great fondness for public holidays and out-of-door sports and enjoyments, the influences surrounding the population of Victoria are of a cheerful and beneficial character.

STATEMENTS OF WORKING PEOPLE.

The Victorian working man is very sensitive to whatever may appear to him as an intrusion upon his domestic privacy, and is, therefore, indisposed to communicate any detailed information relative to his household expenditure unless required to do so before a royal commission. Consequently, I am unable to comply with the suggestions of the Department in this particular, but in lieu thereof I herewith transmit the sworn statements of representative tradesmen made before the royal commission on the tariff, which I trust will prove equally satisfactory

a. Statement of a bootmaker. •

WILLIAM TRENOWITH, bootmaker, sworn and examined.

Question. What were the wages in 1879, and what are they now?—Answer. It is very difficult, of course, to give accurate figures, because some men are so much smarter than others.

Q. Take a smart man, first of all, to compare with the smart man you spoke of who earned high wages under abnormal circumstances?—A. Some men, I am told, now earn as much as four pounds a week. They are a very few and rare exceptions, but I should say the average wages for a fairly competent man—not a slow man, and not a very quick man—are about fifty shillings a week.

Q. How many pairs of boots did that man turn out for his thirty shillings?—A. Twelve pairs of women's boots, at two and sixpence a pair.

Q. If the same man turned out the same twelve pairs of women's boots now, what would his pay be?—A. Twelve pairs of the same boots?

Q. Yes.—A. Eighteen shillings.

Q. Eighteen shillings, instead of thirty shillings?—A. Yes.

Q. You are an operative, and speak from experience and for those whom you represent. Do you find the cost of living increased since the year 1876?—A. No; I think in almost every particular it has decreased.

Q. You show us, by figures, how the operative bootmaker in 1867, before the tariff was introduced, earned about £2 8s. a week. You show us now that after all the competition between various manufacturers an average man may earn 50s. a week in his factory. Now, is his 50s. a week worth as much to him in purchasing power as 50s. was in previous times?—A. From a rough calculation my experience is that 50s. a week is worth nearly as much as three pounds; at any rate, it is worth much more than it was in 1867.

Q. So that taking that into account as well, you have absolutely got an increase of wages?—A. Yes; I can give an illustration of what I mean by purchasing power being greater. In 1867 I gave £2 7s. 6d. for a trousers and vest in Bourke street, and I was unfortunate enough to fall in a waterhole with them, and when I tried to get them on again I could not put them on with pleasure, they were so shrunk up, and now I can get a very good trousers and vest for a pound less.

Q. Then we understand you that considering the increase of value and the purchasing power of your wages now as compared with 1867, you are twelve shillings a week better off under present circumstances than you were before?—A. I think so.

Q. You say you think so; I would like it definitely.—A. I have not gone into figures, and I would not say definitely twelve shillings, but I am sure I am better off. I could not say what was the sum—it might be more or less, but I feel sure at looking back at the cost of everything I use, then, and now, that I must be better off now than then.

Q. Do you pay more for rent now than you did then; that is a large item in an operative's expenses?—A. I could not speak upon that, because at that time I was not a householder.

Q. You only speak of wearing apparel?—A. Wearing apparel and things I use.

Q. They are cheaper than they were?—A. Yes; for instance, a heel shave used to be four and sixpence then, and now the highest price is three and sixpence.

b. Statement of an engineer.

JOHN REYNOLDS, engineer (fitter), sworn and examined.

By the Hon. Mr. LORIMER:

Question. What is the rate of wages of men in your occupation?—Answer. From 10s. to 12s. a day, some 13s.

Q. What were you getting in 1870? Were you here then?—A. I was here then. I know that when I came out first I went to Ballarat, and they were working for very small wages at that time, I believe.

Q. What rate did you get at Ballarat?—A. I got 10s. when I landed first; that was only a week or two. I was employed at Stawell after that, but I had to work ten hours a day for 12s. a day.

Q. You got as much at that time as you do now?—A. Yes.

Q. Was it the high rate of wages that induced you to come out?—A. Yes, undoubtedly; that and the advice of my friends.

Q. What year did you come out in?—A. 1870.

By the CHAIRMAN:

Q. What wages had you at home?—A. Twenty-nine shillings a week.

Q. How many hours a day?—A. Ten.

Q. You did not work sixty hours a week, did you?—A. Yes; we wrought ten hours and a half a day every day, so as to get away on Saturday at 2 o'clock.

Q. You work forty-eight hours here?—A. Yes.

Q. And you wrought sixty hours at home for 29s. a week?—A. Yes.

Q. Could you live any cheaper at home, taking into account rent, food, and clothing?—A. Yes, rent, of course, was cheaper.

Q. Taking everything into consideration, could you live cheaper?—A. I do not know that I could, much.

Q. Better?—A. No better than you can here. I think a man in steady employment can live more comfortably here than at home; that is if he has steady employment.

Q. Is there much difference in the steadiness of employment here and at home?—A. Yes; a great deal.

Q. In which way?—A. At home you may serve your time in a shop, and be in it till you are a very old man. There is one case, perhaps, here out of every hundred where that is the case.

Q. Does the irregularity of employment have any effect upon wages here?—A. I do think it has, because in dull times the wages are not so good. The men cannot command as high a rate of wages as when there is plenty of employment to give a man 1s. a day extra.

c. Statement of a miner.

WILLIAM JOHN COOK sworn and examined.

By the CHAIRMAN:

Question. What are you?—Answer. A miner.

Q. Are you a working miner?—A. A working miner.

Q. Are you a member of the Miners' Association?—A. I am not just now.

Q. Have you ever been a member?—A. I was previously.

Q. What mine have you been working in?—A. In the Ellesmere for about two years.

Q. Are you a shareholder?—A. No, I am sorry to say I am not.

Q. How long have you been a working miner?—A. Since the year 1853.

Q. Is the rate of wages in your calling lower now than it was in 1853?—A. Yes; it is reduced considerably since the year 1853. About 1853 and 1854 wages were about £5 a week and over.

Q. Within the last ten years—1853 was an exceptional period?—A. About the last ten years it has been about the same in Bendigo.

Q. Has the cost of living been reduced during that time?—A. I do not think so.

Q. Do you pay as much for rent now as you did ten years ago?—A. About that time I think the rent about Sandhurst has been about the same as it was; perhaps not quite so much now as it was ten years ago, but I do not know exactly.

Q. Is clothing as expensive as it was ten years ago?—A. No; I do not think so.

Q. It is lower than it was ten years ago?—A. No, I think not. I think miners' clothing is about the same as ten years ago; I do not find very much difference in it.

Q. Do you give as much for a pair of mole trousers now as you did then?—A. I think I gave about the same price; there may 6d. difference, and that is, I think, about the only difference.

Q. Do you mean 6d. higher or lower?—A. I fancy the moles are 6d. dearer than they were ten years ago.

Q. How about boots?—A. Boots are about the same; I do not think there is very much difference in a pair of boots between now and ten years ago, as far as I am concerned.

d. Statement of a jeweler.

CHARLES THOMPSON, journeyman jeweler, sworn and examined.

Question. Is the position of a working jeweler in this colony as good as in England?—Answer. Yes; I think, perhaps, if there is any difference it is in favor of the colonial workman.

Q. Are your hours of labor longer or shorter?—A. Shorter; that is the advantage; we have eight hours here, and we have to work perhaps nine and in some instances nine hours and a half at home.

Q. For about the same rate of wages?—A. No; perhaps wages are a little better here, with eight hours a day labor.

Q. Less hours of labor and a little better wages. Is the rate of living higher here or at home?—A. Yes; it is higher, slightly; still the rate of wages is in favor of the colonial workman.

Q. When you say the rate of living is higher, as you have not been very long in the colony, will you explain to the commission on what lines it is higher—in what department of expenditure is it higher here than at home?—A. Clothing and house rent; clothing is 75 per cent. higher here than at home.

Q. Is that your experience?—A. Yes.

Q. Do you mean to tell the commission that you could walk into a shop in a country town in England, or one of the manufacturing towns—?—A. Take my native town, Birmingham.

Q. Very well, take Birmingham—and buy a suit of tweed clothes, equal in quality to tweed clothes here, for half the price?—A. Say 75 per cent. I can buy a good suit of tweed clothes at home for 42s. that would cost me £3 10s. here. Of course that is cheap suits at home—tourists' suits.

Q. Then in the item of house rent and clothing the colonial expenditure is larger than the home expenditure?—A. Yes.

Q. And in the item of living, is not the colonial expenditure less?—A. No; I think it about the same at home.

Q. Do not we get a better style of living for the same expenditure here?—A. Perhaps we do.

Q. Perhaps we spend as much, I do not dispute that; but would not the kind of living you get here for an equal expenditure be preferable to what you get at home?—A. I think not.

Q. How do you account for that when the price of meat and bread is so much better in the colony?—A. I should prefer one mutton chop at home to a leg of mutton in Victoria.

Q. Have you made any calculation as to the cost of living between Melbourne and Birmingham, so as to tell us how much per week extra you should have here to compensate you for the increase in the cost of living here?—A. You mean to include clothing, house rent, and everything?

Q. Yes; how much more in Melbourne would be the equivalent of your wages in Birmingham?—A. Three pounds a week in this country is not any better than 35s. in the old country.

Q. That is a difference of 25s. a week?—A. Yes.

Q. You consider that you in Melbourne, with 25s. a week extra wages, would be no better off than at home?—A. With 35s.; I have proved that myself; I have gone into that.

Q. You have gone into the calculation, and that is your estimate?—A. Yes.

By Mr. BOSISTO:

Q. What kind of a house were you living in in Birmingham?—A. I had a very nice two-story house, with seven rooms and a good garden, for 6s. a week.

Q. How far was that from Birmingham?—A. I could walk home to dinner between 1 and 2 o'clock, and have my dinner comfortably and enjoy my walk in the garden, too, in an hour and ten minutes.

e. Statement of a die-sinker.

GEORGE PALMER, a jeweler's die-sinker, sworn and examined.

By Mr. TUCKER:

Question. Where did you learn your trade?—Answer. In Birmingham.

Q. How long have you been in the colony?—A. Eight years.

Q. You heard the evidence of the last witness as to the cost of living?—A. Yes.

Q. And the comparison with Victoria; do you agree with him?—A. No; I do not agree with him.

Q. Do you think the cost of living is less here, or more, than in England?—A. It may be a little more; rent is high.

Q. Leave the question of rent out altogether, is it higher then?—A. I doubt it. I doubt whether, if a workman lived up to the standard he does here, it would not cost him as much in the old country.

Q. You think the standard of living is lower in the old country than it is here?—A. As regards the working classes, it is.

Q. Then you do not agree with the statement that £3 a week in Victoria is no better than 35s. in England?—A. I cannot agree with that.

Q. A man getting 35s. a week in Birmingham and coming to Victoria and getting £3 a week, betters his condition?—A. He does.

f. Statement of a smith.

JOSEPH SEDDON sworn and examined.

By the CHAIRMAN:

Question. What are you?—Answer. I am a smith by trade.

Q. What are you employed at now?—A. I am employed at smith work.

Q. In a foundry?—A. In Mr. Thompson's foundry.

Q. How long have you been employed at your present business?—A. I have been about twenty-three years in the colony—mostly employed in Castlemaine.

Q. What is the present rate of wages that you earn?—A. About four pounds eight a week.

Q. What were you earning ten years ago?—A Sixteen shillings a day; in fact, I never had less since I came into the colony.

Q. Never less than what?—A. Sixteen shillings a day.

Q. Are you earning sixteen shillings a day?—A. No.

Q. As a representative working man, do you find the cost of living increased since the duties were imposed?—A. No; I do not see any difference in that respect.

Q. Do you pay any more for your food than you did?—A. No; much about the same.

Q. Do you pay the same for clothing that you did?—A. I think it is much about the same as it was. I have never seen much difference since I came to the colony. Certainly, I think more clothing is made by tailors now than was fifteen years ago.

Q. You buy less slop clothes; you have more made at the tailors, is that it?—A. Exactly.

Q. Do you think you get as good an article as you did?—A. A better article; it lasts longer; in fact, I have seen the time when I bought shoes out of a shop they did not last me three months, they were done lump and stump, and now I get a pair of shoes that lasts me longer than twelve months, and nobody is harder on shoes than I am.

Q. Do you pay more for your shoes now?—A. I used to give about twelve shillings for them imported, and the last I bought I gave sixteen shillings for, and I find that they are much cheaper by far than the others.

Q. Is house rent dearer?—A. I never was one that paid house rent, except about twenty-three years ago. I have property of my own.

Q. Do you have those shoes made to measure for you that you buy now?—A. I have them made to order.

Q. Can you tell us, as a landlord, whether house rent has increased or decreased?—A. I have only the property I live in at present.

Q. If you had let that property fifteen years ago, could you get more for it than you could to-day?—A. Twice as much.

Q. Then as far as your experience goes house rent is twice as cheap as it was?—A. Of course the house has paid for itself long ago, and that is right enough.

Q. Is rent more than it was twenty years ago?—A. No; less by half.

By Mr. McIntire:

Q. You are paid at present four pounds eight a week?—A. Yes.

Q. How many hours do you work for that?—A. Eight hours a day.

Q. The whole week through?—A. The whole week through.

Q. You had five pounds eight a week, how many year ago?—A. No; not five pounds eight. I had sixteen shillings for the eight hours with Mr. Vivian.

Q. When was that?—A. That is within five years ago, previous to going to Mr. Thompson.

Q. In regard to the cost of living, you say that clothing is cheaper than it was?—A. No; I do not see any difference.

Q. You say it is better value?—A. It is a better article.

Q. Does that not mean cheaper?—A. It is.

Q. With regard to boots, the boots you bought before were imported?—A. They were.

Q. Have you bought any ready-made boots in the shops here?—A. I have not bought ready-made boots for ten years.

Q. Your evidence only refers to bespoke goods?—A. Yes.

Q. Is sixteen shillings the average price?—A. It is about the top.

Q. Would you mean to say that, as one pair of boots lasted twelve months, and the other three, the colonial boot was worth four pairs of the imported?—A. If I order a pair of shoes they generally last me two soles after the new ones are worn off.

Q. With regard to provisions, are not candles a great deal cheaper than they were twenty years ago?—A. Yes; a great deal.

Q. Butter, cheese, and all other articles—are they not cheaper?—A. They are.

Q. But you said they were about the same?—A. Taking one with the other, they are about the same.

Q. Is not bread much cheaper?—A. Taking bread and all those things, they are cheaper than when we came, no doubt.

Q. Say ten years ago?—A. There is not much difference from ten years ago.

g. Statement of a baker.

Henry Foley examined.

Question. What are you?—Answer. A baker.

Q. How long have you been in the business?—A. Ever since I was born.

Q. How many years?—A. Twenty-five years as working journeyman.

Q. What are the usual hours that you are called upon to work?—A. When I first came to Victoria, eleven years ago, I was working from 11 o'clock at night to 2 o'clock the next afternoon, with no intermission for meals. I was with Mr. Harrison, of Collingwood.

Q. That is fifteen hours?—A. Yes.

Q. And you still survive?—A. Yes. On Friday night it was twenty hours; we worked till 3 o'clock on Friday afternoon to give enough bread to do over Sunday.

Q. What are the hours now?—A. Since the agitation it is only ten hours.

Q. When did this agitation occur?—A. Since the first of October last year.

Q. You do not complain so much of your hours now?—A. We want to be placed on the same footing as the other tradesmen. We have to pay for their eight hours, and we do not see why they should not pay for our eight hours too. When a contractor takes a contract for a certain amount of work, he does it with eight hours' men, and we have to work ten hours.

Q. You want to be put on an equality with all the other trades?—A. Yes.

Q. What time do you go on as a rule?—A. We have no set time. Some shops go on at 8 o'clock at night, some 9, some 11, and some 1; the principal shops go on at 8 o'clock at night.

Q. And work till when?—A. Ten hours after that.

Q. What hours do you have during that time for meals?—A. None at all; we are allowed half an hour, but as a rule we do not get it. We have got it lately, but before the short hours we had to work fifteen hours right off, and get no hours for our meals at all.

Q. Has the alteration of the hours been general throughout the trade?—A. Yes, I believe it has; we know for a fact it has been general.

Q. Are you connected with any trade association?—A. Only the Operative Bakers' Society; I am the secretary.

Q. You are part of the Amalgamated Trades' Association that meets at the Trades'

Hall?—A. We meet there, but we do not belong to the Amalgamated Trades' Association yet; we have appointed our delegates, but they have not taken their seats yet.

Q. Have there been many disputes between you?—A. Yes; it takes us all our time to maintain the ten hours against the employers; they say they will not benefit by it, but they benefit more by it than we do.

Q. Do you consider that the eight hours' system should be extended to the bakers as well as to the other trades?—A. Certainly; for the reason that the public should pay for our eight hours the same as we pay for theirs.

Q. How do you account for it that you cannot get the eight hours as well as the other trades?—A. The pressure that is brought to bear against us by the public running to the different employers. We have a lot of men working long hours who have set up for themselves and employ no men.

Q. Have you made any appeal to the employers to reduce the hours of labor?—A. Certainly; we have reduced it from fifteen hours to ten.

Q. Have you made a further appeal since that?—A. No; we are trying to maintain the ten hours at present.

Q. Does it make any appreciable difference in the price of bread—the shortning of the hours?—A. It has made no difference as yet—the bread was the same price before as it is now—the master bakers never rose the price of bread.

Q. If the eight hours were conceded, you do not think the change would be felt?—A. It would not make much difference to persons taking bread by the week.

Q. It would not much advance the price of a loaf of bread?—A. No; still they would have to maintain it to give us our eight hours, at a certain price, the same as the confectioners have done.

Q. Then I understand the competition that master bakers who employ labor have to risk is that of men working on their own account as long as hours they please?—A. Yes, that is the idea; men who have worked long hours go into business themselves, and still work long hours. In our late agitation we are asking for less wages than a laboring man gets, working eight hours a day. We are only asking 10d. an hour, and a laboring man gets 1s. an hour for eight hours a day.

Q. Is is not the case sometimes that the bread does not rise sufficiently early to enable you to complete the work within the eight hours?—A. Yes.

Q. How do you propose meeting that?—A. By starting the eight hours from the time we start our work, from the time it does rise.

Q. If you had the eight hours, would the employers require more men?—A. Certainly, and that would absorb the surplus labor in the market.

Q. There are plenty of bakers to be had if the employers want them?—A. Certainly; the very fact of their working the long hours is keeping those men out of work.

Q. Are there many journeymen bakers out of work now?—A. I could not exactly say.

Q. What are the wages of journeymen bakers?—A. The minimum is £2 10s. a week; foremen get as much as they can above that. We only get 10d. an hour for skilled labor, 2d. less than men get working in the street.

h. Statement of a flint-glass worker.

JOSEPH COOKSEY, flint-glass maker, sworn and examined.

By the CHAIRMAN:

Question. You have been eight months away from England?—Answer. I landed here on the 30th October.

Q. May I ask if you have any family?—A. Six. I have one grown up son with me.

Q. Did you bring the six with you?—A. No: only one of my grown up sons.

Q. Then the remainder of your family are able to support themselves, I presume?—A. I have got one married, and one in the army.

Q. I do not want to follow that particularly. They are not dependent upon you to maintain?—A. Some of them are.

Q. What I want to ascertain is, whether you find any difference in the cost of living as a family man here, and the cost of living at home?—A. Yes, a deal. If I had got my family here, it would be dearer for my family to live than it is at home.

Q. Would you live as well in England with a family of six, for a less sum of money than you could live here?—A. Yes; I could.

Q. Is house rent here much dearer?—A. Yes; a great deal. I left a very nice house at home that I paid 4s. a week for, and coal sixpence a hundredweight. You cannot get that here—10s. a ton.

Q. You were in the neighborhood of Birmingham?—A. I was in the neighborhood of Birmingham.

Q. How many rooms would this house at 4s. a week have?—A. Attic high, three stories high.

Q. How many rooms?—A. One bedroom above another, and the one we lived in below; and we make cellars in our houses at home—not like the cellars here.

Q. This house would have three rooms, one above the other, and 4s. a week?—A. Four shillings a week—a nice house.

Q. Did you say a cellar as well?—A. A cellar as well, under the house—arched under the house.

Q. It is four apartments?—A. Yes.

Q. What was the cost of bread. Was it more than it is here?—A. It was fivepence a loaf when I came away.

Q. The average price at home was about sixpence, was it not?—A. Yes; it is about sixpence, average price.

Q. So it is about the same as it is here?—A. Yes.

Q. Meat is dearer at home, is it not?—A. That is the only thing at home that is dearer at present.

Q. Are vegetables cheaper at home than here?—A. You can get a good beefsteak at fourteen or fifteen pence a pound. Chops—the nice mutton chops—cost tenpence or elevenpence a pound.

Q. So that meat is much dearer than it is here?—A. You get beautiful bacon at sixpence a pound, and ham at eightpence: and beautiful ham, not salty and tough, such as you get here, that you cannot eat.

Q. I was asking about the price of vegetables. What could you buy a hundredweight of potatoes for at home when you left?—A. We did not buy a hundredweight, except the shopkeepers.

Q. How did you buy them?—A. You can buy a half-pennyworth. You can buy five pounds for twopence half-penny.

Q. But you as a family man wanting to buy cheaply, of course, would not buy potatoes by the pennyworth?—A. You can buy five pounds for threepence—as cheap as you can buy by the hundredweight.

Q. What did you pay for butter?—A. One and tenpence to two shillings a pound, the best butter.

Q. Was that the usual price all the year round?—A. That is for the very best, but you get all sorts of butter made there: but it must be all marked or else they are fined.

Q. What is the cheese at home?—A. You can get cheese from twopence a pound up to tenpence and a shilling.

Q. Your experience is, then, that living is somewhat dearer here than it was in England?—A. Yes. I am a boarder and I pay 18s. for my board, and could get it for 10s. at home.

Q. Board and lodging?—A. Board and lodging, and mending, and at home I could get it quite as good for 10s.

Q. Would the comfort at home for 10s. be equal to what you get for 18s here?—A. Yes; quite as good.

Q. As good provisions?—A. Yes; quite as good.

Q. So that you lose 8s. on your expenditure?—A. Yes.

Q. And you gain about £2 6s. on your income?—A. Sometimes.

By Mr. GRIMWADE:

Q. It is a fine country, is it not?—A. Yes; a beautiful country. I like the country very much, myself.

By the CHAIRMAN:

Q. So that taking the increase of expenditure on the one hand, and putting the increase of income on the other, you prefer this country to the old country?—A. I do, or I should not have come out. I have had an inclination to come out here for years—to come out to the country. I had my emigration papers signed twice before, and my wife would not sign them, and they would not bring me without her.

By Mr. GRIMWADE:

Q. How did you get out this time?—A. Through the company.

By the CHAIRMAN:

Q. Have you any suggestion to make beside the measurement of glassware?—A. No.

By Mr. McINTYRE:

Q. You say, in America, they get £4 10s. a week wages?—A. Sometimes more.

Q. That is the average?—A. Yes.

Q. Have you any idea of the price of living in America compared with the old country?—A. Not at present, but I believe it is very cheap.

Q. What was the price of a pair of trousers in America—ordinary workmen's clothes?—A. About 2s. 6d. difference.

Q. Not more than that?—A. No.

Q. Would you tell the Commission how much your average wages were since you arrived here eight months ago; you say one week you made £4 15s.?—A. Yes.

Q. How much have your wages averaged since you arrived?—A. I have earned about £3 8s. or £3 10s. a week since I came, but sometimes we were stopped for want of metal.

By Mr. FISHER:

Q. Suppose you were living with your family in this colony in the same comfortable way you did in England, and with the wages you get here at your particular work, in which place would you save the more money?—A. I dare say I should save more here if I had my family here. You must understand that because all my girls are servant girls, they would get more wages. I have three nice girls at service.

i. Statement of a tailor.

JOHN LIVINGSTONE sworn and examined.

Question. Where are you employed?—Answer. Scourfield & Coultas, Collins street.

Q. At what employment?—A. Tailoring.

Q. How many journeymen are employed along with you?—A. From twenty-five to thirty.

Q. That is the number employed upon the premises?—A. Yes, upon the premises.

Q Have your employers put work out to be done as well?—A. There is only one case of that, and that is a man that is in delicate health.

Q. He takes his work home?—A. In this instance he was allowed to do so.

Q. How many apprentices are employed in the establishment?—A. None.

Q. Is your work done by piece-work?—A. Yes.

Q. The whole of it?—A. Yes, with the exception of one man, who does jobbing.

Q. And he is paid by the day?—A. By the week.

Q. What is the average rate of wages that a journeyman can earn in your establishment?—A. We work by a time log; that is, a log framed that allows so many hours for each garment, and according to that garment, whether there is more or less work, it is paid accordingly, and that log is made which both the men and the employers have agreed to, and we are paid by that log at the rate of 10d. per hour.

Q. Coming back to my question, what does the average amount come to that the workmen earn upon this system?—A. That would be rather a difficult question for an ordinary journeyman to answer. I might be able to give an idea of my own, but when men sometimes work irregularly it is difficult to give an average.

Q. I go upon the assumption that a man works for a week—what is the avearge he can earn for a week; of course if he only works half a week he can only expect to earn half the amount—is it £3 a week, or £4 a week, or £3 10s. a week, or what?—A. In our shop about £2 to £3 a week is the range; it would not average £3 a week.

Q. How many hours a day do you work for that wage?—A. We work between ten and eleven hours a day.

Q. You are all good workmen—they employ first-class workmen, do they not?—A. Yes.

Q. And no apprentices are employed at all; you do not teach people?—A. We have no lads in the place sewing.

Q. Is it a fact then that first-class men like you, such as are employed in your shop, working ten or eleven hours a day, cannot average £3 a week?—A. No, we cannot.

Q. And you work ten or eleven hours a day?—A. That is true.

Q. You say 10d. an hour?—A. I say 10d. an hour. I take the case of a fairly average man. There are some men that are very expert at their business, and by constant working they might easily make the £3 a week, but other men could not come near it, but take a fair average man he will not make any more than 10d. an hour.

Q. We have a good deal of evidence from clothing manufacturers and others. I think more than one of them stated that their wages are considerably more than that, some as much as £4 a week?—A. That may be; perhaps I could explain that.

Q. Could not you earn as much as that in your first-class shop?—A. That is not earned upon their premises.

Q. How long have you been in the trade as a tailor?—A. I have been twenty-nine years in the country, and I have been working in Melbourne at the trade ever since, with a short period I was in Sydney.

j. Statement of a tailor.

DUNCAN McIVOR sworn and examined.

Question. Where are you employed?—Answer. At Peers & Frew, 58 Bourke street, east.

Q. At what are you employed?—A. Tailoring.

Q. Any particular branch?—A. Coat making.

Q. Entirely coat making?—A. All coats.

Q. How many journeymen are employed in the same establishment?—A. Five indoors.

Q. And how many out?—A. About the same number—five or six out.

Q. Are they all employed on coat work?—A. No.

Q. How many apprentices are there?—A. There are no apprentices at all.

Q. Do you work piece-work or day work?—A. Piece-work.

Q. Do you work by the log that the previous witness spoke about?—A. Yes.

Q. You heard his evidence about the average wages?—A. Yes.

Q. Do you indorse that, or is your idea different?—A. It is about that; I have not kept a calculation for some time, but I did keep one for several years, and it did not come to £2 10s.

Q. Have you been long in the trade now?—A. I have been for about twenty-six years in Melbourne.

Q. All the time in your trade?—A. Yes.

Q. Do you say that a pair of trousers could be made for 6s. a pair some time ago, and now they are made for 1s. 6d. a pair?—A. I heard a gentleman here give evidence that trousers were made for 1s. 6d.

Q. A pair of moleskin trousers, not tweed trousers?—A. Moleskin trousers.

Q. Those 6s. a pair were of what material?—A. I understood him to say trousers were made in his factories for 1s. 6d., but there is not more than 4d. difference between moles and tweeds.

Q. Then the establishment of factories has tended to reduce the price of the articles from 6s. to 1s. 10d.?—A. As far as the journeymen tailors are concerned, now with the introduction of female labor, now it is.

Q. That is to be attributed to the introduction of machines and female labor?—A. Yes.

Q. I think you said just now the journeymen tailors do not average 50s. a week?—A. No.

Q. And you also stated that their time is not all filled up—do you mean to say that the time as it is—their part time—does not average 50s. a week?—A. According to our earnings, taking the year round, they do not average 40s. to 45s. I think that our weekly wages throughout the year would average from 40s. to 45s.

Q. When they are working full time, what can they earn?—A. Of course, that it is a thing you would require to understand the trade. For instance, I might be working with a party at a job that I could make perhaps 5 or 6 or 10s. a week more than another man could do at his work.

Q. Take the average man at average work?—A. There is not one man in the shop out of employment, and just now they average 50s., I think, the year round.

Q. That is because their time is not filled in?—A. Exactly so.

Q. Suppose you are engaged constantly in coat making throughout the year, what would be your average earnings?—A. If I was employed coat making the year round, and were in good health, I should make £3 a week upon the average. I have done it many times, and could do it now.

Q. Have you any idea of the number of sewing hands now employed in your trade in Melbourne?—A. No.

k. Statement of a female mill-operative.

MARY PEGLER sworn and examined.

By the CHAIRMAN:

Question. What is your employment?—Answer. A weaver.

Q. In the Castlemaine mill?—A. Yes.

Q. How long have you been in the mill?—A. Five years at the end of next week.

Q. Since the commencement?—A. About six months after it commenced.

Q. Have you been weaving all the time?—A. No.

Q. What did you do at first?—A. I was picking wool at first.

Q. What did you earn at that employment?—A. From 3s. to 5s. a week.

Q. How long did you remain at that?—A. I do not know the exact time; six months, I think.

Q. What did you do next?—A. Burling.

Q. What did you earn at that?—A. About the same. I was at that about twelve months.

Q. What was the next stage?—A. Weaving.

Q. Have you been weaving ever since?—A. Yes.

Q. What did you earn at that when first you commenced?—A. About 12s. a week.

Q. What do you earn now?—A. 25s. to 30s.

Q. How do you account for the difference between your earnings at the commencement and now?—A. None can earn as much at first as they do afterwards.

Q. But how do you account for the difference?—A. Only that I got better accomplished at the work.

Q. You can do it faster?—A. Yes.

Q. You say you earn from 25s. to 30s. Do you oftener earn 25s. than you do the 30s.?—A. Yes.

Q. Have you that for yourself after paying your assistant?—A. I have no assistant.

Q. The other witness who just went out has no assistant?—A. Yes, she has.

Q. Could you have one if you chose?—A. Yes.

Q. Could you earn more if you had one?—A. I think not.

Q. Do you attend to two looms or one?—A. Two.

Q. Do you go home to your meals?—A. No.

Q. Do you take your meals in the factory?—A. Yes.

Q. In the room where you work?—A. No.

Q. Is there any special room where you could take meals?—A. No, only I and another girl go to one room.

Q. You could go to any room you like?—A. Yes.

Q. Every employé has the run of the factory at meal times?—A. Yes.

Q. Which room do you select for your meals?—A. The finishing room.

Q. Is that a little room up-stairs?—A. Yes.

Q. Have you conveniences provided for you to cook your dinner if you like?—A. We always take our dinners ready cooked, and sometimes we have it sent to us from home.

Q. You have conveniences for boiling water for tea, and so on?—A. Yes.

Q. Do the employés complain at all of not having a dining-room?—A. I never heard them.

Q. Would you consider it a great convenience to have such a room put up, with a few tables and forms?—A. I do not think so; I would just as soon like it as it is now.

Q. Do you like the occupation?—A. Yes.

Q. Have you good health?—A. Yes.

Q. Have you been ill since you were at it?—A. No.

Q. Do all the other girls who are weavers, and have been as long at the business as yourself and the one just gone out, earn the same wages?—A. Some vary.

Q. What has the lowest weaver? How many have been in the mills, to your knowledge, as long as you, who are weavers?—A. Only three, I think.

Q. Do all earn as much as you do?—A. Yes, they do.

Q. There is another in the mill beside the one examined this morning—that is Mary Ann Smith, the last witness—beside you; does she earn as much as you?—A. Yes.

Q. The others, who have not been so long as you, what do they earn?—A. Twelve shillings to £1 a week.

Q. Are they as good at it as you?—A. Yes, and do it as well as I do.

Q. What they do of it?—A. Yes.

Q. But they cannot do it as quickly?—A. No.

By Mr. MUNRO:

Q. Do not you think the hours are rather long?—A. I have no complaint.

Q. From 6 o'clock in the morning in winter?—A. I do not mind it. It is rather long, but we would not regard as much at 8 hours a day.

Q. Then in summer, the long hot days?—A. But I would not like to go home in the hot sunshine, I would rather go in the evening.

By Mr. TUCKER:

Q. How far do you live away?—A. About a mile.

Q. Are your parents alive?—A. Yes.

Q. What does your father do?—A. He works in Kunnock's tannery.

Q. How many are there in family beside yourself?—A. Three sisters and three brothers.

Q. Do any of them work in the mill?—A. No.

Q. Do any intend to go there?—A. No.

Q. Would you like them to go there?—A. There is only one that could, and that is my sister, and she must stop at home; some one must stop at home.

Q. After your own experience would you like to see your brothers and sisters there at work in the mill?—A. Yes, I would not mind. I like it very well, I am perfectly satisfied, and always have been ever since I went there.

By Mr. McINTYRE:

Q. Are you kindly treated by your employers?—A. Yes.

l. Statement of a female coat-maker.

Miss B. examined.

By the COMMISSION:

Question. You are employed in what capacity?—Answer. Coat-making.

Q. That is the highest branch of the trade?—A. Yes.

Q. Have you been long in that position?—A. About five years.

Q. In what firm?—A. Barthold.

Q. What terms were you engaged on when you entered into that business?—A. I went as apprentice for eighteen months.

Q. On what terms?—A. Two shillings sixpence a week for the first six months and 5s. the next six months and 7s. 6d. the next.

Q. And after the third six months?—A. On piece-work.

Q. What amount, as a general rule, does a fair hand earn on piece-work, after she has served eighteen months?—A. There are two different prices—the sacs and pagets—the pagets make more; about 30s. a week with very good work. At sacs you can make about £1.

Q. What portion of the coat do you make?—A. The paget coat.

Q. And you take it from the hands of the cutter?—A. No, from the forewoman; we get them from the cutter after they are trimmed.

Q. Are they tacked together for you?—A. Yes.

Q. Do you do all?—A. All but the button-holes and the machining.

Q. You do all that a competent hand is expected to do with a coat?—A. Yes.

Q. In the establishment you have been connected with, what proportion have the apprentices borne to the other hands?—A. The apprentices generally serve twelve months now, and we have only two or three now; there are very few hands there.

Q. When you are in full work have you many?—A. No, they do not keep a table at all for apprentices.

Q. Is the log that was agreed to on the strike taking place some few months ago the one that has been adhered to?—A. No, not the first one.

Q. Although it was tendered as a settlement of the question substantially, the employers have not complied with it?—A. The coats are paid by the log, but not the trousers and vests.

Q. And I suppose they are with piece-workers?—A. Yes.

Q. How many coats a week is a competent hand supposed to complete to earn, say 30s. a week or 25s. a week?—A. You have to make nine or ten; with pagets you get about 4s. 6d. for each coat, and you could only make about seven of them and be very smart.

Q. What time does your factory open and close?—A. About nine, and leave off about six.

Q. And how long do you get for lunch?—A. Three-quarters of an hour.

Q. Then you have about eight hours?—A. Yes.

Q. Do you take work home?—A. Very seldom; some of them do, to make any money at it at all.

Q. What time do you consider it would take a fair hand to be a competent coat-maker?—A. It would take two years.

Q. Do you think it is fair that those who have not served two years should enter into competition with those who have?—A. No.

Q. Do they not sometimes do it for less money than competent persons will, and bring the price down?—A. Yes, that is one of our difficulties; they have tried since the log to reduce them, and they give them out-door work to do.

Q. Those who are not thoroughly competent do it for less money?—A. No, they do not do it, but the employer wants them to reduce it.

Q. Did your employers agree to this log?—A. They agreed to it, but they did not keep to it.

Q. What is the reason?—A. I do not know.

Q. What reason have they assigned?—A. They said it was too high, and they agreed to take it, but they have not done so.

Q. How long after signing the agreement did they break it?—A. About three weeks or a month after. He has given most of the work outside to be done—he gets it cheaper.

Q. Those are the "sweaters"?—A. Yes.

Q. Are they members of the union?—A. I do not think all of them are; some might be.

Q. What action did the employés take when they found the employers refused to acknowledge this log?—A. They could not do anything, and when the hands would not take the work for the money they sent it outside.

Q. Do you think that the strike that took place three months ago placed you in a better position than you are in at the present time?—A. It did for a while, but it did not continue, and everywhere the work went out the hands inside had nothing to do.

Q. Do you think the majority of the employés are worse off now than before the strike?—A. The majority of them are.

Q. Then, virtually the strike was a bad thing?—A. It was for some of the hands—the out-door hands made a benefit by it.

Q. The strike prevented the lowering of the prices beyond what they were at the time—temporarily?—A. Yes.

Q. If the employers could have been compelled to have kept up to their agreement, the employés would have been satisfied?—A. Yes.

Q. Though a number of outside persons were brought into competition with the factory hands, was that through the strike?—A. No.

Q. Did they carry on business before?—A. Not so many, nearly.

Q. Then, in consequence of the strike, and the prices being fixed, the threat the employers used was that they could get the work done outside by those "sweaters," and so brought you down to their prices?—A. Yes.

Q. And so more "sweaters" were brought into competition with the factory hands?—A. Yes.

SAFETY OF EMPLOYÉS.

Special provision has been made by the legislature of Victoria for inclosing or otherwise guarding machinery in motion, so as to protect employés in factories from injury or accident. So also in mines, the employment of winding and lifting apparatus of a "safety" character is rendered obligatory upon mine owners; and government inspectors are appointed, whose duty it is to see that such legislative enactments are duly enforced.

A bill has recently been introduced into the Victorian parliament, making employers liable for personal injuries suffered by their employés while engaged in their service, in the following cases:

(1) By reason of any defect in the state or condition of the ways, works, machinery, or plant connected with, or used in, the business of the employer; or

(2) By reason of the negligence of any person in the service of the employer who has any superintendence intrusted to him whilst in the exercise of such superintendence; or

(3) By reason of the negligence of any person in the service of the employer to whose orders or directions the workman at the time of the injury was bound to conform and did conform, where such injury resulted from his having so conformed; or

(4) By reason of the act or omission of any person in the service of the employer done or made in obedience to the rules or by-laws of the employer, or in obedience to particular instructions given by any person delegated with the authority of the employer in that behalf; or

(5) By reason of the negligence of any person in the service of the employer who has the charge or control of any signal points, locomotive engine, or train or trucks upon a railway—the workman, or, in case the injury results in death, the legal personal representatives of the workman and any person entitled in case of death shall have the same right of compensation and remedies against the employer, and may recover from the employer compensation by way of damages as for a tort committed by such employer as if the workman had not been a workman of, nor in the service of, the employer nor engaged in his work.

If an employé is a member of a friendly society or trades union, provision is made for medical aid and monetary relief in case of sickness or disability, and for the payment of a certain sum to his family in the event of his death.

In 1882 there were 32 friendly societies in Victoria, with 776 branches, and 51,399 members, showing a total income of £194,845, and a total expenditure of £165,788.

The law also takes cognizance of all factories and work rooms where more than ten persons are employed, and prescribes that these shall be constructed so as to secure to the employés a sufficient quantity of pure air and efficient ventilation, and a system of inspection has been established with a view to giving adequate effect to these precautions. Measures are also in contemplation for limiting the number of hours during which young persons may be legally employed in shops, factories, and workrooms; official inquiries having demonstrated the necessity for legislative intervention in this matter.

Within the past few years there has arisen, among young girls more particularly, a great competition for employment in factories. Wages in this particular branch of industry have fallen in consequence, and, while there is a great demand for labor in the country districts, there is a good deal of overcrowding in factories and workrooms, much slop work at very low prices, and a good deal of "sweating" on the part of middlemen.

Thus there has arisen a necessity for special legislation of the kind previously referred to. On the other hand there are many large employers who display a laudable consideration for the health and comfort of their employés and the relations of both in all such cases are of an agreeable and harmonious character.

The royal commission on employés in shops, in their report on the operation of the Victorian factory act, submits the following summary of recommendations:

1. That a thoroughly comprehensive measure amending the Victorian factory act 1874 be submitted to parliament during the ensuing session, and which shall embrace the following provisions:

2. All factories, workrooms, and places in which work for hire is executed shall be registered.

3. An annual licensing fee of a nominal amount shall be imposed and payable by the registered person carrying on such establishment or place of business.

4. Factories and workrooms shall be open for inspection during reasonable hours.

5. A heavy penalty shall be imposed for noncompliance with the regulations respecting ventilation, lighting, space, cleanliness, and sanitary accommodation.

6. Wherever possible, the sexes in factories shall be separated.

7. The eight-hours system shall be one of the fundamental principles of the bill.

8. An arrangement may be made by which employés can obtain the Saturday half-holiday, but the hours of work during the six working days of the week shall not exceed forty-eight.

9. Exemption from the regulation as regards hours of labor may be obtained upon application to the chief secretary in cases of great or sudden emergency.

10. The exemption shall only be permitted to meet the particular emergency.

11. A chief inspector shall be appointed as executive officer under the act.

12. The chief inspector shall be an officer under the central government.

13. Assistant inspectors shall be appointed to country districts.

14. Prosecutions for breaches of the act shall be directed by the chief secretary upon the recommendation of the chief inspector.

15. In all factories and workrooms lists shall be kept giving the names, ages, hours of employment, and rate of remuneration of the employés.

16. Truant officers to have access to factories and workrooms, with power to inspect lists and interrogate those employed.

17. Certificates of health and suitability shall be produced by young persons before obtaining employment.

18. Certificates shall be obtainable from a medical officer appointed under the act.

19. A certificate of age shall also be required.

20. Plans and specifications of all premises to be used for the purposes of a factory or workroom, shall be submitted for approval to the chief inspector of factories.

21. Boys under thirteen and girls under fourteen years of age shall not be employed in factories or workrooms.

22. The probationary period for apprentices and improvers shall not exceed six months.

23. Probationers after six months shall be entitled to the payment of a percentage upon their work.

24. The number of apprentices shall not exceed one in five of every adult employed.

25. Apprentices shall be legally indentured in accordance with the custom of the trade or business in which they are engaged.

26. Persons under 16 shall not be allowed to work except between the hours of 6 a. m. and 6 p. m.

27. No person under 20 years shall be allowed to work between midnight and 6 a. m.

28. Newspaper and other printing establishments shall be brought under the provisions of the factory act.

29. Employés shall not work more than four and a half hours consecutively with out an intermission for a meal.

30. Meals shall be taken outside the room in which work is carried on.

31. Employers shall, where necessary, provide the requisite accommodation and appliances for meals.

32. Special precautions shall be taken for the protection of employés where machinery is utilized.

33. Persons placed in charge of steam boilers and engines shall hold certificates of competency.

34. Notices shall be affixed in all factories indicating the hours of work and meals, and for the relays of hands if such are employed.

36. The sweating system shall be prohibited.

37. Employers shall provide all the accommodation necessary in connexion with the premises in which the factory business is conducted.

38. Employés shall be prohibited from taking work home from the factories.

39. If the quantity of work exceeds the capacity of the factory hands, and that the limited period allowed for overtime does not sufficiently meet the temporary pressure the extra work may be transferred to some other registered place of business.

THE SWEATING SYSTEM.

Referring to the " sweating system " the commissioners says :

The sweating system in connection with factories has been represented by every witness examined on the subject as constituting one of the most serious grievances with which the honest and legitimate worker has to contend. It serves to introduce'an element of unfair competition amongst employés. It encourages a surreptitious and dishonorable mode of dealing between employer and employed. It tends to bring down wages and to the production of an inferior article, without any corresponding diminution of price to the public. Further, while it prejudicially affects the comforts and conveniences of the domestic life of the working class, by converting the home into a workshop, it imperils the health of the community by work being frequently executed under unsanitary conditions, and in localities where epidemics are prevalent. The system appears to have originated in some of the employés being allowed to bring work home with them, after the factory closes for the day. A woman may have daughters who assist her, and thereby she is enabled to supplement her ordinary earnings. In time she employs apprentices, who receive no wages for the first six months, and often for a much longer period. Contracts are accepted by the sweaters at a lower rate than that prescribed by the log, and, where the work is superabundant subcontractors are engaged at a still lower rate, until many persons are unable to earn more than a bare subsistence, even though they labor fourteen and sixteen hours a day. In the boot trade also sweating is carried on extensively, and under conditions that seriously militate against the interests of the skilled workman. The sweating system in connection with the tailoring business bids fair to place the entire trade in the hands of females, who can of course work for lower wages than men. The latter are nowconfined to the finer and better class of work, but they are becoming gradually supplanted in the trade by females, despite the protracted hours of labor, the low rate of wages, and the small, badly lighted, and ill-ventilated rooms in which they have to work. Many young girls were found to prefer working for sweaters, alleging as a reason that the conduct and conversation of those employed in factories were objectionable on mora grounds.

POLITICAL RIGHTS.

As has been previously stated, every working man can exercise the suffrage if he is a rate payer, or by taking out an electoral right if he is not. His influence is a preponderating one in the political affairs of the colony, as both branches of the legislature are elective. The assembly is chosen by the adult male population of the colony, and the council or senate by all persons occupying houses or land of the ratable value of $50 per annum. The number of persons coming within the former category is 213,363, of whom 156,611 are on the rolls for the assembly, and 58,735 on those for the council. In legislative bodies thus constituted, all legislation is conformable to the popular will ; that is to say, it reflects the opinions, wishes, and aspirations of the most numerous classes of the community, and its general tendency is to favor labor and to exclude external competition.

With respect to the share of the public burdens borne by the wages earning classes of the country, it is relatively small. There is no poll tax in Victoria, and the gross amount of money yearly raised by impost on the people averages little more than $10 per head. Taxes on real estate are so adjusted as to exempt the cottage of the working man and the land of the small farmer from their operation, and legacy and succession duties leave the bequests of the operative classes untouched. Local taxation is very light. It rarely exceeds one shilling in the pound per annum on the ratable value of the property, and estimating the sum raised in this way every year at $1,800,000, nearly five-sevenths of this amount would be contributed by the wealthy classes. In order to prevent these from being heavily taxed by their poorer neighbors, who might favor a large expenditure of borrowed money in local improvements, for the sake of increasing the demand for labor, and consequently the rate of wages, the method of electing municipal and shire councils is by a cumulative system of voting, which gives the property owner two or three votes as against one of the ordinary rate payer.

EMIGRATION.

This question is irrelevant to the Australian colonies, whose population is being constantly increased by immigration both assisted and otherwise.

Occupation of the people in Victoria.

Occupations.	Males.		Females.	
	Under 20 years.	Over 20 years.	Under 20 years.	Over 20 years.
PROFESSIONAL AND SCHOLASTIC.				
Government officials and clerks	174	4,076	29	215
Clergymen and church officers	8	1,044	7	178
Law court officers, lawyers, &c	186	1,057		
Physicians, surgeons, and druggists	188	1,295	1	111
Authors, literary and scientific persons	25	462		10
Teachers, &c	382	2,238	983	3,192
Students and scholars	91,979	154	92,444	78
Artists	119	472	43	100
Musicians and music teachers	30	450	176	633
Actors, &c	49	403	28	80
DOMESTIC.				
Persons engaged—				
In boarding and lodging	44	3,689	47	3,495
In attendance	1,385	3,348	11,150	15,351
COMMERCIAL.				
Persons engaged—				
In mercantile pursuits	2,534	12,851	379	1,852
In transportation:				
Carriers on railways	195	2,654	10	239
Carriers on roads	1,150	7,127	1	13
Carriers on seas and rivers	204	3,135		24
Engaged in storage	170	1,078	7	2
Messengers and porters	965	523	19	52
AGRICULTURAL AND PASTORAL.				
Persons engaged—				
In agricultural pursuits	15,591	54,123	8,626	30,579
In pastoral pursuits	1,324	6,157	746	2,381
In similar pursuits	763	3,761	3	148

Occupation of the people in Victoria—Continued.

Occupations.	Males.		Females.	
	Under 20 years.	Over 20 years.	Under 20 years.	Over 20 years.

MANUFACTURING AND MECHANICAL.

Persons engaged in working and dealing in—

Books	1,174	2,122	80	116
Musical instruments	26	112		1
Prints and pictures	60	137	2	1
Carving and figures	46	100	5	11
Watches and philosophical instruments	130	423		3
Machines and tools	156	835	1	2
Carriages, harness, and implements	852	2,690	2	12
Ships and boats	26	581		1
Houses and buildings	2,017	13,454	1	290
Furniture	390	1,254	31	73
Chemicals	31	154	20	24
Other industrial pursuits	36	127	17	25
Textile fabrics	1,171	2,829	223	419
Dress	2,354	6,973	7,960	12,312
Fibrous materials	110	134	33	30
Animal food	1,216	4,376	32	1,069
Vegetable food	791	3,208	54	256
Drinks and stimulants	877	3,051	53	291
Animal products	394	1,483	29	44
Vegetable products	1,204	4,978	73	67
Coal	42	401		1
Stone, clay, earthenware, and glass	500	2,986	5	8
Gold, silver, and precious stones	160	474	8	6
Metals other than gold and silver	2,054	5,656	3	5
Water and ice	9	115		

MINING.

Gold miners:

Alluvial	804	11,231	2	
Quartz	870	7,365	1	
Diggers (not otherwise described)	1,447	12,432		2
Quartz crushing, &c., engaged in	264	771		
Miners (other metals and minerals)	6	40		
Others engaged in mining	122	706		3
Laborers and others not classified	6,492	33,051	1,212	4,773

FEMALE WAGES.

Female teachers in the state schools receive from $311 to $1,071 per annum and results, which may amount to an additional compensation equal to one-half the teacher's fixed salary. Postmistresses receive salaries varying from $292 to $876 per annum. The lowest rate of wages is probably paid to tailoresses, mantle-makers, and factory employés, which range from $2.92 to $6.08 per week. It would be extremely difficult to determine accurately the average rate of wages paid to adult females, but it will probably not vary materially from $4 to to $4.50 per week.

HOURS OF LABOR.

Although eight hours has never been recognized by an act of the Victorian parliament as a legal day's work, still in the case of government employés the eight hours standard is practically the prevailing one.

The hours of labor observed by those engaged in the retail trade in drapery, groceries, boots and shoes, and similar articles, are usually from 7 or 8 a. m. to 9 p. m. on ordinary nights, and until midnight on Saturdays. In fruit and confectionery shops, tobacconists', pawnbrokers', restaurants, and places of refreshment generally, the hours of attendance are said to be from fourteen to sixteen hours daily.

Employés in private workrooms generally commence work at 8.30 or 9 a. m., and with half an hour's, and sometimes only a quarter of an hour's, intermission for meals, they continue to labor often far into the night. Some of the hands also carry home the work with them, and labor for many hours after the factories are closed. In millinery and dressmaking there is often a show of complying with the more humane system of eight hours' work daily. As a matter of fact, however, this is the exception rather than the rule. The front doors are closed, but young girls are kept for many hours, and during the busy season all night. at work, in order to execute the orders received.*

Tailoresses, in many instances, have to work from fourteen to sixteen hours daily in order to earn a livelihood, while barmaids are not unfrequently employed from sixteen to nineteen hours out of the twenty-four.

Speaking of the necessity for legislation in connection with the regulation of the hours of labor, the employés in shops commission say:

Your commissioners, having due regard to the evidence elicited both from employers and employés, are convinced of the absolute necessity for legislative action in order to bring about some definite arrangement with respect to closing shops and suspending business at a reasonable hour in the evening. The history of the Early Closing Association and of the Salesmen and Assistants' Union demonstrates incontestably that, in the absence of any legal obligation to close, there will be found some who, from considerations of self-interest, will not be bound by any moral obligation to close early, or even at a reasonable hour. By means of continued agitation shopkeepers in the city and suburbs at various times have assented to the proposal to close early; they did so for a time, but gradually they fell back into the old system. Moral suasion has, no doubt, accomplished much in diminishing the hours of daily labor, but the large majority of the witnesses expressed the opinion that nothing less than an act of parliament would give permanence to the movement. Your commissioners are not unmindful of the consequences of any undue interference with the laws that may be said to govern the relations of employer and employé, but the obligations of humanity are paramount to those of trade, and therefore it is that we consider that the legislature should step in and seek to do for both employer and employed that which, of themselves, they are unable satisfactorily to accomplish.

MORAL AND PHYSICAL CONDITION OF FEMALE EMPLOYÉS.

It is difficult to state in general terms what is the moral and physical condition of female employés, because it varies so much in different places and in different establishments.

The system which prevails so generally in this colony of employing young women as barmaids in public houses is one which must have a prejudicial effect on the morals of females exposed from morning till night to the license of speech and manners indulged in by the frequenters of such places of public resort. On this point the commissioners appointed by the government of Victoria to inquire into the best means of regulating and shortening the hours of employés in shops and other establishments, say:

The employment of young women to serve in the bars of hotels and public houses, in whatever aspect regarded, must be pronounced as the result of a system in every respect objectionable. Apparently its immediate object is to increase the incentive to drink: the effect is the demoralization of the youth of both sexes—the only purpose served being to enhance the value of the property and augment the profits of those interested in the liquor traffic. Your commissioners have not yet completed this branch of their inquiry, but the testimony obtained from several witnesses, and especially from medical practitioners, goes to show that the employment of barmaids is deserving of the earnest attention of parliament. Some licensees are no doubt thoughtful and considerate of the health and feelings of their employés, but there are many and marked exceptions to this rule, whilst many first-class houses do not employ barmaids at all. Barmaids are generally chosen for their superior personal attractions, and their supposed power of inducing expenditure. They are fairly educated, of superior address, active, capable, and trustworthy. The business offers inducements which young girls accept in preference to seeking employment in factories or in domestic service. With the moral aspect of the question your commissioners do not propose to deal, as no evidence has yet been taken on the point ; but from the medical testimony it is undeniable that, in regard to the hours of labor, this class of

* Report of the royal commission on employés in shops.

employés are subjected to hardships more severe and physically distressing than perhaps any other class in the community. Dr. Girdlestone, health officer, declares that the barmaids are shamefully overworked. Mr. Martin Evans, city inspector, states that they work from sixteen to nineteen hours daily, often under extremely insanitary conditions.

Referring, subsequently, to the moral aspects of the question, the commissioners continue:

The employment of young women in bars appears from the evidence to be attended with temptations, to which they not unfrequently fall victims. The language and manners of the habitués of many hotels, as deposed to by witnesses, are offensive at times to every sense of womanly modesty and self-respect. The fatigues which they endure, the class of persons with whom they are compelled to associate, and other circumstances it would be superfluous to mention, induce sometimes habits of intemperance, with their inevitable consequences.

In the opinion of witnesses, barmaids are sometimes employed as decoys. With that view they are usually selected for their youth, agreeable manners, and personal attractions. Their retention depends upon their capacity for increasing business, so that it becomes a matter of self-interest that they shall induce the frequenters of hotels to indulge in excessive drinking. The presence of females naturally attracts young men, and produces habits both of intemperance and extravagance.

It seems to be acknowledged, also, that the congregation of large numbers of young women in sewing-factories and work-rooms, as well as the intermingling of the sexes during work hours, is inimical to public and private morality, and that it has led to a material increase in the ranks of fallen women in Melbourne and other large cities. In this connection the commissioners observe:

Not the least important feature of the case submitted by the employés who tendered their evidence was the absence of proper sanitary arrangements in many places of business. Those which the factories act does not reach are usually small, ill-ventilated, insufficiently lighted, and devoid even of the ordinary conveniences for the observance of decency. * * * While some employers evince a laudable anxiety for the comfort and convenience of their work-people, there are others wholly indifferent to their health and welfare. Employés are sometimes crowded into small rooms, which are suffocating in summer and intolerably cold in winter. Labor is carried on under both physical and moral disadvantages: resulting, there can be no doubt, in premature debility and disease, and the general deterioration of both mind and body of many young females. Upon this point the trades committee urge, "That the necessities of the young are cruelly ignored has been very clearly demonstrated by the evidence of every witness examined : not only have the existing evils tended to swell the ranks of rowdyism, but, what is more inexpressibly sad, they have been the immediate cause of the ruin and downfall of many of the weaker sex, a fact which can be demonstrated to the most skeptical by a stroll through the streets of this city after dark."

On the other hand, domestic servants, who are in receipt of large wages and are under the protection of their employers, are to a great extent removed from temptation, and constitute, as a class, a reputable and respectable portion of the community.

What are the means provided, and by whom, for the improvement of these employés?

There are no specific agencies at work to ameliorate the condition of female employés except a servants' and governess' home for the reception of young persons between the time of their quitting one engagement and obtaining another. It may not be irrelevant, however, to add in this connection that the charitable institutions of the colony include, among others, nine industrial and reformatory schools, seven orphan asylums, five female refuges, five benevolent asylums, a lying in hospital, a children's hospital, an immigrants' home, and an infant asylum.

CARE OF SICK AND DISABLED.

The Victorian factory act imposes certain restrictions on employers with respect to the proper sanitary conditions of factories and workrooms, while the ample provision made for the relief of persons suffering from illness or from accident in the general hospitals, of which there are thirty-five in the colony, by free dispensaries, and by the sick fund of the various friendly societies, is generally considered to be quite sufficient to meet all reasonable demands. Among the provisions of the factory act are the following:

3. No person or persons shall employ in any factory or work-room any female for more than eight hours in any one day in preparing or manufacturing articles for trade or sale.

4. For the purpose of carrying out the provisions hereof any person authorized by the central or local board of health under the second part of Act No. CCCX may enter and inspect any factory or work-room at any time during working hours. And the central or local board of health may from time to time make regulations (subject to the approval of the governor in council) respecting factories or work-rooms, for the purpose of determining the maximum number of persons to be employed in any one room, also for enforcing provisions for all necessary warmth, ventilation, and cleanliness therein, and further to order that all factories or work-rooms shall be provided with proper sanitary requirements; and such factories or work-rooms shall be deemed to be "public buildings" within the meaning of the thirty-first clause of the said act, and the observance of such regulations may be enforced and disobedience thereof punished in the same manner as the observance or infringement of regulations issued under the authority of the said section may be enforced or punished.

PAST AND PRESENT WAGES.

Ordinarily speaking, the labor market in Victoria is rather understocked than otherwise with adult males, and although at the dullest period of the year there is usually an outcry about the unemployed, there is always at the same time an unsatisfied demand for manual labor in the country districts.

Up to the present time the employment of women in various industrial capacities has had, with few exceptions, no appreciable effect on the wages of men, as they do not enter sufficiently into competition with the latter to influence their earnings. Among the exceptions referred to are, notably, journeymen tailors and factory employés. The rate of wages paid to women and the cost of living are substantially the same as they were five years ago.

The two principal causes which operate to lower the rate of wages in the colony are the "sweating system" and the employment of unindentured apprentices. It is the practice of many tradesmen to discharge their apprentices as soon as they begin to earn respectable wages, and to replace them with others who, with no binding agreement that they shall be properly taught, have the option of leaving whenever they choose. Not to speak of the cheap labor thus introduced into the several trades, these imperfectly trained apprentices, on leaving their employers, enter into competition with regular tradesmen, with the result that the rate of wages is lowered to the standard of that of the young and incompetent.

EDUCATION AMONG FEMALE EMPLOYÉS.

The State school system which brings a good elementary education within the reach of the poorest members of the community, and which is compulsory as well as gratuitous, insures the instruction of all young persons in reading, writing, and arithmetic, so that factory girls and other females earning their own livelihood are tolerably well informed. But the effect of such employment on the family circle is anything but a beneficial one. Young girls and boys acquire a position of quasi independence, and they throw off parental authority at the very period of life when their characters require most discipline and restraint. They claim and exercise a freedom of action which is frequently abused. Their evenings are too often unemployed, and are spent in questionable society and amusements. Young factory girls, as a rule, grow up ignorant of household duties, and with an inordinate love of dress. They dislike domestic service, and are restive under the restraints which it necessarily involves. The result is that when they reach a marriageable age they are illy prepared to discharge the duties of a wife and mother, and in many instances are more likely to become an encumbrance to a working-man than a helpmate.

I have not yet received, in response to the labor circular, any reports from the consular agents at Albany and Adelaide, but it may be observed that, with the exception of Queensland, where Kanakas or Polynesians are employed by the sugar planters for a term of three years at the rate of $30 a year, with clothing and rations,* the conditions of labor are substantially the same in all the Australian colonies.

ACKNOWLEDGMENTS.

In conclusion, it affords me great pleasure to acknowledge my indebtedness to H. H. Hayter, esq., government statistician; P. P. Labertonche, esq., secretary for Victorian railways; Capt. R. Fullarton, chief harbor-master; and James Smith, esq., for valuable statistical and other interesting information embraced in this report.

O. M. SPENCER,
Consul-General.

UNITED STATES CONSULATE-GENERAL,
Melbourne, October 8, 1884.

I. GENERAL TRADES.

Wages paid to the general trades in Melbourne.

Occupations.	Lowest.	Highest.	Average.
BUILDING TRADES.			
Bricklayers................................per day...	$2 43	$2 92	$2 67
Hod-carriers................................do....	1 58	1 70	1 64
Masons................................do....	2 43	2 92	2 67
Tenders................................do....	1 70	1 94	1 82
Plasterers................................do....	2 43	2 92	2 55
﹒enders................................do....	1 70	1 94	1 82
Slaters................................do....			2 92
Plumbers................................per week..	14 60	17 03	15 80
Carpenters................................per day..	2 43	2 92	2 55
Gasfitters................................per week..	14 60	17 03	15 80
Painters and glaziers................................per day..	2 19	2 43	2 31
OTHER TRADES.			
Bakers................................per week..	6 08	14 60	7 30
Blacksmiths................................per day..	2 43	3 40	2 92
Bookbinders................................per week..	9 73	14 60	10 94
Brick-makers................................per 1,000..	4 38	4 87	4 50
Butchers................................per week..	9 73	12 16	10 94
Brass-founders................................per day..	1 94	2 92	2 31
Cabinet-makers................................per week..	10 94	19 47	14 60
Confectioners................................do....	3 65	17 03	9 73
Cigar-makers................................per 1,000..			7 30

* Vide my report on the Queensland labor problem with dispatch No. 184, December 23, 1882.

Wages paid to the general trades in Melbourne—Continued.

Occupations.	Lowest.	Highest.	Average.
OTHER TRADES—Continued.			
Coopers..per week..	$10 94	$14 60	$12 16
Distillers ....do....	7 30	14 60	9 73
Draymen and teamsters ....do....	9 73	14 60	10 94
Engravers ....do....	7 30	48 67	21 90
Jewelers ....do....	13 38	38 93	19 47
Laborers, porters, &c ....per day..	1 70	1 04	1 82
Lithographers ....per week..	12 16	18 25	14 60
Maltsters ....do....	10 94	14 60	11 55
Navvies...per day..	1 46	1 70	1 58
Polishers ....per week..	9 73	14 60	10 94
Quarrymen ....per day..	1 94	2 92	2 19
Saddle and harness makers.............................per week...	9 73	14 60	12 16
Stevedores.....................................:.......... per day..	2 43	2 92	2 55
Stone-breakers .... per cubic yard..	36	85	60
Tanners and curriers.................................per week..	8 76	14 60	10 94
Tailors..do....	12 16	14 60	12 81
Tinsmiths...do....	9 73	14 60	13 38
Upholsterers ....do....	12 16	19 47	14 60

II. FACTORIES, MILLS, ETC.

Wages paid in factories and mills in Melbou , Australia.

[Per week of forty-eight hours.]

Occupations.	Lowest.	Highest.	Average.
Carriage and harness:			
Smiths...per week..	$10 94	$19 47	$14 60
Body-makers ....do....	12 16	21 90	19 47
Wheelers...do....	12 16	17 03	15 81
Painters ....do....	11 64	18 24	14 60
Trimmers ....do....	12 16	17 03	15 81
Vycemen ....do....	6 08	7 30	6 56
Clothing:			
Tailors..do....	9 73	12 16	10 94
Mantle-makers ....do....	3 65	6 08	4 25
Milliners, first class ....do....			17 03
Milliners, second class...do....			8 52
Dressmakers and needlewomen..............................do....	3 65	6 08	4 13
Tailoresses...do....	3 04	8 52	3 89
Pressers ....do ..	9 73	13 38	10 94
Shirt-makers ....do....	2 92	6 08	4 38
Machinists ....do....	4 87	8 52	6 08
Boot-makers:			
Riveters children's boots ....per pair..			12
Riveters boys' boots...do....			20
Riveters women's boots ....do....			24
Riveters men's boots ....do....			30
Wellingtons ....do			2 43
Elastics..do ...			1 82
Machinists ....per week..	3 65	7 30	4 87
Hatters:			
Body-makers...per dozen..	2 92	4 87	3 65
Finishers ....do....	2 92	5 84	4 13
Shapers ....do....	97	2 92	1 82
Crown-sewers ....do....	85	1 21	97
Trimmers .... do ..			1 46

III. FOUNDRIES, MACHINE-SHOPS, AND IRON WORKS.

Wages paid in foundries, machine-shops, and iron works in Melbourne.

[Per week of forty-eight hours.]

Occupations.	Lowest.	Highest.	Average.
Blacksmiths................................per day....	$2 43	$3 40	$2 67
Farriers:			
Firemen ....per week..			13 38
Doormen................................do....	7 30	9 73	8 26
Hammermen ....per day..	1 70	1 94	1 82
Fitters ....do....	2 19	2 92	2 43
Turners ....do....	2 43	2 92	2 43
Boiler-makers and platers ....do....	2 43	3 40	2 67
Riveters.................................do....	2 19	2 67	2 31
Molders ....do....	2 43	2 92	2 61
Brass-finishers and coppersmiths ....do	1 94	2 92	2 55
Tinsmiths ....per week..	9 73	14 60	13 38
Iron-workers ....do....	12 16	14 60	12 77
Galvanizers.............................do....			14 60

V. MINES AND MINING.

Wages paid per week of forty eight hours in and in connection with gold mines in Victoria, Australia.

Occupations.	Lowest.	Highest.	Average.
General managers	$12 16	$58 40	$24 33
Legal managers	2 43	73 00	9 73
Mining managers	10 94	34 07	19 47
Engineers	9 73	29 20	19 47
Engine drivers.......................................	9 73	17 03	14 60
Pitmen	6 33	19 47	9 73
Blacksmiths	9 73	19 47	14 60
Carpenters	10 21	19 47	14 60
Foremen of shift.....................................	10 21	14 60	12 16
Miners	9 73	14 60	11 55
Surface men	6 08	12 16	9 73
Boys	3 65	9 73	6 08
Chinese	2 92	8 76	6 56

VI. RAILWAY EMPLOYÉS.

Wages paid per day to railway employés (those engaged about stations as well as those engaged on the engines and cars, linemen, railroad laborers, &c.), in Victoria, Australia.

Occupations.	Lowest.	Highest.	Average.
Carriage cleaners	$1 21	$2 67	$1 70
Examiners	1 94	2 55	2 19
Builders			2 43
Fitters	2 19	2 55	2 43
Trimmers	2 31	2 43	2 37
Engine drivers	2 67	3 65	2 92
Firemen	1 94	2 43	2 06
Cleaners	1 21	1 58	1 33
Lighters-up			2 06
Assistant lighters-up............................			1 82
Fuelmen			1 70
Gate-keepers	12	1 70	1 00
Gangers...	2 19	2 92	2 43
Goods foremen and porters	1 70	2 55	1 94
Guards..	1 70	2 67	2 06
Inspectors of work	3 04	4 87	3 65
Lampmen	1 21	1 94	1 46
Line repairers and plate-layers	1 46	2 92	1 94
Number-takers	73	1 46	1 21
Plate-layers' foremen			2 19
Point cleaners	1 46	1 82	1 70
Porters	73	2 67	1 70
Signalmen	1 21	2 19	1 82
Shunters	1 21	2 06	1 46
Ticket collectors	1 21	1 33	1 70
Wagon builders.....................................			2 43
Yardsmen	1 82	2 92	2 19

VII. Ship-yards and Ship-building.

Wages paid per week of forty-eight hours in ship-yards in Melbourne, Victoria.

Occupations.	Lowest.	Highest.	Average.
Shipwrights			$17 52
Iron-workers	$14 60	$17 52	16 06
Rivet boys	4 38	4 87	4 62
Engineers	14 60	17 52	16 06

VIII. Seamen's Wages.

Wages paid per month to seamen (officers and men)—distinguishing between ocean, coast, and river navigation, and between sail and steam—in Victoria, Australia.

Occupations.	Lowest.	Highest.	Average.
Steamships: COASTING.			
Mates			$58 40
Second mates			43 80
Able seamen			34 07
Sailing vessels:			
Mates	$34 07	$38 93	38 08
Second mates			29 20
Able seamen			24 33
Steamships: OCEAN-GOING.			
Officers	38 40	58 40	
Able seamen	19 47	24 33	21 90
Sailing vessels:			
Mates	34 07	43 80	38 93
Second mates			29 20
Able seamen	19 47	24 33	21 90

IX. Store and Shop Wages.

Wages paid per week of forty-eight hours in drapers' stores, wholesale or retail, to males and females, in Melbourne.

Occupations.	Lowest.	Highest.	Average.
Male assistants	$7 30	$26 76	$14 60
Female assistants	7 30	21 90	9 73
Carpet salesmen	10 94	21 90	17 03

X. Household Wages in Towns and Cities.

Wages paid to household servants (towns and cities) in Melbourne.

Occupations.	Lowest.	Highest.	Average.
Males: HOUSEHOLD.			
Coachmen, grooms, &c........per week..	$4 87	$7 30	$6 08
Gardeners................do...	4 87	7 30	6 08
Butlers..................do....	4 87	9 73	8 50
Females:			
Cooks.................per annum..	194 66	486 65	253 00
Laundresses.............do...	170 33	253 00	194 66
Housemaids.............do....	121 66	194 66	146 00
Nursemaids.............do....	97 33	194 66	121 66
General servants.........do....	146 00	185 00	170 00
Males: HOTEL.			
Barmen................per week..	7 30	10 94	8 50
Waiters.................do...	4 87	9 73	6 10
Boots.................do...	3 65	4 87	4 13
Ostlers.................do...	4 25	4 87	4 38
Cooks.................do....	4 87	15 81	9 73
Female:			
Barmaids..............per week..	3 65	6 08	4 25
Waitresses..............do....	3 65	4 87	4 25
Housemaids.............per annum..	146 00	194 65	170 33
Cooks..................do....	243 33	486 65	292 00

XI. AGRICULTURAL WAGES.

Wages paid to agricultural laborers and household (country) servants in Victoria, Australia.

Occupations.	Lowest.	Highest.	Average.
FARM.			
Plowmen ....per week. and found..	†4 87	$6 08	$5 34
Laborers and milkmen......................................do....	3 65	4 87	4 13
Cheese-makers...do....	6 08	9 73	7 30
Reapers ....per acre, and found..	2 43	3 65	2 92
Mowers...do..	85	1 46	1 21
Thrashers.................................per bushel, and found..	10	14	13
Cooks, male ....per annum, and found..	243 33	292 00	253 00
Dairy-maids...do....	146 00	170 33	156 00
Cooks, female..do....	146 00	243 33	194 70
General servants ....do	146 00	170 33	156 00
Married couples ....do....	292 00	438 00	389 32
Hop-pickers ....per bushel..	7	9	8
Maize-pickers ....per bag...			12
STATION.			
Boundary riders ....per annum, with rations..	194 66	292 00	253 00
Shepherds ....do....	175 19	253 00	194 66
Stockmen...do....	292 00	365 00	340 65
Hut-keepers ....do....	126 53	194 66	146 00
Cooks, male..do....	243 33	292 00	253 00
Laborers ....per week, with rations..	3 65	4 87	4 13
Drovers...do....	6 08	9 73	8 50
Sheep-washers...do	3 65	6 08	5 10
Shearers ...'...per 100..	2 92	3 65	3 40
Cooks, female................................per annum. and found..	146 00	243 33	219 00
General servants ....do ..	97 33	194 66	170 33
Married couples ....per annum, with rations..	292 00	438 00	389 32

XIII. GOVERNMENT DEPARTMENTS AND OFFICES.

Wages paid to employés in Government departments and offices (exclusive of tradesmen and laborers) in Melbourne, Victoria.

[Per month forty-eight hours]

Occupations.	Lowest.	Highest.	Average.
Department of trade and customs.			
Clerk..per annum..	$253 04	$2,516 00	$1,495 00
Warehousekeeper.....................................do....	851 64	2,516 00	....
Landing surveyor.....................................do....	2,511 12	2,944 23	....
Landing waiter..do	1,265 29	2,360 25	2,068 26
Rebonding officer......................................per week..	....	....	23 40
Locker..per annum..	535 32	1,459 95	973 30
Weigher...do....	379 59	973 30	851 64
Watchman...do....	....	....	632 65
Messenger ....per week..	2 92	10 94	....
Tide surveyor.......................................per annum..	....	....	1,703 28
Tide waiter...do ..	608 31	651 64	....
Post-office and electric telegraph.			
Clerk..per annum..	253 06	2,433 25	973 30
Telegraph operators ....do ...	496 38	1,703 28	924 64
Letter-sorters...per week..	10 94	18 73	15 81
Letter-carriers.......................................do....	6 56	13 86	9 73
Letter-stampers ... .do....	10 21	12 86	12 16
Messengers ....do....	2 55	7 30	4 87
Telegraph line repairers ....do....	12 40	14 60	13 38
Female assistants ....per annum..	253 06	467 18	340 66
Treasury Department.			
Receiver and paymaster ....per annum..	438 00	3,041 56	1,459 95
Clerk...do....	97 33	3,041 56	973 30
Dispatch clerk ....do....	....	....	875 97
Messenger..do....	292 00	730 00	....

XV. PRINTERS AND PRINTING OFFICES.

Statement showing the wages paid to printers (compositors, pressmen, proof-readers, &c.) in Melbourne, Victoria.

[Per week of forty-eight hours.]

Occupations.		Lowest.	Highest.	Average.
Printers	per 1,000..	......	......	24
Lithographers	per week..'	$12 16	$14 25	$14 60
Binders	do ..	9 73	14 60	12 16
Paper rulers	do..	14 60	17 03	15 81
Sewers and folders, females	do....	3 65	6 08	4 87
GOVERNMENT PRINTING OFFICE.				
Overseers	per annum..	973 30	1,825 00	1,703 28
Reader	do ..	1,216 63	1,338 29	1,313 96
Compositors	do ..	875 97	1,216 64	921 63
Engineer	per week....	....	....	23 54
Machinist	do...	17 03	21 90	20 68
Warehouseman	do ...	13 40	19 47	14 60
Binders	do ...	8 50	19 47	17 03
Folders and sewers	do ...	6 08	8 50	7 30

The prices paid for the necessaries of life, clothing, rent, &c.

Articles.	Price.	Articles.	Price.
Agricultural produce:		**Garden produce:**	
Wheat.........per bushel..	$0 93 to $0 97	Potatoes ....per cwt..	60 to 97
Barley ....do....	1 03 to 1 13	Onions ....do ..	97 to 1 46
Oats ....do ..	56 to 73	Carrots ...dozen bunches..	12 to 18
Maize ....do....	1 13 to 1 21	Turnips ....do....	12 to 18
Bran ....do ..	22 to 24	Radishes ....do ..	08 to 12
Hay ....ton..	14 60 to 29 30	Cabbages ....each..	03 to 04
Flour .....do....	40 75 to 43 80	Cauliflowers.........do ..	03 to 06
Bread ....4-pound loaf..	11 to 13	Lettuce ....do ..	02
Grazing produce:		Green peas .....per pound..	03 to 08
Cattle-fat ...each ..	19 47 to 63 26	**Miscellaneous articles:**	
Milch cows ....do ...	24 33 to 48 67	Tea ....per pound..	36 to 60
Sheep ....do....	1 94 to 4 62	Coffee ....do....	30 to 36
Lambs ....do....	1 46 to 2 92	Sugar ....do....	06 to 08
Beef ....per pound..	06 to 16	Rice ....do ..	03 to 04
Mutton ....do ..	04 to 10	Jams ....pound tin	10 to 14
Veal ....do ..	10 to 16	**Tobacco:**	
Pork ....do....	12 to 20	Colonial .....per pound..	73
Lamb ....per quarter..	48 to 85	American ....do....	1 21 to 1 46
Dairy produce:		Soap ....do....	06 to 08
Butter:		Candles ....do ..	18 to 24
Fresh ......per pound	32 to 36	Salt ....do ..	2
Potted ....do....	20	Coals.........per ton..	6 08 to 8 72
Cheese ....do....	18 to 24	Firewood ....do....	2 31 to 2 92
Milk ....per quart..	08 to 12	**Clothing:**	
Farm-yard produce:		Tweed suits	9 73 to 14 60
Turkeys ....each..	2 43 to 3 65	Tweed coats	4 50 to 8 50
Geese ....do....	85 to 1 21	Tweed trousers	2 55 to 4 01
Ducks ....do ..	60 to 73	Mole trousers	1 21 to 2 55
Fowls ....do ..	60 to 73	Cotton shirts	48 to 1 09
Rabbits ....per pair..	24 to 36	Wool shirts	1 33 to 2 55
Pigeons ....do ..	60	Flannel shirts	1 09 to 1 58
Sucking pigs....each..	2 43 to 3 40	Felt hats	60 to 2 06
Bacon ....per pound..	16 to 24	Socks	12 to 24
Ham ....do....	20 to 26	Boots and shoes	1 21 to 4 87
Eggs....per dozen..	28 to 36		

WEST AUSTRALIA.

REPORT BY CONSULAR AGENT DYNES, OF ALBANY.

I. GENERAL EMPLOYMENT.

Wages paid in Albany.

Occupations.	Lowest.	Highest.	Average.
	£ s. d.	£ s. d.	
Carpenters ....per day..	10 0	12 0	$2 88
Builders ....do....	8 0	10 0	2 40
Brick-layers ....do....	10 0	12 0	2 88
Brick-layers' laborers ....do....		6 0	1 44
Stone masons.....................................do....	8 0	10 0	2 40
Blacksmiths ....do....	8 0	10 0	2 40
Plasterers ....do....	10 0	12 0	2 88
Plasterers' laborers ....do....		6 0	1 44
Cabinet-makers..................................do....	10 0	12 0	2 88
Drivers ....do....		6 0	1 44
Teamsters ....do....		6 0	1 44
Laborers, general ....per month..		6 0	1 44
Teamsters, public schools.........................do....	4 0 0	10 0 0	48 65
Tanners ....per day..		6 0	1 44
Hod-carriers ....do....		6 0	1 44
Farm laborers ....per month..	2 10 0	4 0 0	19 20
Domestics....................................per year..	15 0 0	40 0 0	194 65
Team drivers ....per month..	3 0 0	4 0 0	19 20

VIII. SEAMEN'S WAGES.

Wages paid per month to seamen (officers and men), distinguishing between sail and steam.

Occupations.	Lowest.	Highest.	Average.
Master, steamer...	£20	£30	$146 60
First officer	12	20	97 32
Second officer...	8	15	73 00
Third officer	7	12	58 41
Chief steward		15	73 00
Second steward		9	43 78
Third steward..		7	34 06
Cook		9	43 78
Firemen...	7	8	38 92
Seamen		6	29 17
Master, sailing ship	12	15	73 00
First officer	7	9	43 78
Second officer	6	8	38 92
Seamen		5	24 33
Cook		6	29 14

IX. STORE AND SHOP WAGES.

Wages paid per week of six days, 7 a. m. to 6 p. m., stores, wholesale or retail, to males and females, in Albany.

Occupations.	Lowest.	Highest.	Average.
Shop-boys	£4	£6	$29 19
Shop-men	7	12	58 38
Shop-clerks	12	18	87 57
Females in shops	4	6	29 19
Yard-men...		7	34 06
Butchers..		12	58 38
Draymen..		7	34 06

NEW ZEALAND.

REPORT BY CONSUL GRIFFIN, OF AUCKLAND.

The average rates of wages paid to laborers of almost every class in New Zealand do not differ greatly from the rates for the same classes of labor in the older States in America. The industrial development of the colony, due to British immigration, began only about fifty years ago, and the opportunities for the profitable employment of labor are so great that no over-supply of laborers has ever been experienced in the colony. The farming and grazing interests are both extensive, supplying a large amount of the food products and woolen goods needed for home consumption, besides which there is yielded a steadily increasing supply of grain for export. The mining interests are likewise extensive. The average annual yield of gold during the last few years, in the North and the South Islands together has been about $5,000,000. The coal-fields, which exist in every district, furnishing the greater part of the fuel used in the cities, give rise to a growing demand for labor. When there are added to these the iron industries, the timber trade, the cement interests, and various forms of manufacturing not referred to above, together with the shipping and fisheries, almost every one of which is on the increase, it will be seen that a large field for labor exists here.

The figures given in the table herewith appended apply to labor in the district of Auckland, in the North Island, where, owing to a greater diversity of industry than in any other district, perhaps, the standard of wages in the trades is fixed. The short notice given me for the preparation of this report precludes a greater definiteness of detail in these tables.

I. GENERAL TRADES.

Wages paid per week of sixty hours in Auckland.

Occupations.	Lowest.	Highest.	Average.
BUILDING TRADES.			
Bricklayers	$14 59	$18 97	$17 51
Hod-carriers	8 75	11 67	10 21
Masons	14 59	20 43	17 51
Tenders	8 75	11 67	10 21
Plasterers	14 59	20 43	17 51
Tenders	8 75	11 67	10 21
Roofers	10 21	17 51	14 59
Plumbers	13 13	17 51	14 59
Carpenters	10 21	17 51	14 59
Gas-fitters	13 13	17 51	14 59
OTHER TRADES.			
Blacksmiths	12 69	17 51	14 59
Book-binders	11 67	14 59	12 16
Butchers	8 75	11 67	10 21
Brass-founders	14 59	20 43	17 51
Cabinet-makers	10 21	17 51	14 59
Confectioners	8 75	11 67	10 21
Cigar-makers	10 21	15 00	13 16
Coopers	11 67	16 05	14 59
Drivers	8 75	11 67	10 21
Draymen and teamsters	8 75	11 67	10 21
Cab and carriage	10 21	13 13	11 67
Dyers	10 21	13 13	12 16
Gardeners	8 75	11 67	10 21
Hatters	10 21	13 13	12 16
Horseshoers	11 67	17 51	14 59
Jewelers	14 59	20 43	17 51
Laborers, porters, &c.	8 75	11 67	10 21

Wages paid per week of sixty hours in Auckland—Continued.

Occupations.	Lowest.	Highest.	Average.
OTHER TRADES—Continued.			
Millwrights.	$14 59	$20 43	$17 51
Nail-makers (hand)	11 67	14 59	12 16
Potters	11 67	16 05	14 59
Printers	15 00	25 00	30 00
Teachers (public schools)	12 00	27 00	22 00
Saddle and harness makers	10 00	13 00	15 00
Sail-makers	10 21	13 13	12 16
Stevedores	10 21	13 13	15 00
Tanners	10 21	17 00	14 00
Tailors	11 67	14 59	12 16
Telegraph operators	18 00	27 00	25 00
Tinsmiths	10 21	13 17	12 15
Weavers (outside of mills)	11 00	17 00	14 00

II. FACTORIES, MILLS, ETC.

Wages paid per week of sixty hours in factories or mills in Auckland.

Occupations.	Lowest.	Highest.	Average.
Timber mills*	$3 25	$18 97	$14 59
Soap factory	6 36	13 13	12 16
Candle and soap factories	8 75	11 67	10 21

*The timber industry in Auckland is the largest in the southern hemisphere, over 8,000 hands being employed in the town and country mills. The Auckland Timber Company, of which Mr. George Holdship is the managing director, gives employment to 1,000 hands.

III. FOUNDRIES, MACHINE-SHOPS, AND IRON WORKS.

Wages paid per week in foundries, machine-shops, and iron works in Auckland.

Occupations	Lowest.	Highest.	Average.
Foundrymen	$10 21	$17 51	$14 59

IV. GLASS-WORKERS.

Wages paid per week of sixty hours to glass-workers in Auckland.

Occupations.	Lowest.	Highest.	Average.
Glass-blowers	$17 02	$23 22	$19 46

V. MINES AND MINING.

Wages paid per week of sixty hours in and in connection with gold and coal mines in Auckland district.

Occupations.	Lowest.	Highest.	Average.
Coal miners	$13 13	$18 16	$17 21
Gold miners	15 13	18 16	17 21
Manganese?	13 13	17 21	17 21

VI. RAILWAY EMPLOYÉS.

Wages paid per week to railway employés (those engaged about stations, as well as those engaged on the engines and cars, linemen, railroad laborers, &c.) in Auckland.

Occupations.	Lowest.	Highest.	Average.
Engine-drivers	$11 13	$17 21	$12 16
Brakemen	9 16	13 14	11 91
Laborers	8 75	11 67	10 21

VII. SHIP-YARDS AND SHIP-BUILDING.

Wages paid per week of sixty hours in ship-yards—distinguishing between iron and wood ship-building—in Auckland.

Occupations.	Lowest.	Highest.	Average.
Wood	$10 21	$17 51	$14 50

VIII. SEAMEN'S WAGES.

Wages paid per month to seamen (officers and men) in Auckland.

Occupations.	Lowest.	Highest.	Average.
Mate	$38 93	$43 79	$38 93
Able seamen	24 33	38 93	29 19

IX. STORE AND SHOP WAGES.

Wages paid per week of sixty hours in stores, wholesale or retail, to males and females, in Auckland.

Occupations.	Lowest.	Highest.	Average.
Dry-goods stores, male	$9 73	$21 16	$12 16
Milliners, female	6 13	8 21	7 29
Dress-makers, female	3 40	4 13	3 65

X. HOUSEHOLD WAGES IN TOWNS AND CITIES.

Wages paid per week to household servants (towns and cities) in Auckland.

Occupations.	Lowest.	Highest.	Average.
General house servants	$1 94	$3 40	$2 67
Cooks	4 86	7 29	6 07
Laundresses	2 92	4 86	3 65
Housemaids	2 43	3 40	2 92
Nursemaids	1 21	2 43	1 94
Needlewomen	2 43	3 40	2 02

XI. AGRICULTURAL WAGES.

Wages paid per week* to agricultural laborers and household (country) servants in Otago, with board and lodging.

Occupations.	Lowest.	Highest.	Average.
Plowmen	$5 10	$6 31	$5 70
Reapers	9 73	10 94	10 33
Mowers	9 73	14 59	12 16
Thrashers	9 73	12 16	10 94
Farm laborers	4 85	6 07	5 46
Shepherds	6 07	9 73	8 90
Stock-keepers	6 07	9 73	8 90
Sheep-washers	6 11	8 51	7 32
Men cooks on farms	5 59	7 20	6 44
Female farm servants	3 04	3 89	3 46

* Laborers are frequently employed by the day, without board, at wages averaging 30 per cent. more than the figures here given.

XII. CORPORATION EMPLOYÉS.

Wages paid per week of forty-eight hours to the corporation employés in the city of Auckland.

Occupations.	Lowest.	Highest	Average.
Book-keepers in banks	$17 02	$28 22	$19 46
Book-keepers, in other corporations	15 32	25 40	17 52
Messengers in banks	4 80	7 20	6 07
Confidential clerks in stores and banks	17 02	28 22	19 46

XIII. GOVERNMENT DEPARTMENTS AND OFFICES.

Wages paid per month of one hundred and fifty-six hours to employés in Government departments and offices, exclusive of tradesmen and laborers, in Auckland.

Occupations.	Lowest.	Highest.	Average.
Government of the colony:			
Custom-house clerks	$60 81	$121 62	$81 25
Post-office clerks*	51 08	91 23	81 25
Letter-carriers†	51 08	91 23	81 25
Clerks in railroad, insurance, and registration offices	60 81	101 09	83 33
Telegraph operators†	63 25	97 20	87 58
Municipal government:			
Mayor			81 25
Town clerk			81 25

* Per month of 260 hours.   † Per month of 208 hours.

XIV. TRADES AND LABOR—GOVERNMENT EMPLOY.

Wages paid by the week of sixty hours to the trades and laborers in Government employ in Auckland.

Occupations.	Lowest.	Highest.	Average.
Porters	$8 71	$11 67	$10 25
Laborers	10 16	14 59	12 16

XV. PRINTERS AND PRINTING OFFICES.

About the same as the Western States of the United States; generally work by the piece.

COST OF LIVING.

The cost of living amongst the laboring classes other than those on farms is such as to enable them in most cases to approximate the condition of the better classes of laborers in the American cities. The farming classes are able generally to supply their tables well from the direct results of their labor. Some idea of the cost of food may be had from the table given below, embracing a range from the manufacturing and agricultural city and district of Auckland to the almost purely agricultural district of Marlborough, which includes no town of importance. The quality of wheat grown in New Zealand is worthy of note. Dr. Schomburgh, an authority on agriculture in Australasia, classes the leading varieties grown here with the very best American varieties. This being a grazing country, also, the beef and mutton used even upon the tables of workingmen, all of whom can afford meat every day, are of a good quality.

Average prices of provisions.

Articles.	Auck-land.	Canter-bury.	Otago.	Nelson.	Marl-borough.
Meat:					
Beef ....per pound..	$0 11	$0 09	$0 10	$0 12	$0 12
Mutton...............................do....	07	08	08	08	08
Pork ....do....	10	11	13	12	12
Wheat ....per bushel..	1 15	88	99	1 09	1 21
Flour ....per 100 pounds..	3 04	2 67	2 79	4 01	3 16
Sugar ....per pound..	09	08	10	11	10
Tea................................do....	52	57	66	60	73
Coffee ....do....	36	46	39	44	48
Rice...............................do....	06	06	07	08	08
Salt.............................. do....	02	02	03	02	02
Milk ....per quart..	10	08	09	12	06
Butter:					
Fresh ....per pound..	26	24	24	26	16
Salt...............................do....	24	18	23	20	12
Cheese:					
Colonial ....do....	16	22	20	16	20
Imported ....do....	24	36	31	56	48
Beer, colonial ....per hogshead..	22 62	25 33	24 33	24 33	24 33
Bottled beer, English..........per dozen quarts..	3 16	4 38	3 40	3 89	3 40
Brandy ....per gallon..	5 57	5 69	5 73	5 69	5 73

NOTE.—The above table is compiled from the New Zealand government statistics for the year ended December 31, 1883. There has been since then a slight decline in some of the articles and a slight increase in others, but upon the whole the prices here given may be regarded as a fair average of the year 1884.

G. W. G.

HABITS OF THE WORKING CLASSES.

The habits of the working classes of New Zealand are better perhaps than in any other colony in Australasia. Beer and spirits are not drunk amongst these classes so much as formerly. Although both are included in the New Zealand lists of provisions, their consumption in many of the districts is so small that it ought not to be taken into consideration. As a class, the working people of the colony are industrious, prudent, and economical. The liberal inducements they have to save their earnings have been taken advantage of very generally, both in the cities and in the rural districts, principally with a view to attracting immigrants, who were formerly deterred from settling in the North Island by a dis-

like of proximity to the Maori, or native population, on account of their
fierce and warlike habits. The Maori race may now be considered
entirely subdued. Their country is gradually being opened up for settlement, and every effort is made, both by the government and people, to cultivate cordial and friendly relations between the two races.
There is a strong disposition on the part of the white laborers in the North
Island to purchase small farms; indeed nearly all of them aspire to become proprietors, which they may do more readily, perhaps, than in any
other country except the United States. The deferred payment system, which applies both to country and city, permits of the purchase of
lands or building lots, to be paid for in a term of years of sufficient
length not to oppress the purchaser.

The existence of numerous savings banks, which pay a liberal rate
(4 to 6 per cent.) upon deposits, has also been a great incentive to the
saving of money by wage-workers. The largest of the private savings
banks is that at Auckland, under the patronage of the governor of the
colony, who is its president. Smaller banks of the same character
exist in all the cities. The Postal Savings Bank, under the auspices of
the government, has its headquarters at Auckland, with branches in
every district in the colony. These various banks contained in deposits,
according to the last published report, $9,166,748.42, to the credit of 68,358
persons, or an average of $127.98 to each. The depositors belong al-
most altogether to the laboring classes. The deferred payment system,
before referred to, permits laboring men in many cases to deposit their
earnings long enough for some interest to accrue upon them before paying for the lands purchased.

Workingmen are very generally heads of families, and it is worthy
of mention that the influence which such a responsibility has to encourage industrious and economical habits is so great that a man with a
family, as a rule, succeeds in getting employment better than others.
The extent of the responsibility referred to will be understood when it
is mentioned that the climate here seems to promote productiveness
amongst women, they becoming developed at an early age and often
giving birth to a child every year for a long period. Families containing a dozen or more children are by no means rare.

FEELING BETWEEN EMPLOYÉ AND EMPLOYER.

The feeling which prevails generally between employés and employers in the colony is a fortunate one for both classes. Generally the two
classes are brought into closer contact than is the case either in England, or in the older States of America, where large corporations often
control the labor of hundreds or thousands of men whose personal condition, wants, or grievances cannot be known to the chief employer.
The result in the latter case is to give rise to the expression so often
heard, that "corporations have no souls." The relation of the two classes
in New Zealand is well illustrated by the fact that in most of the large
mills and factories there is given every year a dinner to all the employés.
On these occasions the proprietor or a foreman delivers an address to
the workingmen, commending them if they have done well and encouraging them to further good efforts. Speeches are made also by the leading employés, both responding to the expressions of good will on the part
of the propreitor and counseling the under-workmen on the value of
habits of industry and economy.

ORGANIZATION OF LABOR.

Trades unions have existed here for the past twenty years, nearly
every trade now being so organized. The general purpose of these

unions is very much the same as with similar organizations in older countries, though little occasion has existed in the past for testing their strength, either as a political factor or as a means of dictating terms to employers or capitalists. Heretofore questions of this character have not reached a sufficient importance to lead to any legislation with reference to the employment of labor or the protection of laborers.

There has arisen of late, however, a workingmen's party, the future of which is being looked forward to with interest. Here suffrage is universal, every male of the age of twenty-one being an elector. The government of New Zealand is like that of other British colonies. It consists of a legislative council appointed for life and a house of representatives containing ninety-one members elected for three years by the people, and four Maori members elected by the Maori race. The governor is appointed by the Crown. The ministry is formed in the same way as that of Great Britain. The people also elect the municipal officers. It must be borne in mind, however, that a man is entitled to a vote in every district in which he owns property. This reference to the government is made here that the character of the movement of the workingmen in New Zealand may be better understood.

This movement had its origin only a few months since, but its strength has grown with a rapidity that can be understood only by those who have been familiar with such uprisings as that of the "Know-Nothing" party in the United States thirty years ago. The new party already sustains a number of newspaper organs, the two leading ones being published at Auckland and Dunedin. In general, these papers are devoted to propagating the views of Henry George, the economic writer who has begun recently to attract so much attention in England and America. The specific demands made by these papers for the classes they represent are:

1. A readjustment of the system of taxation. At present the Maoris are entirely exempt from taxation. The workingmen complain likewise of the high amount of indirect taxation, such as customs dues on articles that cannot be manufactured in New Zealand. They also demand a reduction of the property tax.

2. A curtailment of the power of suffrage of the wealthier classes. While every man is entitled to vote once, property-holders have the right to vote in every district in which they have possessions, thus giving to many citizens two or more votes.

3. More liberal terms for the acquirement of land in fee-simple in the South Island, where the liberal spirit before referred to as existing in the North Island is less known.

4. The enactment of an eight-hour labor law and an act making holidays more frequent.

The workingmen's party has, perhaps, its principal strength in the South Island, where the conditions generally prevailing have been somewhat less favorable for the working classes than in the North Island, particularly with regard to the acquirement of lands by small farmers and factory operatives. Its leader, however, Sir George Grey, resides in the North Island, and his personal popularity has given the party great strength in the city and district of Auckland.

NEW ZEALAND TARIFF.

The tariff or customs dues may be regarded as protective, although it is claimed by the governmental authorities to be levied only for revenue. There is an ad valorem duty of 15 per cent. on nearly all necessaries. Woolen goods pay 15 per cent. ad valorem. This, small as it is, enables the New Zealand manufacturer to compete successfully with the foreign market in many branches of woolens, such as tweeds, blankets, &c.

The boot and shoe manufacturers are protected. The duty charged on boots imported into New Zealand is 12s. ($2.92) per one dozen pairs. Youths, Nos. 1 to 5, 10s. ($2.43) per one dozen pairs. Women's, No. 3 and upwards, 8s. ($1.94) per one dozen pairs. Soap and candle manufactures are also protected. Common soap is taxed at 3s. (73 cents) per cwt. Scented soap pays an ad valorem duty of 25 per cent. Tallow candles pay a half penny (1 cent) per pound. Sperm and paraffine 1½d. (3 cents) per pound. The timber industry is also protected. There is a duty of 2s. (48 cents) charged on every 100 feet of rough timber imported. Sawn timber, dressed timber, and dressed sawn timber pay a duty of 4s. (97 cents) for every 100 superficial feet. There is also a charge of 8s. ($1.94) for every 100 posts imported. Rails pay 4s. (97 cents) for every 100 imported.

Canned fruits are also protected with a specific duty of 1½d. (3 cents) per pound. Jams and jellies pay 3 cents per pound.

Tobacco is taxed at 3s. 6d. (87 cents) per pound. This import duty has been the means of developing the growth and manufacture of tobacco in New Zealand, especially in the North Island, where the soil in many places is said to contain the same chemical ingredients as in the most favored districts in the Island of Cuba.

TAXATION.

A late assessment for property tax shows the total value of private property in New Zealand to be $369,790,910. Annual value, $26,082,605. The property tax, which is about 1 penny (2 cents) in the pound sterling ($4.86), is levied on all persons possessing over £500 ($2.430) worth of property. There are in New Zealand 5,417 paying a tax of £1 ($4.86) and 9,048 persons paying a tax of over £1 ($4.86) and under £5 ($24.33); 2,146 persons of £10 ($48.66) and under £20 ($97.33). The total number of persons paying property tax in New Zealand from £1 ($4.86) to £6,000 ($29.16) is 22,087. A further return shows that there are 902 persons possessing freeholder's interest in land worth £10,000 ($48.66) and over. The same return shows that there are 60,658 in the colony owning freehold titles to farms—about one-eighth of the European population, probably unparalleled in the world. The number of persons owning separate farms in the United States is unexceptionably large, but according to the census of 1880 it was 4,208,907—considerably less in proportion to the population than that of New Zealand.

SOURCES OF REVENUE.

In this connection it will be well enough to mention that the principal source of revenue in New Zealand is derived from the customs. The next largest is from the railways and telegraphs, which are owned and managed by the Government. Then there are other sources, such as the receipts from the postal service, stamp duty, beer duty, judicial fees, property tax (referred to above), judicial fees, land and deeds, marine fees, registration and other fees, disparturing licenses, land sales, &c. The tax actually paid per head in New Zealand is estimated at £3 12s. ($17.51). The gross indebtedness of the colony on account of loans at the end of March, 1883, was $145,714,193, subject to a reduction of $12,344,779 for sinking funds that have accrued. The total expenditure up to the 31st of March, 1883, out of the public works fund, amounted to $91,459,286. The large public debt of the colony, as I have frequently pointed out in my reports to the Department of State, was principally incurred by expenditures on public works. Prior to 1870 the year in which the public works and immigration policy was inaugurated, the indebtedness of the colony was only $35,330,957.

PUBLIC LOANS.

Under the public works and immigration system the sum of $94,560,000 has been borrowed. Bills were passed, during the session of the colonial parliament, of 1882, authorizing loans of $19,200,000; $14,400,000 for the construction of railways and public works, and $4,800,000 for the North Island trunk railway.

These loans were obtained in London at the rate of 4 per cent. per annum. The revenue for the year ending the 31st of March, 1883, was $17,964,264. Of this amount $7,179,422 was received at the customs, $4,582,752 from the railways, $2,133,067 from stamps, and $447,048 from the telegraph, and the remainder from the property tax. The revenue for stamps was $50,000 in excess of the colonial treasurer's estimate. Included in this class are the duties under the stamp act, postal revenue fees, and fines of the law courts, and land transfer fees, for all of which there is now only one description of stamp in use.

The treasury is consequently unable to apportion the money received from sales of stamps to the classes of revenue to which they relate. The same course, that of permitting one kind of stamp to be used for all purposes, has been followed to some extent in other British colonies and in England, and no practical inconvenience has resulted therefrom, while to the public the use of only one stamp has been of very great advantage.

THE WORKINGMEN AND ASSISTED IMMIGRATION.

During the year from the 1st of April, 1882, to the 30th of June, 1883, 3,205 assisted immigrants arrived in New Zealand. Auckland received 556, Taranaki 14, Hawkes Bay 160, Wellington 223, Marlborough 8, Nelson 19, Westland 27, Canterbury 1,074, and Otago 1,114 From July, 1870, when the assisted-immigration policy was inaugurated, to June 30, 1883, 104,419 assisted immigrants have arrived in the colony. The workingmen are opposed very bitterly to the policy of assisting immigrants to New Zealand; they believe in immigration but do not think the people should be taxed for such a purpose. The workingmen argue that the policy operates injuriously to the interest of the workmen in reducing the price paid for labor. It is admitted, however, that a great benefit is conferred upon the immigrant by bringing him out from England, thereby securing to him double the amount of wages and many more comforts than he could get at home. Mr. Hursthouse, who has given much time, thought, and study to the condition of labor in New Zealand, is of the opinion that a workman can support a small family very comfortably on 6s. 6d. ($1.58) per day. He says that the workman in England has to live on less than 3s. 6d. (85 cents) per day, when the price of food is nearly double what it is in New Zealand.

Mr. Hutchison, a member of parliament from Wellington district, has been for a number of years a very earnest opponent to the assisted-immigration policy, and he thinks that if abolished the rate of wages would be unquestionably higher, and moreover that not only the workingman but all classes would be improved by the change.· Mr. Hutchison does not think that the present rate of wages for the workingmen in New Zealand, 6s. 6d. ($1.58) per day, is enough to enable him to live, especially if he should have a family.

COST OF LIVING.

I am indebted to Mr. Hutchison for the following table showing the cost of living in New Zealand for a workingman with a wife and three children:

Items.	Per week.	Per annum.
	s. d.	£ s. d.
Rent and taxes	6 0	18 4 0
Fuel	3 6	9 2 0
Lighting	1 0	2 12 0
Bread, flour, oatmeal	5 0	13 0 0
Butter	3 0	7 16 0
Milk	2 0	5 4 0
Butcher meat	4 6	11 14 0
Potatoes, vegetables	1 6	3 18 0
Fish	1 0	2 12 0
Tea	1 3	3 5 0
Coffee	0 10	2 3 4
Sugar	2 0	5 4 0
Rice and barley	1 0	2 12 0
Soap, soda, starch	0 6	1 6 0
Salt, pepper, mustard, &c.		0 13 8
Clothing, boots, &c.	7 0	18 4 0
Religion and charity	0 6	1 6 0
Newspaper, stationery, and school-books	1 0	2 12 0
Total		111 8 0
Total in American money		$542 12

This expenditure is £10 12s. ($51.57) in excess of the workingman's earnings at the rate of 6s. 6d. ($1.55) per day, supposing he should receive work throughout the year. In the event of illness, his case is deplorable. The table makes no allowance for doctor's bills, medicine, &c. Mr. Hutchison says the reason that there is no pauper class in New Zealand is because the country is so productive that it is able to stand the worst kind of legislation, but this state of affairs, he argues, cannot last much longer. The number of the unemployed, he says, is daily increasing and the bitter cry of the poor is beginning to be heard in all the large towns. The Hon. Major Atkinson, the premier, is of the opinion that the workingmen have little cause of complaint, and that the action of the working classes is making matters worse. He says in his last financial statement to the New Zealand parliament:

I say distinctly, after a most careful consideration of the whole condition of the country, that there are not only no real grounds for taking a despondent view of our position, but on the contrary there is much reason to justify us in looking forward with confidence to a future of great prosperity. We, like other communities, shall have our ups and downs. Unusual prosperity will be followed by unusual depression as is the case all over the world. No one who sees the steady improvements that are going on all over the colony, who observes the very substantial increase in the savings banks deposit, the great increase in life-assurance business, and the rapid development of our manufacturing industries, and who has watched our import and export trade, can doubt that we are producing enough to pay our debts, I ve comfortably and gradually accumulate capital.

Major Atkinson accounts for the present depression in parts of the colony principally from the fact that the colonists were tempted by cheap freights and comparatively easy money, to over-import, forgetting, for the moment, the effect which would follow the contraction in the expenditure of borrowed money. He urges the people to practice self-denial, self-restraint, and to live within their means both publicly and privately.

STRIKES.

Labor strikes have never been prevalent, and, when they have occurred, have been so limited in extent that employers have had but little trouble in filling the places of the strikers with other laborers. Hence the strikes have been usually of short duration, nearly always resulting in the final adoption of the terms of the employer. Within the past few weeks a strike occurred in one of the largest boot manufactories in Auckland, the strikers emphasizing their demand for higher wages by such scenes of violence as have been witnessed in strikes in America. The proprietors had no trouble, however, in filling their factory with new men upon the old terms.

WAGES AND FOOD PURCHASES.

The working people generally are paid their wages once a week in factories and once a month upon farms. The money in use is sterling coin and the notes of the various banks and branch banks of issue in the colony. These notes are not allowed to circulate outside of New Zealand, and there is paid upon the amount issued a yearly tax of 2 per cent. to the Government. The wage-working classes are free to purchase the necessaries of life wherever they choose, the plan of corporation stores, or company stores, such as prevail in the Pennsylvania mining regions being unknown here. Co-operative stores and co-operative purchasing agencies have no general existence as yet among working people.

GENERAL CONDITION OF THE WORKING CLASSES.

In addition to the light thrown upon the condition of the working classes in the preceding statements mention may be made of their homes and the manner in which their homes are furnished. Tenement houses are almost unknown. In the cities certain streets come to be occupied by the cottages of the workingmen, while others live in the suburbs. On the farms, where it is usual for laborers regularly employed to have families, cottages are provided for them. These houses, both in city and country, are usually built of wood, though many of brick and concrete are built. The rental per week is from $1.31 upward; this sum, $1.31 per week, being sufficient to secure a house containing two or three rooms and a kitchen. For $4 to $5 per week (£50 and £60 per year) a house containing eight or ten rooms may be had in Auckland.

The table of an average workingman in Auckland will usually be found to be supplied as follows: For breakfast, meat (beef or lamb), potatoes, oatmeal, bread, and coffee. For dinner, soup, meat (beef or lamb, with pork in winter), vegetables (potatoes, *kumeros* or sweet potatoes, beans, asparagus, cauliflower, cabbage, &c.), wheat bread, and tea. For supper, meat, bread, potatoes, coffee or tea.

Wheat bread here is often made of unbolted flour by the workingmen's families, this being cheaper besides being considered more wholesome, than bolted flour. Since the recent increase in the temperance sentiment the use of tea has largely supplanted that of beer as a table drink.

The fuel used in the cities and towns is coal, the whole country being one vast coal-seam. It is also used upon the farms in the vicinity of the mines. The black coal, similar to the Newcastle coals in England, and harder than the Pittsburgh coals, costs at the mines $2.92 per English ton, and $3.89 per ton delivered in Auckland. There is a cheaper coal—a brown variety—which costs only two-thirds as much as the other, but it is better fitted for manufacturing purposes than for household use.

The male population is greatly in excess of the females. In the European population here the disparity is 49,277, as shown by the most recent statistics, in a population of 500,000. The women are in such demand for wives, therefore, that not only are they not found in factories, but it is difficult often to supply the demand for female house servants. Generally the head of a family is the only member found at work in factories, though boys among people of every class are usually apprenticed to some trade. There is no law against the employment of children in factories, and they are sometimes found at light work. Education is compulsory, some discretion being allowed, however, to the local boards of the district schools, as in some cases the strict enforcement of the law might result in hardships.

Workingmen are generally occupied ten hours per day. Factories heretofore have been lacking in comfort and cleanliness, but some of the new establishments show an improvement in this respect. In some of those which are operated after daylight electric lights are used. Regard is usually had for the safety of employés in factories, a fire-escape being seen in almost all of them.

Operatives in almost every branch of industry aspire to become proprietors or employers themselves, and the facility with which this may be done forms the brightest side of the life of the workingman in New Zealand.

NEW INDUSTRIES.

Amongst the new new industries in New Zealand may be mentioned the manufacture of jewelry. In each of the large towns small jewelry factories have been established, and with a reasonable prospect of permanent success. The annual consumption of gold, however, in New Zealand for this purpose is estimated not to exceed 10,000 ounces. Indeed, the only method as yet for testing the product of the gold mines of the colony is from the quantity entered for export at the customs, &c. Amount of gold exported dured the year ended the 31st of December, 1883, was 248,374 ounces, valued at $4,768,090, against 230,893 ounces, valued at $4,423,987. For the year 1882 the estimate of 10,000 ounces for local consumption may be regarded as correct as it was given to me by the government statist. The largest jewelry factory in the colony is that of Mr. G. Hyndman, at Dunedin. It employs about sixteen hands. The gold and silver used are brought from the Thames gold fields-and even the tools are manufactured on the premises.

The factory is now engaged in making greenstone pendants, brooches, crosses, and ear-rings. It also makes gold and silver rings, chains, necklaces, and lockets. The smelting operations are carried on in a brick furnace, where the metal receives the necessary alloy. The metal is then hammered into any form desired.

When plates are needed the gold is placed between two tempered steel rollers arranged for whatever thickness required. Gold wire is manufactured by means of a draw-bench. The iron screw-presses are worked by hand and cut the metal into various kinds of patterns; the ·

metal always being worked cold. About six or seven men are employed at these presses, and when the jewelry leaves their hands it only requires polishing to be ready for market.

GREENSTONE MERES.

There is a lapidary connected with the establishment, employing eight or nine men. Here a steam-engine is used to work the saw and other implements necessary for cutting and polishing New Zealand greenstone, a species of jade found in various parts of the South Island. This greenstone is hard, clear, and beautiful, and susceptible of an exquisite polish. The natives formerly made their *meres* (battle-axes) out of it. The process of cutting and polishing the axes was a very tedious one, and the natives placed such high value on them that at one time it was very difficult for a European to purchase one. I remember Sir George Grey telling me that when governor of New Zealand he saw a very beautiful *mere* in possession of a Maori chief well known to him, and proposed to buy it. The native, however, agreed to part with it only on condition that Sir George would give him the man-of-war that brought him to New Zealand. Sir George told him that the ship cost the British Government nearly £100,000 sterling. "Even that sum," said the chief, "is not the equivalent in value of my *mere*."

The demand for *meres* and other greenstone ornaments is so great that they are often made out of glass in London and Paris and sent to New Zealand, but the imposture is easily detected.

A well-executed greenstone *mere*, whether made by hand or machinery, will sell readily in New Zealand from $150 to $250.

ACKNOWLEDGMENT.

I have been aided in the preparation of this report by Mr. Hawthorne Hill, the able and scholarly journalist of Louisville, Ky., who has for many years given much study to the material and conditional resources of New Zealand.

G. W. GRIFFIN,
Consul.

UNITED STATES CONSULATE,
  Auckland, New Zealand, May 27th, 1884.

POLYNESIA.

HAWAIIAN ISLANDS.

REPORT BY CONSUL M'KINLEY, OF HONOLULU.

I. GENERAL TRADES.

Wages paid per week of fifty-four hours in Honolulu.

Occupations.	Lowest.	Highest.	Average.
BUILDING TRADES.			
Bricklayers	$24 00	$36 00	$30 00
Hod-carriers	10 00	12 00	11 00
Masons	18 00	30 00	24 00
Tenders	10 00	12 00	11 00
Plasterers	12 00	42 00	27 00
Tenders	9 00	15 00	12 00
Roofers	24 00	24 00	24 00
Tenders	15 00	15 00	15 00
Plumbers	24 00	24 00	24 00
Assistants	6 00	15 00	10 50
Carpenters	15 00	27 00	21 00
Gas-fitters	24 00	24 00	24 00
OTHER TRADES.			
Bakers	16 00	30 00	23 00
Blacksmiths	24 00	30 00	27 00
Strikers	15 00	20 00	17 50
Book-binders	12 00	20 00	16 00
Butchers	10 50	15 00	12 75
Cabinet-makers	15 00	24 00	19 50
Drivers:			
Draymen and teamsters	2 00	3 00	2 50
Cab and carriage	2 00	3 00	2 50
Engravers	18 00	20 00	19 00
Horseshoers			24 00
Jewelers	18 00	20 00	19 00
Laborers, porters, &c	3 00	6 00	4 00
Printers	25 00	25 00	25 00
Teachers public schools	7 00	40 00	23 50
Saddle and harness makers	12 00	27 00	19 05
Stevedores	12 00	12 00	12 00
Tailors	18 00	25 00	21 50
Tinsmiths	15 00	12 00	18 00

III. FOUNDRIES, MACHINE-SHOPS, AND IRON WORKS.

Wages paid per week of fifty-three hours in foundries, machine-shops, and iron works in Honolulu, Hawaiian Islands.

Occupations.	Lowest.	Highest.	Average.
Foundry:			
Loam molders	$30 00	$36 00	$33 00
Green sand molders	27 00		27 00
Core-makers	25 50		25 50
Furnacemen	19 50		19 50
White helpers	15 00	18 00	16 50
Chippers	18 00		18 00
Native helpers	8 00	12 00	10 00

Wages paid per week of fifty-three hours in foundries, &c.—Continued.

Occupations.	Lowest.	Highest.	Average.
Boiler-shop :			
Boiler riveters	$25 50	$30 00	$27 75
Boiler calkers	25 50	30 00	27 75
Boiler helpers	10 00	12 00	11 00
Rivet heaters	7 00	8 00	7 50
Blacksmiths	27 00	....	27 00
Pattern-shop pattern-makers..............................	27 00	36 00	31 50
Machine-shop :			
Lathe hands	24 00	33 00	28 50
Machine hands..	21 00	27 00	24 00
Fitters and erectors......................................	24 00	36 00	30 00
Native helpers	8 00	13 00	10 50
Brass turners	27 00	....	27 00
Blacksmiths	27 00	33 00	30 00
Blacksmiths' helpers.....................................	12 00	18 00	15 00

VI. RAILWAY EMPLOYÉS.

Wages paid to railway employés (those engaged about stations, as well as those engaged on the engines and cars, linemen, railroad laborers, &c.) on Hawaiian Railroad Company.

Occupations.	Lowest.	Highest.	Average.
Superintendent.....................................per year..	....	....	$3,000 00
Book-keeper ....do ...	....	....	1,500 00
Conductor ....do...	....	....	1,000 00
Engine drivers...................................do...	....	....	1,200 00
Section overseers...............................do ...	....	....	900 00
Section laborers ....per day..	....	....	1 00
Warehouse and yard overseer ....per year..	$900 00	....	....
Brakemen ....per month..	40 00	$60 00	50 00
Warehouse laborers ....per day..	....	....	1 50
Carpenters......................................do....	2 50	4 00	....

VII. SHIP-YARDS AND SHIP-BUILDING.

Wages paid per day of nine hours in ship-yards.

Occupations.	Average wages.
Carpenters...	$5 00
Calkers	5 00

VII. SEAMEN'S WAGES.

Wages paid per month to seamen (officers and men), distinguishing between ocean, coast, and river navigation, and between sail and steam.

Occupations.	Lowest.	Highest.	Occupations.	Lowest.	Highest.
OCEAN STEAMERS.			**COASTING STEAMERS—Cont'd.**		
Masters	$100 00	$250 00	Stewards	$30 00	$50 00
Mates	50 00	100 00	Cooks	30 00	50 00
Stewards	50 00	90 00	Engineers	75 00	150 00
Cooks	40 00	60 00	Assistant engineers........	30 00	60 00
Seamen	15 00	30 00	Firemen...................	20 00	30 00
Engineers	100 00	150 00	Seamen...................	15 00	28 00
Assistant engineers........	40 00	80 00			
Firemen..................	20 00	35 00	**SAILING VESSELS.**		
			Masters...................	40 00	125 00
COASTING STEAMERS.			Mates	30 00	50 00
			Cooks	40 00	50 00
Masters	100 00	150 00	Stewards..................	25 00	50 00
Mates	40 00	60 00			

XI. AGRICULTURAL WAGES.

Wages paid per week to agricultural laborers and household (country) servants in Honolulu.

Occupations.	Lowest.	Highest.	Average.
Cook	$5 00	$7 00	$6 00
Steward	3 00	5 00	4 00
Coachman	5 00	7 00	6 00
Gardener	4 00	6 00	5 00

XIII. GOVERNMENT DEPARTMENTS AND OFFICES.

Wages paid per month to employés in Government departments and offices, exclusive of tradesmen and laborers.

Occupations.	Lowest.	Highest.	Average.
Secretaries and chief clerks of departments			$250 00
Associate clerks	$50 00	$150 00	100 00
Jailer of Oahu prison			150 00
Superintendent of public works			250 00
Superintendent of water-works			125 00
Clerk to superintendent of water-works			83 33½
Postmaster-general			333 33½
Civil engineer			333 33½
Collector-general of customs			333 33½
Deputy collector-general of customs			208 33½
Marshal of the Kingdom			333 33½
Collectors at other ports	83 33½	125 00	
Deputy marshal			208 33½
Captain of police			100 00
Sheriffs	166 66⅔	208 33½	
Interpreter:			
Hawaiian			166 66⅔
Chinese			125 00

XV. PRINTERS AND PRINTING OFFICES.

Statement showing the wages paid per week of nine hours per day to printers (compositors, pressmen, proof-readers, &c.).

Occupations.	Lowest.	Highest.	Average.
Foreman		$30 00	
Printers	$20 00	30 00	$25 00
Pressmen		20 00	20 00

D. A. McKINLEY,

Consul.

UNITED STATES CONSULATE,
Honolulu, May 5, 1884.

SAMOA.

REPORT BY CONSUL CANISIUS.

In answer to the labor circular of February 15th, I have the honor to say that the only kind of labor employed in the Samoa Islands is the so-called Polynesian contract labor, concerning which some information will be found in my annual commercial report for 1883.

The wages of these plantation laborers average $3 per month, with food and lodging. White carpenters earn from $3 to $4 per day. There is no fixed rate of wages for seamen.

T. CANISIUS,
Consul.

UNITED STATES CONSULATE,
Apia, May 16, 1884.

LABOR IN SAMOA.

[Extract from Consul Canisius's annual report for 1883.]

As the resources of the Samoan group are developed the question of the labor supply becomes a more momentous one. The immense competition for Polynesian labor from Fiji and Australia is causing the supply for Samoa to become very limited, and at some not very distant day the planters will have to resort to "John Chinaman" for aid.

In Samoa there is only one firm (German) which has any extensive plantations, and they employ between eight and nine hundred laborers. They keep three vessels running between Samoa and the various groups whence the laborers are brought. One of these vessels recently returned with only 107 men after having been out some months.

The usual impression on first seeing the creatures which one of these labor ships brings is that they can never become good laborers. They belong to one of the lowest types of humanity, the greatest cannibals on earth. They arrive filthy, lazy, and ferocious. They are comfortably housed, decently clothed, and well fed. At the end of the three years for which they are generally engaged, they are as unfit to return to their savage homes as they were previously to have contact with civilized beings.

Missionaries, philanthropists, and others have denounced in unmeasured terms the horrible outrages of the labor traffic, indiscriminately accusing all nationalities of the guilt. While it is doubtless true that many outrages have been committed, it is equally true that they have in many instances been greatly exaggerated. If one looks at both sides of the question one cannot but think that the "slavery" so much denounced by those persons must finally turn out to be a blessing. To be convinced of this one has only to compare the difference in the aspect of these cannibal Polynesian laborers when they arrive on the plantations and when they depart for their island homes.

The laborers are paid in "trade," consisting generally of clothing, tobacco, knives, axes, guns, powder, shot, and many other articles which savage races prize. During their three years' service on the plantations these ignorant savages learn the white man's method of cultivating the soil and become acquainted with the use of many valuable plants. Their food consists for the most part of such things as can be grown on the plantation, such as bananas, bread-fruit, yams, and cocoanuts, besides which they have an allowance of rice, corn meal, beans, salt meat or fish. They are also allowed to help themselves to various kinds of fruits and roots which grow wild on the plantations and in the forests.

INDEX.

CONTINENT OF AMERICA.

DOMINION OF CANADA.

PROVINCE OF ONTARIO.

92 A—2 LAB——27

418 INDEX.

SOUTH AMERICA.

UNITED STATES OF COLOMBIA.

VENEZUELA.

INDEX. 425

SYRIA.

PALESTINE.

PERSIA.

CEYLON.

THE PHILIPPINE ISLANDS.

JAPAN.

CHINA.

SOUTHERN CHINA.

CONTINENT OF AFRICA.

MOROCCO.

CAPE COLONY.

SENEGAL.

SIERRA LEONE.

MADEIRA.

AUSTRALASIA.

VICTORIA.

○